AHA Hospital Statistics™

2012 Edition

P/A

RA 981 .A2 A6234 2012
Hospital statistics
(American Hospital
Hospital statistics.

ISSN 0090-6662
ISBN-13: 978-0-87258-892-9

Contents

Acknowledgements & Advisements

Acknowledgments

The 2012 edition of AHA Hospital Statistics is published by Health Forum, an affiliate of the American Hospital Association, Richard J. Umbdenstock, President and CEO.

Advisements

The data published here should be used with the following advisements: The data are based on replies to an annual survey that seeks a variety of information, not all of which is published in this book. The information gathered by the survey includes specific services, but not all of each hospital's services. Therefore, the data do not reflect an exhaustive list of all services offered by all hospitals. For information on the availability of additional data, please contact Health Forum, (800) 821-2039.

Health Forum does not assume responsibility for the accuracy of information voluntarily reported by the individual institutions surveyed. The purpose of this publication is to provide basic data reflecting the delivery of health care in the United States and associated areas, and is not to serve an official and all-inclusive list of services offered by individual hospitals.

Hospitals Strengthen Physician Ties to Gear up for Delivery System Reform

By Caroline Steinberg

Hospital Statistics is a comprehensive compilation of data on trends in the hospital field through 2010 based on the results of the American Hospital Association's (AHA) Annual Survey of Hospitals. Overall, Hospital Statistics identifies both long-standing and emerging trends and offers insights into what the future may hold for hospitals.

The increased focus by public and private payers on accountability for improving quality and reducing costs across the continuum has hospitals looking to align more closely with physicians. Success in value-based purchasing, reducing readmissions and managing costs within a bundled or per capita rate hinges on making physicians full partners in examining and redesigning care processes. While many of these efforts are in their infancy, hospitals are gearing up by employing more physicians of a variety of specialty types. However, the shift to new payment mechanisms remains slow. The 2010 AHA Annual Survey included a series of new questions to better examine these trends.

Rising Number of Physicians Employed by Hospitals

Physician employment has grown by 32 percent over the past decade (Chart 1). Today, hospitals employ 212,000 physicians, representing about 20 percent of those practicing.[1] For physicians, employment represents an opportunity to shield themselves from economic risks—such as reductions in Medicare payment—turn over costly and burdensome administrative tasks, and work more predictable hours. During the recent recession, two-thirds of hospitals reported physicians approaching them for financial support with three-quarters of those noting an uptick in physicians seeking employment.[2] Employment is particularly appealing to young physicians who may carry a large financial burden from student loans and may not have the capital to start a practice.

For hospitals, greater physician integration represents the potential to better align goals and processes across the care continuum. Trying to engage physicians in efforts to reduce costs, improve quality and implement clinical information technologies is difficult given the limited ability of hospitals to provide incentives to physicians to alter their practice patterns. Hospital administrators also must balance the need for hospital service line

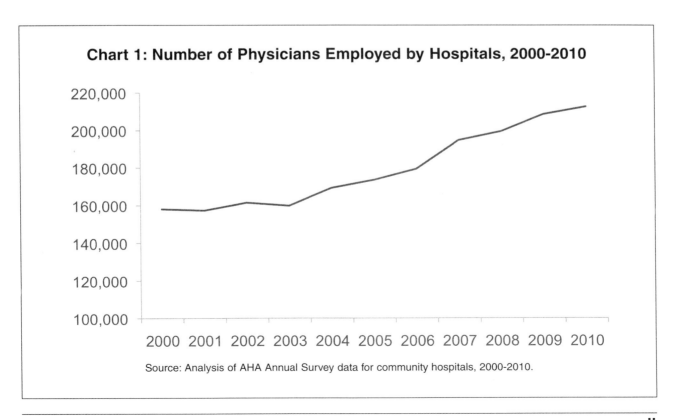

Chart 1: Number of Physicians Employed by Hospitals, 2000-2010

Source: Analysis of AHA Annual Survey data for community hospitals, 2000-2010.

managers to become more involved in clinical decision-making against concerns that any perceived intrusion on the part of community physicians could drive them to competitors. Also, employment poses the fewest legal and regulatory risks among the various approaches, which may account for some of the observed trends. Stark, Anti-kickback, and Civil Monetary Penalty laws with respect to federal health programs and antitrust laws more broadly create barriers to many other clinical integration strategies.

Hospitals Have a Range of Relationships Beyond Employment Through Which to Engage Physicians

In addition to direct employment, hospitals contract with physicians on a group or individual basis (Chart 2). Among specialty types, emergency physicians are the most likely to be employed or under contract; but even among non hospital-based primary care physicians and other specialists, hospitals

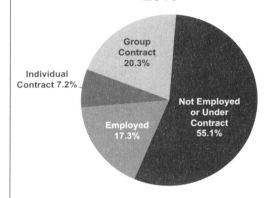

Chart 2: Percent of Privileged Physicians by Type of Relationship, 2010

Source: Analysis of AHA Annual Survey data for community hospitals, 2010. Hospitals were asked to report the total number of physicians on the medical staff except those with courtesy, honorary and provisional privileges. Residents or interns are not included. Employed physicians are either direct hospital employees or employees of a hospital subsidiary corporation. Individual contract physicians are under a formal contract to provide services at the hospital. Group contract physicians are part of a group (group practice, faculty practice plan or medical foundation) under a formal contract to provide services at the hospital.

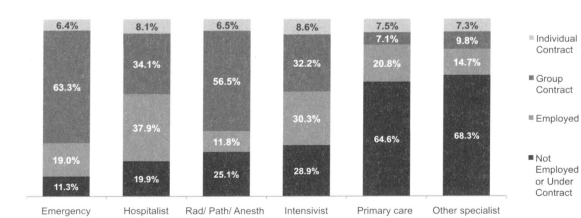

Chart 3: Percent of Hospitals Reporting Physician Relationships by Type by Specialty, 2010

Source: Analysis of AHA Annual Survey data for community hospitals, 2010.

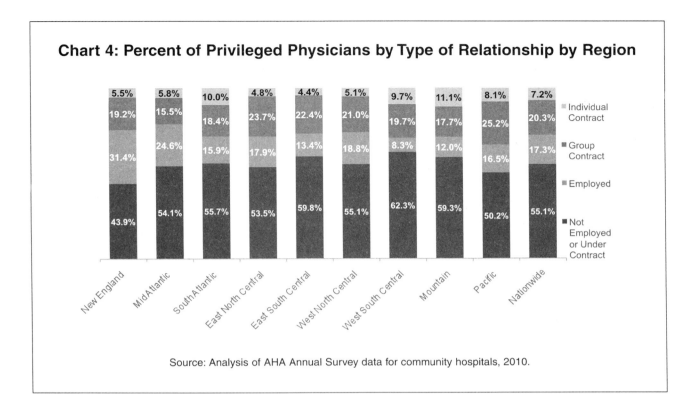

Chart 4: Percent of Privileged Physicians by Type of Relationship by Region

Legend:
- Individual Contract
- Group Contract
- Employed
- Not Employed or Under Contract

Region	Individual Contract	Group Contract	Employed	Not Employed or Under Contract
New England	5.5%	19.2%	31.4%	43.9%
MidAtlantic	5.8%	15.5%	24.6%	54.1%
SouthAtlantic	10.0%	18.4%	15.9%	55.7%
East North Central	4.8%	23.7%	17.9%	53.5%
East South Central	4.4%	22.4%	13.4%	59.8%
West North Central	5.1%	21.0%	18.8%	55.1%
West South Central	9.7%	19.7%	8.3%	62.3%
Mountain	11.1%	17.7%	12.0%	59.3%
Pacific	8.1%	25.2%	16.5%	50.2%
Nationwide	7.2%	20.3%	17.3%	55.1%

Source: Analysis of AHA Annual Survey data for community hospitals, 2010.

report about a third of privileged physicians are employed or under contract (Chart 3). Relationships vary somewhat by region, from a high in New England of 56 percent of privileged physicians either employed or under contract to a low of 38 percent in the West South Central Region. New England is the only region where the majority of privileged physicians is employed or under contract (Chart 4). Some regional variation is due to state corporate practice of medicine laws that prohibit the employment of physicians, such as those in Texas and California.

Hospitals have a range of other organizational models for working with physicians. These include Independent Practice Associations (IPA), Open and Closed Physician Hospital Organizations (PHO) and Equity Models. The types of models that are typically composed of independent physicians or group practices have been declining in prevalence. Meanwhile those in which physicians are salaried by the

hospital or another entity are on the rise. These include the Integrated Salary and Foundation models.[3] Overall, 69 percent of hospitals report having at least one of these types of arrangements.

The rise of more tightly aligned arrangements reflects an increase in the perception by hospital administrators of the degree of future collaboration that will be required to be successful in an environment based on accountability for cost, quality and outcomes. In a recent survey by the American College of Healthcare Executives (ACHE), 72 percent of hospital executives noted that they planned to align more closely with physicians.

Use of Hospitalists and Intensivists is Increasing Rapidly
Beyond the traditional types of hospital-based physicians such as emergency physicians, radiologists, pathologists and anesthesiologists, more and more hospitals are adding hospitalists

Chart 5: Percent of Hospitals Reporting That Hospitalists or Intensivists Provide Care in Their Hospital, 2003-2010

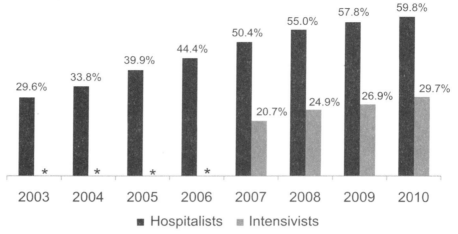

■ Hospitalists　■ Intensivists

*Question not included on survey prior to 2007.
Source: Analysis of AHA Annual Survey data for community hospitals 2003-2010. A hospitalist is a physician whose primary professional focus is the care of hospitalized medical patients (through clinical, education, administrative and research activity). An intensivist is a physician with special training to work with critically ill patients.

and intensivists to their staff (Chart 5). The use of these physicians—who specialize in the care of hospitalized patients—has benefits for admitting physicians, who can turn some or all of the management of hospitalized patients over to these professionals in order to focus their time more efficiently on their office-based practices and avoid hospital calls that interrupt personal time. Patients benefit from having around-the-clock physician care provided by individuals who are fully integrated into the hospital care delivery team. From the hospital's perspective, their use enhances communication between physicians and other members of the care delivery team, which can lead to more efficient care delivery. A recent study found that the use of hospitalists decreases both the length and cost of the hospital stay.[4]

The use of hospitalists and intensivists shows striking differences across regions of the country with the West North Central Region lagging other areas on both fronts (Chart 6).

Majority of Hospitals Use Advanced Practice Nurses in a Variety of Roles

Advanced Practice Registered Nurses (APRN) can fill a range of roles in the hospital setting, from providing primary or specialty care for low-risk patients to care management and patient education. Given the current shortage of primary care physicians, demand for APRNs is expected to increase as people gain coverage under health care reform. Within hospitals, primary care is the most commonly reported role (Chart 7). While more than half

Chart 6: Percent of Hospitals Reporting That Hospitalists and Intensivists Provide Care in Their Hospital by Region, 2010

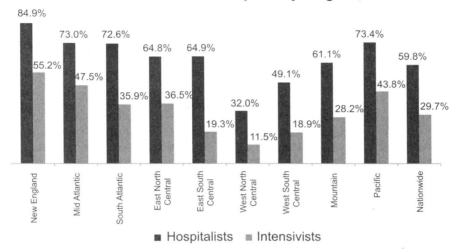

■ Hospitalists ■ Intensivists

Source: Analysis of AHA Annual Survey data for community hospitals, 2010. A hospitalist is a physician whose primary professional focus is the care of hospitalized medical patients (through clinical, education, administrative and research activity). An intensivist is a physician with special training to work with critically ill patients.

Chart 7: Percent of Hospitals Reporting Use of Advanced Practice Nurses by Type of Care Provided, 2010

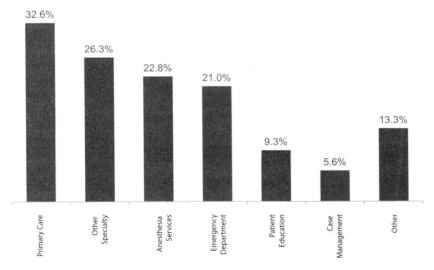

Source: Analysis of AHA Annual Survey data for community hospitals, 2010. Advanced practice registered nurses (APRN) are registered nurses with advanced didactic and clinical education, knowledge, skills, and scope of practice, including physician assistants, nurse practitioners and clinical nurse specialists.

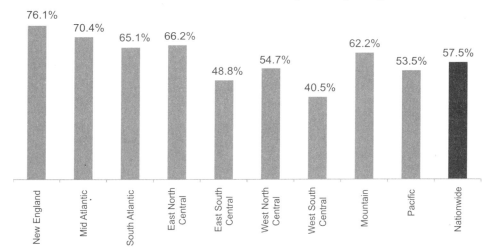

Chart 8: Percent of Hospitals Reporting that Advanced Practice Nurses Provide Care in Their Hospital by Region, 2010

Source: Analysis of AHA Annual Survey data for community hospitals, 2010. Advanced practice nurses (APN) are registered nurses with advanced didactic and clinical education, knowledge, skills, and scope of practice, including physician assistants, nurse practitioners and clinical nurse specialists.

of all hospitals employ APRNs, use varies from a low of 40 percent of hospitals in the West South Central Region to a high of 76 percent in New England (Chart 8). This pattern may reflect the varying APRN scope of practice laws across states, which determine the level of oversight required, prescribing privileges, whether they can admit patients or certify post-acute care stays, and other aspects of their role in care delivery.

Capitation and Shared Risk Models are on the Decline Nationally but Remain Prevalent in Some Regions

Recently the percentage of hospitals engaging in shared risk or capitated contracts has been on the wane (Chart 9). However, some regions are outliers: around 20 percent of hospitals in the Mid-Atlantic and Pacific regions report some revenue paid on a capitated basis and around 15 percent of hospitals in the New England and Pacific regions report some revenue paid on a shared-risk basis (Chart 10). Reform initiatives under the Patient Protection and Affordable Care Act (ACA) such as accountable care organizations, bundled payments, and medical homes should spur growth in this area, but hospital-physician integration will be a necessary ingredient of success.

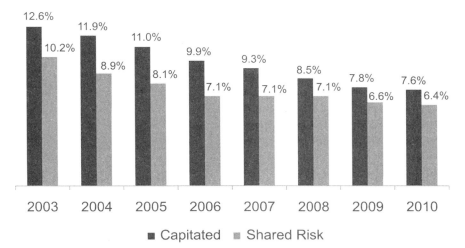

Chart 9: Percent of Hospitals Reporting Some Percent of Their Revenue Is Paid on a Capitated or Shared Risk Basis, 2003-2010

	2003	2004	2005	2006	2007	2008	2009	2010
Capitated	12.6%	11.9%	11.0%	9.9%	9.3%	8.5%	7.8%	7.6%
Shared Risk	10.2%	8.9%	8.1%	7.1%	7.1%	7.1%	6.6%	6.4%

■ Capitated ■ Shared Risk

Source: Analysis of AHA Annual Survey data for community hospitals 2003-2010. Capitation is defined as an at-risk payment arrangement in which an organization receives a fixed prearranged payment and in turn guarantees to deliver or arrange all medically necessary care required by enrollees in the capitated plan.

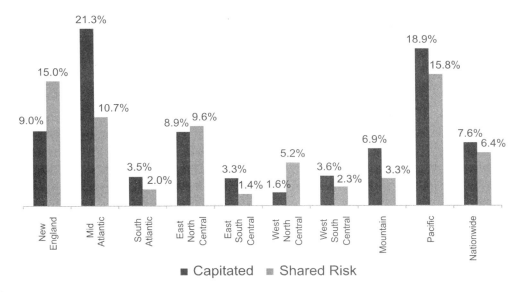

Chart 10: Percent of Hospitals Reporting a Portion of Their Revenue Is Paid on a Capitated or Shared Risk Basis by Region, 2010

	New England	Mid Atlantic	South Atlantic	East North Central	East South Central	West North Central	West South Central	Mountain	Pacific	Nationwide
Capitated	9.0%	21.3%	3.5%	8.9%	3.3%	1.6%	3.6%	6.9%	18.9%	7.6%
Shared Risk	15.0%	10.7%	2.0%	9.6%	1.4%	5.2%	2.3%	3.3%	15.8%	6.4%

■ Capitated ■ Shared Risk

Source: Analysis of AHA Annual Survey data for community hospitals, 2010. Capitation is defined as an at-risk payment arrangement in which an organization receives a fixed prearranged payment and in turn guarantees to deliver or arrange all medically necessary care required by enrollees in the capitated plan.

Conclusion

While the speed of change is uncertain, the direction is clear. Public and private payers will hold providers increasingly accountable for costs and quality across the continuum, and success will depend on hospitals' ability to work with physicians to achieve both greater efficiency and improved outcomes. The nature of hospital-physician ties will change from relationships that shore up the referral base to relationships that allow for the joint establishment of clinical protocols, financial mechanisms that align incentives, tracking of performance across the care continuum, and the integration of information systems. Given the high degree of interdependence required, we are likely to continue to see a move toward hospital employment of physicians.

[1] Number of employed physicians from Health Forum, AHA Annual Survey, 2009 data for all hospitals. Includes full time and part time physicians, dentists, interns and residents.

[2] American Hospital Association. (March 2009). Rapid Response Survey, The Economic Crisis: Ongoing Monitoring of Impact on Hospitals.

[3] See Health Forum, *AHA Statistics 2011*, Table 3.

[4] Peterson, MC. (2009). A Systematic Review of Outcomes and Quality Measures in Adult Patients Cared for by Hospitalists. *Mayo Clinic Proceedings,* 84 (3):248-54.

How to Use this Book

For more than six decades, *AHA Hospital Statistics*™ has reported aggregate hospital data derived from the AHA Annual Survey and is the definitive source when doing trend analysis with data by bed size category, U.S. Census Divisions, States, and Metropolitan Statistical Areas (MSAs). As the health care delivery system changes, so have the data tracked by the survey and presented in this report. Recent additions include:

- **Community health indicators** that offer readers a connection to the community for their analysis and planning: the data are broken down into beds, admissions, inpatient days, ER outpatient visits, and other indicators per 1000 population, as well as expense per capita.

- **Utilization, personnel and finance** by all MSAs in the United States.

- **Five-year trend data** on physician models, insurance products, and managed care contracts enable you to identify changes in relationships between hospitals and other health care systems and providers.

- **Tables 3 through 6 have been organized** to show breakdowns between inpatient and outpatient care to better reflect market shifts toward outpatient-centered care. Additional clarity is gained by the breakdown between total facility data (which includes nursing home type units under the control of the hospital) and hospital units (which exclude the nursing home data).

TABLE 6	**Sample State**				

U.S. Registered Community Hospitals
(Nonfederal, short-term general and other special hospitals)

Overview 2006-2010

	2010	2009	2008	2007	2006
Physician Models					
Independent Practice Association	14	17	17	17	14
Group Practice without Walls	4	5	5	8	4
Open Physician-Hospital Organization	20	21	24	23	18
Closed Physician-Hospital Organization	21	17	18	17	11
Management Service Organization	14	18	20	14	9
Integrated Salary Model	35	29	30	26	24
Equity Model	4	3	4	6	3
Foundation	9	8	23	21	19
Insurance Products					
Health Maintenance Organization	20	22	23	24	19
Preferred Provider Organization	39	47	52	53	37
Indemnity Fee for Service	7	12	14	12	6
Managed Care Contracts					
Health Maintenance Organization	64	67	62	49	42
Preferred Provider Organization	97	93	92	87	72

Example of five-year trend data

- **Facilities and Services information** on more than 100 categories of hospital facilities and services in Table 7. At a glance, you can determine the number and percentage of hospitals offering a specific service such as Oncology, Angioplasty, Palliative Care Program, Complementary Medicine, Women's Health Services and Tobacco Cessation.

- **Plus, System and Network involvement along with Group Purchasing Organizations** that demonstrate ways in which organizations are linked.

The survey instrument and the glossary

A good place to begin your analysis is the AHA Annual Survey instrument. Found on page 215, it includes the instructions, questions, and terms that were used to gather the data for fiscal year 2010. This can be extremely valuable for a clearer understanding of the data we collect and the tables presented in *AHA Hospital Statistics*.

Please also review the glossary in the back of the book. The glossary contains complete definitions for specific terms used in the tables and text of *AHA Hospital Statistics*. These definitions will clarify how terminology is being used.

As mentioned above, it is important to note that the primary focus of the most detailed data contained in *AHA Hospital Statistics* is community hospitals. As defined, community hospitals are all non-federal, short-term general and special hospitals whose facilities and services are available to the public. If the majority of a hospital's patients are admitted to units where the average length of stay is 30 days or less, a hospital may still be classified as short-term even if it includes a nursing- home-type unit. (For a more complete definition of community hospitals, please see the glossary definition, located on page 201.)

Getting the most out of *AHA Hospital Statistics*

This section of the book provides an introduction for getting the most out of your *AHA Hospital Statistics* 2012 edition. Here, you'll find a guide to the book, with insights into each table.

Equity model: An arrangement that allows established practitioners to become shareholders in a professional corporation in exchange for tangible and intangible assets of their existing practices.

Expenses: Includes all expenses for the reporting period including payroll, non-payroll, and all nonoperating expenses. *Payroll expenses* include all salaries and wages. *Non-payroll expenses* are all professional fees and those salary expenditures excluded from payroll. *Labor related expenses* are defined as payroll expenses plus employee benefits. *Non-labor related expenses* are all other non-payroll expenses. *Bad debt* has been reclassified from a "reduction in revenue" to an expense in accordance with the revised AICPA Audit Guide. However, for purposes of historical consistency, the expense total that appears throughout *AHA Hospital Statistics does not include "bad debt" as an expense item.* Note: Financial data may not add due to rounding.

Extracorporeal shock wave lithotripter (ESWL): A medical device used for treating stones in the kidney or urethra. The device disintegrates kidney stones noninvasively through the transmission of acoustic shock waves directed at the stones.

Fitness center: Provides exercise, testing, or evaluation programs and fitness activities to the community and hospital employees.

Example of Glossary definitions.

| Table 1 | Historical Trends in Utilization, Personnel, and Finances for Selected Years from 1946 through 2010 |

CLASSIFICATION	YEAR	HOSPITALS	BEDS (in thousands)	ADMISSIONS (in thousands)	AVERAGE DAILY CENSUS (in thousands)	ADJUSTED AVERAGE DAILY CENSUS (in thousands)
Total United States	1946	6,125	1,436	15,675	1,142	—
	1950	6,788	1,456	18,483	1,253	—
	1955	6,956	1,604	21,073	1,363	—
	1960	6,876	1,658	25,027	1,402	—
	1965	7,123	1,704	28,812	1,403	—
	1970	7,123	1,616	31,759	1,298	—
	1971	7,097	1,556	32,664	1,237	—
	1972	7,061	1,550	33,265	1,209	—
	1973	7,123	1,535	34,352	1,189	—
	1974	7,174	1,513	35,506	1,167	—
	1975	7,156	1,466	36,157	1,125	—
	1976	7,082	1,434	36,776	1,090	—
	1977	7,099	1,407	37,060	1,066	—
	1978	7,015	1,381	37,243	1,042	—
	1979	6,988	1,372	37,802	1,043	—
	1980	6,965	1,365	38,892	1,060	—
	1981	6,933	1,362	39,169	1,061	—
	1982	6,915	1,360	39,095	1,053	—
	1983	6,888	1,350	38,887	1,028	—
	1984	6,872	1,339	37,938	970	—
	1985	6,872	1,318	36,304	910	—
	1986	6,841	1,290	35,219	883	—
	1987	6,821	1,267	34,439	873	—
	1988	6,780	1,248	34,107	863	—
	1989	6,720	1,226	33,742	853	—
	1990	6,649	1,213	33,774	844	—
	1991	6,634	1,202	33,567	827	—
	1992	6,539	1,178	33,536	807	—
	1993	6,467	1,163	33,201	783	—
	1994	6,374	1,128	33,125	745	—
	1995	6,291	1,081	33,282	710	—
	1996	6,201	1,062	33,307	685	—
	1997	6,097	1,035	33,624	673	—
	1998	6,021	1,013	33,766	662	—
	1999	5,890	994	34,181	657	—
	2000	5,810	984	34,891	650	—
	2001	5,801	987	35,644	658	—
	2002	5,794	976	36,326	662	—
	2003	5,764	965	36,611	657	—
	2004	5,759	956	36,942	658	—
	2005	5,756	947	37,006	656	—

Example of Table 1

Table 1 — Historical Trends in Utilization, Personnel and Finances for Selected Years from 1946 through 2010

Table 1 at a Glance
This table is used to evaluate historical data and allows you to examine long-term trends in health care with data dating back more than sixty years. Table 1 reports on all AHA registered hospitals in the United States. One important note: To be considered an AHA-registered hospital, a hospital does not need to be an AHA member. Rather, the hospital must meet particular certification or satisfy a number of requirements. These Registration Requirements immediately follow this section and begin on page (xxiv.)

This table segments the data into various organizational structure categories. Here's a brief look at these different classifications:

- Total United States Hospitals
- Total Non-Federal Short-term and other special hospitals
- Community hospitals
- Non-government not-for-profit community hospitals
- Investor-owned (for-profit) community hospitals
- State and local government community hospitals

Table 1 also provides input on nationwide utilization, personnel and finance trends. You'll find answers to questions such as: *Over the past 25 years, what trends do I see comparing the average length of stay at government and non-government not-for-profit community hospitals and investor-owned for-profit community hospitals?* or *What has been the trend in outpatient visits?*

Table 2 — 2010 U.S. Registered Hospitals: Utilization, Personnel and Finances

Table 2 at a Glance
This table takes a closer look at U.S. Registered Hospitals for 2010. It offers a snapshot of utilization, personnel and finance statistics, and breaks down this information for specialty hospitals. In addition, this is the only table that outlines data on federal hospitals. You'll be able to use this table to better understand the number of beds set-up and staffed, how many personnel and trainees are on the payroll, and what the financial implications of these may be.

TABLE 3

TABLE 3

TOTAL UNITED STATES

U.S. Registered Community Hospitals
(Nonfederal, short-term general and other special hospitals)

Utilization, Personnel, Revenue and Expenses, Community Health Indicators 2006-2010

	2010	2009	2008	2007	2006
TOTAL FACILITY (Includes Hospital and Nursing Home Units)					
Utilization - Inpatient					
Beds	839,988	853,287	862,352	872,736	902,061
Admissions	31,811,673	31,576,960	31,098,959	30,945,357	30,718,136
Inpatient Days	191,430,450	192,504,015	193,747,004	199,876,367	207,180,278
Average Length of Stay	6.0	6.1	6.2	6.5	6.7
Inpatient Surgeries	9,735,705	9,509,081	9,545,612	9,700,613	9,833,938
Births	3,726,233	3,742,191	3,723,871	3,764,698	3,809,367
HOSPITAL UNIT (Excludes Separate Nursing Home Units)					
Utilization - Inpatient					
Beds	758,186	769,505	782,504	794,502	824,969
Admissions	31,265,867	31,047,930	30,652,820	30,577,564	30,403,766
Inpatient Days	165,644,176	165,605,620	168,189,130	174,898,504	182,702,882
Average Length of Stay	5.3	5.3	5.5	5.7	6.0
Personnel					
Total Full Time	3,235,153	3,183,730	3,154,603	3,166,729	3,147,922
Total Part Time	1,213,426	1,214,232	1,153,790	1,146,082	1,122,957
Revenue and Expenses - Totals					
(Includes Inpatient and Outpatient)					
Total Net Revenue	$333,054,828,642	$322,459,942,930	$310,513,291,998	$298,519,717,355	$285,858,018,951
Total Expenses	314,709,758,455	301,905,101,393	290,128,641,153	282,372,557,487	272,840,121,437

Example of Table 3. Helps contrast acute and long-term care

Table 3 — Total United States

Table 3 at a Glance

This table provides a look at all U.S. Registered Community Hospitals, in terms of general overview with utilization by inpatient and outpatient, personnel, revenue, expenses and community health indicators. It provides a snapshot of the past five years, allowing you to track emerging trends.

This national information can be compared to local or regional trends, for benchmarking:

- Both inpatient and outpatient information is included, for better evaluation of data.

- Reporting by total facility *Includes hospital and Nursing Home Units* and hospital unit only *Excludes Separate Nursing Home Units* helps contrast acute and long-term care.

- Community health indicators can help uncover trends and help determine future facility needs.

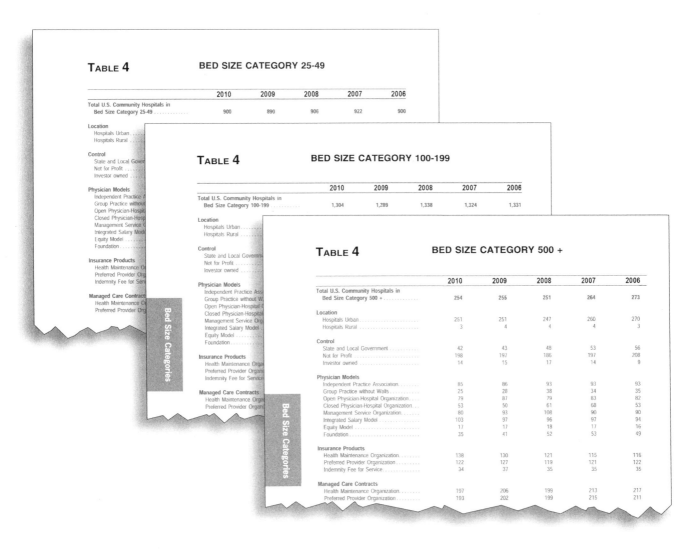

Example of Table 4. Compares facilities with peers.

Table 4 — Bed Size Categories

Table 4 at a Glance
This table provides a look at all U.S. Registered Community Hospitals, broken down by bed size. The table includes general overview, utilization, personnel, and revenue and expense information. These categories of bed sizes were developed by the AHA, and have become an industry standard. By categorizing each facility into a peer group, this table provides a snapshot of the past five years allowing you to compare facilities with their peers.

TABLE 5

U.S. CENSUS DIVISION 2: MIDDLE ATLANTIC

U.S. Registered Community Hospitals
(Nonfederal, short-term general and other special hospitals)

Utilization, Personnel, Revenue and Expenses, Community Health Indicators 2006-2010

	2010	2009	2008	2007	2006
COMMUNITY HEALTH INDICATORS PER 1000 POPULATION					
Total Population (in thousands) . . .	38,292	38,216	38,184	38,147	38,108
Inpatient					
Beds	3.6	3.8	3.9	4.0	4.1
Admissions	135.8	136.7	136.2	138.3	137.4
Inpatient Days	963.5	988.8	1,019.0	1,093.8	1,145.0
Inpatient Surgeries	42.2	41.4	41.2	42.7	43.6
Births	13.0	13.2	13.6	13.7	14.3
Outpatient					
Emergency Outpatient Visits	367.7	362.0	363.4	379.5	360.1
Other Outpatient Visits	1,970.9	1,802.3	1,767.7	1,680.3	1,573.9
Total Outpatient Visits	2,338.6	2,164.3	2,131.1	2,059.8	1,934.0
Outpatient Surgeries	67.8	62.4	59.9	55.4	53.5
Expense per Capita (per person)	$1,494.9	$1,462.7	$1,428.6	$1,429.8	$1,369.2

Example of Table 5. Uncovers trends to determine future facility needs.

Table 5 — U.S. Census Divisions

Table 5 at a Glance

This table provides a look at all U.S. Registered Community Hospitals, broken down by Census Division. The table includes general overview, utilization, personnel, and expenses, and community health indicator information. It provides a snapshot of the past five years, allowing you to track trends on a regional level. In addition, this allows you to compare this data to other population based health indicators, offering a more comprehensive look than the survey data alone. Community health indicators can help uncover trends and help determine future facility needs.

Table 6 — States

Table 6 at a Glance

This table provides a look at all U.S. Registered Community Hospitals, broken down by State. The table includes general overview, utilization, personnel, revenue and expenses, and community health indicator information. It provides a snapshot of the past five years, allowing you to track trends on a state level.

Note:

You can use the information in tables 3, 4, 5 and 6 to make accurate comparisons across Total U.S., Bed Size Category, Census Division and State.

Table 7 — 2010 Facilities and Services in the U.S. Census Divisions and States

Table 7 at a Glance

This table examines facilities and services by both Census Division and State. A comprehensive alphabetical guide helps make each facility or service easy to find. This table will allow you to better understand what service lines are emerging and how many facilities offer a particular service in a discrete state or region.

This collection of facilities and services information data is unique to *AHA Hospital Statistics* and the list is continually growing. Recent additions include:

- Rural health clinic
- Adult cardiology services
- Pediatric cardiology services
- Assistive technology center
- Electrodiagnostic services
- Prosthetic and orthotic services
- Adult cardiac electrophysiology
- Pediatric cardiac electrophysiology
- Optical colonoscopy
- Robot-assisted walking therapy
- Simulated rehabilitation environment

Example of Table 7.

These new categories reflect the trends as hospitals expand their service lines to mirror the needs of their patients. For example, services such as acupuncture or massage therapy are now accounted for in the Complementary Medicine service item.

This table can answer questions such as: *What percentage of hospitals in the United States offer complementary medicine or wound management?* or *How are these new services distributed by state?*

Table 8 — Utilization, Personnel and Finances in Community Hospitals by MSAs for 2010

Table 8 at a Glance

This table provides a look at all U.S. Registered Community Hospitals, broken down by Metropolitan Statistical Area (MSA). The table includes general overview, utilization, personnel, and finance information. It provides a snapshot of the past year.

Additional Resources

Again, in the back of the book you will find the comprehensive glossary and the 2010 annual survey questionnaire. The survey itself can be a valuable resource to understanding what was asked in order to gather the data in the book. This survey is also used to produce the *AHA Guide*® and AHA Annual Survey Database™.

Registration Requirements for Hospitals

AHA-Registered Hospitals

Any institution that can be classified as a hospital according to the requirements may be registered if it so desires. Membership in the American Hospital Association is not a prerequisite.

The American Hospital Association may, at the sole discretion of the Executive Committee of the Board of Trustees, grant, deny, or withdraw the registration of an institution.

An institution may be registered by the American Hospital Association as a hospital if it is accredited as a hospital by The Joint Commission or is certified as a provider of acute services under Title 18 of the Social Security Act and has provided the Association with documents verifying the accreditation or certification.

In lieu of the preceding accreditation or certification, an institution licensed as a hospital by the appropriate state agency may be registered by AHA as a hospital by meeting the following alternative requirements:

Function: The primary function of the institution is to provide patient services, diagnostic and therapeutic, for particular or general medical conditions.

1. The institution shall maintain at least six inpatient beds, which shall be continuously available for the care of patients who are nonrelated and who stay on the average in excess of 24 hours per admission.

2. The institution shall be constructed, equipped, and maintained to ensure the health and safety of patients and to provide uncrowded, sanitary facilities for the treatment of patients.

3. There shall be an identifiable governing authority legally and morally responsible for the conduct of the hospital.

4. There shall be a chief executive to whom the governing authority delegates the continuous responsibility for the operation of the hospital in accordance with established policy.

5. There shall be an organized medical staff of fully licensed physicians* that may include other licensed individuals permitted by law and by the hospital to provide patient care services independently in the hospital. The medical staff shall be accountable to the governing authority for maintaining proper standards of medical care, and it shall be governed by bylaws adopted by said staff and approved by the governing authority.

6. Each patient shall be admitted on the authority of a member of the medical staff who has been granted the privilege to admit patients to inpatient services in accordance with state law and criteria for standards of medical care established by the individual medical staff. Each patient's general medical condition is the responsibility of a qualified physician member of the medical staff. When nonphysician members of the medical staff are granted privileges to admit patients, provision is made for prompt medical evaluation of these patients by a qualified physician. Any graduate of a foreign medical school who is permitted to assume responsibilities for patient care shall possess a valid license to practice medicine, or shall be certified by the Educational Commission for Foreign Medical Graduates, or shall have qualified for and have successfully completed an academic year of supervised clinical training under the direction of a medical school approved by the Liaison Committee on GAT Medical Education.

7. Registered nurse supervision and other nursing services are continuous.

8. A current and complete‡ medical record shall be maintained by the institution for each patient and shall be available for reference.

9. Pharmacy service shall be maintained in the institution and shall be supervised by a registered pharmacist.

10. The institution shall provide patients with food service that meets their nutritional and therapeutic requirements; special diets shall also be available.

Types of Hospitals

In addition to meeting these 10 general registration requirements, hospitals are registered as one of four types of hospitals: general, special, rehabilitation and chronic disease, or psychiatric. The following type of hospital and special requirements for registration are employed:

General

The primary function of the institution is to provide patient services, diagnostic and therapeutic, for a variety of medical conditions. A general hospital also shall provide:

- diagnostic x-ray services with facilities and staff for a variety of procedures
- clinical laboratory service with facilities and staff for a variety of procedures and with anatomical pathology services regularly and conveniently available
- operating room service with facilities and staff.

Special

The primary function of the institution is to provide diagnostic and treatment services for patients who have specified medical conditions, both surgical and nonsurgical. A special hospital also shall provide:

- such diagnostic and treatment services as may be determined by the Executive Committee of the Board of Trustees of the American Hospital Association to be appropriate for the specified medical conditions for which medical services are provided shall be maintained in the institution with suitable facilities and staff. If such conditions do not normally require diagnostic x-ray service, laboratory service, or operating room service, and if any such services are therefore not maintained in the institution, there shall be written arrangements to make them available to patients requiring them.
- clinical laboratory services capable of providing tissue diagnosis when offering pregnancy termination services.

Rehabilitation and Chronic Disease

The primary function of the institution is to provide diagnostic and treatment services to handicapped or disabled individuals requiring restorative and adjustive services. A rehabilitation and chronic disease hospital also shall provide:

- arrangements for diagnostic x-ray services, as required, on a regular and conveniently available basis
- arrangements for clinical laboratory service, as required on a regular and conveniently available basis
- arrangements for operating room service, as required, on a regular and conveniently available basis
- a physical therapy service with suitable facilities and staff in the institution
- an occupational therapy service with suitable facilities and staff in the institution
- arrangements for psychological and social work services on a regular and conveniently available basis

---

* Physician—Term used to describe an individual with an M.D. or D.O. degree who is fully licensed to practice medicine in all its phases.

‡ The completed records in general shall contain at least the following: the patient's identifying data and consent forms, medical history, record of physical examination, physicians' progress notes, operative notes, nurses' notes, routine x-ray and laboratory reports, doctors' orders, and final diagnosis.

- arrangements for educational and vocational services on a regular and conveniently available basis
- written arrangements with a general hospital for the transfer of patients who require medical, obstetrical, or surgical services not available in the institution.

Psychiatric

The primary function of the institution is to provide diagnostic and treatment services for patients who have psychiatric-related illnesses. A psychiatric hospital also shall provide:

- arrangements for clinical laboratory service, as required, on a regular and conveniently available basis
- arrangements for diagnostic x-ray services, as required on a regular and conveniently available basis
- psychiatric, psychological, and social work service with facilities and staff in the institution
- arrangements for electroencephalograph services, as required, on a regular and conveniently available basis.
- written arrangements with a general hospital for the transfer of patients who require medical, obstetrical, or surgical services not available in the institution.

The American Hospital Association may, at the sole discretion of the Executive Committee of the Board of Trustees, grant, deny, or withdraw the registration of an institution.

Data Comparability

The economic climate, demographic characteristics, personnel issues, and health care financing and payment policies differ by region, state, and city across the country. *Differences in these factors must be taken into account when using the data.* In addition, the profiles of hospitals across comparison groups vary. For example, states will differ in terms of the number and percentage of hospitals by size, ownership, services provided, types of patients treated, and so forth. *Differences in these variables also must be taken into consideration when doing a comparative analysis.*

Notes on the Survey

The 2012 edition of *AHA Hospital Statistics*™ draws its data from the 2010 AHA Annual Survey of Hospitals. It is the statistical complement to the 2012 edition of the *AHA Guide®*, which contains selected data about individual hospitals.

The AHA Survey was mailed to all hospitals, both AHA-registered and nonregistered, in the U.S. and its associated areas: American Samoa, Guam, the Marshall Islands, Puerto Rico, and the Virgin Islands. U.S. government hospitals located outside the U.S. were not included. Overall, the average response rate over the past five years has been approximately 83 percent.

Reporting Period

In completing the survey, hospitals were requested to report data for a full year, in accord with their fiscal year, ending in 2010. The statistical table present data reported or estimated for a 12-month period, except for data on personnel, which represent situations as they existed at the end of the reporting period.

Respondents

Data for Tables 1 and 2 include 5,754 AHA-registered hospitals in the U.S. Data on community hospitals (nonfederal, short-term general and other special hospitals) only are presented in Tables 3-6, and Table 8.

It is important to note that the AHA-registered hospitals included in *AHA Hospital Statistics* are not necessarily identical to those included in *AHA Guide*. The institutions listed in the 2012 edition of AHA Guide include all of those institutions CMS certified, Joint Commission accredited, or AHA registered as of September 2010. Tables 1-6 in *AHA Hospital Statistics* present data for AHA-registered hospitals that were in operation during the 12-month reporting period ending 2010.

Estimates

Estimates were made of data for nonreporting hospitals and for reporting hospitals that submitted incomplete AHA Annual Survey questionnaires. Estimates were not made for beds, bassinets and facilities and services. Data for beds and bassinets of nonreporting hospitals were based on the most recent information from those hospitals. (Note that in all statistical tables, whenever bed-size categories are listed, all eight categories appear, whether or not there are hospitals in every category.)

Missing revenue, expenses, admissions, births, inpatient days, surgical operations, outpatient visits, and full-time-equivalent personnel values are estimates from regression models. For all other variables the estimates were based on ratios such as per bed averages derived from data reported by hospitals similar in size, control, major service provided, length of stay, and geographical characteristics to the hospitals that did not report this information.

Tables 1–2

Table

1

Historical Trends in Utilization, Personnel, and Finances for Selected Years from 1946 through 2010

Data are for all AHA-registered hospitals in the United States. Data are estimated for nonreporting hospitals with the exception of newborn and outpatient data before 1972. Personnel data exclude residents, interns, and students from 1952 on; personnel data include full-time personnel and full-time equivalents for part-time personnel from 1954 on. As a result of the AHA Annual Survey validation process, the New York state expense data from 1976 were revised after the 1977 edition was published. The revised figures are included below. In order to provide trend data on a consistent basis, the 1970 and 1971 psychiatric and long-term data have been slightly modified. The 1982 FTE figures have been updated to provide the most accurate data possible.

CLASSIFICATION	YEAR	HOSPITALS	BEDS (in thousands)	ADMISSIONS (in thousands)	AVERAGE DAILY CENSUS (in thousands)	ADJUSTED AVERAGE DAILY CENSUS (in thousands)	AVERAGE STAY (days)	OUTPATIENT VISITS (in thousands)	NEWBORNS		FTE PERSONNEL		TOTAL EXPENSES		
									Bassinets	Births	Number (in thousands)	Per 100 Adjusted Census	Amount (In Millions of dollars)	Adjusted per Inpatient Stay (dollars)	Adjusted per Inpatient Day (dollars)
Total United States	1946	6,125	1,436	15,675	1,142	—	—	—	85,585	2,135,327	830	—	$1,963	—	—
	1950	6,788	1,456	18,483	1,253	—	—	—	90,101	2,742,780	1,058	—	$3,651	—	—
	1955	6,956	1,604	21,073	1,363	—	—	—	98,823	3,476,753	1,301	—	$5,594	—	—
	1960	6,876	1,658	25,027	1,402	—	—	—	102,764	3,835,735	1,598	—	$8,421	—	—
	1965	7,123	1,704	28,812	1,403	—	—	125,793	101,287	3,565,344	1,952	—	$12,948	—	—
	1970	7,123	1,616	31,759	1,298	—	—	181,370	97,128	3,537,000	2,537	—	$25,556	—	—
	1971	7,097	1,556	32,664	1,237	—	—	199,725	94,344	3,464,513	2,589	—	$28,812	—	—
	1972	7,061	1,550	33,265	1,209	—	—	219,182	92,960	3,231,875	2,671	—	$32,667	—	—
	1973	7,123	1,535	34,352	1,189	—	—	233,555	90,071	3,087,210	2,769	—	$36,290	—	—
	1974	7,174	1,513	35,506	1,167	—	—	250,481	88,269	3,043,386	2,919	—	$41,406	—	—
	1975	7,156	1,466	36,157	1,125	—	—	254,844	86,875	3,091,629	3,023	—	$48,706	—	—
	1976	7,082	1,434	36,776	1,090	—	—	270,951	85,284	3,067,063	3,108	—	$56,005	—	—
	1977	7,099	1,407	37,060	1,066	—	—	263,775	83,193	3,223,699	3,213	—	$63,630	—	—
	1978	7,015	1,381	37,243	1,042	—	—	263,606	80,650	3,250,373	3,280	—	$70,927	—	—
	1979	6,988	1,372	37,802	1,043	—	—	262,009	79,720	3,376,467	3,382	—	$79,796	—	—
	1980	6,965	1,365	38,892	1,060	—	—	262,951	79,842	3,500,043	3,492	—	$91,886	—	—
	1981	6,933	1,362	39,169	1,061	—	—	265,332	78,823	3,558,274	3,661	—	$107,146	—	—
	1982	6,915	1,360	39,095	1,053	—	—	313,667	77,998	3,615,751	3,746	—	$123,219	—	—
	1983	6,888	1,350	38,887	1,028	—	—	273,168	77,837	3,596,146	3,707	—	$136,315	—	—
	1984	6,872	1,339	37,938	970	—	—	276,566	77,845	3,563,106	3,630	—	$144,114	—	—
	1985	6,872	1,318	36,304	910	—	—	282,140	77,202	3,630,961	3,625	—	$153,327	—	—
	1986	6,841	1,290	35,219	883	—	—	294,634	76,002	3,680,178	3,647	—	$165,194	—	—
	1987	6,821	1,267	34,439	873	—	—	310,707	74,770	3,698,294	3,742	—	$178,662	—	—
	1988	6,780	1,248	34,107	863	—	—	336,208	72,568	3,794,369	3,839	—	$196,704	—	—
	1989	6,720	1,226	33,742	853	—	—	352,248	71,491	3,920,384	3,937	—	$214,886	—	—
	1990	6,649	1,213	33,774	844	—	—	368,184	70,539	4,046,704	4,063	—	$234,870	—	—
	1991	6,634	1,202	33,567	827	—	—	387,675	69,464	4,047,504	4,165	—	$258,508	—	—
	1992	6,539	1,178	33,536	807	—	—	417,874	69,052	4,007,179	4,236	—	$282,531	—	—
	1993	6,467	1,163	33,201	783	—	—	435,619	67,911	3,949,788	4,289	—	$301,538	—	—
	1994	6,374	1,128	33,125	745	—	—	453,584	67,311	3,886,667	4,270	—	$310,834	—	—
	1995	6,291	1,081	33,282	710	—	—	483,195	66,256	3,833,132	4,273	—	$320,252	—	—
	1996	6,201	1,062	33,307	685	—	—	505,455	65,138	3,790,678	4,276	—	$330,531	—	—
	1997	6,097	1,035	33,624	673	—	—	520,600	64,649	3,811,522	4,333	—	$342,334	—	—
	1998	6,021	1,013	33,766	662	—	—	545,481	63,485	3,795,212	4,407	—	$355,450	—	—
	1999	5,890	994	34,181	657	—	—	573,461	62,714	3,829,881	4,369	—	$372,933	—	—
	2000	5,810	984	34,891	650	—	—	592,673	61,915	3,940,017	4,454	—	$395,391	—	—
	2001	5,801	987	35,644	658	—	—	612,276	61,527	3,929,733	4,535	—	$426,849	—	—
	2002	5,794	976	36,326	662	—	—	640,515	62,151	3,934,421	4,610	—	$462,222	—	—
	2003	5,764	965	36,611	657	—	—	648,560	60,699	3,976,886	4,651	—	$498,104	—	—
	2004	5,759	956	36,942	658	—	—	662,131	59,660	3,965,906	4,696	—	$533,853	—	—
	2005	5,756	947	37,006	656	—	—	673,689	59,073	4,048,442	4,791	—	$570,534	—	—
	2006	5,747	947	37,189	653	—	—	690,425	58,670	4,126,598	4,907	—	$607,355	—	—
	2007	5,708	945	37,120	649	—	—	693,510	58,429	4,128,796	5,024	—	$641,124	—	—
	2008	5,815	951	37,529	649	—	—	709,960	58,133	4,109,081	5,116	—	$690,074	—	—
	2009	5,795	944	37,480	641	—	—	741,551	58,078	4,001,748	5,178	—	$726,671	—	—
	2010	5,754	942	36,915	627	—	—	750,408	57,396	3,871,751	5,184	—	$750,602	—	—

Table 1 (Continued)

CLASSIFICATION: Total nonfederal short-term general and other special

YEAR	HOSPITALS	BEDS (in thousands)	ADMISSIONS (in thousands)	AVERAGE DAILY CENSUS (in thousands)	ADJUSTED AVERAGE DAILY CENSUS (in thousands)	AVERAGE LENGTH OF STAY (days)	OUTPATIENT VISITS (in thousands)	NEWBORNS Bassinets	NEWBORNS Births	FTE PERSONNEL Number (in thousands)	FTE PERSONNEL Per 100 Adjusted Census	EXPENSES Amount (In Millions of dollars)	EXPENSES Adjusted per Inpatient Stay (dollars)	EXPENSES Adjusted per Inpatient Day (dollars)
1946	4,444	473	13,655	341	—	9.1	—	80,987	2,087,503	505	—	$1,169	—	—
1950	5,031	505	16,663	372	—	8.1	—	86,019	2,660,982	662	—	$2,120	—	—
1955	5,237	568	19,100	407	—	7.8	—	93,868	3,304,451	826	—	$3,434	—	—
1960	5,407	639	22,970	477	—	7.6	—	98,127	3,678,051	1,080	—	$5,617	—	—
1965	5,736	741	26,463	563	620	7.8	92,631	96,782	3,413,370	1,386	224	$9,147	$316.37	$40.56
1970	5,859	848	29,252	662	727	8.2	133,545	93,079	3,403,064	1,929	265	$19,560	$604.59	$73.73
1971	5,865	867	30,142	665	736	8.0	148,423	90,444	3,337,605	1,999	272	$22,400	$667.44	$83.43
1972	5,843	884	30,777	664	739	7.9	166,983	89,315	3,119,446	2,056	278	$25,549	$747.42	$94.61
1973	5,891	903	31,761	681	768	7.8	178,939	86,851	2,987,089	2,149	280	$28,496	$793.88	$101.78
1974	5,977	931	32,943	701	793	7.8	194,838	85,208	2,947,342	2,289	289	$32,751	$883.04	$113.21
1975	5,979	947	33,519	708	806	7.7	196,311	83,834	2,998,590	2,399	298	$39,110	$1,024.72	$133.08
1976	5,956	961	34,068	715	816	7.7	207,725	82,307	2,962,305	2,483	304	$45,402	$1,172.25	$152.24
1977	5,973	974	34,353	717	820	7.6	204,238	80,228	3,117,756	2,581	315	$51,832	$1,316.70	$173.25
1978	5,935	980	34,575	720	841	7.6	204,461	78,090	3,156,570	2,662	323	$58,348	$1,470.13	$193.81
1979	5,923	988	35,160	729	841	7.6	203,873	77,277	3,287,157	2,762	328	$66,184	$1,631.16	$215.75
1980	5,904	992	36,198	748	861	7.6	206,752	77,539	3,408,699	2,879	334	$76,970	$1,844.19	$244.44
1981	5,879	1,007	36,494	764	876	7.6	206,729	76,567	3,465,683	3,039	347	$90,739	$2,167.70	$283.94
1982	5,863	1,015	36,429	763	882	7.6	250,888	75,739	3,514,761	3,110	353	$105,094	$2,493.09	$326.68
1983	5,843	1,021	36,201	750	869	7.6	213,995	75,471	3,490,629	3,102	357	$116,632	$2,775.55	$368.01
1984	5,814	1,020	35,202	703	824	7.3	216,474	75,587	3,456,467	3,023	367	$123,550	$2,984.00	$409.85
1985	5,784	1,003	33,501	650	780	7.1	222,773	74,899	3,521,296	3,003	385	$130,700	$3,238.94	$459.57
1986	5,728	982	32,410	631	774	7.1	234,270	73,688	3,584,530	3,032	392	$140,907	$3,529.60	$499.19
1987	5,659	961	31,633	624	780	7.2	247,704	72,516	3,602,416	3,120	400	$152,909	$3,848.79	$536.96
1988	5,579	949	31,480	622	795	7.2	271,436	70,361	3,706,748	3,209	404	$168,941	$4,194.39	$581.08
1989	5,497	936	31,141	619	805	7.3	287,909	69,436	3,831,051	3,307	411	$185,204	$4,572.23	$630.59
1990	5,420	929	31,203	620	820	7.3	302,691	68,443	3,958,646	3,423	417	$203,927	$4,929.93	$681.52
1991	5,370	926	31,084	612	828	7.2	323,202	67,440	3,965,489	3,539	427	$225,230	$5,345.63	$745.37
1992	5,321	923	31,053	606	832	7.1	349,397	67,095	3,925,024	3,624	436	$248,318	$5,788.52	$815.99
1993	5,289	921	30,770	593	834	7.0	368,358	66,060	3,870,392	3,681	441	$266,382	$6,120.94	$874.98
1994	5,256	904	30,739	569	814	6.8	384,880	65,728	3,809,367	3,697	454	$276,148	$6,230.33	$929.65
1995	5,220	874	30,966	549	811	6.5	415,710	64,742	3,764,756	3,718	458	$286,073	$6,220.54	$966.79
1996	5,160	864	31,116	531	800	6.2	440,845	63,646	3,723,907	3,728	466	$293,920	$6,225.95	$1,005.45
1997	5,082	855	31,595	529	813	6.1	450,907	63,247	3,742,240	3,794	467	$306,088	$6,266.24	$1,031.68
1998	5,039	842	31,830	527	821	6.0	474,366	62,162	3,726,234	3,835	467	$319,035	$6,387.53	$1,064.93
1999	4,977	831	32,377	527	835	5.9	495,850	61,534	3,760,295	3,840	460	$335,405	$6,512.44	$1,101.47
2000	4,934	825	33,102	527	850	5.8	522,970	60,845	3,880,166	3,916	461	$356,757	$6,650.68	$1,147.99
2001	4,927	828	33,834	534	866	5.8	539,316	60,454	3,873,395	3,990	461	$383,911	$6,979.29	$1,216.04
2002	4,949	823	34,501	541	887	5.7	557,336	59,974	3,870,191	4,072	459	$416,791	$7,353.17	$1,288.63
2003	4,918	815	34,800	540	895	5.7	563,804	59,662	3,915,842	4,112	459	$451,403	$7,798.19	$1,378.78
2004	4,942	810	35,098	542	910	5.6	573,126	58,710	3,931,508	4,151	456	$481,517	$8,168.06	$1,449.90
2005	4,956	804	35,265	542	930	5.6	587,296	58,195	3,987,766	4,260	458	$516,172	$8,538.30	$1,521.58
2006	4,947	805	35,403	540	940	5.6	599,597	57,832	4,075,193	4,347	462	$552,276	$8,972.85	$1,610.76
2007	4,915	803	35,370	535	944	5.5	603,411	57,546	4,077,962	4,468	473	$583,550	$9,377.82	$1,694.38
2008	5,026	810	35,776	538	963	5.5	624,185	57,301	4,073,724	4,552	473	$626,823	$9,789.69	$1,780.45
2009	5,023	807	35,603	529	973	5.4	643,420	57,302	3,960,432	4,594	472	$657,242	$10,042.56	$1,851.44
2010	4,995	806	35,160	520	974	5.4	651,617	56,610	3,818,399	4,603	473	$678,254	$10,316.07	$1,908.59

Table 1 (Continued)

CLASSIFICATION	YEAR	HOSPITALS	BEDS (in thousands)	ADMISSIONS (in thousands)	AVERAGE DAILY CENSUS (in thousands)	ADJUSTED AVERAGE DAILY CENSUS (in thousands)	AVERAGE LENGTH OF STAY (days)	OUTPATIENT VISITS (in thousands)	NEWBORNS		FTE PERSONNEL		EXPENSES		
									Bassinets	Births	Number (in thousands)	Per 100 Adjusted Census	Amount (In Millions of dollars)	Adjusted per Inpatient Stay (dollars)	Adjusted per Inpatient Day (dollars)
Total community hospitals	1975	5,875	942	33,435	706	798	7.7	190,672	83,829	2,998,552	2,392	300	$38,962	$1,030.34	$133.81
	1976	5,857	956	33,979	713	810	7.7	201,247	82,296	2,962,216	2,475	306	$45,240	$1,176.25	$152.76
	1979	5,842	984	35,099	727	833	7.6	198,778	77,266	3,287,012	2,756	331	$66,004	$1,641.67	$217.34
	1980	5,830	988	36,143	747	857	7.6	202,310	77,522	3,408,482	2,873	335	$76,851	$1,851.04	$245.12
	1981	5,813	1,003	36,438	763	873	7.6	202,768	76,561	3,465,401	3,033	347	$90,572	$2,171.20	$284.33
	1982	5,801	1,012	36,379	762	878	7.6	248,124	75,733	3,514,457	3,103	353	$104,876	$2,500.52	$327.37
	1983	5,783	1,018	36,152	749	864	7.6	210,044	75,465	3,490,254	3,096	358	$116,438	$2,789.18	$369.49
	1984	5,759	1,017	35,155	702	820	7.3	211,961	75,581	3,456,308	3,017	368	$123,336	$2,995.38	$411.10
	1985	5,732	1,001	33,449	649	777	7.1	218,716	74,893	3,521,135	2,997	386	$130,499	$3,244.74	$460.19
	1986	5,678	978	32,379	629	770	7.1	231,912	73,682	3,584,408	3,025	393	$140,654	$3,532.51	$500.81
	1987	5,611	958	31,601	622	776	7.2	245,524	72,510	3,602,296	3,114	401	$152,585	$3,850.16	$538.96
	1988	5,533	947	31,453	620	787	7.2	269,129	70,325	3,706,402	3,205	407	$168,722	$4,206.73	$586.33
	1989	5,455	933	31,116	618	796	7.2	285,712	69,405	3,830,615	3,303	415	$184,898	$4,587.87	$636.96
	1990	5,384	927	31,181	619	813	7.2	301,329	68,412	3,958,263	3,420	421	$203,693	$4,946.68	$686.83
	1991	5,342	924	31,064	611	820	7.2	322,048	67,434	3,965,396	3,535	431	$225,023	$5,359.56	$752.10
	1992	5,292	921	31,034	604	827	7.1	348,522	67,089	3,924,944	3,620	437	$248,095	$5,794.43	$819.83
	1993	5,261	919	30,748	592	828	7.0	366,885	66,054	3,870,376	3,677	444	$266,089	$6,132.06	$880.52
	1994	5,229	902	30,718	568	812	6.7	382,924	65,722	3,809,367	3,692	455	$275,779	$6,229.83	$930.71
	1995	5,194	873	30,945	548	809	6.5	414,345	64,736	3,764,698	3,714	459	$285,588	$6,215.51	$967.69
	1996	5,134	862	31,099	531	799	6.2	439,863	63,640	3,723,871	3,725	466	$293,755	$6,224.94	$1,006.14
	1997	5,057	853	31,577	528	811	6.1	450,140	63,241	3,742,191	3,790	467	$305,763	$6,261.93	$1,032.70
	1998	5,015	840	31,812	525	819	6.0	474,193	62,156	3,726,233	3,831	468	$318,834	$6,385.99	$1,066.96
	1999	4,956	830	32,359	526	833	5.9	495,346	61,528	3,760,295	3,838	461	$335,246	$6,511.72	$1,102.61
	2000	4,915	824	33,089	526	849	5.8	521,404	60,839	3,880,166	3,911	461	$356,564	$6,648.82	$1,149.40
	2001	4,908	826	33,814	533	865	5.7	538,480	60,448	3,873,395	3,987	461	$383,735	$6,979.53	$1,217.27
	2002	4,927	821	34,478	540	886	5.7	556,404	59,974	3,870,191	4,069	459	$416,591	$7,354.60	$1,289.87
	2003	4,895	813	34,783	539	894	5.7	563,186	59,662	3,915,842	4,109	460	$450,124	$7,796.41	$1,379.48
	2004	4,919	808	35,086	541	909	5.6	571,569	58,710	3,931,508	4,148	456	$481,247	$8,165.55	$1,450.35
	2005	4,936	802	35,239	540	929	5.6	584,429	58,195	3,987,766	4,257	458	$515,740	$8,534.90	$1,522.42
	2006	4,927	803	35,378	538	939	5.6	599,553	57,832	4,075,193	4,343	463	$551,835	$8,970.31	$1,612.23
	2007	4,897	801	35,346	533	943	5.5	603,300	57,546	4,077,962	4,465	474	$583,252	$9,377.17	$1,696.10
	2008	5,010	808	35,761	536	962	5.5	624,098	57,301	4,073,724	4,550	473	$626,577	$9,788.25	$1,782.28
	2009	5,008	806	35,527	528	970	5.4	641,953	57,282	3,959,605	4,585	472	$656,156	$10,045.15	$1,852.59
	2010	4,985	805	35,149	520	973	5.4	651,424	56,610	3,818,399	4,600	473	$677,968	$10,313.44	$1,909.64

Table 1 (Continued)

Nongovernment not-for-profit community hospitals

YEAR	HOSPITALS	BEDS (in thousands)	ADMISSIONS (in thousands)	AVERAGE DAILY CENSUS (in thousands)	ADJUSTED AVERAGE DAILY CENSUS (in thousands)	AVERAGE LENGTH OF STAY (days)	OUTPATIENT VISITS (in thousands)	NEWBORNS Bassinets	NEWBORNS Births	FTE PERSONNEL Number (in thousands)	FTE PERSONNEL Per 100 Adjusted Census	EXPENSES Amount (In Millions of dollars)	EXPENSES Adjusted per Inpatient Stay (dollars)	EXPENSES Adjusted per Inpatient Day (dollars)
1975	3,339	658	23,722	510	574	7.8	131,435	57,496	2,131,057	1,712	298	$27,938	$1,040.21	$133.36
1976	3,345	670	24,082	517	586	7.9	140,914	56,442	2,100,917	1,791	306	$32,764	$1,208.23	$152.94
1979	3,330	690	24,874	528	603	7.7	139,565	52,859	2,308,548	1,999	332	$47,937	$1,684.40	$218.06
1980	3,322	692	25,566	542	621	7.7	142,156	52,659	2,389,478	2,086	336	$55,780	$1,901.64	$245.74
1981	3,340	706	25,945	555	636	7.8	143,380	52,302	2,455,033	2,213	399	$66,267	$2,225.17	$285.64
1982	3,338	712	25,898	553	637	7.8	176,245	51,566	2,483,345	2,265	355	$76,806	$2,572.93	$330.41
1983	3,347	718	25,827	544	629	7.7	150,839	51,649	2,465,604	2,270	362	$85,637	$2,868.80	$373.78
1984	3,351	716	25,236	512	598	7.4	153,281	51,491	2,446,540	2,222	372	$90,814	$3,072.51	$415.04
1985	3,349	707	24,179	476	569	7.2	158,953	51,424	2,507,288	2,216	389	$96,150	$3,307.41	$462.69
1986	3,323	689	23,483	460	563	7.2	167,633	50,885	2,547,170	2,241	398	$103,524	$3,589.64	$503.64
1987	3,274	673	22,937	455	566	7.2	177,413	50,133	2,557,294	2,298	406	$112,325	$3,914.23	$543.67
1988	3,242	668	22,939	456	577	7.3	195,363	48,828	2,653,794	2,373	412	$124,703	$4,272.95	$591.13
1989	3,220	661	22,792	455	584	7.3	209,191	48,305	2,751,426	2,454	420	$136,889	$4,649.22	$642.45
1990	3,191	657	22,878	455	596	7.3	221,073	47,441	2,833,204	2,533	424	$150,673	$5,001.24	$692.36
1991	3,175	656	22,964	451	603	7.2	238,204	47,229	2,845,995	2,624	435	$166,806	$5,393.30	$758.21
1992	3,173	656	23,056	445	606	7.1	257,887	47,185	2,846,386	2,692	443	$183,793	$5,808.80	$828.44
1993	3,154	651	22,749	432	602	6.9	270,138	46,214	2,802,164	2,711	451	$197,187	$6,177.69	$897.70
1994	3,139	637	22,704	413	589	6.6	282,653	46,381	2,792,116	2,719	462	$204,219	$6,256.72	$950.31
1995	3,092	610	22,557	393	578	6.4	303,851	45,198	2,725,641	2,702	468	$209,614	$6,279.17	$994.39
1996	3,045	598	22,542	379	567	6.1	320,746	44,650	2,683,750	2,711	478	$215,950	$6,344.05	$1,042.04
1997	3,000	591	22,905	376	575	6.0	330,215	44,484	2,698,086	2,765	481	$225,287	$6,392.74	$1,074.26
1998	3,026	588	23,282	377	587	5.9	352,114	44,087	2,715,958	2,834	483	$237,978	$6,525.68	$1,110.50
1999	3,012	587	23,871	381	605	5.8	370,784	44,172	2,746,453	2,862	473	$251,534	$6,607.51	$1,139.89
2000	3,003	583	24,452	382	618	5.7	393,168	43,655	2,833,615	2,919	472	$267,051	$6,717.48	$1,182.32
2001	2,998	585	24,983	385	628	5.6	404,901	43,640	2,829,691	2,971	473	$287,250	$7,051.76	$1,255.25
2002	3,025	582	25,425	391	646	5.6	416,910	43,241	2,820,159	3,039	471	$312,726	$7,457.84	$1,328.81
2003	2,984	575	25,668	389	647	5.5	424,215	42,965	2,854,764	3,059	473	$337,696	$7,904.93	$1,429.62
2004	2,967	568	25,757	388	655	5.5	430,262	41,968	2,844,617	3,077	470	$359,414	$8,266.64	$1,501.09
2005	2,958	561	25,881	388	667	5.5	441,653	41,585	2,876,677	3,155	473	$385,993	$8,670.83	$1,585.34
2006	2,919	559	25,798	385	671	5.4	453,501	40,888	2,905,275	3,207	478	$412,868	$9,189.58	$1,685.62
2007	2,913	554	25,752	380	673	5.4	455,825	40,681	2,907,002	3,286	488	$436,319	$9,592.93	$1,776.06
2008	2,923	557	25,899	380	683	5.4	469,804	40,567	2,901,854	3,340	489	$468,080	$10,080.50	$1,875.78
2009	2,918	556	25,783	375	690	5.3	485,935	40,467	2,822,527	3,369	488	$492,853	$10,379.09	$1,956.71
2010	2,904	556	25,532	368	691	5.3	494,178	39,946	2,750,163	3,388	490	$510,744	$10,651.81	$2,025.05

Table 1 (Continued)

Investor-owned (for-profit) community hospitals

CLASSIFICATION / YEAR	HOSPITALS	BEDS (in thousands)	ADMISSIONS (in thousands)	AVERAGE DAILY CENSUS (in thousands)	ADJUSTED AVERAGE DAILY CENSUS (in thousands)	AVERAGE LENGTH OF STAY (days)	OUTPATIENT VISITS (in thousands)	NEWBORNS		FTE PERSONNEL		EXPENSES		
								Bassinets	Births	Number (in thousands)	Per 100 Adjusted Census	Amount (In Millions of dollars)	Adjusted per Inpatient Stay (dollars)	Adjusted per Inpatient Day (dollars)
1975	775	73	2,646	48	53	6.6	7,713	4,062	141,392	139	263	$2,561	$876.48	$132.80
1976	752	76	2,734	50	54	6.6	8,048	4,044	144,751	147	272	$3,085	$1,031.91	$156.35
1979	727	83	2,963	53	59	6.6	9,289	4,110	174,843	174	300	$4,820	$1,476.42	$225.87
1980	730	87	3,165	57	62	6.5	9,696	4,439	199,722	189	304	$5,847	$1,675.85	$257.12
1981	729	88	3,239	58	63	6.5	9,961	4,523	207,405	203	322	$6,856	$1,952.56	$299.02
1982	748	91	3,316	60	66	6.6	13,193	4,736	219,675	212	320	$8,177	$2,224.75	$340.03
1983	757	94	3,299	59	66	6.5	10,389	5,039	228,883	213	323	$9,208	$2,517.53	$385.42
1984	786	100	3,314	57	64	6.3	11,090	5,807	242,088	214	335	$10,251	$2,748.51	$438.30
1985	805	104	3,242	54	63	6.1	12,378	6,117	266,839	221	350	$11,486	$3,033.06	$500.48
1986	834	107	3,231	54	65	6.1	14,896	6,305	291,112	229	354	$12,987	$3,341.79	$552.40
1987	828	106	3,157	54	66	6.2	16,566	6,391	306,492	242	367	$14,067	$3,617.19	$585.01
1988	790	104	3,090	53	66	6.2	17,926	6,254	308,828	249	379	$15,545	$4,022.77	$649.33
1989	769	102	3,071	53	67	6.3	19,341	6,354	325,711	261	390	$17,240	$4,406.20	$707.90
1990	749	101	3,066	54	69	6.4	20,110	6,261	340,555	273	396	$18,822	$4,727.27	$751.55
1991	738	100	3,016	52	69	6.3	21,174	6,358	359,115	281	409	$20,516	$5,133.53	$820.19
1992	723	99	2,969	51	69	6.3	22,900	6,519	357,776	285	412	$22,496	$5,548.24	$888.73
1993	717	99	2,946	51	69	6.2	24,936	6,395	363,358	289	417	$23,077	$5,643.21	$914.39
1994	719	101	3,035	50	70	6.1	26,443	6,329	354,477	302	434	$23,445	$5,528.91	$923.90
1995	752	106	3,428	55	77	5.8	31,940	7,164	408,339	343	443	$26,653	$5,425.20	$946.99
1996	759	109	3,684	56	82	5.6	37,347	7,441	444,697	359	437	$28,385	$5,207.44	$945.49
1997	797	115	3,953	60	89	5.5	40,919	8,026	465,919	385	433	$31,179	$5,218.69	$961.96
1998	771	113	3,971	60	90	5.5	42,072	7,895	466,025	383	425	$31,732	$5,262.44	$968.00
1999	747	107	3,905	58	86	5.5	39,896	7,486	467,585	362	422	$31,179	$5,350.07	$999.03
2000	749	110	4,141	61	90	5.4	43,378	7,792	503,497	378	418	$34,969	$5,642.18	$1,057.32
2001	754	109	4,197	63	92	5.4	44,706	7,413	494,669	379	413	$37,348	$5,971.81	$1,121.31
2002	766	108	4,365	64	93	5.3	45,215	7,467	496,988	380	407	$40,082	$6,161.44	$1,180.83
2003	790	110	4,481	65	95	5.3	44,246	7,491	515,693	391	411	$43,953	$6,589.91	$1,264.50
2004	835	113	4,599	68	100	5.4	44,962	7,763	534,503	406	406	$48,971	$7,139.13	$1,362.42
2005	868	114	4,618	68	101	5.3	46,016	7,714	546,307	421	418	$51,833	$7,351.96	$1,412.74
2006	890	115	4,735	68	103	5.2	44,237	8,012	574,113	423	413	$55,030	$7,422.08	$1,471.53
2007	873	116	4,626	66	101	5.2	43,943	7,760	555,670	432	429	$56,405	$7,823.44	$1,535.98
2008	982	121	4,839	70	109	5.3	44,897	7,791	562,711	450	414	$61,762	$7,984.62	$1,555.55
2009	998	122	4,887	70	112	5.3	47,281	7,965	553,233	464	414	$64,367	$8,037.18	$1,573.64
2010	1,013	125	4,925	71	113	5.3	48,201	7,965	525,427	474	420	$67,168	$8,336.16	$1,628.90

Table 1 (Continued)

CLASSIFICATION	YEAR	HOSPITALS	BEDS (in thousands)	ADMISSIONS (in thousands)	AVERAGE DAILY CENSUS (in thousands)	ADJUSTED AVERAGE DAILY CENSUS (in thousands)	AVERAGE LENGTH OF STAY (days)	OUTPATIENT VISITS (in thousands)	NEWBORNS Bassinets	NEWBORNS Births	FTE PERSONNEL Number (in thousands)	FTE PERSONNEL Per 100 Adjusted Census	EXPENSES Amount (in Millions of dollars)	EXPENSES Adjusted per Inpatient Stay (dollars)	EXPENSES Adjusted per Inpatient Day (dollars)
State and local government community hospitals	1975	1,761	210	7,067	148	171	7.6	51,525	22,271	726,103	540	316	$8,463	$1,030.86	$135.64
	1976	1,760	210	7,163	146	170	7.5	52,286	21,810	716,548	537	315	$9,391	$1,132.50	$151.00
	1979	1,785	211	7,262	146	171	7.4	49,924	20,297	803,621	583	341	$13,247	$1,561.04	$211.89
	1980	1,778	209	7,413	149	174	7.3	50,459	20,424	819,282	598	343	$15,204	$1,750.13	$238.63
	1981	1,744	210	7,255	150	174	7.6	49,427	19,736	802,963	618	354	$17,449	$2,071.57	$274.25
	1982	1,715	210	7,165	149	175	7.6	58,685	19,431	811,437	627	320	$19,893	$2,364.09	$311.56
	1983	1,679	207	7,025	145	170	7.6	48,816	18,777	795,767	613	360	$21,593	$2,621.28	$347.56
	1984	1,622	201	6,606	133	158	7.3	47,590	18,283	767,680	581	368	$22,271	$2,823.13	$385.17
	1985	1,578	189	6,028	119	145	7.2	47,386	17,352	747,008	561	387	$22,863	$3,106.14	$432.84
	1986	1,521	182	5,665	114	142	7.4	49,383	16,492	746,126	555	391	$24,143	$3,404.69	$466.17
	1987	1,509	180	5,507	113	144	7.5	51,544	15,986	738,510	573	399	$26,192	$3,717.77	$499.33
	1988	1,501	175	5,424	112	145	7.6	55,840	15,243	743,780	583	403	$28,474	$4,033.67	$538.63
	1989	1,466	170	5,253	110	145	7.7	57,179	14,746	753,478	589	406	$30,769	$4,430.12	$582.15
	1990	1,444	169	5,236	111	148	7.7	60,146	14,710	784,504	614	415	$34,198	$4,837.76	$634.45
	1991	1,429	168	5,084	108	148	7.8	62,670	13,847	760,286	630	424	$37,701	$5,339.75	$695.89
	1992	1,396	166	5,008	108	152	7.9	67,734	13,385	720,782	643	424	$41,806	$5,870.76	$753.92
	1993	1,390	169	5,054	109	157	7.8	71,811	13,445	704,854	676	430	$45,825	$6,205.52	$799.73
	1994	1,371	164	4,979	104	154	7.6	73,828	13,012	662,774	672	438	$48,115	$6,513.39	$858.62
	1995	1,350	157	4,961	100	154	7.4	78,554	12,374	630,718	670	435	$49,322	$6,445.18	$877.85
	1996	1,330	155	4,873	96	150	7.2	81,770	11,549	595,424	654	437	$49,420	$6,418.65	$903.41
	1997	1,260	148	4,720	92	148	7.1	79,007	10,731	578,186	640	433	$49,298	$6,475.07	$913.62
	1998	1,218	139	4,559	87	142	7.0	80,008	10,174	544,250	614	433	$49,123	$6,612.23	$949.36
	1999	1,197	136	4,583	86	143	6.9	84,667	9,870	546,257	614	430	$52,534	$6,923.35	$1,006.91
	2000	1,163	131	4,496	83	140	6.7	84,858	9,392	543,054	614	438	$54,544	$7,106.05	$1,063.75
	2001	1,156	132	4,634	85	145	6.7	88,873	9,395	549,035	637	438	$59,137	$7,400.01	$1,113.79
	2002	1,136	130	4,688	84	147	6.6	94,280	9,266	553,044	651	442	$63,783	$7,772.93	$1,188.12
	2003	1,121	129	4,634	84	152	6.6	94,725	9,206	545,385	658	434	$68,475	$8,205.10	$1,237.64
	2004	1,117	128	4,730	85	154	6.5	96,345	8,979	552,388	666	431	$72,861	$8,473.18	$1,291.06
	2005	1,110	128	4,740	85	161	6.5	96,760	8,896	564,782	681	424	$77,914	$8,793.26	$1,329.64
	2006	1,119	128	4,848	86	165	6.5	101,845	8,932	595,805	713	433	$83,974	$9,147.40	$1,400.09
	2007	1,111	131	4,967	87	169	6.4	103,532	9,105	615,290	747	443	$90,528	$9,523.22	$1,472.26
	2008	1,105	131	5,023	86	170	6.3	109,398	8,943	609,159	760	446	$96,735	$9,826.94	$1,552.32
	2009	1,092	127	4,857	83	168	6.2	108,738	8,850	583,845	751	447	$98,937	$10,067.96	$1,611.31
	2010	1,068	125	4,693	80	169	6.2	109,045	8,699	542,809	738	437	$100,056	$10,283.35	$1,624.93

Table **2**

2010 U.S. Registered Hospitals: Utilization, Personnel, and Finances

Excludes U.S.-Associated Areas, Puerto Rico, and nonregistered hospitals.

CLASSIFICATION	HOSPITALS	BEDS	ADMISSIONS	INPATIENT DAYS	ADJUSTED PATIENT DAYS	AVERAGE DAILY CENSUS	ADJUSTED AVERAGE DAILY CENSUS	AVERAGE STAY (days)	SURGICAL OPERATIONS	OUTPATIENT VISITS Emergency	OUTPATIENT VISITS Total	NEWBORNS Bassinets	NEWBORNS Births
UNITED STATES	5,754	941,995	36,915,331	228,847,095	—	627,092	—	—	28,019,014	131,543,381	750,407,889	57,396	3,871,751
6-24 Beds	465	7,932	227,349	988,879	—	2,718	—	—	314,829	2,153,464	13,156,438	478	14,722
25-49	1,266	41,088	1,257,204	6,998,306	—	19,192	—	—	1,404,252	8,448,913	52,439,575	2,961	117,753
50-99	1,191	85,742	2,531,946	18,214,582	—	49,927	—	—	2,260,034	12,463,317	71,796,010	5,413	242,374
100-199	1,216	173,915	6,610,145	39,882,492	—	109,333	—	—	5,288,694	27,131,343	140,711,627	11,997	714,633
200-299	684	166,866	6,931,876	40,362,514	—	110,581	—	—	5,076,163	25,029,004	131,645,977	10,820	701,256
300-399	399	137,910	5,952,776	34,363,704	—	94,142	—	—	4,039,587	18,996,743	98,063,516	8,883	669,356
400-499	213	94,910	3,976,176	24,359,368	—	66,737	—	—	2,914,219	11,853,928	74,121,007	5,318	408,256
500 or more	320	233,632	9,427,859	63,677,250	—	174,462	—	—	6,721,236	25,476,669	168,473,739	11,526	1,003,401
Psychiatric	446	79,570	809,453	24,596,617	—	67,391	—	—	41,622	229,318	10,559,241	0	0
Hospitals	439	76,131	808,968	23,549,566	—	64,521	—	—	41,622	229,318	10,555,618	0	0
Institutions for mentally retarded	7	3,439	485	1,047,051	—	2,870	—	—	0	0	3,623	0	0
General	4,710	812,796	35,259,683	191,628,693	—	525,085	—	—	27,354,284	130,651,815	723,155,559	56,618	3,818,017
Hospitals	4,697	811,104	35,242,034	191,136,979	—	523,739	—	—	27,353,557	130,601,299	722,567,598	56,618	3,818,017
Hospital units of institutions	13	1,692	17,649	491,714	—	1,346	—	—	727	50,516	587,961	0	0
TB and other respiratory diseases	2	122	151	25,264	—	70	—	—	0	0	204	0	0
Obstetrics and gynecology	9	1,499	77,865	334,790	—	918	—	—	61,603	54,228	774,638	599	49,209
Eye, ear, nose and throat	4	139	3,064	8,341	—	22	—	—	63,359	36,631	759,096	0	0
Rehabilitation	195	15,652	266,686	4,022,896	—	11,032	—	—	25,989	2,106	6,397,384	40	750
Orthopedic	23	1,162	49,025	197,686	—	543	—	—	96,410	18,118	791,302	0	0
Chronic Disease	6	543	5,714	135,470	—	371	—	—	6,381	5,894	163,670	0	0
Surgical	9	330	12,338	54,239	—	149	—	—	43,460	47,748	234,629	0	0
Cancer	13	2,161	96,375	620,745	—	1,702	—	—	84,196	37,649	4,014,896	0	0
Heart	8	842	48,483	210,859	—	577	—	—	38,452	37,943	252,371	0	0
Acute long-term care hospital	290	22,477	218,235	5,734,385	—	15,730	—	—	147,885	267,709	1,931,686	5	135
All other	39	4,702	68,259	1,277,110	—	3,502	—	—	55,373	154,222	1,373,213	134	3,640
Federal	213	44,940	911,050	10,705,617	—	29,332	—	—	670,920	4,044,274	90,134,352	776	53,351
Psychiatric	11	3,638	31,061	897,264	—	2,456	—	—	19,834	47,111	3,186,117	0	0
General and other special	202	41,302	879,989	9,808,353	—	26,876	—	—	651,086	3,997,163	86,948,235	776	53,351
Nonfederal	5,541	897,055	36,004,281	218,141,478	—	597,760	—	—	27,348,094	127,499,107	660,273,537	56,620	3,818,400
Psychiatric	435	75,932	778,392	23,699,353	—	64,935	—	—	21,788	182,207	7,373,124	0	0
Hospitals	428	72,493	777,907	23,652,302	—	62,065	—	—	21,788	182,207	7,369,501	0	0
Institutions for mentally retarded	7	3,439	485	1,047,051	—	2,870	—	—	0	0	3,623	0	0
TB and other respiratory diseases	2	122	151	25,264	25,264	70	70	167.0	0	0	204	0	1
Long-term general and other special	109	14,886	65,399	4,478,169	4,861,335	12,270	13,321	69.0	14,308	67,583	1,283,474	10	1
Short-term general and other special	4,995	806,115	35,160,339	189,938,692	355,368,999	520,485	973,875	5.4	27,311,998	127,249,317	651,616,735	56,610	3,818,399
Hospital units of institutions	10	1,172	10,912	345,343	345,343	945	945	32.0	0	0	193,018	0	0
Community Hospitals	4,985	804,943	35,149,427	189,593,349	355,023,656	519,540	972,930	5.4	27,311,998	127,249,317	651,423,717	56,610	3,818,399
6-24 Beds	424	7,261	198,692	854,226	3,502,813	2,345	9,604	4.3	307,263	1,658,487	9,934,422	413	13,839
25-49	1,167	37,446	1,168,665	6,116,350	18,536,076	16,777	50,847	5.2	1,349,680	7,923,353	43,099,222	2,800	107,380
50-99	970	69,470	2,173,195	13,960,874	33,366,996	38,267	91,518	6.4	2,135,845	11,667,902	57,701,366	5,160	228,035
100-199	1,029	148,090	6,124,987	32,616,034	67,922,624	89,428	186,178	5.3	5,153,819	26,433,098	120,902,323	11,899	706,284
200-299	585	142,616	6,569,492	33,301,779	60,558,707	91,238	165,910	5.1	4,897,972	24,171,792	110,661,274	10,611	681,848
300-399	352	121,749	5,835,325	29,931,672	51,236,840	82,000	140,376	5.1	3,995,396	18,788,786	90,515,053	8,883	669,356
400-499	185	82,071	3,869,124	20,521,474	34,918,000	56,222	95,667	5.3	2,843,566	11,546,221	65,542,563	5,318	408,256
500 or more	273	196,240	9,209,947	52,290,940	84,981,600	143,263	232,830	5.7	6,628,457	25,059,678	153,067,494	11,526	1,003,401
Nongovernment not-for-profit	2,904	555,768	25,531,509	134,363,362	252,212,704	368,146	691,063	5.3	20,026,802	90,143,348	494,177,718	39,946	2,750,163
Investor-owned (for profit)	1,013	124,652	4,924,846	25,961,903	41,235,427	71,166	113,050	5.3	3,759,371	17,064,641	48,201,473	7,965	525,427
State and Local Government	1,068	124,523	4,693,072	29,268,084	61,575,525	80,228	168,817	6.2	3,525,825	20,041,328	109,044,526	8,699	542,809

Table 2 (Continued)

CLASSIFICATION	FULL-TIME EQUIVALENT PERSONNEL — Physicians and Dentists	Registered Nurses	Licensed Practical Nurses	Other Salaried Personnel	Total Personnel	FULL-TIME EQUIVALENT TRAINEES — Medical and Dental Residents	Other Trainees	Total Trainees	EXPENSES / LABOR — Payroll (in thousands)	Employee Benefits (in thousands)	Total (in thousands)	Percent of Total	EXPENSES / TOTAL — Amount (in thousands)	Adjusted per Admission	Adjusted per Inpatient Day
UNITED STATES	135,204	1,398,556	116,273	3,533,867	5,183,900	105,709	14,855	120,564	$309,734,731	$84,534,874	$394,269,605	52.5	$750,602,099	—	—
6-24 Beds	1,458	10,737	2,695	42,403	57,293	13	9	22	$2,709,141	$717,017	$3,426,159	51.1	$6,701,831	—	—
25-49	7,152	53,520	11,760	187,366	259,798	420	762	1,182	$12,314,741	$3,232,056	$15,546,797	52.6	$29,556,288	—	—
50-99	9,663	93,061	15,315	283,870	401,909	912	505	1,417	$20,833,084	$5,589,299	$26,422,383	53.4	$49,465,596	—	—
100-199	18,815	228,554	23,401	600,474	871,244	5,049	1,252	6,301	$49,917,969	$13,468,023	$63,385,992	53.0	$119,538,014	—	—
200-299	21,887	243,084	20,514	608,773	894,258	14,438	4,494	18,932	$53,471,439	$15,013,115	$68,484,554	53.3	$128,419,169	—	—
300-399	13,443	206,080	13,061	492,653	725,237	9,425	842	10,267	$44,109,360	$12,216,975	$56,326,335	51.6	$109,102,277	—	—
400-499	11,471	159,258	9,974	371,476	552,179	15,384	1,022	16,406	$34,736,626	$9,604,523	$44,341,150	52.0	$85,305,301	—	—
500 or more	51,315	404,262	19,553	946,852	1,421,982	60,068	5,969	66,037	$91,642,370	$24,693,865	$116,336,236	52.3	$222,513,623	—	—
Psychiatric	5,602	30,605	8,057	154,154	198,418	426	651	1,077	$9,876,661	$3,098,113	$12,974,774	71.3	$18,190,153	—	—
Hospitals	5,036	29,169	7,723	149,859	191,787	426	632	1,058	$9,578,216	$3,032,298	$12,610,514	70.9	$17,773,861	—	—
Institutions for mentally retarded	566	1,436	334	4,295	6,631	0	19	19	$298,445	$65,814	$364,259	87.5	$416,292	—	—
General	124,067	1,321,562	100,727	3,225,092	4,771,448	104,111	12,775	116,886	$287,293,130	$78,216,013	$365,509,143	52.0	$702,929,622	—	—
Hospitals	124,004	1,320,804	100,541	3,220,598	4,765,947	104,111	12,713	116,824	$287,054,763	$78,138,926	$365,193,689	52.0	$702,427,932	—	—
Hospital units of institutions	63	758	186	4,494	5,501	0	62	62	$238,367	$77,086	$315,453	62.9	$501,690	—	—
TB and other respiratory diseases	0	32	27	158	217	0	0	0	$9,783	$3,125	$12,909	62.0	$20,828	—	—
Obstetrics and gynecology	183	2,906	77	5,199	8,365	65	4	69	$583,165	$143,865	$727,030	56.1	$1,294,944	—	—
Eye, ear, nose and throat	167	392	20	2,358	2,937	83	29	112	$146,669	$42,369	$189,038	46.5	$406,561	—	—
Rehabilitation	520	10,999	2,458	44,218	58,195	170	21	191	$2,831,507	$672,581	$3,504,088	60.2	$5,825,453	—	—
Orthopedic	418	1,911	122	6,434	8,885	42	4	46	$681,983	$192,271	$874,254	48.7	$1,794,658	—	—
Chronic Disease	18	368	85	1,667	2,138	0	9	9	$112,279	$31,475	$143,755	56.2	$255,585	—	—
Surgical	6	488	35	975	1,504	0	0	0	$94,509	$22,650	$117,159	36.8	$318,505	—	—
Cancer	2,932	8,952	268	33,926	46,078	663	1,287	1,950	$3,346,415	$939,693	$4,286,108	49.6	$8,647,192	—	—
Heart	78	1,524	57	3,255	4,914	3	3	6	$372,669	$91,544	$464,213	49.3	$942,550	—	—
Acute long-term care hospital	533	14,492	3,768	42,733	61,526	89	7	96	$3,232,893	$785,208	$4,018,100	53.9	$7,449,647	—	—
All other	680	4,325	572	13,698	19,275	57	65	122	$1,153,069	$295,967	$1,449,036	57.4	$2,526,401	—	—
Federal	26,651	69,274	16,052	247,401	359,378	10,024	6,037	16,061	$24,449,953	$7,273,407	$31,723,360	60.6	$52,365,505	—	—
Psychiatric	878	2,696	1,087	11,788	16,449	16	57	73	$1,106,107	$300,228	$1,406,336	59.0	$2,382,862	—	—
General and other special	25,773	66,578	14,965	235,613	342,929	10,008	5,980	15,988	$23,343,845	$6,973,179	$30,317,024	60.7	$49,982,644	—	—
Nonfederal	108,553	1,329,282	100,221	3,286,466	4,824,522	95,685	8,818	104,503	$285,284,779	$77,261,467	$362,546,246	51.9	$698,236,594	—	—
Psychiatric	4,724	27,909	6,970	142,366	181,969	410	594	1,004	$8,770,554	$2,797,884	$11,568,438	73.2	$15,807,292	—	—
Hospitals	4,158	26,473	6,636	138,071	175,338	410	575	985	$8,472,109	$2,732,070	$11,204,178	72.8	$15,391,000	—	—
Institutions for mentally retarded	566	1,436	334	4,295	6,631	0	19	19	$298,445	$65,814	$364,259	87.5	$416,292	—	—
TB and other respiratory diseases	0	32	27	158	217	0	0	0	$9,783	$3,125	$12,909	62.0	$20,828	$137,933.93	$824.42
Long-term general and other special	487	6,899	2,042	29,833	39,288	5	27	32	$2,059,566	$583,332	$2,642,898	63.6	$4,154,889	$55,940.02	$854.68
Short-term general and other special	103,342	1,294,442	91,182	3,114,109	4,603,075	95,270	8,197	103,467	$274,444,876	$73,877,125	$348,322,001	51.4	$678,253,585	$10,316.07	$1,908.59
Hospital units of institutions	10	497	125	2,691	3,323	0	44	44	$144,867	$45,965	$190,832	66.8	$285,547	$26,168.17	$826.85
Community Hospitals	103,332	1,293,945	91,057	3,111,418	4,599,752	95,270	8,153	103,423	$274,300,010	$73,831,160	$348,131,169	51.3	$677,968,038	$10,313.44	$1,909.64
6-24 Beds	918	9,934	2,552	33,780	47,184	13	8	21	$2,326,881	$585,119	$2,912,000	51.6	$5,644,510	$6,613.18	$1,611.42
25-49	5,045	49,048	10,584	162,891	227,568	205	746	951	$11,354,553	$2,935,274	$14,289,828	52.8	$27,075,731	$7,671.61	$1,460.70
50-99	5,185	77,536	11,754	224,521	318,996	432	229	661	$16,805,677	$4,456,503	$21,262,180	52.5	$40,509,093	$8,410.02	$1,214.05
100-199	12,878	207,182	18,480	516,181	754,721	3,947	474	4,421	$42,557,281	$11,323,494	$53,880,775	51.5	$104,618,605	$9,553.34	$1,540.26
200-299	14,672	221,018	15,267	523,868	774,825	7,922	854	8,776	$45,586,199	$12,314,129	$57,900,329	51.2	$113,049,739	$10,300.63	$1,866.78
300-399	10,693	196,744	10,423	450,631	668,491	9,259	570	9,829	$40,832,424	$11,218,296	$52,050,720	50.9	$102,319,307	$11,861.62	$1,996.99
400-499	8,959	148,415	7,337	333,857	498,568	15,358	730	16,088	$31,328,521	$8,618,526	$39,947,047	51.3	$77,854,509	$13,788.87	$2,229.64
500 or more	44,982	384,068	14,660	865,689	1,309,399	58,134	4,542	62,676	$83,508,473	$22,379,819	$105,888,292	51.2	$206,896,544		$2,434.60
Nongovernment not-for-profit	84,303	945,146	54,366	2,303,688	3,387,503	67,534	6,299	73,833	$204,753,339	$55,165,012	$259,918,351	50.9	$510,743,888	$10,651.81	$2,025.05
Investor-owned (for profit)	2,723	155,583	16,663	299,352	474,321	2,113	223	2,336	$25,997,663	$5,769,406	$31,767,069	47.3	$67,168,429	$8,336.16	$1,628.90
State and Local Government	16,306	193,216	20,028	508,378	737,928	25,623	1,631	27,254	$43,549,008	$12,896,742	$56,445,749	56.4	$100,055,721	$10,283.35	$1,624.93

Tables 3–6

Total U.S.

TABLE 3

TOTAL UNITED STATES

U.S. Registered Community Hospitals
(Nonfederal, short-term general and other special hospitals)

Overview 2006–2010

	2010	2009	2008	2007	2006
TOTAL U.S. Community Hospitals.............	4,985	5,008	5,010	4,897	4,927
Bed Size Category					
6-24....................................	424	402	389	360	375
25-49...................................	1,167	1,164	1,151	1,076	1,066
50-99...................................	970	991	995	971	969
100-199.................................	1,029	1,063	1,070	1,083	1,117
200-299.................................	585	582	596	613	607
300-399.................................	352	348	355	343	354
400-499.................................	185	192	184	191	180
500 +...................................	273	266	270	260	259
Location					
Hospitals Urban..........................	2,998	3,011	3,012	2,900	2,755
Hospitals Rural	1,987	1,997	1,998	1,997	2,172
Control					
State and Local Government...............	1,068	1,092	1,105	1,111	1,119
Not for Profit...........................	2,904	2,918	2,923	2,913	2,919
Investor owned	1,013	998	982	873	889
Physician Models					
Independent Practice Association	563	579	597	654	683
Group Practice without Walls...............	159	175	160	166	166
Open Physician-Hospital Organization	630	649	672	691	715
Closed Physician-Hospital Organization	203	207	213	240	237
Management Service Organization	454	449	436	453	445
Integrated Salary Model....................	1,728	1,664	1,583	1,534	1,486
Equity Model.............................	80	92	97	75	72
Foundation...............................	261	237	248	236	230
Insurance Products					
Health Maintenance Organization	614	587	597	632	663
Preferred Provider Organization..............	740	693	685	842	887
Indemnity Fee for Service	260	235	250	292	289
Managed Care Contracts					
Health Maintenance Organization	2,677	2,702	2,670	2,655	2,667
Preferred Provider Organization..............	3,074	3,137	3,125	3,099	3,163
Affiliations					
Hospitals in a System.....................	2,941	2,921	2,868	2,730	2,755
Hospitals in a Network....................	1,508	1,485	1,490	1,472	1,508
Hospitals in a Group Purchasing Organization..	3,595	3,674	3,677	3,591	3,666

TABLE 3

TOTAL UNITED STATES

U.S. Registered Community Hospitals
(Nonfederal, short-term general and other special hospitals)

Utilization, Personnel, Revenue and Expenses, Community Health Indicators 2006–2010

	2010	2009	2008	2007	2006
TOTAL FACILITY (Includes Hospital and Nursing Home Units)					
Utilization - Inpatient					
Beds	804,943	805,593	808,069	800,892	802,658
Admissions	35,149,427	35,527,377	35,760,750	35,345,986	35,377,659
Inpatient Days	189,593,349	192,656,804	196,078,468	194,549,348	196,366,512
Average Length of Stay	5.4	5.4	5.5	5.5	5.6
Inpatient Surgeries	9,954,821	10,100,980	10,105,156	10,189,630	10,095,683
Births	3,818,399	3,959,605	4,073,724	4,077,962	4,075,193
Utilization - Outpatient					
Emergency Outpatient Visits	127,249,317	127,298,193	123,024,024	120,811,299	118,374,029
Other Outpatient Visits	524,174,400	514,655,249	501,074,272	482,489,075	481,178,996
Total Outpatient Visits	651,423,717	641,953,442	624,098,296	603,300,374	599,553,025
Outpatient Surgeries	17,357,177	17,357,534	17,354,282	17,146,334	17,235,141
Personnel					
Full Time RNs	1,055,118	1,029,828	984,649	950,064	900,326
Full Time LPNs	76,503	82,159	86,750	89,577	93,038
Part Time RNs	477,739	477,699	487,480	482,239	476,549
Part Time LPNs	29,164	31,647	35,602	38,213	39,712
Total Full Time	3,989,587	3,971,118	3,919,415	3,846,287	3,720,405
Total Part Time	1,427,136	1,434,492	1,460,487	1,441,216	1,431,738
Revenue - Inpatient					
Gross Inpatient Revenue	$1,224,790,498,627	$1,154,085,466,645	$1,090,598,012,951	$1,013,168,556,764	$939,459,919,425
Revenue - Outpatient					
Gross Outpatient Revenue	$887,419,059,972	$802,893,402,009	$711,918,761,681	$632,728,034,944	$570,420,556,680
Revenue and Expenses - Totals					
(Includes Inpatient and Outpatient)					
Total Gross Revenue	$2,112,209,558,599	$1,956,978,868,654	$1,802,516,774,632	$1,645,896,591,708	$1,509,880,476,105
Deductions from Revenue	1,435,826,277,742	1,309,916,141,834	1,191,615,889,365	1,072,315,472,850	969,154,780,687
Net Patient Revenue	676,383,280,857	647,062,726,820	610,900,885,267	573,581,118,858	540,725,695,418
Other Operating Revenue	41,269,017,419	38,997,453,520	37,136,577,114	35,765,948,073	34,170,257,365
Other Nonoperating Revenue	13,251,393,842	4,467,480,534	-4,453,107,631	17,000,138,209	12,172,041,974
Total Net Revenue	730,903,692,118	690,527,660,874	643,584,354,750	626,347,205,140	587,050,913,892
Total Expenses	677,968,038,012	656,156,258,314	626,576,957,912	583,252,287,933	551,835,328,219
HOSPITAL UNIT (Excludes Separate Nursing Home Units)					
Utilization - Inpatient					
Beds	755,091	755,286	753,905	743,401	742,652
Admissions	34,935,503	35,304,455	35,522,351	35,087,765	35,095,084
Inpatient Days	173,686,925	176,511,062	179,043,949	176,068,211	177,215,236
Average Length of Stay	5.0	5.0	5.0	5.0	5.0
Personnel					
Total Full Time	3,955,083	3,930,304	3,875,073	3,795,278	3,671,780
Total Part Time	1,407,838	1,413,237	1,436,850	1,416,918	1,406,083
Revenue and Expenses - Totals					
(Includes Inpatient and Outpatient)					
Total Net Revenue	$726,685,542,179	$686,454,003,753	$639,389,781,304	$621,836,200,340	$580,082,238,834
Total Expenses	674,188,184,839	652,470,080,058	622,828,801,705	579,272,589,469	547,742,177,612
COMMUNITY HEALTH INDICATORS PER 1000 POPULATION					
Total Population (in thousands)	309,051	307,007	304,375	301,580	298,593
Inpatient					
Beds	2.6	2.6	2.7	2.7	2.7
Admissions	113.7	115.7	117.5	117.2	118.5
Inpatient Days	613.5	627.5	644.2	645.1	657.6
Inpatient Surgeries	32.2	32.9	33.2	33.8	33.8
Births	12.4	12.9	13.4	13.5	13.6
Outpatient					
Emergency Outpatient Visits	411.7	414.6	404.2	400.6	396.4
Other Outpatient Visits	1,696.1	1,676.4	1,646.2	1,599.9	1,611.5
Total Outpatient Visits	2,107.8	2,091.0	2,050.4	2,000.5	2,007.9
Outpatient Surgeries	56.2	56.5	57.0	56.9	57.7
Expense per Capita (per person)	$2,193.7	$2,137.3	$2,058.6	$1,934.0	$1,848.1

Total U.S.

TABLE **4**

BED SIZE CATEGORY 6-24

U.S. Registered Community Hospitals
(Nonfederal, short-term general and other special hospitals)

Overview 2006–2010

	2010	2009	2008	2007	2006
Total Community Hospitals in					
Bed Size Category 6-24	424	402	389	360	375
Location					
Hospitals Urban	113	111	103	97	79
Hospitals Rural	311	291	286	263	296
Control					
State and Local Government	165	154	148	138	150
Not for Profit	207	194	186	177	174
Investor owned	52	54	55	45	51
Physician Models					
Independent Practice Association	51	57	49	51	54
Group Practice without Walls	10	13	11	11	14
Open Physician-Hospital Organization	29	31	34	33	33
Closed Physician-Hospital Organization	5	6	9	6	8
Management Service Organization	17	20	18	15	16
Integrated Salary Model	120	116	110	99	101
Equity Model	3	2	6	5	2
Foundation	10	11	7	7	10
Insurance Products					
Health Maintenance Organization	40	36	34	35	32
Preferred Provider Organization	44	38	39	52	48
Indemnity Fee for Service	13	11	15	16	13
Managed Care Contracts					
Health Maintenance Organization	156	151	137	120	128
Preferred Provider Organization	218	210	203	190	186
Affiliations					
Hospitals in a System	172	166	158	141	145
Hospitals in a Network	129	122	116	103	113
Hospitals in a Group Purchasing Organization . .	291	286	263	242	263

Bed Size Categories

TABLE 4

BED SIZE CATEGORY 6-24

U.S. Registered Community Hospitals
(Nonfederal, short-term general and other special hospitals)

Utilization, Personnel, Revenue and Expenses, Community Health Indicators 2006–2010

	2010	2009	2008	2007	2006
TOTAL FACILITY (Includes Hospital and Nursing Home Units)					
Utilization - Inpatient					
Beds	7,261	6,894	6,726	6,238	6,446
Admissions	198,692	196,599	204,522	199,900	191,951
Inpatient Days	854,226	846,228	835,702	792,847	772,553
Average Length of Stay	4.3	4.3	4.1	4.0	4.0
Inpatient Surgeries	36,003	33,615	36,519	39,047	37,527
Births	13,839	14,161	13,938	13,267	12,310
Utilization - Outpatient					
Emergency Outpatient Visits	1,658,487	1,558,802	1,505,235	1,399,997	1,269,428
Other Outpatient Visits	8,275,935	7,553,921	6,877,919	6,297,926	6,533,512
Total Outpatient Visits	9,934,422	9,112,723	8,383,154	7,697,923	7,802,940
Outpatient Surgeries	271,260	250,113	249,528	215,459	212,620
Personnel					
Full Time RNs	7,587	6,790	6,382	5,763	5,759
Full Time LPNs	2,113	1,992	1,996	1,633	1,632
Part Time RNs	4,701	4,212	3,931	3,232	3,354
Part Time LPNs	886	918	859	769	800
Total Full Time	38,328	34,290	32,101	29,240	29,489
Total Part Time	17,746	16,301	14,933	12,801	13,707
Revenue - Inpatient					
Gross Inpatient Revenue	$2,786,370,995	$2,627,018,044	$2,459,057,974	$2,173,593,992	$1,828,399,829
Revenue - Outpatient					
Gross Outpatient Revenue	$8,039,286,106	$7,310,737,048	$6,343,851,906	$5,307,718,755	$4,642,506,692
Revenue and Expenses - Totals					
(Includes Inpatient and Outpatient)					
Total Gross Revenue	$10,825,657,101	$9,937,755,092	$8,802,909,880	$7,481,312,747	$6,470,906,521
Deductions from Revenue	5,474,162,402	5,035,910,207	4,391,015,802	3,707,878,289	3,001,843,000
Net Patient Revenue	5,351,494,699	4,901,844,885	4,411,894,078	3,773,434,458	3,469,063,521
Other Operating Revenue	540,121,094	436,638,024	343,522,682	346,123,111	323,188,226
Other Nonoperating Revenue	103,852,868	70,082,709	69,707,381	85,878,584	86,665,700
Total Net Revenue	5,995,468,661	5,408,565,618	4,825,124,141	4,205,436,153	3,891,511,549
Total Expenses	5,644,509,939	5,099,918,468	4,510,451,244	3,898,795,232	3,644,293,348
HOSPITAL UNIT (Excludes Separate Nursing Home Units)					
Utilization - Inpatient					
Beds	7,225	6,852	6,693	6,214	6,355
Admissions	198,651	196,571	204,445	199,884	191,730
Inpatient Days	841,349	829,135	823,878	781,994	740,244
Average Length of Stay	4.2	4.2	4.0	3.9	3.9
Personnel					
Total Full Time	38,313	34,160	31,993	29,116	29,285
Total Part Time	17,743	16,225	14,902	12,723	13,619
Revenue and Expenses - Totals					
(Includes Inpatient and Outpatient)					
Total Net Revenue	$5,990,190,925	$5,395,279,787	$4,821,483,710	$4,200,890,155	$3,882,018,849
Total Expenses	5,642,553,901	5,092,088,584	4,508,680,031	3,896,171,176	3,636,207,924

TABLE **4**

BED SIZE CATEGORY 25-49

U.S. Registered Community Hospitals
(Nonfederal, short-term general and other special hospitals)

Overview 2006–2010

	2010	2009	2008	2007	2006
Total Community Hospitals in					
Bed Size Category 25-49	1,167	1,164	1,151	1,076	1,066
Location					
Hospitals Urban.	408	411	411	334	277
Hospitals Rural	759	753	740	742	789
Control					
State and Local Government.	381	391	397	399	395
Not for Profit	547	536	527	515	506
Investor owned	239	237	227	162	165
Physician Models					
Independent Practice Association	102	108	104	115	134
Group Practice without Walls.	32	32	27	35	32
Open Physician-Hospital Organization	82	94	92	97	95
Closed Physician-Hospital Organization	23	23	24	28	32
Management Service Organization	54	56	54	54	54
Integrated Salary Model	344	350	309	298	292
Equity Model	17	15	14	9	13
Foundation.	39	40	42	37	36
Insurance Products					
Health Maintenance Organization	86	90	83	81	84
Preferred Provider Organization.	134	123	112	140	154
Indemnity Fee for Service	44	41	39	43	48
Managed Care Contracts					
Health Maintenance Organization	471	488	474	451	433
Preferred Provider Organization.	636	658	649	622	633
Affiliations					
Hospitals in a System.	598	593	580	499	507
Hospitals in a Network	302	296	296	297	301
Hospitals in a Group Purchasing Organization. .	791	805	795	775	768

Bed Size Categories

TABLE **4**

BED SIZE CATEGORY 25-49

U.S. Registered Community Hospitals
(Nonfederal, short-term general and other special hospitals)

Utilization, Personnel, Revenue and Expenses, Community Health Indicators 2006–2010

	2010	2009	2008	2007	2006
TOTAL FACILITY (Includes Hospital and Nursing Home Units)					
Utilization - Inpatient					
Beds	37,446	37,338	37,142	34,350	34,217
Admissions	1,168,665	1,217,233	1,218,123	1,169,941	1,187,667
Inpatient Days	6,116,350	6,265,180	6,342,577	5,786,668	5,837,190
Average Length of Stay	5.2	5.1	5.2	4.9	4.9
Inpatient Surgeries	256,940	266,047	242,142	227,059	234,999
Births	107,380	113,460	106,334	109,618	108,279
Utilization - Outpatient					
Emergency Outpatient Visits	7,923,353	8,004,368	7,781,578	7,409,466	7,198,343
Other Outpatient Visits	35,175,869	34,456,501	32,947,438	31,766,431	29,855,259
Total Outpatient Visits	43,099,222	42,460,869	40,729,016	39,175,897	37,053,602
Outpatient Surgeries	1,092,740	1,067,767	1,022,034	927,021	977,191
Personnel					
Full Time RNs	37,943	37,289	34,935	32,045	31,047
Full Time LPNs	8,776	8,901	9,165	8,382	8,551
Part Time RNs	22,187	21,865	20,005	18,171	18,793
Part Time LPNs	3,605	3,815	3,809	3,590	3,803
Total Full Time	187,568	184,562	178,257	165,913	160,152
Total Part Time	81,895	80,350	76,222	69,915	70,714
Revenue - Inpatient					
Gross Inpatient Revenue	$21,382,867,485	$20,489,409,044	$18,764,220,947	$15,192,815,130	$15,288,298,943
Revenue - Outpatient					
Gross Outpatient Revenue	$39,164,706,833	$36,064,974,499	$31,292,050,672	$26,532,671,728	$24,089,062,315
Revenue and Expenses - Totals **(Includes Inpatient and Outpatient)**					
Total Gross Revenue	$60,547,574,318	$56,554,383,543	$50,056,271,619	$41,725,486,858	$39,377,361,258
Deductions from Revenue	34,313,307,874	31,432,916,209	26,923,199,398	21,510,609,136	20,293,853,524
Net Patient Revenue	26,234,266,444	25,121,467,334	23,133,072,221	20,214,877,722	19,083,507,734
Other Operating Revenue	2,209,537,503	2,229,830,552	1,982,012,610	1,814,575,058	1,642,531,689
Other Nonoperating Revenue	523,520,663	299,120,900	142,977,449	580,543,731	402,345,248
Total Net Revenue	28,967,324,610	27,650,418,786	25,258,062,280	22,609,996,511	21,128,384,671
Total Expenses	27,075,731,145	26,281,664,624	24,074,708,651	21,232,861,615	20,009,399,050
HOSPITAL UNIT (Excludes Separate Nursing Home Units)					
Utilization - Inpatient					
Beds	35,924	35,726	35,230	32,433	32,229
Admissions	1,166,430	1,213,515	1,215,522	1,166,976	1,184,151
Inpatient Days	5,638,505	5,745,424	5,747,460	5,198,062	5,222,566
Average Length of Stay	4.8	4.7	4.7	4.5	4.4
Personnel					
Total Full Time	186,670	182,894	176,408	164,033	158,542
Total Part Time	81,286	79,370	75,100	68,994	69,755
Revenue and Expenses - Totals **(Includes Inpatient and Outpatient)**					
Total Net Revenue	$28,881,412,934	$27,550,727,504	$25,153,457,365	$22,466,173,311	$20,973,029,022
Total Expenses	27,009,348,946	26,216,346,135	23,996,899,302	21,157,891,227	19,924,029,677

Bed Size Categories

TABLE 4

BED SIZE CATEGORY 50-99

U.S. Registered Community Hospitals
(Nonfederal, short-term general and other special hospitals)

Overview 2006–2010

	2010	2009	2008	2007	2006
Total Community Hospitals in					
Bed Size Category 50-99	**970**	**991**	**995**	**971**	**969**
Location					
Hospitals Urban.	483	483	480	449	413
Hospitals Rural	487	508	515	522	556
Control					
State and Local Government.	194	210	215	227	219
Not for Profit	485	501	508	506	514
Investor owned	291	280	272	238	236
Physician Models					
Independent Practice Association	84	86	97	112	114
Group Practice without Walls.	21	20	25	28	27
Open Physician-Hospital Organization	93	94	112	123	119
Closed Physician-Hospital Organization	33	29	34	36	30
Management Service Organization	54	54	61	68	61
Integrated Salary Model	288	280	277	268	247
Equity Model	12	13	14	8	7
Foundation.	40	35	45	41	44
Insurance Products					
Health Maintenance Organization	89	80	94	99	83
Preferred Provider Organization.	128	124	135	171	167
Indemnity Fee for Service	49	44	56	56	51
Managed Care Contracts					
Health Maintenance Organization	444	435	456	447	439
Preferred Provider Organization.	533	548	564	566	559
Affiliations					
Hospitals in a System.	584	576	559	536	537
Hospitals in a Network	260	257	271	278	278
Hospitals in a Group Purchasing Organization. .	649	672	682	674	689

TABLE 4

BED SIZE CATEGORY 50-99

U.S. Registered Community Hospitals
(Nonfederal, short-term general and other special hospitals)

Utilization, Personnel, Revenue and Expenses, Community Health Indicators 2006–2010

	2010	2009	2008	2007	2006
TOTAL FACILITY (Includes Hospital and Nursing Home Units)					
Utilization - Inpatient					
Beds	69,470	71,012	71,477	69,974	69,408
Admissions	2,173,195	2,255,591	2,318,730	2,295,002	2,300,638
Inpatient Days	13,960,874	14,494,367	14,775,775	14,354,674	14,534,929
Average Length of Stay............	6.4	6.4	6.4	6.3	6.3
Inpatient Surgeries................	543,313	557,900	573,876	593,650	576,043
Births..........................	228,035	245,282	252,752	257,346	249,458
Utilization - Outpatient					
Emergency Outpatient Visits........	11,667,902	11,702,839	11,523,593	11,373,584	11,175,926
Other Outpatient Visits............	46,033,464	45,633,323	45,219,692	42,938,775	41,798,859
Total Outpatient Visits	57,701,366	57,336,162	56,743,285	54,312,359	52,974,785
Outpatient Surgeries	1,592,532	1,625,749	1,608,622	1,564,443	1,604,168
Personnel					
Full Time RNs	60,774	59,702	58,276	56,028	54,130
Full Time LPNs	9,718	10,384	10,739	10,921	11,263
Part Time RNs...................	33,585	33,613	33,996	34,128	32,746
Part Time LPNs	4,125	4,537	4,911	5,415	5,475
Total Full Time..................	260,463	263,865	264,056	255,144	248,689
Total Part Time	118,372	119,501	121,026	120,860	118,080
Revenue - Inpatient					
Gross Inpatient Revenue...........	$52,180,741,692	$48,434,688,539	$46,010,068,854	$42,120,063,662	$38,928,521,152
Revenue - Outpatient					
Gross Outpatient Revenue	$60,748,431,980	$57,539,780,471	$51,849,631,924	$45,947,957,640	$40,228,937,486
Revenue and Expenses - Totals					
(Includes Inpatient and Outpatient)					
Total Gross Revenue..............	$112,929,173,672	$105,974,469,010	$97,859,700,778	$88,068,021,302	$79,157,458,638
Deductions from Revenue..........	71,250,437,701	65,093,252,794	59,144,961,432	52,387,575,211	46,042,196,389
Net Patient Revenue	41,678,735,971	40,881,216,216	38,714,739,346	35,680,446,091	33,115,262,249
Other Operating Revenue	1,566,850,196	1,628,159,436	1,598,169,545	1,434,537,429	1,534,330,530
Other Nonoperating Revenue	677,949,955	358,788,581	248,970,994	970,524,605	523,502,772
Total Net Revenue................	43,923,536,122	42,868,164,233	40,561,879,885	38,085,508,125	35,173,095,551
Total Expenses..................	40,509,092,623	39,918,181,789	38,332,175,201	35,148,034,292	32,959,605,126
HOSPITAL UNIT (Excludes Separate Nursing Home Units)					
Utilization - Inpatient					
Beds..........................	60,417	60,783	60,983	58,916	58,329
Admissions.....................	2,152,715	2,233,384	2,293,835	2,271,564	2,273,677
Inpatient Days	11,108,738	11,303,044	11,528,634	10,951,518	11,041,775
Average Length of Stay............	5.2	5.1	5.0	4.8	4.9
Personnel					
Total Full Time..................	255,262	257,466	257,784	248,223	241,410
Total Part Time	114,674	115,249	116,770	115,925	113,258
Revenue and Expenses - Totals					
(Includes Inpatient and Outpatient)					
Total Net Revenue................	$43,379,453,757	$42,231,656,619	$39,967,178,977	$37,463,316,808	$34,506,004,025
Total Expenses..................	40,049,446,577	39,405,302,301	37,833,276,129	34,678,598,342	32,492,030,193

TABLE 4

BED SIZE CATEGORY 100-199

U.S. Registered Community Hospitals
(Nonfederal, short-term general and other special hospitals)

Overview 2006–2010

	2010	2009	2008	2007	2006
Total Community Hospitals in					
Bed Size Category 100-199...............	1,029	1,063	1,070	1,083	1,117
Location					
Hospitals Urban...........................	707	726	726	729	724
Hospitals Rural	322	337	344	354	393
Control					
State and Local Government................	149	159	162	166	176
Not for Profit............................	633	656	660	670	681
Investor owned	247	248	248	247	260
Physician Models					
Independent Practice Association	120	122	124	144	161
Group Practice without Walls...............	36	44	33	33	34
Open Physician-Hospital Organization	152	166	167	176	181
Closed Physician-Hospital Organization	47	53	53	63	61
Management Service Organization	103	102	91	97	96
Integrated Salary Model....................	332	317	308	302	301
Equity Model............................	17	25	26	20	21
Foundation..............................	56	49	43	43	41
Insurance Products					
Health Maintenance Organization	124	116	108	126	154
Preferred Provider Organization..............	136	134	122	169	182
Indemnity Fee for Service	52	46	44	60	68
Managed Care Contracts					
Health Maintenance Organization	587	621	591	620	642
Preferred Provider Organization..............	641	675	668	677	722
Affiliations					
Hospitals in a System......................	655	665	661	652	668
Hospitals in a Network.....................	278	298	296	302	314
Hospitals in a Group Purchasing Organization..	724	779	792	800	830

TABLE 4

BED SIZE CATEGORY 100-199

U.S. Registered Community Hospitals
(Nonfederal, short-term general and other special hospitals)

Utilization, Personnel, Revenue and Expenses, Community Health Indicators 2006–2010

	2010	2009	2008	2007	2006
TOTAL FACILITY (Includes Hospital and Nursing Home Units)					
Utilization - Inpatient					
Beds	148,090	152,655	153,488	155,291	160,426
Admissions	6,124,987	6,337,184	6,304,036	6,341,170	6,661,921
Inpatient Days	32,616,034	34,162,392	34,742,992	35,016,507	36,835,335
Average Length of Stay	5.3	5.4	5.5	5.5	5.5
Inpatient Surgeries	1,602,340	1,687,965	1,670,856	1,728,464	1,830,464
Births	706,284	747,784	765,495	777,562	806,893
Utilization - Outpatient					
Emergency Outpatient Visits	26,433,098	27,527,025	26,601,799	26,879,730	27,389,126
Other Outpatient Visits	94,469,225	99,739,947	93,178,685	92,574,821	97,037,200
Total Outpatient Visits	120,902,323	127,266,972	119,780,484	119,454,551	124,426,326
Outpatient Surgeries	3,551,479	3,694,985	3,653,497	3,645,361	3,799,265
Personnel					
Full Time RNs	163,437	161,715	154,376	150,102	149,572
Full Time LPNs	15,414	16,777	17,825	19,168	20,951
Part Time RNs	87,526	90,352	89,500	89,687	92,656
Part Time LPNs	6,135	6,982	7,788	8,822	9,517
Total Full Time	624,072	634,361	623,645	625,608	633,024
Total Part Time	270,145	275,686	274,371	277,630	285,739
Revenue - Inpatient					
Gross Inpatient Revenue	$177,873,737,781	$172,022,467,282	$161,279,571,502	$149,688,308,624	$146,940,017,410
Revenue - Outpatient					
Gross Outpatient Revenue	$160,748,748,573	$148,908,204,845	$131,980,398,456	$119,230,252,656	$112,299,803,462
Revenue and Expenses - Totals					
(Includes Inpatient and Outpatient)					
Total Gross Revenue	$338,622,486,354	$320,930,672,127	$293,259,969,958	$268,918,561,280	$259,239,820,872
Deductions from Revenue	231,276,346,434	216,014,370,801	195,921,601,786	175,628,976,504	167,765,995,762
Net Patient Revenue	107,346,139,920	104,916,301,326	97,338,368,172	93,289,584,776	91,473,825,110
Other Operating Revenue	4,194,548,704	3,845,471,488	3,635,678,864	3,559,652,278	3,276,140,856
Other Nonoperating Revenue	1,589,574,499	773,148,510	-86,795,995	2,031,003,137	1,781,503,506
Total Net Revenue	113,130,263,123	109,534,921,324	100,887,251,041	98,880,240,191	96,531,469,472
Total Expenses	104,618,604,747	103,165,948,166	96,955,948,353	92,365,463,660	90,741,587,854
HOSPITAL UNIT (Excludes Separate Nursing Home Units)					
Utilization - Inpatient					
Beds	134,182	138,351	137,233	137,797	141,656
Admissions	6,074,709	6,284,177	6,247,190	6,276,370	6,591,271
Inpatient Days	28,160,867	29,540,921	29,546,134	29,443,800	30,891,705
Average Length of Stay	4.6	4.7	4.7	4.7	4.7
Personnel					
Total Full Time	614,788	624,258	612,571	613,811	620,505
Total Part Time	264,091	269,719	267,530	270,208	278,049
Revenue and Expenses - Totals					
(Includes Inpatient and Outpatient)					
Total Net Revenue	$112,109,514,588	$108,564,165,998	$99,832,442,896	$97,743,593,245	$94,798,499,907
Total Expenses	103,732,105,185	102,320,666,510	95,982,012,829	91,367,396,890	89,519,669,886

TABLE 4

BED SIZE CATEGORY 200-299

U.S. Registered Community Hospitals
(Nonfederal, short-term general and other special hospitals)

Overview 2006–2010

	2010	2009	2008	2007	2006
Total Community Hospitals in					
Bed Size Category 200-299	**585**	**582**	**596**	**613**	**607**
Location					
Hospitals Urban.	505	503	515	526	506
Hospitals Rural	80	79	81	87	101
Control					
State and Local Government.	63	58	62	61	63
Not for Profit	422	427	435	448	440
Investor owned	100	97	99	104	104
Physician Models					
Independent Practice Association	67	68	72	78	81
Group Practice without Walls.	18	23	26	21	26
Open Physician-Hospital Organization	111	104	110	102	122
Closed Physician-Hospital Organization	28	26	27	37	39
Management Service Organization	76	74	84	85	84
Integrated Salary Model.	223	211	206	200	198
Equity Model.	17	17	14	13	13
Foundation.	40	35	35	32	33
Insurance Products					
Health Maintenance Organization	93	89	93	96	107
Preferred Provider Organization.	105	88	95	114	123
Indemnity Fee for Service	35	36	33	46	47
Managed Care Contracts					
Health Maintenance Organization	380	382	400	410	426
Preferred Provider Organization.	402	406	421	425	447
Affiliations					
Hospitals in a System.	386	381	377	378	382
Hospitals in a Network.	192	185	195	192	204
Hospitals in a Group Purchasing Organization. .	448	452	475	460	475

TABLE 4

BED SIZE CATEGORY 200-299

U.S. Registered Community Hospitals
(Nonfederal, short-term general and other special hospitals)

Utilization, Personnel, Revenue and Expenses, Community Health Indicators 2006–2010

	2010	2009	2008	2007	2006
TOTAL FACILITY (Includes Hospital and Nursing Home Units)					
Utilization - Inpatient					
Beds	142,616	141,920	144,895	149,546	148,541
Admissions	6,569,492	6,684,169	6,866,533	7,009,011	7,007,798
Inpatient Days	33,301,779	33,902,236	35,165,769	36,324,208	36,681,087
Average Length of Stay	5.1	5.1	5.1	5.2	5.2
Inpatient Surgeries	1,896,663	1,871,675	1,945,775	2,006,491	1,981,815
Births	681,848	739,459	794,470	806,019	803,495
Utilization - Outpatient					
Emergency Outpatient Visits	24,171,792	24,181,322	24,185,692	23,913,978	23,583,282
Other Outpatient Visits	86,489,482	83,087,309	83,791,081	82,621,482	79,848,179
Total Outpatient Visits	110,661,274	107,268,631	107,976,773	106,535,460	103,431,461
Outpatient Surgeries	3,001,309	3,015,075	3,224,033	3,281,300	3,255,244
Personnel					
Full Time RNs	178,567	172,868	171,515	167,333	161,572
Full Time LPNs	12,698	13,435	14,215	15,105	15,865
Part Time RNs	84,923	85,762	88,610	92,245	92,421
Part Time LPNs	5,133	5,396	6,221	6,952	6,919
Total Full Time	657,452	650,138	651,645	656,376	641,525
Total Part Time	252,299	256,501	265,981	271,077	271,052
Revenue - Inpatient					
Gross Inpatient Revenue	$216,302,711,528	$203,207,782,786	$197,533,594,288	$192,707,619,825	$180,028,152,728
Revenue - Outpatient					
Gross Outpatient Revenue	$152,845,016,955	$136,999,646,724	$124,669,613,502	$116,124,524,652	$103,386,338,141
Revenue and Expenses - Totals (Includes Inpatient and Outpatient)					
Total Gross Revenue	$369,147,728,483	$340,207,429,510	$322,203,207,790	$308,832,144,477	$283,414,490,869
Deductions from Revenue	254,962,232,713	230,420,211,811	215,803,795,922	205,589,245,758	186,023,673,013
Net Patient Revenue	114,185,495,770	109,787,217,699	106,399,411,868	103,242,898,719	97,390,817,856
Other Operating Revenue	5,345,831,411	4,960,901,489	5,082,400,440	4,909,405,746	5,003,781,859
Other Nonoperating Revenue	2,413,672,808	869,665,589	-782,268,587	2,859,845,478	2,257,123,002
Total Net Revenue	121,944,999,989	115,617,784,777	110,699,543,721	111,012,149,943	104,622,047,660
Total Expenses	113,049,739,427	109,876,595,200	108,021,530,166	103,273,675,370	98,273,430,973
HOSPITAL UNIT (Excludes Separate Nursing Home Units)					
Utilization - Inpatient					
Beds	133,765	133,463	136,050	140,265	138,521
Admissions	6,516,545	6,624,904	6,806,537	6,944,618	6,933,995
Inpatient Days	30,497,421	31,155,392	32,384,629	33,356,376	33,409,499
Average Length of Stay	4.7	4.7	4.8	4.8	4.8
Personnel					
Total Full Time	650,650	642,802	642,916	649,221	633,780
Total Part Time	248,794	252,441	261,723	267,280	267,116
Revenue and Expenses - Totals (Includes Inpatient and Outpatient)					
Total Net Revenue	$121,195,426,366	$114,847,552,059	$109,893,167,266	$110,282,485,903	$103,386,452,224
Total Expenses	112,407,841,598	109,171,734,399	107,333,326,624	102,575,812,740	97,628,510,565

Bed Size Categories

TABLE 4

BED SIZE CATEGORY 300-399

U.S. Registered Community Hospitals
(Nonfederal, short-term general and other special hospitals)

Overview 2006–2010

	2010	2009	2008	2007	2006
Total Community Hospitals in Bed Size Category 300-399	352	348	355	343	354
Location					
Hospitals Urban..........................	329	327	331	321	327
Hospitals Rural	23	21	24	22	27
Control					
State and Local Government................	41	49	47	45	50
Not for Profit............................	261	252	259	253	259
Investor owned	50	47	49	45	45
Physician Models					
Independent Practice Association	52	55	65	63	59
Group Practice without Walls...............	15	11	11	13	13
Open Physician-Hospital Organization	66	60	61	64	65
Closed Physician-Hospital Organization	28	29	29	23	21
Management Service Organization	57	54	50	52	53
Integrated Salary Model....................	161	143	140	133	132
Equity Model............................	5	5	8	6	3
Foundation..............................	27	20	25	24	23
Insurance Products					
Health Maintenance Organization	61	62	69	70	78
Preferred Provider Organization..............	66	65	67	65	78
Indemnity Fee for Service	18	19	22	27	23
Managed Care Contracts					
Health Maintenance Organization	263	251	250	242	254
Preferred Provider Organization..............	269	266	260	256	263
Affiliations					
Hospitals in a System.....................	234	228	227	217	220
Hospitals in a Network....................	147	139	141	124	129
Hospitals in a Group Purchasing Organization..	296	287	287	272	283

TABLE 4

BED SIZE CATEGORY 300-399

U.S. Registered Community Hospitals
(Nonfederal, short-term general and other special hospitals)

Utilization, Personnel, Revenue and Expenses, Community Health Indicators 2006–2010

	2010	2009	2008	2007	2006
TOTAL FACILITY (Includes Hospital and Nursing Home Units)					
Utilization - Inpatient					
Beds..........................	121,749	120,201	122,363	118,160	121,747
Admissions.....................	5,835,325	5,761,848	5,894,366	5,637,441	5,720,821
Inpatient Days	29,931,672	29,771,668	31,089,796	30,016,302	30,853,206
Average Length of Stay...........	5.1	5.2	5.3	5.3	5.4
Inpatient Surgeries...............	1,594,088	1,638,540	1,679,276	1,626,862	1,634,694
Births..........................	669,356	669,093	678,865	676,761	682,838
Utilization - Outpatient					
Emergency Outpatient Visits........	18,788,786	18,319,154	17,724,755	17,121,428	17,144,271
Other Outpatient Visits...........	71,726,267	68,364,695	72,894,987	64,549,780	65,772,041
Total Outpatient Visits	90,515,053	86,683,849	90,619,742	81,671,208	82,916,312
Outpatient Surgeries	2,401,308	2,371,683	2,340,405	2,279,223	2,345,497
Personnel					
Full Time RNs	159,878	157,652	151,208	143,484	139,473
Full Time LPNs	8,875	10,238	10,864	11,311	12,244
Part Time RNs..................	73,727	71,718	75,014	69,901	69,952
Part Time LPNs	3,090	3,461	4,125	4,365	4,932
Total Full Time..................	572,775	571,380	575,521	554,813	554,388
Total Part Time	211,094	206,711	215,729	204,796	212,170
Revenue - Inpatient					
Gross Inpatient Revenue...........	$209,508,102,124	$192,767,208,267	$188,790,420,618	$169,713,323,276	$159,727,014,412
Revenue - Outpatient					
Gross Outpatient Revenue	$133,493,602,189	$118,085,940,332	$107,500,249,231	$91,813,591,084	$85,030,303,818
Revenue and Expenses - Totals					
(Includes Inpatient and Outpatient)					
Total Gross Revenue..............	$343,001,704,313	$310,853,148,599	$296,290,669,849	$261,526,914,360	$244,757,318,230
Deductions from Revenue..........	239,740,752,936	213,449,294,445	201,399,629,121	176,791,285,927	161,994,484,185
Net Patient Revenue	103,260,951,377	97,403,854,154	94,891,040,728	84,735,628,433	82,762,834,045
Other Operating Revenue	5,624,897,632	5,833,232,696	5,496,095,330	4,775,900,317	4,311,575,332
Other Nonoperating Revenue	2,187,362,723	421,501,249	-735,779,905	2,352,647,862	1,820,794,415
Total Net Revenue................	111,073,211,732	103,658,588,099	99,651,356,153	91,864,176,612	88,895,203,792
Total Expenses..................	102,319,306,727	97,985,067,095	96,680,861,169	85,991,812,527	83,742,334,417
HOSPITAL UNIT (Excludes Separate Nursing Home Units)					
Utilization - Inpatient					
Beds..........................	115,138	114,177	115,956	111,008	114,872
Admissions.....................	5,794,184	5,722,480	5,852,894	5,593,182	5,673,915
Inpatient Days	27,890,368	27,966,432	29,131,108	27,762,180	28,602,063
Average Length of Stay...........	4.8	4.9	5.0	5.0	5.0
Personnel					
Total Full Time..................	567,683	565,928	570,294	548,396	548,927
Total Part Time	208,623	204,570	212,975	201,430	209,541
Revenue and Expenses - Totals					
(Includes Inpatient and Outpatient)					
Total Net Revenue................	$110,402,770,436	$102,987,034,415	$98,992,882,329	$91,064,513,405	$87,874,129,969
Total Expenses..................	101,715,147,145	97,429,327,288	96,149,983,308	85,383,983,393	83,178,661,808

Bed Size Categories

TABLE **4**

BED SIZE CATEGORY 400-499

U.S. Registered Community Hospitals
(Nonfederal, short-term general and other special hospitals)

Overview 2006–2010

	2010	2009	2008	2007	2006
Total Community Hospitals in					
Bed Size Category 400-499	185	192	184	191	180
Location					
Hospitals Urban	182	187	180	188	173
Hospitals Rural	3	5	4	3	7
Control					
State and Local Government	28	23	24	26	24
Not for Profit	139	148	142	149	141
Investor owned	18	21	18	16	15
Physician Models					
Independent Practice Association	27	28	34	35	27
Group Practice without Walls	13	16	15	11	8
Open Physician-Hospital Organization	35	41	39	45	45
Closed Physician-Hospital Organization	13	15	15	17	21
Management Service Organization	30	30	29	33	31
Integrated Salary Model	94	86	79	89	81
Equity Model	4	4	4	3	2
Foundation	24	22	23	25	17
Insurance Products					
Health Maintenance Organization	38	33	36	41	42
Preferred Provider Organization	41	37	40	54	64
Indemnity Fee for Service	15	9	12	17	14
Managed Care Contracts					
Health Maintenance Organization	149	147	134	148	137
Preferred Provider Organization	147	149	135	149	147
Affiliations					
Hospitals in a System	128	128	122	131	121
Hospitals in a Network	78	70	65	72	74
Hospitals in a Group Purchasing Organization . .	158	159	154	154	155

TABLE 4

BED SIZE CATEGORY 400-499

U.S. Registered Community Hospitals
(Nonfederal, short-term general and other special hospitals)

Utilization, Personnel, Revenue and Expenses, Community Health Indicators 2006–2010

	2010	2009	2008	2007	2006
TOTAL FACILITY (Includes Hospital and Nursing Home Units)					
Utilization - Inpatient					
Beds	82,071	84,783	80,815	84,136	79,732
Admissions	3,869,124	4,049,002	3,895,152	4,043,595	3,871,574
Inpatient Days	20,521,474	21,675,972	20,830,426	21,561,191	20,851,846
Average Length of Stay	5.3	5.4	5.3	5.3	5.4
Inpatient Surgeries	1,178,350	1,220,457	1,133,598	1,241,437	1,158,386
Births	408,256	431,706	435,954	436,346	450,952
Utilization - Outpatient					
Emergency Outpatient Visits	11,546,221	12,078,252	10,828,538	11,467,478	10,442,303
Other Outpatient Visits	53,996,342	51,649,202	46,814,290	49,136,174	49,997,574
Total Outpatient Visits	65,542,563	63,727,454	57,642,828	60,603,652	60,439,877
Outpatient Surgeries	1,665,216	1,804,693	1,739,961	1,764,315	1,679,079
Personnel					
Full Time RNs	121,762	123,770	113,628	115,451	105,572
Full Time LPNs	6,176	6,578	7,035	7,749	7,645
Part Time RNs	53,293	55,922	52,946	57,353	55,876
Part Time LPNs	2,317	2,330	2,903	3,355	2,893
Total Full Time	441,431	458,527	435,911	450,198	423,369
Total Part Time	146,459	155,793	152,140	157,418	150,778
Revenue - Inpatient					
Gross Inpatient Revenue	$150,837,747,313	$154,483,680,751	$134,562,622,630	$133,204,086,152	$117,571,183,567
Revenue - Outpatient					
Gross Outpatient Revenue	$98,160,076,960	$94,037,031,898	$77,496,854,013	$72,665,010,884	$63,147,077,256
Revenue and Expenses - Totals					
(Includes Inpatient and Outpatient)					
Total Gross Revenue	$248,997,824,273	$248,520,712,649	$212,059,476,643	$205,869,097,036	$180,718,260,823
Deductions from Revenue	172,382,284,117	170,485,791,464	144,218,038,992	137,448,298,436	117,343,128,467
Net Patient Revenue	76,615,540,156	78,034,921,185	67,841,437,651	68,420,798,600	63,375,132,356
Other Operating Revenue	4,922,929,664	4,809,356,943	4,570,160,760	4,690,966,723	3,949,229,017
Other Nonoperating Revenue	1,471,629,299	576,751,753	-823,396,082	2,572,380,989	1,734,466,487
Total Net Revenue	83,010,099,119	83,421,029,881	71,588,202,329	75,684,146,312	69,058,827,860
Total Expenses	77,854,509,046	79,447,824,942	70,515,262,080	70,823,523,589	65,100,973,378
HOSPITAL UNIT (Excludes Separate Nursing Home Units)					
Utilization - Inpatient					
Beds	79,722	82,330	77,661	80,693	76,731
Admissions	3,854,485	4,034,937	3,878,278	4,023,773	3,850,518
Inpatient Days	19,770,661	20,873,864	19,817,710	20,501,012	19,955,104
Average Length of Stay	5.1	5.2	5.1	5.1	5.2
Personnel					
Total Full Time	439,282	455,941	431,434	446,149	419,376
Total Part Time	145,585	154,827	150,412	156,426	149,020
Revenue and Expenses - Totals					
(Includes Inpatient and Outpatient)					
Total Net Revenue	$82,724,653,206	$83,143,956,566	$71,316,876,706	$75,352,413,590	$68,387,154,288
Total Expenses	77,613,265,522	79,186,633,408	70,261,647,760	70,461,579,770	64,709,737,350

TABLE 4

BED SIZE CATEGORY 500 +

U.S. Registered Community Hospitals
(Nonfederal, short-term general and other special hospitals)

Overview 2006–2010

	2010	2009	2008	2007	2006
Total Community Hospitals in					
Bed Size Category 500 +.................	273	266	270	260	259
Location					
Hospitals Urban..........................	271	263	266	256	256
Hospitals Rural	2	3	4	4	3
Control					
State and Local Government................	47	48	50	49	42
Not for Profit............................	210	204	206	195	204
Investor owned	16	14	14	16	13
Physician Models					
Independent Practice Association	60	55	52	56	53
Group Practice without Walls...............	14	16	12	14	12
Open Physician-Hospital Organization	62	59	57	51	55
Closed Physician-Hospital Organization	26	26	22	30	25
Management Service Organization	63	59	49	49	50
Integrated Salary Model....................	166	161	154	145	134
Equity Model............................	5	11	11	11	11
Foundation..............................	25	25	28	27	26
Insurance Products					
Health Maintenance Organization	83	81	80	84	83
Preferred Provider Organization..............	86	84	75	77	71
Indemnity Fee for Service	34	29	29	27	25
Managed Care Contracts					
Health Maintenance Organization	227	227	228	217	208
Preferred Provider Organization..............	228	225	225	214	206
Affiliations					
Hospitals in a System.....................	184	184	184	176	175
Hospitals in a Network....................	122	118	110	104	95
Hospitals in a Group Purchasing Organization..	238	234	229	214	203

TABLE 4

BED SIZE CATEGORY 500 +

U.S. Registered Community Hospitals
(Nonfederal, short-term general and other special hospitals)

Utilization, Personnel, Revenue and Expenses, Community Health Indicators 2006–2010

	2010	2009	2008	2007	2006
TOTAL FACILITY (Includes Hospital and Nursing Home Units)					
Utilization - Inpatient					
Beds	196,240	190,790	191,163	183,197	182,141
Admissions	9,209,947	9,025,751	9,059,288	8,649,926	8,435,289
Inpatient Days	52,290,940	51,538,761	52,295,431	50,696,951	50,000,366
Average Length of Stay.	5.7	5.7	5.8	5.9	5.9
Inpatient Surgeries.	2,847,124	2,824,781	2,823,114	2,726,620	2,641,755
Births.	1,003,401	998,660	1,025,916	1,001,043	960,968
Utilization - Outpatient					
Emergency Outpatient Visits	25,059,678	23,926,431	22,872,834	21,245,638	20,171,350
Other Outpatient Visits.	128,007,816	124,170,351	119,350,180	112,603,686	110,336,372
Total Outpatient Visits	153,067,494	148,096,782	142,223,014	133,849,324	130,507,722
Outpatient Surgeries	3,781,333	3,527,469	3,516,202	3,469,212	3,362,077
Personnel					
Full Time RNs	325,170	310,042	294,329	279,858	253,201
Full Time LPNs	12,733	13,854	14,911	15,308	14,887
Part Time RNs.	117,797	114,255	123,478	117,522	110,751
Part Time LPNs	3,873	4,208	4,986	4,945	5,373
Total Full Time.	1,207,498	1,173,995	1,158,279	1,108,995	1,029,769
Total Part Time	329,126	323,649	340,085	326,719	309,498
Revenue - Inpatient					
Gross Inpatient Revenue.	$393,918,219,709	$360,053,211,932	$341,198,456,138	$308,368,746,103	$279,148,331,384
Revenue - Outpatient					
Gross Outpatient Revenue	$234,219,190,376	$203,947,086,192	$180,786,111,977	$155,106,307,545	$137,596,527,510
Revenue and Expenses - Totals					
(Includes Inpatient and Outpatient)					
Total Gross Revenue.	$628,137,410,085	$564,000,298,124	$521,984,568,115	$463,475,053,648	$416,744,858,894
Deductions from Revenue.	426,426,753,565	377,984,394,103	343,813,646,912	299,251,603,589	266,689,606,347
Net Patient Revenue	201,710,656,520	186,015,904,021	178,170,921,203	164,223,450,059	150,055,252,547
Other Operating Revenue	16,864,301,215	15,253,862,892	14,428,536,883	14,234,787,411	14,129,479,856
Other Nonoperating Revenue	4,283,831,027	1,098,421,243	-2,486,522,886	5,547,313,823	3,565,640,844
Total Net Revenue.	222,858,788,762	202,368,188,156	190,112,935,200	184,005,551,293	167,750,373,337
Total Expenses.	206,896,544,358	194,381,058,030	187,486,021,048	170,518,121,648	157,363,704,073
HOSPITAL UNIT (Excludes Separate Nursing Home Units)					
Utilization - Inpatient					
Beds	188,718	183,604	184,099	176,075	173,959
Admissions	9,177,784	8,994,487	9,023,650	8,611,398	8,395,827
Inpatient Days	49,779,016	49,096,850	50,064,396	48,073,269	47,352,280
Average Length of Stay.	5.4	5.5	5.5	5.6	5.6
Personnel					
Total Full Time.	1,202,435	1,166,855	1,151,673	1,096,329	1,019,955
Total Part Time	327,042	320,836	337,438	323,932	305,725
Revenue and Expenses - Totals					
(Includes Inpatient and Outpatient)					
Total Net Revenue.	$222,002,119,967	$201,733,630,805	$189,412,292,055	$183,262,813,923	$166,274,950,550
Total Expenses.	206,018,475,965	193,647,981,433	186,762,975,722	169,751,155,931	156,653,330,209

Bed Size Categories

Census Divisions

Census Division 1

New England
Connecticut, Maine, Massachusetts, New Hampshire, Rhode Island, Vermont

Census Division 2

Middle Atlantic
New Jersey, New York, Pennsylvania

Census Division 3

South Atlantic
Delaware, District of Columbia, Florida, Georgia, Maryland, North Carolina, South Carolina, Virginia, West Virginia

Census Division 4

East North Central
Illinois, Indiana, Michigan, Ohio, Wisconsin

Census Division 5

East South Central
Alabama, Kentucky, Mississippi, Tennessee

Census Division 6

West North Central
Iowa, Kansas, Minnesota, Missouri, Nebraska, North Dakota, South Dakota

Census Division 7

West South Central
Arkansas, Louisiana, Oklahoma, Texas

Census Division 8

Mountain
Arizona, Colorado, Idaho, Montana, Nevada, New Mexico, Utah, Wyoming

Census Division 9

Pacific
Alaska, California, Hawaii, Oregon, Washington

TABLE 5

U.S. CENSUS DIVISION 1: NEW ENGLAND

U.S. Registered Community Hospitals
(Nonfederal, short-term general and other special hospitals)

Overview 2006–2010

	2010	2009	2008	2007	2006
Total Community Hospitals					
in Census Division 1, New England	203	203	200	202	205
Bed Size Category					
6-24	10	10	10	8	9
25-49	39	40	38	39	38
50-99	40	41	42	45	44
100-199	59	57	54	54	56
200-299	25	22	22	23	26
300-399	14	17	17	16	16
400-499	4	4	5	5	3
500 + ...	12	12	12	12	13
Location					
Hospitals Urban	145	145	142	144	128
Hospitals Rural	58	58	58	58	77
Control					
State and Local Government	4	5	5	6	6
Not for Profit	182	184	180	182	183
Investor owned	17	14	15	14	16
Physician Models					
Independent Practice Association	44	40	40	46	50
Group Practice without Walls	11	8	7	7	8
Open Physician-Hospital Organization	52	51	50	51	58
Closed Physician-Hospital Organization	14	12	11	16	17
Management Service Organization	24	21	20	23	21
Integrated Salary Model	107	98	98	92	101
Equity Model	4	6	6	5	5
Foundation	13	10	8	12	11
Insurance Products					
Health Maintenance Organization	19	17	19	22	20
Preferred Provider Organization	9	8	9	21	21
Indemnity Fee for Service	6	4	4	12	9
Managed Care Contracts					
Health Maintenance Organization	141	133	132	139	149
Preferred Provider Organization	136	132	127	131	142
Affiliations					
Hospitals in a System	89	77	74	75	79
Hospitals in a Network	75	69	69	74	77
Hospitals in a Group Purchasing Organization . .	166	159	164	171	174

TABLE **5**

U.S. CENSUS DIVISION 1: NEW ENGLAND

U.S. Registered Community Hospitals
(Nonfederal, short-term general and other special hospitals)

Utilization, Personnel, Revenue and Expenses, Community Health Indicators 2006–2010

	2010	2009	2008	2007	2006
TOTAL FACILITY (Includes Hospital and Nursing Home Units)					
Utilization - Inpatient					
Beds	33,974	33,672	33,743	34,140	34,353
Admissions	1,668,378	1,678,176	1,660,654	1,691,347	1,688,920
Inpatient Days	8,813,799	8,987,254	8,992,337	9,029,013	9,240,145
Average Length of Stay	5.3	5.4	5.4	5.3	5.5
Inpatient Surgeries	439,721	454,138	457,144	469,330	444,881
Births	152,389	156,346	163,857	165,858	182,170
Utilization - Outpatient					
Emergency Outpatient Visits	7,120,183	7,004,583	6,848,347	6,732,398	6,691,531
Other Outpatient Visits	39,615,363	38,999,668	37,188,267	34,540,452	33,649,121
Total Outpatient Visits	46,735,546	46,004,251	44,036,614	41,272,850	40,340,652
Outpatient Surgeries	1,018,591	980,423	996,495	1,010,447	1,056,911
Personnel					
Full Time RNs	44,258	44,777	43,571	42,761	39,126
Full Time LPNs	1,811	1,898	1,972	2,052	2,069
Part Time RNs	39,689	38,236	39,421	39,108	37,918
Part Time LPNs	1,359	1,508	1,768	1,863	1,706
Total Full Time	223,298	223,553	217,995	212,334	198,629
Total Part Time	123,799	118,235	121,345	120,603	116,013
Revenue - Inpatient					
Gross Inpatient Revenue	$47,986,647,777	$46,367,979,779	$44,041,639,373	$41,786,910,589	$37,170,857,983
Revenue - Outpatient					
Gross Outpatient Revenue	$52,517,753,883	$49,137,348,602	$43,645,548,924	$38,945,410,783	$35,925,073,139
Revenue and Expenses - Totals					
(Includes Inpatient and Outpatient)					
Total Gross Revenue	$100,504,401,660	$95,505,328,381	$87,687,188,297	$80,732,321,372	$73,095,931,122
Deductions from Revenue	59,098,902,583	55,719,745,134	50,488,459,964	45,898,543,565	40,515,901,458
Net Patient Revenue	41,405,499,077	39,785,583,247	37,198,728,333	34,833,777,807	32,580,029,664
Other Operating Revenue	4,151,761,895	3,962,230,864	3,637,620,235	3,373,305,081	3,113,979,625
Other Nonoperating Revenue	426,472,039	-167,328,782	-272,745,680	1,107,269,692	748,697,662
Total Net Revenue	45,983,733,011	43,580,485,329	40,563,602,888	39,314,352,580	36,442,706,951
Total Expenses	44,366,268,718	42,351,771,503	39,734,569,287	36,994,342,737	34,779,690,838
HOSPITAL UNIT (Excludes Separate Nursing Home Units)					
Utilization - Inpatient					
Beds	32,710	32,524	32,109	32,789	32,825
Admissions	1,662,431	1,673,090	1,654,586	1,682,524	1,675,178
Inpatient Days	8,377,660	8,601,239	8,442,410	8,577,083	8,728,611
Average Length of Stay	5.0	5.1	5.1	5.1	5.2
Personnel					
Total Full Time	222,354	222,494	215,906	210,754	197,029
Total Part Time	123,029	117,563	119,472	119,412	114,872
Revenue and Expenses - Totals					
(Includes Inpatient and Outpatient)					
Total Net Revenue	$45,855,486,664	$43,455,515,086	$40,395,735,597	$39,176,727,876	$36,238,128,346
Total Expenses	44,254,639,824	42,232,006,786	39,589,865,862	36,879,337,539	34,618,507,186
COMMUNITY HEALTH INDICATORS PER 1000 POPULATION					
Total Population (in thousands)	14,474	14,430	14,363	14,298	14,259
Inpatient					
Beds	2.3	2.3	2.3	2.4	2.4
Admissions	115.3	116.3	115.6	118.3	118.4
Inpatient Days	608.9	622.8	626.1	631.5	648.0
Inpatient Surgeries	30.4	31.5	31.8	32.8	31.2
Births	10.5	10.8	11.4	11.6	12.8
Outpatient					
Emergency Outpatient Visits	491.9	485.4	476.8	470.9	469.3
Other Outpatient Visits	2,737.0	2,702.7	2,589.2	2,415.7	2,359.9
Total Outpatient Visits	3,228.9	3,188.2	3,066.1	2,886.6	2,829.2
Outpatient Surgeries	70.4	67.9	69.4	70.7	74.1
Expense per Capita (per person)	$3,065.2	$2,935.0	$2,766.5	$2,587.4	$2,439.2

TABLE 5

U.S. CENSUS DIVISION 2: MIDDLE ATLANTIC

U.S. Registered Community Hospitals
(Nonfederal, short-term general and other special hospitals)

Overview 2006–2010

	2010	2009	2008	2007	2006
Total Community Hospitals					
in Census Division 2, Middle Atlantic.......	454	457	468	462	470
Bed Size Category					
6-24...................................	8	7	7	8	8
25-49..................................	38	39	41	29	30
50-99..................................	66	64	65	60	59
100-199................................	102	111	115	119	130
200-299................................	98	93	95	98	96
300-399................................	53	53	56	57	58
400-499................................	33	36	34	38	32
500 +..................................	56	54	55	53	57
Location					
Hospitals Urban........................	367	369	379	374	390
Hospitals Rural........................	87	88	89	88	80
Control					
State and Local Government................	30	30	33	31	26
Not for Profit.............................	373	381	388	397	412
Investor owned..........................	51	46	47	34	32
Physician Models					
Independent Practice Association............	54	54	63	69	64
Group Practice without Walls................	17	20	20	19	19
Open Physician-Hospital Organization........	40	41	55	55	55
Closed Physician-Hospital Organization.......	15	18	15	18	15
Management Service Organization...........	51	54	52	51	55
Integrated Salary Model....................	172	158	142	150	143
Equity Model.............................	2	5	6	6	7
Foundation..............................	14	12	11	12	8
Insurance Products					
Health Maintenance Organization............	80	66	83	78	74
Preferred Provider Organization..............	79	66	80	76	70
Indemnity Fee for Service..................	42	28	33	31	27
Managed Care Contracts					
Health Maintenance Organization............	286	279	283	289	290
Preferred Provider Organization..............	277	264	270	271	276
Affiliations					
Hospitals in a System.....................	242	235	231	218	231
Hospitals in a Network....................	157	151	154	152	151
Hospitals in a Group Purchasing Organization..	321	305	308	315	324

TABLE 5

U.S. CENSUS DIVISION 2: MIDDLE ATLANTIC

U.S. Registered Community Hospitals
(Nonfederal, short-term general and other special hospitals)

Utilization, Personnel, Revenue and Expenses, Community Health Indicators 2006–2010

	2010	2009	2008	2007	2006
TOTAL FACILITY (Includes Hospital and Nursing Home Units)					
Utilization - Inpatient					
Beds	120,495	120,666	122,511	123,639	125,252
Admissions	5,387,182	5,469,937	5,516,053	5,505,319	5,548,934
Inpatient Days	32,429,928	32,905,796	33,922,806	34,215,129	34,456,727
Average Length of Stay	6.0	6.0	6.1	6.2	6.2
Inpatient Surgeries	1,472,258	1,444,280	1,475,219	1,495,234	1,535,961
Births	473,143	481,966	493,580	498,628	500,614
Utilization - Outpatient					
Emergency Outpatient Visits	17,544,922	18,036,427	17,471,705	17,141,299	16,764,369
Other Outpatient Visits	90,638,433	92,532,690	91,694,245	89,970,276	89,966,865
Total Outpatient Visits	108,183,355	110,569,117	109,165,950	107,111,575	106,731,234
Outpatient Surgeries	2,662,613	2,672,246	2,667,312	2,673,530	2,759,965
Personnel					
Full Time RNs	159,336	157,599	154,609	153,296	145,453
Full Time LPNs	9,477	10,498	11,135	11,648	11,916
Part Time RNs	61,970	58,758	59,586	61,316	59,512
Part Time LPNs	3,392	3,492	3,915	4,192	4,433
Total Full Time	641,848	649,700	652,192	645,979	623,974
Total Part Time	193,048	188,250	187,630	190,730	186,861
Revenue - Inpatient					
Gross Inpatient Revenue	$214,875,701,636	$207,428,274,807	$204,106,922,337	$191,802,352,802	$177,688,048,241
Revenue - Outpatient					
Gross Outpatient Revenue	$131,067,665,392	$119,608,818,446	$108,338,945,283	$97,230,945,480	$90,009,081,885
Revenue and Expenses - Totals					
(Includes Inpatient and Outpatient)					
Total Gross Revenue	$345,943,367,028	$327,037,093,253	$312,445,867,620	$289,033,298,282	$267,697,130,126
Deductions from Revenue	241,791,805,319	226,954,454,439	217,335,551,911	198,289,740,098	181,556,755,763
Net Patient Revenue	104,151,561,709	100,082,638,814	95,110,315,709	90,743,558,184	86,140,374,363
Other Operating Revenue	6,773,917,247	6,240,458,318	5,905,669,784	6,338,357,464	6,577,538,742
Other Nonoperating Revenue	1,636,895,627	1,079,935,145	-522,530,088	2,136,486,090	1,764,422,561
Total Net Revenue	112,562,374,583	107,403,032,277	100,493,455,405	99,218,401,738	94,482,335,756
Total Expenses	107,964,477,816	104,601,314,499	101,341,325,573	94,889,661,651	91,387,151,168
HOSPITAL UNIT (Excludes Separate Nursing Home Units)					
Utilization - Inpatient					
Beds	112,240	112,737	114,721	115,326	117,117
Admissions	5,349,564	5,432,647	5,477,486	5,465,485	5,508,450
Inpatient Days	29,691,180	30,267,570	31,398,678	31,360,166	31,721,535
Average Length of Stay	5.6	5.6	5.7	5.7	5.8
Personnel					
Total Full Time	636,513	642,529	644,394	638,846	617,422
Total Part Time	189,998	184,726	184,048	187,399	183,604
Revenue and Expenses - Totals					
(Includes Inpatient and Outpatient)					
Total Net Revenue	$111,642,685,649	$106,605,542,714	$99,744,284,282	$98,469,053,061	$93,800,512,716
Total Expenses	107,117,179,018	103,815,232,446	100,633,830,609	94,212,728,480	90,738,596,774
COMMUNITY HEALTH INDICATORS PER 1000 POPULATION					
Total Population (in thousands)	40,943	40,854	40,698	40,581	40,451
Inpatient					
Beds	2.9	3.0	3.0	3.0	3.1
Admissions	131.6	133.9	135.5	135.7	137.2
Inpatient Days	792.1	805.4	833.5	843.1	851.8
Inpatient Surgeries	36.0	35.4	36.2	36.8	38.0
Births	11.6	11.8	12.1	12.3	12.4
Outpatient					
Emergency Outpatient Visits	428.5	441.5	429.3	422.4	414.4
Other Outpatient Visits	2,213.8	2,265.0	2,253.1	2,217.0	2,224.1
Total Outpatient Visits	2,642.3	2,706.4	2,682.4	2,639.4	2,638.5
Outpatient Surgeries	65.0	65.4	65.5	65.9	68.2
Expense per Capita (per person)	$2,636.9	$2,560.4	$2,490.1	$2,338.3	$2,259.2

TABLE 5

U.S. CENSUS DIVISION 3: SOUTH ATLANTIC

U.S. Registered Community Hospitals
(Nonfederal, short-term general and other special hospitals)

Overview 2006–2010

	2010	2009	2008	2007	2006
Total Community Hospitals					
in Census Division 3, South Atlantic	758	759	762	735	741
Bed Size Category					
6-24	21	20	18	17	17
25-49	129	127	129	112	111
50-99	133	133	128	120	128
100-199	196	202	209	203	203
200-299	115	115	116	122	118
300-399	65	62	67	66	72
400-499	34	37	30	33	33
500 + ...	65	63	65	62	59
Location					
Hospitals Urban	514	516	516	489	454
Hospitals Rural	244	243	246	246	287
Control					
State and Local Government	141	144	147	148	145
Not for Profit	398	402	406	394	396
Investor owned	219	213	209	193	200
Physician Models					
Independent Practice Association	52	51	52	51	57
Group Practice without Walls	23	26	24	24	24
Open Physician-Hospital Organization	79	77	80	81	89
Closed Physician-Hospital Organization	38	36	39	40	40
Management Service Organization	67	56	51	50	53
Integrated Salary Model	287	256	255	249	228
Equity Model	21	20	20	18	17
Foundation	20	16	21	20	18
Insurance Products					
Health Maintenance Organization	74	72	62	64	83
Preferred Provider Organization	94	85	75	97	124
Indemnity Fee for Service	29	27	24	37	46
Managed Care Contracts					
Health Maintenance Organization	417	412	402	407	406
Preferred Provider Organization	448	452	435	446	463
Affiliations					
Hospitals in a System	504	493	479	443	451
Hospitals in a Network	215	205	211	219	219
Hospitals in a Group Purchasing Organization . .	538	535	542	490	497

TABLE 5

U.S. CENSUS DIVISION 3: SOUTH ATLANTIC

U.S. Registered Community Hospitals
(Nonfederal, short-term general and other special hospitals)

Utilization, Personnel, Revenue and Expenses, Community Health Indicators 2006–2010

	2010	2009	2008	2007	2006
TOTAL FACILITY (Includes Hospital and Nursing Home Units)					
Utilization - Inpatient					
Beds	156,678	156,435	156,622	154,101	153,115
Admissions	6,970,769	7,001,234	6,958,360	6,913,804	6,862,970
Inpatient Days	37,775,346	37,871,460	38,331,279	38,540,724	38,694,981
Average Length of Stay	5.4	5.4	5.5	5.6	5.6
Inpatient Surgeries	1,978,051	2,014,276	2,003,768	1,998,114	2,008,456
Births	718,161	736,030	764,298	771,074	754,948
Utilization - Outpatient					
Emergency Outpatient Visits	25,132,194	25,680,948	24,482,937	24,095,446	23,813,876
Other Outpatient Visits	70,980,844	71,516,908	69,838,160	67,864,346	66,355,974
Total Outpatient Visits	96,113,038	97,197,856	94,321,097	91,959,792	90,169,850
Outpatient Surgeries	3,275,089	3,347,083	3,346,983	3,262,710	3,294,862
Personnel					
Full Time RNs	214,222	209,172	195,655	191,207	182,267
Full Time LPNs	14,299	15,153	16,133	17,055	17,858
Part Time RNs	73,321	75,692	79,445	77,184	75,586
Part Time LPNs	4,092	4,515	5,177	5,470	5,540
Total Full Time	753,621	746,119	731,835	716,204	697,654
Total Part Time	204,742	211,449	219,295	214,064	211,258
Revenue - Inpatient					
Gross Inpatient Revenue	$221,881,724,341	$206,158,157,529	$190,255,383,250	$179,774,493,773	$165,578,390,457
Revenue - Outpatient					
Gross Outpatient Revenue	$156,997,699,889	$141,704,232,345	$123,592,865,886	$110,871,408,881	$97,769,350,198
Revenue and Expenses - Totals					
(Includes Inpatient and Outpatient)					
Total Gross Revenue	$378,879,424,230	$347,862,389,874	$313,848,249,136	$290,645,902,654	$263,347,740,655
Deductions from Revenue	257,534,395,622	231,360,708,001	204,204,305,242	186,436,266,133	165,215,098,511
Net Patient Revenue	121,345,028,608	116,501,681,873	109,643,943,894	104,209,636,521	98,132,642,144
Other Operating Revenue	5,739,614,294	5,340,444,911	5,395,566,187	4,847,826,689	4,785,098,906
Other Nonoperating Revenue	2,153,138,363	702,305,382	-1,072,116,225	2,512,438,728	1,821,994,128
Total Net Revenue	129,237,781,265	122,544,432,166	113,967,393,856	111,569,901,938	104,739,735,178
Total Expenses	118,053,521,062	115,183,239,713	109,762,268,873	103,137,798,170	97,065,907,476
HOSPITAL UNIT (Excludes Separate Nursing Home Units)					
Utilization - Inpatient					
Beds	145,304	146,162	145,784	142,648	140,818
Admissions	6,925,183	6,957,697	6,913,674	6,864,373	6,814,310
Inpatient Days	34,041,050	34,447,166	34,834,753	34,608,173	34,675,520
Average Length of Stay	4.9	5.0	5.0	5.0	5.1
Personnel					
Total Full Time	745,348	737,233	723,355	706,613	686,079
Total Part Time	201,603	208,120	216,083	210,620	207,340
Revenue and Expenses - Totals					
(Includes Inpatient and Outpatient)					
Total Net Revenue	$128,322,166,959	$121,761,391,092	$113,171,813,994	$110,708,005,981	$101,638,027,688
Total Expenses	117,214,899,415	114,453,158,594	109,002,752,761	102,312,602,232	96,238,962,477
COMMUNITY HEALTH INDICATORS PER 1000 POPULATION					
Total Population (in thousands)	59,659	59,196	58,607	57,916	57,128
Inpatient					
Beds	2.6	2.6	2.7	2.7	2.7
Admissions	116.8	118.3	118.7	119.4	120.1
Inpatient Days	633.2	639.8	654.0	665.5	677.3
Inpatient Surgeries	33.2	34.0	34.2	34.5	35.2
Births	12.0	12.4	13.0	13.3	13.2
Outpatient					
Emergency Outpatient Visits	421.3	433.8	417.7	416.0	416.8
Other Outpatient Visits	1,189.8	1,208.1	1,191.6	1,171.8	1,161.5
Total Outpatient Visits	1,611.0	1,642.0	1,609.4	1,587.8	1,578.4
Outpatient Surgeries	54.9	56.5	57.1	56.3	57.7
Expense per Capita (per person)	$1,978.8	$1,945.8	$1,872.8	$1,780.8	$1,699.1

TABLE 5

U.S. CENSUS DIVISION 4: EAST NORTH CENTRAL

U.S. Registered Community Hospitals
(Nonfederal, short-term general and other special hospitals)

Overview 2006–2010

	2010	2009	2008	2007	2006
Total Community Hospitals					
in Census Division 4, East North Central....	777	779	774	742	741
Bed Size Category					
6-24	43	40	37	31	33
25-49	198	196	193	171	161
50-99	163	166	162	150	148
100-199	151	161	159	169	178
200-299	100	96	99	101	100
300-399	56	52	56	50	51
400-499	26	29	29	33	30
500 + ...	40	39	39	37	40
Location					
Hospitals Urban.	503	504	499	469	454
Hospitals Rural	274	275	275	273	287
Control					
State and Local Government.	96	99	103	107	108
Not for Profit	590	593	589	583	580
Investor owned	91	87	82	52	53
Physician Models					
Independent Practice Association	73	86	88	88	90
Group Practice without Walls.	25	23	28	27	28
Open Physician-Hospital Organization	164	163	151	156	152
Closed Physician-Hospital Organization	51	45	47	67	69
Management Service Organization	87	93	96	94	94
Integrated Salary Model.	312	303	295	281	257
Equity Model.	22	26	30	15	16
Foundation.	59	52	49	44	49
Insurance Products					
Health Maintenance Organization	145	143	140	154	157
Preferred Provider Organization.	165	167	155	197	197
Indemnity Fee for Service	57	59	57	71	58
Managed Care Contracts					
Health Maintenance Organization	531	552	529	491	518
Preferred Provider Organization.	568	597	576	535	564
Affiliations					
Hospitals in a System.	475	467	452	421	405
Hospitals in a Network	277	276	271	252	264
Hospitals in a Group Purchasing Organization. .	632	645	643	598	634

TABLE 5

U.S. CENSUS DIVISION 4: EAST NORTH CENTRAL

U.S. Registered Community Hospitals
(Nonfederal, short-term general and other special hospitals)

Utilization, Personnel, Revenue and Expenses, Community Health Indicators 2006–2010

	2010	2009	2008	2007	2006
TOTAL FACILITY (Includes Hospital and Nursing Home Units)					
Utilization - Inpatient					
Beds	124,528	124,648	124,957	123,858	125,144
Admissions	5,573,945	5,631,570	5,730,456	5,656,902	5,666,562
Inpatient Days	28,088,741	28,659,008	29,237,134	28,818,795	29,071,025
Average Length of Stay	5.0	5.1	5.1	5.1	5.1
Inpatient Surgeries	1,598,684	1,629,031	1,641,475	1,611,589	1,570,026
Births	549,668	569,683	590,869	595,181	596,871
Utilization - Outpatient					
Emergency Outpatient Visits	21,645,563	21,143,963	20,682,680	20,641,691	20,042,357
Other Outpatient Visits	110,255,848	106,866,440	102,419,976	100,771,454	99,366,389
Total Outpatient Visits	131,901,411	128,010,403	123,102,656	121,413,145	119,408,746
Outpatient Surgeries	3,207,896	3,184,812	3,147,665	3,131,378	3,160,980
Personnel					
Full Time RNs	166,190	159,198	154,002	148,084	141,688
Full Time LPNs	8,792	9,506	10,480	10,888	11,206
Part Time RNs	97,309	97,165	96,817	94,856	98,318
Part Time LPNs	5,200	5,538	6,489	6,726	7,058
Total Full Time	656,411	652,503	647,246	631,125	616,060
Total Part Time	305,777	309,198	306,273	296,396	307,330
Revenue - Inpatient					
Gross Inpatient Revenue	$169,254,285,621	$159,626,875,101	$149,698,495,809	$138,385,536,623	$128,438,375,170
Revenue - Outpatient					
Gross Outpatient Revenue	$153,605,458,204	$139,937,321,698	$125,559,569,848	$112,453,910,765	$101,789,022,674
Revenue and Expenses - Totals					
(Includes Inpatient and Outpatient)					
Total Gross Revenue	$322,859,743,825	$299,564,196,799	$275,258,065,657	$250,839,447,388	$230,227,397,844
Deductions from Revenue	206,741,773,300	188,295,725,972	169,876,753,425	151,738,136,454	137,355,334,545
Net Patient Revenue	116,117,970,525	111,268,470,827	105,381,312,232	99,101,310,934	92,872,063,299
Other Operating Revenue	6,838,675,527	6,706,843,261	6,300,528,903	5,973,060,158	5,159,399,104
Other Nonoperating Revenue	2,812,190,226	360,822,911	-2,457,450,887	3,688,479,320	2,568,302,789
Total Net Revenue	125,768,836,278	118,336,136,999	109,224,390,248	108,762,850,412	100,599,765,192
Total Expenses	116,021,099,796	112,388,231,445	108,029,056,637	100,228,770,592	94,345,981,361
HOSPITAL UNIT (Excludes Separate Nursing Home Units)					
Utilization - Inpatient					
Beds	118,315	118,136	118,085	116,254	116,691
Admissions	5,532,131	5,587,798	5,687,064	5,612,602	5,612,044
Inpatient Days	26,193,965	26,630,592	27,072,122	26,485,828	26,473,334
Average Length of Stay	4.7	4.8	4.8	4.7	4.7
Personnel					
Total Full Time	652,317	647,481	642,131	620,539	610,220
Total Part Time	302,371	305,428	302,441	292,478	302,984
Revenue and Expenses - Totals					
(Includes Inpatient and Outpatient)					
Total Net Revenue	$125,272,982,180	$117,798,388,335	$108,726,765,462	$108,179,483,196	$99,932,380,489
Total Expenses	115,557,672,594	111,947,643,021	107,600,938,852	99,700,838,980	93,726,813,114
COMMUNITY HEALTH INDICATORS PER 1000 POPULATION					
Total Population (in thousands)	46,522	46,501	46,389	46,299	46,166
Inpatient					
Beds	2.7	2.7	2.7	2.7	2.7
Admissions	119.8	121.1	123.5	122.2	122.7
Inpatient Days	603.8	616.3	630.3	622.5	629.7
Inpatient Surgeries	34.4	35.0	35.4	34.8	34.0
Births	11.8	12.3	12.7	12.9	12.9
Outpatient					
Emergency Outpatient Visits	465.3	454.7	445.8	445.8	434.1
Other Outpatient Visits	2,370.0	2,298.2	2,207.8	2,176.5	2,152.4
Total Outpatient Visits	2,835.3	2,752.9	2,653.7	2,622.4	2,586.5
Outpatient Surgeries	69.0	68.5	67.9	67.6	68.5
Expense per Capita (per person)	$2,493.9	$2,416.9	$2,328.7	$2,164.8	$2,043.6

U.S. Census Divisions

TABLE 5

U.S. CENSUS DIVISION 5: EAST SOUTH CENTRAL

U.S. Registered Community Hospitals
(Nonfederal, short-term general and other special hospitals)

Overview 2006–2010

	2010	2009	2008	2007	2006
Total Community Hospitals					
in Census Division 5, East South Central . . .	441	446	449	441	437
Bed Size Category					
6-24	16	16	18	16	15
25-49	128	128	126	115	109
50-99	100	104	107	109	107
100-199	104	104	99	103	112
200-299	35	35	39	41	36
300-399	25	26	26	23	26
400-499	14	15	14	14	14
500 + ...	19	18	20	20	18
Location					
Hospitals Urban.	208	211	211	203	176
Hospitals Rural	233	235	238	238	261
Control					
State and Local Government.	112	115	119	118	119
Not for Profit	182	186	188	190	186
Investor owned	147	145	142	133	132
Physician Models					
Independent Practice Association	36	36	35	36	34
Group Practice without Walls.	7	10	10	12	9
Open Physician-Hospital Organization	43	41	49	55	51
Closed Physician-Hospital Organization	8	11	17	14	10
Management Service Organization	39	34	34	39	37
Integrated Salary Model	114	102	94	84	76
Equity Model	1	3	2	1	1
Foundation.	22	23	22	21	16
Insurance Products					
Health Maintenance Organization	32	26	39	44	50
Preferred Provider Organization.	75	70	83	90	100
Indemnity Fee for Service	21	15	28	27	30
Managed Care Contracts					
Health Maintenance Organization	165	164	176	160	153
Preferred Provider Organization.	215	211	233	211	212
Affiliations					
Hospitals in a System.	289	289	286	275	276
Hospitals in a Network	101	105	111	108	109
Hospitals in a Group Purchasing Organization. .	205	224	240	242	244

TABLE 5

U.S. CENSUS DIVISION 5: EAST SOUTH CENTRAL

U.S. Registered Community Hospitals
(Nonfederal, short-term general and other special hospitals)

Utilization, Personnel, Revenue and Expenses, Community Health Indicators 2006–2010

	2010	2009	2008	2007	2006
TOTAL FACILITY (Includes Hospital and Nursing Home Units)					
Utilization - Inpatient					
Beds.........................	63,079	63,252	63,626	64,505	63,514
Admissions.....................	2,486,454	2,535,115	2,587,919	2,695,512	2,565,449
Inpatient Days	13,614,893	13,973,205	14,460,015	14,787,799	14,300,824
Average Length of Stay...........	5.5	5.5	5.6	5.5	5.6
Inpatient Surgeries...............	728,125	746,929	736,745	773,623	755,751
Births........................	221,646	233,974	245,061	253,405	237,866
Utilization - Outpatient					
Emergency Outpatient Visits........	9,527,974	9,630,514	9,557,382	9,547,437	8,840,824
Other Outpatient Visits............	25,726,751	25,948,613	25,382,539	24,408,334	23,078,091
Total Outpatient Visits............	35,254,725	35,579,127	34,939,921	33,955,771	31,918,915
Outpatient Surgeries	1,344,976	1,337,590	1,309,219	1,361,522	1,289,816
Personnel					
Full Time RNs	73,350	73,191	70,022	71,100	65,926
Full Time LPNs	7,457	8,025	8,614	9,593	9,818
Part Time RNs..................	25,319	24,568	25,507	28,291	24,318
Part Time LPNs.................	2,052	2,168	2,568	2,954	2,901
Total Full Time.................	262,113	265,884	263,757	275,742	260,548
Total Part Time	72,591	71,457	74,148	81,297	72,460
Revenue - Inpatient					
Gross Inpatient Revenue...........	$73,345,815,567	$70,177,022,070	$67,429,348,071	$64,100,535,279	$57,208,623,237
Revenue - Outpatient					
Gross Outpatient Revenue	$56,798,252,271	$52,231,598,393	$46,662,139,027	$43,516,710,261	$37,377,336,043
Revenue and Expenses - Totals (Includes Inpatient and Outpatient)					
Total Gross Revenue..............	$130,144,067,838	$122,408,620,463	$114,091,487,098	$107,617,245,540	$94,585,959,280
Deductions from Revenue..........	92,627,817,898	85,830,854,030	79,115,671,773	72,599,542,258	62,204,265,707
Net Patient Revenue	37,516,249,940	36,577,766,433	34,975,815,325	35,017,703,282	32,381,693,573
Other Operating Revenue	1,479,335,426	1,540,908,813	1,625,010,586	1,664,289,342	1,346,242,721
Other Nonoperating Revenue	696,071,058	193,864,288	-19,706,728	964,949,462	658,282,487
Total Net Revenue...............	39,691,656,424	38,312,539,534	36,581,119,183	37,646,942,086	34,386,218,781
Total Expenses..................	36,471,494,399	36,466,730,541	34,933,934,594	35,466,530,096	32,228,480,833
HOSPITAL UNIT (Excludes Separate Nursing Home Units)					
Utilization - Inpatient					
Beds	58,946	58,982	59,075	59,580	58,500
Admissions.....................	2,471,184	2,518,083	2,569,243	2,673,641	2,543,509
Inpatient Days	12,327,182	12,606,657	12,982,972	13,211,639	12,688,369
Average Length of Stay............	5.0	5.0	5.1	4.9	5.0
Personnel					
Total Full Time..................	258,805	262,043	259,932	271,754	256,346
Total Part Time	71,637	70,556	73,231	·80,147	71,329
Revenue and Expenses - Totals (Includes Inpatient and Outpatient)					
Total Net Revenue...............	$39,425,199,072	$38,036,670,123	$36,298,364,734	$37,341,333,037	$34,060,819,744
Total Expenses..................	36,231,662,045	36,228,704,518	34,698,028,587	35,232,988,561	31,986,666,215
COMMUNITY HEALTH INDICATORS PER 1000 POPULATION					
Total Population (in thousands)	18,368	18,271	18,146	17,989	17,804
Inpatient					
Beds	3.4	3.5	3.5	3.6	3.6
Admissions.....................	135.4	138.8	142.6	149.8	144.1
Inpatient Days	741.2	764.8	796.9	822.1	803.3
Inpatient Surgeries...............	39.6	40.9	40.6	43.0	42.4
Births........................	12.1	12.8	13.5	14.1	13.4
Outpatient					
Emergency Outpatient Visits........	518.7	527.1	526.7	530.7	496.6
Other Outpatient Visits............	1,400.7	1,420.2	1,398.8	1,356.9	1,296.3
Total Outpatient Visits	1,919.4	1,947.3	1,925.5	1,887.6	1,792.8
Outpatient Surgeries	73.2	73.2	72.1	75.7	72.4
**Expense per Capita (per person)..... **	$1,985.6	$1,995.9	$1,925.2	$1,971.6	$1,810.2

TABLE 5

U.S. CENSUS DIVISION 6: WEST NORTH CENTRAL

U.S. Registered Community Hospitals
(Nonfederal, short-term general and other special hospitals)

Overview 2006–2010

	2010	2009	2008	2007	2006
Total Community Hospitals					
in Census Division 6, West North Central ...	685	689	683	670	674
Bed Size Category					
6-24	113	108	103	94	93
25-49	220	217	214	212	213
50-99	164	167	166	163	167
100-199	97	104	105	106	106
200-299	35	38	38	40	41
300-399	28	25	26	23	23
400-499	12	14	15	15	15
500 + ...	16	16	16	17	16
Location					
Hospitals Urban.........................	223	224	220	207	180
Hospitals Rural	462	465	463	463	494
Control					
State and Local Government................	235	237	236	241	241
Not for Profit.............................	398	399	395	391	396
Investor owned	52	53	52	38	37
Physician Models					
Independent Practice Association	70	77	82	86	97
Group Practice without Walls................	11	14	13	15	21
Open Physician-Hospital Organization	70	84	89	88	89
Closed Physician-Hospital Organization	23	27	26	30	32
Management Service Organization	17	19	25	28	31
Integrated Salary Model....................	317	339	315	305	306
Equity Model.............................	2	5	6	6	6
Foundation...............................	17	14	21	20	20
Insurance Products					
Health Maintenance Organization	59	56	59	62	69
Preferred Provider Organization..............	88	84	93	121	133
Indemnity Fee for Service	27	29	32	27	31
Managed Care Contracts					
Health Maintenance Organization	310	320	313	312	312
Preferred Provider Organization..............	446	469	471	471	488
Affiliations					
Hospitals in a System.....................	348	347	339	326	326
Hospitals in a Network....................	277	282	280	279	296
Hospitals in a Group Purchasing Organization..	552	573	570	571	587

TABLE 5

U.S. CENSUS DIVISION 6: WEST NORTH CENTRAL

U.S. Registered Community Hospitals
(Nonfederal, short-term general and other special hospitals)

Utilization, Personnel, Revenue and Expenses, Community Health Indicators 2006–2010

	2010	2009	2008	2007	2006
TOTAL FACILITY (Includes Hospital and Nursing Home Units)					
Utilization - Inpatient					
Beds	68,830	70,039	70,208	70,058	70,501
Admissions	2,464,267	2,523,626	2,589,852	2,565,443	2,560,628
Inpatient Days	14,928,227	15,492,237	15,912,612	15,932,234	16,030,245
Average Length of Stay	6.1	6.1	6.1	6.2	6.3
Inpatient Surgeries	683,170	705,862	722,817	721,238	714,989
Births	264,621	274,101	279,320	281,227	278,721
Utilization - Outpatient					
Emergency Outpatient Visits	8,260,672	8,272,930	8,056,684	7,704,372	7,485,813
Other Outpatient Visits	50,003,264	48,365,884	45,865,406	43,815,430	42,934,077
Total Outpatient Visits	58,263,936	56,638,814	53,922,090	51,519,802	50,419,890
Outpatient Surgeries	1,322,974	1,367,598	1,420,972	1,413,357	1,420,795
Personnel					
Full Time RNs	73,425	70,664	67,029	64,883	61,457
Full Time LPNs	7,282	7,481	7,692	7,799	8,037
Part Time RNs	52,648	54,581	55,475	51,436	51,894
Part Time LPNs	4,485	4,775	5,225	5,731	5,880
Total Full Time	297,067	289,975	285,576	278,512	271,798
Total Part Time	164,985	169,233	171,973	161,850	162,593
Revenue - Inpatient					
Gross Inpatient Revenue	$71,077,555,297	$68,351,872,323	$65,013,165,311	$59,939,612,338	$55,534,317,918
Revenue - Outpatient					
Gross Outpatient Revenue	$62,710,234,207	$58,193,971,919	$50,949,559,907	$45,736,849,741	$41,298,026,667
Revenue and Expenses - Totals (Includes Inpatient and Outpatient)					
Total Gross Revenue	$133,787,789,504	$126,545,844,242	$115,962,725,218	$105,676,462,079	$96,832,344,585
Deductions from Revenue	82,115,750,561	76,480,891,243	67,883,978,998	61,925,172,023	55,264,598,641
Net Patient Revenue	51,672,038,943	50,064,952,999	48,078,746,220	43,751,290,056	41,567,745,944
Other Operating Revenue	2,830,841,723	2,646,149,834	2,675,404,595	2,616,805,771	2,479,210,752
Other Nonoperating Revenue	1,318,194,215	557,107,759	-524,235,863	1,412,620,373	1,109,745,510
Total Net Revenue	55,821,074,881	53,268,210,592	50,229,914,952	47,780,716,200	45,156,702,206
Total Expenses	51,771,367,599	50,238,229,445	48,227,547,446	44,256,405,517	41,972,965,544
HOSPITAL UNIT (Excludes Separate Nursing Home Units)					
Utilization - Inpatient					
Beds	59,661	59,833	58,879	58,121	58,156
Admissions	2,443,671	2,498,928	2,561,317	2,534,429	2,526,301
Inpatient Days	12,018,243	12,233,218	12,328,044	12,109,078	12,011,373
Average Length of Stay	4.9	4.9	4.8	4.8	4.8
Personnel					
Total Full Time	291,819	283,837	279,159	271,540	264,519
Total Part Time	160,316	164,037	166,260	155,511	156,092
Revenue and Expenses - Totals (Includes Inpatient and Outpatient)					
Total Net Revenue	$55,268,629,929	$52,624,057,167	$49,501,040,808	$47,065,541,644	$44,374,251,964
Total Expenses	51,251,683,260	49,653,268,189	47,573,291,977	43,615,288,526	41,265,906,225
COMMUNITY HEALTH INDICATORS PER 1000 POPULATION					
Total Population (in thousands)	20,451	20,336	20,206	20,060	19,916
Inpatient					
Beds	3.4	3.4	3.5	3.5	3.5
Admissions	120.5	124.1	128.2	127.9	128.6
Inpatient Days	729.9	761.8	787.5	794.2	804.9
Inpatient Surgeries	33.4	34.7	35.8	36.0	35.9
Births	12.9	13.5	13.8	14.0	14.0
Outpatient					
Emergency Outpatient Visits	403.9	406.8	398.7	384.1	375.9
Other Outpatient Visits	2,445.0	2,378.3	2,269.9	2,184.2	2,155.8
Total Outpatient Visits	2,848.9	2,785.1	2,668.6	2,568.2	2,531.7
Outpatient Surgeries	64.7	67.2	70.3	70.5	71.3
Expense per Capita (per person)	$2,531.4	$2,470.4	$2,386.8	$2,206.1	$2,107.5

U.S. Census Divisions

TABLE 5

U.S. CENSUS DIVISION 7: WEST SOUTH CENTRAL

U.S. Registered Community Hospitals
(Nonfederal, short-term general and other special hospitals)

Overview 2006–2010

	2010	2009	2008	2007	2006
Total Community Hospitals					
in Census Division 7, West South Central...	750	758	757	735	745
Bed Size Category					
6-24	119	112	112	105	105
25-49	220	223	219	213	217
50-99	146	147	151	147	149
100-199	115	124	124	118	122
200-299	61	61	61	65	64
300-399	35	35	37	39	39
400-499	20	22	21	20	21
500 + ...	34	34	32	28	28
Location					
Hospitals Urban.........................	436	440	442	422	411
Hospitals Rural	314	318	315	313	334
Control					
State and Local Government................	221	230	225	226	230
Not for Profit...........................	267	263	273	268	266
Investor owned	262	265	259	241	249
Physician Models					
Independent Practice Association	109	109	103	122	129
Group Practice without Walls................	33	41	28	32	27
Open Physician-Hospital Organization	128	137	143	146	150
Closed Physician-Hospital Organization	30	31	32	28	30
Management Service Organization	94	99	92	93	85
Integrated Salary Model....................	181	168	155	142	150
Equity Model.............................	16	17	19	14	11
Foundation...............................	43	44	50	49	47
Insurance Products					
Health Maintenance Organization	96	90	78	84	83
Preferred Provider Organization..............	118	105	93	116	124
Indemnity Fee for Service	36	30	32	30	35
Managed Care Contracts					
Health Maintenance Organization	449	458	453	445	429
Preferred Provider Organization..............	540	544	551	551	536
Affiliations					
Hospitals in a System......................	434	457	454	432	432
Hospitals in a Network.....................	184	175	177	181	182
Hospitals in a Group Purchasing Organization..	623	624	622	600	602

TABLE 5

U.S. CENSUS DIVISION 7: WEST SOUTH CENTRAL

U.S. Registered Community Hospitals
(Nonfederal, short-term general and other special hospitals)

Utilization, Personnel, Revenue and Expenses, Community Health Indicators 2006–2010

	2010	2009	2008	2007	2006
TOTAL FACILITY (Includes Hospital and Nursing Home Units)					
Utilization - Inpatient					
Beds	97,399	98,807	97,720	94,072	94,910
Admissions	4,005,387	4,083,758	4,061,559	3,919,411	3,979,239
Inpatient Days	20,922,699	21,466,556	21,234,945	20,533,725	20,852,125
Average Length of Stay.	5.2	5.3	5.2	5.2	5.2
Inpatient Surgeries.	1,150,547	1,181,045	1,169,284	1,187,576	1,173,512
Births.	528,045	561,702	546,219	536,959	540,951
Utilization - Outpatient					
Emergency Outpatient Visits.	15,392,542	14,987,499	14,148,116	13,551,624	13,210,287
Other Outpatient Visits.	45,924,148	44,027,580	42,236,693	39,885,211	39,010,692
Total Outpatient Visits	61,316,690	59,015,079	56,384,809	53,436,835	52,220,979
Outpatient Surgeries	1,707,264	1,671,570	1,642,752	1,624,911	1,625,425
Personnel					
Full Time RNs	123,112	120,752	110,558	107,131	102,597
Full Time LPNs	15,573	16,584	17,702	17,350	18,288
Part Time RNs.	33,058	33,815	33,899	32,312	31,471
Part Time LPNs	3,961	4,411	4,592	4,559	5,154
Total Full Time.	434,296	436,301	419,150	413,130	403,194
Total Part Time	99,628	101,491	102,483	96,722	99,179
Revenue - Inpatient					
Gross Inpatient Revenue.	$139,926,153,510	$132,565,357,014	$122,760,036,602	$109,628,591,480	$101,979,867,848
Revenue - Outpatient					
Gross Outpatient Revenue	$95,633,086,065	$84,978,216,080	$73,261,517,369	$63,422,381,320	$57,034,788,275
Revenue and Expenses - Totals					
(Includes Inpatient and Outpatient)					
Total Gross Revenue.	$235,559,239,575	$217,543,573,094	$196,021,553,971	$173,050,972,800	$159,014,656,123
Deductions from Revenue	169,768,881,745	154,142,249,102	136,945,981,599	118,940,845,500	106,872,525,570
Net Patient Revenue	65,790,357,830	63,401,323,992	59,075,572,372	54,110,127,300	52,142,130,553
Other Operating Revenue	5,622,273,906	5,328,857,978	4,942,957,894	4,713,837,579	4,747,889,502
Other Nonoperating Revenue	1,791,442,768	267,367,879	412,762,180	1,530,873,066	895,311,146
Total Net Revenue.	73,204,074,504	68,997,549,849	64,431,292,446	60,354,837,945	57,797,925,303
Total Expenses.	65,549,933,822	64,399,048,894	60,693,798,710	55,938,005,973	53,806,425,890
HOSPITAL UNIT (Excludes Separate Nursing Home Units)					
Utilization - Inpatient					
Beds	95,427	96,504	95,219	91,393	91,780
Admissions	3,991,294	4,068,586	4,044,358	3,902,159	3,957,541
Inpatient Days	20,336,517	20,737,974	20,585,465	19,711,788	19,937,670
Average Length of Stay.	5.1	5.1	5.1	5.1	5.0
Personnel					
Total Full Time.	432,842	433,900	416,608	410,704	400,215
Total Part Time	99,156	100,856	101,661	96,037	98,302
Revenue and Expenses - Totals					
(Includes Inpatient and Outpatient)					
Total Net Revenue.	$73,043,779,992	$68,839,731,724	$64,269,536,853	$60,143,040,802	$57,559,802,328
Total Expenses.	65,399,265,396	64,241,260,529	60,516,951,798	55,631,442,741	53,542,353,988
COMMUNITY HEALTH INDICATORS PER 1000 POPULATION					
Total Population (in thousands)	36,378	35,851	35,268	34,668	33,999
Inpatient					
Beds	2.7	2.8	2.8	2.7	2.8
Admissions	110.1	113.9	115.2	113.1	117.0
Inpatient Days	575.2	598.8	602.1	592.3	613.3
Inpatient Surgeries.	31.6	32.9	33.2	34.3	34.5
Births.	14.5	15.7	15.5	15.5	15.9
Outpatient					
Emergency Outpatient Visits.	423.1	418.1	401.2	390.9	388.6
Other Outpatient Visits.	1,262.4	1,228.1	1,197.6	1,150.5	1,147.4
Total Outpatient Visits	1,685.6	1,646.1	1,598.8	1,541.4	1,536.0
Outpatient Surgeries	46.9	46.6	46.6	46.9	47.8
Expense per Capita (per person).	$1,801.9	$1,796.3	$1,721.0	$1,613.5	$1,582.6

TABLE 5

U.S. CENSUS DIVISION 8: MOUNTAIN

U.S. Registered Community Hospitals
(Nonfederal, short-term general and other special hospitals)

Overview 2006–2010

	2010	2009	2008	2007	2006
Total Community Hospitals					
in Census Division 8, Mountain............	382	382	374	365	365
Bed Size Category					
6-24..	53	50	48	46	57
25-49.......................................	98	96	94	90	88
50-99.......................................	88	96	92	92	82
100-199.....................................	66	61	66	66	66
200-299.....................................	32	35	34	34	35
300-399.....................................	21	21	17	15	17
400-499.....................................	11	8	9	9	10
500 +.......................................	13	15	14	13	10
Location					
Hospitals Urban............................	189	189	183	169	155
Hospitals Rural	193	193	191	196	210
Control					
State and Local Government................	94	97	96	95	100
Not for Profit.............................	195	191	189	192	184
Investor owned	93	94	89	78	81
Physician Models					
Independent Practice Association	42	48	46	48	45
Group Practice without Walls................	8	9	8	10	9
Open Physician-Hospital Organization	34	36	33	33	40
Closed Physician-Hospital Organization	14	16	16	17	15
Management Service Organization	27	26	22	24	18
Integrated Salary Model....................	125	130	122	120	112
Equity Model..............................	5	5	6	6	6
Foundation................................	13	11	14	14	13
Insurance Products					
Health Maintenance Organization	54	53	53	55	57
Preferred Provider Organization..............	56	54	49	61	63
Indemnity Fee for Service	27	29	25	36	32
Managed Care Contracts					
Health Maintenance Organization	147	153	156	155	152
Preferred Provider Organization..............	185	198	199	196	197
Affiliations					
Hospitals in a System......................	230	232	225	211	213
Hospitals in a Network.....................	112	111	110	107	104
Hospitals in a Group Purchasing Organization..	248	257	255	258	254

TABLE 5

U.S. CENSUS DIVISION 8: MOUNTAIN

U.S. Registered Community Hospitals
(Nonfederal, short-term general and other special hospitals)

Utilization, Personnel, Revenue and Expenses, Community Health Indicators 2006–2010

	2010	2009	2008	2007	2006
TOTAL FACILITY (Includes Hospital and Nursing Home Units)					
Utilization - Inpatient					
Beds	46,872	47,028	46,293	44,564	43,792
Admissions	2,091,454	2,089,087	2,098,239	2,033,246	2,013,762
Inpatient Days	10,379,491	10,509,716	10,533,261	10,290,695	10,300,681
Average Length of Stay	5.0	5.0	5.0	5.1	5.1
Inpatient Surgeries	662,412	673,176	638,455	633,790	640,838
Births	278,694	300,722	314,340	313,570	312,461
Utilization - Outpatient					
Emergency Outpatient Visits	7,497,043	7,485,406	7,302,452	7,077,571	6,901,098
Other Outpatient Visits	29,432,803	28,867,801	28,396,866	26,578,776	25,201,852
Total Outpatient Visits	36,929,846	36,353,207	35,699,318	33,656,347	32,102,950
Outpatient Surgeries	982,327	962,734	936,167	856,886	842,579
Personnel					
Full Time RNs	66,717	64,343	62,485	57,336	52,261
Full Time LPNs	3,511	4,372	4,011	4,199	4,308
Part Time RNs	23,141	24,303	24,804	22,170	23,766
Part Time LPNs	1,170	1,401	1,594	1,768	1,982
Total Full Time	233,880	229,182	224,101	218,760	204,327
Total Part Time	68,863	73,288	75,630	68,111	73,473
Revenue - Inpatient					
Gross Inpatient Revenue	$74,568,371,912	$69,773,749,237	$65,876,774,754	$58,788,545,403	$53,107,976,721
Revenue - Outpatient					
Gross Outpatient Revenue	$53,530,101,037	$47,901,898,628	$41,380,379,213	$35,716,383,231	$30,552,510,790
Revenue and Expenses - Totals					
(Includes Inpatient and Outpatient)					
Total Gross Revenue	$128,098,472,949	$117,675,647,865	$107,257,153,967	$94,504,928,634	$83,660,487,511
Deductions from Revenue	86,894,343,376	78,561,440,721	70,987,810,766	61,088,641,713	53,002,070,673
Net Patient Revenue	41,204,129,573	39,114,207,144	36,269,343,201	33,416,286,921	30,658,416,838
Other Operating Revenue	1,804,886,179	1,641,533,021	1,612,417,661	1,585,270,393	1,599,894,899
Other Nonoperating Revenue	550,761,263	383,043,417	-20,098,533	870,215,218	481,150,834
Total Net Revenue	43,559,777,015	41,138,783,582	37,861,662,329	35,871,772,532	32,739,462,571
Total Expenses	38,771,182,258	37,489,628,683	35,816,821,042	32,708,537,125	29,827,199,413
HOSPITAL UNIT (Excludes Separate Nursing Home Units)					
Utilization - Inpatient					
Beds	43,563	43,572	42,780	40,648	39,887
Admissions	2,081,194	2,078,283	2,087,447	2,022,366	2,001,347
Inpatient Days	9,356,938	9,453,606	9,502,108	9,123,808	9,089,752
Average Length of Stay	4.5	4.5	4.6	4.5	4.5
Personnel					
Total Full Time	231,537	226,895	220,221	214,707	201,619
Total Part Time	67,617	72,075	74,179	66,557	72,021
Revenue and Expenses - Totals					
(Includes Inpatient and Outpatient)					
Total Net Revenue	$43,323,260,876	$40,917,090,747	$37,657,242,332	$35,656,821,227	$32,520,772,718
Total Expenses	38,565,221,584	37,287,396,355	35,628,245,086	32,520,257,859	29,635,161,921
COMMUNITY HEALTH INDICATORS PER 1000 POPULATION					
Total Population (in thousands)	22,379	22,123	21,793	21,385	20,888
Inpatient					
Beds	2.1	2.1	2.1	2.1	2.1
Admissions	93.5	94.4	96.3	95.1	96.4
Inpatient Days	463.8	475.1	483.3	481.2	493.1
Inpatient Surgeries	29.6	30.4	29.3	29.6	30.7
Births	12.5	13.6	14.4	14.7	15.0
Outpatient					
Emergency Outpatient Visits	335.0	338.4	335.1	331.0	330.4
Other Outpatient Visits	1,315.2	1,304.9	1,303.0	1,242.9	1,206.5
Total Outpatient Visits	1,650.2	1,643.2	1,638.1	1,573.9	1,536.9
Outpatient Surgeries	43.9	43.5	43.0	40.1	40.3
Expense per Capita (per person)	$1,732.5	$1,694.6	$1,643.5	$1,529.5	$1,427.9

TABLE 5

U.S. CENSUS DIVISION 9: PACIFIC

U.S. Registered Community Hospitals
(Nonfederal, short-term general and other special hospitals)

Overview 2006–2010

	2010	2009	2008	2007	2006
Total Community Hospitals in Census Division 9, Pacific	535	535	543	545	549
Bed Size Category					
6-24	41	39	36	35	38
25-49	97	98	97	95	99
50-99	70	73	82	85	85
100-199	139	139	139	145	144
200-299	84	87	92	89	91
300-399	55	57	53	54	52
400-499	31	27	27	24	22
500 +	18	15	17	18	18
Location					
Hospitals Urban	413	413	420	423	407
Hospitals Rural	122	122	123	122	142
Control					
State and Local Government	135	135	141	139	144
Not for Profit	319	319	315	316	316
Investor owned	81	81	87	90	89
Physician Models					
Independent Practice Association	83	78	88	108	117
Group Practice without Walls	24	24	22	20	21
Open Physician-Hospital Organization	20	19	22	26	31
Closed Physician-Hospital Organization	10	11	10	10	9
Management Service Organization	48	47	44	51	51
Integrated Salary Model	113	110	107	111	113
Equity Model	7	5	2	4	3
Foundation	60	55	52	44	48
Insurance Products					
Health Maintenance Organization	55	64	64	69	70
Preferred Provider Organization	56	54	48	63	55
Indemnity Fee for Service	15	14	15	21	21
Managed Care Contracts					
Health Maintenance Organization	231	231	226	257	258
Preferred Provider Organization	259	270	263	287	285
Affiliations					
Hospitals in a System	330	324	328	329	342
Hospitals in a Network	110	111	107	100	106
Hospitals in a Group Purchasing Organization	310	352	333	346	350

TABLE 5

U.S. CENSUS DIVISION 9: PACIFIC

U.S. Registered Community Hospitals
(Nonfederal, short-term general and other special hospitals)

Utilization, Personnel, Revenue and Expenses, Community Health Indicators 2006–2010

	2010	2009	2008	2007	2006
TOTAL FACILITY (Includes Hospital and Nursing Home Units)					
Utilization - Inpatient					
Beds	93,088	91,046	92,389	91,955	92,077
Admissions	4,501,591	4,514,874	4,557,658	4,365,002	4,491,195
Inpatient Days	22,640,225	22,791,572	23,454,079	22,401,234	23,419,759
Average Length of Stay	5.0	5.0	5.1	5.1	5.2
Inpatient Surgeries	1,241,853	1,252,243	1,260,249	1,299,136	1,251,269
Births	632,032	645,081	676,180	662,060	670,591
Utilization - Outpatient					
Emergency Outpatient Visits	15,128,224	15,055,923	14,473,721	14,319,461	14,623,874
Other Outpatient Visits	61,596,946	57,529,665	58,052,120	54,654,796	61,615,935
Total Outpatient Visits	76,725,170	72,585,588	72,525,841	68,974,257	76,239,809
Outpatient Surgeries	1,835,447	1,833,478	1,886,717	1,811,593	1,783,808
Personnel					
Full Time RNs	134,508	130,132	126,718	114,266	109,551
Full Time LPNs	8,301	8,642	9,011	8,993	9,538
Part Time RNs	71,284	70,581	72,526	75,566	73,766
Part Time LPNs	3,453	3,839	4,274	4,950	5,058
Total Full Time	487,053	477,901	477,563	454,501	444,221
Total Part Time	193,703	191,891	201,710	211,443	202,571
Revenue - Inpatient					
Gross Inpatient Revenue	$211,874,242,966	$193,636,178,785	$181,416,247,444	$168,961,978,477	$162,753,461,850
Revenue - Outpatient					
Gross Outpatient Revenue	$124,558,809,024	$109,199,995,898	$98,528,236,224	$84,834,034,482	$78,665,367,009
Revenue and Expenses - Totals					
(Includes Inpatient and Outpatient)					
Total Gross Revenue	$336,433,051,990	$302,836,174,683	$279,944,483,668	$253,796,012,959	$241,418,828,859
Deductions from Revenue	239,252,607,338	212,570,073,192	194,777,375,687	175,398,585,106	167,168,229,819
Net Patient Revenue	97,180,444,652	90,266,101,491	85,167,107,981	78,397,427,853	74,250,599,040
Other Operating Revenue	6,027,711,222	5,590,026,520	5,041,401,269	4,653,195,596	4,361,003,114
Other Nonoperating Revenue	1,866,228,283	1,090,362,535	23,014,193	2,776,806,260	2,124,134,857
Total Net Revenue	105,074,384,157	96,946,490,546	90,231,523,443	85,827,429,709	80,706,061,954
Total Expenses	98,998,692,542	93,038,063,591	88,037,635,750	79,632,236,072	76,421,525,696
HOSPITAL UNIT (Excludes Separate Nursing Home Units)					
Utilization - Inpatient					
Beds	88,925	86,836	87,253	86,642	86,878
Admissions	4,478,851	4,489,343	4,527,176	4,330,186	4,456,404
Inpatient Days	21,344,190	21,533,040	21,897,397	20,880,648	21,889,072
Average Length of Stay	4.8	4.8	4.8	4.8	4.9
Personnel					
Total Full Time	483,548	473,892	473,367	449,821	438,331
Total Part Time	192,111	189,876	199,475	208,757	199,539
Revenue and Expenses - Totals					
(Includes Inpatient and Outpatient)					
Total Net Revenue	$104,531,350,858	$96,415,616,765	$89,624,997,242	$85,096,193,516	$79,957,542,841
Total Expenses	98,595,961,703	92,611,409,620	87,584,896,173	79,167,104,551	75,989,209,712
COMMUNITY HEALTH INDICATORS PER 1000 POPULATION					
Total Population (in thousands)	49,877	49,445	48,905	48,383	47,982
Inpatient					
Beds	1.9	1.8	1.9	1.9	1.9
Admissions	90.3	91.3	93.2	90.2	93.6
Inpatient Days	453.9	460.9	479.6	463.0	488.1
Inpatient Surgeries	24.9	25.3	25.8	26.9	26.1
Births	12.7	13.0	13.8	13.7	14.0
Outpatient					
Emergency Outpatient Visits	303.3	304.5	296.0	296.0	304.8
Other Outpatient Visits	1,235.0	1,163.5	1,187.0	1,129.6	1,284.1
Total Outpatient Visits	1,538.3	1,468.0	1,483.0	1,425.6	1,588.9
Outpatient Surgeries	36.8	37.1	38.6	37.4	37.2
Expense per Capita (per person)	$1,984.8	$1,881.6	$1,800.2	$1,645.9	$1,592.7

TABLE 6

ALABAMA

U.S. Registered Community Hospitals
(Nonfederal, short-term general and other special hospitals)

Overview 2006–2010

	2010	2009	2008	2007	2006
Total Community Hospitals in Alabama	105	108	109	109	109
Bed Size Category					
6-24	7	7	8	6	6
25-49	27	27	25	25	22
50-99	22	24	27	26	24
100-199	28	28	25	29	34
200-299	9	9	11	11	11
300-399	6	7	7	6	7
400-499	3	3	3	2	1
500 + ...	3	3	3	4	4
Location					
Hospitals Urban..........................	58	60	60	60	58
Hospitals Rural	47	48	49	49	51
Control					
State and Local Government................	40	42	42	42	41
Not for Profit............................	24	26	27	27	26
Investor owned	41	40	40	40	42
Physician Models					
Independent Practice Association	7	8	8	7	7
Group Practice without Walls................	1	2	2	3	1
Open Physician-Hospital Organization	7	3	3	5	3
Closed Physician-Hospital Organization	0	1	2	2	1
Management Service Organization	7	5	10	12	7
Integrated Salary Model....................	18	16	14	14	12
Equity Model.............................	0	0	0	1	0
Foundation...............................	7	5	5	6	2
Insurance Products					
Health Maintenance Organization	7	10	13	12	9
Preferred Provider Organization..............	8	9	10	8	8
Indemnity Fee for Service	1	1	3	2	2
Managed Care Contracts					
Health Maintenance Organization	37	36	35	32	27
Preferred Provider Organization..............	51	49	49	42	39
Affiliations					
Hospitals in a System.....................	64	67	68	67	65
Hospitals in a Network....................	9	11	12	12	10
Hospitals in a Group Purchasing Organization..	56	70	68	64	55

TABLE 6

ALABAMA

U.S. Registered Community Hospitals
(Nonfederal, short-term general and other special hospitals)

Utilization, Personnel, Revenue and Expenses, Community Health Indicators 2006–2010

	2010	2009	2008	2007	2006
TOTAL FACILITY (Includes Hospital and Nursing Home Units)					
Utilization - Inpatient					
Beds	15,086	15,290	15,250	15,682	15,639
Admissions	642,309	665,788	687,446	696,131	683,726
Inpatient Days	3,336,285	3,459,946	3,524,687	3,551,293	3,556,939
Average Length of Stay	5.2	5.2	5.1	5.1	5.2
Inpatient Surgeries	197,605	203,945	202,900	221,162	223,876
Births	58,287	62,819	62,436	62,617	59,456
Utilization - Outpatient					
Emergency Outpatient Visits	2,304,682	2,286,343	2,271,755	2,253,215	2,192,221
Other Outpatient Visits	6,496,039	6,905,010	6,746,766	5,934,478	5,831,133
Total Outpatient Visits	8,800,721	9,191,353	9,018,521	8,187,693	8,023,354
Outpatient Surgeries	372,359	380,226	364,648	365,487	373,688
Personnel					
Full Time RNs	19,033	18,906	17,930	17,077	17,308
Full Time LPNs	1,533	1,587	1,795	2,005	2,225
Part Time RNs	6,521	6,495	6,708	7,708	6,677
Part Time LPNs	544	584	755	885	890
Total Full Time	63,565	64,706	64,821	63,949	65,120
Total Part Time	17,485	17,181	18,103	20,423	18,703
Revenue - Inpatient					
Gross Inpatient Revenue	$20,382,077,101	$19,226,829,885	$18,436,910,861	$17,301,065,902	$16,275,203,299
Revenue - Outpatient					
Gross Outpatient Revenue	$15,107,168,189	$13,746,107,465	$11,949,849,370	$10,302,085,003	$9,484,229,706
Revenue and Expenses - Totals					
(Includes Inpatient and Outpatient)					
Total Gross Revenue	$35,489,245,290	$32,972,937,350	$30,386,760,231	$27,603,150,905	$25,759,433,005
Deductions from Revenue	26,885,327,851	24,887,051,667	22,550,588,921	19,968,905,297	18,197,677,398
Net Patient Revenue	8,603,917,439	8,085,885,683	7,836,171,310	7,634,245,608	7,561,755,607
Other Operating Revenue	398,593,891	476,168,844	499,586,864	522,333,646	441,333,070
Other Nonoperating Revenue	180,032,402	209,998,612	-56,405,573	268,802,396	203,736,118
Total Net Revenue	9,182,543,732	8,772,053,139	8,279,352,601	8,425,381,650	8,206,824,795
Total Expenses	8,334,444,846	8,276,604,492	8,288,702,647	7,960,186,498	7,550,751,275
HOSPITAL UNIT (Excludes Separate Nursing Home Units)					
Utilization - Inpatient					
Beds	14,569	14,861	14,824	15,042	14,917
Admissions	641,118	664,534	686,256	693,215	680,564
Inpatient Days	3,188,617	3,314,802	3,377,540	3,347,267	3,335,678
Average Length of Stay	5.0	5.0	4.9	4.8	4.9
Personnel					
Total Full Time	63,159	64,371	64,502	63,572	64,631
Total Part Time	17,373	17,120	18,073	20,305	18,617
Revenue and Expenses - Totals					
(Includes Inpatient and Outpatient)					
Total Net Revenue	$9,160,325,136	$8,749,089,004	$8,258,544,123	$8,397,411,188	$8,172,214,723
Total Expenses	8,308,793,595	8,249,699,883	8,268,150,713	7,937,260,895	7,526,811,142
COMMUNITY HEALTH INDICATORS PER 1000 POPULATION					
Total Population (in thousands)	4,730	4,709	4,677	4,638	4,598
Inpatient					
Beds	3.2	3.2	3.3	3.4	3.4
Admissions	135.8	141.4	147.0	150.1	148.7
Inpatient Days	705.4	734.8	753.5	765.7	773.6
Inpatient Surgeries	41.8	43.3	43.4	47.7	48.7
Births	12.3	13.3	13.3	13.5	12.9
Outpatient					
Emergency Outpatient Visits	487.3	485.6	485.7	485.8	476.8
Other Outpatient Visits	1,373.5	1,466.4	1,442.4	1,279.6	1,268.3
Total Outpatient Visits	1,860.8	1,952.0	1,928.1	1,765.4	1,745.1
Outpatient Surgeries	78.7	80.7	78.0	78.8	81.3
Expense per Capita (per person)	$1,762.2	$1,757.7	$1,772.1	$1,716.3	$1,642.3

TABLE 6

ALASKA

U.S. Registered Community Hospitals
(Nonfederal, short-term general and other special hospitals)

Overview 2006–2010

	2010	2009	2008	2007	2006
Total Community Hospitals in Alaska	22	22	22	22	22
Bed Size Category					
6-24	6	6	6	6	7
25-49	7	8	7	7	7
50-99	4	3	4	4	4
100-199	3	3	3	3	2
200-299	1	1	1	1	1
300-399	1	1	1	1	1
400-499	0	0	0	0	0
500 + ...	0	0	0	0	0
Location					
Hospitals Urban	5	5	5	5	3
Hospitals Rural	17	17	17	17	19
Control					
State and Local Government	7	6	7	7	7
Not for Profit	13	14	13	13	13
Investor owned	2	2	2	2	2
Physician Models					
Independent Practice Association	1	0	0	2	2
Group Practice without Walls	0	0	0	0	1
Open Physician-Hospital Organization	2	2	2	3	2
Closed Physician-Hospital Organization	1	1	0	0	0
Management Service Organization	0	1	0	0	0
Integrated Salary Model	4	3	4	4	6
Equity Model	0	0	0	0	0
Foundation	0	0	0	0	1
Insurance Products					
Health Maintenance Organization	0	0	0	0	0
Preferred Provider Organization	1	2	2	3	2
Indemnity Fee for Service	0	0	1	0	0
Managed Care Contracts					
Health Maintenance Organization	0	0	0	0	0
Preferred Provider Organization	5	7	8	9	8
Affiliations					
Hospitals in a System	9	8	8	8	8
Hospitals in a Network	3	5	3	4	4
Hospitals in a Group Purchasing Organization . .	8	12	11	11	13

States

TABLE 6

ALASKA

U.S. Registered Community Hospitals
(Nonfederal, short-term general and other special hospitals)

Utilization, Personnel, Revenue and Expenses, Community Health Indicators 2006–2010

	2010	2009	2008	2007	2006
TOTAL FACILITY (Includes Hospital and Nursing Home Units)					
Utilization - Inpatient					
Beds	1,543	1,532	1,553	1,554	1,551
Admissions	57,005	57,227	58,204	56,584	52,357
Inpatient Days	342,960	338,547	346,837	337,028	304,978
Average Length of Stay	6.0	5.9	6.0	6.0	5.8
Inpatient Surgeries	17,999	20,294	20,522	18,924	26,787
Births	8,919	9,358	8,882	9,047	9,128
Utilization - Outpatient					
Emergency Outpatient Visits	296,573	296,524	328,164	328,947	610,324
Other Outpatient Visits	1,486,369	1,470,894	1,365,178	1,455,616	1,165,596
Total Outpatient Visits	1,782,942	1,767,418	1,693,342	1,784,563	1,775,920
Outpatient Surgeries	47,417	50,469	43,567	44,193	34,522
Personnel					
Full Time RNs	2,238	2,348	2,090	2,091	2,071
Full Time LPNs	178	163	163	197	191
Part Time RNs	906	816	848	512	826
Part Time LPNs	28	27	48	45	56
Total Full Time	9,608	9,421	8,809	8,712	8,668
Total Part Time	2,584	2,125	2,435	1,661	2,304
Revenue - Inpatient					
Gross Inpatient Revenue	$2,340,223,028	$1,920,419,380	$2,045,394,009	$1,688,213,313	$1,619,128,443
Revenue - Outpatient					
Gross Outpatient Revenue	$2,263,620,240	$1,956,296,065	$1,623,182,947	$1,379,909,276	$1,283,765,424
Revenue and Expenses - Totals					
(Includes Inpatient and Outpatient)					
Total Gross Revenue	$4,603,843,268	$3,876,715,445	$3,668,576,956	$3,068,122,589	$2,902,893,867
Deductions from Revenue	2,836,623,088	2,198,399,661	2,054,343,109	1,623,832,318	1,529,429,013
Net Patient Revenue	1,767,220,180	1,678,315,784	1,614,233,847	1,444,290,271	1,373,464,854
Other Operating Revenue	146,570,128	65,784,620	66,832,290	78,687,582	73,602,633
Other Nonoperating Revenue	21,027,327	18,948,295	16,635,452	41,367,990	27,681,282
Total Net Revenue	1,934,817,635	1,763,048,699	1,697,701,589	1,564,345,843	1,474,748,769
Total Expenses	1,590,214,704	1,753,736,940	1,570,873,845	1,458,281,758	1,424,479,572
HOSPITAL UNIT (Excludes Separate Nursing Home Units)					
Utilization - Inpatient					
Beds	1,334	1,300	1,381	1,280	1,359
Admissions	56,797	56,918	58,081	56,310	51,957
Inpatient Days	275,518	263,515	293,939	252,315	242,591
Average Length of Stay	4.9	4.6	5.1	4.5	4.7
Personnel					
Total Full Time	9,428	9,174	8,712	8,469	8,483
Total Part Time	2,443	1,990	2,350	1,546	2,203
Revenue and Expenses - Totals					
(Includes Inpatient and Outpatient)					
Total Net Revenue	$1,900,578,038	$1,724,497,539	$1,678,203,874	$1,502,363,012	$1,446,879,893
Total Expenses	1,564,596,210	1,726,965,040	1,560,050,288	1,432,798,379	1,402,317,116
COMMUNITY HEALTH INDICATORS PER 1000 POPULATION					
Total Population (in thousands)	709	698	688	682	677
Inpatient					
Beds	2.2	2.2	2.3	2.3	2.3
Admissions	80.4	81.9	84.6	82.9	77.3
Inpatient Days	483.8	484.7	504.0	494.0	450.3
Inpatient Surgeries	25.4	29.1	29.8	27.7	39.5
Births	12.6	13.4	12.9	13.3	13.5
Outpatient					
Emergency Outpatient Visits	418.4	424.5	476.9	482.1	901.1
Other Outpatient Visits	2,096.8	2,105.9	1,983.9	2,133.4	1,720.9
Total Outpatient Visits	2,515.2	2,530.4	2,460.8	2,615.5	2,622.0
Outpatient Surgeries	66.9	72.3	63.3	64.8	51.0
Expense per Capita (per person)	$2,243.3	$2,510.8	$2,282.8	$2,137.3	$2,103.1

States

TABLE 6

ARIZONA

U.S. Registered Community Hospitals
(Nonfederal, short-term general and other special hospitals)

Overview 2006–2010

	2010	2009	2008	2007	2006
Total Community Hospitals in Arizona	73	72	71	66	66
Bed Size Category					
6-24	5	4	4	4	5
25-49	10	10	10	10	9
50-99	18	18	18	14	14
100-199	13	11	12	13	13
200-299	11	12	11	11	12
300-399	5	8	7	6	6
400-499	6	4	4	3	2
500 + ...	5	5	5	5	5
Location					
Hospitals Urban.	58	58	57	48	51
Hospitals Rural	15	14	14	18	15
Control					
State and Local Government.	5	7	4	4	5
Not for Profit	46	43	44	43	41
Investor owned	22	22	23	19	20
Physician Models					
Independent Practice Association	8	9	10	9	6
Group Practice without Walls.	1	1	2	3	2
Open Physician-Hospital Organization	6	6	5	7	9
Closed Physician-Hospital Organization	3	4	4	4	5
Management Service Organization	8	4	3	4	2
Integrated Salary Model.	15	16	12	12	11
Equity Model	0	0	0	0	1
Foundation.	2	2	3	3	4
Insurance Products					
Health Maintenance Organization	9	8	10	11	10
Preferred Provider Organization.	7	5	3	10	9
Indemnity Fee for Service	5	4	3	9	7
Managed Care Contracts					
Health Maintenance Organization	32	32	33	33	28
Preferred Provider Organization.	31	33	31	33	32
Affiliations					
Hospitals in a System.	48	49	48	44	45
Hospitals in a Network	19	14	14	11	12
Hospitals in a Group Purchasing Organization. .	45	41	43	39	37

States

TABLE 6

ARIZONA

U.S. Registered Community Hospitals
(Nonfederal, short-term general and other special hospitals)

Utilization, Personnel, Revenue and Expenses, Community Health Indicators 2006–2010

	2010	2009	2008	2007	2006
TOTAL FACILITY (Includes Hospital and Nursing Home Units)					
Utilization - Inpatient					
Beds	13,385	13,455	13,138	12,157	11,947
Admissions	711,901	705,371	716,136	675,216	664,773
Inpatient Days	3,160,244	3,203,551	3,235,063	3,041,795	3,023,329
Average Length of Stay.	4.4	4.5	4.5	4.5	4.5
Inpatient Surgeries.	247,886	249,404	225,735	209,707	218,604
Births.	80,960	88,943	96,193	97,159	96,797
Utilization - Outpatient					
Emergency Outpatient Visits	2,240,946	2,137,007	2,172,149	2,122,695	2,073,320
Other Outpatient Visits.	5,886,520	4,965,037	5,542,202	5,190,865	4,482,315
Total Outpatient Visits	8,127,466	7,102,044	7,714,351	7,313,560	6,555,635
Outpatient Surgeries	257,530	264,098	254,546	221,754	224,424
Personnel					
Full Time RNs	22,440	21,733	20,898	18,124	16,858
Full Time LPNs	807	1,428	957	920	1,041
Part Time RNs	5,419	6,207	6,462	6,140	5,535
Part Time LPNs	135	217	251	274	298
Total Full Time.	71,092	68,218	65,568	64,315	61,165
Total Part Time	14,521	16,938	18,272	17,536	16,607
Revenue - Inpatient					
Gross Inpatient Revenue.	$26,745,329,251	$25,403,304,711	$23,681,284,471	$21,143,464,204	$19,051,058,791
Revenue - Outpatient					
Gross Outpatient Revenue	$15,678,580,294	$14,088,508,773	$12,097,995,360	$10,534,254,958	$9,001,251,090
Revenue and Expenses - Totals					
(Includes Inpatient and Outpatient)					
Total Gross Revenue.	$42,423,909,545	$39,491,813,484	$35,779,279,831	$31,677,719,162	$28,052,309,881
Deductions from Revenue.	30,579,491,050	28,395,520,445	25,364,507,854	21,946,070,382	19,016,673,089
Net Patient Revenue	11,844,418,495	11,096,293,039	10,414,771,977	9,731,648,780	9,035,636,792
Other Operating Revenue	504,651,779	405,351,865	363,332,345	367,303,347	512,917,408
Other Nonoperating Revenue	65,552,870	146,545,191	-141,211,261	203,652,122	103,114,887
Total Net Revenue.	12,414,623,144	11,648,190,095	10,636,893,061	10,302,604,249	9,651,669,087
Total Expenses.	11,271,574,937	10,838,466,876	10,461,227,615	9,586,339,104	8,959,776,857
HOSPITAL UNIT (Excludes Separate Nursing Home Units)					
Utilization - Inpatient					
Beds	13,265	13,311	12,954	11,949	11,739
Admissions	709,606	703,074	713,487	672,878	662,251
Inpatient Days	3,120,611	3,154,344	3,189,855	2,981,340	2,953,137
Average Length of Stay.	4.4	4.5	4.5	4.4	4.5
Personnel					
Total Full Time.	70,791	68,133	63,940	62,623	61,087
Total Part Time	14,477	16,909	17,993	17,258	16,567
Revenue and Expenses - Totals					
(Includes Inpatient and Outpatient)					
Total Net Revenue.	$12,377,572,952	$11,622,780,339	$10,627,564,240	$10,291,634,189	$9,632,434,792
Total Expenses.	11,256,388,031	10,821,151,582	10,447,130,955	9,573,110,290	8,946,668,918
COMMUNITY HEALTH INDICATORS PER 1000 POPULATION					
Total Population (in thousands)	6,677	6,596	6,499	6,362	6,192
Inpatient					
Beds	2.0	2.0	2.0	1.9	1.9
Admissions	106.6	106.9	110.2	106.1	107.4
Inpatient Days	473.3	485.7	497.7	478.1	488.3
Inpatient Surgeries.	37.1	37.8	34.7	33.0	35.3
Births.	12.1	13.5	14.8	15.3	15.6
Outpatient					
Emergency Outpatient Visits	335.6	324.0	334.2	333.6	334.8
Other Outpatient Visits.	881.7	752.8	852.7	815.9	723.9
Total Outpatient Visits	1,217.3	1,076.8	1,186.9	1,149.5	1,058.7
Outpatient Surgeries	38.6	40.0	39.2	34.9	36.2
Expense per Capita (per person).	$1,688.2	$1,643.2	$1,609.6	$1,506.8	$1,447.0

States

TABLE 6

ARKANSAS

U.S. Registered Community Hospitals
(Nonfederal, short-term general and other special hospitals)

Overview 2006–2010

	2010	2009	2008	2007	2006
Total Community Hospitals in Arkansas.......	85	86	86	84	84
Bed Size Category					
6-24	6	7	7	5	5
25-49	32	31	30	30	29
50-99	16	18	18	17	20
100-199	18	17	18	19	16
200-299	6	5	6	6	7
300-399	4	5	5	5	5
400-499	2	2	0	0	0
500 + ...	1	1	2	2	2
Location					
Hospitals Urban...........................	37	37	37	35	31
Hospitals Rural	48	49	49	49	53
Control					
State and Local Government................	14	15	13	14	15
Not for Profit	45	45	46	45	45
Investor owned	26	26	27	25	24
Physician Models					
Independent Practice Association	16	16	17	17	20
Group Practice without Walls................	6	6	6	6	5
Open Physician-Hospital Organization	25	28	28	28	32
Closed Physician-Hospital Organization	6	6	4	3	4
Management Service Organization	10	10	10	12	13
Integrated Salary Model....................	21	20	18	16	18
Equity Model	1	2	2	2	2
Foundation...............................	7	8	11	8	8
Insurance Products					
Health Maintenance Organization	14	14	15	14	14
Preferred Provider Organization..............	14	14	13	14	11
Indemnity Fee for Service	4	3	4	4	4
Managed Care Contracts					
Health Maintenance Organization	46	50	47	49	45
Preferred Provider Organization..............	62	66	65	68	62
Affiliations					
Hospitals in a System......................	46	47	46	45	47
Hospitals in a Network.....................	26	28	29	27	28
Hospitals in a Group Purchasing Organization..	67	78	80	82	78

TABLE 6

ARKANSAS

U.S. Registered Community Hospitals
(Nonfederal, short-term general and other special hospitals)

Utilization, Personnel, Revenue and Expenses, Community Health Indicators 2006–2010

	2010	2009	2008	2007	2006
TOTAL FACILITY (Includes Hospital and Nursing Home Units)					
Utilization - Inpatient					
Beds...........................	9,451	9,565	9,686	9,502	9,309
Admissions......................	370,401	380,478	376,158	366,452	373,067
Inpatient Days	1,908,843	1,957,556	1,989,969	1,908,909	1,943,363
Average Length of Stay............	5.2	5.1	5.3	5.2	5.2
Inpatient Surgeries................	104,912	101,681	102,681	116,019	108,651
Births............................	36,913	38,556	39,013	39,602	39,232
Utilization - Outpatient					
Emergency Outpatient Visits........	1,376,649	1,355,032	1,301,330	1,294,119	1,267,198
Other Outpatient Visits............	3,645,562	3,692,949	3,671,422	3,942,397	3,818,276
Total Outpatient Visits	5,022,211	5,047,981	4,972,752	5,236,516	5,085,474
Outpatient Surgeries	155,784	143,094	136,565	147,222	144,619
Personnel					
Full Time RNs	11,059	10,620	9,700	9,678	9,699
Full Time LPNs	1,890	2,080	2,455	2,313	2,572
Part Time RNs...................	4,068	4,030	3,596	3,478	3,309
Part Time LPNs	663	809	824	824	859
Total Full Time..................	38,553	38,571	38,483	37,486	37,651
Total Part Time	11,921	11,981	11,549	10,872	10,845
Revenue - Inpatient					
Gross Inpatient Revenue...........	$9,211,448,957	$8,800,185,973	$8,250,771,568	$7,750,748,662	$7,346,539,305
Revenue - Outpatient					
Gross Outpatient Revenue	$7,084,460,315	$6,421,124,915	$5,568,220,057	$5,054,791,861	$4,655,737,561
Revenue and Expenses - Totals					
(Includes Inpatient and Outpatient)					
Total Gross Revenue..............	$16,295,909,272	$15,221,310,888	$13,818,991,625	$12,805,540,523	$12,002,276,866
Deductions from Revenue..........	11,007,346,255	10,164,398,525	9,011,385,599	8,220,632,392	7,572,665,742
Net Patient Revenue	5,288,563,017	5,056,912,363	4,807,606,026	4,584,908,131	4,429,611,124
Other Operating Revenue	221,189,649	193,955,665	169,341,834	162,135,731	154,744,439
Other Nonoperating Revenue	69,605,801	73,678,302	31,674,701	56,666,788	74,174,385
Total Net Revenue................	5,579,358,467	5,324,546,330	5,008,622,561	4,803,710,650	4,658,529,948
Total Expenses..................	5,246,234,974	5,161,176,256	4,921,858,438	4,585,732,810	4,437,596,804
HOSPITAL UNIT (Excludes Separate Nursing Home Units)					
Utilization - Inpatient					
Beds...........................	9,228	9,132	9,250	9,067	8,855
Admissions......................	368,895	378,746	374,159	364,431	371,143
Inpatient Days	1,830,615	1,824,645	1,854,685	1,767,173	1,799,422
Average Length of Stay............	5.0	4.8	5.0	4.8	4.8
Personnel					
Total Full Time...................	38,362	38,050	38,028	37,156	37,231
Total Part Time	11,881	11,767	11,398	10,768	10,671
Revenue and Expenses - Totals					
(Includes Inpatient and Outpatient)					
Total Net Revenue................	$5,558,657,844	$5,301,946,109	$4,986,288,187	$4,782,794,055	$4,637,882,611
Total Expenses..................	5,234,362,445	5,141,870,990	4,902,909,300	4,567,507,045	4,419,957,774
COMMUNITY HEALTH INDICATORS PER 1000 POPULATION					
Total Population (in thousands)	2,910	2,889	2,868	2,842	2,815
Inpatient					
Beds...........................	3.2	3.3	3.4	3.3	3.3
Admissions......................	127.3	131.7	131.2	128.9	132.5
Inpatient Days	655.9	677.5	693.9	671.6	690.3
Inpatient Surgeries................	36.0	35.2	35.8	40.8	38.6
Births............................	12.7	13.3	13.6	13.9	13.9
Outpatient					
Emergency Outpatient Visits........	473.0	469.0	453.8	455.3	450.1
Other Outpatient Visits............	1,252.7	1,278.1	1,280.2	1,387.1	1,356.4
Total Outpatient Visits	1,725.7	1,747.0	1,734.0	1,842.4	1,806.5
Outpatient Surgeries	53.5	49.5	47.6	51.8	51.4
Expense per Capita (per person).....	$1,802.7	$1,786.2	$1,716.3	$1,613.4	$1,576.4

TABLE 6

CALIFORNIA

U.S. Registered Community Hospitals
(Nonfederal, short-term general and other special hospitals)

Overview 2006–2010

	2010	2009	2008	2007	2006
Total Community Hospitals in California	343	343	352	355	357
Bed Size Category					
6-24	13	13	14	14	11
25-49	38	37	36	34	39
50-99	42	42	50	53	53
100-199	104	106	107	111	109
200-299	61	64	66	66	71
300-399	47	50	44	45	43
400-499	24	20	22	18	16
500 + ...	14	11	13	14	15
Location					
Hospitals Urban..........................	312	313	321	323	318
Hospitals Rural	31	30	31	32	39
Control					
State and Local Government................	69	69	71	71	76
Not for Profit	202	202	202	203	202
Investor owned	72	72	79	81	79
Physician Models					
Independent Practice Association	66	62	72	89	93
Group Practice without Walls................	11	12	12	12	13
Open Physician-Hospital Organization	5	5	6	10	12
Closed Physician-Hospital Organization	6	7	7	4	3
Management Service Organization	28	26	27	33	38
Integrated Salary Model....................	24	25	30	32	36
Equity Model	3	0	1	4	2
Foundation...............................	50	40	39	39	41
Insurance Products					
Health Maintenance Organization	35	42	46	48	52
Preferred Provider Organization..............	22	22	19	27	25
Indemnity Fee for Service	11	9	10	15	15
Managed Care Contracts					
Health Maintenance Organization	156	157	154	179	182
Preferred Provider Organization..............	157	159	158	183	184
Affiliations					
Hospitals in a System.....................	226	225	231	235	240
Hospitals in a Network....................	59	59	59	55	61
Hospitals in a Group Purchasing Organization..	182	210	206	206	212

TABLE 6

CALIFORNIA

U.S. Registered Community Hospitals
(Nonfederal, short-term general and other special hospitals)

Utilization, Personnel, Revenue and Expenses, Community Health Indicators 2006–2010

	2010	2009	2008	2007	2006
TOTAL FACILITY (Includes Hospital and Nursing Home Units)					
Utilization - Inpatient					
Beds	70,440	68,745	69,587	69,325	70,021
Admissions	3,423,820	3,433,319	3,460,688	3,276,372	3,428,885
Inpatient Days	17,443,427	17,582,055	18,044,888	17,154,514	18,278,223
Average Length of Stay	5.1	5.1	5.2	5.2	5.3
Inpatient Surgeries	907,650	899,439	904,722	951,529	913,228
Births	493,712	500,085	526,946	514,164	524,279
Utilization - Outpatient					
Emergency Outpatient Visits	10,945,256	10,554,310	10,068,613	10,006,018	10,276,370
Other Outpatient Visits	40,784,007	37,700,623	38,808,536	35,930,559	43,662,065
Total Outpatient Visits	51,729,263	48,254,933	48,877,149	45,936,577	53,938,435
Outpatient Surgeries	1,261,889	1,248,053	1,309,864	1,250,377	1,238,695
Personnel					
Full Time RNs	103,010	98,905	98,152	86,556	82,703
Full Time LPNs	6,817	7,145	7,531	7,494	7,835
Part Time RNs	48,553	48,356	49,205	54,152	52,774
Part Time LPNs	2,625	2,900	3,281	3,948	4,023
Total Full Time	358,559	353,440	356,834	338,268	328,016
Total Part Time	129,897	130,048	134,602	150,145	141,985
Revenue - Inpatient					
Gross Inpatient Revenue	$176,241,777,468	$160,482,118,425	$150,337,219,745	$141,494,365,112	$137,778,920,000
Revenue - Outpatient					
Gross Outpatient Revenue	$93,211,672,697	$81,537,158,136	$74,357,000,289	$63,410,673,627	$59,664,515,444
Revenue and Expenses - Totals					
(Includes Inpatient and Outpatient)					
Total Gross Revenue	$269,453,450,165	$242,019,276,561	$224,694,220,034	$204,905,038,739	$197,443,435,444
Deductions from Revenue	198,665,132,469	176,891,970,909	162,955,378,616	147,778,238,783	142,916,546,652
Net Patient Revenue	70,788,317,696	65,127,305,652	61,738,841,418	57,126,799,956	54,526,888,792
Other Operating Revenue	4,549,376,153	4,239,820,033	3,808,102,197	3,501,284,745	3,340,457,320
Other Nonoperating Revenue	1,405,680,400	900,886,474	139,168,261	2,141,531,027	1,675,375,040
Total Net Revenue	76,743,374,249	70,268,012,159	65,686,111,876	62,769,615,728	59,513,046,095
Total Expenses	72,279,546,582	67,532,620,386	64,441,142,995	58,050,140,085	56,137,019,009
HOSPITAL UNIT (Excludes Separate Nursing Home Units)					
Utilization - Inpatient					
Beds	67,288	65,699	65,773	65,169	65,789
Admissions	3,404,159	3,411,915	3,435,099	3,246,140	3,398,774
Inpatient Days	16,480,612	16,688,765	16,911,379	15,982,046	17,052,324
Average Length of Stay	4.8	4.9	4.9	4.9	5.0
Personnel					
Total Full Time	355,707	350,441	353,564	334,625	323,030
Total Part Time	128,661	128,548	132,907	147,999	139,310
Revenue and Expenses - Totals					
(Includes Inpatient and Outpatient)					
Total Net Revenue	$76,308,938,222	$69,852,937,155	$65,179,794,371	$62,185,142,736	$58,848,516,663
Total Expenses	71,979,685,381	67,204,581,934	64,094,102,118	57,679,563,342	55,775,213,595
COMMUNITY HEALTH INDICATORS PER 1000 POPULATION					
Total Population (in thousands)	37,267	36,962	36,580	36,226	35,979
Inpatient					
Beds	1.9	1.9	1.9	1.9	1.9
Admissions	91.9	92.9	94.6	90.4	95.3
Inpatient Days	468.1	475.7	493.3	473.5	508.0
Inpatient Surgeries	24.4	24.3	24.7	26.3	25.4
Births	13.2	13.5	14.4	14.2	14.6
Outpatient					
Emergency Outpatient Visits	293.7	285.5	275.2	276.2	285.6
Other Outpatient Visits	1,094.4	1,020.0	1,060.9	991.8	1,213.5
Total Outpatient Visits	1,388.1	1,305.5	1,336.2	1,268.1	1,499.2
Outpatient Surgeries	33.9	33.8	35.8	34.5	34.4
Expense per Capita (per person)	$1,939.5	$1,827.1	$1,761.6	$1,602.4	$1,560.3

States

TABLE **6**

COLORADO

U.S. Registered Community Hospitals
(Nonfederal, short-term general and other special hospitals)

Overview 2006–2010

	2010	2009	2008	2007	2006
Total Community Hospitals in Colorado.......	**80**	**81**	**78**	**75**	**73**
Bed Size Category					
6-24	11	13	10	10	13
25-49	21	19	21	18	18
50-99	16	18	16	17	13
100-199	14	11	13	12	11
200-299	6	10	9	9	8
300-399	8	5	4	4	5
400-499	2	3	3	4	4
500 + ...	2	2	2	1	1
Location					
Hospitals Urban...........................	43	43	41	38	36
Hospitals Rural	37	38	37	37	37
Control					
State and Local Government................	27	28	28	28	27
Not for Profit	37	37	37	37	35
Investor owned	16	16	13	10	11
Physician Models					
Independent Practice Association	10	9	9	7	6
Group Practice without Walls...............	2	1	1	2	3
Open Physician-Hospital Organization	13	12	12	8	7
Closed Physician-Hospital Organization	3	3	2	3	2
Management Service Organization	4	3	3	3	2
Integrated Salary Model....................	34	33	32	29	26
Equity Model.............................	2	1	2	3	2
Foundation...............................	4	1	2	2	1
Insurance Products					
Health Maintenance Organization	10	11	9	8	6
Preferred Provider Organization..............	10	10	9	10	8
Indemnity Fee for Service	2	3	3	4	2
Managed Care Contracts					
Health Maintenance Organization	46	47	48	40	41
Preferred Provider Organization..............	52	53	54	46	47
Affiliations					
Hospitals in a System.....................	46	46	44	41	38
Hospitals in a Network....................	27	24	25	23	25
Hospitals in a Group Purchasing Organization..	60	58	57	53	51

States

TABLE 6

COLORADO

U.S. Registered Community Hospitals
(Nonfederal, short-term general and other special hospitals)

Utilization, Personnel, Revenue and Expenses, Community Health Indicators 2006–2010

	2010	2009	2008	2007	2006
TOTAL FACILITY (Includes Hospital and Nursing Home Units)					
Utilization - Inpatient					
Beds	10,208	10,364	10,053	9,708	9,518
Admissions	449,369	445,291	442,161	425,959	420,547
Inpatient Days	2,234,925	2,237,893	2,210,340	2,169,902	2,164,588
Average Length of Stay	5.0	5.0	5.0	5.1	5.1
Inpatient Surgeries	141,751	143,822	141,724	139,125	134,773
Births	63,653	65,130	68,659	66,512	66,612
Utilization - Outpatient					
Emergency Outpatient Visits	1,677,353	1,725,417	1,621,056	1,548,319	1,496,363
Other Outpatient Visits	6,572,791	7,134,664	6,786,916	6,206,101	5,768,007
Total Outpatient Visits	8,250,144	8,860,081	8,407,972	7,754,420	7,264,370
Outpatient Surgeries	211,730	206,315	204,045	185,515	174,314
Personnel					
Full Time RNs	15,787	15,411	15,300	14,201	11,937
Full Time LPNs	551	684	775	823	866
Part Time RNs	5,235	5,377	5,123	3,543	4,957
Part Time LPNs	179	215	240	181	300
Total Full Time	55,072	54,311	53,002	53,751	47,656
Total Part Time	15,268	15,782	16,290	10,814	14,718
Revenue - Inpatient					
Gross Inpatient Revenue	$19,013,208,766	$17,525,068,092	$16,296,367,033	$14,291,552,936	$13,112,287,510
Revenue - Outpatient					
Gross Outpatient Revenue	$14,766,810,304	$13,322,614,754	$11,343,750,441	$9,499,093,812	$8,259,901,579
Revenue and Expenses - Totals **(Includes Inpatient and Outpatient)**					
Total Gross Revenue	$33,780,019,070	$30,847,682,846	$27,640,117,474	$23,790,646,748	$21,372,189,089
Deductions from Revenue	23,450,147,224	21,100,773,225	18,781,874,571	15,715,614,730	13,916,531,235
Net Patient Revenue	10,329,871,846	9,746,909,621	8,858,242,903	8,075,032,018	7,455,657,854
Other Operating Revenue	501,184,086	489,463,546	518,570,378	603,828,098	499,204,326
Other Nonoperating Revenue	196,854,806	146,646,198	-27,071,112	258,400,086	185,613,712
Total Net Revenue	11,027,910,738	10,383,019,365	9,349,742,169	8,937,260,202	8,140,475,892
Total Expenses	9,590,946,802	9,244,357,277	8,889,584,362	8,011,595,534	7,269,883,043
HOSPITAL UNIT (Excludes Separate Nursing Home Units)					
Utilization - Inpatient					
Beds	9,537	9,777	9,518	9,016	8,968
Admissions	447,782	443,718	441,061	424,899	419,404
Inpatient Days	2,026,168	2,056,115	2,076,120	1,986,909	1,990,815
Average Length of Stay	4.5	4.6	4.7	4.7	4.7
Personnel					
Total Full Time	54,554	53,795	52,602	53,421	47,280
Total Part Time	14,960	15,572	16,131	10,670	14,548
Revenue and Expenses - Totals **(Includes Inpatient and Outpatient)**					
Total Net Revenue	$10,984,832,365	$10,343,931,411	$9,321,879,151	$8,905,534,902	$8,111,396,372
Total Expenses	9,546,862,102	9,207,018,816	8,862,237,046	7,977,887,275	7,245,463,125
COMMUNITY HEALTH INDICATORS PER 1000 POPULATION					
Total Population (in thousands)	5,095	5,025	4,935	4,842	4,753
Inpatient					
Beds	2.0	2.1	2.0	2.0	2.0
Admissions	88.2	88.6	89.6	88.0	88.5
Inpatient Days	438.6	445.4	447.9	448.1	455.4
Inpatient Surgeries	27.8	28.6	28.7	28.7	28.4
Births	12.5	13.0	13.9	13.7	14.0
Outpatient					
Emergency Outpatient Visits	329.2	343.4	328.5	319.8	314.8
Other Outpatient Visits	1,290.0	1,419.9	1,375.2	1,281.7	1,213.5
Total Outpatient Visits	1,619.2	1,763.3	1,703.7	1,601.4	1,528.4
Outpatient Surgeries	41.6	41.1	41.3	38.3	36.7
Expense per Capita (per person)	$1,882.3	$1,839.8	$1,801.3	$1,654.5	$1,529.5

States

TABLE **6**

CONNECTICUT

U.S. Registered Community Hospitals
(Nonfederal, short-term general and other special hospitals)

Overview 2006–2010

	2010	2009	2008	2007	2006
Total Community Hospitals in Connecticut	34	35	35	34	35
Bed Size Category					
6-24	0	0	0	0	0
25-49	1	1	1	1	1
50-99	8	8	8	8	8
100-199	10	12	12	11	11
200-299	5	3	4	5	5
300-399	5	6	5	5	5
400-499	2	2	2	1	1
500 + ...	3	3	3	3	4
Location					
Hospitals Urban..........................	29	30	30	29	29
Hospitals Rural	5	5	5	5	6
Control					
State and Local Government................	1	1	1	1	1
Not for Profit...........................	32	33	32	32	33
Investor owned	1	1	2	1	1
Physician Models					
Independent Practice Association	7	8	8	8	6
Group Practice without Walls................	2	0	1	1	0
Open Physician-Hospital Organization	5	6	3	5	9
Closed Physician-Hospital Organization	2	2	2	2	2
Management Service Organization	5	4	3	4	2
Integrated Salary Model....................	17	15	18	13	14
Equity Model	1	1	1	0	0
Foundation...............................	5	1	0	1	0
Insurance Products					
Health Maintenance Organization	2	2	3	2	1
Preferred Provider Organization..............	0	0	0	3	4
Indemnity Fee for Service	0	0	1	0	0
Managed Care Contracts					
Health Maintenance Organization	23	22	22	22	22
Preferred Provider Organization..............	22	23	22	23	22
Affiliations					
Hospitals in a System.....................	14	12	9	9	10
Hospitals in a Network....................	11	12	13	14	12
Hospitals in a Group Purchasing Organization..	28	28	28	29	29

States

TABLE 6

CONNECTICUT

U.S. Registered Community Hospitals
(Nonfederal, short-term general and other special hospitals)

Utilization, Personnel, Revenue and Expenses, Community Health Indicators 2006–2010

	2010	2009	2008	2007	2006
TOTAL FACILITY (Includes Hospital and Nursing Home Units)					
Utilization - Inpatient					
Beds	8,091	7,935	7,906	7,483	7,988
Admissions	406,718	407,710	400,632	396,895	406,498
Inpatient Days	2,290,323	2,345,878	2,296,558	2,128,239	2,303,485
Average Length of Stay	5.6	5.8	5.7	5.4	5.7
Inpatient Surgeries	108,070	109,334	107,611	111,119	114,762
Births	37,483	38,932	40,963	41,620	41,476
Utilization - Outpatient					
Emergency Outpatient Visits	1,661,088	1,607,670	1,524,545	1,461,985	1,463,125
Other Outpatient Visits	6,605,714	6,567,848	6,550,089	6,088,953	6,315,889
Total Outpatient Visits	8,266,802	8,175,518	8,074,634	7,550,938	7,779,014
Outpatient Surgeries	201,480	198,390	192,544	198,022	194,238
Personnel					
Full Time RNs	10,483	10,831	10,057	9,736	9,636
Full Time LPNs	264	311	348	363	367
Part Time RNs	6,609	6,512	6,883	7,422	7,200
Part Time LPNs	194	229	361	353	277
Total Full Time	43,689	44,091	42,558	41,918	41,961
Total Part Time	21,507	20,842	23,152	22,594	21,899
Revenue - Inpatient					
Gross Inpatient Revenue	$13,295,787,334	$12,736,578,199	$11,484,375,092	$10,507,210,277	$9,889,922,333
Revenue - Outpatient					
Gross Outpatient Revenue	$10,537,030,956	$9,767,664,004	$8,402,315,796	$7,345,514,961	$6,623,255,839
Revenue and Expenses - Totals					
(Includes Inpatient and Outpatient)					
Total Gross Revenue	$23,832,818,290	$22,504,242,203	$19,886,690,888	$17,852,725,238	$16,513,178,172
Deductions from Revenue	15,121,712,588	14,125,599,354	12,234,710,097	10,801,568,841	9,681,601,278
Net Patient Revenue	8,711,105,702	8,378,642,849	7,651,980,791	7,051,156,397	6,831,576,894
Other Operating Revenue	455,355,109	420,171,188	368,547,369	303,008,601	288,671,225
Other Nonoperating Revenue	115,215,987	-1,279,820	-125,823,897	157,150,928	141,753,252
Total Net Revenue	9,281,676,798	8,797,534,217	7,894,704,263	7,511,315,926	7,262,001,371
Total Expenses	8,928,296,028	8,565,211,235	7,906,958,696	7,221,249,850	7,066,962,056
HOSPITAL UNIT (Excludes Separate Nursing Home Units)					
Utilization - Inpatient					
Beds	7,676	7,648	7,237	7,196	7,699
Admissions	405,842	407,207	399,384	396,101	405,883
Inpatient Days	2,146,637	2,245,293	2,060,023	2,028,334	2,198,706
Average Length of Stay	5.3	5.5	5.2	5.1	5.4
Personnel					
Total Full Time	43,306	44,052	41,790	41,538	41,600
Total Part Time	21,256	20,826	22,313	22,178	21,794
Revenue and Expenses - Totals					
(Includes Inpatient and Outpatient)					
Total Net Revenue	$9,235,623,435	$8,759,788,307	$7,822,208,146	$7,478,024,431	$7,230,095,664
Total Expenses	8,888,242,578	8,530,306,215	7,846,566,914	7,189,144,542	7,031,531,481
COMMUNITY HEALTH INDICATORS PER 1000 POPULATION					
Total Population (in thousands)	3,527	3,518	3,503	3,489	3,485
Inpatient					
Beds	2.3	2.3	2.3	2.1	2.3
Admissions	115.3	115.9	114.4	113.8	116.6
Inpatient Days	649.4	666.8	655.6	610.0	660.9
Inpatient Surgeries	30.6	31.1	30.7	31.9	32.9
Births	10.6	11.1	11.7	11.9	11.9
Outpatient					
Emergency Outpatient Visits	471.0	456.9	435.2	419.1	419.8
Other Outpatient Visits	1,872.9	1,866.8	1,869.9	1,745.4	1,812.2
Total Outpatient Visits	2,343.9	2,323.7	2,305.1	2,164.4	2,232.0
Outpatient Surgeries	57.1	56.4	55.0	56.8	55.7
Expense per Capita (per person)	$2,531.5	$2,434.5	$2,257.2	$2,069.9	$2,027.7

States

Overview 2006–2010

	2010	2009	2008	2007	2006
Total Community Hospitals in Delaware.......	7	7	7	6	6
Bed Size Category					
6-24	0	0	0	0	0
25-49	1	1	1	0	0
50-99	0	0	0	0	0
100-199	2	2	3	1	1
200-299	2	2	1	3	2
300-399	1	1	1	1	2
400-499	0	0	0	0	0
500 + ...	1	1	1	1	1
Location					
Hospitals Urban...........................	5	5	5	4	4
Hospitals Rural	2	2	2	2	2
Control					
State and Local Government................	0	0	0	0	0
Not for Profit	6	6	6	6	6
Investor owned	1	1	1	0	0
Physician Models					
Independent Practice Association	0	0	0	0	1
Group Practice without Walls................	0	0	0	0	0
Open Physician-Hospital Organization	0	0	0	1	1
Closed Physician-Hospital Organization	0	0	0	0	0
Management Service Organization	0	0	0	1	1
Integrated Salary Model....................	3	3	2	3	4
Equity Model.............................	0	0	0	0	0
Foundation...............................	1	1	1	1	0
Insurance Products					
Health Maintenance Organization	1	1	0	0	0
Preferred Provider Organization..............	1	1	0	0	0
Indemnity Fee for Service	1	1	0	0	1
Managed Care Contracts					
Health Maintenance Organization	4	5	5	5	4
Preferred Provider Organization..............	4	5	5	5	4
Affiliations					
Hospitals in a System.....................	3	3	3	2	2
Hospitals in a Network....................	0	0	—	—	—
Hospitals in a Group Purchasing Organization..	6	6	6	5	5

States

TABLE 6

DELAWARE

U.S. Registered Community Hospitals
(Nonfederal, short-term general and other special hospitals)

Utilization, Personnel, Revenue and Expenses, Community Health Indicators 2006–2010

	2010	2009	2008	2007	2006
TOTAL FACILITY (Includes Hospital and Nursing Home Units)					
Utilization - Inpatient					
Beds	2,155	2,125	2,071	2,288	2,138
Admissions	101,735	102,153	103,726	107,037	105,164
Inpatient Days	580,261	597,993	613,049	671,628	669,392
Average Length of Stay	5.7	5.9	5.9	6.3	6.4
Inpatient Surgeries	28,828	29,930	30,845	32,039	31,881
Births	11,486	12,158	12,536	12,312	12,361
Utilization - Outpatient					
Emergency Outpatient Visits	406,652	392,660	363,979	343,713	382,935
Other Outpatient Visits	1,380,658	1,351,824	1,317,097	1,495,036	1,456,973
Total Outpatient Visits	1,787,310	1,744,484	1,681,076	1,838,749	1,839,908
Outpatient Surgeries	67,852	70,362	60,343	63,526	62,593
Personnel					
Full Time RNs	3,689	3,485	3,334	3,010	2,995
Full Time LPNs	126	135	164	179	212
Part Time RNs	2,195	2,486	2,326	2,021	2,107
Part Time LPNs	125	133	156	148	126
Total Full Time	13,885	13,707	13,954	12,707	12,774
Total Part Time	5,846	6,406	6,340	5,485	5,541
Revenue - Inpatient					
Gross Inpatient Revenue	$2,671,560,601	$2,528,530,549	$2,385,974,140	$2,244,196,638	$2,060,178,931
Revenue - Outpatient					
Gross Outpatient Revenue	$2,026,156,087	$1,797,902,276	$1,569,559,056	$1,352,820,078	$1,315,656,776
Revenue and Expenses - Totals					
(Includes Inpatient and Outpatient)					
Total Gross Revenue	$4,697,716,688	$4,326,432,825	$3,955,533,196	$3,597,016,716	$3,375,835,707
Deductions from Revenue	2,394,621,807	2,111,070,905	1,865,226,783	1,679,045,929	1,626,506,667
Net Patient Revenue	2,303,094,881	2,215,361,920	2,090,306,413	1,917,970,787	1,749,329,040
Other Operating Revenue	165,608,644	159,598,810	121,047,453	167,718,247	144,361,451
Other Nonoperating Revenue	77,555,669	-156,561,766	81,948,435	62,950,703	52,564,940
Total Net Revenue	2,546,259,194	2,218,398,964	2,293,302,301	2,148,639,737	1,946,255,431
Total Expenses	2,344,087,243	2,264,467,218	2,119,860,075	1,949,799,885	1,802,837,132
HOSPITAL UNIT (Excludes Separate Nursing Home Units)					
Utilization - Inpatient					
Beds	1,941	1,911	1,967	1,892	1,742
Admissions	101,130	101,502	103,438	105,462	104,253
Inpatient Days	509,077	525,133	577,278	538,981	532,566
Average Length of Stay	5.0	5.2	5.6	5.1	5.1
Personnel					
Total Full Time	13,670	13,553	13,883	12,391	12,551
Total Part Time	5,705	6,246	6,316	5,297	5,450
Revenue and Expenses - Totals					
(Includes Inpatient and Outpatient)					
Total Net Revenue	$2,525,583,028	$2,197,822,141	$2,283,604,301	$2,109,958,350	$1,913,476,298
Total Expenses	2,323,082,005	2,243,045,075	2,110,993,075	1,902,038,450	1,760,866,423
COMMUNITY HEALTH INDICATORS PER 1000 POPULATION					
Total Population (in thousands)	891	885	876	865	853
Inpatient					
Beds	2.4	2.4	2.4	2.6	2.5
Admissions	114.1	115.4	118.4	123.8	123.3
Inpatient Days	650.9	675.6	699.7	776.5	784.7
Inpatient Surgeries	32.3	33.8	35.2	37.0	37.4
Births	12.9	13.7	14.3	14.2	14.5
Outpatient					
Emergency Outpatient Visits	456.2	443.6	415.4	397.4	448.9
Other Outpatient Visits	1,548.8	1,527.3	1,503.2	1,728.6	1,708.0
Total Outpatient Visits	2,004.9	1,970.9	1,918.6	2,126.0	2,156.9
Outpatient Surgeries	76.1	79.5	68.9	73.4	73.4
Expense per Capita (per person)	$2,629.5	$2,558.4	$2,419.3	$2,254.4	$2,113.5

States

TABLE 6

DISTRICT OF COLUMBIA

U.S. Registered Community Hospitals
(Nonfederal, short-term general and other special hospitals)

Overview 2006–2010

	2010	2009	2008	2007	2006
Total Community Hospitals in District of Columbia	11	10	10	10	11
Bed Size Category					
6-24	0	0	0	0	0
25-49	0	0	0	0	0
50-99	1	1	1	1	1
100-199	2	1	1	1	2
200-299	4	3	3	2	2
300-399	1	2	3	4	4
400-499	1	1	0	0	0
500 +	2	2	2	2	2
Location					
Hospitals Urban	11	10	10	10	11
Hospitals Rural	0	0	0	0	0
Control					
State and Local Government	1	0	0	0	0
Not for Profit	7	7	7	7	7
Investor owned	3	3	3	3	4
Physician Models					
Independent Practice Association	1	0	1	0	0
Group Practice without Walls	0	1	1	1	1
Open Physician-Hospital Organization	0	0	0	1	1
Closed Physician-Hospital Organization	1	1	1	1	1
Management Service Organization	1	1	1	1	1
Integrated Salary Model	5	5	4	5	6
Equity Model	0	0	0	0	0
Foundation	1	1	1	1	1
Insurance Products					
Health Maintenance Organization	2	3	3	4	4
Preferred Provider Organization	0	0	0	1	1
Indemnity Fee for Service	0	0	0	1	1
Managed Care Contracts					
Health Maintenance Organization	7	7	7	7	8
Preferred Provider Organization	6	7	7	5	8
Affiliations					
Hospitals in a System	9	7	7	7	8
Hospitals in a Network	5	4	2	2	—
Hospitals in a Group Purchasing Organization	8	8	8	7	8

TABLE 6

DISTRICT OF COLUMBIA

U.S. Registered Community Hospitals
(Nonfederal, short-term general and other special hospitals)

Utilization, Personnel, Revenue and Expenses, Community Health Indicators 2006–2010

	2010	2009	2008	2007	2006
TOTAL FACILITY (Includes Hospital and Nursing Home Units)					
Utilization - Inpatient					
Beds	3,458	3,452	3,358	3,418	3,601
Admissions	131,976	138,456	137,260	136,488	139,515
Inpatient Days	926,254	927,419	954,416	908,940	979,850
Average Length of Stay	7.0	6.7	7.0	6.7	7.0
Inpatient Surgeries	41,736	42,667	43,173	42,870	42,206
Births	13,814	14,507	14,901	14,871	14,120
Utilization - Outpatient					
Emergency Outpatient Visits	430,637	457,292	436,918	461,465	396,343
Other Outpatient Visits	1,888,245	1,954,514	1,919,145	1,905,247	1,212,621
Total Outpatient Visits	2,318,882	2,411,806	2,356,063	2,366,712	1,608,964
Outpatient Surgeries	58,907	62,497	65,742	59,336	57,955
Personnel					
Full Time RNs	5,458	5,222	4,447	4,357	4,374
Full Time LPNs	267	304	215	296	362
Part Time RNs	1,966	1,845	1,796	1,796	1,648
Part Time LPNs	46	35	38	46	84
Total Full Time	22,654	22,371	21,247	20,507	20,779
Total Part Time	5,259	4,666	4,463	4,946	4,811
Revenue - Inpatient					
Gross Inpatient Revenue	$6,016,677,081	$5,895,449,855	$5,686,127,872	$5,672,805,649	$5,144,465,380
Revenue - Outpatient					
Gross Outpatient Revenue	$3,476,432,807	$3,108,162,999	$2,835,491,356	$2,666,461,627	$2,288,315,622
Revenue and Expenses - Totals					
(Includes Inpatient and Outpatient)					
Total Gross Revenue	$9,493,109,888	$9,003,612,854	$8,521,619,228	$8,339,267,276	$7,432,781,002
Deductions from Revenue	5,971,324,649	5,592,219,614	5,300,645,413	5,229,606,649	4,529,081,776
Net Patient Revenue	3,521,785,239	3,411,393,240	3,220,973,815	3,109,660,627	2,903,699,226
Other Operating Revenue	205,891,415	214,814,678	192,446,948	187,903,112	174,433,561
Other Nonoperating Revenue	33,913,566	32,415,954	-139,712,361	67,564,569	69,896,434
Total Net Revenue	3,761,590,220	3,658,623,872	3,273,708,402	3,365,128,308	3,148,029,221
Total Expenses	3,582,285,072	3,585,829,997	3,392,800,661	3,224,779,035	2,998,369,380
HOSPITAL UNIT (Excludes Separate Nursing Home Units)					
Utilization - Inpatient					
Beds	3,161	3,157	3,061	3,123	3,161
Admissions	130,125	136,578	135,521	134,769	137,343
Inpatient Days	822,314	822,965	850,769	805,786	827,871
Average Length of Stay	6.3	6.0	6.3	6.0	6.0
Personnel					
Total Full Time	22,327	22,067	21,151	20,210	20,365
Total Part Time	5,181	4,595	4,437	4,882	4,666
Revenue and Expenses - Totals					
(Includes Inpatient and Outpatient)					
Total Net Revenue	$3,726,836,744	$3,624,105,283	$3,244,092,304	$3,331,993,244	$3,094,272,498
Total Expenses	3,552,676,361	3,556,839,618	3,363,055,134	3,196,280,439	2,959,472,207
COMMUNITY HEALTH INDICATORS PER 1000 POPULATION					
Total Population (in thousands)	611	600	590	586	584
Inpatient					
Beds	5.7	5.8	5.7	5.8	6.2
Admissions	216.1	230.9	232.6	232.8	238.9
Inpatient Days	1,517.0	1,546.6	1,617.5	1,550.0	1,677.9
Inpatient Surgeries	68.4	71.2	73.2	73.1	72.3
Births	22.6	24.2	25.3	25.4	24.2
Outpatient					
Emergency Outpatient Visits	705.3	762.6	740.4	786.9	678.7
Other Outpatient Visits	3,092.5	3,259.4	3,252.4	3,249.0	2,076.5
Total Outpatient Visits	3,797.8	4,022.0	3,992.8	4,035.9	2,755.2
Outpatient Surgeries	96.5	104.2	111.4	101.2	99.2
Expense per Capita (per person)	$5,866.9	$5,979.8	$5,749.8	$5,499.2	$5,134.4

States

TABLE 6

FLORIDA

U.S. Registered Community Hospitals
(Nonfederal, short-term general and other special hospitals)

Overview 2006–2010

	2010	2009	2008	2007	2006
Total Community Hospitals in Florida.........	210	210	211	200	203
Bed Size Category					
6-24	2	2	3	2	2
25-49	21	21	23	18	16
50-99	39	39	35	33	32
100-199	50	51	55	53	57
200-299	38	37	37	35	35
300-399	27	25	25	27	28
400-499	9	12	11	10	10
500 +..................................	24	23	22	22	23
Location					
Hospitals Urban...........................	181	181	181	169	170
Hospitals Rural	29	29	30	31	33
Control					
State and Local Government................	27	25	25	26	24
Not for Profit.............................	79	82	86	82	84
Investor owned	104	103	100	92	95
Physician Models					
Independent Practice Association	5	4	6	6	8
Group Practice without Walls................	7	9	3	3	2
Open Physician-Hospital Organization	19	19	12	9	14
Closed Physician-Hospital Organization	7	6	10	7	7
Management Service Organization	14	8	5	6	8
Integrated Salary Model....................	59	52	52	59	44
Equity Model.............................	1	0	0	1	0
Foundation...............................	4	4	2	5	4
Insurance Products					
Health Maintenance Organization	11	13	8	9	19
Preferred Provider Organization..............	16	17	10	8	19
Indemnity Fee for Service	5	6	5	5	10
Managed Care Contracts					
Health Maintenance Organization	98	88	81	98	102
Preferred Provider Organization..............	101	91	82	97	103
Affiliations					
Hospitals in a System......................	160	160	159	149	155
Hospitals in a Network.....................	35	35	38	38	40
Hospitals in a Group Purchasing Organization..	106	116	118	123	123

TABLE 6

FLORIDA

U.S. Registered Community Hospitals
(Nonfederal, short-term general and other special hospitals)

Utilization, Personnel, Revenue and Expenses, Community Health Indicators 2006–2010

	2010	2009	2008	2007	2006
TOTAL FACILITY (Includes Hospital and Nursing Home Units)					
Utilization - Inpatient					
Beds	53,318	53,293	52,836	51,648	51,423
Admissions	2,452,089	2,452,546	2,396,691	2,387,525	2,373,712
Inpatient Days	12,191,209	12,261,161	12,192,327	12,351,368	12,432,951
Average Length of Stay............	5.0	5.0	5.1	5.2	5.2
Inpatient Surgeries...............	650,557	655,203	659,237	660,217	672,998
Births..........................	202,862	206,284	218,035	223,202	225,049
Utilization - Outpatient					
Emergency Outpatient Visits........	7,559,853	7,477,209	7,161,108	7,085,930	7,165,036
Other Outpatient Visits............	16,683,248	17,396,409	17,268,832	16,410,090	15,593,993
Total Outpatient Visits	24,243,101	24,873,618	24,429,940	23,496,020	22,759,029
Outpatient Surgeries	798,189	822,841	846,551	796,945	783,330
Personnel					
Full Time RNs	69,840	68,581	62,639	62,349	59,518
Full Time LPNs	4,111	4,470	4,563	5,159	5,212
Part Time RNs...................	16,844	17,495	20,188	18,904	18,411
Part Time LPNs	901	1,092	1,154	1,318	1,310
Total Full Time..................	232,349	229,515	220,165	220,065	213,259
Total Part Time	47,580	49,670	54,335	54,010	53,611
Revenue - Inpatient					
Gross Inpatient Revenue...........	$98,439,589,940	$90,412,617,613	$80,168,815,722	$76,599,198,509	$70,860,708,525
Revenue - Outpatient					
Gross Outpatient Revenue	$58,858,434,042	$52,572,001,561	$44,224,777,407	$39,745,819,297	$34,594,178,527
Revenue and Expenses - Totals					
(Includes Inpatient and Outpatient)					
Total Gross Revenue..............	$157,298,023,982	$142,984,619,174	$124,393,593,129	$116,345,017,806	$105,454,887,052
Deductions from Revenue..........	119,355,324,858	107,498,135,646	91,084,229,921	84,506,636,341	75,260,615,364
Net Patient Revenue	37,942,699,124	35,486,483,528	33,309,363,208	31,838,381,465	30,194,271,688
Other Operating Revenue	2,190,285,623	1,811,268,561	2,104,002,109	1,913,000,678	1,737,406,049
Other Nonoperating Revenue	562,284,781	483,113,737	64,179,556	592,244,508	431,835,226
Total Net Revenue................	40,695,269,528	37,780,865,826	35,477,544,873	34,343,626,651	32,363,512,963
Total Expenses..................	36,318,160,204	34,922,141,446	33,117,894,364	31,504,674,840	30,009,185,777
HOSPITAL UNIT (Excludes Separate Nursing Home Units)					
Utilization - Inpatient					
Beds	52,415	52,361	51,863	50,444	50,173
Admissions	2,448,276	2,448,331	2,392,911	2,382,000	2,368,632
Inpatient Days	11,888,876	11,942,896	11,874,879	11,954,597	12,062,565
Average Length of Stay............	4.9	4.9	5.0	5.0	5.1
Personnel					
Total Full Time...................	231,450	228,263	219,027	218,802	209,939
Total Part Time	47,423	49,227	54,203	53,792	52,895
Revenue and Expenses - Totals					
(Includes Inpatient and Outpatient)					
Total Net Revenue................	$40,594,960,399	$37,709,543,480	$35,402,114,525	$34,260,176,558	$32,235,490,697
Total Expenses..................	36,197,864,998	34,839,959,163	33,027,271,463	31,421,178,984	29,908,580,552
COMMUNITY HEALTH INDICATORS PER 1000 POPULATION					
Total Population (in thousands)	18,678	18,538	18,424	18,278	18,089
Inpatient					
Beds	2.9	2.9	2.9	2.8	2.8
Admissions	131.3	132.3	130.1	130.6	131.2
Inpatient Days	652.7	661.4	661.8	675.8	687.3
Inpatient Surgeries...............	34.8	35.3	35.8	36.1	37.2
Births..........................	10.9	11.1	11.8	12.2	12.4
Outpatient					
Emergency Outpatient Visits........	404.7	403.3	388.7	387.7	396.1
Other Outpatient Visits............	893.2	938.4	937.3	897.8	862.1
Total Outpatient Visits	1,297.9	1,341.8	1,326.0	1,285.5	1,258.2
Outpatient Surgeries	42.7	44.4	45.9	43.6	43.3
Expense per Capita (per person).....	$1,944.4	$1,883.8	$1,797.6	$1,723.6	$1,659.0

TABLE 6

GEORGIA

U.S. Registered Community Hospitals
(Nonfederal, short-term general and other special hospitals)

Overview 2006–2010

	2010	2009	2008	2007	2006
Total Community Hospitals in Georgia........	154	152	153	147	147
Bed Size Category					
6-24	6	6	4	3	4
25-49	39	38	41	35	35
50-99	24	24	22	22	24
100-199	42	42	44	42	40
200-299	17	16	15	18	17
300-399	7	8	9	8	8
400-499	10	10	9	11	13
500 + ...	9	8	9	8	6
Location					
Hospitals Urban...........................	89	87	87	82	65
Hospitals Rural	65	65	66	65	82
Control					
State and Local Government................	52	53	56	57	56
Not for Profit	66	63	63	59	59
Investor owned	36	36	34	31	32
Physician Models					
Independent Practice Association	8	10	10	8	12
Group Practice without Walls...............	0	1	2	1	2
Open Physician-Hospital Organization	18	15	19	22	19
Closed Physician-Hospital Organization	17	16	15	17	16
Management Service Organization	8	7	8	8	8
Integrated Salary Model....................	41	37	35	34	33
Equity Model.............................	5	5	6	4	4
Foundation...............................	4	3	5	5	5
Insurance Products					
Health Maintenance Organization	9	12	10	6	9
Preferred Provider Organization..............	20	21	20	24	35
Indemnity Fee for Service	5	7	7	6	10
Managed Care Contracts					
Health Maintenance Organization	81	83	79	67	67
Preferred Provider Organization..............	94	95	89	83	91
Affiliations					
Hospitals in a System.....................	81	79	81	74	72
Hospitals in a Network....................	40	39	42	42	50
Hospitals in a Group Purchasing Organization..	104	105	100	92	100

TABLE 6

GEORGIA

U.S. Registered Community Hospitals
(Nonfederal, short-term general and other special hospitals)

Utilization, Personnel, Revenue and Expenses, Community Health Indicators 2006–2010

	2010	2009	2008	2007	2006
TOTAL FACILITY (Includes Hospital and Nursing Home Units)					
Utilization - Inpatient					
Beds	25,513	25,419	25,583	25,483	24,772
Admissions	961,391	956,870	959,375	963,583	956,395
Inpatient Days	6,138,828	6,059,475	6,172,510	6,278,894	6,221,330
Average Length of Stay	6.4	6.3	6.4	6.5	6.5
Inpatient Surgeries	265,789	267,788	269,766	277,885	273,420
Births	128,531	135,505	142,382	146,746	140,741
Utilization - Outpatient					
Emergency Outpatient Visits	4,095,951	4,081,812	3,843,244	3,747,532	3,629,453
Other Outpatient Visits	10,195,629	10,308,523	10,340,848	10,010,319	10,153,274
Total Outpatient Visits	14,291,580	14,390,335	14,184,092	13,757,851	13,782,727
Outpatient Surgeries	497,929	511,272	487,070	491,459	504,293
Personnel					
Full Time RNs	30,393	29,719	27,823	27,684	25,671
Full Time LPNs	3,276	3,506	3,651	3,738	3,965
Part Time RNs	10,469	11,965	11,963	13,312	12,286
Part Time LPNs	857	977	1,035	1,253	1,230
Total Full Time	112,040	111,451	108,871	107,711	104,111
Total Part Time	29,110	32,522	32,169	35,093	32,617
Revenue - Inpatient					
Gross Inpatient Revenue	$28,768,523,466	$26,548,862,459	$25,139,478,750	$24,285,401,220	$22,163,780,319
Revenue - Outpatient					
Gross Outpatient Revenue	$22,700,713,568	$20,738,855,918	$18,392,697,423	$16,838,734,295	$14,777,650,188
Revenue and Expenses - Totals					
(Includes Inpatient and Outpatient)					
Total Gross Revenue	$51,469,237,034	$47,287,718,377	$43,532,176,173	$41,124,135,515	$36,941,430,507
Deductions from Revenue	35,169,736,402	31,401,538,356	28,602,816,610	26,341,808,978	23,269,007,568
Net Patient Revenue	16,299,500,632	15,886,180,021	14,929,359,563	14,782,326,537	13,672,422,939
Other Operating Revenue	773,260,104	755,206,277	788,733,742	594,706,811	830,795,303
Other Nonoperating Revenue	324,122,628	128,720,872	-102,237,534	373,626,935	257,847,975
Total Net Revenue	17,396,883,364	16,770,107,170	15,615,855,771	15,750,660,283	14,761,066,217
Total Expenses	16,079,597,038	15,616,820,380	15,098,639,746	14,769,627,733	13,846,913,245
HOSPITAL UNIT (Excludes Separate Nursing Home Units)					
Utilization - Inpatient					
Beds	21,605	21,868	22,332	22,171	21,036
Admissions	953,677	949,070	953,328	957,240	950,054
Inpatient Days	4,826,637	4,890,754	5,113,980	5,168,328	4,942,793
Average Length of Stay	5.1	5.2	5.4	5.4	5.2
Personnel					
Total Full Time	109,514	108,900	106,600	105,488	101,590
Total Part Time	28,416	31,885	31,471	34,314	31,890
Revenue and Expenses - Totals					
(Includes Inpatient and Outpatient)					
Total Net Revenue	$17,166,588,760	$16,591,803,789	$15,449,511,224	$15,588,075,384	$14,592,684,941
Total Expenses	15,896,591,116	15,452,332,194	14,947,753,769	14,621,668,884	13,687,516,954
COMMUNITY HEALTH INDICATORS PER 1000 POPULATION					
Total Population (in thousands)	9,908	9,829	9,698	9,534	9,330
Inpatient					
Beds	2.6	2.6	2.6	2.7	2.7
Admissions	97.0	97.3	98.9	101.1	102.5
Inpatient Days	619.6	616.5	636.5	658.6	666.8
Inpatient Surgeries	26.8	27.2	27.8	29.1	29.3
Births	13.0	13.8	14.7	15.4	15.1
Outpatient					
Emergency Outpatient Visits	413.4	415.3	396.3	393.1	389.0
Other Outpatient Visits	1,029.0	1,048.8	1,066.3	1,050.0	1,088.2
Total Outpatient Visits	1,442.4	1,464.0	1,462.6	1,443.1	1,477.2
Outpatient Surgeries	50.3	52.0	50.2	51.5	54.1
Expense per Capita (per person)	$1,622.8	$1,588.8	$1,556.9	$1,549.2	$1,484.1

States

TABLE 6

HAWAII

U.S. Registered Community Hospitals
(Nonfederal, short-term general and other special hospitals)

Overview 2006–2010

	2010	2009	2008	2007	2006
Total Community Hospitals in Hawaii	26	25	25	23	24
Bed Size Category					
6-24	6	5	4	3	4
25-49	3	4	4	4	4
50-99	4	5	5	3	3
100-199	7	5	6	7	7
200-299	5	5	5	5	5
300-399	0	0	0	0	0
400-499	1	1	1	1	1
500 + ...	0	0	0	0	0
Location					
Hospitals Urban............................	14	13	14	13	13
Hospitals Rural	12	12	11	10	11
Control					
State and Local Government................	8	7	8	7	7
Not for Profit	18	18	17	16	17
Investor owned	0	0	0	0	0
Physician Models					
Independent Practice Association	2	1	1	0	1
Group Practice without Walls................	0	0	0	0	0
Open Physician-Hospital Organization	2	2	3	2	2
Closed Physician-Hospital Organization	1	1	1	1	1
Management Service Organization	0	0	0	0	0
Integrated Salary Model	7	5	4	4	5
Equity Model	0	0	0	0	0
Foundation................................	0	2	1	1	1
Insurance Products					
Health Maintenance Organization	1	2	0	1	1
Preferred Provider Organization..............	3	3	1	1	1
Indemnity Fee for Service	1	1	0	0	0
Managed Care Contracts					
Health Maintenance Organization	7	9	9	11	11
Preferred Provider Organization..............	8	9	9	10	9
Affiliations					
Hospitals in a System......................	21	20	21	18	20
Hospitals in a Network	2	3	1	1	4
Hospitals in a Group Purchasing Organization..	15	14	13	12	14

States

TABLE 6

HAWAII

U.S. Registered Community Hospitals
(Nonfederal, short-term general and other special hospitals)

Utilization, Personnel, Revenue and Expenses, Community Health Indicators 2006–2010

	2010	2009	2008	2007	2006
TOTAL FACILITY (Includes Hospital and Nursing Home Units)					
Utilization - Inpatient					
Beds	3,148	2,966	3,087	2,920	2,969
Admissions	110,577	111,706	111,310	110,788	111,713
Inpatient Days	827,977	772,508	846,756	796,898	841,667
Average Length of Stay	7.5	6.9	7.6	7.2	7.5
Inpatient Surgeries	30,626	32,340	30,723	32,305	32,495
Births	9,271	11,031	10,522	9,921	11,543
Utilization - Outpatient					
Emergency Outpatient Visits	365,903	383,778	361,068	339,004	339,863
Other Outpatient Visits	1,828,179	1,773,550	1,658,064	1,538,987	1,543,551
Total Outpatient Visits	2,194,082	2,157,328	2,019,132	1,877,991	1,883,414
Outpatient Surgeries	58,602	61,508	59,191	57,484	54,946
Personnel					
Full Time RNs	3,858	3,860	3,776	3,724	3,656
Full Time LPNs	292	252	298	302	339
Part Time RNs	974	1,136	1,254	1,052	1,029
Part Time LPNs	53	82	78	57	75
Total Full Time	14,755	14,505	14,550	14,045	13,537
Total Part Time	3,083	3,514	3,712	3,186	3,436
Revenue - Inpatient					
Gross Inpatient Revenue	$3,433,349,265	$3,279,585,271	$3,209,458,842	$2,947,813,604	$2,786,116,929
Revenue - Outpatient					
Gross Outpatient Revenue	$2,820,300,482	$2,476,907,535	$2,484,934,032	$2,190,455,686	$1,971,471,114
Revenue and Expenses - Totals					
(Includes Inpatient and Outpatient)					
Total Gross Revenue	$6,253,649,747	$5,756,492,806	$5,694,392,874	$5,138,269,290	$4,757,588,043
Deductions from Revenue	3,827,427,740	3,433,368,063	3,484,200,407	3,151,824,643	2,884,449,692
Net Patient Revenue	2,426,222,007	2,323,124,743	2,210,192,467	1,986,444,647	1,873,138,351
Other Operating Revenue	171,665,631	174,637,723	150,555,239	137,045,681	131,661,720
Other Nonoperating Revenue	48,234,523	40,300,553	21,263,753	67,676,101	89,618,454
Total Net Revenue	2,646,122,161	2,538,063,019	2,382,011,459	2,191,166,429	2,094,418,525
Total Expenses	2,611,062,195	2,576,059,889	2,321,587,503	2,144,699,750	2,017,583,352
HOSPITAL UNIT (Excludes Separate Nursing Home Units)					
Utilization - Inpatient					
Beds	2,688	2,635	2,589	2,706	2,706
Admissions	108,956	109,467	108,918	108,877	109,755
Inpatient Days	660,450	657,887	667,147	716,562	754,872
Average Length of Stay	6.1	6.0	6.1	6.6	6.9
Personnel					
Total Full Time	14,428	14,178	14,172	13,832	13,278
Total Part Time	3,047	3,446	3,610	3,146	3,405
Revenue and Expenses - Totals					
(Includes Inpatient and Outpatient)					
Total Net Revenue	$2,601,754,091	$2,512,905,897	$2,353,764,329	$2,164,235,821	$2,079,708,741
Total Expenses	2,561,364,433	2,550,665,438	2,275,182,714	2,126,689,282	2,005,122,969
COMMUNITY HEALTH INDICATORS PER 1000 POPULATION					
Total Population (in thousands)	1,300	1,295	1,287	1,277	1,276
Inpatient					
Beds	2.4	2.3	2.4	2.3	2.3
Admissions	85.1	86.2	86.5	86.8	87.6
Inpatient Days	636.9	596.4	657.7	624.1	659.8
Inpatient Surgeries	23.6	25.0	23.9	25.3	25.5
Births	7.1	8.5	8.2	7.8	9.0
Outpatient					
Emergency Outpatient Visits	281.4	296.3	280.4	265.5	266.4
Other Outpatient Visits	1,406.2	1,369.3	1,287.8	1,205.3	1,210.1
Total Outpatient Visits	1,687.6	1,665.7	1,568.3	1,470.8	1,476.5
Outpatient Surgeries	45.1	47.5	46.0	45.0	43.1
Expense per Capita (per person)	$2,008.4	$1,989.0	$1,803.2	$1,679.7	$1,581.7

States

TABLE **6**

IDAHO

U.S. Registered Community Hospitals
(Nonfederal, short-term general and other special hospitals)

Overview 2006–2010

	2010	2009	2008	2007	2006
Total Community Hospitals in Idaho	41	41	39	39	38
Bed Size Category					
6-24	11	11	11	10	11
25-49	12	11	10	10	9
50-99	9	10	9	9	8
100-199	5	5	5	6	5
200-299	1	1	2	2	3
300-399	2	2	1	1	1
400-499	0	0	0	0	1
500 + ...	1	1	1	1	0
Location					
Hospitals Urban.	15	15	14	14	7
Hospitals Rural	26	26	25	25	31
Control					
State and Local Government.	20	20	22	21	21
Not for Profit	16	16	14	15	14
Investor owned	5	5	3	3	3
Physician Models					
Independent Practice Association	5	5	7	9	7
Group Practice without Walls.	1	2	2	2	1
Open Physician-Hospital Organization	4	4	3	3	5
Closed Physician-Hospital Organization	2	3	4	5	4
Management Service Organization	3	4	4	5	3
Integrated Salary Model	13	13	11	10	7
Equity Model	0	0	1	1	2
Foundation.	1	1	1	2	2
Insurance Products					
Health Maintenance Organization	2	2	2	2	2
Preferred Provider Organization.	2	4	4	3	3
Indemnity Fee for Service	0	1	1	1	1
Managed Care Contracts					
Health Maintenance Organization	14	15	16	15	11
Preferred Provider Organization.	19	22	21	22	18
Affiliations					
Hospitals in a System.	23	23	22	19	20
Hospitals in a Network	13	15	15	19	16
Hospitals in a Group Purchasing Organization. .	25	28	26	30	27

States

TABLE 6

IDAHO

U.S. Registered Community Hospitals
(Nonfederal, short-term general and other special hospitals)

Utilization, Personnel, Revenue and Expenses, Community Health Indicators 2006–2010

	2010	2009	2008	2007	2006
TOTAL FACILITY (Includes Hospital and Nursing Home Units)					
Utilization - Inpatient					
Beds	3,376	3,382	3,311	3,296	3,303
Admissions	131,375	129,645	135,697	133,895	141,839
Inpatient Days	628,840	627,077	643,039	654,818	678,059
Average Length of Stay	4.8	4.8	4.7	4.9	4.8
Inpatient Surgeries	39,614	40,358	41,234	42,964	43,284
Births	18,941	20,126	23,014	23,236	21,341
Utilization - Outpatient					
Emergency Outpatient Visits	489,718	514,299	520,941	521,382	511,381
Other Outpatient Visits	2,672,240	2,558,653	2,419,470	2,346,680	2,192,224
Total Outpatient Visits	3,161,958	3,072,952	2,940,411	2,868,062	2,703,605
Outpatient Surgeries	73,409	68,339	70,154	65,946	63,077
Personnel					
Full Time RNs	4,103	3,898	3,739	3,634	3,375
Full Time LPNs	403	399	421	429	402
Part Time RNs	2,245	2,119	2,641	2,228	2,265
Part Time LPNs	166	169	215	226	204
Total Full Time	18,010	16,594	16,336	15,868	14,449
Total Part Time	7,175	6,408	7,728	7,213	7,177
Revenue - Inpatient					
Gross Inpatient Revenue	$2,899,758,710	$2,707,480,791	$2,561,301,943	$2,248,997,324	$2,059,962,522
Revenue - Outpatient					
Gross Outpatient Revenue	$3,113,164,805	$2,775,500,660	$2,451,235,258	$2,086,866,647	$1,843,045,507
Revenue and Expenses - Totals					
(Includes Inpatient and Outpatient)					
Total Gross Revenue	$6,012,923,515	$5,482,981,451	$5,012,537,201	$4,335,863,971	$3,903,008,029
Deductions from Revenue	3,190,452,073	2,796,704,816	2,484,822,454	1,983,781,556	1,717,092,865
Net Patient Revenue	2,822,471,442	2,686,276,635	2,527,714,747	2,352,082,415	2,185,915,164
Other Operating Revenue	96,182,670	83,202,052	90,838,094	82,800,813	75,440,778
Other Nonoperating Revenue	47,366,046	-11,931,355	15,092,420	77,705,507	39,175,538
Total Net Revenue	2,966,020,158	2,757,547,332	2,633,645,261	2,512,588,735	2,300,531,480
Total Expenses	2,546,624,205	2,563,109,938	2,406,259,158	2,224,117,950	2,083,181,465
HOSPITAL UNIT (Excludes Separate Nursing Home Units)					
Utilization - Inpatient					
Beds	3,027	3,013	3,004	2,895	2,857
Admissions	129,900	127,927	134,364	132,563	140,455
Inpatient Days	525,428	518,291	553,925	541,539	554,457
Average Length of Stay	4.0	4.1	4.1	4.1	3.9
Personnel					
Total Full Time	17,803	16,327	16,134	15,619	14,134
Total Part Time	7,040	6,227	7,599	7,060	6,963
Revenue and Expenses - Totals					
(Includes Inpatient and Outpatient)					
Total Net Revenue	$2,934,932,796	$2,730,768,774	$2,607,116,770	$2,485,446,404	$2,270,617,640
Total Expenses	2,524,919,767	2,541,756,270	2,389,059,009	2,205,976,897	2,056,627,846
COMMUNITY HEALTH INDICATORS PER 1000 POPULATION					
Total Population (in thousands)	1,560	1,546	1,528	1,499	1,464
Inpatient					
Beds	2.2	2.2	2.2	2.2	2.3
Admissions	84.2	83.9	88.8	89.3	96.9
Inpatient Days	403.2	405.7	421.0	436.8	463.0
Inpatient Surgeries	25.4	26.1	27.0	28.7	29.6
Births	12.1	13.0	15.1	15.5	14.6
Outpatient					
Emergency Outpatient Visits	314.0	332.7	341.0	347.8	349.2
Other Outpatient Visits	1,713.2	1,655.2	1,583.9	1,565.2	1,497.0
Total Outpatient Visits	2,027.2	1,987.9	1,925.0	1,913.0	1,846.2
Outpatient Surgeries	47.1	44.2	45.9	44.0	43.1
Expense per Capita (per person)	$1,632.7	$1,658.1	$1,575.3	$1,483.5	$1,422.5

States

TABLE 6

ILLINOIS

U.S. Registered Community Hospitals
(Nonfederal, short-term general and other special hospitals)

Overview 2006–2010

	2010	2009	2008	2007	2006
Total Community Hospitals in Illinois	189	189	191	190	190
Bed Size Category					
6-24	10	8	6	3	3
25-49	32	31	33	34	34
50-99	36	37	34	32	34
100-199	50	49	50	53	53
200-299	25	29	30	34	31
300-399	19	17	21	16	17
400-499	9	10	9	10	9
500 + ...	8	8	8	8	9
Location					
Hospitals Urban.........................	125	125	127	126	119
Hospitals Rural	64	64	64	64	71
Control					
State and Local Government...............	26	26	26	27	27
Not for Profit	143	147	149	150	150
Investor owned	20	16	16	13	13
Physician Models					
Independent Practice Association	28	30	29	32	33
Group Practice without Walls................	4	5	8	7	6
Open Physician-Hospital Organization	43	47	41	41	41
Closed Physician-Hospital Organization	13	11	8	10	13
Management Service Organization	22	27	24	26	27
Integrated Salary Model	62	64	61	57	52
Equity Model	2	4	3	3	1
Foundation..............................	13	6	7	7	8
Insurance Products					
Health Maintenance Organization	19	18	20	22	21
Preferred Provider Organization..............	17	16	18	22	24
Indemnity Fee for Service	7	7	10	7	6
Managed Care Contracts					
Health Maintenance Organization	123	127	120	120	127
Preferred Provider Organization..............	134	142	133	131	140
Affiliations					
Hospitals in a System.....................	108	104	105	103	100
Hospitals in a Network....................	47	47	45	44	43
Hospitals in a Group Purchasing Organization..	157	158	149	144	151

TABLE 6

ILLINOIS

U.S. Registered Community Hospitals
(Nonfederal, short-term general and other special hospitals)

Utilization, Personnel, Revenue and Expenses, Community Health Indicators 2006–2010

	2010	2009	2008	2007	2006
TOTAL FACILITY (Includes Hospital and Nursing Home Units)					
Utilization - Inpatient					
Beds	33,310	33,856	34,506	34,560	34,178
Admissions	1,542,958	1,557,816	1,610,844	1,606,241	1,583,620
Inpatient Days	7,552,956	7,769,059	8,069,859	8,107,743	8,072,145
Average Length of Stay	4.9	5.0	5.0	5.0	5.1
Inpatient Surgeries	403,226	399,042	406,437	412,696	407,498
Births	159,563	166,005	176,458	172,896	170,858
Utilization - Outpatient					
Emergency Outpatient Visits	5,366,010	5,312,763	5,123,091	5,068,338	5,079,148
Other Outpatient Visits	27,192,086	26,780,252	25,863,666	25,579,122	24,485,471
Total Outpatient Visits	32,558,096	32,093,015	30,986,757	30,647,460	29,564,619
Outpatient Surgeries	738,783	723,461	728,072	723,558	729,602
Personnel					
Full Time RNs	41,948	39,989	39,613	39,478	36,521
Full Time LPNs	1,769	1,882	2,142	2,308	2,271
Part Time RNs	23,493	24,237	23,785	22,555	24,837
Part Time LPNs	808	827	1,051	1,086	1,220
Total Full Time	163,519	162,002	164,936	165,962	158,757
Total Part Time	74,448	76,241	73,769	72,865	79,025
Revenue - Inpatient					
Gross Inpatient Revenue	$50,630,716,983	$48,011,580,288	$45,587,537,606	$42,978,477,154	$38,493,305,193
Revenue - Outpatient					
Gross Outpatient Revenue	$41,884,636,238	$38,198,138,940	$34,572,195,642	$30,813,226,194	$26,754,990,338
Revenue and Expenses - Totals					
(Includes Inpatient and Outpatient)					
Total Gross Revenue	$92,515,353,221	$86,209,719,228	$80,159,733,248	$73,791,703,348	$65,248,295,531
Deductions from Revenue	63,248,692,053	58,012,296,593	53,322,130,324	47,626,354,101	42,114,856,257
Net Patient Revenue	29,266,661,168	28,197,422,635	26,837,602,924	26,165,349,247	23,133,439,274
Other Operating Revenue	1,918,358,653	1,923,701,500	1,822,911,841	1,776,488,686	1,399,916,299
Other Nonoperating Revenue	712,723,108	-244,005,396	38,822,875	1,235,227,543	713,723,481
Total Net Revenue	31,897,742,929	29,877,118,739	28,699,337,640	29,177,065,476	25,247,079,054
Total Expenses	29,193,599,201	28,870,203,691	27,982,801,609	26,624,446,808	24,077,972,512
HOSPITAL UNIT (Excludes Separate Nursing Home Units)					
Utilization - Inpatient					
Beds	31,615	32,096	32,847	32,590	31,932
Admissions	1,526,371	1,540,936	1,597,722	1,593,560	1,565,855
Inpatient Days	7,117,426	7,294,792	7,595,924	7,592,769	7,450,541
Average Length of Stay	4.7	4.7	4.8	4.8	4.8
Personnel					
Total Full Time	162,567	160,793	163,669	159,417	157,039
Total Part Time	73,868	75,623	73,011	72,017	77,948
Revenue and Expenses - Totals					
(Includes Inpatient and Outpatient)					
Total Net Revenue	$31,785,482,525	$29,750,884,315	$28,605,435,197	$29,063,650,445	$25,089,859,015
Total Expenses	29,102,876,687	28,774,155,633	27,899,476,892	26,479,602,469	23,875,608,006
COMMUNITY HEALTH INDICATORS PER 1000 POPULATION					
Total Population (in thousands)	12,944	12,910	12,843	12,779	12,718
Inpatient					
Beds	2.6	2.6	2.7	2.7	2.7
Admissions	119.2	120.7	125.4	125.7	124.5
Inpatient Days	583.5	601.8	628.3	634.4	634.7
Inpatient Surgeries	31.2	30.9	31.6	32.3	32.0
Births	12.3	12.9	13.7	13.5	13.4
Outpatient					
Emergency Outpatient Visits	414.5	411.5	398.9	396.6	399.4
Other Outpatient Visits	2,100.7	2,074.3	2,013.8	2,001.6	1,925.3
Total Outpatient Visits	2,515.2	2,485.8	2,412.7	2,398.2	2,324.6
Outpatient Surgeries	57.1	56.0	56.7	56.6	57.4
Expense per Capita (per person)	$2,255.3	$2,236.2	$2,178.8	$2,083.4	$1,893.2

States

TABLE 6

INDIANA

U.S. Registered Community Hospitals
(Nonfederal, short-term general and other special hospitals)

Overview 2006–2010

	2010	2009	2008	2007	2006
Total Community Hospitals in Indiana	125	123	123	114	114
Bed Size Category					
6-24	5	5	6	5	5
25-49	41	41	40	37	35
50-99	28	27	28	23	20
100-199	21	23	20	18	22
200-299	16	14	16	18	17
300-399	5	4	4	3	3
400-499	3	2	2	3	5
500 + ...	6	7	7	7	7
Location					
Hospitals Urban..........................	85	83	83	74	70
Hospitals Rural	40	40	40	40	44
Control					
State and Local Government...............	33	34	39	39	39
Not for Profit	67	64	59	56	56
Investor owned	25	25	25	19	19
Physician Models					
Independent Practice Association	6	9	8	6	8
Group Practice without Walls...............	2	2	4	4	4
Open Physician-Hospital Organization	26	26	25	28	26
Closed Physician-Hospital Organization	8	9	9	11	9
Management Service Organization	9	9	9	13	12
Integrated Salary Model	55	53	49	48	41
Equity Model	2	3	2	1	1
Foundation..............................	5	7	6	4	6
Insurance Products					
Health Maintenance Organization	29	26	26	30	29
Preferred Provider Organization..............	33	27	25	43	42
Indemnity Fee for Service	6	4	5	7	9
Managed Care Contracts					
Health Maintenance Organization	65	69	64	68	60
Preferred Provider Organization..............	77	84	80	82	75
Affiliations					
Hospitals in a System.....................	85	82	79	70	68
Hospitals in a Network....................	46	44	42	41	41
Hospitals in a Group Purchasing Organization..	97	98	103	101	94

TABLE 6

INDIANA

U.S. Registered Community Hospitals
(Nonfederal, short-term general and other special hospitals)

Utilization, Personnel, Revenue and Expenses, Community Health Indicators 2006–2010

	2010	2009	2008	2007	2006
TOTAL FACILITY (Includes Hospital and Nursing Home Units)					
Utilization - Inpatient					
Beds	17,759	17,298	17,612	17,055	18,076
Admissions	718,348	713,456	732,627	690,866	726,020
Inpatient Days	3,756,021	3,687,549	3,829,835	3,513,575	3,801,325
Average Length of Stay	5.2	5.2	5.2	5.1	5.2
Inpatient Surgeries	206,124	206,101	217,917	196,104	201,896
Births	77,124	78,371	82,040	82,852	85,960
Utilization - Outpatient					
Emergency Outpatient Visits	3,185,166	3,004,721	3,041,160	3,080,110	2,704,727
Other Outpatient Visits	15,543,606	14,446,277	13,981,154	13,641,278	13,815,730
Total Outpatient Visits	18,728,772	17,450,998	17,022,314	16,721,388	16,520,457
Outpatient Surgeries	423,827	430,435	433,467	420,587	443,997
Personnel					
Full Time RNs	22,345	21,653	20,417	17,979	18,592
Full Time LPNs	1,664	1,742	2,092	2,075	2,197
Part Time RNs	14,136	13,502	14,045	14,638	14,729
Part Time LPNs	874	995	1,275	1,348	1,381
Total Full Time	86,266	86,530	83,800	79,310	81,503
Total Part Time	41,019	40,675	43,202	42,633	43,210
Revenue - Inpatient					
Gross Inpatient Revenue	$21,889,172,836	$19,297,952,821	$18,735,608,044	$16,424,288,617	$15,861,935,722
Revenue - Outpatient					
Gross Outpatient Revenue	$20,791,179,952	$18,451,255,529	$16,228,904,838	$14,405,730,848	$13,095,278,016
Revenue and Expenses - Totals					
(Includes Inpatient and Outpatient)					
Total Gross Revenue	$42,680,352,788	$37,749,208,350	$34,964,512,882	$30,830,019,465	$28,957,213,738
Deductions from Revenue	26,936,969,969	22,765,297,520	20,658,195,492	17,923,123,410	16,266,448,623
Net Patient Revenue	15,743,382,819	14,983,910,830	14,306,317,390	12,906,896,055	12,690,765,115
Other Operating Revenue	881,745,072	769,461,090	837,647,729	847,569,677	729,382,635
Other Nonoperating Revenue	434,805,381	282,345,047	-665,292,556	543,156,760	394,167,657
Total Net Revenue	17,059,933,272	16,035,716,967	14,478,672,563	14,297,622,492	13,814,315,407
Total Expenses	15,349,922,777	14,724,925,283	14,654,457,324	13,178,097,122	12,642,920,543
HOSPITAL UNIT (Excludes Separate Nursing Home Units)					
Utilization - Inpatient					
Beds	17,208	16,879	16,911	16,295	17,194
Admissions	713,224	707,886	724,499	682,827	716,630
Inpatient Days	3,584,106	3,567,515	3,612,957	3,287,612	3,532,765
Average Length of Stay	5.0	5.0	5.0	4.8	4.9
Personnel					
Total Full Time	85,948	85,900	82,933	78,394	80,597
Total Part Time	40,630	40,280	42,676	42,129	42,664
Revenue and Expenses - Totals					
(Includes Inpatient and Outpatient)					
Total Net Revenue	$17,017,380,655	$15,997,778,555	$14,424,793,981	$14,228,510,655	$13,752,934,410
Total Expenses	15,311,258,669	14,696,533,580	14,603,238,942	13,123,516,451	12,580,110,810
COMMUNITY HEALTH INDICATORS PER 1000 POPULATION					
Total Population (in thousands)	6,445	6,423	6,388	6,346	6,302
Inpatient					
Beds	2.8	2.7	2.8	2.7	2.9
Admissions	111.5	111.1	114.7	108.9	115.2
Inpatient Days	582.8	574.1	599.5	553.7	603.2
Inpatient Surgeries	32.0	32.1	34.1	30.9	32.0
Births	12.0	12.2	12.8	13.1	13.6
Outpatient					
Emergency Outpatient Visits	494.2	467.8	476.1	485.4	429.2
Other Outpatient Visits	2,411.6	2,249.1	2,188.6	2,149.5	2,192.4
Total Outpatient Visits	2,905.8	2,716.9	2,664.6	2,634.9	2,621.6
Outpatient Surgeries	65.8	67.0	67.9	66.3	70.5
Expense per Capita (per person)	$2,381.6	$2,292.5	$2,293.9	$2,076.6	$2,006.3

States

TABLE 6

IOWA

U.S. Registered Community Hospitals
(Nonfederal, short-term general and other special hospitals)

Overview 2006–2010

	2010	2009	2008	2007	2006
Total Community Hospitals in Iowa...........	118	118	118	117	117
Bed Size Category					
6-24	18	15	13	13	13
25-49	49	51	53	50	51
50-99	27	26	26	28	26
100-199	10	12	11	11	12
200-299	6	6	6	6	7
300-399	5	5	5	5	4
400-499	1	1	2	2	2
500 + ...	2	2	2	2	2
Location					
Hospitals Urban..........................	34	34	34	33	22
Hospitals Rural	84	84	84	84	95
Control					
State and Local Government................	59	59	59	59	59
Not for Profit	57	58	58	58	58
Investor owned	2	1	1	0	0
Physician Models					
Independent Practice Association	13	13	15	15	17
Group Practice without Walls................	4	3	3	3	3
Open Physician-Hospital Organization	20	24	27	26	26
Closed Physician-Hospital Organization	10	10	10	11	11
Management Service Organization	8	9	12	12	12
Integrated Salary Model....................	72	70	65	64	62
Equity Model	0	0	0	1	1
Foundation..............................	4	4	6	5	6
Insurance Products					
Health Maintenance Organization	8	9	9	13	13
Preferred Provider Organization..............	23	22	20	26	29
Indemnity Fee for Service	5	6	4	6	7
Managed Care Contracts					
Health Maintenance Organization	73	71	70	69	66
Preferred Provider Organization..............	99	98	97	97	99
Affiliations					
Hospitals in a System......................	66	64	64	63	64
Hospitals in a Network	73	72	70	70	73
Hospitals in a Group Purchasing Organization..	115	112	112	111	110

States

TABLE 6

IOWA

U.S. Registered Community Hospitals
(Nonfederal, short-term general and other special hospitals)

Utilization, Personnel, Revenue and Expenses, Community Health Indicators 2006–2010

	2010	2009	2008	2007	2006
TOTAL FACILITY (Includes Hospital and Nursing Home Units)					
Utilization - Inpatient					
Beds	10,075	10,276	10,531	10,515	10,500
Admissions	341,744	354,534	373,330	368,272	363,077
Inpatient Days	2,058,304	2,185,446	2,248,874	2,266,094	2,267,449
Average Length of Stay	6.0	6.2	6.0	6.2	6.2
Inpatient Surgeries	87,343	92,154	101,343	100,151	99,335
Births	38,193	39,522	39,060	40,274	39,560
Utilization - Outpatient					
Emergency Outpatient Visits	1,223,271	1,230,737	1,226,568	1,165,305	1,122,636
Other Outpatient Visits	9,805,308	9,724,268	9,154,060	9,390,580	9,172,457
Total Outpatient Visits	11,028,579	10,955,005	10,380,628	10,555,885	10,295,093
Outpatient Surgeries	253,148	265,368	337,632	337,757	335,367
Personnel					
Full Time RNs	10,516	10,657	10,589	10,263	10,218
Full Time LPNs	775	814	902	915	904
Part Time RNs	6,988	7,147	7,573	7,388	7,211
Part Time LPNs	548	587	734	824	759
Total Full Time	43,589	43,659	45,177	44,058	43,563
Total Part Time	23,392	24,045	26,052	25,304	25,228
Revenue - Inpatient					
Gross Inpatient Revenue	$7,478,207,382	$7,402,854,971	$7,173,320,596	$6,622,133,635	$6,041,189,863
Revenue - Outpatient					
Gross Outpatient Revenue	$8,615,345,555	$7,932,610,080	$7,008,785,229	$6,341,069,890	$5,765,745,834
Revenue and Expenses - Totals					
(Includes Inpatient and Outpatient)					
Total Gross Revenue	$16,093,552,937	$15,335,465,051	$14,182,105,825	$12,963,203,525	$11,806,935,697
Deductions from Revenue	9,374,915,563	8,788,605,112	7,919,893,373	7,059,676,768	6,158,463,230
Net Patient Revenue	6,718,637,374	6,546,859,939	6,262,212,452	5,903,526,757	5,648,472,467
Other Operating Revenue	483,246,348	490,608,985	479,246,797	468,286,796	423,197,979
Other Nonoperating Revenue	236,093,511	9,177,812	-17,782,222	235,126,914	141,353,867
Total Net Revenue	7,437,977,233	7,046,646,736	6,723,677,027	6,606,940,467	6,213,024,313
Total Expenses	6,934,527,799	6,824,533,485	6,518,050,247	6,082,343,644	5,830,164,533
HOSPITAL UNIT (Excludes Separate Nursing Home Units)					
Utilization - Inpatient					
Beds	8,341	8,385	8,524	8,486	8,491
Admissions	337,483	348,765	365,727	360,207	354,676
Inpatient Days	1,521,829	1,602,497	1,616,630	1,626,922	1,605,060
Average Length of Stay	4.5	4.6	4.4	4.5	4.5
Personnel					
Total Full Time	42,836	42,865	44,290	43,130	42,578
Total Part Time	22,670	23,241	25,160	24,397	24,254
Revenue and Expenses - Totals					
(Includes Inpatient and Outpatient)					
Total Net Revenue	$7,354,382,506	$6,945,244,251	$6,614,103,911	$6,497,382,484	$6,108,192,223
Total Expenses	6,860,708,589	6,739,111,985	6,429,352,282	5,997,176,987	5,746,268,857
COMMUNITY HEALTH INDICATORS PER 1000 POPULATION					
Total Population (in thousands)	3,023	3,008	2,994	2,979	2,964
Inpatient					
Beds	3.3	3.4	3.5	3.5	3.5
Admissions	113.0	117.9	124.7	123.6	122.5
Inpatient Days	680.9	726.6	751.1	760.8	764.9
Inpatient Surgeries	28.9	30.6	33.8	33.6	33.5
Births	12.6	13.1	13.0	13.5	13.3
Outpatient					
Emergency Outpatient Visits	404.6	409.2	409.7	391.2	378.7
Other Outpatient Visits	3,243.5	3,233.0	3,057.5	3,152.6	3,094.2
Total Outpatient Visits	3,648.1	3,642.1	3,467.2	3,543.8	3,472.9
Outpatient Surgeries	83.7	88.2	112.8	113.4	113.1
Expense per Capita (per person)	$2,293.9	$2,268.9	$2,177.0	$2,041.9	$1,966.7

States

TABLE 6

KANSAS

U.S. Registered Community Hospitals
(Nonfederal, short-term general and other special hospitals)

Overview 2006–2010

	2010	2009	2008	2007	2006
Total Community Hospitals in Kansas	130	133	132	128	129
Bed Size Category					
6-24	19	18	15	14	15
25-49	49	50	51	51	52
50-99	37	40	39	38	38
100-199	16	15	17	14	13
200-299	4	5	5	6	6
300-399	2	2	2	2	2
400-499	0	0	0	0	1
500 + ...	3	3	3	3	2
Location					
Hospitals Urban...........................	33	33	33	29	24
Hospitals Rural	97	100	99	99	105
Control					
State and Local Government................	62	62	62	62	61
Not for Profit	51	54	53	55	57
Investor owned	17	17	17	11	11
Physician Models					
Independent Practice Association	13	14	14	13	17
Group Practice without Walls................	2	2	3	2	5
Open Physician-Hospital Organization	11	14	15	15	14
Closed Physician-Hospital Organization	0	2	2	2	2
Management Service Organization	3	4	4	4	6
Integrated Salary Model	69	71	65	62	66
Equity Model	0	0	1	1	1
Foundation...............................	5	3	3	4	5
Insurance Products					
Health Maintenance Organization	1	2	5	6	5
Preferred Provider Organization..............	9	8	11	28	31
Indemnity Fee for Service	1	2	3	5	4
Managed Care Contracts					
Health Maintenance Organization	56	52	51	46	44
Preferred Provider Organization..............	109	111	112	107	113
Affiliations					
Hospitals in a System.....................	53	54	52	47	48
Hospitals in a Network....................	83	83	82	79	81
Hospitals in a Group Purchasing Organization..	128	126	126	124	124

TABLE 6

KANSAS

U.S. Registered Community Hospitals
(Nonfederal, short-term general and other special hospitals)

Utilization, Personnel, Revenue and Expenses, Community Health Indicators 2006–2010

	2010	2009	2008	2007	2006
TOTAL FACILITY (Includes Hospital and Nursing Home Units)					
Utilization - Inpatient					
Beds	9,965	10,127	10,269	10,079	10,019
Admissions	304,769	315,820	328,279	325,355	332,524
Inpatient Days	1,960,261	2,014,165	2,079,667	2,025,564	2,024,257
Average Length of Stay.	6.4	6.4	6.3	6.2	6.1
Inpatient Surgeries.	79,305	79,857	82,907	84,061	82,929
Births.	39,777	41,092	41,592	41,753	40,729
Utilization - Outpatient					
Emergency Outpatient Visits	1,019,521	1,042,407	1,028,706	1,003,181	972,761
Other Outpatient Visits.	5,660,293	5,687,308	5,497,497	5,394,624	5,173,496
Total Outpatient Visits	6,679,814	6,729,715	6,526,203	6,397,805	6,146,257
Outpatient Surgeries	157,746	160,653	162,784	158,129	160,808
Personnel					
Full Time RNs	10,852	10,517	9,924	9,353	8,599
Full Time LPNs	1,056	1,132	1,104	1,085	1,055
Part Time RNs.	4,535	4,550	4,448	4,483	4,671
Part Time LPNs	441	495	502	533	484
Total Full Time.	38,881	38,833	38,038	36,715	35,113
Total Part Time	14,183	14,585	14,394	14,215	14,162
Revenue - Inpatient					
Gross Inpatient Revenue.	$9,158,840,266	$8,857,616,660	$8,347,025,856	$7,570,341,842	$7,121,171,892
Revenue - Outpatient					
Gross Outpatient Revenue	$7,804,133,580	$7,296,946,111	$6,341,227,760	$5,585,998,443	$5,152,612,930
Revenue and Expenses - Totals					
(Includes Inpatient and Outpatient)					
Total Gross Revenue.	$16,962,973,846	$16,154,562,771	$14,688,253,616	$13,156,340,285	$12,273,784,822
Deductions from Revenue	11,147,817,611	10,508,920,047	9,366,195,974	8,521,152,481	7,575,131,231
Net Patient Revenue	5,815,156,235	5,645,642,724	5,322,057,642	4,635,187,804	4,698,653,591
Other Operating Revenue	203,257,460	212,360,609	194,026,086	190,949,651	183,451,488
Other Nonoperating Revenue	128,773,371	25,755,861	33,604,548	143,977,328	92,775,123
Total Net Revenue.	6,147,187,066	5,883,759,194	5,549,688,276	4,970,114,783	4,974,880,202
Total Expenses.	5,759,373,331	5,603,169,760	5,330,135,811	4,536,195,594	4,612,906,605
HOSPITAL UNIT (Excludes Separate Nursing Home Units)					
Utilization - Inpatient					
Beds	8,338	8,418	8,435	8,287	8,313
Admissions	302,003	313,046	325,383	322,629	329,818
Inpatient Days	1,447,040	1,507,027	1,551,696	1,496,858	1,498,214
Average Length of Stay.	4.8	4.8	4.8	4.6	4.5
Personnel					
Total Full Time.	37,806	37,721	36,923	35,595	34,042
Total Part Time	13,660	13,972	13,775	13,608	13,650
Revenue and Expenses - Totals					
(Includes Inpatient and Outpatient)					
Total Net Revenue.	$6,068,771,082	$5,807,209,303	$5,472,326,781	$4,898,350,636	$4,908,181,882
Total Expenses.	5,694,269,627	5,536,264,786	5,262,852,507	4,478,090,750	4,558,169,540
COMMUNITY HEALTH INDICATORS PER 1000 POPULATION					
Total Population (in thousands)	2,841	2,819	2,797	2,776	2,756
Inpatient					
Beds	3.5	3.6	3.7	3.6	3.6
Admissions	107.3	112.0	117.4	117.2	120.7
Inpatient Days	690.0	714.6	743.4	729.8	734.6
Inpatient Surgeries.	27.9	28.3	29.6	30.3	30.1
Births.	14.0	14.6	14.9	15.0	14.8
Outpatient					
Emergency Outpatient Visits	358.8	369.8	367.7	361.4	353.0
Other Outpatient Visits.	1,992.3	2,017.7	1,965.2	1,943.6	1,877.4
Total Outpatient Visits	2,351.1	2,387.5	2,333.0	2,305.0	2,230.4
Outpatient Surgeries	55.5	57.0	58.2	57.0	58.4
Expense per Capita (per person).	$2,027.1	$1,987.8	$1,905.4	$1,634.3	$1,674.0

TABLE **6**

KENTUCKY

U.S. Registered Community Hospitals
(Nonfederal, short-term general and other special hospitals)

Overview 2006–2010

	2010	2009	2008	2007	2006
Total Community Hospitals in Kentucky.......	106	104	105	104	104
Bed Size Category					
6-24	1	1	1	1	2
25-49	34	33	34	32	31
50-99	24	24	23	24	24
100-199	24	23	22	19	19
200-299	8	8	10	14	13
300-399	10	9	9	8	8
400-499	3	3	3	3	5
500 + ...	2	3	3	3	2
Location					
Hospitals Urban...........................	43	42	41	40	34
Hospitals Rural	63	62	64	64	70
Control					
State and Local Government................	11	11	14	12	13
Not for Profit	75	73	71	73	71
Investor owned	20	20	20	19	20
Physician Models					
Independent Practice Association	5	6	7	7	7
Group Practice without Walls................	0	2	2	3	2
Open Physician-Hospital Organization	9	12	11	11	11
Closed Physician-Hospital Organization	3	4	5	5	4
Management Service Organization	8	3	2	3	3
Integrated Salary Model.....................	43	38	39	38	34
Equity Model	0	1	1	0	0
Foundation................................	4	3	3	2	3
Insurance Products					
Health Maintenance Organization	10	5	4	9	17
Preferred Provider Organization..............	15	9	9	17	23
Indemnity Fee for Service	8	2	3	2	3
Managed Care Contracts					
Health Maintenance Organization	48	46	41	43	45
Preferred Provider Organization..............	59	57	60	63	67
Affiliations					
Hospitals in a System......................	79	76	72	68	74
Hospitals in a Network.....................	22	23	24	27	26
Hospitals in a Group Purchasing Organization..	80	77	82	83	83

TABLE 6

KENTUCKY

U.S. Registered Community Hospitals
(Nonfederal, short-term general and other special hospitals)

Utilization, Personnel, Revenue and Expenses, Community Health Indicators 2006–2010

	2010	2009	2008	2007	2006
TOTAL FACILITY (Includes Hospital and Nursing Home Units)					
Utilization - Inpatient					
Beds	14,238	14,124	14,180	14,423	14,574
Admissions	608,644	597,224	610,449	611,689	612,842
Inpatient Days	3,141,502	3,113,326	3,216,149	3,188,902	3,239,168
Average Length of Stay	5.2	5.2	5.3	5.2	5.3
Inpatient Surgeries	173,656	173,196	176,178	178,549	178,264
Births	53,630	50,085	54,872	56,096	54,614
Utilization - Outpatient					
Emergency Outpatient Visits	2,386,673	2,321,519	2,339,390	2,305,046	2,191,969
Other Outpatient Visits	8,050,866	7,798,087	7,319,408	7,219,771	6,623,337
Total Outpatient Visits	10,437,539	10,119,606	9,658,798	9,524,817	8,815,306
Outpatient Surgeries	385,960	372,057	385,428	376,310	373,174
Personnel					
Full Time RNs	17,666	16,592	16,222	15,410	15,106
Full Time LPNs	1,648	1,849	1,807	2,045	2,146
Part Time RNs	6,087	6,016	6,151	6,335	6,400
Part Time LPNs	397	419	445	539	547
Total Full Time	63,493	61,699	61,610	60,572	59,725
Total Part Time	18,309	18,144	18,576	18,836	18,967
Revenue - Inpatient					
Gross Inpatient Revenue	$15,503,184,961	$14,536,872,535	$13,943,782,950	$13,031,881,310	$12,527,888,281
Revenue - Outpatient					
Gross Outpatient Revenue	$14,305,855,765	$12,460,315,729	$11,459,995,978	$10,354,782,898	$9,475,429,030
Revenue and Expenses - Totals					
(Includes Inpatient and Outpatient)					
Total Gross Revenue	$29,809,040,726	$26,997,188,264	$25,403,778,928	$23,386,664,208	$22,003,317,311
Deductions from Revenue	19,784,508,926	17,477,244,235	16,462,600,038	14,766,322,595	13,658,377,781
Net Patient Revenue	10,024,531,800	9,519,944,029	8,941,178,890	8,620,341,613	8,344,939,530
Other Operating Revenue	338,831,936	353,366,856	309,734,161	282,137,777	257,873,549
Other Nonoperating Revenue	145,526,221	-11,001,226	-81,140,239	206,333,489	190,808,469
Total Net Revenue	10,508,889,957	9,862,309,659	9,169,772,812	9,108,812,879	8,793,621,548
Total Expenses	9,801,870,954	9,424,000,735	8,831,617,722	8,398,874,713	7,943,139,511
HOSPITAL UNIT (Excludes Separate Nursing Home Units)					
Utilization - Inpatient					
Beds	13,367	13,243	13,383	13,437	13,581
Admissions	602,635	591,112	603,967	604,725	606,435
Inpatient Days	2,889,658	2,843,189	2,975,158	2,886,705	2,928,444
Average Length of Stay	4.8	4.8	4.9	4.8	4.8
Personnel					
Total Full Time	62,730	60,717	60,776	59,665	58,711
Total Part Time	17,998	17,826	18,322	18,550	18,596
Revenue and Expenses - Totals					
(Includes Inpatient and Outpatient)					
Total Net Revenue	$10,416,730,891	$9,778,913,020	$9,092,827,775	$9,023,023,649	$8,703,572,762
Total Expenses	9,715,872,866	9,348,520,481	8,766,577,356	8,337,062,529	7,869,950,752
COMMUNITY HEALTH INDICATORS PER 1000 POPULATION					
Total Population (in thousands)	4,339	4,314	4,288	4,256	4,219
Inpatient					
Beds	3.3	3.3	3.3	3.4	3.5
Admissions	140.3	138.4	142.4	143.7	145.2
Inpatient Days	723.9	721.7	750.0	749.2	767.7
Inpatient Surgeries	40.0	40.1	41.1	41.9	42.2
Births	12.4	11.6	12.8	13.2	12.9
Outpatient					
Emergency Outpatient Visits	550.0	538.1	545.6	541.6	519.5
Other Outpatient Visits	1,855.3	1,807.6	1,707.0	1,696.3	1,569.7
Total Outpatient Visits	2,405.3	2,345.7	2,252.6	2,237.8	2,089.2
Outpatient Surgeries	88.9	86.2	89.9	88.4	88.4
Expense per Capita (per person)	$2,258.8	$2,184.5	$2,059.6	$1,973.3	$1,882.5

TABLE 6

LOUISIANA

U.S. Registered Community Hospitals
(Nonfederal, short-term general and other special hospitals)

Overview 2006–2010

	2010	2009	2008	2007	2006
Total Community Hospitals in Louisiana	126	128	130	129	132
Bed Size Category					
6-24	18	16	19	16	16
25-49	40	39	37	39	40
50-99	22	24	22	24	27
100-199	21	26	28	28	27
200-299	12	10	9	9	10
300-399	6	5	7	6	4
400-499	3	3	5	5	4
500 + ...	4	5	3	2	4
Location					
Hospitals Urban	76	77	80	79	81
Hospitals Rural	50	51	50	50	51
Control					
State and Local Government	50	54	50	50	51
Not for Profit	38	35	38	38	38
Investor owned	38	39	42	41	43
Physician Models					
Independent Practice Association	7	9	8	9	14
Group Practice without Walls	6	5	4	5	4
Open Physician-Hospital Organization	12	14	14	14	14
Closed Physician-Hospital Organization	5	7	8	5	6
Management Service Organization	4	4	8	3	7
Integrated Salary Model	29	27	24	22	18
Equity Model	2	2	4	2	1
Foundation	1	2	4	3	4
Insurance Products					
Health Maintenance Organization	8	7	9	5	7
Preferred Provider Organization	10	8	6	7	12
Indemnity Fee for Service	2	1	2	2	6
Managed Care Contracts					
Health Maintenance Organization	47	47	51	50	41
Preferred Provider Organization	57	55	61	58	54
Affiliations					
Hospitals in a System	57	64	70	70	72
Hospitals in a Network	22	22	24	20	19
Hospitals in a Group Purchasing Organization ..	71	71	72	63	64

TABLE 6

LOUISIANA

U.S. Registered Community Hospitals
(Nonfederal, short-term general and other special hospitals)

Utilization, Personnel, Revenue and Expenses, Community Health Indicators 2006–2010

	2010	2009	2008	2007	2006
TOTAL FACILITY (Includes Hospital and Nursing Home Units)					
Utilization - Inpatient					
Beds	15,421	15,857	16,007	15,516	15,864
Admissions	625,489	639,450	636,767	630,873	623,144
Inpatient Days	3,341,419	3,517,185	3,378,368	3,448,099	3,556,169
Average Length of Stay............	5.3	5.5	5.3	5.5	5.7
Inpatient Surgeries................	174,853	180,909	184,754	187,991	176,644
Births...........................	61,525	71,711	67,081	69,359	69,455
Utilization - Outpatient					
Emergency Outpatient Visits........	2,514,006	2,450,514	2,381,889	2,194,465	2,096,962
Other Outpatient Visits.............	9,840,934	9,922,624	8,779,479	8,233,730	7,764,689
Total Outpatient Visits	12,354,940	12,373,138	11,161,368	10,428,195	9,861,651
Outpatient Surgeries	283,987	279,065	278,141	288,118	281,956
Personnel					
Full Time RNs	18,458	18,666	17,187	16,261	15,502
Full Time LPNs	2,884	2,803	3,034	2,675	2,761
Part Time RNs...................	4,899	5,230	5,039	4,942	5,545
Part Time LPNs..................	628	686	773	616	778
Total Full Time...................	71,458	73,220	70,862	69,031	65,516
Total Part Time	15,447	16,165	15,367	14,004	17,124
Revenue - Inpatient					
Gross Inpatient Revenue...........	$17,480,238,475	$16,516,892,572	$15,609,477,577	$14,226,935,015	$12,833,233,745
Revenue - Outpatient					
Gross Outpatient Revenue	$13,195,535,770	$11,720,385,666	$10,443,222,809	$8,622,281,370	$7,529,943,140
Revenue and Expenses - Totals					
(Includes Inpatient and Outpatient)					
Total Gross Revenue..............	$30,675,774,245	$28,237,278,238	$26,052,700,386	$22,849,216,385	$20,363,176,885
Deductions from Revenue..........	21,158,064,386	19,280,756,846	17,411,142,732	15,075,589,108	13,060,049,470
Net Patient Revenue	9,517,709,859	8,956,521,392	8,641,557,654	7,773,627,277	7,303,127,415
Other Operating Revenue	672,891,456	549,360,404	521,425,542	530,981,708	495,512,730
Other Nonoperating Revenue	498,721,170	-74,290,469	33,327,586	276,902,027	168,610,943
Total Net Revenue...............	10,689,322,485	9,431,591,327	9,196,310,782	8,581,511,012	7,979,845,190
Total Expenses..................	9,593,366,678	9,451,348,220	9,014,212,755	8,192,722,277	7,552,791,081
HOSPITAL UNIT (Excludes Separate Nursing Home Units)					
Utilization - Inpatient					
Beds	14,721	15,199	15,323	14,832	14,964
Admissions	623,661	638,013	634,313	629,620	621,068
Inpatient Days	3,134,514	3,306,229	3,273,703	3,236,493	3,276,461
Average Length of Stay............	5.0	5.2	5.2	5.1	5.3
Personnel					
Total Full Time...................	70,950	72,664	70,017	68,659	64,629
Total Part Time	15,241	15,946	15,147	13,879	16,905
Revenue and Expenses - Totals					
(Includes Inpatient and Outpatient)					
Total Net Revenue...............	$10,655,165,063	$9,395,699,394	$9,161,979,219	$8,548,109,513	$7,947,920,310
Total Expenses..................	9,556,204,131	9,410,102,839	8,973,038,466	8,161,833,462	7,514,898,181
COMMUNITY HEALTH INDICATORS PER 1000 POPULATION					
Total Population (in thousands)	4,529	4,492	4,452	4,376	4,240
Inpatient					
Beds	3.4	3.5	3.6	3.5	3.7
Admissions	138.1	142.4	143.0	144.2	147.0
Inpatient Days	737.7	783.0	758.9	787.9	838.7
Inpatient Surgeries................	38.6	40.3	41.5	43.0	41.7
Births...........................	13.6	16.0	15.1	15.8	16.4
Outpatient					
Emergency Outpatient Visits........	555.0	545.5	535.1	501.5	494.5
Other Outpatient Visits.............	2,172.7	2,208.9	1,972.2	1,881.5	1,831.2
Total Outpatient Visits	2,727.7	2,754.4	2,507.3	2,383.0	2,325.7
Outpatient Surgeries	62.7	62.1	62.5	65.8	66.5
Expense per Capita (per person).....	$2,118.0	$2,104.0	$2,025.0	$1,872.1	$1,781.2

TABLE **6**

MAINE

U.S. Registered Community Hospitals
(Nonfederal, short-term general and other special hospitals)

Overview 2006–2010

	2010	2009	2008	2007	2006
Total Community Hospitals in Maine..........	37	37	37	37	37
Bed Size Category					
6-24	2	2	2	2	2
25-49	15	16	16	16	15
50-99	10	9	9	9	10
100-199	7	7	7	7	7
200-299	1	1	1	1	1
300-399	1	1	1	1	1
400-499	0	0	0	0	0
500 + ...	1	1	1	1	1
Location					
Hospitals Urban..........................	15	15	15	15	8
Hospitals Rural	22	22	22	22	29
Control					
State and Local Government...............	2	2	2	2	2
Not for Profit	34	34	34	34	34
Investor owned	1	1	1	1	1
Physician Models					
Independent Practice Association	4	4	3	4	4
Group Practice without Walls...............	4	4	2	2	2
Open Physician-Hospital Organization	10	10	12	12	14
Closed Physician-Hospital Organization	4	1	0	0	0
Management Service Organization	5	5	5	4	3
Integrated Salary Model....................	24	23	20	21	21
Equity Model............................	1	1	1	1	1
Foundation..............................	1	1	0	0	0
Insurance Products					
Health Maintenance Organization	5	3	5	4	3
Preferred Provider Organization.............	4	3	4	5	5
Indemnity Fee for Service	3	2	2	3	3
Managed Care Contracts					
Health Maintenance Organization	23	20	21	22	21
Preferred Provider Organization.............	26	22	20	17	20
Affiliations					
Hospitals in a System.....................	20	12	14	15	15
Hospitals in a Network....................	18	18	17	18	20
Hospitals in a Group Purchasing Organization..	33	32	31	34	33

TABLE 6

MAINE

U.S. Registered Community Hospitals
(Nonfederal, short-term general and other special hospitals)

Utilization, Personnel, Revenue and Expenses, Community Health Indicators 2006–2010

	2010	2009	2008	2007	2006
TOTAL FACILITY (Includes Hospital and Nursing Home Units)					
Utilization - Inpatient					
Beds	3,571	3,583	3,504	3,509	3,489
Admissions	145,806	150,199	148,635	151,877	150,990
Inpatient Days	808,166	822,849	845,428	839,900	851,520
Average Length of Stay.	5.5	5.5	5.7	5.5	5.6
Inpatient Surgeries.	42,190	43,395	44,812	43,205	44,380
Births.	12,874	13,146	13,489	13,707	13,736
Utilization - Outpatient					
Emergency Outpatient Visits	790,243	792,592	780,874	718,242	757,685
Other Outpatient Visits.	5,174,906	4,967,837	4,312,504	3,982,761	3,447,664
Total Outpatient Visits	5,965,149	5,760,429	5,093,378	4,701,003	4,205,349
Outpatient Surgeries	137,762	115,503	130,708	128,931	125,183
Personnel					
Full Time RNs	4,813	4,909	4,707	4,702	4,337
Full Time LPNs	248	262	234	222	270
Part Time RNs	3,658	3,232	3,384	3,571	3,596
Part Time LPNs	116	153	159	143	150
Total Full Time.	22,775	23,628	23,172	22,259	21,285
Total Part Time	12,597	10,590	11,058	11,809	11,494
Revenue - Inpatient					
Gross Inpatient Revenue.	$3,184,130,431	$3,177,081,239	$3,043,869,279	$2,773,541,415	$2,679,113,113
Revenue - Outpatient					
Gross Outpatient Revenue	$4,265,543,968	$3,904,796,010	$3,446,970,975	$3,066,834,815	$2,828,799,712
Revenue and Expenses - Totals					
(Includes Inpatient and Outpatient)					
Total Gross Revenue.	$7,449,674,399	$7,081,877,249	$6,490,840,254	$5,840,376,230	$5,507,912,825
Deductions from Revenue.	3,559,422,414	3,352,561,094	2,989,235,436	2,569,231,346	2,428,063,405
Net Patient Revenue	3,890,251,985	3,729,316,155	3,501,604,818	3,271,144,884	3,079,849,420
Other Operating Revenue	106,225,360	98,806,755	93,262,738	95,971,646	90,802,554
Other Nonoperating Revenue	36,578,921	24,828,817	13,684,134	74,855,385	61,676,959
Total Net Revenue.	4,033,056,266	3,852,951,727	3,608,551,690	3,441,971,915	3,232,328,933
Total Expenses.	4,238,756,324	3,725,426,220	3,516,496,379	3,265,842,064	3,060,867,876
HOSPITAL UNIT (Excludes Separate Nursing Home Units)					
Utilization - Inpatient					
Beds	3,185	3,189	3,108	3,090	3,099
Admissions	144,564	148,985	147,524	150,702	149,665
Inpatient Days	673,425	685,582	712,754	709,283	721,622
Average Length of Stay.	4.7	4.6	4.8	4.7	4.8
Personnel					
Total Full Time.	22,465	23,103	22,480	21,683	20,709
Total Part Time	12,310	10,299	10,596	11,516	11,123
Revenue and Expenses - Totals					
(Includes Inpatient and Outpatient)					
Total Net Revenue.	$4,000,528,653	$3,820,585,488	$3,580,910,825	$3,413,422,605	$3,203,268,060
Total Expenses.	4,208,922,953	3,694,875,984	3,486,675,727	3,236,639,252	3,034,440,927
COMMUNITY HEALTH INDICATORS PER 1000 POPULATION					
Total Population (in thousands)	1,313	1,318	1,320	1,317	1,315
Inpatient					
Beds	2.7	2.7	2.7	2.7	2.7
Admissions	111.1	113.9	112.6	115.3	114.8
Inpatient Days	615.5	624.2	640.6	637.6	647.6
Inpatient Surgeries.	32.1	32.9	34.0	32.8	33.7
Births.	9.8	10.0	10.2	10.4	10.4
Outpatient					
Emergency Outpatient Visits	601.9	601.2	591.7	545.2	576.2
Other Outpatient Visits.	3,941.5	3,768.4	3,267.8	3,023.4	2,621.9
Total Outpatient Visits	4,543.4	4,369.6	3,859.5	3,568.6	3,198.1
Outpatient Surgeries	104.9	87.6	99.0	97.9	95.2
Expense per Capita (per person).	$3,228.4	$2,825.9	$2,664.6	$2,479.2	$2,327.7

States

TABLE **6**

MARYLAND

U.S. Registered Community Hospitals
(Nonfederal, short-term general and other special hospitals)

Overview 2006–2010

	2010	2009	2008	2007	2006
Total Community Hospitals in Maryland.......	47	49	50	49	50
Bed Size Category					
6-24	0	0	0	0	0
25-49	2	2	2	3	3
50-99	6	6	6	5	7
100-199	13	13	13	13	13
200-299	11	15	15	14	16
300-399	9	6	8	8	6
400-499	4	5	3	3	2
500 + ...	2	2	3	3	3
Location					
Hospitals Urban...........................	41	43	44	43	41
Hospitals Rural	6	6	6	6	9
Control					
State and Local Government................	0	0	0	0	0
Not for Profit	45	47	48	47	48
Investor owned	2	2	2	2	2
Physician Models					
Independent Practice Association	7	5	3	3	4
Group Practice without Walls................	3	3	3	4	2
Open Physician-Hospital Organization	6	4	4	5	7
Closed Physician-Hospital Organization	1	2	2	3	4
Management Service Organization	10	7	6	6	6
Integrated Salary Model.....................	30	29	27	25	26
Equity Model..............................	3	3	4	3	2
Foundation................................	6	4	5	2	2
Insurance Products					
Health Maintenance Organization	16	14	12	10	8
Preferred Provider Organization..............	5	5	5	6	4
Indemnity Fee for Service	2	2	2	3	2
Managed Care Contracts					
Health Maintenance Organization	32	34	36	36	36
Preferred Provider Organization..............	29	32	33	34	32
Affiliations					
Hospitals in a System......................	30	33	32	30	32
Hospitals in a Network	17	17	15	13	10
Hospitals in a Group Purchasing Organization..	42	42	44	45	46

States

TABLE 6

MARYLAND

U.S. Registered Community Hospitals
(Nonfederal, short-term general and other special hospitals)

Utilization, Personnel, Revenue and Expenses, Community Health Indicators 2006–2010

	2010	2009	2008	2007	2006
TOTAL FACILITY (Includes Hospital and Nursing Home Units)					
Utilization - Inpatient					
Beds	11,682	11,887	12,018	11,743	11,479
Admissions	707,549	715,496	711,267	698,057	690,371
Inpatient Days	3,160,045	3,252,959	3,298,930	3,243,033	3,167,502
Average Length of Stay	4.5	4.5	4.6	4.6	4.6
Inpatient Surgeries	195,577	201,144	196,641	195,341	192,341
Births	69,042	70,210	73,595	72,022	69,138
Utilization - Outpatient					
Emergency Outpatient Visits	2,460,678	2,429,724	2,282,417	2,285,417	2,299,181
Other Outpatient Visits	5,912,927	5,864,175	5,800,698	5,016,402	4,708,636
Total Outpatient Visits	8,373,605	8,293,899	8,083,115	7,301,819	7,007,817
Outpatient Surgeries	352,770	354,443	355,489	350,768	349,370
Personnel					
Full Time RNs	17,338	16,670	16,216	15,333	14,709
Full Time LPNs	429	472	554	592	578
Part Time RNs	8,448	9,291	8,857	8,651	8,972
Part Time LPNs	185	236	271	257	264
Total Full Time	68,011	66,942	66,471	63,954	62,875
Total Part Time	26,604	28,595	27,048	25,034	25,458
Revenue - Inpatient					
Gross Inpatient Revenue	$9,444,745,728	$9,330,184,751	$8,955,048,928	$8,470,935,614	$7,817,701,056
Revenue - Outpatient					
Gross Outpatient Revenue	$5,942,458,212	$5,482,610,364	$4,920,676,123	$4,305,767,399	$4,043,062,566
Revenue and Expenses - Totals					
(Includes Inpatient and Outpatient)					
Total Gross Revenue	$15,387,203,940	$14,812,795,115	$13,875,725,051	$12,776,703,013	$11,860,763,622
Deductions from Revenue	3,358,927,214	3,011,679,371	2,596,608,560	2,295,774,013	2,108,964,137
Net Patient Revenue	12,028,276,726	11,801,115,744	11,279,116,491	10,480,929,000	9,751,799,485
Other Operating Revenue	481,101,758	477,892,272	462,807,673	432,880,309	395,195,238
Other Nonoperating Revenue	134,850,598	-253,477,709	-106,798,785	189,549,902	132,820,364
Total Net Revenue	12,644,229,082	12,025,530,307	11,635,125,379	11,103,359,211	10,279,815,087
Total Expenses	12,132,497,694	11,898,147,143	11,389,973,159	10,520,002,176	9,794,446,454
HOSPITAL UNIT (Excludes Separate Nursing Home Units)					
Utilization - Inpatient					
Beds	11,113	11,318	11,272	10,986	10,733
Admissions	700,707	708,844	704,669	690,355	682,097
Inpatient Days	2,998,068	3,079,527	3,104,039	3,007,468	2,948,727
Average Length of Stay	4.3	4.3	4.4	4.4	4.3
Personnel					
Total Full Time	67,425	66,271	65,813	63,276	62,242
Total Part Time	26,242	28,247	26,682	24,731	25,092
Revenue and Expenses - Totals					
(Includes Inpatient and Outpatient)					
Total Net Revenue	$12,543,530,248	$11,912,050,531	$11,517,892,326	$10,987,997,184	$10,172,144,312
Total Expenses	12,026,632,893	11,787,009,932	11,280,192,702	10,409,152,064	9,685,250,847
COMMUNITY HEALTH INDICATORS PER 1000 POPULATION					
Total Population (in thousands)	5,737	5,699	5,659	5,634	5,612
Inpatient					
Beds	2.0	2.1	2.1	2.1	2.0
Admissions	123.3	125.5	125.7	123.9	123.0
Inpatient Days	550.8	570.7	583.0	575.6	564.4
Inpatient Surgeries	34.1	35.3	34.8	34.7	34.3
Births	12.0	12.3	13.0	12.8	12.3
Outpatient					
Emergency Outpatient Visits	428.9	426.3	403.3	405.6	409.7
Other Outpatient Visits	1,030.6	1,028.9	1,025.1	890.3	839.0
Total Outpatient Visits	1,459.5	1,455.2	1,428.5	1,296.0	1,248.7
Outpatient Surgeries	61.5	62.2	62.8	62.3	62.3
Expense per Capita (per person)	$2,114.7	$2,087.6	$2,012.8	$1,867.2	$1,745.2

TABLE 6

MASSACHUSETTS

U.S. Registered Community Hospitals
(Nonfederal, short-term general and other special hospitals)

Overview 2006–2010

	2010	2009	2008	2007	2006
Total Community Hospitals in Massachusetts..	79	78	75	78	80
Bed Size Category					
6-24	6	6	6	5	6
25-49	8	8	7	7	7
50-99	10	12	11	14	12
100-199	29	25	22	23	25
200-299	12	11	11	11	14
300-399	6	8	9	8	8
400-499	1	1	2	3	1
500 + ...	7	7	7	7	7
Location					
Hospitals Urban..........................	77	76	73	76	69
Hospitals Rural	2	2	2	2	11
Control					
State and Local Government................	1	2	2	3	3
Not for Profit	67	68	65	67	67
Investor owned	11	8	8	8	10
Physician Models					
Independent Practice Association	26	22	21	25	30
Group Practice without Walls................	3	2	2	2	6
Open Physician-Hospital Organization	19	17	15	15	15
Closed Physician-Hospital Organization	7	7	6	10	11
Management Service Organization	12	9	10	10	10
Integrated Salary Model....................	35	32	30	30	37
Equity Model	2	4	4	4	4
Foundation..............................	5	6	4	7	7
Insurance Products					
Health Maintenance Organization	9	8	6	11	11
Preferred Provider Organization..............	5	5	3	9	8
Indemnity Fee for Service	3	2	1	6	4
Managed Care Contracts					
Health Maintenance Organization	59	52	48	53	64
Preferred Provider Organization..............	55	51	45	52	59
Affiliations					
Hospitals in a System.....................	43	41	39	39	42
Hospitals in a Network....................	25	20	22	24	25
Hospitals in a Group Purchasing Organization..	62	55	58	60	62

TABLE 6

MASSACHUSETTS

U.S. Registered Community Hospitals
(Nonfederal, short-term general and other special hospitals)

Utilization, Personnel, Revenue and Expenses, Community Health Indicators 2006–2010

	2010	2009	2008	2007	2006
TOTAL FACILITY (Includes Hospital and Nursing Home Units)					
Utilization - Inpatient					
Beds	15,694	15,483	15,710	16,496	16,344
Admissions	823,246	819,625	808,489	842,417	834,895
Inpatient Days	4,164,008	4,187,076	4,190,441	4,391,528	4,432,313
Average Length of Stay	5.1	5.1	5.2	5.2	5.3
Inpatient Surgeries	209,277	213,059	216,569	229,481	201,727
Births	72,306	73,363	77,002	77,250	94,228
Utilization - Outpatient					
Emergency Outpatient Visits	3,153,290	3,116,535	3,119,580	3,187,172	3,139,255
Other Outpatient Visits	18,597,755	18,237,800	17,340,178	16,393,033	16,404,673
Total Outpatient Visits	21,751,045	21,354,335	20,459,758	19,580,205	19,543,928
Outpatient Surgeries	471,811	446,779	451,925	462,064	515,027
Personnel					
Full Time RNs	20,665	20,920	20,635	20,433	17,773
Full Time LPNs	797	825	857	935	873
Part Time RNs	22,332	21,508	21,666	21,460	20,521
Part Time LPNs	707	745	814	905	827
Total Full Time	112,453	112,122	108,893	106,269	95,358
Total Part Time	67,465	64,882	64,047	64,652	61,747
Revenue - Inpatient					
Gross Inpatient Revenue	$22,838,917,130	$22,083,175,335	$21,768,649,075	$21,032,291,099	$18,131,480,820
Revenue - Outpatient					
Gross Outpatient Revenue	$26,120,785,816	$24,897,792,185	$22,264,309,254	$20,101,218,739	$18,765,595,188
Revenue and Expenses - Totals					
(Includes Inpatient and Outpatient)					
Total Gross Revenue	$48,959,702,946	$46,980,967,520	$44,032,958,329	$41,133,509,838	$36,897,076,008
Deductions from Revenue	28,469,292,992	27,289,257,271	25,449,205,856	23,579,085,229	20,747,996,172
Net Patient Revenue	20,490,409,954	19,691,710,249	18,583,752,473	17,554,424,609	16,149,079,836
Other Operating Revenue	3,161,300,000	3,056,380,254	2,794,111,079	2,603,492,463	2,378,723,094
Other Nonoperating Revenue	180,218,312	-134,832,543	-71,544,749	710,404,019	410,670,072
Total Net Revenue	23,831,928,266	22,613,257,960	21,306,318,803	20,868,321,091	18,938,473,002
Total Expenses	22,819,002,547	22,049,297,978	20,772,347,640	19,480,349,556	18,075,916,295
HOSPITAL UNIT (Excludes Separate Nursing Home Units)					
Utilization - Inpatient					
Beds	15,569	15,374	15,586	16,311	15,959
Admissions	820,368	817,254	805,960	837,201	824,881
Inpatient Days	4,125,806	4,153,746	4,156,756	4,324,089	4,316,301
Average Length of Stay	5.0	5.1	5.2	5.2	5.2
Personnel					
Total Full Time	112,401	112,051	108,805	106,159	95,080
Total Part Time	67,389	64,777	63,855	64,470	61,339
Revenue and Expenses - Totals					
(Includes Inpatient and Outpatient)					
Total Net Revenue	$23,814,188,986	$22,595,437,262	$21,279,253,160	$20,834,366,846	$18,830,494,898
Total Expenses	22,805,667,399	22,031,539,336	20,753,005,237	19,457,179,959	18,007,708,627
COMMUNITY HEALTH INDICATORS PER 1000 POPULATION					
Total Population (in thousands)	6,631	6,594	6,544	6,499	6,466
Inpatient					
Beds	2.4	2.3	2.4	2.5	2.5
Admissions	124.1	124.3	123.6	129.6	129.1
Inpatient Days	627.9	635.0	640.4	675.7	685.4
Inpatient Surgeries	31.6	32.3	33.1	35.3	31.2
Births	10.9	11.1	11.8	11.9	14.6
Outpatient					
Emergency Outpatient Visits	475.5	472.7	476.7	490.4	485.5
Other Outpatient Visits	2,804.5	2,766.0	2,649.9	2,522.3	2,536.9
Total Outpatient Visits	3,280.1	3,238.7	3,126.7	3,012.7	3,022.4
Outpatient Surgeries	71.1	67.8	69.1	71.1	79.6
Expense per Capita (per person)	$3,441.1	$3,344.1	$3,174.5	$2,997.3	$2,795.4

States

TABLE 6

MICHIGAN

U.S. Registered Community Hospitals
(Nonfederal, short-term general and other special hospitals)

Overview 2006–2010

	2010	2009	2008	2007	2006
Total Community Hospitals in Michigan.......	156	158	153	143	142
Bed Size Category					
6-24..................................	12	11	9	8	10
25-49.................................	44	42	40	30	25
50-99.................................	35	38	39	42	41
100-199...............................	18	21	20	18	21
200-299...............................	18	17	15	15	16
300-399...............................	15	14	14	13	12
400-499...............................	3	4	6	7	6
500 +.................................	11	11	10	10	11
Location					
Hospitals Urban..........................	97	99	94	84	84
Hospitals Rural..........................	59	59	59	59	58
Control					
State and Local Government...............	14	15	15	16	17
Not for Profit...........................	125	126	123	123	120
Investor owned.........................	17	17	15	4	5
Physician Models					
Independent Practice Association...........	15	15	13	13	12
Group Practice without Walls..............	9	5	5	4	6
Open Physician-Hospital Organization........	39	41	41	40	36
Closed Physician-Hospital Organization.......	17	13	14	17	19
Management Service Organization...........	19	15	12	15	16
Integrated Salary Model....................	86	88	85	81	70
Equity Model...........................	0	0	0	2	2
Foundation.............................	8	9	7	7	8
Insurance Products					
Health Maintenance Organization...........	41	44	40	42	49
Preferred Provider Organization.............	41	45	42	49	61
Indemnity Fee for Service.................	13	17	16	15	17
Managed Care Contracts					
Health Maintenance Organization...........	114	120	117	110	111
Preferred Provider Organization.............	119	124	123	116	113
Affiliations					
Hospitals in a System.....................	96	96	89	79	74
Hospitals in a Network....................	70	72	71	66	64
Hospitals in a Group Purchasing Organization..	127	130	132	128	128

TABLE 6

MICHIGAN

U.S. Registered Community Hospitals
(Nonfederal, short-term general and other special hospitals)

Utilization, Personnel, Revenue and Expenses, Community Health Indicators 2006–2010

	2010	2009	2008	2007	2006
TOTAL FACILITY (Includes Hospital and Nursing Home Units)					
Utilization - Inpatient					
Beds	25,623	25,863	25,272	25,396	25,945
Admissions	1,207,546	1,219,893	1,221,970	1,204,263	1,205,481
Inpatient Days	6,214,588	6,332,816	6,350,025	6,275,096	6,245,033
Average Length of Stay	5.1	5.2	5.2	5.2	5.2
Inpatient Surgeries	355,358	359,169	370,118	347,370	349,826
Births	111,192	113,883	118,965	122,072	123,600
Utilization - Outpatient					
Emergency Outpatient Visits	4,550,617	4,538,588	4,428,070	4,468,623	4,326,912
Other Outpatient Visits	25,699,720	24,759,189	23,570,226	23,417,840	23,798,191
Total Outpatient Visits	30,250,337	29,297,777	27,998,296	27,886,463	28,125,103
Outpatient Surgeries	704,866	694,079	707,236	726,158	755,353
Personnel					
Full Time RNs	36,166	34,530	33,536	32,510	30,490
Full Time LPNs	1,377	1,591	1,770	1,772	1,770
Part Time RNs	18,803	18,878	18,989	19,064	19,793
Part Time LPNs	916	949	1,156	1,151	1,241
Total Full Time	144,577	141,897	139,918	139,154	135,402
Total Part Time	64,909	65,113	65,331	63,156	65,321
Revenue - Inpatient					
Gross Inpatient Revenue	$32,307,141,469	$31,376,243,717	$29,869,338,749	$27,912,729,445	$26,450,363,373
Revenue - Outpatient					
Gross Outpatient Revenue	$30,177,541,390	$28,205,271,055	$26,487,242,565	$24,527,347,942	$22,637,487,899
Revenue and Expenses - Totals					
(Includes Inpatient and Outpatient)					
Total Gross Revenue	$62,484,682,859	$59,581,514,772	$56,356,581,314	$52,440,077,387	$49,087,851,272
Deductions from Revenue	38,000,334,594	35,829,939,127	33,607,413,797	31,030,821,925	28,905,181,590
Net Patient Revenue	24,484,348,265	23,751,575,645	22,749,167,517	21,409,255,462	20,182,669,682
Other Operating Revenue	1,105,518,315	1,092,750,061	1,094,570,561	1,094,719,240	1,018,637,486
Other Nonoperating Revenue	555,064,648	-550,883,455	-268,360,656	919,654,570	566,746,298
Total Net Revenue	26,144,931,228	24,293,442,251	23,575,377,422	23,423,629,272	21,768,053,466
Total Expenses	24,872,817,460	24,366,675,781	23,392,920,738	21,728,603,773	20,701,788,855
HOSPITAL UNIT (Excludes Separate Nursing Home Units)					
Utilization - Inpatient					
Beds	24,243	24,499	23,838	23,682	24,542
Admissions	1,203,343	1,215,211	1,217,600	1,199,366	1,201,976
Inpatient Days	5,761,918	5,877,775	5,868,107	5,699,371	5,766,423
Average Length of Stay	4.8	4.8	4.8	4.8	4.8
Personnel					
Total Full Time	143,514	140,743	138,950	138,010	134,441
Total Part Time	64,019	64,048	64,550	62,250	64,532
Revenue and Expenses - Totals					
(Includes Inpatient and Outpatient)					
Total Net Revenue	$26,022,486,264	$24,172,162,834	$23,455,611,994	$23,302,680,432	$21,641,889,153
Total Expenses	24,753,757,439	24,287,466,409	23,316,518,420	21,640,135,083	20,619,312,307
COMMUNITY HEALTH INDICATORS PER 1000 POPULATION					
Total Population (in thousands)	9,931	9,970	10,002	10,051	10,082
Inpatient					
Beds	2.6	2.6	2.5	2.5	2.6
Admissions	121.6	122.4	122.2	119.8	119.6
Inpatient Days	625.8	635.2	634.8	624.3	619.4
Inpatient Surgeries	35.8	36.0	37.0	34.6	34.7
Births	11.2	11.4	11.9	12.1	12.3
Outpatient					
Emergency Outpatient Visits	458.2	455.2	442.7	444.6	429.2
Other Outpatient Visits	2,587.8	2,483.4	2,356.4	2,329.9	2,360.4
Total Outpatient Visits	3,046.0	2,938.7	2,799.1	2,774.5	2,789.5
Outpatient Surgeries	71.0	69.6	70.7	72.2	74.9
Expense per Capita (per person)	$2,504.5	$2,444.1	$2,338.7	$2,161.9	$2,053.3

TABLE 6

MINNESOTA

U.S. Registered Community Hospitals
(Nonfederal, short-term general and other special hospitals)

Overview 2006–2010

	2010	2009	2008	2007	2006
Total Community Hospitals in Minnesota......	133	132	130	131	131
Bed Size Category					
6-24	19	19	17	18	17
25-49	29	26	25	25	23
50-99	38	37	37	36	40
100-199	30	34	35	36	35
200-299	5	4	4	4	4
300-399	5	4	4	3	4
400-499	4	5	5	6	5
500 + ...	3	3	3	3	3
Location					
Hospitals Urban..........................	51	50	49	49	46
Hospitals Rural	82	82	81	82	85
Control					
State and Local Government...............	36	38	37	40	40
Not for Profit	96	93	93	91	91
Investor owned	1	1	0	0	0
Physician Models					
Independent Practice Association	18	20	20	25	28
Group Practice without Walls...............	3	4	2	4	5
Open Physician-Hospital Organization	9	10	11	9	9
Closed Physician-Hospital Organization	3	3	3	5	5
Management Service Organization	1	1	2	1	3
Integrated Salary Model....................	49	52	47	44	42
Equity Model	0	1	1	1	1
Foundation...............................	1	1	2	1	1
Insurance Products					
Health Maintenance Organization	14	11	9	8	11
Preferred Provider Organization..............	15	13	14	12	16
Indemnity Fee for Service	6	3	4	1	3
Managed Care Contracts					
Health Maintenance Organization	46	54	51	53	53
Preferred Provider Organization..............	52	57	55	58	59
Affiliations					
Hospitals in a System.....................	77	73	69	70	70
Hospitals in a Network....................	27	22	24	25	28
Hospitals in a Group Purchasing Organization..	90	93	91	92	95

States

TABLE 6

MINNESOTA

U.S. Registered Community Hospitals
(Nonfederal, short-term general and other special hospitals)

Utilization, Personnel, Revenue and Expenses, Community Health Indicators 2006–2010

	2010	2009	2008	2007	2006
TOTAL FACILITY (Includes Hospital and Nursing Home Units)					
Utilization - Inpatient					
Beds...........................	15,346	15,589	15,621	15,809	15,843
Admissions.....................	591,919	623,504	640,976	635,133	633,225
Inpatient Days..................	3,596,879	3,726,573	3,873,690	3,929,879	3,955,503
Average Length of Stay...........	6.1	6.0	6.0	6.2	6.2
Inpatient Surgeries................	177,600	186,593	186,775	186,218	182,856
Births.........................	62,885	67,064	69,360	70,789	71,999
Utilization - Outpatient					
Emergency Outpatient Visits........	1,832,257	1,873,419	1,772,982	1,727,682	1,711,528
Other Outpatient Visits.............	9,232,626	8,906,635	8,233,087	8,125,800	8,397,658
Total Outpatient Visits.............	11,064,883	10,780,054	10,006,069	9,853,482	10,109,186
Outpatient Surgeries..............	303,839	311,336	294,628	299,076	300,661
Personnel					
Full Time RNs...................	11,163	9,976	9,744	9,704	8,980
Full Time LPNs	1,467	1,361	1,365	1,429	1,481
Part Time RNs..................	21,198	22,208	22,355	20,379	20,193
Part Time LPNs.................	1,767	1,862	2,031	2,206	2,300
Total Full Time.................	56,863	51,952	51,432	50,937	48,647
Total Part Time	62,186	64,411	64,764	58,808	59,057
Revenue - Inpatient					
Gross Inpatient Revenue...........	$18,410,175,974	$17,936,453,916	$17,008,252,322	$15,698,619,417	$14,591,084,241
Revenue - Outpatient					
Gross Outpatient Revenue	$15,401,043,442	$13,869,730,845	$12,005,677,625	$11,064,301,671	$10,131,993,797
Revenue and Expenses - Totals					
(Includes Inpatient and Outpatient)					
Total Gross Revenue..............	$33,811,219,416	$31,806,184,761	$29,013,929,947	$26,762,921,088	$24,723,078,038
Deductions from Revenue..........	20,208,906,364	18,729,750,687	16,742,727,027	15,261,878,579	13,936,215,046
Net Patient Revenue	13,602,313,052	13,076,434,074	12,271,202,920	11,501,042,509	10,786,862,992
Other Operating Revenue	627,863,165	654,722,103	615,406,723	596,121,525	579,265,096
Other Nonoperating Revenue	222,331,201	35,427,093	-172,569,600	316,210,452	241,843,240
Total Net Revenue................	14,452,507,418	13,766,583,270	12,714,040,043	12,413,374,486	11,607,971,328
Total Expenses..................	13,507,569,053	12,894,812,345	12,401,406,555	11,693,354,628	10,886,427,005
HOSPITAL UNIT (Excludes Separate Nursing Home Units)					
Utilization - Inpatient					
Beds...........................	13,128	13,443	12,837	12,895	12,729
Admissions.....................	588,566	620,484	637,183	631,175	629,069
Inpatient Days..................	2,835,161	2,987,272	2,943,441	2,927,784	2,901,267
Average Length of Stay...........	4.8	4.8	4.6	4.6	4.6
Personnel					
Total Full Time...................	55,794	51,026	50,078	49,542	47,079
Total Part Time	60,461	62,837	62,661	56,612	56,638
Revenue and Expenses - Totals					
(Includes Inpatient and Outpatient)					
Total Net Revenue...............	$14,309,968,863	$13,627,368,247	$12,531,828,490	$12,245,206,091	$11,431,135,431
Total Expenses..................	13,362,374,519	12,751,881,151	12,221,469,706	11,521,791,897	10,704,577,635
COMMUNITY HEALTH INDICATORS PER 1000 POPULATION					
Total Population (in thousands)	5,290	5,266	5,231	5,191	5,148
Inpatient					
Beds...........................	2.9	3.0	3.0	3.0	3.1
Admissions.....................	111.9	118.4	122.5	122.3	123.0
Inpatient Days..................	679.9	707.6	740.6	757.0	768.3
Inpatient Surgeries................	33.6	35.4	35.7	35.9	35.5
Births.........................	11.9	12.7	13.3	13.6	14.0
Outpatient					
Emergency Outpatient Visits........	346.3	355.7	339.0	332.8	332.4
Other Outpatient Visits............	1,745.2	1,691.3	1,574.0	1,565.3	1,631.1
Total Outpatient Visits.............	2,091.5	2,047.0	1,913.0	1,898.1	1,963.6
Outpatient Surgeries	57.4	59.1	56.3	57.6	58.4
Expense per Capita (per person).....	$2,553.2	$2,448.6	$2,370.9	$2,252.5	$2,114.5

TABLE **6**   MISSISSIPPI

U.S. Registered Community Hospitals
(Nonfederal, short-term general and other special hospitals)

Overview 2006–2010

	2010	2009	2008	2007	2006
Total Community Hospitals in Mississippi.....	96	97	98	95	94
Bed Size Category					
6-24	2	2	2	2	1
25-49	32	32	31	30	28
50-99	22	24	25	25	26
100-199	23	23	23	22	24
200-299	6	5	6	4	4
300-399	3	3	3	4	3
400-499	3	3	3	3	3
500 + ...	5	5	5	5	5
Location					
Hospitals Urban...........................	29	28	29	26	20
Hospitals Rural	67	69	69	69	74
Control					
State and Local Government................	41	40	41	42	41
Not for Profit	27	28	30	29	29
Investor owned	28	29	27	24	24
Physician Models					
Independent Practice Association	5	5	6	6	7
Group Practice without Walls................	2	3	2	2	4
Open Physician-Hospital Organization	16	15	16	18	18
Closed Physician-Hospital Organization	2	3	5	2	2
Management Service Organization	8	8	7	7	9
Integrated Salary Model....................	22	22	22	16	19
Equity Model	1	2	1	0	1
Foundation...............................	7	8	6	7	7
Insurance Products					
Health Maintenance Organization	7	6	8	7	7
Preferred Provider Organization..............	35	36	38	40	43
Indemnity Fee for Service	9	10	12	9	10
Managed Care Contracts					
Health Maintenance Organization	14	15	14	8	6
Preferred Provider Organization..............	33	30	37	26	28
Affiliations					
Hospitals in a System.....................	45	43	42	39	39
Hospitals in a Network....................	29	30	30	31	32
Hospitals in a Group Purchasing Organization..	0	0	1	10	24

TABLE 6   MISSISSIPPI

U.S. Registered Community Hospitals
(Nonfederal, short-term general and other special hospitals)

Utilization, Personnel, Revenue and Expenses, Community Health Indicators 2006–2010

	2010	2009	2008	2007	2006
TOTAL FACILITY (Includes Hospital and Nursing Home Units)					
Utilization - Inpatient					
Beds	12,925	12,879	13,094	12,712	12,973
Admissions	402,947	412,912	430,680	417,929	415,577
Inpatient Days	2,557,704	2,600,075	2,807,964	2,675,307	2,697,952
Average Length of Stay	6.3	6.3	6.5	6.4	6.5
Inpatient Surgeries	107,497	114,231	113,847	115,564	122,509
Births	39,044	41,266	43,775	44,650	42,729
Utilization - Outpatient					
Emergency Outpatient Visits	1,705,959	1,720,780	1,694,645	1,736,141	1,650,523
Other Outpatient Visits	2,880,177	2,964,042	3,320,962	2,688,325	2,567,848
Total Outpatient Visits	4,586,136	4,684,822	5,015,607	4,424,466	4,218,371
Outpatient Surgeries	174,969	172,105	173,799	176,076	162,127
Personnel					
Full Time RNs	12,176	11,847	11,143	10,987	10,092
Full Time LPNs	1,570	1,651	1,726	1,799	1,803
Part Time RNs	3,489	3,543	3,757	3,670	3,583
Part Time LPNs	344	423	487	502	475
Total Full Time	46,910	46,451	46,424	45,895	43,338
Total Part Time	11,258	11,656	12,158	11,902	11,648
Revenue - Inpatient					
Gross Inpatient Revenue	$10,614,195,531	$11,045,652,557	$11,036,455,713	$9,436,579,499	$8,470,744,247
Revenue - Outpatient					
Gross Outpatient Revenue	$8,108,639,171	$8,571,533,053	$7,520,162,560	$6,352,192,000	$5,402,234,688
Revenue and Expenses - Totals (Includes Inpatient and Outpatient)					
Total Gross Revenue	$18,722,834,702	$19,617,185,610	$18,556,618,273	$15,788,771,499	$13,872,978,935
Deductions from Revenue	13,026,769,588	13,518,559,893	12,632,981,913	10,466,830,159	8,822,388,239
Net Patient Revenue	5,696,065,114	6,098,625,717	5,923,636,360	5,321,941,340	5,050,590,696
Other Operating Revenue	332,166,296	279,046,585	319,430,782	335,839,429	231,893,393
Other Nonoperating Revenue	101,837,598	76,839,630	36,224,687	126,182,224	62,006,706
Total Net Revenue	6,130,069,008	6,454,511,932	6,279,291,829	5,783,962,993	5,344,490,795
Total Expenses	5,635,912,981	6,071,620,664	5,817,368,267	5,702,007,832	5,237,172,195
HOSPITAL UNIT (Excludes Separate Nursing Home Units)					
Utilization - Inpatient					
Beds	11,260	11,196	11,401	11,013	11,247
Admissions	402,148	412,159	429,960	417,221	414,554
Inpatient Days	2,004,002	2,048,068	2,233,999	2,088,193	2,123,492
Average Length of Stay	5.0	5.0	5.2	5.0	5.1
Personnel					
Total Full Time	45,658	45,069	45,125	44,537	41,925
Total Part Time	10,899	11,336	11,832	11,547	11,290
Revenue and Expenses - Totals (Includes Inpatient and Outpatient)					
Total Net Revenue	$6,056,564,286	$6,377,178,448	$6,211,348,322	$5,699,630,012	$5,251,964,574
Total Expenses	5,576,805,214	6,011,102,605	5,767,228,058	5,640,280,980	5,189,913,198
COMMUNITY HEALTH INDICATORS PER 1000 POPULATION					
Total Population (in thousands)	2,960	2,952	2,940	2,922	2,897
Inpatient					
Beds	4.4	4.4	4.5	4.4	4.5
Admissions	136.1	139.9	146.5	143.0	143.4
Inpatient Days	864.0	880.8	955.0	915.7	931.2
Inpatient Surgeries	36.3	38.7	38.7	39.6	42.3
Births	13.2	14.0	14.9	15.3	14.7
Outpatient					
Emergency Outpatient Visits	576.2	582.9	576.4	594.2	569.7
Other Outpatient Visits	972.9	1,004.1	1,129.5	920.1	886.3
Total Outpatient Visits	1,549.1	1,587.0	1,705.9	1,514.3	1,456.0
Outpatient Surgeries	59.1	58.3	59.1	60.3	56.0
Expense per Capita (per person)	$1,903.7	$2,056.8	$1,978.6	$1,951.6	$1,807.7

States

TABLE 6

MISSOURI

U.S. Registered Community Hospitals
(Nonfederal, short-term general and other special hospitals)

Overview 2006–2010

	2010	2009	2008	2007	2006
Total Community Hospitals in Missouri	122	125	123	117	119
Bed Size Category					
6-24	7	8	8	5	5
25-49	41	39	38	36	36
50-99	21	22	19	17	18
100-199	22	24	26	27	28
200-299	11	12	12	15	13
300-399	11	9	9	7	9
400-499	3	5	5	4	4
500 + ...	6	6	6	6	6
Location					
Hospitals Urban.........................	69	72	70	64	60
Hospitals Rural	53	53	53	53	59
Control					
State and Local Government................	35	35	35	35	36
Not for Profit	64	64	62	61	62
Investor owned	23	26	26	21	21
Physician Models					
Independent Practice Association	8	8	10	13	13
Group Practice without Walls................	0	0	0	0	1
Open Physician-Hospital Organization	14	15	14	14	19
Closed Physician-Hospital Organization	8	8	8	7	9
Management Service Organization	1	1	2	4	5
Integrated Salary Model....................	67	69	66	65	59
Equity Model	1	1	1	0	0
Foundation..............................	4	2	3	3	2
Insurance Products					
Health Maintenance Organization	16	15	16	16	19
Preferred Provider Organization..............	14	13	14	14	14
Indemnity Fee for Service	4	4	5	5	7
Managed Care Contracts					
Health Maintenance Organization	95	99	97	99	99
Preferred Provider Organization..............	103	107	106	107	107
Affiliations					
Hospitals in a System.....................	72	73	72	66	68
Hospitals in a Network	37	38	38	40	40
Hospitals in a Group Purchasing Organization..	114	115	115	114	114

TABLE 6

MISSOURI

U.S. Registered Community Hospitals
(Nonfederal, short-term general and other special hospitals)

Utilization, Personnel, Revenue and Expenses, Community Health Indicators 2006–2010

	2010	2009	2008	2007	2006
TOTAL FACILITY (Includes Hospital and Nursing Home Units)					
Utilization - Inpatient					
Beds	18,745	19,101	18,968	18,454	18,888
Admissions	821,322	825,090	841,118	833,114	830,882
Inpatient Days	4,196,865	4,256,929	4,396,779	4,310,130	4,331,742
Average Length of Stay	5.1	5.2	5.2	5.2	5.2
Inpatient Surgeries	213,685	219,835	222,378	220,098	219,027
Births	74,903	77,799	80,282	79,940	79,240
Utilization - Outpatient					
Emergency Outpatient Visits	2,871,884	2,894,040	2,860,410	2,677,716	2,641,586
Other Outpatient Visits	16,929,041	16,319,944	15,968,175	14,297,938	13,696,600
Total Outpatient Visits	19,800,925	19,213,984	18,828,585	16,975,654	16,338,186
Outpatient Surgeries	374,120	382,232	377,592	378,013	384,189
Personnel					
Full Time RNs	26,334	25,768	24,084	23,139	21,839
Full Time LPNs	2,398	2,508	2,711	2,719	2,811
Part Time RNs	11,453	12,399	12,367	11,264	11,942
Part Time LPNs	719	826	837	922	1,001
Total Full Time	100,265	98,635	96,722	93,628	92,126
Total Part Time	36,219	37,004	36,336	34,771	35,565
Revenue - Inpatient					
Gross Inpatient Revenue	$24,578,843,364	$23,360,022,165	$22,713,673,771	$20,986,021,738	$19,488,280,323
Revenue - Outpatient					
Gross Outpatient Revenue	$20,597,557,308	$19,480,819,585	$17,415,385,697	$15,502,302,919	$13,820,205,178
Revenue and Expenses - Totals					
(Includes Inpatient and Outpatient)					
Total Gross Revenue	$45,176,400,672	$42,840,841,750	$40,129,059,468	$36,488,324,657	$33,308,485,501
Deductions from Revenue	28,944,744,487	27,014,970,190	24,102,018,264	22,479,673,810	20,127,195,935
Net Patient Revenue	16,231,656,185	15,825,871,560	16,027,041,204	14,008,650,847	13,181,289,566
Other Operating Revenue	1,085,534,981	875,169,162	985,155,809	969,705,284	882,120,238
Other Nonoperating Revenue	529,984,875	522,159,166	-360,477,386	443,559,855	414,857,246
Total Net Revenue	17,847,176,041	17,223,199,888	16,651,719,627	15,421,915,986	14,478,267,050
Total Expenses	16,521,828,978	16,235,293,324	15,824,162,545	14,391,329,687	13,503,914,459
HOSPITAL UNIT (Excludes Separate Nursing Home Units)					
Utilization - Inpatient					
Beds	17,754	18,188	17,970	17,293	17,664
Admissions	816,764	818,739	834,653	824,907	820,375
Inpatient Days	3,946,461	3,999,089	4,109,631	3,971,643	3,966,608
Average Length of Stay	4.8	4.9	4.9	4.8	4.8
Personnel					
Total Full Time	99,631	97,598	96,023	92,704	91,235
Total Part Time	35,866	36,601	35,963	34,258	35,082
Revenue and Expenses - Totals					
(Includes Inpatient and Outpatient)					
Total Net Revenue	$17,771,368,041	$17,122,754,301	$16,539,007,342	$15,292,838,772	$14,267,051,695
Total Expenses	16,444,776,729	16,149,196,359	15,727,570,466	14,270,140,082	13,315,304,412
COMMUNITY HEALTH INDICATORS PER 1000 POPULATION					
Total Population (in thousands)	6,012	5,988	5,956	5,910	5,862
Inpatient					
Beds	3.1	3.2	3.2	3.1	3.2
Admissions	136.6	137.8	141.2	141.0	141.8
Inpatient Days	698.1	711.0	738.2	729.3	739.0
Inpatient Surgeries	35.5	36.7	37.3	37.2	37.4
Births	12.5	13.0	13.5	13.5	13.5
Outpatient					
Emergency Outpatient Visits	477.7	483.3	480.2	453.1	450.7
Other Outpatient Visits	2,816.0	2,725.6	2,680.9	2,419.4	2,336.7
Total Outpatient Visits	3,293.7	3,209.0	3,161.1	2,872.4	2,787.3
Outpatient Surgeries	62.2	63.8	63.4	64.0	65.5
Expense per Capita (per person)	$2,748.3	$2,711.5	$2,656.7	$2,435.2	$2,303.8

TABLE 6

MONTANA

U.S. Registered Community Hospitals
(Nonfederal, short-term general and other special hospitals)

Overview 2006–2010

	2010	2009	2008	2007	2006
Total Community Hospitals in Montana	48	48	48	52	52
Bed Size Category					
6-24	10	8	9	9	10
25-49	15	16	14	15	15
50-99	12	13	15	17	14
100-199	8	8	7	8	10
200-299	1	1	1	1	1
300-399	1	1	1	1	1
400-499	1	0	1	1	1
500 + ...	0	1	0	0	0
Location					
Hospitals Urban.	6	6	5	6	3
Hospitals Rural	42	42	43	46	49
Control					
State and Local Government.	8	7	8	9	9
Not for Profit	39	40	39	42	42
Investor owned	1	1	1	1	1
Physician Models					
Independent Practice Association	7	9	9	10	9
Group Practice without Walls.	3	3	3	3	2
Open Physician-Hospital Organization	5	5	6	7	8
Closed Physician-Hospital Organization	1	1	2	2	1
Management Service Organization	6	7	6	6	8
Integrated Salary Model	27	28	29	30	28
Equity Model	2	2	2	1	0
Foundation.	4	3	5	5	3
Insurance Products					
Health Maintenance Organization	4	4	4	5	7
Preferred Provider Organization.	8	8	9	9	9
Indemnity Fee for Service	6	6	4	6	7
Managed Care Contracts					
Health Maintenance Organization	11	11	13	14	15
Preferred Provider Organization.	22	25	27	31	29
Affiliations					
Hospitals in a System.	12	12	11	11	12
Hospitals in a Network	22	22	24	24	24
Hospitals in a Group Purchasing Organization. .	39	44	47	48	48

TABLE 6

MONTANA

U.S. Registered Community Hospitals
(Nonfederal, short-term general and other special hospitals)

Utilization, Personnel, Revenue and Expenses, Community Health Indicators 2006–2010

	2010	2009	2008	2007	2006
TOTAL FACILITY (Includes Hospital and Nursing Home Units)					
Utilization - Inpatient					
Beds	3,692	3,820	3,765	4,002	4,089
Admissions	97,453	101,327	103,840	106,860	106,826
Inpatient Days	848,356	869,897	903,981	957,251	975,390
Average Length of Stay...........	8.7	8.6	8.7	9.0	9.1
Inpatient Surgeries...............	29,136	30,167	30,697	32,021	32,099
Births...........................	10,217	10,432	10,708	10,714	10,681
Utilization - Outpatient					
Emergency Outpatient Visits........	357,543	357,066	346,670	354,943	333,504
Other Outpatient Visits............	3,146,841	2,973,218	2,807,604	2,680,087	2,568,374
Total Outpatient Visits	3,504,384	3,330,284	3,154,274	3,035,030	2,901,878
Outpatient Surgeries	48,043	45,364	45,012	43,987	44,129
Personnel					
Full Time RNs	2,946	2,843	2,496	2,654	2,508
Full Time LPNs	478	508	497	530	490
Part Time RNs...................	1,930	2,067	1,936	1,847	1,882
Part Time LPNs	257	283	328	330	315
Total Full Time..................	14,816	14,621	13,974	14,098	13,081
Total Part Time	7,138	7,470	7,358	7,091	7,059
Revenue - Inpatient					
Gross Inpatient Revenue...........	$2,049,917,318	$2,001,422,796	$1,868,192,302	$1,749,392,120	$1,669,626,014
Revenue - Outpatient					
Gross Outpatient Revenue	$2,452,151,901	$2,187,645,447	$1,879,526,779	$1,692,878,144	$1,490,075,406
Revenue and Expenses - Totals					
(Includes Inpatient and Outpatient)					
Total Gross Revenue..............	$4,502,069,219	$4,189,068,243	$3,747,719,081	$3,442,270,264	$3,159,701,420
Deductions from Revenue..........	2,145,913,313	1,939,387,748	1,670,030,190	1,497,426,748	1,333,944,188
Net Patient Revenue	2,356,155,906	2,249,680,495	2,077,688,891	1,944,843,516	1,825,757,232
Other Operating Revenue	93,578,995	90,423,031	80,597,184	82,175,840	69,888,745
Other Nonoperating Revenue	64,235,515	-5,428,277	16,554,468	73,552,521	54,093,518
Total Net Revenue...............	2,513,970,416	2,334,675,249	2,174,840,543	2,100,571,877	1,949,739,495
Total Expenses..................	2,379,151,295	2,263,313,965	2,077,753,777	1,933,325,734	1,800,736,855
HOSPITAL UNIT (Excludes Separate Nursing Home Units)					
Utilization - Inpatient					
Beds	2,398	2,421	2,292	2,426	2,484
Admissions	95,238	99,163	101,233	103,637	103,686
Inpatient Days	442,106	435,087	440,713	465,512	471,793
Average Length of Stay...........	4.6	4.4	4.4	4.5	4.6
Personnel					
Total Full Time...................	14,038	13,813	12,999	13,047	11,960
Total Part Time	6,602	6,946	6,770	6,498	6,352
Revenue and Expenses - Totals					
(Includes Inpatient and Outpatient)					
Total Net Revenue...............	$2,441,209,709	$2,259,366,824	$2,092,696,080	$2,015,682,825	$1,870,972,965
Total Expenses..................	2,306,425,879	2,191,842,514	2,002,337,963	1,859,283,771	1,727,928,485
COMMUNITY HEALTH INDICATORS PER 1000 POPULATION					
Total Population (in thousands)	980	975	968	957	946
Inpatient					
Beds	3.8	3.9	3.9	4.2	4.3
Admissions	99.4	103.9	107.3	111.6	112.9
Inpatient Days	865.5	892.2	933.8	1,000.0	1,030.8
Inpatient Surgeries...............	29.7	30.9	31.7	33.5	33.9
Births...........................	10.4	10.7	11.1	11.2	11.3
Outpatient					
Emergency Outpatient Visits........	364.8	366.2	358.1	370.8	352.5
Other Outpatient Visits............	3,210.6	3,049.5	2,900.3	2,799.9	2,714.3
Total Outpatient Visits	3,575.3	3,415.7	3,258.4	3,170.7	3,066.8
Outpatient Surgeries	49.0	46.5	46.5	46.0	46.6
Expense per Capita (per person).....	$2,427.3	$2,321.4	$2,146.4	$2,019.7	$1,903.1

States

TABLE **6**

NEBRASKA

U.S. Registered Community Hospitals
(Nonfederal, short-term general and other special hospitals)

Overview 2006–2010

	2010	2009	2008	2007	2006
Total Community Hospitals in Nebraska.......	88	87	86	85	85
Bed Size Category					
6-24	23	22	21	18	19
25-49	23	22	23	26	24
50-99	23	22	23	22	23
100-199	9	10	7	8	8
200-299	4	6	7	4	6
300-399	4	4	4	5	3
400-499	1	0	0	1	1
500 + ...	1	1	1	1	1
Location					
Hospitals Urban............................	17	16	16	16	14
Hospitals Rural	71	71	70	69	71
Control					
State and Local Government................	39	40	38	40	40
Not for Profit	46	45	46	43	43
Investor owned	3	2	2	2	2
Physician Models					
Independent Practice Association	6	6	8	6	7
Group Practice without Walls................	1	2	2	3	3
Open Physician-Hospital Organization	12	13	13	13	13
Closed Physician-Hospital Organization	0	1	0	0	0
Management Service Organization	3	2	3	3	3
Integrated Salary Model....................	27	33	32	31	37
Equity Model	0	0	0	0	0
Foundation...............................	0	1	2	2	0
Insurance Products					
Health Maintenance Organization	3	2	3	4	5
Preferred Provider Organization..............	11	13	14	19	20
Indemnity Fee for Service	3	3	4	4	3
Managed Care Contracts					
Health Maintenance Organization	16	17	19	21	23
Preferred Provider Organization..............	43	50	53	53	58
Affiliations					
Hospitals in a System.....................	26	28	29	28	26
Hospitals in a Network....................	28	33	36	38	44
Hospitals in a Group Purchasing Organization..	47	54	56	57	66

States

TABLE 6

NEBRASKA

U.S. Registered Community Hospitals
(Nonfederal, short-term general and other special hospitals)

Utilization, Personnel, Revenue and Expenses, Community Health Indicators 2006–2010

	2010	2009	2008	2007	2006
TOTAL FACILITY (Includes Hospital and Nursing Home Units)					
Utilization - Inpatient					
Beds	7,246	7,442	7,264	7,468	7,375
Admissions	208,949	209,750	214,808	214,628	215,219
Inpatient Days	1,461,558	1,552,206	1,562,960	1,619,546	1,666,078
Average Length of Stay	7.0	7.4	7.3	7.5	7.7
Inpatient Surgeries	65,316	67,275	71,248	68,537	67,255
Births	24,575	26,224	26,802	26,659	26,226
Utilization - Outpatient					
Emergency Outpatient Visits	700,818	688,519	639,756	630,134	551,914
Other Outpatient Visits	3,870,823	3,969,589	3,987,333	3,569,670	3,497,191
Total Outpatient Visits	4,571,641	4,658,108	4,627,089	4,199,804	4,049,105
Outpatient Surgeries	112,213	120,310	130,440	133,820	131,698
Personnel					
Full Time RNs	8,038	7,653	7,104	6,962	6,799
Full Time LPNs	856	876	913	906	1,039
Part Time RNs	4,286	4,111	4,477	4,018	3,646
Part Time LPNs	489	512	530	550	590
Total Full Time	29,024	28,451	27,407	27,636	27,907
Total Part Time	14,502	13,922	15,212	13,899	13,082
Revenue - Inpatient					
Gross Inpatient Revenue	$6,579,976,131	$6,240,788,042	$5,994,545,329	$5,595,875,292	$5,152,084,912
Revenue - Outpatient					
Gross Outpatient Revenue	$5,335,861,059	$4,923,545,533	$4,349,628,655	$3,960,071,473	$3,474,072,754
Revenue and Expenses - Totals					
(Includes Inpatient and Outpatient)					
Total Gross Revenue	$11,915,837,190	$11,164,333,575	$10,344,173,984	$9,555,946,765	$8,626,157,666
Deductions from Revenue	7,060,882,109	6,451,826,044	5,885,164,745	5,361,837,259	4,630,561,170
Net Patient Revenue	4,854,955,081	4,712,507,531	4,459,009,239	4,194,109,506	3,995,596,496
Other Operating Revenue	211,231,348	209,020,415	210,752,208	186,903,385	192,326,079
Other Nonoperating Revenue	132,518,504	-28,338,616	-24,908,037	165,706,153	132,919,108
Total Net Revenue	5,198,704,933	4,893,189,330	4,644,853,410	4,546,719,044	4,320,841,683
Total Expenses	4,710,906,183	4,471,302,656	4,380,337,731	4,013,619,694	3,862,460,549
HOSPITAL UNIT (Excludes Separate Nursing Home Units)					
Utilization - Inpatient					
Beds	6,168	6,102	5,793	5,929	5,734
Admissions	206,235	206,131	211,021	211,109	211,591
Inpatient Days	1,128,398	1,144,790	1,117,877	1,157,386	1,151,365
Average Length of Stay	5.5	5.6	5.3	5.5	5.4
Personnel					
Total Full Time	28,177	27,569	26,467	26,664	26,795
Total Part Time	13,927	13,239	14,524	13,150	12,430
Revenue and Expenses - Totals					
(Includes Inpatient and Outpatient)					
Total Net Revenue	$5,123,202,118	$4,790,650,335	$4,527,469,170	$4,444,144,173	$4,235,396,340
Total Expenses	4,634,581,746	4,379,557,407	4,274,392,152	3,932,011,095	3,778,967,078
COMMUNITY HEALTH INDICATORS PER 1000 POPULATION					
Total Population (in thousands)	1,811	1,797	1,782	1,770	1,760
Inpatient					
Beds	4.0	4.1	4.1	4.2	4.2
Admissions	115.4	116.7	120.5	121.3	122.3
Inpatient Days	807.0	864.0	877.1	915.0	946.4
Inpatient Surgeries	36.1	37.4	40.0	38.7	38.2
Births	13.6	14.6	15.0	15.1	14.9
Outpatient					
Emergency Outpatient Visits	387.0	383.2	359.0	356.0	313.5
Other Outpatient Visits	2,137.3	2,209.5	2,237.6	2,016.9	1,986.5
Total Outpatient Visits	2,524.3	2,592.7	2,596.6	2,372.9	2,300.1
Outpatient Surgeries	62.0	67.0	73.2	75.6	74.8
Expense per Capita (per person)	$2,601.2	$2,488.7	$2,458.2	$2,267.7	$2,194.0

States

TABLE 6

NEVADA

U.S. Registered Community Hospitals
(Nonfederal, short-term general and other special hospitals)

Overview 2006–2010

	2010	2009	2008	2007	2006
Total Community Hospitals in Nevada	36	35	35	33	33
Bed Size Category					
6-24	4	4	4	3	6
25-49	6	6	6	6	5
50-99	12	11	11	10	9
100-199	6	6	6	6	5
200-299	3	3	3	3	3
300-399	2	2	2	2	2
400-499	0	0	0	0	0
500 + ...	3	3	3	3	3
Location					
Hospitals Urban.	25	24	24	23	22
Hospitals Rural	11	11	11	10	11
Control					
State and Local Government.	6	6	6	6	7
Not for Profit	13	13	13	13	11
Investor owned	17	16	16	14	15
Physician Models					
Independent Practice Association	2	3	3	3	4
Group Practice without Walls.	0	0	0	0	0
Open Physician-Hospital Organization	1	1	0	1	3
Closed Physician-Hospital Organization	2	2	1	1	1
Management Service Organization	2	4	3	2	1
Integrated Salary Model	2	3	4	3	3
Equity Model	0	0	0	0	0
Foundation.	0	0	0	0	1
Insurance Products					
Health Maintenance Organization	7	5	4	4	3
Preferred Provider Organization.	7	6	5	4	4
Indemnity Fee for Service	4	3	3	3	2
Managed Care Contracts					
Health Maintenance Organization	13	12	11	13	12
Preferred Provider Organization.	15	15	14	13	16
Affiliations					
Hospitals in a System.	25	24	24	22	21
Hospitals in a Network	5	5	5	6	4
Hospitals in a Group Purchasing Organization. .	16	18	18	17	17

States

TABLE 6

NEVADA

U.S. Registered Community Hospitals
(Nonfederal, short-term general and other special hospitals)

Utilization, Personnel, Revenue and Expenses, Community Health Indicators 2006–2010

	2010	2009	2008	2007	2006
TOTAL FACILITY (Includes Hospital and Nursing Home Units)					
Utilization - Inpatient					
Beds	5,192	5,119	5,144	5,051	4,826
Admissions	241,296	245,866	247,232	244,187	245,649
Inpatient Days	1,296,929	1,311,084	1,300,514	1,275,671	1,307,303
Average Length of Stay	5.4	5.3	5.3	5.2	5.3
Inpatient Surgeries	69,928	72,737	68,365	71,526	71,718
Births	24,844	30,373	29,248	30,441	32,737
Utilization - Outpatient					
Emergency Outpatient Visits	820,675	820,980	780,500	751,845	697,906
Other Outpatient Visits	1,849,263	1,988,669	2,135,809	1,903,945	1,689,902
Total Outpatient Visits	2,669,938	2,809,649	2,916,309	2,655,790	2,387,808
Outpatient Surgeries	103,406	104,340	100,526	90,820	83,381
Personnel					
Full Time RNs	6,436	6,357	6,457	6,112	5,317
Full Time LPNs	406	404	452	445	452
Part Time RNs	1,439	1,340	1,521	1,617	1,633
Part Time LPNs	68	74	83	88	111
Total Full Time	20,948	20,386	21,672	20,043	17,567
Total Part Time	3,779	3,636	3,766	4,061	4,255
Revenue - Inpatient					
Gross Inpatient Revenue	$10,608,864,288	$10,439,117,032	$10,133,945,714	$9,157,234,146	$8,318,719,056
Revenue - Outpatient					
Gross Outpatient Revenue	$5,826,489,194	$5,312,533,278	$4,647,890,751	$3,939,962,372	$3,245,923,076
Revenue and Expenses - Totals					
(Includes Inpatient and Outpatient)					
Total Gross Revenue	$16,435,353,482	$15,751,650,310	$14,781,836,465	$13,097,196,518	$11,564,642,132
Deductions from Revenue	12,559,876,799	11,866,367,378	10,926,597,214	9,514,175,359	8,554,764,914
Net Patient Revenue	3,875,476,683	3,885,282,932	3,855,239,251	3,583,021,159	3,009,877,218
Other Operating Revenue	97,417,940	98,119,383	94,718,637	93,358,804	79,167,789
Other Nonoperating Revenue	93,314,155	73,065,405	49,631,516	86,652,018	31,991,694
Total Net Revenue	4,066,208,778	4,056,467,720	3,999,589,404	3,763,031,981	3,121,036,701
Total Expenses	3,940,182,337	3,957,622,058	3,912,575,991	3,536,781,905	2,930,773,692
HOSPITAL UNIT (Excludes Separate Nursing Home Units)					
Utilization - Inpatient					
Beds	5,174	5,076	5,119	5,026	4,670
Admissions	241,287	245,844	247,208	244,175	245,070
Inpatient Days	1,291,351	1,298,643	1,293,475	1,267,602	1,257,697
Average Length of Stay	5.4	5.3	5.2	5.2	5.1
Personnel					
Total Full Time	20,939	20,368	21,651	20,025	17,471
Total Part Time	3,779	3,630	3,763	4,056	4,236
Revenue and Expenses - Totals					
(Includes Inpatient and Outpatient)					
Total Net Revenue	$4,065,636,650	$4,053,142,416	$3,997,480,744	$3,760,531,168	$3,112,151,041
Total Expenses	3,939,711,041	3,956,074,612	3,911,278,159	3,535,439,430	2,922,980,821
COMMUNITY HEALTH INDICATORS PER 1000 POPULATION					
Total Population (in thousands)	2,655	2,643	2,616	2,568	2,493
Inpatient					
Beds	2.0	1.9	2.0	2.0	1.9
Admissions	90.9	93.0	94.5	95.1	98.5
Inpatient Days	488.5	496.0	497.2	496.8	524.3
Inpatient Surgeries	26.3	27.5	26.1	27.9	28.8
Births	9.4	11.5	11.2	11.9	13.1
Outpatient					
Emergency Outpatient Visits	309.1	310.6	298.4	292.8	279.9
Other Outpatient Visits	696.6	752.4	816.5	741.5	677.7
Total Outpatient Visits	1,005.7	1,063.0	1,114.9	1,034.3	957.6
Outpatient Surgeries	39.0	39.5	38.4	35.4	33.4
Expense per Capita (per person)	$1,484.2	$1,497.3	$1,495.8	$1,377.4	$1,175.4

States

TABLE 6

NEW HAMPSHIRE

U.S. Registered Community Hospitals
(Nonfederal, short-term general and other special hospitals)

Overview 2006–2010

	2010	2009	2008	2007	2006
Total Community Hospitals in New Hampshire	28	28	28	28	28
Bed Size Category					
6-24	1	1	1	1	1
25-49	9	9	8	8	8
50-99	7	7	9	9	9
100-199	7	7	6	6	6
200-299	3	3	3	3	3
300-399	1	1	1	1	1
400-499	0	0	0	0	0
500 +	0	0	0	0	0
Location					
Hospitals Urban	11	11	11	11	10
Hospitals Rural	17	17	17	17	18
Control					
State and Local Government	0	0	0	0	0
Not for Profit	24	24	24	24	24
Investor owned	4	4	4	4	4
Physician Models					
Independent Practice Association	2	2	2	3	3
Group Practice without Walls	2	2	2	2	0
Open Physician-Hospital Organization	9	10	10	10	10
Closed Physician-Hospital Organization	0	0	1	2	2
Management Service Organization	0	1	0	2	3
Integrated Salary Model	17	16	16	16	15
Equity Model	0	0	0	0	0
Foundation	0	0	1	1	1
Insurance Products					
Health Maintenance Organization	0	0	0	0	0
Preferred Provider Organization	0	0	1	0	0
Indemnity Fee for Service	0	0	0	0	0
Managed Care Contracts					
Health Maintenance Organization	23	26	25	25	24
Preferred Provider Organization	21	25	24	24	23
Affiliations					
Hospitals in a System	6	6	6	6	6
Hospitals in a Network	10	11	11	12	12
Hospitals in a Group Purchasing Organization	26	27	26	27	26

TABLE 6

NEW HAMPSHIRE

U.S. Registered Community Hospitals
(Nonfederal, short-term general and other special hospitals)

Utilization, Personnel, Revenue and Expenses, Community Health Indicators 2006–2010

	2010	2009	2008	2007	2006
TOTAL FACILITY (Includes Hospital and Nursing Home Units)					
Utilization - Inpatient					
Beds	2,851	2,863	2,858	2,841	2,825
Admissions	119,971	122,959	124,184	121,747	118,956
Inpatient Days	624,399	655,015	664,659	659,511	644,096
Average Length of Stay	5.2	5.3	5.4	5.4	5.4
Inpatient Surgeries	33,622	33,041	35,022	34,217	33,612
Births	12,630	13,261	13,636	13,995	13,615
Utilization - Outpatient					
Emergency Outpatient Visits	667,605	627,769	623,814	619,714	604,317
Other Outpatient Visits	4,109,910	4,097,077	3,844,709	3,479,378	3,266,700
Total Outpatient Visits	4,777,515	4,724,846	4,468,523	4,099,092	3,871,017
Outpatient Surgeries	92,450	91,495	91,320	85,548	86,761
Personnel					
Full Time RNs	4,298	4,191	4,181	4,070	3,852
Full Time LPNs	278	250	223	199	208
Part Time RNs	3,008	3,017	3,102	2,604	2,453
Part Time LPNs	139	176	156	151	123
Total Full Time	22,066	21,046	20,853	19,705	18,632
Total Part Time	10,151	10,294	10,452	9,465	8,674
Revenue - Inpatient					
Gross Inpatient Revenue	$3,890,334,236	$3,730,906,874	$3,458,246,012	$3,409,556,142	$2,702,075,606
Revenue - Outpatient					
Gross Outpatient Revenue	$5,494,839,267	$4,960,506,458	$4,446,890,786	$3,772,204,893	$3,488,005,564
Revenue and Expenses - Totals					
(Includes Inpatient and Outpatient)					
Total Gross Revenue	$9,385,173,503	$8,691,413,332	$7,905,136,798	$7,181,761,035	$6,190,081,170
Deductions from Revenue	5,410,431,600	4,934,553,834	4,413,714,285	3,943,723,858	3,195,298,030
Net Patient Revenue	3,974,741,903	3,756,859,498	3,491,422,513	3,238,037,177	2,994,783,140
Other Operating Revenue	106,982,372	93,662,673	87,274,249	83,643,504	79,223,066
Other Nonoperating Revenue	52,157,491	-52,943,319	-67,525,945	99,299,362	57,646,499
Total Net Revenue	4,133,881,766	3,797,578,852	3,511,170,817	3,420,980,043	3,131,652,705
Total Expenses	3,781,620,257	3,539,365,267	3,330,628,143	3,070,122,158	2,848,299,424
HOSPITAL UNIT (Excludes Separate Nursing Home Units)					
Utilization - Inpatient					
Beds	2,721	2,683	2,678	2,661	2,645
Admissions	119,391	122,334	123,622	121,196	118,323
Inpatient Days	577,175	602,460	605,089	600,484	584,931
Average Length of Stay	4.8	4.9	4.9	5.0	4.9
Personnel					
Total Full Time	22,003	20,963	20,767	19,612	18,545
Total Part Time	10,110	10,246	10,380	9,388	8,594
Revenue and Expenses - Totals					
(Includes Inpatient and Outpatient)					
Total Net Revenue	$4,120,469,030	$3,781,637,703	$3,496,911,705	$3,407,280,709	$3,118,367,395
Total Expenses	3,770,403,066	3,528,118,615	3,319,098,045	3,059,851,657	2,837,832,481
COMMUNITY HEALTH INDICATORS PER 1000 POPULATION					
Total Population (in thousands)	1,324	1,325	1,322	1,317	1,312
Inpatient					
Beds	2.2	2.2	2.2	2.2	2.2
Admissions	90.6	92.8	93.9	92.4	90.7
Inpatient Days	471.8	494.5	502.8	500.6	491.0
Inpatient Surgeries	25.4	24.9	26.5	26.0	25.6
Births	9.5	10.0	10.3	10.6	10.4
Outpatient					
Emergency Outpatient Visits	504.4	473.9	471.9	470.4	460.6
Other Outpatient Visits	3,105.3	3,093.1	2,908.5	2,641.2	2,490.1
Total Outpatient Visits	3,609.7	3,567.1	3,380.5	3,111.6	2,950.7
Outpatient Surgeries	69.9	69.1	69.1	64.9	66.1
Expense per Capita (per person)	$2,857.2	$2,672.1	$2,519.6	$2,330.5	$2,171.1

States

TABLE 6

NEW JERSEY

U.S. Registered Community Hospitals
(Nonfederal, short-term general and other special hospitals)

Overview 2006–2010

	2010	2009	2008	2007	2006
Total Community Hospitals in New Jersey.....	73	74	73	73	79
Bed Size Category					
6-24	0	0	0	0	0
25-49	2	3	3	0	0
50-99	6	5	4	6	7
100-199	16	19	19	18	23
200-299	20	16	16	17	17
300-399	11	12	13	14	15
400-499	9	11	11	12	11
500 + ...	9	8	7	6	6
Location					
Hospitals Urban..........................	73	74	73	73	79
Hospitals Rural	0	0	0	0	0
Control					
State and Local Government................	3	3	4	3	1
Not for Profit............................	62	64	61	65	74
Investor owned	8	7	8	5	4
Physician Models					
Independent Practice Association	12	14	16	17	24
Group Practice without Walls...............	3	3	2	2	2
Open Physician-Hospital Organization	4	7	10	6	5
Closed Physician-Hospital Organization	2	4	2	2	2
Management Service Organization	12	13	12	10	11
Integrated Salary Model....................	23	22	17	19	17
Equity Model............................	0	2	0	1	0
Foundation..............................	4	3	3	1	1
Insurance Products					
Health Maintenance Organization	6	3	4	7	10
Preferred Provider Organization..............	7	5	6	12	12
Indemnity Fee for Service	3	4	3	5	4
Managed Care Contracts					
Health Maintenance Organization	53	53	52	48	52
Preferred Provider Organization..............	53	54	53	49	49
Affiliations					
Hospitals in a System.....................	42	43	42	41	45
Hospitals in a Network....................	26	28	33	29	31
Hospitals in a Group Purchasing Organization..	54	55	61	52	52

States

TABLE 6

NEW JERSEY

U.S. Registered Community Hospitals
(Nonfederal, short-term general and other special hospitals)

Utilization, Personnel, Revenue and Expenses, Community Health Indicators 2006–2010

	2010	2009	2008	2007	2006
TOTAL FACILITY (Includes Hospital and Nursing Home Units)					
Utilization - Inpatient					
Beds	21,096	21,054	20,867	21,544	22,094
Admissions	1,067,267	1,094,810	1,086,445	1,084,226	1,111,101
Inpatient Days	5,433,359	5,565,763	5,595,966	5,613,126	5,835,422
Average Length of Stay	5.1	5.1	5.2	5.2	5.3
Inpatient Surgeries	254,003	250,689	255,641	266,546	284,822
Births	100,677	105,841	107,580	107,824	108,995
Utilization - Outpatient					
Emergency Outpatient Visits	3,360,970	3,484,463	3,350,786	3,175,910	3,256,298
Other Outpatient Visits	12,619,644	14,948,039	14,789,129	14,013,705	13,734,887
Total Outpatient Visits	15,980,614	18,432,502	18,139,915	17,189,615	16,991,185
Outpatient Surgeries	378,695	385,028	378,011	379,519	407,085
Personnel					
Full Time RNs	26,849	27,096	26,330	27,020	26,071
Full Time LPNs	976	948	988	1,239	1,400
Part Time RNs	12,933	11,792	11,559	12,682	11,367
Part Time LPNs	342	313	341	446	478
Total Full Time	101,574	102,243	100,758	106,135	104,148
Total Part Time	39,829	37,722	37,240	39,675	37,053
Revenue - Inpatient					
Gross Inpatient Revenue	$53,676,558,488	$53,769,546,685	$55,005,071,849	$49,634,356,051	$45,310,317,960
Revenue - Outpatient					
Gross Outpatient Revenue	$25,954,408,517	$23,718,074,694	$21,188,946,872	$18,690,116,226	$17,267,735,947
Revenue and Expenses - Totals					
(Includes Inpatient and Outpatient)					
Total Gross Revenue	$79,630,967,005	$77,487,621,379	$76,194,018,721	$68,324,472,277	$62,578,053,907
Deductions from Revenue	62,268,213,291	60,433,181,540	60,144,230,629	53,091,395,932	47,643,352,686
Net Patient Revenue	17,362,753,714	17,054,439,839	16,049,788,092	15,233,076,345	14,934,701,221
Other Operating Revenue	991,173,520	937,712,136	843,164,744	994,975,114	1,010,071,748
Other Nonoperating Revenue	355,140,452	506,772,443	-674,159,972	387,392,141	283,078,006
Total Net Revenue	18,709,067,686	18,498,924,418	16,218,792,864	16,615,443,600	16,227,850,975
Total Expenses	17,953,893,599	17,724,384,287	17,087,597,199	16,016,305,676	15,863,979,000
HOSPITAL UNIT (Excludes Separate Nursing Home Units)					
Utilization - Inpatient					
Beds	20,533	20,583	20,358	21,151	21,663
Admissions	1,061,552	1,091,384	1,082,467	1,080,885	1,107,354
Inpatient Days	5,258,495	5,408,363	5,429,164	5,482,670	5,706,480
Average Length of Stay	5.0	5.0	5.0	5.1	5.2
Personnel					
Total Full Time	100,902	101,537	99,958	105,444	103,669
Total Part Time	39,482	37,475	36,951	39,453	36,787
Revenue and Expenses - Totals					
(Includes Inpatient and Outpatient)					
Total Net Revenue	$18,584,183,240	$18,453,887,888	$16,159,968,959	$16,577,766,424	$16,177,529,982
Total Expenses	17,859,249,404	17,680,544,335	17,039,861,968	15,991,283,969	15,839,497,100
COMMUNITY HEALTH INDICATORS PER 1000 POPULATION					
Total Population (in thousands)	8,733	8,708	8,663	8,636	8,624
Inpatient					
Beds	2.4	2.4	2.4	2.5	2.6
Admissions	122.2	125.7	125.4	125.5	128.8
Inpatient Days	622.2	639.2	645.9	650.0	676.7
Inpatient Surgeries	29.1	28.8	29.5	30.9	33.0
Births	11.5	12.2	12.4	12.5	12.6
Outpatient					
Emergency Outpatient Visits	384.9	400.2	386.8	367.8	377.6
Other Outpatient Visits	1,445.1	1,716.6	1,707.1	1,622.7	1,592.7
Total Outpatient Visits	1,830.0	2,116.8	2,093.9	1,990.5	1,970.3
Outpatient Surgeries	43.4	44.2	43.6	43.9	47.2
Expense per Capita (per person)	$2,055.9	$2,035.5	$1,972.4	$1,854.6	$1,839.6

States

TABLE 6

NEW MEXICO

U.S. Registered Community Hospitals
(Nonfederal, short-term general and other special hospitals)

Overview 2006–2010

	2010	2009	2008	2007	2006
Total Community Hospitals in New Mexico	36	37	36	35	36
Bed Size Category					
6-24	4	4	4	4	6
25-49	8	8	9	9	8
50-99	12	14	10	10	9
100-199	8	8	10	9	10
200-299	2	1	1	1	1
300-399	0	0	0	0	1
400-499	0	0	0	0	0
500 + ...	2	2	2	2	1
Location					
Hospitals Urban............................	14	15	14	13	14
Hospitals Rural	22	22	22	22	22
Control					
State and Local Government................	6	7	7	7	8
Not for Profit.............................	16	14	14	15	15
Investor owned	14	16	15	13	13
Physician Models					
Independent Practice Association	4	4	3	5	8
Group Practice without Walls................	0	1	0	0	0
Open Physician-Hospital Organization	3	4	4	4	4
Closed Physician-Hospital Organization	0	0	1	0	0
Management Service Organization	0	0	1	2	0
Integrated Salary Model....................	11	13	10	11	9
Equity Model.............................	0	1	1	1	1
Foundation...............................	1	2	2	2	2
Insurance Products					
Health Maintenance Organization	6	7	7	8	8
Preferred Provider Organization..............	6	7	6	5	6
Indemnity Fee for Service	5	5	4	4	4
Managed Care Contracts					
Health Maintenance Organization	14	19	17	21	21
Preferred Provider Organization..............	15	19	19	22	23
Affiliations					
Hospitals in a System......................	28	30	28	26	29
Hospitals in a Network.....................	11	10	7	6	6
Hospitals in a Group Purchasing Organization..	20	26	22	25	24

TABLE 6

NEW MEXICO

U.S. Registered Community Hospitals
(Nonfederal, short-term general and other special hospitals)

Utilization, Personnel, Revenue and Expenses, Community Health Indicators 2006–2010

	2010	2009	2008	2007	2006
TOTAL FACILITY (Includes Hospital and Nursing Home Units)					
Utilization - Inpatient					
Beds	3,975	3,913	3,935	3,695	3,525
Admissions	186,092	183,116	174,169	170,081	160,792
Inpatient Days	831,384	844,787	809,916	764,458	762,267
Average Length of Stay	4.5	4.6	4.7	4.5	4.7
Inpatient Surgeries	49,435	51,319	48,698	52,350	57,642
Births	23,767	26,224	24,127	24,530	24,275
Utilization - Outpatient					
Emergency Outpatient Visits	844,650	829,138	770,475	650,026	777,671
Other Outpatient Visits	3,795,337	3,814,530	3,481,084	3,458,967	3,566,448
Total Outpatient Visits	4,639,987	4,643,668	4,251,559	4,108,993	4,344,119
Outpatient Surgeries	92,079	92,936	84,596	85,918	78,948
Personnel					
Full Time RNs	6,022	5,579	5,151	4,690	4,555
Full Time LPNs	391	455	401	415	484
Part Time RNs	2,065	2,213	1,997	2,025	2,726
Part Time LPNs	124	145	143	220	338
Total Full Time	20,493	21,568	19,610	18,112	18,746
Total Part Time	5,559	6,609	5,789	5,808	8,132
Revenue - Inpatient					
Gross Inpatient Revenue	$5,597,578,195	$5,011,641,495	$4,955,498,423	$4,068,780,483	$3,696,095,782
Revenue - Outpatient					
Gross Outpatient Revenue	$5,288,644,232	$4,601,410,841	$4,098,164,016	$3,553,788,776	$3,022,732,688
Revenue and Expenses - Totals					
(Includes Inpatient and Outpatient)					
Total Gross Revenue	$10,886,222,427	$9,613,052,336	$9,053,662,439	$7,622,569,259	$6,718,828,470
Deductions from Revenue	6,965,889,535	5,938,985,924	5,863,897,074	4,772,970,882	4,102,007,203
Net Patient Revenue	3,920,332,892	3,674,066,412	3,189,765,365	2,849,598,377	2,616,821,267
Other Operating Revenue	193,738,359	179,587,865	201,317,481	147,824,626	141,948,486
Other Nonoperating Revenue	32,566,260	22,192,097	25,179,087	67,325,548	29,409,340
Total Net Revenue	4,146,637,511	3,875,846,374	3,416,261,933	3,064,748,551	2,788,179,093
Total Expenses	3,540,766,412	3,378,281,656	3,078,569,624	2,857,121,542	2,532,320,664
HOSPITAL UNIT (Excludes Separate Nursing Home Units)					
Utilization - Inpatient					
Beds	3,928	3,863	3,838	3,582	3,478
Admissions	186,058	182,956	173,883	169,533	160,746
Inpatient Days	818,802	841,637	788,033	736,788	751,554
Average Length of Stay	4.4	4.6	4.5	4.3	4.7
Personnel					
Total Full Time	20,450	21,545	19,566	18,009	18,692
Total Part Time	5,554	6,606	5,778	5,765	8,122
Revenue and Expenses - Totals					
(Includes Inpatient and Outpatient)					
Total Net Revenue	$4,145,724,111	$3,872,546,211	$3,409,480,468	$3,054,320,532	$2,785,047,800
Total Expenses	3,537,873,415	3,375,982,169	3,074,660,998	2,852,899,697	2,530,199,604
COMMUNITY HEALTH INDICATORS PER 1000 POPULATION					
Total Population (in thousands)	2,034	2,010	1,987	1,969	1,943
Inpatient					
Beds	2.0	1.9	2.0	1.9	1.8
Admissions	91.5	91.1	87.7	86.4	82.8
Inpatient Days	408.8	420.4	407.7	388.3	392.4
Inpatient Surgeries	24.3	25.5	24.5	26.6	29.7
Births	11.7	13.0	12.1	12.5	12.5
Outpatient					
Emergency Outpatient Visits	415.3	412.6	387.8	330.2	400.3
Other Outpatient Visits	1,866.1	1,898.1	1,752.1	1,757.0	1,835.9
Total Outpatient Visits	2,281.4	2,310.7	2,139.9	2,087.1	2,236.2
Outpatient Surgeries	45.3	46.2	42.6	43.6	40.6
Expense per Capita (per person)	$1,740.9	$1,681.0	$1,549.5	$1,451.3	$1,303.6

TABLE 6

NEW YORK

U.S. Registered Community Hospitals
(Nonfederal, short-term general and other special hospitals)

Overview 2006–2010

	2010	2009	2008	2007	2006
Total Community Hospitals in New York	185	189	194	202	203
Bed Size Category					
6-24	5	4	5	6	5
25-49	7	7	9	8	8
50-99	18	19	19	21	23
100-199	40	45	47	48	50
200-299	44	40	38	41	42
300-399	25	28	29	31	28
400-499	13	15	14	14	9
500 + ...	33	31	33	33	38
Location					
Hospitals Urban..........................	147	150	154	162	167
Hospitals Rural	38	39	40	40	36
Control					
State and Local Government................	25	25	26	26	23
Not for Profit	160	164	167	174	177
Investor owned	0	0	1	2	3
Physician Models					
Independent Practice Association	35	32	38	43	31
Group Practice without Walls................	6	4	5	5	5
Open Physician-Hospital Organization	12	9	13	18	20
Closed Physician-Hospital Organization	10	10	9	11	7
Management Service Organization	18	15	13	16	14
Integrated Salary Model....................	74	63	56	56	54
Equity Model	0	0	4	3	3
Foundation...............................	2	3	2	6	2
Insurance Products					
Health Maintenance Organization	45	39	50	42	35
Preferred Provider Organization..............	30	22	30	23	19
Indemnity Fee for Service	22	12	15	14	10
Managed Care Contracts					
Health Maintenance Organization	116	111	115	119	113
Preferred Provider Organization..............	109	101	105	105	106
Affiliations					
Hospitals in a System......................	82	80	73	76	79
Hospitals in a Network....................	82	76	73	74	68
Hospitals in a Group Purchasing Organization..	128	116	116	125	130

TABLE 6

NEW YORK

U.S. Registered Community Hospitals
(Nonfederal, short-term general and other special hospitals)

Utilization, Personnel, Revenue and Expenses, Community Health Indicators 2006–2010

	2010	2009	2008	2007	2006
TOTAL FACILITY (Includes Hospital and Nursing Home Units)					
Utilization - Inpatient					
Beds	59,510	60,400	61,237	62,367	63,591
Admissions	2,509,980	2,533,577	2,528,191	2,540,711	2,571,572
Inpatient Days	17,226,868	17,474,823	17,973,047	18,344,398	18,510,969
Average Length of Stay	6.9	6.9	7.1	7.2	7.2
Inpatient Surgeries	683,336	653,545	660,660	679,506	698,078
Births	238,062	238,647	242,326	247,523	249,648
Utilization - Outpatient					
Emergency Outpatient Visits	8,063,821	8,542,392	8,114,078	8,193,513	7,924,843
Other Outpatient Visits	45,586,391	45,702,429	44,455,562	44,944,035	46,104,567
Total Outpatient Visits	53,650,212	54,244,821	52,569,640	53,137,548	54,029,410
Outpatient Surgeries	1,369,360	1,369,632	1,340,449	1,362,222	1,354,724
Personnel					
Full Time RNs	79,270	79,073	76,900	76,438	72,165
Full Time LPNs	5,095	5,781	5,964	6,184	6,174
Part Time RNs	24,090	21,651	22,118	22,590	22,604
Part Time LPNs	1,492	1,442	1,561	1,696	1,850
Total Full Time	333,121	344,168	340,045	335,364	319,765
Total Part Time	80,711	76,142	74,972	75,084	74,473
Revenue - Inpatient					
Gross Inpatient Revenue	$83,446,219,992	$79,742,230,648	$76,153,885,959	$73,373,569,851	$71,010,568,325
Revenue - Outpatient					
Gross Outpatient Revenue	$52,554,490,709	$48,142,548,531	$43,198,790,671	$38,929,448,202	$37,230,180,894
Revenue and Expenses - Totals (Includes Inpatient and Outpatient)					
Total Gross Revenue	$136,000,710,701	$127,884,779,179	$119,352,676,630	$112,303,018,053	$108,240,749,219
Deductions from Revenue	83,151,232,467	77,411,417,932	71,744,138,399	66,207,959,482	64,798,876,462
Net Patient Revenue	52,849,478,234	50,473,361,247	47,608,538,231	46,095,058,571	43,441,872,757
Other Operating Revenue	4,222,330,075	3,824,228,913	3,624,584,884	3,905,891,729	4,156,988,495
Other Nonoperating Revenue	925,916,282	1,020,046,507	-31,698,081	1,052,459,422	959,995,822
Total Net Revenue	57,997,724,591	55,317,636,667	51,201,425,034	51,053,409,722	48,558,857,074
Total Expenses	56,081,000,844	54,164,979,905	52,930,511,542	50,122,518,825	47,808,815,271
HOSPITAL UNIT (Excludes Separate Nursing Home Units)					
Utilization - Inpatient					
Beds	53,436	54,708	55,922	56,413	58,005
Admissions	2,494,952	2,518,427	2,514,606	2,525,283	2,557,311
Inpatient Days	15,107,729	15,475,231	16,133,356	16,221,721	16,556,677
Average Length of Stay	6.1	6.1	6.4	6.4	6.5
Personnel					
Total Full Time	329,655	339,060	334,474	330,451	315,355
Total Part Time	78,770	73,758	72,541	72,893	72,457
Revenue and Expenses - Totals (Includes Inpatient and Outpatient)					
Total Net Revenue	$57,401,240,974	$54,761,298,914	$50,719,366,889	$50,534,703,285	$48,111,502,694
Total Expenses	55,490,108,946	53,587,952,457	52,469,154,258	49,634,461,793	47,414,611,530
COMMUNITY HEALTH INDICATORS PER 1000 POPULATION					
Total Population (in thousands)	19,578	19,541	19,468	19,423	19,357
Inpatient					
Beds	3.0	3.1	3.1	3.2	3.3
Admissions	128.2	129.7	129.9	130.8	132.9
Inpatient Days	879.9	894.2	923.2	944.5	956.9
Inpatient Surgeries	34.9	33.4	33.9	35.0	36.1
Births	12.2	12.2	12.4	12.7	12.9
Outpatient					
Emergency Outpatient Visits	411.9	437.1	416.8	421.9	409.4
Other Outpatient Visits	2,328.5	2,338.7	2,283.5	2,314.0	2,381.9
Total Outpatient Visits	2,740.4	2,775.9	2,700.3	2,735.8	2,791.3
Outpatient Surgeries	69.9	70.1	68.9	70.1	70.0
Expense per Capita (per person)	$2,864.5	$2,771.8	$2,718.9	$2,580.6	$2,469.9

States

TABLE 6

NORTH CAROLINA

U.S. Registered Community Hospitals
(Nonfederal, short-term general and other special hospitals)

Overview 2006–2010

	2010	2009	2008	2007	2006
Total Community Hospitals in North Carolina ..	117	115	116	113	114
Bed Size Category					
6-24	4	4	4	4	3
25-49	19	18	16	14	15
50-99	25	20	22	19	22
100-199	35	39	40	40	38
200-299	13	13	12	14	13
300-399	6	6	7	7	9
400-499	2	2	2	2	1
500 + ...	13	13	13	13	13
Location					
Hospitals Urban..........................	59	58	58	55	53
Hospitals Rural	58	57	58	58	61
Control					
State and Local Government...............	32	32	32	32	32
Not for Profit	73	74	74	75	75
Investor owned	12	9	10	6	7
Physician Models					
Independent Practice Association	10	11	11	13	13
Group Practice without Walls...............	2	3	2	2	3
Open Physician-Hospital Organization	10	11	10	11	14
Closed Physician-Hospital Organization	6	7	6	7	8
Management Service Organization	12	14	16	13	14
Integrated Salary Model...................	54	50	57	48	45
Equity Model............................	4	5	3	2	3
Foundation.............................	3	2	5	4	4
Insurance Products					
Health Maintenance Organization	7	4	7	9	12
Preferred Provider Organization.............	14	10	10	20	21
Indemnity Fee for Service	5	2	2	3	4
Managed Care Contracts					
Health Maintenance Organization	70	71	80	78	74
Preferred Provider Organization.............	75	80	89	88	86
Affiliations					
Hospitals in a System.....................	78	70	69	60	59
Hospitals in a Network....................	41	39	41	40	43
Hospitals in a Group Purchasing Organization..	90	90	102	102	102

TABLE **6**

NORTH CAROLINA

U.S. Registered Community Hospitals
(Nonfederal, short-term general and other special hospitals)

Utilization, Personnel, Revenue and Expenses, Community Health Indicators 2006–2010

	2010	2009	2008	2007	2006
TOTAL FACILITY (Includes Hospital and Nursing Home Units)					
Utilization - Inpatient					
Beds	23,012	22,830	23,140	23,158	23,441
Admissions	1,038,337	1,034,112	1,041,918	1,027,909	1,015,594
Inpatient Days	5,852,967	5,788,671	6,019,401	6,069,660	6,131,924
Average Length of Stay	5.6	5.6	5.8	5.9	6.0
Inpatient Surgeries	293,323	296,668	292,208	292,262	294,298
Births	117,422	122,588	126,934	125,276	120,778
Utilization - Outpatient					
Emergency Outpatient Visits	4,259,853	4,249,375	4,166,718	4,068,389	3,849,736
Other Outpatient Visits	14,026,042	14,071,173	13,566,350	13,699,957	13,363,083
Total Outpatient Visits	18,285,895	18,320,548	17,733,068	17,768,346	17,212,819
Outpatient Surgeries	558,068	561,072	561,677	548,944	561,285
Personnel					
Full Time RNs	37,461	36,051	33,527	32,542	31,642
Full Time LPNs	1,585	1,567	1,847	1,867	2,000
Part Time RNs	13,790	13,892	15,014	13,391	13,498
Part Time LPNs	509	560	717	765	761
Total Full Time	130,456	128,117	127,114	124,066	121,023
Total Part Time	35,766	37,093	39,645	36,185	36,764
Revenue - Inpatient					
Gross Inpatient Revenue	$28,197,730,702	$25,877,825,356	$23,694,080,318	$22,069,980,664	$20,338,755,428
Revenue - Outpatient					
Gross Outpatient Revenue	$24,683,456,547	$22,124,796,442	$19,809,416,116	$17,851,201,525	$15,852,323,132
Revenue and Expenses - Totals					
(Includes Inpatient and Outpatient)					
Total Gross Revenue	$52,881,187,249	$48,002,621,798	$43,503,496,434	$39,921,182,189	$36,191,078,560
Deductions from Revenue	33,708,237,290	29,458,448,362	26,008,781,838	23,217,172,845	20,163,280,987
Net Patient Revenue	19,172,949,959	18,544,173,436	17,494,714,596	16,704,009,344	16,027,797,573
Other Operating Revenue	1,122,729,376	1,094,994,175	988,309,628	844,581,143	774,858,487
Other Nonoperating Revenue	492,730,856	213,265,535	-560,668,606	571,143,345	556,662,511
Total Net Revenue	20,788,410,191	19,852,433,146	17,922,355,618	18,119,733,832	17,359,318,571
Total Expenses	18,847,920,294	18,590,518,185	17,662,604,664	16,635,094,264	15,721,863,715
HOSPITAL UNIT (Excludes Separate Nursing Home Units)					
Utilization - Inpatient					
Beds	20,841	20,811	20,496	20,302	20,428
Admissions	1,030,472	1,026,457	1,031,609	1,016,854	1,004,707
Inpatient Days	5,150,233	5,133,526	5,128,782	5,093,680	5,164,167
Average Length of Stay	5.0	5.0	5.0	5.0	5.1
Personnel					
Total Full Time	128,958	126,542	125,088	121,526	118,627
Total Part Time	35,100	36,425	38,721	35,164	35,802
Revenue and Expenses - Totals					
(Includes Inpatient and Outpatient)					
Total Net Revenue	$20,648,909,546	$19,725,156,052	$17,753,404,722	$17,925,776,886	$17,183,454,204
Total Expenses	18,715,167,064	18,471,921,787	17,488,022,607	16,444,335,265	15,526,247,079
COMMUNITY HEALTH INDICATORS PER 1000 POPULATION					
Total Population (in thousands)	9,459	9,381	9,247	9,064	8,867
Inpatient					
Beds	2.4	2.4	2.5	2.6	2.6
Admissions	109.8	110.2	112.7	113.4	114.5
Inpatient Days	618.8	617.1	650.9	669.6	691.5
Inpatient Surgeries	31.0	31.6	31.6	32.2	33.2
Births	12.4	13.1	13.7	13.8	13.6
Outpatient					
Emergency Outpatient Visits	450.4	453.0	450.6	448.8	434.2
Other Outpatient Visits	1,482.8	1,500.0	1,467.1	1,511.5	1,507.1
Total Outpatient Visits	1,933.2	1,953.0	1,917.7	1,960.3	1,941.2
Outpatient Surgeries	59.0	59.8	60.7	60.6	63.3
Expense per Capita (per person)	$1,992.6	$1,981.7	$1,910.1	$1,835.3	$1,773.1

States

TABLE 6

NORTH DAKOTA

U.S. Registered Community Hospitals
(Nonfederal, short-term general and other special hospitals)

Overview 2006–2010

	2010	2009	2008	2007	2006
Total Community Hospitals in North Dakota...	41	41	41	41	41
Bed Size Category					
6-24	10	10	11	11	9
25-49	15	15	12	11	13
50-99	8	9	11	12	12
100-199	3	2	2	2	2
200-299	3	3	3	3	3
300-399	0	0	0	0	0
400-499	1	1	1	1	1
500 +	1	1	1	1	1
Location					
Hospitals Urban	8	8	7	6	6
Hospitals Rural	33	33	34	35	35
Control					
State and Local Government	0	0	0	0	0
Not for Profit	39	39	39	40	41
Investor owned	2	2	2	1	0
Physician Models					
Independent Practice Association	4	4	4	4	4
Group Practice without Walls	0	0	0	0	1
Open Physician-Hospital Organization	1	2	3	3	2
Closed Physician-Hospital Organization	0	0	0	1	2
Management Service Organization	0	0	0	1	0
Integrated Salary Model	10	16	15	14	16
Equity Model	0	1	1	1	1
Foundation	1	2	4	3	5
Insurance Products					
Health Maintenance Organization	1	0	0	0	1
Preferred Provider Organization	5	5	7	4	5
Indemnity Fee for Service	2	2	4	1	1
Managed Care Contracts					
Health Maintenance Organization	1	3	1	2	4
Preferred Provider Organization	13	17	16	17	19
Affiliations					
Hospitals in a System	17	17	15	16	14
Hospitals in a Network	8	12	8	7	10
Hospitals in a Group Purchasing Organization	19	28	25	29	32

TABLE **6**

NORTH DAKOTA

U.S. Registered Community Hospitals
(Nonfederal, short-term general and other special hospitals)

Utilization, Personnel, Revenue and Expenses, Community Health Indicators 2006–2010

	2010	2009	2008	2007	2006
TOTAL FACILITY (Includes Hospital and Nursing Home Units)					
Utilization - Inpatient					
Beds	3,345	3,362	3,442	3,488	3,550
Admissions	94,436	92,593	89,225	89,010	88,737
Inpatient Days	718,950	751,653	744,876	772,643	762,500
Average Length of Stay	7.6	8.1	8.3	8.7	8.6
Inpatient Surgeries	29,558	27,732	26,451	28,861	28,577
Births	12,851	10,552	9,966	9,687	9,587
Utilization - Outpatient					
Emergency Outpatient Visits	353,557	303,190	289,070	274,223	263,144
Other Outpatient Visits	2,722,180	2,059,310	1,406,490	1,474,224	1,446,140
Total Outpatient Visits	3,075,737	2,362,500	1,695,560	1,748,447	1,709,284
Outpatient Surgeries	54,165	56,128	46,734	45,328	44,257
Personnel					
Full Time RNs	2,889	2,497	2,424	2,356	2,110
Full Time LPNs	514	599	512	556	544
Part Time RNs	2,452	2,163	2,002	2,030	2,244
Part Time LPNs	392	361	460	566	602
Total Full Time	13,962	13,326	12,312	12,036	11,623
Total Part Time	8,187	7,909	7,148	7,666	8,050
Revenue - Inpatient					
Gross Inpatient Revenue	$2,092,135,268	$2,019,340,609	$1,483,180,662	$1,414,871,895	$1,334,432,797
Revenue - Outpatient					
Gross Outpatient Revenue	$2,551,094,052	$2,583,127,227	$1,953,610,192	$1,687,925,226	$1,527,971,411
Revenue and Expenses - Totals					
(Includes Inpatient and Outpatient)					
Total Gross Revenue	$4,643,229,320	$4,602,467,836	$3,436,790,854	$3,102,797,121	$2,862,404,208
Deductions from Revenue	2,493,872,027	2,518,310,749	1,680,883,923	1,444,698,089	1,303,212,416
Net Patient Revenue	2,149,357,293	2,084,157,087	1,755,906,931	1,658,099,032	1,559,191,792
Other Operating Revenue	96,921,743	91,082,749	87,201,376	83,258,147	78,157,365
Other Nonoperating Revenue	33,585,013	13,376,054	-13,097,663	43,988,926	38,911,418
Total Net Revenue	2,279,864,049	2,188,615,890	1,830,010,644	1,785,346,105	1,676,260,575
Total Expenses	2,142,846,297	2,133,367,717	1,853,693,024	1,748,248,300	1,630,169,448
HOSPITAL UNIT (Excludes Separate Nursing Home Units)					
Utilization - Inpatient					
Beds	3,063	2,569	2,649	2,610	2,589
Admissions	92,796	90,862	86,795	86,408	85,589
Inpatient Days	634,164	485,393	479,593	472,732	446,177
Average Length of Stay	6.8	5.3	5.5	5.5	5.2
Personnel					
Total Full Time	13,822	12,820	11,728	11,350	10,927
Total Part Time	8,048	7,540	6,808	7,147	7,481
Revenue and Expenses - Totals					
(Includes Inpatient and Outpatient)					
Total Net Revenue	$2,258,523,169	$2,145,215,671	$1,780,423,431	$1,729,923,488	$1,621,940,757
Total Expenses	2,126,714,369	2,094,921,706	1,809,203,400	1,702,249,310	1,587,820,886
COMMUNITY HEALTH INDICATORS PER 1000 POPULATION					
Total Population (in thousands)	654	647	641	638	637
Inpatient					
Beds	5.1	5.2	5.4	5.5	5.6
Admissions	144.4	143.1	139.1	139.5	139.4
Inpatient Days	1,099.7	1,162.0	1,161.3	1,210.7	1,197.4
Inpatient Surgeries	45.2	42.9	41.2	45.2	44.9
Births	19.7	16.3	15.5	15.2	15.1
Outpatient					
Emergency Outpatient Visits	540.8	468.7	450.7	429.7	413.2
Other Outpatient Visits	4,163.8	3,183.6	2,192.8	2,310.0	2,271.1
Total Outpatient Visits	4,704.6	3,652.3	2,643.4	2,739.6	2,684.3
Outpatient Surgeries	82.8	86.8	72.9	71.0	69.5
Expense per Capita (per person)	$3,277.6	$3,298.1	$2,890.0	$2,739.3	$2,560.1

States

TABLE 6

OHIO

U.S. Registered Community Hospitals
(Nonfederal, short-term general and other special hospitals)

Overview 2006–2010

	2010	2009	2008	2007	2006
Total Community Hospitals in Ohio..........	183	183	181	171	171
Bed Size Category					
6-24	3	4	4	3	4
25-49	44	45	44	37	36
50-99	33	32	29	26	26
100-199	41	43	45	47	45
200-299	28	25	25	24	26
300-399	12	11	11	12	14
400-499	9	11	10	11	8
500 + ...	13	12	13	11	12
Location					
Hospitals Urban..........................	128	128	126	117	121
Hospitals Rural	55	55	55	54	50
Control					
State and Local Government................	21	22	21	23	23
Not for Profit	138	138	139	137	136
Investor owned	24	23	21	11	12
Physician Models					
Independent Practice Association	15	19	25	27	26
Group Practice without Walls...............	7	8	9	11	11
Open Physician-Hospital Organization	52	46	41	41	45
Closed Physician-Hospital Organization	9	10	13	25	24
Management Service Organization	35	39	49	39	38
Integrated Salary Model....................	71	64	68	65	64
Equity Model............................	9	7	8	6	7
Foundation..............................	31	28	27	24	25
Insurance Products					
Health Maintenance Organization	36	32	31	35	35
Preferred Provider Organization..............	43	44	34	45	45
Indemnity Fee for Service	16	15	11	26	17
Managed Care Contracts					
Health Maintenance Organization	113	120	112	110	109
Preferred Provider Organization..............	120	129	120	120	122
Affiliations					
Hospitals in a System.....................	114	111	107	99	93
Hospitals in a Network....................	77	77	74	70	74
Hospitals in a Group Purchasing Organization..	133	143	141	139	144

TABLE 6

OHIO

U.S. Registered Community Hospitals
(Nonfederal, short-term general and other special hospitals)

Utilization, Personnel, Revenue and Expenses, Community Health Indicators 2006–2010

	2010	2009	2008	2007	2006
TOTAL FACILITY (Includes Hospital and Nursing Home Units)					
Utilization - Inpatient					
Beds	34,316	33,994	33,860	32,866	32,822
Admissions	1,516,501	1,531,076	1,547,720	1,542,176	1,542,333
Inpatient Days	7,598,267	7,744,235	7,814,849	7,753,839	7,742,312
Average Length of Stay	5.0	5.1	5.0	5.0	5.0
Inpatient Surgeries	405,507	407,777	413,959	416,220	414,838
Births	133,946	141,295	143,941	146,861	147,992
Utilization - Outpatient					
Emergency Outpatient Visits	6,383,429	6,207,290	6,023,705	5,918,218	5,840,398
Other Outpatient Visits	29,375,819	28,033,655	26,868,157	27,167,211	26,846,119
Total Outpatient Visits	35,759,248	34,240,945	32,891,862	33,085,429	32,686,517
Outpatient Surgeries	817,556	800,882	787,850	763,623	782,568
Personnel					
Full Time RNs	51,255	48,681	45,914	44,637	43,114
Full Time LPNs	3,309	3,580	3,769	4,022	4,279
Part Time RNs	25,325	24,409	24,600	23,100	23,277
Part Time LPNs	1,808	1,859	2,080	2,113	2,122
Total Full Time	198,795	198,906	194,709	185,526	181,475
Total Part Time	76,929	75,934	76,454	69,946	70,557
Revenue - Inpatient					
Gross Inpatient Revenue	$49,069,396,749	$45,306,391,429	$41,893,875,454	$38,144,462,997	$35,776,947,886
Revenue - Outpatient					
Gross Outpatient Revenue	$44,283,440,488	$40,277,248,420	$35,108,967,663	$30,960,953,256	$28,562,090,312
Revenue and Expenses - Totals					
(Includes Inpatient and Outpatient)					
Total Gross Revenue	$93,352,837,237	$85,583,639,849	$77,002,843,117	$69,105,416,253	$64,339,038,198
Deductions from Revenue	61,559,545,620	55,069,727,140	48,579,748,500	42,732,933,128	39,005,578,638
Net Patient Revenue	31,793,291,617	30,513,912,709	28,423,094,617	26,372,483,125	25,333,459,560
Other Operating Revenue	2,302,711,954	2,204,346,362	1,902,066,455	1,781,044,376	1,572,944,936
Other Nonoperating Revenue	824,057,575	899,809,957	-1,531,882,065	696,280,084	665,928,838
Total Net Revenue	34,920,061,146	33,618,069,028	28,793,279,007	28,849,807,585	27,572,333,334
Total Expenses	32,374,139,783	30,929,648,514	29,074,986,966	26,781,375,793	25,712,641,988
HOSPITAL UNIT (Excludes Separate Nursing Home Units)					
Utilization - Inpatient					
Beds	33,157	32,613	32,422	31,350	30,827
Admissions	1,503,171	1,517,223	1,532,848	1,526,090	1,521,553
Inpatient Days	7,219,041	7,292,581	7,365,607	7,283,480	7,158,331
Average Length of Stay	4.8	4.8	4.8	4.8	4.7
Personnel					
Total Full Time	197,828	197,669	193,511	184,300	179,982
Total Part Time	76,311	75,222	75,671	69,255	69,778
Revenue and Expenses - Totals					
(Includes Inpatient and Outpatient)					
Total Net Revenue	$34,807,563,235	$33,478,190,434	$28,664,373,342	$28,691,701,961	$27,333,636,562
Total Expenses	32,265,651,508	30,795,620,302	28,951,022,330	26,629,876,388	25,525,939,444
COMMUNITY HEALTH INDICATORS PER 1000 POPULATION					
Total Population (in thousands)	11,532	11,543	11,528	11,521	11,492
Inpatient					
Beds	3.0	2.9	2.9	2.9	2.9
Admissions	131.5	132.6	134.3	133.9	134.2
Inpatient Days	658.9	670.9	677.9	673.0	673.7
Inpatient Surgeries	35.2	35.3	35.9	36.1	36.1
Births	11.6	12.2	12.5	12.7	12.9
Outpatient					
Emergency Outpatient Visits	553.5	537.8	522.5	513.7	508.2
Other Outpatient Visits	2,547.3	2,428.7	2,330.7	2,358.1	2,336.0
Total Outpatient Visits	3,100.8	2,966.5	2,853.2	2,871.8	2,844.2
Outpatient Surgeries	70.9	69.4	68.3	66.3	68.1
Expense per Capita (per person)	$2,807.3	$2,679.6	$2,522.1	$2,324.6	$2,237.3

States

TABLE 6

OKLAHOMA

U.S. Registered Community Hospitals
(Nonfederal, short-term general and other special hospitals)

Overview 2006–2010

	2010	2009	2008	2007	2006
Total Community Hospitals in Oklahoma	113	116	115	113	112
Bed Size Category					
6-24	22	20	23	24	23
25-49	41	42	41	38	37
50-99	22	26	24	25	25
100-199	15	15	14	12	13
200-299	2	3	2	4	3
300-399	5	4	5	4	5
400-499	1	1	2	2	2
500 + ...	5	5	4	4	4
Location					
Hospitals Urban.	48	49	50	48	41
Hospitals Rural	65	67	65	65	71
Control					
State and Local Government.	44	45	45	45	44
Not for Profit	36	36	37	35	35
Investor owned	33	35	33	33	33
Physician Models					
Independent Practice Association	14	15	11	16	15
Group Practice without Walls.	6	6	4	7	3
Open Physician-Hospital Organization	9	11	11	16	17
Closed Physician-Hospital Organization	0	0	3	3	5
Management Service Organization	7	11	11	13	10
Integrated Salary Model.	34	26	22	17	25
Equity Model.	0	0	1	1	1
Foundation.	0	1	1	0	1
Insurance Products					
Health Maintenance Organization	8	7	5	9	7
Preferred Provider Organization.	10	8	8	12	13
Indemnity Fee for Service	4	4	3	3	3
Managed Care Contracts					
Health Maintenance Organization	38	38	41	41	35
Preferred Provider Organization.	63	62	64	68	60
Affiliations					
Hospitals in a System.	53	60	57	58	56
Hospitals in a Network.	22	19	20	25	24
Hospitals in a Group Purchasing Organization. .	87	89	85	86	85

States

TABLE 6

OKLAHOMA

U.S. Registered Community Hospitals
(Nonfederal, short-term general and other special hospitals)

Utilization, Personnel, Revenue and Expenses, Community Health Indicators 2006–2010

	2010	2009	2008	2007	2006
TOTAL FACILITY (Includes Hospital and Nursing Home Units)					
Utilization - Inpatient					
Beds	11,170	11,316	10,988	10,862	10,773
Admissions	429,096	442,394	462,954	453,977	454,085
Inpatient Days	2,340,946	2,401,771	2,436,253	2,359,878	2,307,539
Average Length of Stay	5.5	5.4	5.3	5.2	5.1
Inpatient Surgeries	109,345	117,362	117,982	115,503	112,716
Births	48,569	53,456	49,851	49,623	47,489
Utilization - Outpatient					
Emergency Outpatient Visits	1,762,821	1,743,802	1,645,625	1,618,741	1,554,914
Other Outpatient Visits	3,895,891	3,827,100	3,785,996	3,654,371	3,779,892
Total Outpatient Visits	5,658,712	5,570,902	5,431,621	5,273,112	5,334,806
Outpatient Surgeries	206,440	200,043	198,007	197,718	188,902
Personnel					
Full Time RNs	11,105	10,929	10,585	10,229	9,638
Full Time LPNs	1,686	1,903	1,986	2,275	2,209
Part Time RNs	3,984	3,654	3,684	3,523	3,508
Part Time LPNs	567	500	508	650	690
Total Full Time	43,629	43,977	43,201	43,508	42,811
Total Part Time	13,056	12,159	12,279	12,348	12,270
Revenue - Inpatient					
Gross Inpatient Revenue	$12,758,064,725	$12,064,230,137	$11,758,611,895	$10,320,519,778	$9,412,503,176
Revenue - Outpatient					
Gross Outpatient Revenue	$9,221,121,763	$8,258,194,596	$7,423,183,911	$6,214,687,591	$5,508,080,380
Revenue and Expenses - Totals					
(Includes Inpatient and Outpatient)					
Total Gross Revenue	$21,979,186,488	$20,322,424,733	$19,181,795,806	$16,535,207,369	$14,920,583,556
Deductions from Revenue	15,258,319,649	13,635,382,267	12,656,733,800	10,641,812,711	9,331,819,127
Net Patient Revenue	6,720,866,839	6,687,042,466	6,525,062,006	5,893,394,658	5,588,764,429
Other Operating Revenue	235,730,490	201,195,524	211,578,156	234,090,824	247,484,700
Other Nonoperating Revenue	102,371,200	-36,278,624	37,213,785	137,588,524	86,916,871
Total Net Revenue	7,058,968,529	6,851,959,366	6,773,853,947	6,265,074,006	5,923,166,000
Total Expenses	6,484,581,837	6,376,319,309	6,361,690,040	5,731,142,311	5,384,898,786
HOSPITAL UNIT (Excludes Separate Nursing Home Units)					
Utilization - Inpatient					
Beds	10,981	11,013	10,699	10,542	10,392
Admissions	427,982	440,886	461,577	452,687	451,626
Inpatient Days	2,280,666	2,277,293	2,339,600	2,256,043	2,204,009
Average Length of Stay	5.3	5.2	5.1	5.0	4.9
Personnel					
Total Full Time	43,532	43,684	42,916	43,203	42,351
Total Part Time	12,983	12,110	12,202	12,267	12,075
Revenue and Expenses - Totals					
(Includes Inpatient and Outpatient)					
Total Net Revenue	$7,049,646,928	$6,836,200,847	$6,759,273,857	$6,249,707,579	$5,904,273,214
Total Expenses	6,475,775,258	6,361,745,192	6,348,305,959	5,658,213,009	5,367,863,128
COMMUNITY HEALTH INDICATORS PER 1000 POPULATION					
Total Population (in thousands)	3,724	3,687	3,644	3,612	3,574
Inpatient					
Beds	3.0	3.1	3.0	3.0	3.0
Admissions	115.2	120.0	127.0	125.7	127.0
Inpatient Days	628.5	651.4	668.6	653.3	645.6
Inpatient Surgeries	29.4	31.8	32.4	32.0	31.5
Births	13.0	14.5	13.7	13.7	13.3
Outpatient					
Emergency Outpatient Visits	473.3	473.0	451.6	448.1	435.0
Other Outpatient Visits	1,046.0	1,038.0	1,039.0	1,011.7	1,057.5
Total Outpatient Visits	1,519.3	1,510.9	1,490.6	1,459.8	1,492.5
Outpatient Surgeries	55.4	54.3	54.3	54.7	52.8
Expense per Capita (per person)	$1,741.1	$1,729.4	$1,745.8	$1,586.6	$1,506.5

States

TABLE 6

OREGON

U.S. Registered Community Hospitals
(Nonfederal, short-term general and other special hospitals)

Overview 2006–2010

	2010	2009	2008	2007	2006
Total Community Hospitals in Oregon	58	58	58	58	58
Bed Size Category					
6-24	9	8	8	7	8
25-49	20	19	19	20	19
50-99	10	12	11	11	12
100-199	9	9	9	9	9
200-299	4	4	5	4	4
300-399	1	1	0	1	0
400-499	3	3	4	4	5
500 + ...	2	2	2	2	1
Location					
Hospitals Urban..........................	29	29	29	29	26
Hospitals Rural	29	29	29	29	32
Control					
State and Local Government...............	12	12	13	13	13
Not for Profit	44	44	43	43	42
Investor owned	2	2	2	2	3
Physician Models					
Independent Practice Association	12	13	13	13	14
Group Practice without Walls...............	9	8	8	7	6
Open Physician-Hospital Organization	6	6	6	6	10
Closed Physician-Hospital Organization	2	2	2	3	3
Management Service Organization	14	14	14	14	9
Integrated Salary Model...................	39	35	35	36	31
Equity Model	0	1	1	0	1
Foundation..............................	5	6	5	3	4
Insurance Products					
Health Maintenance Organization	15	15	14	16	13
Preferred Provider Organization..............	19	15	14	21	19
Indemnity Fee for Service	3	3	3	5	6
Managed Care Contracts					
Health Maintenance Organization	34	29	30	34	34
Preferred Provider Organization..............	51	51	51	47	46
Affiliations					
Hospitals in a System.....................	39	39	37	37	34
Hospitals in a Network....................	27	25	25	24	22
Hospitals in a Group Purchasing Organization..	57	56	56	57	57

States

TABLE 6

OREGON

U.S. Registered Community Hospitals
(Nonfederal, short-term general and other special hospitals)

Utilization, Personnel, Revenue and Expenses, Community Health Indicators 2006–2010

	2010	2009	2008	2007	2006
TOTAL FACILITY (Includes Hospital and Nursing Home Units)					
Utilization - Inpatient					
Beds	6,420	6,481	6,814	6,841	6,609
Admissions	321,334	323,733	348,600	347,089	341,540
Inpatient Days	1,387,082	1,437,561	1,551,894	1,534,999	1,508,314
Average Length of Stay	4.3	4.4	4.5	4.4	4.4
Inpatient Surgeries	114,683	114,337	120,048	119,933	117,402
Births	41,914	43,940	47,273	48,230	47,369
Utilization - Outpatient					
Emergency Outpatient Visits	1,229,539	1,312,068	1,330,142	1,301,629	1,250,008
Other Outpatient Visits	7,982,714	7,587,931	7,228,022	6,877,816	7,007,868
Total Outpatient Visits	9,212,253	8,899,999	8,558,164	8,179,445	8,257,876
Outpatient Surgeries	205,542	207,341	210,333	213,159	206,125
Personnel					
Full Time RNs	9,293	9,230	9,498	9,248	8,633
Full Time LPNs	189	212	214	179	219
Part Time RNs	7,003	7,068	7,753	7,217	7,901
Part Time LPNs	131	165	171	212	240
Total Full Time	35,968	35,768	37,581	36,209	35,767
Total Part Time	18,954	19,325	20,437	19,627	20,862
Revenue - Inpatient					
Gross Inpatient Revenue	$8,342,718,826	$7,965,180,365	$7,942,127,860	$7,305,555,599	$6,636,156,491
Revenue - Outpatient					
Gross Outpatient Revenue	$7,669,159,468	$7,028,661,629	$6,403,379,909	$5,753,564,088	$5,193,062,718
Revenue and Expenses - Totals					
(Includes Inpatient and Outpatient)					
Total Gross Revenue	$16,011,878,294	$14,993,841,994	$14,345,507,769	$13,059,119,687	$11,829,219,209
Deductions from Revenue	8,389,072,711	7,773,324,462	7,249,042,014	6,506,212,357	5,737,941,726
Net Patient Revenue	7,622,805,583	7,220,517,532	7,096,465,755	6,552,907,330	6,091,277,483
Other Operating Revenue	356,073,198	354,503,423	351,902,221	303,815,392	299,687,588
Other Nonoperating Revenue	164,944,836	-58,115,473	-55,685,102	238,442,802	138,893,278
Total Net Revenue	8,143,823,617	7,516,905,482	7,392,682,874	7,095,165,524	6,529,858,349
Total Expenses	7,875,937,042	7,402,240,332	7,376,298,400	6,704,406,099	6,192,331,481
HOSPITAL UNIT (Excludes Separate Nursing Home Units)					
Utilization - Inpatient					
Beds	6,233	6,228	6,551	6,577	6,345
Admissions	321,153	323,516	348,313	346,747	341,242
Inpatient Days	1,338,597	1,373,086	1,485,018	1,464,066	1,437,308
Average Length of Stay	4.2	4.2	4.3	4.2	4.2
Personnel					
Total Full Time	35,872	35,629	37,436	36,068	35,615
Total Part Time	18,863	19,243	20,381	19,561	20,784
Revenue and Expenses - Totals					
(Includes Inpatient and Outpatient)					
Total Net Revenue	$8,133,821,379	$7,504,259,729	$7,380,524,478	$7,083,566,291	$6,520,330,928
Total Expenses	7,866,577,239	7,391,642,279	7,366,061,834	6,693,285,719	6,183,003,680
COMMUNITY HEALTH INDICATORS PER 1000 POPULATION					
Total Population (in thousands)	3,856	3,826	3,783	3,733	3,678
Inpatient					
Beds	1.7	1.7	1.8	1.8	1.8
Admissions	83.3	84.6	92.1	93.0	92.9
Inpatient Days	359.8	375.8	410.2	411.2	410.1
Inpatient Surgeries	29.7	29.9	31.7	32.1	31.9
Births	10.9	11.5	12.5	12.9	12.9
Outpatient					
Emergency Outpatient Visits	318.9	343.0	351.6	348.7	339.9
Other Outpatient Visits	2,070.5	1,983.4	1,910.7	1,842.5	1,905.6
Total Outpatient Visits	2,389.4	2,326.4	2,262.3	2,191.1	2,245.5
Outpatient Surgeries	53.3	54.2	55.6	57.1	56.0
Expense per Capita (per person)	$2,042.8	$1,934.9	$1,949.9	$1,796.0	$1,683.8

TABLE 6

PENNSYLVANIA

U.S. Registered Community Hospitals
(Nonfederal, short-term general and other special hospitals)

Overview 2006–2010

	2010	2009	2008	2007	2006
Total Community Hospitals in Pennsylvania ...	196	194	201	187	188
Bed Size Category					
6-24	3	3	2	2	3
25-49	29	29	29	21	22
50-99	42	40	42	33	29
100-199	46	47	49	53	57
200-299	34	37	41	40	37
300-399	17	13	14	12	15
400-499	11	10	9	12	12
500 + ...	14	15	15	14	13
Location					
Hospitals Urban..........................	147	145	152	139	144
Hospitals Rural	49	49	49	48	44
Control					
State and Local Government................	2	2	3	2	2
Not for Profit	151	153	160	158	161
Investor owned	43	39	38	27	25
Physician Models					
Independent Practice Association	7	8	9	9	9
Group Practice without Walls................	8	13	13	12	12
Open Physician-Hospital Organization	24	25	32	31	30
Closed Physician-Hospital Organization	3	4	4	5	6
Management Service Organization	21	26	27	25	30
Integrated Salary Model....................	75	73	69	75	72
Equity Model.............................	2	3	2	2	4
Foundation...............................	8	6	6	5	5
Insurance Products					
Health Maintenance Organization	29	24	29	29	29
Preferred Provider Organization..............	42	39	44	41	39
Indemnity Fee for Service	17	12	15	12	13
Managed Care Contracts					
Health Maintenance Organization	117	115	116	122	125
Preferred Provider Organization..............	115	109	112	117	121
Affiliations					
Hospitals in a System.....................	118	112	116	101	107
Hospitals in a Network....................	49	47	48	49	52
Hospitals in a Group Purchasing Organization..	139	134	131	138	142

TABLE 6

PENNSYLVANIA

U.S. Registered Community Hospitals
(Nonfederal, short-term general and other special hospitals)

Utilization, Personnel, Revenue and Expenses, Community Health Indicators 2006–2010

	2010	2009	2008	2007	2006
TOTAL FACILITY (Includes Hospital and Nursing Home Units)					
Utilization - Inpatient					
Beds	39,889	39,212	40,407	39,728	39,567
Admissions	1,809,935	1,841,550	1,901,417	1,880,382	1,866,261
Inpatient Days	9,769,701	9,865,210	10,353,793	10,257,605	10,110,336
Average Length of Stay	5.4	5.4	5.4	5.5	5.4
Inpatient Surgeries	534,919	540,046	558,918	549,182	553,061
Births	134,404	137,478	143,674	143,281	141,971
Utilization - Outpatient					
Emergency Outpatient Visits	6,120,131	6,009,572	6,006,841	5,771,876	5,583,228
Other Outpatient Visits	32,432,398	31,882,222	32,449,554	31,012,536	30,127,411
Total Outpatient Visits	38,552,529	37,891,794	38,456,395	36,784,412	35,710,639
Outpatient Surgeries	914,558	917,586	948,852	931,789	998,156
Personnel					
Full Time RNs	53,217	51,430	51,379	49,838	47,217
Full Time LPNs	3,406	3,769	4,183	4,225	4,342
Part Time RNs	24,947	25,315	25,909	26,044	25,541
Part Time LPNs	1,558	1,737	2,013	2,050	2,105
Total Full Time	207,153	203,289	211,389	204,480	200,061
Total Part Time	72,508	74,386	75,418	75,971	75,335
Revenue - Inpatient					
Gross Inpatient Revenue	$77,752,923,156	$73,916,497,474	$72,947,964,529	$68,794,426,900	$61,367,161,956
Revenue - Outpatient					
Gross Outpatient Revenue	$52,558,766,166	$47,748,195,221	$43,951,207,740	$39,611,381,052	$35,511,165,044
Revenue and Expenses - Totals					
(Includes Inpatient and Outpatient)					
Total Gross Revenue	$130,311,689,322	$121,664,692,695	$116,899,172,269	$108,405,807,952	$96,878,327,000
Deductions from Revenue	96,372,359,561	89,109,854,967	85,447,182,883	78,990,384,684	69,114,526,615
Net Patient Revenue	33,939,329,761	32,554,837,728	31,451,989,386	29,415,423,268	27,763,800,385
Other Operating Revenue	1,560,413,652	1,478,517,269	1,437,920,156	1,437,490,621	1,410,478,499
Other Nonoperating Revenue	355,838,893	-446,883,805	183,327,965	696,634,527	521,348,733
Total Net Revenue	35,855,582,306	33,586,471,192	33,073,237,507	31,549,548,416	29,695,627,707
Total Expenses	33,929,583,373	32,711,950,307	31,323,216,832	28,750,837,150	27,714,356,897
HOSPITAL UNIT (Excludes Separate Nursing Home Units)					
Utilization - Inpatient					
Beds	38,271	37,446	38,441	37,762	37,449
Admissions	1,793,060	1,822,836	1,880,413	1,859,317	1,843,785
Inpatient Days	9,324,956	9,383,976	9,836,158	9,655,775	9,458,378
Average Length of Stay	5.2	5.1	5.2	5.2	5.1
Personnel					
Total Full Time	205,956	201,932	209,962	202,951	198,398
Total Part Time	71,746	73,493	74,556	75,053	74,360
Revenue and Expenses - Totals					
(Includes Inpatient and Outpatient)					
Total Net Revenue	$35,657,261,435	$33,390,355,912	$32,864,948,434	$31,356,583,352	$29,511,480,040
Total Expenses	33,767,820,668	32,546,735,654	31,124,814,383	28,586,982,718	27,484,488,144
COMMUNITY HEALTH INDICATORS PER 1000 POPULATION					
Total Population (in thousands)	12,633	12,605	12,566	12,523	12,471
Inpatient					
Beds	3.2	3.1	3.2	3.2	3.2
Admissions	143.3	146.1	151.3	150.2	149.6
Inpatient Days	773.4	782.7	823.9	819.1	810.7
Inpatient Surgeries	42.3	42.8	44.5	43.9	44.3
Births	10.6	10.9	11.4	11.4	11.4
Outpatient					
Emergency Outpatient Visits	484.5	476.8	478.0	460.9	447.7
Other Outpatient Visits	2,567.3	2,529.4	2,582.3	2,476.5	2,415.8
Total Outpatient Visits	3,051.8	3,006.1	3,060.3	2,937.5	2,863.5
Outpatient Surgeries	72.4	72.8	75.5	74.4	80.0
Expense per Capita (per person)	$2,685.8	$2,595.2	$2,492.6	$2,295.9	$2,222.3

TABLE **6**

RHODE ISLAND

U.S. Registered Community Hospitals
(Nonfederal, short-term general and other special hospitals)

Overview 2006–2010

	2010	2009	2008	2007	2006
Total Community Hospitals in Rhode Island . . .	11	11	11	11	11
Bed Size Category					
6-24	0	0	0	0	0
25-49	0	0	0	0	0
50-99	1	1	1	1	1
100-199	5	5	6	6	6
200-299	3	3	2	2	2
300-399	1	1	1	1	1
400-499	0	0	0	0	0
500 + ...	1	1	1	1	1
Location					
Hospitals Urban.	11	11	11	11	10
Hospitals Rural	0	0	0	0	1
Control					
State and Local Government.	0	0	0	0	0
Not for Profit	11	11	11	11	11
Investor owned	0	0	0	0	0
Physician Models					
Independent Practice Association	5	4	6	6	6
Group Practice without Walls.	0	0	0	0	0
Open Physician-Hospital Organization	6	6	7	7	7
Closed Physician-Hospital Organization	0	1	1	1	1
Management Service Organization	2	2	2	2	2
Integrated Salary Model.	6	5	5	5	5
Equity Model.	0	0	0	0	0
Foundation.	2	2	3	3	3
Insurance Products					
Health Maintenance Organization	1	1	2	2	2
Preferred Provider Organization.	0	0	1	2	2
Indemnity Fee for Service	0	0	0	1	1
Managed Care Contracts					
Health Maintenance Organization	7	7	9	10	10
Preferred Provider Organization.	7	7	10	9	10
Affiliations					
Hospitals in a System.	5	5	5	5	5
Hospitals in a Network.	6	3	1	1	3
Hospitals in a Group Purchasing Organization. .	7	7	9	10	10

TABLE 6

RHODE ISLAND

U.S. Registered Community Hospitals
(Nonfederal, short-term general and other special hospitals)

Utilization, Personnel, Revenue and Expenses, Community Health Indicators 2006–2010

	2010	2009	2008	2007	2006
TOTAL FACILITY (Includes Hospital and Nursing Home Units)					
Utilization - Inpatient					
Beds	2,479	2,512	2,463	2,449	2,394
Admissions	123,188	126,761	127,413	128,519	127,179
Inpatient Days	621,614	654,695	666,745	672,831	680,881
Average Length of Stay	5.0	5.2	5.2	5.2	5.4
Inpatient Surgeries	32,612	39,752	38,970	37,084	36,517
Births	11,492	11,815	12,785	13,305	13,171
Utilization - Outpatient					
Emergency Outpatient Visits	495,149	502,224	494,817	485,624	466,720
Other Outpatient Visits	2,127,266	2,131,290	2,139,409	2,082,179	1,973,903
Total Outpatient Visits	2,622,415	2,633,514	2,634,226	2,567,803	2,440,623
Outpatient Surgeries	66,930	79,583	82,597	91,082	92,416
Personnel					
Full Time RNs	2,251	2,255	2,301	2,269	2,074
Full Time LPNs	58	87	92	119	128
Part Time RNs	2,771	2,705	3,147	2,840	2,862
Part Time LPNs	54	95	118	149	148
Total Full Time	12,686	12,928	12,908	12,810	12,612
Total Part Time	8,001	7,707	8,873	8,459	8,239
Revenue - Inpatient					
Gross Inpatient Revenue	$3,623,363,473	$3,585,072,822	$3,383,235,261	$3,157,359,726	$2,969,325,063
Revenue - Outpatient					
Gross Outpatient Revenue	$3,560,931,543	$3,292,773,520	$3,067,731,603	$2,874,889,949	$2,667,727,132
Revenue and Expenses - Totals					
(Includes Inpatient and Outpatient)					
Total Gross Revenue	$7,184,295,016	$6,877,846,342	$6,450,966,864	$6,032,249,675	$5,637,052,195
Deductions from Revenue	4,555,181,118	4,297,920,625	4,018,043,505	3,748,195,534	3,451,826,897
Net Patient Revenue	2,629,113,898	2,579,925,717	2,432,923,359	2,284,054,141	2,185,225,298
Other Operating Revenue	265,788,290	241,675,005	247,620,663	241,675,507	233,392,317
Other Nonoperating Revenue	6,408,073	6,908,048	6,024,220	26,894,546	15,205,663
Total Net Revenue	2,901,310,261	2,828,508,770	2,686,568,242	2,552,624,194	2,433,823,278
Total Expenses	2,883,693,916	2,812,067,020	2,649,565,524	2,504,792,635	2,395,122,194
HOSPITAL UNIT (Excludes Separate Nursing Home Units)					
Utilization - Inpatient					
Beds	2,479	2,512	2,439	2,425	2,370
Admissions	123,188	126,761	127,095	127,928	126,326
Inpatient Days	621,614	654,695	662,377	665,265	669,632
Average Length of Stay	5.0	5.2	5.2	5.2	5.3
Personnel					
Total Full Time	12,686	12,928	12,846	12,799	12,601
Total Part Time	8,001	7,707	8,790	8,451	8,231
Revenue and Expenses - Totals					
(Includes Inpatient and Outpatient)					
Total Net Revenue	$2,901,310,261	$2,828,508,770	$2,679,872,351	$2,549,240,364	$2,429,083,387
Total Expenses	2,883,693,916	2,812,067,020	2,643,600,577	2,501,997,062	2,391,044,858
COMMUNITY HEALTH INDICATORS PER 1000 POPULATION					
Total Population (in thousands)	1,057	1,053	1,054	1,055	1,060
Inpatient					
Beds	2.3	2.4	2.3	2.3	2.3
Admissions	116.6	120.4	120.9	121.8	120.0
Inpatient Days	588.2	621.6	632.9	637.7	642.2
Inpatient Surgeries	30.9	37.7	37.0	35.2	34.4
Births	10.9	11.2	12.1	12.6	12.4
Outpatient					
Emergency Outpatient Visits	468.5	476.9	469.7	460.3	440.2
Other Outpatient Visits	2,012.8	2,023.6	2,030.8	1,973.6	1,861.8
Total Outpatient Visits	2,481.3	2,500.5	2,500.4	2,433.9	2,302.0
Outpatient Surgeries	63.3	75.6	78.4	86.3	87.2
Expense per Capita (per person)	$2,728.5	$2,670.0	$2,515.0	$2,374.2	$2,259.1

TABLE **6**

SOUTH CAROLINA

U.S. Registered Community Hospitals
(Nonfederal, short-term general and other special hospitals)

Overview 2006–2010

	2010	2009	2008	2007	2006
Total Community Hospitals in South Carolina..	67	70	69	67	66
Bed Size Category					
6-24	1	2	0	1	0
25-49	19	18	18	16	16
50-99	10	13	12	11	11
100-199	13	13	14	14	15
200-299	9	10	12	14	12
300-399	7	7	7	5	7
400-499	3	2	1	2	1
500 + ...	5	5	5	4	4
Location					
Hospitals Urban..........................	42	45	44	42	38
Hospitals Rural	25	25	25	25	28
Control					
State and Local Government................	17	20	20	19	19
Not for Profit	24	25	25	23	22
Investor owned	26	25	24	25	25
Physician Models					
Independent Practice Association	5	5	6	3	2
Group Practice without Walls................	1	1	3	0	2
Open Physician-Hospital Organization	4	7	8	7	9
Closed Physician-Hospital Organization	1	0	1	1	1
Management Service Organization	2	1	0	1	4
Integrated Salary Model....................	19	15	14	13	12
Equity Model.............................	0	0	0	0	0
Foundation...............................	0	0	0	0	0
Insurance Products					
Health Maintenance Organization	7	7	2	2	4
Preferred Provider Organization..............	10	10	5	7	9
Indemnity Fee for Service	6	6	1	1	2
Managed Care Contracts					
Health Maintenance Organization	39	45	37	33	40
Preferred Provider Organization..............	38	46	36	36	46
Affiliations					
Hospitals in a System......................	44	47	45	43	42
Hospitals in a Network.....................	12	12	15	16	14
Hospitals in a Group Purchasing Organization..	59	58	52	1	—

TABLE 6

SOUTH CAROLINA

U.S. Registered Community Hospitals
(Nonfederal, short-term general and other special hospitals)

Utilization, Personnel, Revenue and Expenses, Community Health Indicators 2006–2010

	2010	2009	2008	2007	2006
TOTAL FACILITY (Includes Hospital and Nursing Home Units)					
Utilization - Inpatient					
Beds	12,495	12,483	12,498	12,032	11,790
Admissions	522,793	528,204	528,872	518,994	521,773
Inpatient Days	3,002,541	2,960,134	2,962,830	3,006,247	3,083,647
Average Length of Stay............	5.7	5.6	5.6	5.8	5.9
Inpatient Surgeries...............	194,895	205,119	196,304	190,349	189,509
Births..........................	54,894	57,559	56,068	56,616	52,676
Utilization - Outpatient					
Emergency Outpatient Visits........	1,453,696	2,171,925	1,954,264	1,890,731	1,893,605
Other Outpatient Visits.............	4,922,633	4,147,745	3,969,951	4,151,591	4,200,091
Total Outpatient Visits	6,376,329	6,319,670	5,924,215	6,042,322	6,093,696
Outpatient Surgeries	289,794	300,093	294,280	280,735	288,804
Personnel					
Full Time RNs	17,476	17,451	16,203	15,120	14,900
Full Time LPNs	1,062	1,170	1,292	1,363	1,462
Part Time RNs	5,184	5,246	5,834	5,826	5,429
Part Time LPNs	347	395	510	514	491
Total Full Time..................	58,567	58,933	58,372	54,571	53,886
Total Part Time	14,343	14,332	16,302	16,040	15,478
Revenue - Inpatient					
Gross Inpatient Revenue..........	$18,371,422,174	$17,448,319,308	$16,743,319,395	$14,774,254,035	$13,760,712,078
Revenue - Outpatient					
Gross Outpatient Revenue	$12,660,946,189	$11,900,471,047	$10,266,244,867	$8,994,634,785	$7,918,853,975
Revenue and Expenses - Totals					
(Includes Inpatient and Outpatient)					
Total Gross Revenue..............	$31,032,368,363	$29,348,790,355	$27,009,564,262	$23,768,888,820	$21,679,566,053
Deductions from Revenue..........	21,049,743,519	19,883,727,173	18,082,987,646	15,526,589,717	13,957,650,045
Net Patient Revenue	9,982,624,844	9,465,063,182	8,926,576,616	8,242,299,103	7,721,916,008
Other Operating Revenue	249,339,525	236,614,730	262,341,118	224,352,076	222,065,204
Other Nonoperating Revenue	210,607,769	190,176,135	85,822,937	161,793,047	12,894,836
Total Net Revenue...............	10,442,572,138	9,891,854,047	9,274,740,671	8,628,444,226	7,956,876,048
Total Expenses..................	9,349,824,264	9,264,970,348	8,890,465,525	7,888,982,140	7,522,995,957
HOSPITAL UNIT (Excludes Separate Nursing Home Units)					
Utilization - Inpatient					
Beds	11,611	11,739	11,728	11,080	10,695
Admissions	518,130	524,147	524,838	514,618	516,307
Inpatient Days	2,729,473	2,685,104	2,750,321	2,686,337	2,717,463
Average Length of Stay............	5.3	5.1	5.2	5.2	5.3
Personnel					
Total Full Time..................	57,811	58,169	57,714	53,761	52,914
Total Part Time	14,118	13,998	16,043	15,737	15,161
Revenue and Expenses - Totals					
(Includes Inpatient and Outpatient)					
Total Net Revenue...............	$10,354,825,713	$9,821,499,987	$9,217,872,804	$8,562,824,215	$5,684,998,987
Total Expenses..................	9,272,925,368	9,204,773,809	8,842,007,632	7,826,701,269	7,443,633,754
COMMUNITY HEALTH INDICATORS PER 1000 POPULATION					
Total Population (in thousands)	4,597	4,561	4,503	4,424	4,339
Inpatient					
Beds	2.7	2.7	2.8	2.7	2.7
Admissions	113.7	115.8	117.4	117.3	120.2
Inpatient Days	653.2	649.0	657.9	679.5	710.6
Inpatient Surgeries...............	42.4	45.0	43.6	43.0	43.7
Births..........................	11.9	12.6	12.5	12.8	12.1
Outpatient					
Emergency Outpatient Visits........	316.2	476.2	434.0	427.4	436.4
Other Outpatient Visits............	1,070.8	909.3	881.6	938.4	967.9
Total Outpatient Visits	1,387.1	1,385.5	1,315.5	1,365.7	1,404.3
Outpatient Surgeries	63.0	65.8	65.3	63.5	66.6
Expense per Capita (per person).....	$2,033.9	$2,031.2	$1,974.2	$1,783.1	$1,733.6

States

TABLE 6

SOUTH DAKOTA

U.S. Registered Community Hospitals
(Nonfederal, short-term general and other special hospitals)

Overview 2006–2010

	2010	2009	2008	2007	2006
Total Community Hospitals in South Dakota...	53	53	53	51	52
Bed Size Category					
6-24	17	16	18	15	15
25-49	14	14	12	13	14
50-99	10	11	11	10	10
100-199	7	7	7	8	8
200-299	2	2	1	2	2
300-399	1	1	2	1	1
400-499	2	2	2	1	1
500 +	0	0	0	1	1
Location					
Hospitals Urban	11	11	11	10	8
Hospitals Rural	42	42	42	41	44
Control					
State and Local Government	4	3	5	5	5
Not for Profit	45	46	44	43	44
Investor owned	4	4	4	3	3
Physician Models					
Independent Practice Association	8	12	11	10	11
Group Practice without Walls	1	3	3	3	3
Open Physician-Hospital Organization	3	6	6	8	6
Closed Physician-Hospital Organization	2	3	3	4	3
Management Service Organization	1	2	2	3	2
Integrated Salary Model	23	28	25	25	24
Equity Model	1	2	2	2	2
Foundation	2	1	1	2	1
Insurance Products					
Health Maintenance Organization	16	17	17	15	15
Preferred Provider Organization	11	10	13	18	18
Indemnity Fee for Service	6	9	8	5	6
Managed Care Contracts					
Health Maintenance Organization	23	24	24	22	23
Preferred Provider Organization	27	29	32	32	33
Affiliations					
Hospitals in a System	37	38	38	36	36
Hospitals in a Network	21	22	22	20	20
Hospitals in a Group Purchasing Organization..	39	45	45	44	46

States

TABLE 6

SOUTH DAKOTA

U.S. Registered Community Hospitals
(Nonfederal, short-term general and other special hospitals)

Utilization, Personnel, Revenue and Expenses, Community Health Indicators 2006–2010

	2010	2009	2008	2007	2006
TOTAL FACILITY (Includes Hospital and Nursing Home Units)					
Utilization - Inpatient					
Beds	4,108	4,142	4,113	4,245	4,326
Admissions	101,128	102,335	102,116	99,931	96,964
Inpatient Days	935,410	1,005,265	1,005,766	1,008,378	1,022,716
Average Length of Stay	9.2	9.8	9.8	10.1	10.5
Inpatient Surgeries	30,363	32,416	31,715	33,312	35,010
Births	11,437	11,848	12,258	12,125	11,380
Utilization - Outpatient					
Emergency Outpatient Visits	259,364	240,618	239,192	226,131	222,244
Other Outpatient Visits	1,782,993	1,698,830	1,618,764	1,562,594	1,550,535
Total Outpatient Visits	2,042,357	1,939,448	1,857,956	1,788,725	1,772,779
Outpatient Surgeries	67,743	71,571	71,162	61,234	63,815
Personnel					
Full Time RNs	3,633	3,596	3,160	3,106	2,912
Full Time LPNs	216	191	185	189	203
Part Time RNs	1,736	2,003	2,253	1,874	1,987
Part Time LPNs	129	132	131	130	144
Total Full Time	14,483	15,119	14,488	13,502	12,819
Total Part Time	6,316	7,357	8,067	7,187	7,449
Revenue - Inpatient					
Gross Inpatient Revenue	$2,779,376,912	$2,534,795,960	$2,293,166,775	$2,051,748,519	$1,806,073,890
Revenue - Outpatient					
Gross Outpatient Revenue	$2,405,199,211	$2,107,192,538	$1,875,244,749	$1,595,180,119	$1,425,424,763
Revenue and Expenses - Totals					
(Includes Inpatient and Outpatient)					
Total Gross Revenue	$5,184,576,123	$4,641,988,498	$4,168,411,524	$3,646,928,638	$3,231,498,653
Deductions from Revenue	2,884,612,400	2,468,508,414	2,187,095,692	1,796,255,037	1,533,819,613
Net Patient Revenue	2,299,963,723	2,173,480,084	1,981,315,832	1,850,673,601	1,697,679,040
Other Operating Revenue	122,786,678	113,185,811	103,615,596	121,580,983	140,692,507
Other Nonoperating Revenue	34,907,740	-20,449,611	30,994,497	64,050,745	47,085,508
Total Net Revenue	2,457,658,141	2,266,216,284	2,115,925,925	2,036,305,329	1,885,457,055
Total Expenses	2,194,315,958	2,075,750,158	1,919,761,533	1,791,313,970	1,646,922,945
HOSPITAL UNIT (Excludes Separate Nursing Home Units)					
Utilization - Inpatient					
Beds	2,869	2,728	2,671	2,621	2,636
Admissions	99,824	100,901	100,555	97,994	95,183
Inpatient Days	505,190	507,150	509,176	455,753	442,682
Average Length of Stay	5.1	5.0	5.1	4.7	4.7
Personnel					
Total Full Time	13,753	14,238	13,650	12,555	11,863
Total Part Time	5,684	6,607	7,369	6,339	6,557
Revenue and Expenses - Totals					
(Includes Inpatient and Outpatient)					
Total Net Revenue	$2,382,414,150	$2,185,615,059	$2,035,881,683	$1,957,696,000	$1,802,353,636
Total Expenses	2,128,257,681	2,002,334,795	1,848,451,464	1,713,828,405	1,574,797,817
COMMUNITY HEALTH INDICATORS PER 1000 POPULATION					
Total Population (in thousands)	820	812	805	797	789
Inpatient					
Beds	5.0	5.1	5.1	5.3	5.5
Admissions	123.3	126.0	126.9	125.4	123.0
Inpatient Days	1,140.6	1,237.4	1,250.1	1,265.2	1,297.0
Inpatient Surgeries	37.0	39.9	39.4	41.8	44.4
Births	13.9	14.6	15.2	15.2	14.4
Outpatient					
Emergency Outpatient Visits	316.3	296.2	297.3	283.7	281.8
Other Outpatient Visits	2,174.2	2,091.2	2,012.1	1,960.5	1,966.4
Total Outpatient Visits	2,490.4	2,387.4	2,309.4	2,244.2	2,248.2
Outpatient Surgeries	82.6	88.1	88.5	76.8	80.9
Expense per Capita (per person)	$2,675.7	$2,555.1	$2,386.2	$2,247.5	$2,088.6

TABLE **6**

TENNESSEE

U.S. Registered Community Hospitals
(Nonfederal, short-term general and other special hospitals)

Overview 2006–2010

	2010	2009	2008	2007	2006
Total Community Hospitals in Tennessee	134	137	137	133	130
Bed Size Category					
6-24	6	6	7	7	6
25-49	35	36	36	28	28
50-99	32	32	32	34	33
100-199	29	30	29	33	35
200-299	12	13	12	12	8
300-399	6	7	7	5	8
400-499	5	6	5	6	5
500 + ...	9	7	9	8	7
Location					
Hospitals Urban............................	78	81	81	77	64
Hospitals Rural	56	56	56	56	66
Control					
State and Local Government.................	20	22	22	22	24
Not for Profit	56	59	60	61	60
Investor owned	58	56	55	50	46
Physician Models					
Independent Practice Association	19	17	14	16	13
Group Practice without Walls................	4	3	4	4	2
Open Physician-Hospital Organization	11	11	19	21	19
Closed Physician-Hospital Organization	3	3	5	5	3
Management Service Organization	16	18	15	17	18
Integrated Salary Model....................	31	26	19	16	11
Equity Model.............................	0	0	0	0	0
Foundation...............................	4	7	8	6	4
Insurance Products					
Health Maintenance Organization	8	5	14	16	17
Preferred Provider Organization..............	17	16	26	25	26
Indemnity Fee for Service	3	2	10	14	15
Managed Care Contracts					
Health Maintenance Organization	66	67	86	77	75
Preferred Provider Organization..............	72	75	87	80	78
Affiliations					
Hospitals in a System.....................	101	103	104	101	98
Hospitals in a Network....................	41	41	45	38	41
Hospitals in a Group Purchasing Organization..	69	77	89	85	82

TABLE 6

TENNESSEE

U.S. Registered Community Hospitals
(Nonfederal, short-term general and other special hospitals)

Utilization, Personnel, Revenue and Expenses, Community Health Indicators 2006–2010

	2010	2009	2008	2007	2006
TOTAL FACILITY (Includes Hospital and Nursing Home Units)					
Utilization - Inpatient					
Beds	20,830	20,959	21,102	21,688	20,328
Admissions	832,554	859,191	859,344	969,763	853,304
Inpatient Days	4,579,402	4,799,858	4,911,215	5,372,297	4,806,765
Average Length of Stay	5.5	5.6	5.7	5.5	5.6
Inpatient Surgeries	249,367	255,557	243,820	258,348	231,102
Births	70,685	79,804	83,978	90,042	81,067
Utilization - Outpatient					
Emergency Outpatient Visits	3,130,660	3,301,872	3,251,592	3,253,035	2,806,111
Other Outpatient Visits	8,299,669	8,281,474	7,995,403	8,565,760	8,055,773
Total Outpatient Visits	11,430,329	11,583,346	11,246,995	11,818,795	10,861,884
Outpatient Surgeries	411,688	413,202	385,344	443,649	380,827
Personnel					
Full Time RNs	24,475	25,846	24,727	27,626	23,420
Full Time LPNs	2,706	2,938	3,286	3,744	3,644
Part Time RNs	9,222	8,514	8,891	10,578	7,658
Part Time LPNs	767	742	881	1,028	989
Total Full Time	88,145	93,028	90,902	105,326	92,365
Total Part Time	25,539	24,476	25,311	30,136	23,142
Revenue - Inpatient					
Gross Inpatient Revenue	$26,846,357,974	$25,367,667,093	$24,012,198,547	$24,331,008,568	$19,934,787,410
Revenue - Outpatient					
Gross Outpatient Revenue	$19,276,589,146	$17,453,642,146	$15,732,131,119	$16,507,650,360	$13,015,442,619
Revenue and Expenses - Totals					
(Includes Inpatient and Outpatient)					
Total Gross Revenue	$46,122,947,120	$42,821,309,239	$39,744,329,666	$40,838,658,928	$32,950,230,029
Deductions from Revenue	32,931,211,533	29,947,998,235	27,469,500,901	27,397,484,207	21,525,822,289
Net Patient Revenue	13,191,735,587	12,873,311,004	12,274,828,765	13,441,174,721	11,424,407,740
Other Operating Revenue	409,743,303	432,326,528	496,258,779	523,978,490	415,142,709
Other Nonoperating Revenue	268,674,837	-81,972,728	81,614,397	363,631,353	201,731,194
Total Net Revenue	13,870,153,727	13,223,664,804	12,852,701,941	14,328,784,564	12,041,281,643
Total Expenses	12,699,265,618	12,694,504,650	11,996,245,958	13,405,461,053	11,497,417,852
HOSPITAL UNIT (Excludes Separate Nursing Home Units)					
Utilization - Inpatient					
Beds	19,750	19,682	19,467	20,088	18,755
Admissions	825,283	850,278	849,060	958,480	841,956
Inpatient Days	4,244,905	4,400,598	4,396,275	4,889,474	4,300,755
Average Length of Stay	5.1	5.2	5.2	5.1	5.1
Personnel					
Total Full Time	87,258	91,886	89,529	103,980	91,079
Total Part Time	25,367	24,274	25,004	29,745	22,826
Revenue and Expenses - Totals					
(Includes Inpatient and Outpatient)					
Total Net Revenue	$13,791,578,759	$13,131,489,651	$12,735,644,514	$14,221,268,188	$11,933,067,685
Total Expenses	12,630,190,370	12,619,381,549	11,896,072,460	13,318,384,157	11,399,991,123
COMMUNITY HEALTH INDICATORS PER 1000 POPULATION					
Total Population (in thousands)	6,338	6,296	6,240	6,173	6,089
Inpatient					
Beds	3.3	3.3	3.4	3.5	3.3
Admissions	131.4	136.5	137.7	157.1	140.1
Inpatient Days	722.5	762.3	787.0	870.3	789.4
Inpatient Surgeries	39.3	40.6	39.1	41.9	38.0
Births	11.2	12.7	13.5	14.6	13.3
Outpatient					
Emergency Outpatient Visits	493.9	524.4	521.1	527.0	460.8
Other Outpatient Visits	1,309.5	1,315.3	1,281.2	1,387.6	1,322.9
Total Outpatient Visits	1,803.4	1,839.7	1,802.3	1,914.6	1,783.7
Outpatient Surgeries	65.0	65.6	61.7	71.9	62.5
Expense per Capita (per person)	$2,003.6	$2,016.2	$1,922.3	$2,171.7	$1,888.1

States

TABLE **6**

TEXAS

U.S. Registered Community Hospitals
(Nonfederal, short-term general and other special hospitals)

Overview 2006–2010

	2010	2009	2008	2007	2006
Total Community Hospitals in Texas..........	426	428	426	409	417
Bed Size Category					
6-24	73	69	63	60	61
25-49	107	111	111	106	111
50-99	86	79	87	81	77
100-199	61	66	64	59	66
200-299	41	43	44	46	44
300-399	20	21	20	24	25
400-499	14	16	14	13	15
500 + ...	24	23	23	20	18
Location					
Hospitals Urban..........................	275	277	275	260	258
Hospitals Rural	151	151	151	149	159
Control					
State and Local Government................	113	116	117	117	120
Not for Profit	148	147	152	150	148
Investor owned	165	165	157	142	149
Physician Models					
Independent Practice Association	72	69	67	80	80
Group Practice without Walls................	15	24	14	14	15
Open Physician-Hospital Organization	82	84	90	88	87
Closed Physician-Hospital Organization	19	18	17	17	15
Management Service Organization	73	74	63	65	55
Integrated Salary Model....................	97	95	91	87	89
Equity Model.............................	13	13	12	9	7
Foundation...............................	35	33	34	38	34
Insurance Products					
Health Maintenance Organization	66	62	49	56	55
Preferred Provider Organization..............	84	75	66	83	88
Indemnity Fee for Service	26	22	23	21	22
Managed Care Contracts					
Health Maintenance Organization	318	323	314	305	308
Preferred Provider Organization..............	358	361	361	357	360
Affiliations					
Hospitals in a System.....................	278	286	281	259	257
Hospitals in a Network....................	114	106	104	109	111
Hospitals in a Group Purchasing Organization..	398	386	385	369	375

TABLE 6

TEXAS

U.S. Registered Community Hospitals
(Nonfederal, short-term general and other special hospitals)

Utilization, Personnel, Revenue and Expenses, Community Health Indicators 2006–2010

	2010	2009	2008	2007	2006
TOTAL FACILITY (Includes Hospital and Nursing Home Units)					
Utilization - Inpatient					
Beds	61,357	62,069	61,039	58,192	58,964
Admissions	2,580,401	2,621,436	2,585,680	2,468,109	2,528,943
Inpatient Days	13,331,491	13,590,044	13,430,355	12,816,839	13,045,054
Average Length of Stay	5.2	5.2	5.2	5.2	5.2
Inpatient Surgeries	761,437	781,093	763,867	768,063	775,501
Births	381,038	397,979	390,274	378,375	384,775
Utilization - Outpatient					
Emergency Outpatient Visits	9,739,066	9,438,151	8,819,272	8,444,299	8,291,213
Other Outpatient Visits	28,541,761	26,584,907	25,999,796	24,054,713	23,647,835
Total Outpatient Visits	38,280,827	36,023,058	34,819,068	32,499,012	31,939,048
Outpatient Surgeries	1,061,053	1,049,368	1,030,039	991,853	1,009,948
Personnel					
Full Time RNs	82,490	80,537	73,086	70,963	67,758
Full Time LPNs	9,113	9,798	10,227	10,087	10,746
Part Time RNs	20,107	20,901	21,580	20,369	19,109
Part Time LPNs	2,103	2,416	2,487	2,469	2,827
Total Full Time	280,656	280,533	266,604	263,105	257,216
Total Part Time	59,204	61,186	63,288	59,498	58,940
Revenue - Inpatient					
Gross Inpatient Revenue	$100,476,401,353	$95,184,048,332	$87,141,175,562	$77,330,388,025	$72,387,591,622
Revenue - Outpatient					
Gross Outpatient Revenue	$66,131,968,217	$58,578,510,903	$49,826,890,592	$43,530,620,498	$39,341,027,194
Revenue and Expenses - Totals (Includes Inpatient and Outpatient)					
Total Gross Revenue	$166,608,369,570	$153,762,559,235	$136,968,066,154	$120,861,008,523	$111,728,618,816
Deductions from Revenue	122,345,151,455	111,061,711,464	97,866,719,468	85,002,811,289	76,907,991,231
Net Patient Revenue	44,263,218,115	42,700,847,771	39,101,346,686	35,858,197,234	34,820,627,585
Other Operating Revenue	4,492,462,311	4,384,346,385	4,040,612,362	3,786,629,316	3,850,147,633
Other Nonoperating Revenue	1,120,744,597	304,258,670	310,546,108	1,059,715,727	565,608,947
Total Net Revenue	49,876,425,023	47,389,452,826	43,452,505,156	40,704,542,277	39,236,384,165
Total Expenses	44,225,750,333	43,410,205,109	40,396,037,477	37,428,408,575	36,431,139,219
HOSPITAL UNIT (Excludes Separate Nursing Home Units)					
Utilization - Inpatient					
Beds	60,497	61,160	59,947	56,952	57,569
Admissions	2,570,756	2,610,941	2,574,309	2,455,421	2,513,704
Inpatient Days	13,090,722	13,329,807	13,117,477	12,452,079	12,657,778
Average Length of Stay	5.1	5.1	5.1	5.1	5.0
Personnel					
Total Full Time	279,998	279,502	265,647	261,686	256,004
Total Part Time	59,051	61,033	62,914	59,123	58,651
Revenue and Expenses - Totals (Includes Inpatient and Outpatient)					
Total Net Revenue	$49,780,310,157	$47,305,885,374	$43,361,995,590	$40,562,429,655	$39,069,726,193
Total Expenses	44,132,923,562	43,327,541,508	40,292,698,073	37,243,889,225	36,239,634,905
COMMUNITY HEALTH INDICATORS PER 1000 POPULATION					
Total Population (in thousands)	25,213	24,782	24,304	23,838	23,369
Inpatient					
Beds	2.4	2.5	2.5	2.4	2.5
Admissions	102.3	105.8	106.4	103.5	108.2
Inpatient Days	528.7	548.4	552.6	537.7	558.2
Inpatient Surgeries	30.2	31.5	31.4	32.2	33.2
Births	15.1	16.1	16.1	15.9	16.5
Outpatient					
Emergency Outpatient Visits	386.3	380.8	362.9	354.2	354.8
Other Outpatient Visits	1,132.0	1,072.7	1,069.8	1,009.1	1,011.9
Total Outpatient Visits	1,518.3	1,453.6	1,432.6	1,363.3	1,366.7
Outpatient Surgeries	42.1	42.3	42.4	41.6	43.2
Expense per Capita (per person)	$1,754.1	$1,751.7	$1,662.1	$1,570.1	$1,558.9

States

TABLE 6

UTAH

U.S. Registered Community Hospitals
(Nonfederal, short-term general and other special hospitals)

Overview 2006–2010

	2010	2009	2008	2007	2006
Total Community Hospitals in Utah...........	44	44	43	41	43
Bed Size Category					
6-24	8	6	6	6	6
25-49	15	15	14	12	14
50-99	3	6	6	8	8
100-199	8	8	9	8	8
200-299	5	4	4	4	4
300-399	3	3	2	1	1
400-499	2	1	1	1	2
500 + ...	0	1	1	1	0
Location					
Hospitals Urban..........................	26	26	26	25	20
Hospitals Rural	18	18	17	16	23
Control					
State and Local Government................	6	6	5	4	6
Not for Profit............................	23	23	23	22	22
Investor owned	15	15	15	15	15
Physician Models					
Independent Practice Association	4	6	2	2	2
Group Practice without Walls................	1	1	0	0	1
Open Physician-Hospital Organization	1	3	2	2	3
Closed Physician-Hospital Organization	2	2	1	1	1
Management Service Organization	2	2	1	1	1
Integrated Salary Model....................	13	13	13	14	17
Equity Model............................	1	1	0	0	0
Foundation..............................	1	2	1	0	0
Insurance Products					
Health Maintenance Organization	15	15	16	16	20
Preferred Provider Organization..............	13	13	12	15	19
Indemnity Fee for Service	5	7	7	9	9
Managed Care Contracts					
Health Maintenance Organization	14	13	14	15	21
Preferred Provider Organization..............	17	17	19	17	21
Affiliations					
Hospitals in a System.....................	36	36	37	36	36
Hospitals in a Network....................	11	16	15	14	13
Hospitals in a Group Purchasing Organization..	22	21	19	23	27

TABLE 6

UTAH

U.S. Registered Community Hospitals
(Nonfederal, short-term general and other special hospitals)

Utilization, Personnel, Revenue and Expenses, Community Health Indicators 2006–2010

	2010	2009	2008	2007	2006
TOTAL FACILITY (Includes Hospital and Nursing Home Units)					
Utilization - Inpatient					
Beds	5,086	4,973	4,874	4,584	4,528
Admissions	224,264	226,239	226,376	223,971	220,750
Inpatient Days	979,963	1,003,710	1,015,945	1,003,917	968,656
Average Length of Stay	4.4	4.4	4.5	4.5	4.4
Inpatient Surgeries	70,503	71,568	67,840	71,541	68,590
Births	49,392	52,189	55,088	53,731	53,194
Utilization - Outpatient					
Emergency Outpatient Visits	834,897	865,286	856,277	900,975	789,653
Other Outpatient Visits	4,642,827	4,609,086	4,449,171	4,062,804	4,192,042
Total Outpatient Visits	5,477,724	5,474,372	5,305,448	4,963,779	4,981,695
Outpatient Surgeries	166,870	155,162	152,105	138,824	149,004
Personnel					
Full Time RNs	7,303	6,961	6,780	6,318	6,125
Full Time LPNs	358	367	378	500	413
Part Time RNs	4,353	4,454	4,620	4,170	4,311
Part Time LPNs	187	222	277	380	359
Total Full Time	26,111	26,390	26,648	25,903	24,814
Total Part Time	13,418	14,135	14,535	13,269	13,536
Revenue - Inpatient					
Gross Inpatient Revenue	$6,581,097,114	$5,718,543,491	$5,428,255,474	$5,250,442,289	$4,396,532,960
Revenue - Outpatient					
Gross Outpatient Revenue	$5,300,499,527	$4,667,222,276	$4,060,507,024	$3,704,805,862	$3,068,647,875
Revenue and Expenses - Totals					
(Includes Inpatient and Outpatient)					
Total Gross Revenue	$11,881,596,641	$10,385,765,767	$9,488,762,498	$8,955,248,151	$7,465,180,835
Deductions from Revenue	6,906,546,426	5,568,409,487	5,093,986,033	4,961,871,950	3,754,113,535
Net Patient Revenue	4,975,050,215	4,817,356,280	4,394,776,465	3,993,376,201	3,711,067,300
Other Operating Revenue	243,975,154	228,925,055	207,762,710	158,758,359	175,237,458
Other Nonoperating Revenue	31,741,257	12,752,174	20,119,824	39,067,658	16,047,892
Total Net Revenue	5,250,766,626	5,059,033,509	4,622,658,999	4,191,202,218	3,902,352,650
Total Expenses	4,470,510,613	4,263,844,434	4,041,481,901	3,710,391,899	3,437,079,268
HOSPITAL UNIT (Excludes Separate Nursing Home Units)					
Utilization - Inpatient					
Beds	4,931	4,808	4,720	4,431	4,383
Admissions	223,117	224,928	225,065	223,089	218,711
Inpatient Days	935,962	961,475	976,402	960,104	929,668
Average Length of Stay	4.2	4.3	4.3	4.3	4.3
Personnel					
Total Full Time	26,037	26,296	26,562	25,822	24,704
Total Part Time	13,364	14,068	14,449	13,158	13,437
Revenue and Expenses - Totals					
(Includes Inpatient and Outpatient)					
Total Net Revenue	$5,239,992,029	$5,050,316,084	$4,612,854,633	$4,183,929,529	$3,892,595,169
Total Expenses	4,461,414,330	4,255,351,046	4,034,303,806	3,704,812,297	3,430,215,718
COMMUNITY HEALTH INDICATORS PER 1000 POPULATION					
Total Population (in thousands)	2,831	2,785	2,727	2,664	2,584
Inpatient					
Beds	1.8	1.8	1.8	1.7	1.8
Admissions	79.2	81.2	83.0	84.1	85.4
Inpatient Days	346.2	360.5	372.5	376.9	374.9
Inpatient Surgeries	24.9	25.7	24.9	26.9	26.5
Births	17.4	18.7	20.2	20.2	20.6
Outpatient					
Emergency Outpatient Visits	294.9	310.7	314.0	338.2	305.6
Other Outpatient Visits	1,640.1	1,655.2	1,631.3	1,525.2	1,622.5
Total Outpatient Visits	1,935.1	1,966.0	1,945.3	1,863.4	1,928.1
Outpatient Surgeries	58.9	55.7	55.8	52.1	57.7
Expense per Capita (per person)	$1,579.3	$1,531.2	$1,481.8	$1,392.9	$1,330.3

States

TABLE 6

VERMONT

U.S. Registered Community Hospitals
(Nonfederal, short-term general and other special hospitals)

Overview 2006–2010

	2010	2009	2008	2007	2006
Total Community Hospitals in Vermont	14	14	14	14	14
Bed Size Category					
6-24	1	1	1	0	0
25-49	6	6	6	7	7
50-99	4	4	4	4	4
100-199	1	1	1	1	1
200-299	1	1	1	1	1
300-399	0	0	0	0	0
400-499	1	1	1	1	1
500 + ...	0	0	0	0	0
Location					
Hospitals Urban...........................	2	2	2	2	2
Hospitals Rural	12	12	12	12	12
Control					
State and Local Government................	0	0	0	0	0
Not for Profit	14	14	14	14	14
Investor owned	0	0	0	0	0
Physician Models					
Independent Practice Association	0	0	0	0	1
Group Practice without Walls................	0	0	0	0	0
Open Physician-Hospital Organization	3	2	3	2	3
Closed Physician-Hospital Organization	1	1	1	1	1
Management Service Organization	0	0	0	1	1
Integrated Salary Model....................	8	7	9	7	9
Equity Model.............................	0	0	0	0	0
Foundation...............................	0	0	0	0	0
Insurance Products					
Health Maintenance Organization	2	3	3	3	3
Preferred Provider Organization..............	0	0	0	2	2
Indemnity Fee for Service	0	0	0	2	1
Managed Care Contracts					
Health Maintenance Organization	6	6	7	7	8
Preferred Provider Organization..............	5	4	6	6	8
Affiliations					
Hospitals in a System.....................	1	1	1	1	1
Hospitals in a Network.....................	5	5	5	5	5
Hospitals in a Group Purchasing Organization..	10	10	12	11	14

States

TABLE 6

VERMONT

U.S. Registered Community Hospitals
(Nonfederal, short-term general and other special hospitals)

Utilization, Personnel, Revenue and Expenses, Community Health Indicators 2006–2010

	2010	2009	2008	2007	2006
TOTAL FACILITY (Includes Hospital and Nursing Home Units)					
Utilization - Inpatient					
Beds	1,288	1,296	1,302	1,362	1,313
Admissions	49,449	50,922	51,301	49,892	50,402
Inpatient Days	305,289	321,741	328,506	337,004	327,850
Average Length of Stay	6.2	6.3	6.4	6.8	6.5
Inpatient Surgeries	13,950	15,557	14,160	14,224	13,883
Births	5,604	5,829	5,982	5,981	5,944
Utilization - Outpatient					
Emergency Outpatient Visits	352,808	357,793	304,717	259,661	260,429
Other Outpatient Visits	2,999,812	2,997,816	3,001,378	2,514,148	2,240,292
Total Outpatient Visits	3,352,620	3,355,609	3,306,095	2,773,809	2,500,721
Outpatient Surgeries	48,158	48,673	47,401	44,800	43,286
Personnel					
Full Time RNs	1,748	1,671	1,690	1,551	1,454
Full Time LPNs	166	163	218	214	223
Part Time RNs	1,311	1,262	1,239	1,211	1,286
Part Time LPNs	149	110	160	162	181
Total Full Time	9,629	9,738	9,611	9,373	8,781
Total Part Time	4,078	3,920	3,763	3,624	3,960
Revenue - Inpatient					
Gross Inpatient Revenue	$1,154,115,173	$1,055,165,310	$903,264,654	$906,951,930	$798,941,048
Revenue - Outpatient					
Gross Outpatient Revenue	$2,538,622,333	$2,313,816,425	$2,017,330,510	$1,784,747,426	$1,551,689,704
Revenue and Expenses - Totals					
(Includes Inpatient and Outpatient)					
Total Gross Revenue	$3,692,737,506	$3,368,981,735	$2,920,595,164	$2,691,699,356	$2,350,630,752
Deductions from Revenue	1,982,861,871	1,719,852,956	1,383,550,785	1,256,738,757	1,011,115,676
Net Patient Revenue	1,709,875,635	1,649,128,779	1,537,044,379	1,434,960,599	1,339,515,076
Other Operating Revenue	56,110,764	51,534,989	46,804,137	45,513,360	43,167,369
Other Nonoperating Revenue	35,893,255	-10,009,965	-27,559,443	38,665,452	61,745,217
Total Net Revenue	1,801,879,654	1,690,653,803	1,556,289,073	1,519,139,411	1,444,427,662
Total Expenses	1,714,899,646	1,660,403,783	1,558,572,905	1,451,986,474	1,332,522,993
HOSPITAL UNIT (Excludes Separate Nursing Home Units)					
Utilization - Inpatient					
Beds	1,080	1,118	1,061	1,106	1,053
Admissions	49,078	50,549	51,001	49,396	50,100
Inpatient Days	233,003	259,463	245,411	249,628	237,419
Average Length of Stay	4.7	5.1	4.8	5.1	4.7
Personnel					
Total Full Time	9,493	9,397	9,218	8,963	8,494
Total Part Time	3,963	3,708	3,538	3,409	3,791
Revenue and Expenses - Totals					
(Includes Inpatient and Outpatient)					
Total Net Revenue	$1,783,366,299	$1,669,557,556	$1,536,579,410	$1,494,392,921	$1,426,818,942
Total Expenses	1,697,709,912	1,635,099,616	1,540,919,362	1,434,525,067	1,315,948,812
COMMUNITY HEALTH INDICATORS PER 1000 POPULATION					
Total Population (in thousands)	622	622	621	620	620
Inpatient					
Beds	2.1	2.1	2.1	2.2	2.1
Admissions	79.4	81.9	82.6	80.4	81.3
Inpatient Days	490.5	517.5	529.0	543.2	528.8
Inpatient Surgeries	22.4	25.0	22.8	22.9	22.4
Births	9.0	9.4	9.6	9.6	9.6
Outpatient					
Emergency Outpatient Visits	566.8	575.5	490.6	418.5	420.1
Other Outpatient Visits	4,819.5	4,821.5	4,832.8	4,052.1	3,613.5
Total Outpatient Visits	5,386.3	5,397.0	5,323.4	4,470.6	4,033.5
Outpatient Surgeries	77.4	78.3	76.3	72.2	69.8
Expense per Capita (per person)	$2,755.2	$2,670.5	$2,509.6	$2,340.2	$2,149.3

States

TABLE 6

VIRGINIA

U.S. Registered Community Hospitals
(Nonfederal, short-term general and other special hospitals)

Overview 2006–2010

	2010	2009	2008	2007	2006
Total Community Hospitals in Virginia	89	90	90	87	88
Bed Size Category					
6-24	5	3	4	4	5
25-49	14	15	15	13	12
50-99	15	17	16	15	17
100-199	25	27	25	25	24
200-299	12	11	13	15	13
300-399	6	5	5	3	6
400-499	5	5	4	4	5
500 + ...	7	7	8	8	6
Location					
Hospitals Urban	59	60	60	57	53
Hospitals Rural	30	30	30	30	35
Control					
State and Local Government	4	4	4	4	4
Not for Profit	64	66	65	64	64
Investor owned	21	20	21	19	20
Physician Models					
Independent Practice Association	13	12	11	12	11
Group Practice without Walls	10	8	10	11	10
Open Physician-Hospital Organization	9	7	13	11	9
Closed Physician-Hospital Organization	2	1	1	2	2
Management Service Organization	18	15	10	9	7
Integrated Salary Model	51	40	39	37	30
Equity Model	8	7	7	7	7
Foundation	1	1	2	2	2
Insurance Products					
Health Maintenance Organization	15	13	17	19	21
Preferred Provider Organization	18	12	18	22	26
Indemnity Fee for Service	2	1	5	14	13
Managed Care Contracts					
Health Maintenance Organization	55	48	50	56	50
Preferred Provider Organization	59	54	56	60	56
Affiliations					
Hospitals in a System	70	69	60	55	57
Hospitals in a Network	44	37	38	45	38
Hospitals in a Group Purchasing Organization . .	70	57	60	63	61

States

TABLE **6**

VIRGINIA

U.S. Registered Community Hospitals
(Nonfederal, short-term general and other special hospitals)

Utilization, Personnel, Revenue and Expenses, Community Health Indicators 2006–2010

	2010	2009	2008	2007	2006
TOTAL FACILITY (Includes Hospital and Nursing Home Units)					
Utilization - Inpatient					
Beds	17,747	17,538	17,648	16,895	17,274
Admissions	776,678	793,145	795,578	787,319	778,680
Inpatient Days	4,310,430	4,375,451	4,452,740	4,354,340	4,416,114
Average Length of Stay	5.5	5.5	5.6	5.5	5.7
Inpatient Surgeries	223,354	234,981	235,678	229,376	233,922
Births	99,623	96,209	98,991	98,733	98,948
Utilization - Outpatient					
Emergency Outpatient Visits	3,256,956	3,199,466	3,091,131	3,040,762	3,060,052
Other Outpatient Visits	10,524,980	10,959,387	10,223,288	9,892,129	10,592,692
Total Outpatient Visits	13,781,936	14,158,853	13,314,419	12,932,891	13,652,744
Outpatient Surgeries	439,146	448,650	463,342	463,212	473,915
Personnel					
Full Time RNs	24,035	23,711	23,382	22,863	21,187
Full Time LPNs	2,226	2,231	2,460	2,445	2,645
Part Time RNs	11,030	10,025	10,075	9,823	9,948
Part Time LPNs	703	684	861	777	793
Total Full Time	82,310	82,332	83,178	80,744	78,169
Total Part Time	30,091	28,083	28,749	27,126	26,965
Revenue - Inpatient					
Gross Inpatient Revenue	$24,373,894,322	$22,941,847,825	$22,555,481,294	$21,113,593,014	$19,234,761,450
Revenue - Outpatient					
Gross Outpatient Revenue	$21,205,056,723	$18,818,269,487	$17,042,951,627	$15,015,219,220	$13,231,876,352
Revenue and Expenses - Totals					
(Includes Inpatient and Outpatient)					
Total Gross Revenue	$45,578,951,045	$41,760,117,312	$39,598,432,921	$36,128,812,234	$32,466,637,802
Deductions from Revenue	30,139,978,214	26,616,556,088	25,464,931,182	23,062,020,224	20,174,935,834
Net Patient Revenue	15,438,972,831	15,143,561,224	14,133,501,739	13,066,792,010	12,291,701,968
Other Operating Revenue	425,128,846	422,020,787	404,136,415	356,732,830	379,912,278
Other Nonoperating Revenue	253,492,718	10,537,285	-269,241,513	393,479,251	245,713,096
Total Net Revenue	16,117,594,395	15,576,119,296	14,268,396,641	13,817,004,091	12,917,327,342
Total Expenses	14,709,796,266	14,456,123,508	13,800,772,246	12,626,089,380	11,554,705,543
HOSPITAL UNIT (Excludes Separate Nursing Home Units)					
Utilization - Inpatient					
Beds	16,163	16,422	16,478	16,097	16,411
Admissions	770,195	788,427	790,203	782,324	775,367
Inpatient Days	3,775,706	3,995,348	4,052,958	3,977,976	4,129,270
Average Length of Stay	4.9	5.1	5.1	5.1	5.3
Personnel					
Total Full Time	81,441	81,316	82,241	79,956	77,634
Total Part Time	29,637	27,710	28,385	26,940	26,744
Revenue and Expenses - Totals					
(Includes Inpatient and Outpatient)					
Total Net Revenue	$15,986,427,239	$15,479,330,448	$14,180,093,186	$13,715,806,678	$12,814,301,298
Total Expenses	14,592,391,811	14,367,593,188	13,713,829,141	12,526,340,640	11,498,207,599
COMMUNITY HEALTH INDICATORS PER 1000 POPULATION					
Total Population (in thousands)	7,952	7,883	7,795	7,720	7,647
Inpatient					
Beds	2.2	2.2	2.3	2.2	2.3
Admissions	97.7	100.6	102.1	102.0	101.8
Inpatient Days	542.0	555.1	571.2	564.1	577.5
Inpatient Surgeries	28.1	29.8	30.2	29.7	30.6
Births	12.5	12.2	12.7	12.8	12.9
Outpatient					
Emergency Outpatient Visits	409.6	405.9	396.5	393.9	400.2
Other Outpatient Visits	1,323.5	1,390.3	1,311.4	1,281.4	1,385.2
Total Outpatient Visits	1,733.1	1,796.2	1,708.0	1,675.3	1,785.4
Outpatient Surgeries	55.2	56.9	59.4	60.0	62.0
Expense per Capita (per person)	$1,849.8	$1,833.9	$1,770.4	$1,635.6	$1,511.0

States

TABLE 6

WASHINGTON

U.S. Registered Community Hospitals
(Nonfederal, short-term general and other special hospitals)

Overview 2006–2010

	2010	2009	2008	2007	2006
Total Community Hospitals in Washington	86	87	86	87	88
Bed Size Category					
6-24	7	7	4	5	8
25-49	29	30	31	30	30
50-99	10	11	12	14	13
100-199	16	16	14	15	17
200-299	13	13	15	13	10
300-399	6	5	8	7	8
400-499	3	3	0	1	0
500 + ...	2	2	2	2	2
Location					
Hospitals Urban..........................	53	53	51	53	47
Hospitals Rural	33	34	35	34	41
Control					
State and Local Government................	39	41	42	41	41
Not for Profit............................	42	41	40	41	42
Investor owned	5	5	4	5	5
Physician Models					
Independent Practice Association	2	2	2	4	7
Group Practice without Walls................	4	4	2	1	1
Open Physician-Hospital Organization	5	4	5	5	5
Closed Physician-Hospital Organization	0	0	0	2	2
Management Service Organization	6	6	3	4	4
Integrated Salary Model....................	39	42	34	35	35
Equity Model............................	4	4	0	0	0
Foundation..............................	5	7	7	1	1
Insurance Products					
Health Maintenance Organization	4	5	4	4	4
Preferred Provider Organization..............	11	12	12	11	8
Indemnity Fee for Service	0	1	1	1	0
Managed Care Contracts					
Health Maintenance Organization	34	36	33	33	31
Preferred Provider Organization..............	38	44	37	38	38
Affiliations					
Hospitals in a System......................	35	32	31	31	40
Hospitals in a Network.....................	19	19	19	16	15
Hospitals in a Group Purchasing Organization..	48	60	47	60	54

TABLE **6**

WASHINGTON

U.S. Registered Community Hospitals
(Nonfederal, short-term general and other special hospitals)

Utilization, Personnel, Revenue and Expenses, Community Health Indicators 2006–2010

	2010	2009	2008	2007	2006
TOTAL FACILITY (Includes Hospital and Nursing Home Units)					
Utilization - Inpatient					
Beds	11,537	11,322	11,348	11,315	10,927
Admissions	588,855	588,889	578,856	574,169	556,700
Inpatient Days	2,638,779	2,660,901	2,663,704	2,577,795	2,486,577
Average Length of Stay	4.5	4.5	4.6	4.5	4.5
Inpatient Surgeries	170,895	185,833	184,234	176,445	161,357
Births	78,216	80,667	82,557	80,698	78,272
Utilization - Outpatient					
Emergency Outpatient Visits	2,290,953	2,509,243	2,385,734	2,343,863	2,147,309
Other Outpatient Visits	9,515,677	8,996,667	8,992,320	8,851,818	8,236,855
Total Outpatient Visits	11,806,630	11,505,910	11,378,054	11,195,681	10,384,164
Outpatient Surgeries	261,997	266,107	263,762	246,380	249,520
Personnel					
Full Time RNs	16,109	15,789	13,202	12,647	12,488
Full Time LPNs	825	870	805	821	954
Part Time RNs	13,848	13,205	13,466	12,633	11,236
Part Time LPNs	616	665	696	688	664
Total Full Time	68,163	64,767	59,789	57,267	58,233
Total Part Time	39,185	36,879	40,524	36,824	33,984
Revenue - Inpatient					
Gross Inpatient Revenue	$21,516,174,379	$19,988,875,344	$17,882,046,988	$15,526,030,849	$13,933,139,987
Revenue - Outpatient					
Gross Outpatient Revenue	$18,594,056,137	$16,200,972,533	$13,659,739,047	$12,099,431,805	$10,552,552,309
Revenue and Expenses - Totals **(Includes Inpatient and Outpatient)**					
Total Gross Revenue	$40,110,230,516	$36,189,847,877	$31,541,786,035	$27,625,462,654	$24,485,692,296
Deductions from Revenue	25,534,351,330	22,273,010,097	19,034,411,541	16,338,477,005	14,099,862,736
Net Patient Revenue	14,575,879,186	13,916,837,780	12,507,374,494	11,286,985,649	10,385,829,560
Other Operating Revenue	804,026,112	755,280,721	664,009,322	632,362,196	515,593,853
Other Nonoperating Revenue	226,341,197	188,342,686	-98,368,171	287,788,340	192,566,803
Total Net Revenue	15,606,246,495	14,860,461,187	13,073,015,645	12,207,136,185	11,093,990,216
Total Expenses	14,641,932,019	13,773,406,044	12,327,733,007	11,274,708,380	10,650,112,282
HOSPITAL UNIT (Excludes Separate Nursing Home Units)					
Utilization - Inpatient					
Beds	11,382	10,974	10,959	10,910	10,679
Admissions	587,786	587,527	576,765	572,112	554,676
Inpatient Days	2,589,013	2,549,787	2,539,914	2,465,659	2,401,977
Average Length of Stay	4.4	4.3	4.4	4.3	4.3
Personnel					
Total Full Time	68,113	64,470	59,483	56,827	57,925
Total Part Time	39,097	36,649	40,227	36,505	33,837
Revenue and Expenses - Totals **(Includes Inpatient and Outpatient)**					
Total Net Revenue	$15,586,259,128	$14,821,016,445	$13,032,710,190	$12,160,885,656	$11,062,106,616
Total Expenses	14,623,738,440	13,737,554,929	12,289,499,219	11,234,767,829	10,623,552,352
COMMUNITY HEALTH INDICATORS PER 1000 POPULATION					
Total Population (in thousands)	6,746	6,664	6,566	6,465	6,372
Inpatient					
Beds	1.7	1.7	1.7	1.8	1.7
Admissions	87.3	88.4	88.2	88.8	87.4
Inpatient Days	391.2	399.3	405.7	398.7	390.2
Inpatient Surgeries	25.3	27.9	28.1	27.3	25.3
Births	11.6	12.1	12.6	12.5	12.3
Outpatient					
Emergency Outpatient Visits	339.6	376.5	363.3	362.5	337.0
Other Outpatient Visits	1,410.5	1,350.0	1,369.5	1,369.2	1,292.6
Total Outpatient Visits	1,750.1	1,726.5	1,732.9	1,731.7	1,629.6
Outpatient Surgeries	38.8	39.9	40.2	38.1	39.2
Expense per Capita (per person)	$2,170.4	$2,066.8	$1,877.5	$1,744.0	$1,671.3

States

TABLE 6

WEST VIRGINIA

U.S. Registered Community Hospitals
(Nonfederal, short-term general and other special hospitals)

Overview 2006–2010

	2010	2009	2008	2007	2006
Total Community Hospitals in West Virginia . . .	56	56	56	56	56
Bed Size Category					
6-24	3	3	3	3	3
25-49	14	14	13	13	14
50-99	13	13	14	14	14
100-199	14	14	14	14	13
200-299	9	8	8	7	8
300-399	1	2	2	3	2
400-499	0	0	0	1	1
500 + ...	2	2	2	1	1
Location					
Hospitals Urban.	27	27	27	27	19
Hospitals Rural	29	29	29	29	37
Control					
State and Local Government.	8	10	10	10	10
Not for Profit	34	32	32	31	31
Investor owned	14	14	14	15	15
Physician Models					
Independent Practice Association	3	4	4	6	6
Group Practice without Walls.	0	0	0	2	2
Open Physician-Hospital Organization	13	14	14	14	15
Closed Physician-Hospital Organization	3	3	3	2	1
Management Service Organization	2	3	5	5	4
Integrated Salary Model.	25	25	25	25	28
Equity Model	0	0	0	1	1
Foundation.	0	0	0	0	0
Insurance Products					
Health Maintenance Organization	6	5	3	5	6
Preferred Provider Organization.	10	9	7	9	9
Indemnity Fee for Service	3	2	2	4	3
Managed Care Contracts					
Health Maintenance Organization	31	31	27	27	25
Preferred Provider Organization.	42	42	38	38	37
Affiliations					
Hospitals in a System.	29	25	23	23	24
Hospitals in a Network	21	22	20	23	24
Hospitals in a Group Purchasing Organization. .	53	53	52	52	52

States

TABLE 6

WEST VIRGINIA

U.S. Registered Community Hospitals
(Nonfederal, short-term general and other special hospitals)

Utilization, Personnel, Revenue and Expenses, Community Health Indicators 2006–2010

	2010	2009	2008	2007	2006
TOTAL FACILITY (Includes Hospital and Nursing Home Units)					
Utilization - Inpatient					
Beds	7,298	7,408	7,470	7,436	7,197
Admissions	278,221	280,252	283,673	286,892	281,766
Inpatient Days	1,612,811	1,648,197	1,665,076	1,656,614	1,592,271
Average Length of Stay	5.8	5.9	5.9	5.8	5.7
Inpatient Surgeries	83,992	80,776	79,916	77,775	77,881
Births	20,487	21,010	20,856	21,296	21,137
Utilization - Outpatient					
Emergency Outpatient Visits	1,207,918	1,221,485	1,183,158	1,171,507	1,137,535
Other Outpatient Visits	5,446,482	5,463,158	5,431,951	5,283,575	5,074,611
Total Outpatient Visits	6,654,400	6,684,643	6,615,109	6,455,082	6,212,146
Outpatient Surgeries	212,434	215,853	212,489	207,785	213,317
Personnel					
Full Time RNs	8,532	8,282	8,084	7,949	7,271
Full Time LPNs	1,217	1,298	1,387	1,416	1,422
Part Time RNs	3,395	3,447	3,392	3,460	3,287
Part Time LPNs	419	403	435	392	481
Total Full Time	33,349	32,751	32,463	31,879	30,778
Total Part Time	10,143	10,082	10,244	10,145	10,013
Revenue - Inpatient					
Gross Inpatient Revenue	$5,597,580,327	$5,174,519,813	$4,927,056,831	$4,544,128,430	$4,197,327,290
Revenue - Outpatient					
Gross Outpatient Revenue	$5,444,045,714	$5,161,162,251	$4,531,051,911	$4,100,750,655	$3,747,433,060
Revenue and Expenses - Totals					
(Includes Inpatient and Outpatient)					
Total Gross Revenue	$11,041,626,041	$10,335,682,064	$9,458,108,742	$8,644,879,085	$7,944,760,350
Deductions from Revenue	6,386,501,669	5,787,332,486	5,198,077,289	4,577,611,437	4,125,056,133
Net Patient Revenue	4,655,124,372	4,548,349,578	4,260,031,453	4,067,267,648	3,819,704,217
Other Operating Revenue	126,269,003	168,034,621	71,741,101	125,951,483	126,071,335
Other Nonoperating Revenue	63,579,778	54,115,339	-125,408,354	100,086,468	61,758,746
Total Net Revenue	4,844,973,153	4,770,499,538	4,206,364,200	4,293,305,599	4,007,534,298
Total Expenses	4,689,352,987	4,584,221,488	4,289,258,433	4,018,748,717	3,814,590,273
HOSPITAL UNIT (Excludes Separate Nursing Home Units)					
Utilization - Inpatient					
Beds	6,454	6,575	6,587	6,553	6,439
Admissions	272,471	274,341	277,157	280,751	275,550
Inpatient Days	1,340,666	1,371,913	1,381,747	1,375,020	1,350,098
Average Length of Stay	4.9	5.0	5.0	4.9	4.9
Personnel					
Total Full Time	32,752	32,152	31,838	31,203	30,217
Total Part Time	9,781	9,787	9,825	9,763	9,640
Revenue and Expenses - Totals					
(Includes Inpatient and Outpatient)					
Total Net Revenue	$4,774,505,282	$4,700,079,381	$4,123,228,602	$4,225,397,482	$3,947,204,453
Total Expenses	4,637,567,799	4,529,683,828	4,229,627,238	3,964,906,237	3,769,187,062
COMMUNITY HEALTH INDICATORS PER 1000 POPULATION					
Total Population (in thousands)	1,826	1,820	1,815	1,811	1,807
Inpatient					
Beds	4.0	4.1	4.1	4.1	4.0
Admissions	152.4	154.0	156.3	158.4	155.9
Inpatient Days	883.5	905.7	917.5	914.7	881.1
Inpatient Surgeries	46.0	44.4	44.0	42.9	43.1
Births	11.2	11.5	11.5	11.8	11.7
Outpatient					
Emergency Outpatient Visits	661.7	671.2	651.9	646.8	629.4
Other Outpatient Visits	2,983.5	3,002.1	2,993.0	2,917.2	2,807.9
Total Outpatient Visits	3,645.2	3,673.3	3,644.9	3,564.0	3,437.4
Outpatient Surgeries	116.4	118.6	117.1	114.7	118.0
Expense per Capita (per person)	$2,568.8	$2,519.1	$2,363.4	$2,218.8	$2,110.7

TABLE 6   WISCONSIN

U.S. Registered Community Hospitals
(Nonfederal, short-term general and other special hospitals)

Overview 2006–2010

	2010	2009	2008	2007	2006
Total Community Hospitals in Wisconsin......	**124**	**126**	**126**	**124**	**124**
Bed Size Category					
6-24	13	12	12	12	11
25-49	37	37	36	33	31
50-99	31	32	32	27	27
100-199	21	25	24	33	37
200-299	13	11	13	10	10
300-399	5	6	6	6	5
400-499	2	2	2	2	2
500 + ...	2	1	1	1	1
Location					
Hospitals Urban...........................	68	69	69	68	60
Hospitals Rural	56	57	57	56	64
Control					
State and Local Government................	2	2	2	2	2
Not for Profit	117	118	119	117	118
Investor owned	5	6	5	5	4
Physician Models					
Independent Practice Association	9	13	13	10	11
Group Practice without Walls................	3	3	2	1	1
Open Physician-Hospital Organization	4	3	3	6	4
Closed Physician-Hospital Organization	4	2	3	4	4
Management Service Organization	2	3	2	1	1
Integrated Salary Model....................	38	34	32	30	30
Equity Model.............................	9	12	17	3	5
Foundation...............................	2	2	2	2	2
Insurance Products					
Health Maintenance Organization	20	23	23	25	23
Preferred Provider Organization..............	31	35	36	38	25
Indemnity Fee for Service	15	16	15	16	9
Managed Care Contracts					
Health Maintenance Organization	116	116	116	83	111
Preferred Provider Organization..............	118	118	120	86	114
Affiliations					
Hospitals in a System.....................	72	74	72	70	70
Hospitals in a Network....................	37	36	39	31	42
Hospitals in a Group Purchasing Organization..	118	116	118	86	117

States

TABLE 6

WISCONSIN

U.S. Registered Community Hospitals
(Nonfederal, short-term general and other special hospitals)

Utilization, Personnel, Revenue and Expenses, Community Health Indicators 2006–2010

	2010	2009	2008	2007	2006
TOTAL FACILITY (Includes Hospital and Nursing Home Units)					
Utilization - Inpatient					
Beds	13,520	13,637	13,707	13,981	14,123
Admissions	588,592	609,329	617,295	613,356	609,108
Inpatient Days	2,966,909	3,125,349	3,172,566	3,168,542	3,210,210
Average Length of Stay	5.0	5.1	5.1	5.2	5.3
Inpatient Surgeries	228,469	256,942	233,044	239,199	195,968
Births	67,843	70,129	69,465	70,500	68,461
Utilization - Outpatient					
Emergency Outpatient Visits	2,160,341	2,080,601	2,066,654	2,106,402	2,091,172
Other Outpatient Visits	12,444,617	12,847,067	12,136,773	10,966,003	10,420,878
Total Outpatient Visits	14,604,958	14,927,668	14,203,427	13,072,405	12,512,050
Outpatient Surgeries	522,864	535,955	491,040	497,452	449,460
Personnel					
Full Time RNs	14,476	14,345	14,522	13,480	12,971
Full Time LPNs	673	711	707	711	689
Part Time RNs	15,552	16,139	15,398	15,499	15,682
Part Time LPNs	794	908	927	1,028	1,094
Total Full Time	63,254	63,168	63,883	61,173	58,923
Total Part Time	48,472	51,235	47,517	47,796	49,217
Revenue - Inpatient					
Gross Inpatient Revenue	$15,357,857,584	$15,634,706,846	$13,612,135,956	$12,925,578,410	$11,855,822,996
Revenue - Outpatient					
Gross Outpatient Revenue	$16,468,660,136	$14,805,407,754	$13,162,259,140	$11,746,652,525	$10,739,176,109
Revenue and Expenses - Totals					
(Includes Inpatient and Outpatient)					
Total Gross Revenue	$31,826,517,720	$30,440,114,600	$26,774,395,096	$24,672,230,935	$22,594,999,105
Deductions from Revenue	16,996,231,064	16,618,465,592	13,709,265,312	12,424,903,890	11,063,269,437
Net Patient Revenue	14,830,286,656	13,821,649,008	13,065,129,784	12,247,327,045	11,531,729,668
Other Operating Revenue	630,341,533	716,584,248	643,332,317	473,238,179	438,517,748
Other Nonoperating Revenue	285,539,514	-26,443,242	-30,738,485	294,160,363	227,736,515
Total Net Revenue	15,746,167,703	14,511,790,014	13,677,723,616	13,014,725,587	12,197,983,931
Total Expenses	14,230,620,575	13,496,778,176	12,923,890,000	11,916,247,096	11,210,657,463
HOSPITAL UNIT (Excludes Separate Nursing Home Units)					
Utilization - Inpatient					
Beds	12,092	12,049	12,067	12,337	12,196
Admissions	586,022	606,542	614,395	610,759	606,030
Inpatient Days	2,511,474	2,597,929	2,629,527	2,622,596	2,565,274
Average Length of Stay	4.3	4.3	4.3	4.3	4.2
Personnel					
Total Full Time	62,460	62,376	63,068	60,418	58,161
Total Part Time	47,543	50,255	46,533	46,827	48,062
Revenue and Expenses - Totals					
(Includes Inpatient and Outpatient)					
Total Net Revenue	$15,640,069,501	$14,399,372,197	$13,576,550,948	$12,892,939,703	$12,114,061,349
Total Expenses	14,124,128,291	13,393,867,097	12,830,682,268	11,827,708,589	11,125,842,547
COMMUNITY HEALTH INDICATORS PER 1000 POPULATION					
Total Population (in thousands)	5,669	5,655	5,628	5,602	5,572
Inpatient					
Beds	2.4	2.4	2.4	2.5	2.5
Admissions	103.8	107.8	109.7	109.5	109.3
Inpatient Days	523.4	552.7	563.8	565.7	576.2
Inpatient Surgeries	40.3	45.4	41.4	42.7	35.2
Births	12.0	12.4	12.3	12.6	12.3
Outpatient					
Emergency Outpatient Visits	381.1	367.9	367.2	376.0	375.3
Other Outpatient Visits	2,195.4	2,271.9	2,156.6	1,957.7	1,870.3
Total Outpatient Visits	2,576.5	2,639.8	2,523.9	2,333.7	2,245.7
Outpatient Surgeries	92.2	94.8	87.3	88.8	80.7
Expense per Capita (per person)	$2,510.5	$2,386.8	$2,296.5	$2,127.3	$2,012.1

States

TABLE 6

WYOMING

U.S. Registered Community Hospitals
(Nonfederal, short-term general and other special hospitals)

Overview 2006–2010

	2010	2009	2008	2007	2006
Total Community Hospitals in Wyoming.......	24	24	24	24	24
Bed Size Category					
6-24	0	0	0	0	0
25-49	11	11	10	10	10
50-99	6	6	7	7	7
100-199	4	4	4	4	4
200-299	3	3	3	3	3
300-399	0	0	0	0	0
400-499	0	0	0	0	0
500 + ...	0	0	0	0	0
Location					
Hospitals Urban...........................	2	2	2	2	2
Hospitals Rural	22	22	22	22	22
Control					
State and Local Government................	16	16	16	16	17
Not for Profit	5	5	5	5	4
Investor owned	3	3	3	3	3
Physician Models					
Independent Practice Association	2	3	3	3	3
Group Practice without Walls................	0	0	0	0	0
Open Physician-Hospital Organization	1	1	1	1	1
Closed Physician-Hospital Organization	1	1	1	1	1
Management Service Organization	2	2	1	1	1
Integrated Salary Model....................	10	11	11	11	11
Equity Model.............................	0	0	0	0	0
Foundation...............................	0	0	0	0	0
Insurance Products					
Health Maintenance Organization	1	1	1	1	1
Preferred Provider Organization..............	3	1	1	5	5
Indemnity Fee for Service	0	0	0	0	0
Managed Care Contracts					
Health Maintenance Organization	3	4	4	4	3
Preferred Provider Organization..............	14	14	14	12	11
Affiliations					
Hospitals in a System......................	12	12	11	12	12
Hospitals in a Network.....................	4	5	5	4	4
Hospitals in a Group Purchasing Organization..	21	21	23	23	23

States

TABLE 6

WYOMING

U.S. Registered Community Hospitals
(Nonfederal, short-term general and other special hospitals)

Utilization, Personnel, Revenue and Expenses, Community Health Indicators 2006–2010

	2010	2009	2008	2007	2006
TOTAL FACILITY (Includes Hospital and Nursing Home Units)					
Utilization - Inpatient					
Beds	1,958	2,002	2,073	2,071	2,056
Admissions	49,704	52,232	52,628	53,077	52,586
Inpatient Days	398,850	411,717	414,463	422,883	421,089
Average Length of Stay.	8.0	7.9	7.9	8.0	8.0
Inpatient Surgeries.	14,159	13,801	14,162	14,556	14,128
Births.	6,920	7,305	7,303	7,247	6,824
Utilization - Outpatient					
Emergency Outpatient Visits.	231,261	236,213	234,384	227,386	221,300
Other Outpatient Visits.	866,984	823,944	774,610	729,327	742,540
Total Outpatient Visits	1,098,245	1,060,157	1,008,994	956,713	963,840
Outpatient Surgeries	29,260	26,180	25,183	24,122	25,302
Personnel					
Full Time RNs	1,680	1,561	1,664	1,603	1,586
Full Time LPNs	117	127	130	137	160
Part Time RNs.	455	526	504	600	457
Part Time LPNs	54	76	57	69	57
Total Full Time.	7,338	7,094	7,291	6,670	6,849
Total Part Time	2,005	2,310	1,892	2,319	1,989
Revenue - Inpatient					
Gross Inpatient Revenue.	$1,072,618,270	$967,170,829	$951,929,394	$878,681,901	$803,694,086
Revenue - Outpatient					
Gross Outpatient Revenue	$1,103,760,780	$946,462,599	$801,309,584	$704,732,660	$620,933,569
Revenue and Expenses - Totals					
(Includes Inpatient and Outpatient)					
Total Gross Revenue.	$2,176,379,050	$1,913,633,428	$1,753,238,978	$1,583,414,561	$1,424,627,655
Deductions from Revenue.	1,096,026,956	955,291,698	802,095,376	696,730,106	606,943,644
Net Patient Revenue	1,080,352,094	958,341,730	951,143,602	886,684,455	817,684,011
Other Operating Revenue	74,157,196	66,460,224	55,280,832	49,220,506	46,089,909
Other Nonoperating Revenue	19,130,354	-798,016	21,606,525	63,859,758	21,704,253
Total Net Revenue.	1,173,639,644	1,024,003,938	1,028,030,959	999,764,719	885,478,173
Total Expenses.	1,031,425,657	980,632,479	949,368,614	848,863,457	813,447,569
HOSPITAL UNIT (Excludes Separate Nursing Home Units)					
Utilization - Inpatient					
Beds	1,303	1,303	1,335	1,323	1,308
Admissions	48,206	50,673	51,146	51,592	51,024
Inpatient Days	196,510	188,014	183,585	184,014	180,631
Average Length of Stay.	4.1	3.7	3.6	3.6	3.5
Personnel					
Total Full Time.	6,925	6,618	6,767	6,141	6,291
Total Part Time	1,841	2,117	1,696	2,092	1,796
Revenue and Expenses - Totals					
(Includes Inpatient and Outpatient)					
Total Net Revenue.	$1,133,360,264	$984,238,688	$988,170,246	$959,741,678	$845,556,939
Total Expenses.	991,627,019	938,219,346	907,237,150	810,848,202	775,077,404
COMMUNITY HEALTH INDICATORS PER 1000 POPULATION					
Total Population (in thousands)	548	544	533	523	513
Inpatient					
Beds	3.6	3.7	3.9	4.0	4.0
Admissions	90.8	96.0	98.7	101.4	102.5
Inpatient Days	728.3	756.5	777.6	807.9	821.1
Inpatient Surgeries.	25.9	25.4	26.6	27.8	27.5
Births.	12.6	13.4	13.7	13.8	13.3
Outpatient					
Emergency Outpatient Visits.	422.3	434.0	439.8	434.4	431.5
Other Outpatient Visits.	1,583.1	1,513.9	1,453.4	1,393.4	1,447.9
Total Outpatient Visits	2,005.4	1,947.9	1,893.1	1,827.8	1,879.4
Outpatient Surgeries	53.4	48.1	47.2	46.1	49.3
Expense per Capita (per person).	$1,883.4	$1,801.7	$1,781.2	$1,621.8	$1,586.2

Table 7

The facilities and services presented in Table 7 are listed below in alphabetical order by major heading (where applicable).

2010 Facilities and Services in the U.S. Census Divisions and States

Table 7

These data include only hospital-based facilities and services as reported by responding hospitals in Section C of the 2010 AHA Annual Survey, beginning on page 215. All hospitals are represented with Community Hospitals listed separately under United States. No estimates have been made for nonresponding hospitals. Definitions of facilities and services are listed in the Glossary, page 201.

CLASSIFICATION	HOSPITALS REPORTING	ADULT DAY CARE PROGRAM Number	Percent	AIRBORNE INFECTION ISOLATION ROOM Number	Percent	ALCOHOL/DRUG ABUSE OR DEPENDENCY INPATIENT CARE UNITS Number	Percent	ALCOHOL/DRUG ABUSE OR DEPENDENCY OUTPATIENT SERVICES Number	Percent	ALZHEIMER CENTER Number	Percent	AMBULANCE SERVICE Number	Percent	AMBULATORY SURGERY CENTER Number	Percent	ARTHRITIS TREATMENT CENTER Number	Percent	ASSISTED LIVING Number	Percent
UNITED STATES	4,782	235	4.9	3,481	72.8	463	9.7	712	14.9	195	4.1	754	15.8	1,171	24.5	272	5.7	205	4.3
COMMUNITY HOSPITALS	4,079	199	4.9	3,187	78.1	310	7.6	543	13.3	173	4.2	725	17.8	1,108	27.2	258	6.3	186	4.6
CENSUS DIVISION 1, NEW ENGLAND	198	14	7.1	151	76.3	21	10.6	58	29.3	15	7.6	29	14.6	75	37.9	17	8.6	10	5.1
Connecticut	32	3	9.4	26	81.3	7	21.9	13	40.6	3	9.4	4	12.5	19	59.4	4	12.5	2	6.3
Maine	40	2	5.0	29	72.5	6	15.0	14	35.0	4	10.0	8	20.0	12	30.0	0	0.0	3	7.5
Massachusetts	74	3	4.1	53	71.6	5	6.8	23	31.1	5	6.8	9	12.2	24	32.4	9	12.2	1	1.4
New Hampshire	28	5	17.9	25	89.3	0	0.0	2	7.1	1	3.6	6	21.4	7	25.0	2	7.1	2	7.1
Rhode Island	12	0	0.0	8	66.7	2	16.7	4	33.3	1	8.3	1	8.3	7	58.3	0	0.0	1	8.3
Vermont	12	1	8.3	10	83.3	1	8.3	2	16.7	1	8.3	1	8.3	6	50.0	2	16.7	1	8.3
CENSUS DIVISION 2, MIDDLE ATLANTIC	414	34	8.2	310	74.9	76	18.4	111	26.8	30	7.2	76	18.4	175	42.3	57	13.8	14	3.4
New Jersey	73	8	11.0	54	74.0	11	15.1	23	31.5	6	8.2	19	26.0	18	24.7	8	11.0	3	4.1
New York	168	20	11.9	124	73.8	49	29.2	65	38.7	11	6.5	31	18.5	104	61.9	30	17.9	3	1.8
Pennsylvania	173	6	3.5	132	76.3	16	9.2	23	13.3	13	7.5	26	15.0	53	30.6	19	11.0	8	4.6
CENSUS DIVISION 3, SOUTH ATLANTIC	715	26	3.6	542	75.8	75	10.5	112	15.7	31	4.3	102	14.3	167	23.4	40	5.6	24	3.4
Delaware	11	2	18.2	6	54.5	2	18.2	3	27.3	1	9.1	3	27.3	5	45.5	0	0.0	0	0.0
District of Columbia	12	0	0.0	9	75.0	2	16.7	5	41.7	2	16.7	2	16.7	3	25.0	2	16.7	1	8.3
Florida	160	5	3.1	119	74.4	14	8.8	13	8.1	8	5.0	14	8.8	41	25.6	5	3.1	4	2.5
Georgia	128	3	2.3	93	72.7	12	9.4	16	12.5	5	3.9	24	18.8	27	21.1	4	3.1	7	5.5
Maryland	58	4	6.9	46	79.3	7	12.1	21	36.2	3	5.2	5	8.6	18	31.0	7	12.1	5	8.6
North Carolina	115	4	3.5	92	80.0	13	11.3	17	14.8	5	4.3	24	20.9	33	28.7	7	6.1	3	2.6
South Carolina	79	2	2.5	59	74.7	15	19.0	11	13.9	3	3.8	12	15.2	9	11.4	3	3.8	0	0.0
Virginia	89	5	5.6	72	80.9	8	9.0	19	21.3	4	4.5	12	13.5	25	28.1	8	9.0	4	4.5
West Virginia	63	1	1.6	46	73.0	2	3.2	7	11.1	0	0.0	6	9.5	6	9.5	4	6.3	0	0.0
CENSUS DIVISION 4, EAST NORTH CENTRAL	721	46	6.4	555	77.0	99	13.7	161	22.3	53	7.4	120	16.6	203	28.2	66	9.2	33	4.6
Illinois	173	17	9.8	144	83.2	18	10.4	42	24.3	9	5.2	25	14.5	41	23.7	17	9.8	2	1.2
Indiana	108	3	2.8	82	75.9	14	13.0	20	18.5	1	0.9	31	28.7	37	34.3	4	3.7	4	3.7
Michigan	147	6	4.1	120	81.6	15	10.2	30	20.4	6	4.1	22	15.0	35	23.8	12	8.2	8	5.4
Ohio	152	9	5.9	126	82.9	15	9.9	32	21.1	11	7.2	25	16.4	57	37.5	15	9.9	7	4.6
Wisconsin	141	11	7.8	83	58.9	37	26.2	37	26.2	26	18.4	17	12.1	33	23.4	18	12.8	12	8.5
CENSUS DIVISION 5, EAST SOUTH CENTRAL	419	11	2.6	257	61.3	40	9.5	35	8.4	6	1.4	51	12.2	65	15.5	7	1.7	7	1.7
Alabama	120	3	2.5	73	60.8	10	8.3	7	5.8	3	2.5	10	8.3	22	18.3	2	1.7	3	2.5
Kentucky	98	5	5.1	78	79.6	7	7.1	11	11.2	2	2.0	13	13.3	17	17.3	3	3.1	2	2.0
Mississippi	110	0	0.0	34	30.9	16	14.5	7	6.4	0	0.0	13	11.8	9	8.2	0	0.0	0	0.0
Tennessee	91	3	3.3	72	79.1	7	7.7	10	11.0	1	1.1	15	16.5	17	18.7	2	2.2	2	2.2
CENSUS DIVISION 6, WEST NORTH CENTRAL	649	39	6.0	443	68.3	50	7.7	73	11.2	22	3.4	166	25.6	110	16.9	29	4.5	61	9.4
Iowa	125	3	2.4	73	58.4	12	9.6	17	13.6	3	2.4	56	44.8	22	17.6	3	2.4	10	8.0
Kansas	153	11	7.2	100	65.4	4	2.6	5	3.3	2	1.3	23	15.0	12	7.8	2	1.3	12	7.8
Minnesota	102	15	14.7	77	75.5	7	6.9	17	16.7	6	5.9	35	34.3	27	26.5	7	6.9	15	14.7
Missouri	149	1	0.7	112	75.2	21	14.1	21	14.1	6	4.0	28	18.8	22	14.8	12	8.1	2	1.3
Nebraska	52	3	5.8	37	71.2	3	5.8	6	11.5	3	5.8	8	15.4	10	19.2	1	1.9	6	11.5
North Dakota	24	2	8.3	18	75.0	2	8.3	2	8.3	0	0.0	7	29.2	8	33.3	3	12.5	2	8.3
South Dakota	44	4	9.1	26	59.1	1	2.3	5	11.4	2	4.5	9	20.5	9	20.5	1	2.3	14	31.8
CENSUS DIVISION 7, WEST SOUTH CENTRAL	883	15	1.7	651	73.7	43	4.9	59	6.7	6	0.7	101	11.4	137	15.5	21	2.4	22	2.5
Arkansas	91	4	4.4	67	73.6	4	4.4	4	4.4	1	1.1	12	13.2	17	18.7	3	3.3	1	1.1
Louisiana	102	5	4.9	67	65.7	3	2.9	5	4.9	1	1.0	10	9.8	22	21.6	6	5.9	4	3.9
Oklahoma	123	1	0.8	87	70.7	3	2.4	6	4.9	1	0.8	12	9.8	25	20.3	2	1.6	3	2.4
Texas	567	5	0.9	430	75.8	33	5.8	44	7.8	3	0.5	67	11.8	73	12.9	10	1.8	14	2.5
CENSUS DIVISION 8, MOUNTAIN	335	25	7.5	240	71.6	25	7.5	38	11.3	14	4.2	65	19.4	93	27.8	11	3.3	22	6.6
Arizona	59	0	0.0	45	76.3	3	5.1	8	13.6	2	3.4	3	5.1	18	30.5	1	1.7	1	1.7
Colorado	71	3	4.2	53	74.6	7	9.9	8	11.3	2	2.8	15	21.1	19	26.8	3	4.2	4	5.6
Idaho	30	7	23.3	25	83.3	2	6.7	4	13.3	0	0.0	8	26.7	12	40.0	2	6.7	3	10.0
Montana	53	13	24.5	34	64.2	2	3.8	3	5.7	4	7.5	15	28.3	11	20.8	1	1.9	11	20.8
Nevada	27	0	0.0	15	55.6	1	3.7	4	14.8	0	0.0	2	7.4	6	22.2	0	0.0	0	0.0
New Mexico	36	0	0.0	22	61.1	4	11.1	3	8.3	0	0.0	6	16.7	13	36.1	2	5.6	2	5.6
Utah	32	1	3.1	26	81.3	3	9.4	5	15.6	2	6.3	6	18.8	10	31.3	2	6.3	0	0.0
Wyoming	27	1	3.7	20	74.1	3	11.1	4	14.8	4	14.8	10	37.0	4	14.8	0	0.0	2	7.4
CENSUS DIVISION 9, PACIFIC	448	25	5.6	332	74.1	34	7.6	65	14.5	18	4.0	44	9.8	146	32.6	24	5.4	12	2.7
Alaska	13	0	0.0	9	69.2	2	15.4	3	23.1	0	0.0	2	15.4	3	23.1	0	0.0	0	0.0
California	284	17	6.0	209	73.6	22	7.7	40	14.1	16	5.6	22	7.7	94	33.1	17	6.0	3	1.1
Hawaii	20	1	5.0	11	55.0	1	5.0	2	10.0	0	0.0	1	5.0	3	15.0	1	5.0	0	0.0
Oregon	61	4	6.6	55	90.2	3	4.9	6	9.8	1	1.6	7	11.5	16	26.2	4	6.6	2	3.3
Washington	70	3	4.3	48	68.6	6	8.6	14	20.0	1	1.4	12	17.1	30	42.9	2	2.9	7	10.0

Table 7 (Continued)

These data include only hospital-based facilities and services as reported by responding hospitals in Section C of the 2010 AHA Annual Survey, beginning on page 215. All hospitals are represented with Community Hospitals listed separately under United States. No estimates have been made for nonresponding hospitals. Definitions of facilities and services are listed in the Glossary, page 201.

CLASSIFICATION	HOSPITALS REPORTING	AUXILIARY Number	AUXILIARY Percent	BARIATRIC/WEIGHT CONTROL SERVICES Number	BARIATRIC/WEIGHT CONTROL SERVICES Percent	BIRTHING/LDR/LDRP ROOM Number	BIRTHING/LDR/LDRP ROOM Percent	BLOOD DONOR CENTER Number	BLOOD DONOR CENTER Percent	BREAST CANCER SCREENING Number	BREAST CANCER SCREENING Percent	BURN CARE UNITS Number	BURN CARE UNITS Percent	CASE MANAGEMENT Number	CASE MANAGEMENT Percent	CHAPLAINCY/PASTORAL CARE SERVICES Number	CHAPLAINCY/PASTORAL CARE SERVICES Percent	CHEMOTHERAPY Number	CHEMOTHERAPY Percent
UNITED STATES	4,782	2,776	58.1	1,127	23.6	2,590	54.2	322	6.7	3,317	69.4	172	3.6	4,020	84.1	3,108	65.0	2,391	50.0
COMMUNITY HOSPITALS	4,079	2,709	66.4	1,055	25.9	2,555	62.6	312	7.6	3,226	79.1	163	4.0	3,577	87.7	2,816	69.0	2,309	56.6
CENSUS DIVISION 1. NEW ENGLAND	198	121	61.1	63	31.8	130	65.7	32	16.2	156	78.8	11	5.6	184	92.9	166	83.8	143	72.2
Connecticut	32	21	65.6	16	50.0	25	78.1	4	12.5	25	78.1	1	3.1	30	93.8	31	96.9	23	71.9
Maine	40	26	65.0	7	17.5	29	72.5	0	0.0	34	85.0	2	5.0	38	95.0	29	72.5	26	65.0
Massachusetts	74	38	51.4	28	37.8	42	56.8	23	31.1	55	74.3	5	6.8	67	90.5	62	83.8	54	73.0
New Hampshire	28	19	67.9	6	21.4	19	67.9	4	14.3	22	78.6	1	3.6	27	96.4	22	78.6	20	71.4
Rhode Island	12	8	66.7	4	33.3	6	50.0	0	0.0	10	83.3	1	8.3	11	91.7	10	83.3	11	91.7
Vermont	12	9	75.0	2	16.7	9	75.0	1	8.3	10	83.3	1	8.3	11	91.7	12	100.0	9	75.0
CENSUS DIVISION 2. MIDDLE ATLANTIC	414	274	66.2	164	39.6	238	57.5	65	15.7	320	77.3	23	5.6	374	90.3	327	79.0	270	65.2
New Jersey	73	55	75.3	39	53.4	46	63.0	10	13.7	52	71.2	4	5.5	64	87.7	61	83.6	54	74.0
New York	168	108	64.3	66	39.3	107	63.7	34	20.2	139	82.7	13	7.7	158	94.0	139	82.7	116	69.0
Pennsylvania	173	111	64.2	59	34.1	85	49.1	21	12.1	129	74.6	6	3.5	152	87.9	127	73.4	100	57.8
CENSUS DIVISION 3. SOUTH ATLANTIC	715	446	62.4	173	24.2	381	53.3	54	7.6	528	73.8	22	3.1	634	88.7	547	76.5	378	52.9
Delaware	11	5	45.5	5	45.5	5	45.5	0	0.0	6	54.5	1	9.1	7	63.6	8	72.7	7	63.6
District of Columbia	12	5	16.7	5	41.7	6	50.0	2	16.7	6	50.0	1	8.3	10	83.3	11	91.7	6	50.0
Florida	160	96	60.0	46	28.8	73	45.6	11	6.9	114	71.3	5	3.1	149	93.1	116	72.5	92	57.5
Georgia	128	87	68.0	68	20.3	68	53.1	5	3.9	98	76.6	2	1.6	114	89.1	92	71.9	56	43.8
Maryland	58	41	70.7	17	29.3	33	56.9	12	20.7	41	70.7	2	3.4	52	89.7	51	87.9	43	74.1
North Carolina	115	73	63.5	30	26.1	75	65.2	9	7.8	87	75.7	4	3.5	103	89.6	97	84.3	67	58.3
South Carolina	79	46	58.2	14	17.7	41	51.9	5	6.3	56	70.9	2	2.5	68	86.1	49	62.0	31	39.2
Virginia	89	60	67.4	24	27.0	51	57.3	10	11.2	72	80.9	4	4.5	78	87.6	78	87.6	52	58.4
West Virginia	63	36	57.1	6	9.5	29	46.0	0	0.0	48	76.2	1	1.6	53	84.1	45	71.4	24	38.1
CENSUS DIVISION 4. EAST NORTH CENTRAL	721	466	64.6	191	26.5	454	63.0	37	5.1	589	81.7	37	5.1	641	88.9	518	71.8	440	61.0
Illinois	173	116	67.1	57	32.9	108	62.4	12	6.9	147	85.0	6	3.5	160	92.5	140	80.9	117	67.6
Indiana	108	55	50.9	23	21.3	74	68.5	2	1.9	88	81.5	3	2.8	99	91.7	86	79.6	65	60.2
Michigan	147	107	72.8	43	29.3	82	55.8	9	6.1	121	82.3	8	5.4	130	88.4	112	76.2	93	63.3
Ohio	152	106	69.7	37	24.3	96	63.2	12	7.9	127	83.6	10	6.6	139	91.4	120	78.9	107	70.4
Wisconsin	141	82	58.2	31	22.0	94	66.7	2	1.4	106	75.2	10	7.1	113	80.1	60	42.6	58	41.1
CENSUS DIVISION 5. EAST SOUTH CENTRAL	419	170	40.6	72	17.2	184	43.9	14	3.3	284	67.8	13	3.1	332	79.2	238	56.8	127	30.3
Alabama	120	50	41.7	26	21.7	51	42.5	5	4.2	76	63.3	6	5.0	95	79.2	67	55.8	38	31.7
Kentucky	98	63	64.3	25	25.5	48	49.0	4	4.1	78	79.6	4	4.1	88	89.8	79	80.6	43	43.9
Mississippi	110	19	17.3	5	4.5	42	38.2	1	0.9	59	53.6	1	0.9	64	58.2	21	19.1	12	10.9
Tennessee	91	38	41.8	16	17.6	43	47.3	4	4.4	71	78.0	2	2.2	85	93.4	71	78.0	34	37.4
CENSUS DIVISION 6. WEST NORTH CENTRAL	649	435	67.0	107	16.5	356	54.9	22	3.4	460	70.9	26	4.0	452	69.6	345	53.2	351	54.1
Iowa	125	110	88.0	14	11.2	81	64.8	5	3.2	112	89.6	5	4.0	98	78.4	58	46.4	84	67.2
Kansas	153	82	53.6	21	13.7	70	45.8	5	3.9	79	51.6	6	3.9	82	53.6	67	43.8	50	32.7
Minnesota	102	77	75.5	26	25.5	73	71.6	5	5.9	87	85.3	6	2.0	72	70.6	58	56.9	72	70.6
Missouri	149	101	67.8	25	16.8	71	47.7	9	4.9	103	69.1	9	6.0	125	83.9	102	68.5	69	46.3
Nebraska	52	25	48.1	10	19.2	34	65.4	0	0.0	38	73.1	2	3.8	34	65.4	27	51.9	35	67.3
North Dakota	24	19	79.2	6	25.0	9	37.5	1	4.2	15	62.5	2	8.3	19	79.2	18	75.0	14	58.3
South Dakota	44	21	47.7	5	11.4	18	40.9	2	4.5	26	59.1	0	0.0	22	50.0	15	34.1	27	61.4
CENSUS DIVISION 7. WEST SOUTH CENTRAL	883	422	47.8	168	19.0	363	41.1	29	3.3	429	48.6	20	2.3	745	84.4	455	51.5	254	28.8
Arkansas	91	57	62.6	10	11.0	40	44.0	3	3.3	53	58.2	1	1.1	78	85.7	43	47.3	31	34.1
Louisiana	102	47	46.1	23	22.5	47	46.1	6	5.9	66	64.7	4	3.9	91	89.2	48	47.1	41	40.2
Oklahoma	123	60	48.8	15	12.2	54	43.9	5	4.1	65	52.8	3	2.4	101	82.1	72	58.5	30	24.4
Texas	567	258	45.5	120	21.2	222	39.2	15	2.6	245	43.2	12	2.1	475	83.8	292	51.5	152	26.8
CENSUS DIVISION 8. MOUNTAIN	335	188	56.1	70	20.9	205	61.2	23	6.9	234	69.9	7	2.1	270	80.6	194	57.9	163	48.7
Arizona	59	36	61.0	16	27.1	32	54.2	4	6.8	38	64.4	1	1.7	57	96.6	47	79.7	35	59.3
Colorado	71	45	63.4	23	32.4	47	66.2	13	18.3	54	76.1	2	2.8	60	84.5	48	67.6	46	64.8
Idaho	30	23	76.7	9	30.0	22	73.3	2	6.7	19	63.3	0	0.0	22	73.3	18	60.0	13	43.3
Montana	53	30	56.6	3	5.7	28	52.8	1	1.9	38	71.7	0	0.0	30	56.6	21	39.6	18	34.0
Nevada	27	7	25.9	6	22.2	12	44.4	0	0.0	16	59.3	1	3.7	24	88.9	14	51.9	13	48.1
New Mexico	36	19	52.8	1	2.8	20	55.6	1	2.8	24	66.7	1	2.8	30	83.3	22	61.1	9	25.0
Utah	32	12	37.5	8	25.0	25	78.1	2	6.3	25	78.1	1	3.1	26	81.3	11	34.4	16	50.0
Wyoming	27	16	59.3	4	14.8	19	70.4	0	0.0	20	74.1	0	0.0	21	77.8	13	48.1	13	48.1
CENSUS DIVISION 9. PACIFIC	448	254	56.7	119	26.6	279	62.3	46	10.3	317	70.8	13	2.9	388	86.6	318	71.0	265	59.2
Alaska	13	6	46.2	3	23.1	9	69.2	1	7.7	10	76.9	0	0.0	11	84.6	7	69.2	8	61.5
California	284	156	54.9	76	26.8	166	58.5	42	14.8	190	66.9	9	3.2	251	88.4	200	70.4	171	60.2
Hawaii	20	6	30.0	5	25.0	6	30.0	2	10.0	11	55.0	1	5.0	14	70.0	7	35.0	11	55.0
Oregon	61	46	75.4	17	27.9	51	83.6	0	0.0	53	86.9	1	1.6	52	85.2	48	78.7	38	62.3
Washington	70	40	57.1	18	25.7	47	67.1	1	1.4	53	75.7	2	2.9	60	85.7	54	77.1	37	52.9

Table 7 (Continued)

These data include only hospital-based facilities and services as reported by responding hospitals in Section C of the 2010 AHA Annual Survey, beginning on page 215. All hospitals are represented with Community Hospitals listed separately under United States. No estimates have been made for nonresponding hospitals. Definitions of facilities and services are listed in the Glossary, page 201.

CLASSIFICATION	HOSPITALS REPORTING	CHILDREN'S WELLNESS PROGRAM Number	Percent	CHIROPRACTIC SERVICES Number	Percent	COMMUNITY OUTREACH Number	Percent	COMPLEMENTARY AND ALTERNATIVE MEDICINE SERVICES Number	Percent	COMPUTER ASSISTED ORTHOPEDIC SURGERY (CAOS) Number	Percent	CRISIS PREVENTION Number	Percent	DENTAL SERVICES Number	Percent	ENABLING SERVICES Number	Percent	ENROLLMENT ASSISTANCE SERVICES Number	Percent	EXTRACORPOREAL SHOCK WAVE LITHOTRIPTER (ESWL) Number	Percent
UNITED STATES	4,782	911	19.1	128	2.7	3,119	65.2	899	18.8	657	13.7	1,015	21.2	1,072	22.4	1,111	23.2	2,274	47.6	1,244	26.0
COMMUNITY HOSPITALS	4,079	877	21.5	91	2.2	2,902	71.1	845	20.7	638	15.6	873	21.4	899	22.0	1,036	25.4	2,107	51.7	1,193	29.2
CENSUS DIVISION 1, NEW ENGLAND	198	68	34.3	8	4.0	169	85.4	86	43.4	32	16.2	70	35.4	56	28.3	72	36.4	150	75.8	103	52.0
Connecticut	32	14	43.8	2	6.3	29	90.6	21	65.6	6	18.8	18	56.3	12	37.5	13	40.6	24	75.0	18	56.3
Maine	40	9	22.5	1	2.5	33	82.5	14	35.0	3	7.5	7	17.5	5	12.5	10	25.0	24	60.0	16	40.0
Massachusetts	74	26	35.1	2	2.7	62	83.8	28	37.8	13	17.6	28	37.8	18	24.3	29	39.2	64	86.5	41	55.4
New Hampshire	28	12	42.9	1	3.6	23	82.1	14	50.0	6	21.4	11	39.3	12	42.9	12	42.9	21	75.0	14	50.0
Rhode Island	12	3	25.0	0	0.0	12	100.0	3	25.0	2	16.7	4	33.3	5	41.7	3	25.0	8	66.7	9	75.0
Vermont	12	4	33.3	2	16.7	10	83.3	6	50.0	2	16.7	2	16.7	4	33.3	5	41.7	9	75.0	5	41.7
CENSUS DIVISION 2, MIDDLE ATLANTIC	414	149	36.0	19	4.6	319	77.1	122	29.5	82	19.8	172	41.5	160	38.6	146	35.3	252	60.9	139	33.6
New Jersey	73	31	42.5	3	4.1	54	74.0	24	32.9	13	17.8	39	53.4	23	31.5	30	41.1	40	54.8	21	28.8
New York	168	67	39.9	13	7.7	140	83.3	60	35.7	36	21.4	82	48.8	81	48.2	51	30.4	104	61.9	55	32.7
Pennsylvania	173	51	29.5	3	1.7	125	72.3	38	22.0	33	19.1	51	29.5	56	32.4	65	37.6	108	62.4	63	36.4
CENSUS DIVISION 3, SOUTH ATLANTIC	715	123	17.2	11	1.5	508	71.0	122	17.1	125	17.5	154	21.5	175	24.5	195	27.3	383	53.6	226	31.6
Delaware	11	5	45.5	0	0.0	6	54.5	3	27.3	2	18.2	4	36.4	4	36.4	2	18.2	6	54.5	3	27.3
District of Columbia	12	3	25.0	0	0.0	9	75.0	3	25.0	3	25.0	3	25.0	5	41.7	4	33.3	6	50.0	3	25.0
Florida	160	17	10.6	3	1.9	104	65.0	22	13.8	37	23.1	20	12.5	25	15.6	34	21.3	76	47.5	68	42.5
Georgia	128	11	8.6	2	1.6	86	67.2	12	9.4	24	18.8	29	22.7	23	18.0	32	25.0	72	56.3	33	25.8
Maryland	58	17	29.3	2	3.4	44	75.9	24	41.4	12	20.7	25	43.1	25	43.1	29	50.0	39	67.2	27	46.6
North Carolina	115	22	19.1	1	0.9	83	72.2	20	17.4	15	13.0	22	19.1	31	27.0	35	30.4	54	47.0	19	16.5
South Carolina	79	16	20.3	0	0.0	66	83.5	4	5.1	8	10.1	9	11.4	17	21.5	11	13.9	37	46.8	18	22.8
Virginia	89	17	19.1	2	2.2	68	76.4	26	29.2	21	23.6	31	34.8	30	33.7	36	40.4	61	68.5	38	42.7
West Virginia	63	15	23.8	1	1.6	42	66.7	8	12.7	3	4.8	11	17.5	15	23.8	12	19.0	32	50.8	17	27.0
CENSUS DIVISION 4, EAST NORTH CENTRAL	721	183	25.4	31	4.3	525	72.8	233	32.3	131	18.2	207	28.7	182	25.2	237	32.9	405	56.2	210	29.1
Illinois	173	51	29.5	10	5.8	134	77.5	53	30.6	38	22.0	62	35.8	47	27.2	57	32.9	100	57.8	42	24.3
Indiana	108	27	25.0	0	0.0	89	82.4	25	23.1	9	8.3	25	23.1	22	20.4	24	22.2	69	63.9	28	25.9
Michigan	147	48	32.7	7	4.8	113	76.9	55	37.4	24	16.3	45	30.6	43	29.3	62	42.2	99	67.3	53	36.1
Ohio	152	37	24.3	10	6.6	122	80.3	42	27.6	36	23.7	41	27.0	49	32.2	58	38.2	82	53.9	54	35.5
Wisconsin	141	20	14.2	4	2.8	67	47.5	58	41.1	24	17.0	34	24.1	21	14.9	36	25.5	55	39.0	33	23.4
CENSUS DIVISION 5, EAST SOUTH CENTRAL	419	35	8.4	5	1.2	241	57.5	27	6.4	31	7.4	48	11.5	79	18.9	53	12.6	136	32.5	94	22.4
Alabama	120	11	9.2	2	1.7	56	46.7	6	5.0	9	7.5	14	11.7	7	5.8	11	9.2	41	34.2	26	21.7
Kentucky	98	13	13.3	2	2.0	66	67.3	16	16.3	10	10.2	13	13.3	20	20.4	22	22.4	48	49.0	27	27.6
Mississippi	110	4	3.6	1	0.9	62	56.4	2	1.8	2	1.8	4	3.6	34	30.9	3	2.7	11	10.0	19	17.3
Tennessee	91	7	7.7	0	0.0	57	62.6	3	3.3	10	11.0	17	18.7	18	19.8	17	18.7	36	39.6	22	24.2
CENSUS DIVISION 6, WEST NORTH CENTRAL	649	113	17.4	17	2.6	402	61.9	102	15.7	52	8.0	121	18.6	124	19.1	129	19.9	247	38.1	110	16.9
Iowa	125	26	20.8	2	1.6	94	75.2	26	20.8	12	9.6	30	24.0	24	19.2	32	25.6	61	48.8	15	12.0
Kansas	153	13	8.5	1	0.7	56	36.6	8	5.2	13	8.5	7	4.6	16	10.5	13	8.5	37	24.2	22	14.4
Minnesota	102	26	25.5	6	5.9	69	67.6	28	27.5	9	8.8	26	25.5	18	17.6	18	17.6	40	39.2	17	16.7
Missouri	149	27	18.1	5	3.4	99	66.4	26	17.4	12	8.1	37	24.8	46	30.9	47	31.5	73	49.0	40	26.8
Nebraska	52	10	19.2	0	0.0	40	76.9	7	13.5	2	3.8	12	23.1	10	19.2	9	17.3	18	34.6	9	17.3
North Dakota	24	6	25.0	2	8.3	16	66.7	3	12.5	2	8.3	4	16.7	3	12.5	6	25.0	10	41.7	3	12.5
South Dakota	44	5	11.4	1	2.3	28	63.6	4	9.1	2	4.5	5	11.4	7	15.9	4	9.1	8	18.2	4	9.1
CENSUS DIVISION 7, WEST SOUTH CENTRAL	883	103	11.7	7	0.8	416	47.1	47	5.3	82	9.3	78	8.8	137	15.5	117	13.3	324	36.7	168	19.0
Arkansas	91	8	8.8	0	0.0	48	52.7	3	3.3	4	4.4	11	12.1	12	13.2	9	9.9	37	40.7	15	16.5
Louisiana	102	17	16.7	0	0.0	52	51.0	6	5.9	14	13.7	14	13.7	13	12.7	11	10.8	49	48.0	18	17.6
Oklahoma	123	13	10.6	2	1.6	55	44.7	3	2.4	6	4.9	7	5.7	22	17.9	8	6.5	29	23.6	25	20.3
Texas	567	65	11.5	5	0.9	261	46.0	35	6.2	58	10.2	46	8.1	90	15.9	89	15.7	209	36.9	110	19.4
CENSUS DIVISION 8, MOUNTAIN	335	60	17.9	11	3.3	215	64.2	69	20.6	50	14.9	73	21.8	69	20.6	57	17.0	151	45.1	67	20.0
Arizona	59	14	23.7	5	8.5	36	61.0	18	30.5	14	23.7	14	23.7	12	20.3	10	16.9	30	50.8	16	27.1
Colorado	71	9	12.7	2	2.8	53	74.6	23	32.4	15	21.1	13	18.3	13	18.3	15	21.1	34	47.9	14	19.7
Idaho	30	7	23.3	1	3.3	25	83.3	7	23.3	8	26.7	5	16.7	11	36.7	6	20.0	16	53.3	5	16.7
Montana	53	10	18.9	1	1.9	32	60.4	9	17.0	5	9.4	6	11.3	4	7.5	4	7.5	27	50.9	4	7.5
Nevada	27	6	22.2	0	0.0	15	55.6	1	3.7	1	3.7	6	22.2	6	22.2	6	22.2	10	37.0	4	14.8
New Mexico	36	4	11.1	2	5.6	22	61.1	3	8.3	2	5.6	5	13.9	6	16.7	4	11.1	13	36.1	9	25.0
Utah	32	7	21.9	0	0.0	19	59.4	5	15.6	5	15.6	14	43.8	14	43.8	11	34.4	17	53.1	11	34.4
Wyoming	27	3	11.1	0	0.0	13	48.1	3	11.1	0	0.0	6	22.2	3	11.1	0	0.0	4	14.8	4	14.8
CENSUS DIVISION 9, PACIFIC	448	77	17.2	19	4.2	324	72.3	91	20.3	72	16.1	92	20.5	90	20.1	105	23.4	226	50.4	127	28.3
Alaska	13	3	23.1	1	7.7	7	53.8	2	15.4	1	7.7	5	38.5	2	15.4	2	15.4	7	53.8	5	38.5
California	284	45	15.8	11	3.9	207	72.9	55	19.4	42	14.8	52	18.3	65	22.9	62	21.8	135	47.5	81	28.5
Hawaii	20	2	10.0	1	5.0	10	50.0	3	15.0	2	10.0	2	10.0	3	15.0	3	15.0	6	30.0	4	20.0
Oregon	61	13	21.3	3	4.9	50	82.0	14	23.0	16	26.2	11	18.0	5	8.2	19	31.1	44	72.1	18	29.5
Washington	70	14	20.0	3	4.3	50	71.4	17	24.3	11	15.7	22	31.4	14	20.0	19	27.1	34	48.6	19	27.1

Table 7 (Continued)

These data include only hospital-based facilities and services as reported by responding hospitals in Section C of the 2010 AHA Annual Survey, beginning on page 215. All hospitals are represented with Community Hospitals listed separately under United States. No estimates have been made for nonresponding hospitals. Definitions of facilities and services are listed in the Glossary, page 201.

CLASSIFICATION	HOSPITALS REPORTING	FERTILITY CLINIC Number	FERTILITY CLINIC Percent	FITNESS CENTER Number	FITNESS CENTER Percent	FREESTANDING OUTPATIENT CARE CENTER Number	FREESTANDING OUTPATIENT CARE CENTER Percent	GENETIC TESTING/COUNSELING Number	GENETIC TESTING/COUNSELING Percent	GERIATRIC SERVICES Number	GERIATRIC SERVICES Percent	HEALTH FAIR Number	HEALTH FAIR Percent	COMMUNITY HEALTH EDUCATION Number	COMMUNITY HEALTH EDUCATION Percent	HEALTH RESEARCH Number	HEALTH RESEARCH Percent	HEALTH SCREENINGS Number	HEALTH SCREENINGS Percent	HEMODIALYSIS Number	HEMODIALYSIS Percent	HIV/AIDS SERVICES Number	HIV/AIDS SERVICES Percent
UNITED STATES	4,782	238	5.0	1,325	27.7	1,420	29.7	609	12.7	1,797	37.6	3,417	71.5	3,333	69.7	1,048	21.9	3,490	73.0	1,450	30.3	1,116	23.3
COMMUNITY HOSPITALS	4,079	234	5.7	1,224	30.0	1,305	32.0	590	14.5	1,626	39.9	3,219	78.9	3,109	76.2	965	23.7	3,275	80.3	1,356	33.2	1,021	25.0
CENSUS DIVISION 1, NEW ENGLAND	198	25	12.6	53	26.8	86	43.4	50	25.3	102	51.5	161	81.3	173	87.4	75	37.9	175	88.4	70	35.4	91	46.0
Connecticut	32	5	15.6	12	37.5	17	53.1	14	43.8	18	56.3	25	78.1	29	90.6	20	62.5	29	90.6	11	34.4	21	65.6
Maine	40	2	5.0	13	32.5	16	40.0	7	17.5	14	35.0	30	75.0	32	80.0	10	25.0	34	85.0	7	17.5	14	35.0
Massachusetts	74	12	16.2	9	12.2	30	40.5	20	27.0	38	51.4	62	83.8	63	85.1	26	35.1	65	87.8	37	50.0	35	47.3
New Hampshire	28	3	10.7	10	35.7	12	42.9	5	17.9	16	57.1	26	92.9	25	89.3	6	21.4	24	85.7	4	14.3	12	42.9
Rhode Island	12	1	8.3	4	33.3	7	58.3	3	25.0	11	91.7	10	83.3	12	100.0	8	66.7	12	100.0	8	66.7	7	58.3
Vermont	12	2	16.7	5	41.7	4	33.3	1	8.3	5	41.7	8	66.7	12	100.0	5	41.7	11	91.7	3	25.0	2	16.7
CENSUS DIVISION 2, MIDDLE ATLANTIC	414	45	10.9	123	29.7	208	50.2	119	28.7	229	55.3	330	79.7	328	79.2	150	36.2	343	82.9	201	48.6	184	44.4
New Jersey	73	7	9.6	21	28.8	28	38.4	30	41.1	46	63.0	52	71.2	55	75.3	33	45.2	58	79.5	45	61.6	37	50.7
New York	168	25	14.9	43	25.6	104	61.9	56	33.3	98	58.3	146	86.9	149	88.7	68	40.5	145	86.3	104	61.9	88	52.4
Pennsylvania	173	13	7.5	59	34.1	76	43.9	33	19.1	85	49.1	132	76.3	124	71.7	49	28.3	140	80.9	52	30.1	59	34.1
CENSUS DIVISION 3, SOUTH ATLANTIC	715	34	4.8	202	28.3	260	36.4	103	14.4	264	36.9	551	77.1	528	73.8	180	25.2	559	78.2	273	38.2	214	29.9
Delaware	11	0	0.0	4	36.4	6	54.5	4	36.4	5	45.5	5	45.5	8	72.7	5	45.5	6	54.5	5	45.5	6	54.5
District of Columbia	12	2	16.7	2	16.7	4	33.3	4	33.3	4	33.3	6	50.0	8	66.7	6	50.0	6	50.0	4	33.3	6	50.0
Florida	160	9	5.6	50	31.3	58	36.3	28	17.5	56	35.0	116	72.5	117	73.1	49	30.6	122	76.3	78	48.8	45	28.1
Georgia	128	3	2.3	34	26.6	46	35.9	12	9.4	40	31.3	97	75.8	92	71.9	27	21.1	101	78.9	43	33.6	35	27.3
Maryland	58	6	10.3	14	24.1	25	43.1	21	36.2	33	56.9	46	79.3	47	81.0	28	48.3	47	81.0	33	56.9	25	43.1
North Carolina	115	6	5.2	37	32.2	40	34.8	10	8.7	42	36.5	91	79.1	90	78.3	24	20.9	93	80.9	38	33.0	27	23.5
South Carolina	79	2	2.5	18	22.8	25	31.6	5	6.3	35	44.3	63	79.7	54	68.4	14	17.7	58	73.4	29	36.7	28	35.4
Virginia	89	4	4.5	23	25.8	38	42.7	16	18.0	31	34.8	72	80.9	67	75.3	21	23.6	73	82.0	29	32.6	30	33.7
West Virginia	63	2	3.2	20	31.7	18	28.6	3	4.8	18	28.6	55	87.3	45	71.4	6	9.5	53	84.1	14	22.2	12	19.0
CENSUS DIVISION 4, EAST NORTH CENTRAL	721	44	6.1	249	34.5	280	38.8	108	15.0	368	51.0	554	76.8	594	82.4	213	29.5	577	80.0	234	32.5	179	24.8
Illinois	173	12	6.9	52	30.1	65	37.6	26	15.0	91	52.6	143	82.7	141	81.5	57	32.9	151	87.3	51	29.5	52	30.1
Indiana	108	5	4.6	35	32.4	39	36.1	13	12.0	42	38.9	93	86.1	88	81.5	24	22.2	93	86.1	22	20.4	19	17.6
Michigan	147	11	7.5	50	34.0	67	45.6	23	15.6	75	51.0	115	78.2	117	79.6	56	38.1	123	83.7	54	36.7	51	34.7
Ohio	152	11	7.2	60	39.5	64	42.1	27	17.8	60	39.5	132	86.8	130	85.5	56	36.8	135	88.8	72	47.4	50	32.9
Wisconsin	141	5	3.5	52	36.9	45	31.9	19	13.5	100	70.9	71	50.4	118	83.7	20	14.2	75	53.2	35	24.8	7	5.0
CENSUS DIVISION 5, EAST SOUTH CENTRAL	419	8	1.9	103	24.6	81	19.3	27	6.4	115	27.4	257	61.3	230	54.9	54	12.9	250	59.7	87	20.8	70	16.7
Alabama	120	4	3.3	33	27.5	22	18.3	5	4.2	34	28.3	84	65.0	67	55.8	15	12.5	74	61.7	34	28.3	25	12.5
Kentucky	98	2	2.0	23	23.5	31	31.6	9	9.2	29	29.6	84	85.7	78	79.6	18	18.4	80	81.6	23	23.5	16	16.3
Mississippi	110	1	0.9	30	27.3	5	4.5	3	2.7	21	19.1	29	26.4	28	25.5	4	3.6	28	25.5	0	0.0	22	20.0
Tennessee	91	1	1.1	17	18.7	23	25.3	10	11.0	31	34.1	66	72.5	57	62.6	17	18.7	68	74.7	30	33.0	17	18.7
CENSUS DIVISION 6, WEST NORTH CENTRAL	649	29	4.5	234	36.1	105	16.2	52	8.0	237	36.5	458	70.6	435	67.0	85	13.1	495	76.3	135	20.8	114	17.6
Iowa	125	3	2.4	48	38.4	16	12.8	6	4.8	56	44.8	105	84.0	99	79.2	14	11.2	118	94.4	26	20.8	24	19.2
Kansas	153	2	1.3	41	26.8	10	6.5	8	5.2	45	29.4	82	53.6	67	43.8	8	5.2	79	51.6	16	10.5	17	11.1
Minnesota	102	6	5.9	40	39.2	22	21.6	11	10.8	42	41.2	77	75.5	83	81.4	18	17.6	81	79.4	18	17.6	20	19.6
Missouri	149	10	6.7	53	35.6	40	26.8	19	12.8	53	35.6	107	71.8	101	67.8	27	18.1	116	77.9	47	31.5	36	24.2
Nebraska	52	3	5.8	24	46.2	9	17.3	4	7.7	15	28.8	40	76.9	39	75.0	8	13.5	43	82.7	10	19.2	7	13.5
North Dakota	24	4	16.7	11	45.8	4	16.7	2	8.3	12	50.0	15	62.5	16	66.7	6	25.0	18	75.0	8	33.3	5	20.8
South Dakota	44	1	2.3	17	38.6	4	9.1	2	4.5	14	31.8	32	72.7	30	68.2	5	11.4	40	90.9	10	22.7	5	11.4
CENSUS DIVISION 7, WEST SOUTH CENTRAL	883	19	2.2	177	20.0	167	18.9	52	5.9	236	26.7	544	61.6	479	54.2	100	11.3	522	59.1	188	21.3	106	12.0
Arkansas	91	0	0.0	18	19.8	13	14.3	4	4.4	27	29.7	66	72.5	51	56.0	8	8.8	67	73.6	16	17.6	12	13.2
Louisiana	102	3	2.9	19	18.6	28	27.5	9	8.8	33	32.4	66	64.7	62	60.8	19	18.6	62	60.8	31	30.4	21	20.6
Oklahoma	123	2	1.6	20	16.3	18	14.6	4	3.3	27	22.0	71	57.7	66	53.7	14	11.4	66	53.7	20	16.3	12	9.8
Texas	567	14	2.5	120	21.2	108	19.0	35	6.2	149	26.3	341	60.1	300	52.9	59	10.4	327	57.7	121	21.3	61	10.8
CENSUS DIVISION 8, MOUNTAIN	335	13	3.9	90	26.9	84	25.1	36	10.7	104	31.0	252	75.2	234	69.9	65	19.4	242	72.2	95	28.4	57	17.0
Arizona	59	4	6.8	20	33.9	20	33.9	6	10.2	16	27.1	38	64.4	42	71.2	20	33.9	38	64.4	35	59.3	13	22.0
Colorado	71	2	2.8	24	33.8	21	29.6	16	22.5	18	25.4	53	74.6	53	74.6	15	21.1	52	73.2	16	22.5	14	19.7
Idaho	30	1	3.3	11	36.7	9	30.0	4	13.3	10	33.3	27	90.0	25	83.3	4	13.3	25	83.3	6	20.0	5	16.7
Montana	53	1	1.9	7	13.2	5	9.4	4	7.5	24	45.3	43	81.1	34	64.2	6	11.3	43	81.1	6	11.3	8	15.1
Nevada	27	0	0.0	2	7.4	7	25.9	0	0.0	5	18.5	16	59.3	17	63.0	8	29.6	15	55.6	7	25.9	5	18.5
New Mexico	36	1	2.8	8	22.2	9	25.0	1	2.8	8	22.2	26	72.2	18	50.0	2	5.6	23	63.9	6	16.7	2	5.6
Utah	32	4	12.5	14	43.8	12	37.5	5	15.6	13	40.6	26	81.3	26	81.3	10	31.3	26	81.3	12	37.5	8	25.0
Wyoming	27	0	0.0	4	14.8	1	3.7	0	0.0	10	37.0	23	85.2	19	70.4	0	0.0	20	74.1	7	25.9	2	7.4
CENSUS DIVISION 9, PACIFIC	448	21	4.7	94	21.0	149	33.3	62	13.8	142	31.7	310	69.2	332	74.1	126	28.1	327	73.0	167	37.3	101	22.5
Alaska	13	0	0.0	2	15.4	1	7.7	2	15.4	2	15.4	8	61.5	10	76.9	2	15.4	10	76.9	3	23.1	3	23.1
California	284	16	5.6	54	19.0	97	34.2	46	16.2	94	33.1	190	66.9	200	70.4	86	30.3	193	68.0	119	41.9	69	24.3
Hawaii	20	1	5.0	3	15.0	3	15.0	2	10.0	5	25.0	11	55.0	11	55.0	3	15.0	13	65.0	4	20.0	3	15.0
Oregon	61	1	1.6	22	36.1	21	34.4	2	3.3	20	32.8	49	80.3	55	90.2	13	21.3	53	86.9	18	29.5	11	18.0
Washington	70	3	4.3	13	18.6	27	38.6	10	14.3	21	30.0	52	74.3	56	80.0	21	30.0	58	82.9	23	32.9	15	21.4

Table 7 (Continued)

These data include only hospital-based facilities and services as reported by responding hospitals in Section C of the 2010 AHA Annual Survey, beginning on page 215. All hospitals are represented with Community Hospitals listed separately under United States. No estimates have been made for nonresponding hospitals. Definitions of facilities and services are listed in the Glossary, page 201.

CLASSIFICATION	HOSPITALS REPORTING	HOME HEALTH SERVICES		HOSPICE		HOSPITAL-BASED OUTPATIENT CARE CENTER SERVICES		IMMUNIZATION PROGRAM		INDIGENT CARE CLINIC		LINGUISTIC/ TRANSLATION SERVICES		MEALS ON WHEELS		MOBILE HEALTH SERVICES		NEONATAL INTERMEDIATE CARE UNITS		NEUROLOGICAL SERVICES		NUTRITION PROGRAMS CENTER	
		Number	Percent	Number	Percent	Number	Percent	Number	Percent	Number	Percent	Number	Percent	Number	Percent	Number	Percent	Number	Percent	Number	Percent	Number	Percent
UNITED STATES	4,782	1,336	27.9	992	20.7	3,395	71.0	1,724	36.1	738	15.4	2,589	54.1	440	9.2	487	10.2	705	14.7	2,248	47.0	3,497	73.1
COMMUNITY HOSPITALS	4,079	1,269	31.1	930	22.8	3,161	77.5	1,586	38.9	713	17.5	2,369	58.1	428	10.5	461	11.3	693	17.0	2,086	51.1	3,159	77.4
CENSUS DIVISION 1, NEW ENGLAND	198	46	23.2	53	26.8	171	86.4	115	58.1	53	26.8	139	70.2	10	5.1	25	12.6	31	15.7	142	71.7	190	96.0
Connecticut	32	7	21.9	13	40.6	28	87.5	17	53.1	15	46.9	23	71.9	2	6.3	7	21.9	5	15.6	27	84.4	29	90.6
Maine	40	7	17.5	7	17.5	30	75.0	26	65.0	9	22.5	20	50.0	3	7.5	2	5.0	4	10.0	19	47.5	38	95.0
Massachusetts	74	22	29.7	19	25.7	66	89.2	41	55.4	13	17.6	61	82.4	2	2.7	8	10.8	16	21.6	57	77.0	72	97.3
New Hampshire	28	5	17.9	7	25.0	25	89.3	14	50.0	7	25.0	17	60.7	1	3.6	6	21.4	3	10.7	20	71.4	28	100.0
Rhode Island	12	3	25.0	2	16.7	11	91.7	9	75.0	6	50.0	10	83.3	1	8.3	1	8.3	2	16.7	11	91.7	11	91.7
Vermont	12	2	16.7	5	41.7	11	91.7	8	66.7	3	25.0	8	66.7	1	8.3	1	8.3	1	8.3	8	66.7	12	100.0
CENSUS DIVISION 2, MIDDLE ATLANTIC	414	124	30.0	116	28.0	329	79.5	222	53.6	154	37.2	283	68.4	38	9.2	66	15.9	117	28.3	293	70.8	348	84.1
New Jersey	73	18	24.7	19	26.0	56	76.7	38	52.1	43	58.9	59	80.8	10	13.7	15	20.5	39	53.4	57	78.1	63	86.3
New York	168	45	26.8	49	29.2	139	82.7	100	59.5	70	41.7	122	72.6	16	9.5	38	22.6	52	31.0	128	76.2	140	83.3
Pennsylvania	173	61	35.3	48	27.7	134	77.5	84	48.6	41	23.7	102	59.0	12	6.9	13	7.5	26	15.0	108	62.4	145	83.8
CENSUS DIVISION 3, SOUTH ATLANTIC	715	170	23.8	134	18.7	526	73.6	237	33.1	107	15.0	393	55.0	29	4.1	96	13.4	140	19.6	402	56.2	547	76.5
Delaware	11	1	8.3	2	18.2	5	45.5	6	54.5	2	18.2	9	81.8	1	9.1	1	9.1	2	18.2	6	54.5	6	54.5
District of Columbia	12	1	8.3	2	16.7	9	75.0	8	66.7	3	25.0	8	66.7	1	8.3	3	25.0	3	25.0	10	83.3	10	83.3
Florida	160	32	20.0	24	15.0	113	70.6	41	25.6	24	15.0	83	51.9	1	0.6	18	11.3	23	14.4	118	73.8	118	73.8
Georgia	128	17	13.3	20	15.6	90	70.3	30	23.4	18	14.1	70	54.7	2	1.6	15	11.7	33	25.8	57	44.5	97	75.8
Maryland	58	11	19.0	13	22.4	45	77.6	34	58.6	17	29.3	38	65.5	2	3.4	11	19.0	6	10.3	44	75.9	47	81.0
North Carolina	115	38	33.0	24	20.9	90	78.3	36	31.3	18	15.7	65	56.5	6	5.2	19	16.5	32	27.8	57	49.6	89	77.4
South Carolina	79	15	19.0	9	11.4	59	74.7	21	26.6	5	6.3	38	48.1	4	5.1	8	10.1	26	32.9	35	44.3	62	78.5
Virginia	89	33	37.1	31	34.8	68	76.4	29	32.6	14	15.7	59	66.3	9	10.1	18	20.2	13	14.6	53	59.6	70	78.7
West Virginia	63	18	28.6	9	14.3	47	74.6	32	50.8	6	9.5	23	36.5	4	6.3	3	4.8	2	3.2	30	47.6	48	76.2
CENSUS DIVISION 4, EAST NORTH CENTRAL	721	236	32.7	198	27.5	581	80.6	302	41.9	152	21.1	439	60.9	133	18.4	84	11.7	95	13.2	401	55.6	616	85.4
Illinois	173	61	35.3	50	28.9	138	79.8	69	39.9	35	20.2	112	64.7	29	16.8	18	10.4	33	19.1	109	63.0	141	81.5
Indiana	108	39	36.1	27	25.0	83	76.9	38	35.2	18	16.7	62	57.4	26	24.1	11	10.2	19	17.6	58	53.7	92	85.2
Michigan	147	52	35.4	56	38.1	121	82.3	85	57.8	38	25.9	99	67.3	13	8.8	15	10.2	16	10.9	88	59.9	125	85.0
Ohio	152	56	36.8	47	30.9	125	82.2	65	42.8	47	30.9	100	65.8	24	15.8	26	17.1	27	17.8	102	67.1	136	89.5
Wisconsin	141	28	19.9	18	12.8	114	80.9	45	31.9	14	9.9	66	46.8	41	29.1	14	9.9	0	0.0	44	31.2	122	86.5
CENSUS DIVISION 5, EAST SOUTH CENTRAL	419	96	22.9	50	11.9	216	51.6	68	16.2	26	6.2	156	37.2	14	3.3	28	6.7	66	15.8	144	34.4	228	54.4
Alabama	120	34	28.3	12	10.0	72	60.0	20	16.7	7	5.8	46	38.3	5	4.2	5	4.2	9	7.5	43	35.8	57	47.5
Kentucky	98	33	33.7	14	14.3	75	76.5	18	18.4	11	11.2	52	53.1	7	7.1	13	13.3	17	17.3	48	49.0	72	73.5
Mississippi	110	11	10.0	11	10.0	19	17.3	13	11.8	3	2.7	16	14.5	0	0.0	1	0.9	30	27.3	14	12.7	37	33.6
Tennessee	91	18	19.8	13	14.3	50	54.9	17	18.7	5	5.5	42	46.2	2	2.2	9	9.9	10	11.0	39	42.9	62	68.1
CENSUS DIVISION 6, WEST NORTH CENTRAL	649	272	41.9	185	28.5	491	75.7	250	38.5	51	7.9	319	49.2	116	17.9	61	9.4	69	10.6	194	29.9	454	70.0
Iowa	125	62	49.6	55	44.0	111	88.8	61	48.8	13	10.4	72	57.6	36	28.8	12	9.6	10	8.0	35	28.0	111	88.8
Kansas	153	52	34.0	18	11.8	103	67.3	33	21.6	3	2.0	53	34.6	32	20.9	5	3.3	12	7.8	27	17.6	75	49.0
Minnesota	102	47	46.1	46	45.1	81	79.4	43	42.2	10	9.8	57	55.9	17	16.7	8	7.8	8	7.8	29	28.4	77	75.5
Missouri	149	56	37.6	27	18.1	112	75.2	63	42.3	16	10.7	87	58.4	18	12.1	22	14.8	27	18.1	72	48.3	115	77.2
Nebraska	52	25	48.1	18	34.6	38	73.1	16	30.8	4	7.7	28	53.8	5	9.6	3	5.8	5	9.6	18	34.6	37	71.2
North Dakota	24	10	41.7	8	33.3	16	66.7	11	45.8	2	8.3	9	37.5	5	20.8	3	12.5	5	20.8	6	25.0	15	62.5
South Dakota	44	20	45.5	13	29.5	30	68.2	23	52.3	3	6.8	13	29.5	5	11.4	8	18.2	2	4.5	7	15.9	24	54.5
CENSUS DIVISION 7, WEST SOUTH CENTRAL	883	182	20.6	74	8.4	529	59.9	226	25.6	74	8.4	395	44.7	44	5.0	51	5.8	91	10.3	310	35.1	550	62.3
Arkansas	91	39	42.9	11	12.1	62	68.1	14	15.4	1	1.1	44	48.4	5	5.5	6	6.6	6	6.6	27	29.7	59	64.8
Louisiana	102	12	11.8	6	5.9	58	56.9	29	28.4	16	15.7	37	36.3	2	2.0	6	5.9	8	7.8	37	36.3	69	67.6
Oklahoma	123	37	30.1	10	8.1	62	50.4	30	24.4	6	4.9	52	42.3	15	12.2	6	4.9	5	4.1	36	29.3	58	47.2
Texas	567	94	16.6	47	8.3	347	61.2	153	27.0	51	9.0	262	46.2	22	3.9	31	5.5	72	12.7	210	37.0	364	64.2
CENSUS DIVISION 8, MOUNTAIN	335	89	26.6	79	23.6	231	69.0	112	33.4	39	11.6	179	53.4	29	8.7	25	7.5	47	14.0	135	40.3	236	70.4
Arizona	59	14	23.7	11	18.6	39	66.1	18	30.5	7	11.9	43	72.9	8	13.6	5	8.5	11	18.6	34	57.6	46	78.0
Colorado	71	17	23.9	11	15.5	51	71.8	15	21.1	11	15.5	40	56.3	7	9.9	5	7.0	10	14.1	34	47.9	53	74.6
Idaho	30	6	20.0	9	30.0	23	76.7	14	46.7	4	13.3	20	66.7	3	10.0	4	13.3	0	0.0	10	33.3	23	76.7
Montana	53	21	39.6	21	39.6	40	75.5	24	45.3	6	11.3	16	30.2	8	15.1	2	3.8	4	7.5	14	26.4	33	62.3
Nevada	27	4	14.8	3	11.1	18	66.7	10	37.0	3	11.1	14	51.9	0	0.0	1	3.7	4	14.8	12	44.4	18	66.7
New Mexico	36	10	27.8	7	19.4	24	66.7	13	36.1	2	5.6	15	41.7	1	2.8	1	2.8	8	22.2	13	36.1	19	52.8
Utah	32	10	31.3	9	28.1	22	68.8	10	31.3	4	12.5	19	59.4	1	3.1	2	6.3	8	25.0	13	40.6	26	81.3
Wyoming	27	7	25.9	8	29.6	14	51.9	8	29.6	2	7.4	12	44.4	1	3.7	3	11.1	2	7.4	8	29.6	18	66.7
CENSUS DIVISION 9, PACIFIC	448	121	27.0	103	23.0	321	71.7	192	42.9	82	18.3	286	63.8	27	6.0	51	11.4	49	10.9	227	50.7	328	73.2
Alaska	13	5	38.5	1	7.7	6	46.2	4	30.8	1	7.7	8	61.5	0	0.0	1	7.7	1	7.7	4	30.8	10	76.9
California	284	63	22.2	56	19.7	197	69.4	124	43.7	57	20.1	182	64.1	20	7.0	34	12.0	30	10.6	157	55.3	196	69.0
Hawaii	20	5	25.0	2	10.0	11	55.0	5	25.0	1	5.0	9	45.0	1	5.0	1	5.0	1	5.0	8	40.0	13	65.0
Oregon	61	29	47.5	26	42.6	54	88.5	25	41.0	12	19.7	40	65.6	1	1.6	7	11.5	4	6.6	24	39.3	54	88.5
Washington	70	19	27.1	18	25.7	53	75.7	34	48.6	11	15.7	47	67.1	5	7.1	8	11.4	13	18.6	34	48.6	55	78.6

Facilities and Services

Table 7 (Continued)

These data include only hospital-based facilities and services as reported by responding hospitals in Section C of the 2010 AHA Annual Survey, beginning on page 215. All hospitals are represented with Community Hospitals listed separately under United States. No estimates have been made for nonresponding hospitals. Definitions of facilities and services are listed in the Glossary, page 201.

CLASSIFICATION	HOSPITALS REPORTING	OBSTETRICS INPATIENT CARE UNITS Number	Percent	OCCUPATIONAL HEALTH SERVICES Number	Percent	ONCOLOGY SERVICES Number	Percent	ORTHOPEDIC SERVICES Number	Percent	OTHER SPECIAL CARE UNITS Number	Percent	OUTPATIENT SURGERY Number	Percent	PAIN MANAGEMENT PROGRAM Number	Percent	PALLIATIVE CARE PROGRAM Number	Percent	PALLIATIVE CARE INPATIENT UNIT Number	Percent	PATIENT CONTROLLED ANALGESIA (PCA) Number	Percent	PATIENT EDUCATION CENTER Number	Percent
UNITED STATES	4,782	2,613	54.6	3,003	62.8	2,446	51.2	3,210	67.1	705	14.7	3,837	80.2	2,383	49.8	1,505	31.5	443	9.3	3,092	64.7	2,619	54.8
COMMUNITY HOSPITALS	4,079	2,570	63.0	2,781	68.2	2,354	57.7	3,010	73.8	661	16.2	3,622	88.8	2,185	53.6	1,406	34.5	384	9.4	2,881	70.6	2,378	58.3
CENSUS DIVISION 1, NEW ENGLAND	198	126	63.6	156	78.8	150	75.8	170	85.9	20	10.1	167	84.3	137	69.2	93	47.0	31	15.7	159	80.3	139	70.2
Connecticut	32	25	78.1	22	68.8	26	81.3	25	78.1	8	25.0	26	81.3	26	81.3	20	62.5	5	15.6	24	75.0	21	65.6
Maine	40	29	72.5	27	67.5	27	67.5	36	90.0	3	7.5	35	87.5	21	52.5	17	42.5	7	17.5	32	80.0	25	62.5
Massachusetts	74	40	54.1	62	83.8	57	77.0	64	86.5	4	5.4	59	79.7	56	75.7	25	33.8	9	12.2	60	81.1	56	75.7
New Hampshire	28	19	67.9	25	89.3	20	71.4	25	89.3	5	17.9	24	85.7	17	60.7	15	53.6	7	25.0	24	85.7	19	67.9
Rhode Island	12	6	50.0	9	75.0	11	91.7	10	83.3	0	0.0	12	100.0	9	75.0	7	58.3	1	8.3	9	75.0	11	91.7
Vermont	12	7	58.3	11	91.7	9	75.0	10	83.3	0	0.0	11	91.7	8	66.7	9	75.0	2	16.7	10	83.3	7	58.3
CENSUS DIVISION 2, MIDDLE ATLANTIC	414	242	58.5	312	75.4	289	69.8	334	80.7	76	18.4	346	83.6	284	68.6	199	48.1	71	17.1	290	70.0	276	66.7
New Jersey	73	45	61.6	51	69.9	54	74.0	55	75.3	9	12.3	58	79.5	54	74.0	39	53.4	12	16.4	47	64.4	49	67.1
New York	168	110	65.5	129	76.8	127	75.6	143	85.1	37	22.0	149	88.7	117	69.6	94	56.0	38	22.6	122	72.6	115	68.5
Pennsylvania	173	87	50.3	132	76.3	108	62.4	136	78.6	30	17.3	139	80.3	113	65.3	66	38.2	21	12.1	121	69.9	112	64.7
CENSUS DIVISION 3, SOUTH ATLANTIC	715	393	55.0	479	67.0	385	53.8	526	73.6	137	19.2	569	79.6	372	52.0	240	33.6	65	9.1	491	68.7	429	60.0
Delaware	11	6	54.5	8	54.5	6	54.5	7	63.6	3	27.3	7	63.6	4	36.4	2	18.2	1	9.1	7	63.6	5	45.5
District of Columbia	12	6	50.0	8	66.7	6	50.0	6	50.0	3	25.0	7	58.3	7	58.3	7	58.3	2	16.7	8	66.7	8	66.7
Florida	160	76	47.5	101	63.1	97	60.6	122	76.3	40	25.0	129	80.6	83	51.9	49	30.6	17	10.6	111	69.4	97	60.6
Georgia	128	81	63.3	81	63.3	59	46.1	88	68.8	17	13.3	104	81.3	60	46.9	27	21.1	9	7.0	74	57.8	71	55.5
Maryland	58	48	82.8	48	82.8	42	72.4	47	81.0	14	24.1	46	79.3	43	74.1	29	50.0	7	12.1	46	79.3	36	62.1
North Carolina	115	76	66.1	83	72.2	68	59.1	89	77.4	27	23.5	98	85.2	76	66.1	43	37.4	13	11.3	90	78.3	64	55.7
South Carolina	79	44	55.7	53	67.1	30	38.0	57	72.2	20	25.3	57	72.2	32	40.5	19	24.1	2	2.5	51	64.6	53	67.1
Virginia	89	53	59.6	65	73.0	54	60.7	69	77.5	11	12.4	73	82.0	46	51.7	41	46.1	9	10.1	68	76.4	58	65.2
West Virginia	63	29	46.0	34	54.0	23	36.5	41	65.1	2	3.2	48	76.2	21	33.3	23	36.5	5	7.9	36	57.1	37	58.7
CENSUS DIVISION 4, EAST NORTH CENTRAL	721	457	63.4	504	69.9	479	66.4	546	75.7	196	27.2	643	89.2	474	65.7	266	36.9	75	10.4	535	74.2	511	70.9
Illinois	173	107	61.8	108	62.4	123	71.1	137	79.2	17	9.8	157	90.8	118	68.2	67	38.7	11	6.4	138	79.8	108	62.4
Indiana	108	73	67.6	75	69.4	65	60.2	88	81.5	19	17.6	96	88.9	61	56.5	30	27.8	5	4.6	82	75.9	68	63.0
Michigan	147	85	57.8	115	78.2	96	65.3	117	79.6	26	17.7	127	86.4	85	57.8	64	43.5	21	14.3	113	76.9	95	64.6
Ohio	152	97	63.8	118	77.6	111	73.0	139	91.4	27	17.8	142	93.4	113	74.3	62	40.8	27	17.8	130	85.5	110	72.4
Wisconsin	141	95	67.4	88	62.4	84	59.6	65	46.1	107	75.9	121	85.8	97	68.8	43	30.5	11	7.8	72	51.1	130	92.2
CENSUS DIVISION 5, EAST SOUTH CENTRAL	419	185	44.2	205	48.9	154	36.8	208	49.6	51	12.2	308	73.5	119	28.4	73	17.4	22	5.3	190	45.3	190	45.3
Alabama	120	53	44.2	51	42.5	41	34.2	66	55.0	10	8.3	85	70.8	46	38.3	18	15.0	5	4.2	51	42.5	47	39.2
Kentucky	98	45	45.9	64	65.3	48	49.0	66	67.3	10	10.2	79	80.6	47	48.0	27	27.6	9	9.2	66	67.3	59	60.2
Mississippi	110	43	39.1	37	33.6	28	25.5	18	16.4	15	13.6	69	62.7	0	0.0	10	9.1	0	0.0	20	18.2	41	37.3
Tennessee	91	44	48.4	53	58.2	37	40.7	58	63.7	16	17.6	75	82.4	26	28.6	18	19.8	8	8.8	53	58.2	43	47.3
CENSUS DIVISION 6, WEST NORTH CENTRAL	649	347	53.5	423	65.2	299	46.1	388	59.8	68	10.5	554	85.4	281	43.3	194	29.9	53	8.2	403	62.1	317	48.8
Iowa	125	79	63.2	93	74.4	76	60.8	92	73.6	8	6.4	118	94.4	60	48.0	36	28.8	7	5.6	89	71.2	68	54.4
Kansas	153	68	44.4	78	51.0	43	28.1	64	41.8	10	6.5	120	78.4	54	35.3	30	19.6	6	3.9	75	49.0	52	34.0
Minnesota	102	72	70.6	80	78.4	41	40.2	66	64.7	8	7.8	99	97.1	44	43.1	40	39.2	16	15.7	67	65.7	52	51.0
Missouri	149	72	48.3	99	66.4	71	47.7	101	67.8	28	18.8	111	74.5	74	49.7	48	32.2	12	8.1	106	71.1	87	58.4
Nebraska	52	28	53.8	34	65.4	28	53.8	39	75.0	6	11.5	47	90.4	26	50.0	20	38.5	5	9.6	32	61.5	27	51.9
North Dakota	24	11	45.8	11	45.8	12	50.0	9	37.5	4	16.7	22	91.7	7	29.2	7	29.2	4	16.7	15	62.5	12	50.0
South Dakota	44	17	38.6	28	63.6	15	34.1	17	38.6	4	9.1	37	84.1	16	36.4	10	22.7	3	6.8	19	43.2	19	43.2
CENSUS DIVISION 7, WEST SOUTH CENTRAL	883	363	41.1	430	48.7	269	30.5	478	54.1	86	9.7	595	67.4	307	34.8	139	15.7	33	3.7	511	57.9	366	41.4
Arkansas	91	40	44.0	47	51.6	32	35.2	46	50.5	6	6.6	65	71.4	21	23.1	14	15.4	4	4.4	52	57.1	52	39.6
Louisiana	102	44	43.1	50	49.0	41	40.2	56	54.9	8	7.8	77	75.5	33	32.4	18	17.6	1	1.0	56	54.9	39	38.2
Oklahoma	123	54	43.9	53	43.1	27	22.0	68	55.3	9	7.3	94	76.4	47	38.2	15	12.2	8	6.5	68	55.3	37	30.1
Texas	567	225	39.7	280	49.4	169	29.8	308	54.3	63	11.1	359	63.3	206	36.3	92	16.2	20	3.5	335	59.1	254	44.8
CENSUS DIVISION 8, MOUNTAIN	335	204	60.9	198	59.1	160	47.8	221	66.0	25	7.5	273	81.5	170	50.7	101	30.1	33	9.9	213	63.6	151	45.1
Arizona	59	39	55.9	37	62.7	34	57.6	44	74.6	2	3.4	50	84.7	33	55.9	23	39.0	9	15.3	39	66.1	29	49.2
Colorado	71	47	66.2	50	70.4	42	59.2	53	74.6	12	16.9	63	88.7	35	49.3	25	35.2	4	5.6	53	74.6	32	45.1
Idaho	30	19	63.3	20	66.7	11	36.7	24	80.0	1	3.3	28	93.3	10	33.3	10	33.3	6	20.0	22	73.3	19	63.3
Montana	53	27	50.9	28	52.8	18	34.0	25	47.2	2	3.8	36	67.9	23	43.4	14	26.4	5	9.4	22	41.5	20	37.7
Nevada	27	13	48.1	17	63.0	14	51.9	18	66.7	1	3.7	19	70.4	13	48.1	8	29.6	2	7.4	18	66.7	14	51.9
New Mexico	36	21	58.3	12	33.3	14	38.9	18	50.0	1	2.8	28	77.8	10	27.8	6	16.7	4	11.1	22	61.1	8	22.2
Utah	32	25	78.1	20	62.5	16	50.0	21	65.6	4	12.5	28	87.5	20	62.5	10	31.3	2	6.3	22	68.8	19	59.4
Wyoming	27	19	70.4	14	51.9	11	40.7	18	66.7	2	7.4	21	77.8	14	51.9	5	18.5	1	3.7	15	55.6	10	37.0
CENSUS DIVISION 9, PACIFIC	448	296	66.1	296	66.1	261	58.3	339	75.7	46	10.3	382	85.3	239	53.3	200	44.6	60	13.4	300	67.0	240	53.6
Alaska	13	7	53.8	8	61.5	7	53.8	8	61.5	1	7.7	9	69.2	5	38.5	2	15.4	1	7.7	7	53.8	6	46.2
California	284	183	64.4	189	66.5	173	60.9	218	76.8	27	9.5	242	85.2	155	54.6	132	46.5	37	13.0	186	65.5	148	52.1
Hawaii	20	9	45.0	14	70.0	9	45.0	12	60.0	1	5.0	12	60.0	7	35.0	6	30.0	0	0.0	8	40.0	8	40.0
Oregon	61	51	83.6	38	62.3	34	55.7	50	82.0	5	8.2	57	93.4	34	55.7	31	50.8	9	14.8	51	83.6	34	55.7
Washington	70	46	65.7	47	67.1	38	54.3	51	72.9	12	17.1	62	88.6	38	54.3	29	41.4	13	18.6	48	68.6	44	62.9

Table 7 (Continued)

These data include only hospital-based facilities and services as reported by responding hospitals in Section C of the 2010 AHA Annual Survey, beginning on page 215. All hospitals are represented with Community Hospitals listed separately under United States. No estimates have been made for nonresponding hospitals. Definitions of facilities and services are listed in the Glossary, page 201.

CLASSIFICATION	HOSPITALS REPORTING	PATIENT REPRESENTATIVE SERVICES Number	Percent	PHYSICAL REHABILITATION INPATIENT CARE UNITS Number	Percent	PRIMARY CARE DEPARTMENT Number	Percent	PSYCHIATRIC INPATIENT CARE UNITS Number	Percent	RETIREMENT HOUSING Number	Percent	ROBOTIC SURGERY Number	Percent	RURAL HEALTH CLINIC Number	Percent	SLEEP CENTER Number	Percent	SOCIAL WORK SERVICES Number	Percent	SPORTS MEDICINE Number	Percent	SUPPORT GROUPS Number	Percent
UNITED STATES	4,782	3,118	65.2	1,400	29.3	1,787	37.4	1,606	33.6	148	3.1	819	17.1	903	18.9	2,195	45.9	4,028	84.2	1,785	37.3	2,960	61.9
COMMUNITY HOSPITALS	4,079	2,806	68.8	1,309	32.1	1,655	40.6	1,234	30.3	143	3.5	798	19.6	833	20.4	2,105	51.6	3,520	86.3	1,725	42.3	2,706	66.3
CENSUS DIVISION 1, NEW ENGLAND	198	159	80.3	49	24.7	123	62.1	101	51.0	8	4.0	47	23.7	28	14.1	112	56.6	195	98.5	118	59.6	180	90.9
Connecticut	32	26	81.3	9	28.1	19	59.4	25	78.1	3	9.4	16	50.0	0	0.0	22	68.8	30	93.8	20	62.5	32	100.0
Maine	40	28	70.0	11	27.5	30	75.0	13	32.5	3	7.5	3	7.5	15	37.5	22	55.0	39	97.5	17	42.5	36	90.0
Massachusetts	74	64	86.5	14	18.9	37	50.0	44	59.5	0	0.0	18	24.3	2	2.7	42	56.8	74	100.0	45	60.8	66	89.2
New Hampshire	28	23	82.1	8	28.6	19	67.9	9	32.1	1	3.6	6	21.4	5	17.9	15	53.6	28	100.0	21	75.0	24	85.7
Rhode Island	12	9	75.0	4	33.3	10	83.3	8	66.7	0	0.0	3	25.0	1	8.3	7	58.3	12	100.0	6	50.0	12	100.0
Vermont	12	9	75.0	3	25.0	8	66.7	2	16.7	1	8.3	1	8.3	5	41.7	4	33.3	12	100.0	9	75.0	10	83.3
CENSUS DIVISION 2, MIDDLE ATLANTIC	414	316	76.3	160	38.6	226	54.6	238	57.5	9	2.2	111	26.8	30	7.2	229	55.3	389	94.0	188	45.4	323	78.0
New Jersey	73	61	83.6	21	28.8	47	64.4	45	61.6	3	4.1	27	37.0	2	2.7	47	64.4	69	94.5	26	35.6	54	74.0
New York	168	137	81.5	70	41.7	111	66.1	104	61.9	4	2.4	45	26.8	16	9.5	80	47.6	158	94.0	91	54.2	136	81.0
Pennsylvania	173	118	68.2	69	39.9	68	39.3	89	51.4	2	1.2	39	22.5	12	6.9	102	59.0	162	93.6	71	41.0	133	76.9
CENSUS DIVISION 3, SOUTH ATLANTIC	715	498	69.7	225	31.5	239	33.4	257	35.9	10	1.4	152	21.3	87	12.2	362	50.6	604	84.5	278	38.9	472	66.0
Delaware	11	7	63.6	5	45.5	5	45.5	6	54.5	0	0.0	2	18.2	0	0.0	5	45.5	9	81.8	3	27.3	6	54.5
District of Columbia	12	7	58.3	4	33.3	5	41.7	9	75.0	0	0.0	4	33.3	0	0.0	6	50.0	11	91.7	7	58.3	7	58.3
Florida	160	107	66.9	41	25.6	44	27.5	48	30.0	2	1.3	50	31.3	13	8.1	72	45.0	121	75.6	68	42.5	109	68.1
Georgia	128	87	68.0	37	28.9	37	28.9	32	25.0	5	3.9	18	14.1	20	15.6	69	53.9	103	80.5	40	31.3	66	51.6
Maryland	58	48	82.8	14	24.2	25	43.1	37	63.8	1	1.7	15	25.9	3	5.2	40	69.0	55	94.8	25	43.1	49	84.5
North Carolina	115	81	70.4	33	28.7	44	38.3	48	41.7	0	0.0	29	25.2	14	12.2	66	57.4	98	85.2	47	40.9	78	67.8
South Carolina	79	52	65.8	19	24.1	22	27.8	26	32.9	1	1.1	11	13.9	13	16.5	33	41.8	70	88.6	27	34.2	50	63.3
Virginia	89	67	75.3	63	70.9	31	34.8	34	38.2	1	1.1	18	20.2	7	7.9	42	47.2	79	88.8	40	44.9	67	75.3
West Virginia	63	42	66.7	9	14.3	26	41.3	17	27.0	0	0.0	5	7.9	17	27.0	29	46.0	58	92.1	21	33.3	40	63.5
CENSUS DIVISION 4, EAST NORTH CENTRAL	721	551	76.4	254	35.2	341	47.3	276	38.3	28	3.9	146	20.2	120	16.6	432	59.9	660	91.5	380	52.7	539	74.8
Illinois	173	127	73.4	50	28.9	81	46.8	68	39.3	7	4.0	39	22.5	39	22.5	114	65.9	158	91.3	89	51.4	144	83.2
Indiana	108	83	76.9	36	33.3	47	43.5	37	34.3	2	1.9	17	15.7	11	10.2	72	66.7	91	84.3	45	41.7	88	81.5
Michigan	147	113	76.9	48	32.7	89	60.5	62	42.2	4	2.7	36	24.5	45	30.6	95	64.6	137	93.2	84	57.1	119	81.0
Ohio	152	123	80.9	54	35.5	80	52.6	67	44.1	7	4.6	38	25.0	11	7.2	101	66.4	141	92.8	86	56.6	115	75.7
Wisconsin	141	105	74.5	66	46.8	44	31.2	42	29.8	8	5.7	16	11.3	14	9.9	50	35.5	133	94.3	76	53.9	73	51.8
CENSUS DIVISION 5, EAST SOUTH CENTRAL	419	240	57.3	116	27.7	104	24.8	150	35.8	4	1.0	56	13.4	55	13.1	166	39.6	330	78.8	122	29.1	204	48.7
Alabama	120	55	45.8	22	18.3	20	16.7	42	35.0	3	2.5	18	15.0	11	9.2	48	40.0	77	64.2	39	32.5	51	42.5
Kentucky	98	66	67.3	23	23.5	36	36.7	33	33.7	0	0.0	16	16.3	25	25.5	54	55.1	86	87.8	29	29.6	65	66.3
Mississippi	110	63	57.3	49	44.5	24	21.8	42	38.2	0	0.0	7	6.4	15	13.6	16	14.5	99	90.0	21	19.1	40	36.4
Tennessee	91	56	61.5	22	24.2	24	26.4	33	36.3	1	1.1	15	16.5	4	4.4	48	52.7	68	74.7	33	36.3	48	52.7
CENSUS DIVISION 6, WEST NORTH CENTRAL	649	362	55.8	186	28.7	263	40.5	169	26.0	63	9.7	56	8.6	244	37.6	304	46.8	523	80.6	261	40.2	392	60.4
Iowa	125	67	53.6	25	20.0	63	50.4	36	28.8	19	15.2	11	8.8	61	48.8	70	56.0	106	84.8	54	43.2	97	77.6
Kansas	153	64	41.8	30	19.6	47	30.7	26	17.0	10	6.5	7	4.6	24	15.7	41	26.8	104	68.0	40	26.1	57	37.3
Minnesota	102	63	61.8	26	25.5	45	44.1	28	27.5	16	15.7	9	8.8	59	57.8	55	53.9	94	92.2	42	41.2	80	78.4
Missouri	149	109	73.2	82	55.0	58	38.9	58	38.9	2	1.3	17	11.4	66	44.3	86	57.7	132	88.6	70	47.0	94	63.1
Nebraska	52	27	51.9	9	17.3	20	38.5	9	17.3	3	5.8	9	17.3	12	23.1	29	55.8	40	76.9	23	44.2	13	25.0
North Dakota	24	16	66.7	7	29.2	12	50.0	7	29.2	3	12.5	1	4.2	12	50.0	7	29.2	21	87.5	12	50.0	21	87.5
South Dakota	44	16	36.4	7	15.9	18	40.9	5	11.4	10	22.7	2	4.5	21	47.7	16	36.4	26	59.1	20	45.5	30	68.2
CENSUS DIVISION 7, WEST SOUTH CENTRAL	883	493	55.8	220	24.9	194	22.0	213	24.1	11	1.2	92	10.4	173	19.6	300	34.0	670	75.9	201	22.8	378	42.8
Arkansas	91	51	56.0	26	28.6	22	24.2	34	37.4	2	2.2	12	13.2	20	22.0	40	44.0	64	70.3	22	24.2	43	47.3
Louisiana	102	52	51.0	33	32.4	28	27.5	42	41.2	3	2.9	12	11.8	20	19.6	32	31.4	81	79.4	24	23.5	43	42.2
Oklahoma	123	64	52.0	31	25.2	23	18.7	32	26.0	1	0.8	10	8.1	18	14.6	58	47.2	82	66.7	32	26.0	43	35.0
Texas	567	326	57.5	130	22.9	121	21.3	105	18.5	5	0.9	58	10.2	115	20.3	170	30.0	443	78.1	123	21.7	249	43.9
CENSUS DIVISION 8, MOUNTAIN	335	205	61.2	85	25.4	134	40.0	72	21.5	9	2.7	61	18.2	94	28.1	149	44.5	270	80.6	120	35.8	177	52.8
Arizona	59	40	67.8	19	32.2	13	22.0	15	25.4	0	0.0	21	35.6	4	6.8	21	35.6	53	89.8	17	28.8	37	62.7
Colorado	71	49	69.0	24	33.8	34	47.9	13	18.3	2	2.8	18	25.4	14	19.7	45	63.4	53	74.6	32	45.1	40	56.3
Idaho	30	22	73.3	7	23.3	14	46.7	6	20.0	0	0.0	4	13.3	8	26.7	15	50.0	25	83.3	17	56.7	18	60.0
Montana	53	24	45.3	10	18.9	30	56.6	8	15.1	5	9.4	5	9.4	31	58.5	18	34.0	44	83.0	22	41.5	22	41.5
Nevada	27	15	55.6	5	18.5	7	25.9	5	19.4	1	3.7	4	14.8	3	11.1	5	18.5	23	85.2	6	22.2	12	44.4
New Mexico	36	16	44.4	8	22.2	13	36.1	7	19.4	0	0.0	2	5.6	23	63.9	10	27.8	23	63.9	2	5.6	16	44.4
Utah	32	24	75.0	10	31.3	13	40.6	11	34.4	1	3.1	6	18.8	3	9.4	20	62.5	24	75.0	17	53.1	19	59.4
Wyoming	27	15	55.6	2	7.4	10	37.0	7	25.9	0	0.0	1	3.7	8	29.6	15	55.6	25	92.6	7	25.9	13	48.1
CENSUS DIVISION 9, PACIFIC	448	294	65.6	105	23.4	163	36.4	130	29.0	6	1.3	98	21.9	72	16.1	141	31.5	387	86.4	117	26.1	295	65.8
Alaska	13	9	69.2	2	15.4	2	15.4	6	46.2	0	0.0	1	7.7	1	7.7	7	53.8	11	84.6	3	23.1	7	53.8
California	284	180	63.4	72	25.4	91	32.0	82	28.9	4	1.4	66	23.2	41	14.4	64	22.5	252	88.7	61	21.5	181	63.7
Hawaii	20	10	50.0	2	10.0	5	25.0	6	30.0	0	0.0	2	10.0	2	10.0	5	25.0	15	75.0	5	25.0	10	50.0
Oregon	61	44	72.1	11	18.0	31	50.8	17	27.9	1	1.6	13	21.3	13	21.3	29	47.5	50	82.0	22	36.1	54	88.5
Washington	70	51	72.9	18	25.7	34	48.6	19	27.1	1	1.4	16	22.9	15	21.4	36	51.4	59	84.3	26	37.1	43	61.4

Table 7 (Continued)

These data include only hospital-based facilities and services as reported by responding hospitals in Section C of the 2009 AHA Annual Survey, beginning on page 215. All hospitals are represented with Community Hospitals listed separately under United States. No estimates have been made for nonresponding hospitals. Definitions of facilities and services are listed in the Glossary, page 201.

CLASSIFICATION	HOSPITALS REPORTING	SWING BED SERVICES Number	Percent	TEEN OUTREACH SERVICES Number	Percent	TOBACCO TREATMENT/ CESSATION PROGRAM Number	Percent	TRANSPORTATION TO HEALTH FACILITIES Number	Percent	URGENT CARE CENTER Number	Percent	VIRTUAL COLONOSCOPY Number	Percent	VOLUNTEER SERVICES DEPARTMENT Number	Percent	WOMEN'S HEALTH SERVICES Number	Percent	WOUND MANAGEMENT SERVICES Number	Percent
UNITED STATES	4,782	1,469	30.7	616	12.9	2,340	48.9	1,151	24.1	1,013	21.2	735	15.4	3,485	72.9	2,250	47.1	2,961	61.9
COMMUNITY HOSPITALS	4,079	1,423	34.9	586	14.4	2,148	52.7	992	24.3	952	23.3	713	17.5	3,235	79.3	2,137	52.4	2,732	67.0
CENSUS DIVISION 1, NEW ENGLAND	198	43	21.7	55	27.8	144	72.7	66	33.3	68	34.3	42	21.2	187	94.4	143	72.2	149	75.3
Connecticut	32	4	12.5	13	40.6	22	68.8	6	18.8	16	50.0	15	46.9	29	90.6	21	65.6	26	81.3
Maine	40	12	30.0	8	20.0	30	75.0	11	27.5	10	25.0	6	15.0	37	92.5	30	75.0	29	72.5
Massachusetts	74	4	5.4	22	29.7	48	64.9	32	43.2	26	35.1	16	21.6	70	94.6	52	70.3	56	75.7
New Hampshire	28	15	53.6	8	28.6	22	78.6	9	32.1	9	32.1	4	14.3	27	96.4	24	85.7	20	71.4
Rhode Island	12	1	8.3	3	25.0	10	83.3	4	33.3	4	33.3	0	0.0	12	100.0	9	75.0	9	75.0
Vermont	12	7	58.3	1	8.3	12	100.0	4	33.3	3	25.0	1	8.3	12	100.0	7	58.3	9	75.0
CENSUS DIVISION 2, MIDDLE ATLANTIC	414	68	16.4	108	26.1	277	66.9	151	36.5	99	23.9	97	23.4	369	89.1	270	65.2	295	71.3
New Jersey	73	7	9.6	24	32.9	42	57.5	43	58.9	19	26.0	11	15.1	64	87.7	50	68.5	60	82.2
New York	168	29	17.3	46	27.4	126	75.0	57	33.9	48	28.6	55	32.7	154	91.7	122	72.6	116	69.0
Pennsylvania	173	32	18.5	38	22.0	109	63.0	51	29.5	32	18.5	31	17.9	151	87.3	98	56.6	119	68.8
CENSUS DIVISION 3, SOUTH ATLANTIC	715	143	20.0	91	12.7	380	53.1	180	25.2	146	20.4	123	17.2	589	82.4	380	53.1	460	64.3
Delaware	11	0	0.0	3	27.3	7	63.6	4	36.4	1	9.1	1	9.1	7	63.6	7	63.6	7	63.6
District of Columbia	12	1	8.3	4	33.3	6	50.0	6	50.0	2	16.7	3	25.0	9	75.0	7	58.3	8	66.7
Florida	160	13	8.1	17	10.6	77	48.1	36	22.5	36	22.5	25	15.6	127	79.4	79	49.4	107	66.9
Georgia	128	44	34.4	14	10.9	56	43.8	28	21.9	25	19.5	13	10.2	101	78.9	62	48.4	77	60.2
Maryland	58	2	3.4	14	24.1	39	67.2	18	31.0	17	29.3	14	24.1	51	87.9	35	60.3	42	72.4
North Carolina	115	32	27.8	12	10.4	68	59.1	39	33.9	29	25.2	26	22.6	101	87.8	61	53.0	77	67.0
South Carolina	79	10	12.7	10	12.7	38	48.1	11	13.9	9	11.4	11	13.9	63	79.7	42	53.2	46	58.2
Virginia	89	18	20.2	10	11.2	52	58.4	23	25.8	15	16.9	17	19.1	81	91.0	51	57.3	62	69.7
West Virginia	63	23	36.5	7	11.1	37	58.7	15	23.8	12	19.0	13	20.6	49	77.8	36	57.1	34	54.0
CENSUS DIVISION 4, EAST NORTH CENTRAL	721	188	26.1	125	17.3	443	61.4	203	28.2	279	38.7	141	19.6	588	81.6	399	55.3	485	67.3
Illinois	173	52	30.1	33	19.1	97	56.1	55	31.8	47	27.2	47	27.2	146	84.4	98	56.6	123	71.1
Indiana	108	35	32.4	18	16.7	84	77.8	23	21.3	36	33.3	20	18.5	93	86.1	61	56.5	73	67.6
Michigan	147	29	19.7	30	20.4	98	66.7	45	30.6	63	42.9	25	17.0	132	89.8	84	57.1	111	75.5
Ohio	152	31	20.4	28	18.4	111	73.0	54	35.5	52	34.2	29	19.1	141	92.8	95	62.5	104	68.4
Wisconsin	141	41	29.1	16	11.3	53	37.6	26	18.4	81	57.4	20	14.2	76	53.9	61	43.3	74	52.5
CENSUS DIVISION 5, EAST SOUTH CENTRAL	419	145	34.6	34	8.1	162	38.7	59	14.1	41	9.8	34	8.1	255	60.9	157	37.5	172	41.1
Alabama	120	22	18.3	8	6.7	40	33.3	14	11.7	12	10.0	7	5.8	74	61.7	40	33.3	47	39.2
Kentucky	98	39	39.8	9	9.2	60	61.2	18	18.4	12	12.2	12	12.2	80	81.6	48	49.0	52	53.1
Mississippi	110	53	48.2	8	7.3	22	20.0	16	14.5	9	8.2	3	2.7	31	28.2	31	28.2	24	21.8
Tennessee	91	31	34.1	9	9.9	40	44.0	11	12.1	8	8.8	12	13.2	70	76.9	38	41.8	49	53.8
CENSUS DIVISION 6, WEST NORTH CENTRAL	649	391	60.2	60	9.2	307	47.3	162	25.0	106	16.3	90	13.9	421	64.9	229	35.3	372	57.3
Iowa	125	92	73.6	17	13.6	81	64.8	25	20.0	21	16.8	15	12.0	96	76.8	49	39.2	79	63.2
Kansas	153	102	66.7	5	3.3	44	28.8	34	22.2	10	6.5	20	13.1	73	47.7	39	25.5	84	54.9
Minnesota	102	56	54.9	14	13.7	52	51.0	24	23.5	31	30.4	21	20.6	78	76.5	40	39.2	58	56.9
Missouri	149	54	36.2	16	10.7	79	53.0	52	34.9	32	21.5	18	12.1	106	71.1	65	43.6	87	58.4
Nebraska	52	32	61.5	6	11.5	26	50.0	12	23.1	4	7.7	9	17.3	33	63.5	18	34.6	30	57.7
North Dakota	24	18	75.0	0	0.0	10	41.7	8	33.3	5	20.8	3	12.5	14	58.3	8	33.3	10	41.7
South Dakota	44	37	84.1	2	4.5	15	34.1	7	15.9	3	6.8	4	9.1	21	47.7	10	22.7	24	54.5
CENSUS DIVISION 7, WEST SOUTH CENTRAL	883	242	27.4	46	5.2	273	30.9	130	14.7	95	10.8	87	9.9	483	54.7	292	33.1	506	57.3
Arkansas	91	35	38.5	5	5.5	34	37.4	15	16.5	10	11.0	6	6.6	56	61.5	30	33.0	47	51.6
Louisiana	102	26	25.5	7	6.9	45	44.1	18	17.6	17	16.7	9	8.8	60	58.8	39	38.2	55	53.9
Oklahoma	123	46	37.4	6	4.9	41	33.3	20	16.3	17	13.8	12	9.8	74	60.2	42	34.1	64	52.0
Texas	567	135	23.8	28	4.9	153	27.0	77	13.6	51	9.0	60	10.6	293	51.7	181	31.9	340	60.0
CENSUS DIVISION 8, MOUNTAIN	335	145	43.3	40	11.9	161	48.1	78	23.3	76	22.7	48	14.3	235	70.1	158	47.2	214	63.9
Arizona	59	13	22.0	9	15.3	36	61.0	17	28.8	12	20.3	11	18.6	45	76.3	28	47.5	44	74.6
Colorado	71	29	40.8	8	11.3	32	45.1	11	15.5	13	18.3	9	12.7	53	74.6	38	53.5	52	73.2
Idaho	30	17	56.7	7	23.3	16	53.3	10	33.3	10	33.3	3	10.0	25	83.3	16	53.3	18	60.0
Montana	53	44	83.0	3	5.7	21	39.6	21	39.6	15	28.3	9	17.0	33	62.3	16	30.2	26	49.1
Nevada	27	4	14.8	2	7.4	10	37.0	7	14.8	5	18.5	4	14.8	17	63.0	12	44.4	21	70.4
New Mexico	36	7	19.4	3	8.3	18	50.0	7	19.4	7	19.4	3	8.3	17	47.2	16	44.4	21	58.3
Utah	32	11	34.4	6	18.8	14	43.8	4	12.5	7	21.9	3	9.4	26	81.3	20	62.5	22	68.8
Wyoming	27	20	74.1	2	7.4	14	51.9	4	14.8	7	25.9	6	22.2	19	70.4	12	44.4	12	44.4
CENSUS DIVISION 9, PACIFIC	448	104	23.2	57	12.7	193	43.1	122	27.2	103	23.0	73	16.3	358	79.9	222	49.6	308	68.8
Alaska	13	4	30.8	2	15.4	8	61.5	2	15.4	0	0.0	4	30.8	8	61.5	4	30.8	4	69.2
California	284	42	14.8	34	12.0	94	33.1	83	29.2	63	22.2	45	15.8	222	78.2	129	45.4	185	65.1
Hawaii	20	7	35.0	2	10.0	9	45.0	4	20.0	2	10.0	3	15.0	15	75.0	9	45.0	14	70.0
Oregon	61	28	45.9	6	9.8	44	72.1	18	29.5	16	26.2	12	19.7	54	88.5	40	65.6	52	85.2
Washington	70	23	32.9	13	18.6	38	54.3	15	21.4	22	31.4	9	12.9	59	84.3	40	57.1	48	68.6

Table 7 (Continued)

These data include only hospital-based facilities and services as reported by responding hospitals in Section C of the 2010 AHA Annual Survey, beginning on page 215. All hospitals are represented with Community Hospitals listed separately under United States. No estimates have been made for nonresponding hospitals. Definitions of facilities and services are listed in the Glossary, page 201.

CLASSIFICATION	HOSPITALS REPORTING	GENERAL MEDICAL SURGICAL CARE — ADULT UNITS Number	ADULT UNITS Percent	PEDIATRIC UNITS Number	PEDIATRIC UNITS Percent	INTENSIVE CARE UNITS — CARDIAC UNITS Number	CARDIAC UNITS Percent	MEDICAL SURGICAL UNITS Number	MEDICAL SURGICAL UNITS Percent	NEONATAL UNITS Number	NEONATAL UNITS Percent	OTHER UNITS Number	OTHER UNITS Percent	PEDIATRIC UNITS Number	PEDIATRIC UNITS Percent	ACUTE LONG-TERM CARE UNITS Number	ACUTE LONG-TERM CARE UNITS Percent	LONG-TERM CARE UNITS — SKILLED NURSING CARE UNITS Number	SKILLED NURSING CARE UNITS Percent	INTERMEDIATE NURSING CARE UNITS Number	INTERMEDIATE NURSING CARE UNITS Percent	OTHER LONG-TERM CARE UNITS Number	OTHER LONG-TERM CARE UNITS Percent
UNITED STATES	4,782	4,014	83.9	2,020	42.2	1,351	28.3	2,964	62.0	938	19.6	484	10.1	423	8.8	336	7.0	1,148	24.0	371	7.8	232	4.9
COMMUNITY HOSPITALS	4,079	3,756	92.1	1,971	48.3	1,316	32.3	2,829	69.4	923	22.6	465	11.4	415	10.2	215	5.3	1,055	25.9	328	8.0	191	4.7
CENSUS DIVISION 1, NEW ENGLAND	198	164	82.8	107	54.0	55	27.8	152	76.8	36	18.2	14	7.1	15	7.6	11	5.6	34	17.2	18	9.1	6	3.0
Connecticut	32	25	78.1	18	56.3	13	40.6	25	78.1	15	46.9	1	3.1	3	9.4	2	6.3	3	9.4	1	3.1	0	0.0
Maine	40	35	87.5	21	52.5	5	12.5	32	80.0	3	7.5	5	12.5	3	7.5	2	5.0	10	25.0	8	20.0	4	10.0
Massachusetts	74	57	77.0	43	58.1	25	33.8	53	71.6	13	17.6	4	5.4	6	8.1	6	8.1	8	10.8	1	1.4	2	2.7
New Hampshire	28	24	85.7	15	53.6	6	21.4	22	78.6	3	10.7	2	7.1	1	3.6	1	3.6	9	32.1	7	25.0	0	0.0
Rhode Island	12	11	91.7	6	50.0	4	33.3	10	83.3	1	8.3	2	16.7	1	8.3	0	0.0	0	0.0	0	0.0	0	0.0
Vermont	12	12	100.0	4	33.3	2	16.7	10	83.3	1	8.3	0	0.0	1	8.3	0	0.0	4	33.3	1	8.3	0	0.0
CENSUS DIVISION 2, MIDDLE ATLANTIC	414	349	84.3	206	49.8	186	44.9	318	76.8	118	28.5	46	11.1	55	13.3	16	3.9	105	25.4	10	2.4	23	5.6
New Jersey	73	58	79.5	43	58.9	36	49.3	58	79.5	23	31.5	6	8.2	16	21.9	4	5.5	15	20.5	5	6.8	7	9.6
New York	168	153	91.1	98	58.3	88	52.4	137	81.5	57	33.9	21	12.5	32	19.0	10	6.0	46	27.4	4	2.4	14	8.3
Pennsylvania	173	138	79.8	65	37.6	62	35.8	123	71.1	38	22.0	19	11.0	7	4.0	2	1.2	44	25.4	1	0.6	2	1.2
CENSUS DIVISION 3, SOUTH ATLANTIC	715	590	82.5	304	42.5	230	32.2	505	70.6	155	21.7	100	14.0	69	9.7	63	8.8	193	27.0	64	9.0	43	6.0
Delaware	11	6	54.5	6	54.5	7	63.6	6	54.5	5	45.5	2	18.2	4	36.4	1	9.1	2	18.2	2	18.2	2	18.2
District of Columbia	12	6	50.0	3	25.0	6	50.0	7	58.3	5	41.7	1	8.3	2	16.7	2	16.7	3	25.0	2	16.7	1	8.3
Florida	160	132	82.5	56	35.0	64	40.0	123	76.9	43	26.9	18	11.3	24	15.0	8	5.0	38	23.8	7	4.4	4	2.5
Georgia	128	112	87.5	44	34.4	29	22.7	81	63.3	27	21.1	15	11.7	6	4.7	9	7.0	15	11.7	13	10.2	4	3.1
Maryland	58	46	79.3	34	58.6	22	37.9	45	77.6	17	29.3	9	15.5	5	8.6	4	6.9	15	25.9	3	5.2	2	3.4
North Carolina	115	101	87.8	53	46.1	32	27.8	85	73.9	22	19.1	14	12.2	12	10.4	6	5.2	39	33.9	14	12.2	1	0.9
South Carolina	79	60	75.9	46	58.2	27	34.2	52	65.8	10	12.7	30	38.0	7	8.9	29	36.7	33	41.8	8	10.1	25	31.6
Virginia	89	74	83.1	35	39.3	25	28.1	70	78.7	22	24.7	7	7.9	6	6.7	2	2.2	19	21.3	9	10.1	2	2.2
West Virginia	63	53	84.1	27	42.9	18	28.6	36	57.1	4	6.3	4	6.3	3	4.8	2	3.2	29	46.0	6	9.5	2	3.2
CENSUS DIVISION 4, EAST NORTH CENTRAL	721	636	88.2	383	53.1	249	34.5	501	69.5	128	17.8	129	17.9	80	11.1	40	5.5	165	22.9	43	6.0	38	5.3
Illinois	173	154	89.0	95	54.9	48	27.7	124	71.7	31	17.9	12	6.9	19	11.0	7	4.0	53	30.6	7	4.0	8	4.6
Indiana	108	95	88.0	54	50.0	27	25.0	74	68.5	19	17.6	11	10.2	9	8.3	4	3.7	20	18.5	9	8.3	5	4.6
Michigan	147	128	87.1	72	49.0	48	32.7	101	68.7	23	15.6	16	10.9	12	8.2	9	6.1	31	21.1	8	5.4	8	5.4
Ohio	152	139	91.4	60	39.5	55	36.2	122	80.3	29	19.1	18	11.8	11	7.2	7	4.6	36	23.7	10	6.6	12	7.9
Wisconsin	141	120	85.1	102	72.3	71	50.4	80	56.7	26	18.4	72	51.1	29	20.6	13	9.2	25	17.7	9	6.4	5	3.5
CENSUS DIVISION 5, EAST SOUTH CENTRAL	419	358	85.4	172	41.1	116	27.7	227	54.2	65	15.5	41	9.8	32	7.6	16	3.8	83	19.8	21	5.0	29	6.9
Alabama	120	94	78.3	34	28.3	29	24.2	67	55.8	17	14.2	14	11.7	8	6.7	4	3.3	13	10.8	6	5.0	3	2.5
Kentucky	98	80	81.6	36	36.7	25	25.5	60	61.2	15	15.3	7	7.1	4	4.1	9	9.2	25	25.5	5	5.1	5	5.1
Mississippi	110	105	95.5	73	66.4	39	35.5	45	40.9	16	14.5	7	6.4	13	11.8	0	0.0	25	22.7	2	1.8	19	17.3
Tennessee	91	79	86.8	29	31.9	23	25.3	55	60.4	17	18.7	13	14.3	7	7.7	3	3.3	20	22.0	8	8.8	2	2.2
CENSUS DIVISION 6, WEST NORTH CENTRAL	649	585	90.1	283	43.6	139	21.4	326	50.2	84	12.9	40	6.2	45	6.9	39	6.0	261	40.2	124	19.1	54	8.3
Iowa	125	119	95.2	58	46.4	23	18.4	72	57.6	17	13.6	7	5.6	10	8.0	6	4.8	56	44.8	42	33.6	14	11.2
Kansas	153	137	89.5	47	30.7	15	9.8	54	35.3	16	10.5	7	4.6	9	5.9	6	3.9	65	42.5	44	28.8	15	9.8
Minnesota	102	96	94.1	54	52.9	28	27.5	62	60.8	10	9.8	4	3.9	8	7.8	9	8.8	42	41.2	6	5.9	2	2.0
Missouri	149	118	79.2	79	53.0	41	27.5	86	57.7	20	13.4	16	10.7	8	5.4	12	8.1	36	24.2	15	10.1	9	6.0
Nebraska	52	49	94.2	18	34.6	14	26.9	20	38.5	11	21.2	3	5.8	3	5.8	1	1.9	25	48.1	5	9.6	6	11.5
North Dakota	24	23	95.8	11	45.8	9	37.5	12	50.0	7	29.2	2	8.3	4	16.7	3	12.5	12	50.0	4	16.7	2	8.3
South Dakota	44	43	97.7	16	36.4	9	20.5	20	45.5	3	6.8	1	2.3	3	6.8	2	4.5	25	56.8	8	18.2	6	13.6
CENSUS DIVISION 7, WEST SOUTH CENTRAL	883	647	73.3	264	29.9	148	16.8	410	46.4	150	17.0	60	6.8	56	6.3	111	12.6	99	11.2	21	2.4	12	1.4
Arkansas	91	69	75.8	25	27.5	26	28.6	42	46.2	10	11.0	5	5.5	2	2.2	8	8.8	15	16.5	1	1.1	0	0.0
Louisiana	102	78	76.5	46	45.1	18	17.6	59	57.8	28	27.5	8	7.8	12	11.8	10	9.8	19	18.6	4	3.9	3	2.9
Oklahoma	123	101	82.1	32	26.0	21	17.1	50	40.7	11	8.9	8	6.5	5	4.1	10	8.1	22	17.9	4	3.3	2	1.6
Texas	567	399	70.4	161	28.4	83	14.6	259	45.7	101	17.8	39	6.9	37	6.5	84	14.8	43	7.6	12	2.1	7	1.2
CENSUS DIVISION 8, MOUNTAIN	335	297	88.7	134	40.0	70	20.9	202	60.3	70	20.9	21	6.3	29	8.7	19	5.7	91	27.2	39	11.6	16	4.8
Arizona	59	50	84.7	18	30.5	17	28.8	43	72.9	13	22.0	4	6.8	8	13.6	2	3.4	3	5.1	6	10.2	3	5.1
Colorado	71	65	91.5	32	45.1	15	21.1	45	63.4	24	33.8	6	8.5	6	8.5	3	4.2	14	19.7	5	7.0	3	4.2
Idaho	30	30	100.0	13	43.3	6	20.0	17	56.7	5	16.7	2	6.7	2	6.7	1	3.3	12	40.0	9	30.0	0	0.0
Montana	53	51	96.2	21	39.6	11	20.8	23	43.4	7	13.2	2	3.8	3	5.7	5	9.4	34	64.2	5	9.4	6	11.3
Nevada	27	19	70.4	6	22.2	6	22.2	17	63.0	6	22.2	4	14.8	4	14.8	4	14.8	1	3.7	4	14.8	1	3.7
New Mexico	36	30	83.3	15	41.7	4	11.1	22	61.1	4	11.1	4	11.1	2	5.6	2	5.6	5	13.9	6	16.7	2	5.6
Utah	32	27	84.4	18	56.3	11	34.4	17	53.1	11	34.4	2	6.3	3	9.4	1	3.1	10	31.3	0	0.0	1	3.1
Wyoming	27	25	92.6	11	40.7	0	0.0	18	66.7	0	0.0	1	3.7	1	3.7	1	3.7	12	44.4	4	14.8	0	0.0
CENSUS DIVISION 9, PACIFIC	448	388	86.6	167	37.3	158	35.3	323	72.1	132	29.5	33	7.4	42	9.4	21	4.7	117	26.1	31	6.9	11	2.5
Alaska	13	10	76.9	2	15.4	1	7.7	9	69.2	2	15.4	0	0.0	2	15.4	1	7.7	4	30.8	4	30.8	1	7.7
California	284	240	84.5	108	38.0	113	39.8	207	72.9	110	38.7	22	7.7	32	11.3	15	5.3	84	29.6	7	2.5	8	2.8
Hawaii	20	16	80.0	2	10.0	6	30.0	11	55.0	1	5.0	0	0.0	1	5.0	1	5.0	8	40.0	7	35.0	0	0.0
Oregon	61	59	96.7	25	41.0	18	29.5	51	83.6	7	11.5	4	6.6	2	3.3	1	1.6	10	16.4	9	14.8	0	0.0
Washington	70	63	90.0	30	42.9	20	28.6	45	64.3	12	17.1	7	10.0	5	7.1	3	4.3	11	15.7	4	5.7	2	2.9

Table 7 (Continued)

These data include only hospital-based facilities and services as reported by responding hospitals in Section C of the 2010 AHA Annual Survey, beginning on page 215. All hospitals are represented with Community Hospitals listed separately under United States. No estimates have been made for nonresponding hospitals. Definitions of facilities and services are listed in the Glossary, page 201.

CARDIOLOGY AND CARDIAC SERVICES

CLASSIFICATION	HOSPITALS REPORTING	ADULT CARDIOLOGY SERVICES Number	Percent	PEDIATRIC CARDIOLOGY SERVICES Number	Percent	ADULT DIAGNOSTIC CATHETERIZATION Number	Percent	PEDIATRIC DIAGNOSTIC CATHETERIZATION Number	Percent	ADULT INTERVENTIONAL CARDIAC CATHETERIZATION Number	Percent	PEDIATRIC INTERVENTIONAL CARDIAC CATHETERIZATION Number	Percent	ADULT CARDIAC SURGERY Number	Percent	PEDIATRIC CARDIAC SURGERY Number	Percent	ADULT CARDIAC ELECTRO-PHYSIOLOGY Number	Percent	PEDIATRIC CARDIAC ELECTRO-PHYSIOLOGY Number	Percent	CARDIAC REHABILITATION Number	Percent
UNITED STATES	4,782	2,135	44.6	389	8.1	1,769	37.0	199	4.2	1,456	30.4	187	3.9	1,112	23.3	181	3.8	1,217	25.4	189	4.0	2,411	50.4
COMMUNITY HOSPITALS	4,079	2,037	49.9	382	9.4	1,704	41.8	195	4.8	1,402	34.4	186	4.6	1,072	26.3	179	4.4	1,171	28.7	186	4.6	2,348	57.6
CENSUS DIVISION 1, NEW ENGLAND	198	120	60.6	19	9.6	81	40.9	10	5.1	56	28.3	9	4.5	38	19.2	9	4.5	54	27.3	10	5.1	135	68.2
Connecticut	32	21	65.6	4	12.5	17	53.1	3	9.4	15	46.9	3	9.4	12	37.5	3	9.4	12	37.5	4	12.5	24	75.0
Maine	40	20	50.0	4	10.0	11	27.5	1	2.5	5	12.5	1	2.5	4	10.0	1	2.5	7	17.5	2	5.0	29	72.5
Massachusetts	74	51	68.9	8	10.8	36	48.6	2	2.7	25	33.8	2	2.7	16	21.6	3	4.1	21	28.4	3	4.1	45	60.8
New Hampshire	28	16	57.1	1	3.6	9	32.1	2	7.1	7	25.0	1	3.6	3	10.7	1	3.6	8	28.6	1	3.6	20	71.4
Rhode Island	12	8	66.7	1	8.3	6	50.0	1	8.3	3	25.0	1	8.3	2	16.7	0	0.0	4	33.3	0	0.0	8	66.7
Vermont	12	4	33.3	1	8.3	2	16.7	1	8.3	1	8.3	1	8.3	1	8.3	1	8.3	2	16.7	0	0.0	9	75.0
CENSUS DIVISION 2, MIDDLE ATLANTIC	414	272	65.7	72	17.4	206	49.8	23	5.6	162	39.1	22	5.3	112	27.1	22	5.3	140	33.8	24	5.8	233	56.3
New Jersey	73	53	72.6	16	21.9	50	68.5	2	2.7	38	52.1	3	4.1	17	23.3	2	2.7	25	34.2	4	5.5	45	61.6
New York	168	117	69.6	40	23.8	73	43.5	17	10.1	55	32.7	15	8.9	36	21.4	13	7.7	56	33.3	14	8.3	82	48.8
Pennsylvania	173	102	59.0	16	9.2	83	48.0	4	2.3	69	39.9	4	2.3	59	34.1	7	4.0	59	34.1	6	3.5	106	61.3
CENSUS DIVISION 3, SOUTH ATLANTIC	715	370	51.7	59	8.3	333	46.6	28	3.9	248	34.7	27	3.8	166	23.2	27	3.8	230	32.2	30	4.2	360	50.3
Delaware	11	6	54.5	1	9.1	5	45.5	1	9.1	5	45.5	1	9.1	5	45.5	1	9.1	4	36.4	1	9.1	6	54.5
District of Columbia	12	5	41.7	1	8.3	6	50.0	1	8.3	5	41.7	1	8.3	2	16.7	1	8.3	4	33.3	2	16.7	4	33.3
Florida	160	100	62.5	16	10.0	91	56.9	9	5.6	77	48.1	8	5.0	60	37.5	10	6.3	67	41.9	10	6.3	67	41.9
Georgia	128	53	41.4	6	4.7	51	39.8	3	1.6	37	28.9	2	1.6	19	14.8	2	1.6	35	27.3	2	1.6	52	40.6
Maryland	58	41	70.7	7	12.1	35	60.3	3	5.2	28	48.3	3	5.2	10	17.2	2	3.4	32	55.2	3	5.2	34	58.6
North Carolina	115	58	50.4	10	8.7	52	45.2	5	4.3	32	27.8	6	5.2	24	20.9	5	4.3	35	30.4	6	5.2	72	62.6
South Carolina	79	34	43.0	4	5.1	31	39.2	1	1.3	19	24.1	1	1.3	19	24.1	1	1.3	15	19.0	1	1.3	37	46.8
Virginia	89	51	57.3	11	12.4	40	44.9	4	4.5	33	37.1	4	4.5	21	23.6	4	4.5	31	34.8	4	4.5	57	64.0
West Virginia	63	22	34.9	3	4.8	22	34.9	2	3.2	12	19.0	1	1.6	6	9.5	1	1.6	7	11.1	1	1.6	31	49.2
CENSUS DIVISION 4, EAST NORTH CENTRAL	721	379	52.6	71	9.8	321	44.5	28	3.9	267	37.0	28	3.9	214	29.7	30	4.2	242	33.6	30	4.2	508	70.5
Illinois	173	113	65.3	32	18.5	91	52.6	9	5.2	84	48.6	10	5.8	64	37.0	9	5.2	69	39.9	10	5.8	132	76.3
Indiana	108	52	48.1	7	6.5	42	38.9	3	2.8	37	34.3	3	2.8	29	26.9	5	4.6	31	28.7	5	4.6	74	68.5
Michigan	147	75	51.0	11	7.5	61	41.5	3	2.0	46	31.3	3	2.0	38	25.9	5	3.4	55	37.4	4	2.7	92	62.6
Ohio	152	96	63.2	12	7.9	81	53.3	8	5.3	61	40.1	7	4.6	53	34.9	8	5.3	57	37.5	7	4.6	105	69.1
Wisconsin	141	43	30.5	9	6.4	46	32.6	5	3.5	39	27.7	5	3.5	30	21.3	5	3.5	30	21.3	4	2.8	105	74.5
CENSUS DIVISION 5, EAST SOUTH CENTRAL	419	137	32.7	16	3.8	124	29.6	13	3.1	97	23.2	11	2.6	77	18.4	9	2.1	70	16.7	11	2.6	135	32.2
Alabama	120	35	29.2	5	4.2	37	30.8	4	3.3	33	27.5	3	2.5	25	20.8	2	1.7	24	20.0	3	2.5	39	32.5
Kentucky	98	43	43.9	2	2.0	38	38.8	2	2.0	27	27.6	2	2.0	21	21.4	3	3.1	20	20.4	3	3.1	47	48.0
Mississippi	110	16	14.5	2	1.8	12	10.9	1	0.9	9	8.2	1	0.9	9	8.2	0	0.0	7	6.4	2	1.8	13	11.8
Tennessee	91	43	47.3	7	7.7	37	40.7	6	6.6	28	30.8	5	5.5	22	24.2	5	5.5	19	20.9	4	4.4	36	39.6
CENSUS DIVISION 6, WEST NORTH CENTRAL	649	208	32.0	34	5.2	140	21.6	14	2.2	133	20.5	15	2.3	94	14.5	15	2.3	103	15.9	16	2.5	451	69.5
Iowa	125	39	31.2	4	3.2	26	20.8	1	0.7	26	20.8	1	0.7	12	9.6	2	1.6	23	18.4	3	2.4	107	85.6
Kansas	153	33	21.6	5	3.3	24	15.7	1	0.7	23	15.0	1	0.7	17	11.1	1	0.7	15	9.8	3	2.0	73	47.7
Minnesota	132	32	31.4	9	8.8	16	15.7	4	2.0	15	14.7	4	2.0	13	12.7	3	2.0	15	14.7	4	3.9	84	82.4
Missouri	149	70	47.0	8	5.4	52	34.9	4	2.7	48	32.2	4	2.7	37	24.8	6	4.0	36	24.2	4	2.7	87	58.4
Nebraska	52	20	38.5	3	5.8	12	23.1	2	3.8	11	21.2	2	3.8	7	13.5	1	1.9	9	17.3	1	1.9	40	76.9
North Dakota	24	7	29.2	2	8.3	5	20.8	1	4.2	5	20.8	2	8.3	5	20.8	2	8.3	3	12.5	1	4.2	21	87.5
South Dakota	44	7	15.9	3	6.8	5	11.4	0	0.0	5	11.4	2	4.5	3	6.8	1	2.3	2	4.5	1	2.3	39	88.6
CENSUS DIVISION 7, WEST SOUTH CENTRAL	883	308	34.9	40	4.5	263	29.8	31	3.5	228	25.8	29	3.3	196	22.2	23	2.6	166	18.8	20	2.3	282	31.9
Arkansas	91	29	31.9	2	2.2	25	27.5	1	1.1	23	25.3	1	1.1	18	19.8	1	1.1	12	13.2	1	1.1	35	38.5
Louisiana	102	52	51.0	11	10.8	42	41.2	8	7.8	37	36.3	7	6.9	29	28.4	5	4.9	26	25.5	5	4.9	40	39.2
Oklahoma	123	37	30.1	3	2.4	29	23.6	2	1.6	24	19.5	3	2.4	20	16.3	2	1.6	12	9.8	2	1.6	34	27.6
Texas	567	190	33.5	24	4.2	167	29.5	20	3.5	144	25.4	18	3.2	129	22.8	15	2.6	116	20.5	12	2.1	173	30.5
CENSUS DIVISION 8, MOUNTAIN	335	121	36.1	28	8.4	110	32.8	19	5.7	102	30.4	17	5.1	74	22.1	17	5.1	71	21.2	17	5.1	145	43.3
Arizona	59	34	57.6	7	11.9	33	55.9	3	6.8	32	54.2	3	5.1	22	39.0	4	6.8	22	37.3	6	10.2	31	52.5
Colorado	71	30	42.3	7	9.9	31	43.7	3	4.2	31	43.7	3	4.2	17	23.9	4	5.6	18	25.4	3	4.2	39	54.9
Idaho	30	9	30.0	2	6.7	6	20.0	1	3.3	8	26.7	2	6.7	5	16.7	1	3.3	4	13.3	1	3.3	9	30.0
Montana	53	9	17.0	3	5.7	7	13.2	1	1.9	6	11.3	1	1.9	6	11.3	1	1.9	6	11.3	1	1.9	27	50.9
Nevada	27	13	48.1	4	14.8	12	44.4	4	14.8	9	33.3	3	11.1	9	33.3	2	7.4	10	37.0	3	11.1	8	29.6
New Mexico	36	10	27.8	2	5.6	8	22.2	2	5.6	9	13.9	2	5.6	4	11.1	2	5.6	5	13.9	2	5.6	8	22.2
Utah	32	14	43.8	3	9.4	11	34.4	2	6.3	8	28.1	3	9.4	8	25.0	3	9.4	5	15.6	1	3.1	12	37.5
Wyoming	27	2	7.4	0	0.0	2	7.4	0	0.0	2	7.4	0	0.0	2	7.4	0	0.0	1	3.7	0	0.0	11	40.7
CENSUS DIVISION 9, PACIFIC	448	220	49.1	50	11.2	191	42.6	33	7.4	163	36.4	29	6.5	141	31.5	29	6.5	141	31.5	31	6.9	162	36.2
Alaska	13	3	23.1	2	15.4	3	23.1	1	15.4	2	15.4	1	7.7	1	7.7	0	0.0	1	7.7	1	7.7	4	30.8
California	284	151	53.2	35	12.3	130	45.8	21	7.4	109	38.4	19	6.7	101	35.6	21	7.4	100	35.2	20	7.0	104	36.6
Hawaii	20	7	35.0	1	5.0	7	35.0	1	5.0	6	30.0	1	5.0	4	20.0	1	5.0	5	25.0	1	5.0	3	15.0
Oregon	61	26	42.6	6	9.8	23	37.7	6	9.8	20	32.8	6	9.8	16	26.2	4	6.6	15	24.6	6	9.8	23	37.7
Washington	70	33	47.1	6	8.6	28	40.0	3	4.3	26	37.1	2	2.9	19	27.1	3	4.3	20	28.6	3	4.3	28	40.0

Table 7 (Continued)

These data include only hospital-based facilities and services as reported by responding hospitals in Section C of the 2010 AHA Annual Survey, beginning on page 215. All hospitals are represented with Community Hospitals listed separately under United States. No estimates have been made for nonresponding hospitals. Definitions of facilities and services are listed in the Glossary, page 201.

CLASSIFICATION	HOSPITALS REPORTING	EMERGENCY SERVICES						ENDOSCOPIC SERVICES										
		Emergency Department		Freestanding/Satellite Emergency Department		Trauma Center (Certified)		Endoscopic Ultrasound		Ablation of Barrett's Esophagus		Esophageal Impedance Study		Endoscopic Retrograde Cholangiopancreatography		Optical Colonoscopy	
		Number	Percent	Number	Percent	Number	Percent	Number	Percent	Number	Percent	Number	Percent	Number	Percent	Number	Percent
UNITED STATES	4,782	3,964	82.9	284	5.9	1,570	32.8	1,382	28.9	924	19.3	885	18.5	1,858	38.9	2,626	54.9
COMMUNITY HOSPITALS	4,079	3,729	91.4	268	6.6	1,541	37.8	1,319	32.3	884	21.7	845	20.7	1,791	43.9	2,479	60.8
CENSUS DIVISION 1, NEW ENGLAND	198	164	82.8	15	7.6	62	31.3	72	36.4	50	25.3	54	27.3	103	52.0	123	62.1
Connecticut	32	26	81.3	3	9.4	12	37.5	16	50.0	13	40.6	13	40.6	22	68.8	20	62.5
Maine	40	35	87.5	3	7.5	13	32.5	9	22.5	7	17.5	9	22.5	11	27.5	25	62.5
Massachusetts	74	55	74.3	4	5.4	18	24.3	27	36.5	17	23.0	22	29.7	39	52.7	44	59.5
New Hampshire	28	24	85.7	5	17.9	12	42.9	11	39.3	8	28.6	6	21.4	15	53.6	18	64.3
Rhode Island	12	12	100.0	0	0.0	3	25.0	6	50.0	4	33.3	3	25.0	9	75.0	6	50.0
Vermont	12	12	100.0	0	0.0	4	33.3	3	25.0	1	8.3	1	8.3	7	58.3	10	83.3
CENSUS DIVISION 2, MIDDLE ATLANTIC	414	339	81.9	23	5.6	111	26.8	171	41.3	98	23.7	97	23.4	247	59.7	250	60.4
New Jersey	73	58	79.5	7	9.6	12	16.4	37	50.7	30	41.1	23	31.5	46	63.0	44	60.3
New York	168	145	86.3	7	4.2	65	38.7	77	45.8	39	23.2	34	20.2	105	62.5	105	62.5
Pennsylvania	173	136	78.6	9	5.2	34	19.7	57	32.9	29	16.8	40	23.1	96	55.5	101	58.4
CENSUS DIVISION 3, SOUTH ATLANTIC	715	578	80.8	45	6.3	150	21.0	228	31.9	159	22.2	178	24.9	339	47.4	424	59.3
Delaware	11	7	63.6	1	9.1	6	54.5	3	27.3	4	27.3	4	36.4	7	63.6	4	36.4
District of Columbia	7	7	100.0	2	16.7	4	33.3	6	50.0	4	33.3	5	41.7	4	33.3	6	50.0
Florida	160	128	80.0	12	7.5	27	16.9	63	39.4	47	29.4	42	26.3	98	61.3	109	68.1
Georgia	128	109	85.2	1	0.8	16	12.5	38	29.7	22	17.2	28	21.9	51	39.8	69	53.9
Maryland	58	44	75.9	5	8.6	10	17.2	27	46.6	16	27.6	16	27.6	37	63.8	36	62.1
North Carolina	115	99	86.1	9	7.8	18	15.7	35	30.4	28	24.3	32	27.8	48	41.7	80	69.6
South Carolina	79	57	72.2	3	3.8	19	24.1	18	22.8	15	19.0	15	19.0	28	35.4	32	40.5
Virginia	89	75	84.3	11	12.4	18	20.2	25	28.1	16	18.0	24	27.0	46	51.7	55	61.8
West Virginia	63	52	82.5	1	1.6	32	50.8	13	20.6	8	12.7	12	19.0	20	31.7	33	52.4
CENSUS DIVISION 4, EAST NORTH CENTRAL	721	628	87.1	64	8.9	263	36.5	240	33.3	171	23.7	151	20.9	327	45.4	426	59.1
Illinois	173	159	91.9	9	5.2	68	39.3	65	37.6	49	28.3	41	23.7	101	58.4	113	65.3
Indiana	108	90	83.3	5	4.6	14	13.0	35	32.4	26	24.1	18	16.7	47	43.5	71	65.7
Michigan	147	124	84.4	17	11.6	42	28.6	55	37.4	23	15.6	25	17.0	63	42.9	96	65.3
Ohio	152	135	88.8	26	17.1	45	29.6	55	36.2	46	30.3	40	26.3	77	50.7	96	63.2
Wisconsin	141	120	85.1	7	5.0	94	66.7	30	21.3	27	19.1	27	19.1	39	27.7	50	35.5
CENSUS DIVISION 5, EAST SOUTH CENTRAL	419	339	80.9	32	7.6	137	32.7	77	18.4	59	14.1	63	15.0	106	25.3	167	39.9
Alabama	120	92	76.7	1	0.8	35	29.2	17	14.2	15	12.5	14	11.7	32	26.7	45	37.5
Kentucky	98	83	84.7	5	5.1	21	21.4	26	26.5	18	18.4	20	20.4	38	38.8	50	51.0
Mississippi	110	88	80.0	23	20.9	68	61.8	9	8.2	7	6.4	9	8.2	10	9.1	24	21.8
Tennessee	91	76	83.5	3	3.3	13	14.3	25	27.5	19	20.9	20	22.0	26	28.6	48	52.7
CENSUS DIVISION 6, WEST NORTH CENTRAL	649	573	88.3	24	3.7	231	35.6	119	18.3	68	10.5	79	12.2	143	22.0	355	54.7
Iowa	119	119	95.2	4	3.2	86	68.8	25	20.0	11	8.8	17	13.6	21	16.8	75	60.0
Kansas	153	126	82.4	5	3.3	12	7.8	14	9.2	13	8.5	11	7.2	24	15.7	75	49.0
Minnesota	102	96	94.1	2	2.0	59	57.8	27	26.5	10	9.8	12	11.8	25	24.5	58	56.9
Missouri	149	118	79.2	8	5.4	28	18.8	32	21.5	25	16.8	22	14.8	53	35.6	76	51.0
Nebraska	52	48	92.3	3	5.8	22	42.3	14	26.9	5	9.6	7	13.5	11	21.2	29	55.8
North Dakota	24	24	100.0	1	4.2	13	54.2	2	8.3	2	8.3	5	20.8	5	20.8	17	70.8
South Dakota	44	42	95.5	1	2.3	11	25.0	5	11.4	2	4.5	5	11.4	4	9.1	25	56.8
CENSUS DIVISION 7, WEST SOUTH CENTRAL	883	681	77.1	43	4.9	313	35.4	193	21.9	133	15.1	103	11.7	265	30.0	413	46.8
Arkansas	91	71	78.0	6	6.6	24	26.4	20	22.0	10	11.0	10	11.0	22	24.2	46	50.5
Louisiana	102	75	73.5	3	2.9	17	16.7	28	27.5	20	19.6	18	17.6	38	37.3	55	53.9
Oklahoma	123	111	90.2	1	0.8	42	34.1	16	13.0	16	13.0	10	8.1	34	27.6	62	50.4
Texas	567	424	74.8	33	5.8	230	40.6	129	22.8	87	15.3	65	11.5	171	30.2	250	44.1
CENSUS DIVISION 8, MOUNTAIN	335	288	86.0	24	7.2	142	42.4	101	30.1	61	18.2	69	20.6	113	33.7	200	59.7
Arizona	59	47	79.7	5	8.5	19	32.2	29	49.2	20	33.9	16	27.1	33	55.9	34	57.6
Colorado	71	63	88.7	7	9.9	51	71.8	20	28.2	14	19.7	17	23.9	30	42.3	47	66.2
Idaho	30	28	93.3	1	3.3	6	20.0	10	33.3	7	23.3	6	20.0	9	30.0	20	66.7
Montana	53	49	92.5	1	1.9	23	43.4	6	11.3	3	5.7	5	9.4	7	13.2	27	50.9
Nevada	27	20	74.1	2	7.4	4	14.8	9	33.3	4	11.1	3	11.1	10	37.0	12	44.4
New Mexico	36	29	80.6	4	11.1	7	19.4	8	22.2	4	11.1	4	11.1	7	19.4	20	55.6
Utah	32	28	87.5	3	9.4	15	46.9	11	34.4	8	25.0	13	40.6	14	43.8	24	75.0
Wyoming	27	24	88.9	1	3.7	17	63.0	8	29.6	2	7.4	5	18.5	3	11.1	16	59.3
CENSUS DIVISION 9, PACIFIC	448	374	83.5	14	3.1	161	35.9	181	40.4	125	27.9	91	20.3	215	48.0	268	59.8
Alaska	13	9	69.2	0	0.0	1	7.7	5	38.5	2	15.4	2	15.4	4	30.8	8	61.5
California	284	227	79.9	6	2.1	68	23.9	118	41.5	84	29.6	63	22.2	149	52.5	162	57.0
Hawaii	20	15	75.0	1	5.0	2	10.0	4	20.0	3	15.0	2	10.0	7	35.0	7	35.0
Oregon	61	59	96.7	3	4.9	42	68.9	26	42.6	19	31.1	10	16.4	22	36.1	46	75.4
Washington	70	64	91.4	4	5.7	48	68.6	28	40.0	17	24.3	14	20.0	33	47.1	45	64.3

Table 7 (Continued)

These data include only hospital-based facilities and services as reported by responding hospitals in Section C of the 2009 AHA Annual Survey, beginning on page 215. All hospitals are represented with Community Hospitals listed separately under United States. No estimates have been made for nonresponding hospitals. Definitions of facilities and services are listed in the Glossary, page 201.

Classification	Hospitals Reporting	PHYSICAL REHABILITATION SERVICES												PSYCHIATRIC SERVICES									
		Assistive Technology Center		Electro-Diagnostic Services		Physical Rehabilitation Outpatient Services		Prosthetic Orthotic Services		Robot Assisted Walking Therapy		Simulated Rehabilitation Environment		Child/Adolescent Services		Consultation/Liaison Services		Education Services		Emergency Services		Geriatric Services	
		Number	Percent	Number	Percent	Number	Percent	Number	Percent	Number	Percent	Number	Percent	Number	Percent	Number	Percent	Number	Percent	Number	Percent	Number	Percent
UNITED STATES	4,782	741	15.5	1,008	21.1	3,501	73.2	826	17.3	170	3.6	1,084	22.7	852	17.8	1,501	31.4	1,166	24.4	1,565	32.7	1,432	29.9
COMMUNITY HOSPITALS	4,079	635	15.6	939	23.0	3,320	81.4	727	17.8	154	3.8	1,004	24.6	641	15.7	1,257	30.8	900	22.1	1,357	33.3	1,169	28.7
CENSUS DIVISION 1. NEW ENGLAND	198	42	21.2	54	27.3	173	87.4	53	26.8	12	6.1	59	29.8	64	32.3	110	55.6	82	41.4	107	54.0	92	46.5
Connecticut	32	10	31.3	12	37.5	25	78.1	13	40.6	3	9.4	15	46.9	16	50.0	23	71.9	20	62.5	25	78.1	20	62.5
Maine	40	4	10.0	6	15.0	34	85.0	5	12.5	1	2.5	9	22.5	11	27.5	14	35.0	11	27.5	13	32.5	11	27.5
Massachusetts	74	20	27.0	23	31.1	67	90.5	21	28.4	5	6.8	19	25.7	25	33.8	48	64.9	35	47.3	43	58.1	41	55.4
New Hampshire	28	4	14.3	5	17.9	26	92.9	8	28.6	2	7.1	8	28.6	8	28.6	13	46.4	8	28.6	12	42.9	10	35.7
Rhode Island	12	2	16.7	5	41.7	9	75.0	2	16.7	0	0.0	3	25.0	2	16.7	8	66.7	6	50.0	10	83.3	8	66.7
Vermont	12	2	16.7	3	25.0	12	100.0	4	33.3	1	8.3	5	41.7	2	16.7	4	33.3	2	16.7	4	33.3	2	16.7
CENSUS DIVISION 2. MIDDLE ATLANTIC	414	98	23.7	180	43.5	339	81.9	119	28.7	23	5.6	121	29.2	133	32.1	238	57.5	164	39.6	220	53.1	200	48.3
New Jersey	73	17	23.3	34	46.6	61	83.6	19	26.0	5	6.8	22	30.1	29	39.7	47	64.4	29	39.7	43	58.9	34	46.6
New York	168	36	21.4	71	42.3	140	83.3	59	35.1	8	4.8	46	27.4	63	37.5	106	63.1	71	42.3	100	59.5	89	53.0
Pennsylvania	173	45	26.0	75	43.4	138	79.8	41	23.7	10	5.8	53	30.6	41	23.7	85	49.1	64	37.0	77	44.5	77	44.5
CENSUS DIVISION 3. SOUTH ATLANTIC	715	113	15.8	180	25.2	539	75.4	169	23.6	43	6.0	200	28.0	126	17.6	235	32.9	186	26.0	260	36.4	212	29.7
Delaware	11	1	9.1	4	36.4	7	63.6	4	36.4	0	0.0	3	27.3	3	27.3	5	45.5	3	27.3	1	9.1	5	45.5
District of Columbia	12	3	25.0	5	41.7	8	66.7	6	50.0	2	16.7	6	50.0	3	25.0	8	66.7	7	58.3	7	58.3	6	50.0
Florida	160	42	26.3	40	25.0	129	80.6	31	19.4	13	8.1	55	34.4	27	16.9	44	27.5	34	21.3	53	33.1	44	27.5
Georgia	128	10	7.8	18	14.1	96	75.0	15	11.7	3	2.3	31	24.2	12	9.4	35	27.3	25	19.5	32	25.0	29	22.7
Maryland	58	13	22.4	25	43.1	43	74.1	19	32.8	3	5.2	20	34.5	20	34.5	37	63.8	26	44.8	40	69.0	29	50.0
North Carolina	115	21	18.3	33	28.7	94	81.7	19	16.5	7	6.1	32	27.8	20	17.4	36	31.3	32	27.8	44	38.3	37	32.2
South Carolina	79	5	6.3	8	10.1	44	55.7	40	50.6	5	6.3	12	15.2	15	19.0	22	27.8	17	21.5	23	29.1	20	25.3
Virginia	89	12	13.5	32	36.0	74	83.1	28	31.5	7	7.9	29	32.6	14	15.7	32	36.0	26	29.2	45	50.6	27	30.3
West Virginia	63	6	9.5	15	23.8	44	69.8	7	11.1	3	4.8	12	19.0	12	19.0	16	25.4	16	25.4	15	23.8	15	23.8
CENSUS DIVISION 4. EAST NORTH CENTRAL	721	114	15.8	222	30.8	591	82.0	157	21.8	22	3.1	243	33.7	155	21.5	295	40.9	245	34.0	285	39.5	257	35.6
Illinois	173	27	15.6	60	34.7	146	84.4	37	21.4	6	3.5	62	35.8	47	27.2	71	41.0	64	37.0	75	43.4	70	40.5
Indiana	108	15	13.9	25	23.1	86	79.6	16	14.8	1	0.9	29	26.9	19	17.6	31	28.7	27	25.0	31	28.7	29	26.9
Michigan	147	33	22.4	55	37.4	118	80.3	34	23.1	8	5.4	56	38.1	28	19.0	69	46.9	56	38.1	68	46.3	57	38.8
Ohio	152	30	19.7	62	40.8	127	83.6	42	27.6	5	3.3	62	40.8	25	16.4	67	44.1	54	35.5	65	42.8	54	35.5
Wisconsin	141	9	6.4	20	14.2	114	80.9	28	19.9	2	1.4	34	24.1	36	25.5	57	40.4	44	31.2	46	32.6	47	33.3
CENSUS DIVISION 5. EAST SOUTH CENTRAL	419	42	10.0	52	12.4	277	66.1	34	8.1	14	3.3	55	13.1	44	10.5	89	21.2	70	16.7	95	22.7	134	32.0
Alabama	120	6	5.0	10	8.3	75	62.5	13	10.8	6	5.0	14	11.7	12	10.0	21	17.5	17	14.2	24	20.0	36	30.0
Kentucky	98	11	11.2	14	14.3	73	74.5	7	7.1	4	4.1	14	14.3	12	12.2	29	29.6	22	22.4	34	34.7	27	27.6
Mississippi	110	10	9.1	9	8.2	59	53.6	6	5.5	1	0.9	8	7.3	9	8.2	19	17.3	15	13.6	16	14.5	40	36.4
Tennessee	91	15	16.5	19	20.9	70	76.9	8	8.8	3	3.3	19	20.9	11	12.1	20	22.0	16	17.6	21	23.1	31	34.1
CENSUS DIVISION 6. WEST NORTH CENTRAL	649	79	12.2	99	15.3	512	78.9	96	14.8	10	1.5	111	17.1	105	16.2	155	23.9	135	20.8	179	27.6	163	25.1
Iowa	125	20	16.0	19	15.2	105	84.0	14	11.2	0	0.0	26	20.8	27	21.6	35	28.0	34	27.2	46	36.8	35	28.0
Kansas	153	12	7.8	11	7.2	115	75.2	12	7.8	2	1.3	17	11.1	8	5.2	14	9.2	14	9.2	26	17.0	25	16.3
Minnesota	102	13	12.7	15	14.7	89	87.3	15	14.7	2	2.0	17	16.7	23	22.5	34	33.3	27	26.5	31	30.4	33	32.4
Missouri	149	13	8.7	25	16.8	107	71.8	32	21.5	4	2.7	32	21.5	31	20.8	52	34.9	44	29.5	54	36.2	50	33.6
Nebraska	52	7	13.5	10	19.2	41	78.8	10	19.2	1	1.9	8	15.4	9	17.3	11	21.2	8	15.4	9	17.3	12	23.1
North Dakota	24	10	41.7	11	45.8	20	83.3	4	16.7	1	4.2	4	16.7	4	16.7	4	16.7	4	16.7	5	20.8	4	16.7
South Dakota	44	4	9.1	8	18.2	35	79.5	9	20.5	0	0.0	7	15.9	3	6.8	5	11.4	4	9.1	8	18.2	4	9.1
CENSUS DIVISION 7. WEST SOUTH CENTRAL	883	128	14.5	75	8.5	520	58.9	83	9.4	25	2.8	157	17.8	89	10.1	157	17.8	123	13.9	167	18.9	201	22.8
Arkansas	91	12	13.2	6	6.6	57	62.6	6	6.6	2	2.2	12	13.2	14	15.4	22	24.2	15	16.5	20	22.0	26	28.6
Louisiana	102	10	9.8	9	8.8	53	52.0	9	8.8	2	2.0	24	23.5	9	8.8	19	18.6	16	15.7	27	26.5	34	33.3
Oklahoma	123	15	12.2	8	6.5	78	63.4	11	8.9	1	0.8	20	16.3	10	8.1	21	17.1	17	13.8	29	23.6	24	19.5
Texas	567	91	16.0	52	9.2	332	58.6	57	10.1	20	3.5	101	17.8	56	9.9	95	16.8	75	13.2	91	16.0	117	20.6
CENSUS DIVISION 8. MOUNTAIN	335	54	16.1	54	16.1	238	71.0	36	10.7	9	2.7	54	16.1	56	16.7	83	24.8	63	18.8	108	32.2	73	21.8
Arizona	59	11	18.6	12	20.3	40	67.8	5	8.5	2	3.4	11	18.6	8	13.6	20	33.9	13	22.0	19	32.2	17	28.8
Colorado	71	11	15.5	15	21.1	56	78.9	8	11.3	3	4.2	15	21.1	10	14.1	13	18.3	12	16.9	21	29.6	12	16.9
Idaho	30	4	13.3	4	13.3	21	70.0	3	10.0	0	0.0	5	16.7	6	20.0	7	23.3	7	23.3	9	30.0	5	16.7
Montana	53	5	9.4	6	11.3	40	75.5	3	5.7	0	0.0	5	9.4	6	11.3	11	20.8	7	13.2	16	30.2	7	13.2
Nevada	27	6	22.2	2	7.4	18	66.7	1	3.7	1	3.7	5	18.5	3	11.1	5	18.5	3	11.1	8	29.6	7	25.9
New Mexico	36	7	19.4	5	13.9	25	69.4	4	11.1	2	5.6	6	16.7	12	33.3	11	30.6	8	22.2	11	30.6	10	27.8
Utah	32	10	31.3	9	28.1	23	71.9	9	28.1	1	3.1	5	15.6	5	15.6	10	31.3	8	25.0	15	46.9	8	25.0
Wyoming	27	0	0.0	1	3.7	15	55.6	3	11.1	0	0.0	2	7.4	6	22.2	6	22.2	5	18.5	9	33.3	7	25.9
CENSUS DIVISION 9. PACIFIC	448	71	15.8	92	20.5	312	69.6	79	17.6	12	2.7	84	18.8	80	17.9	139	31.0	98	21.9	144	32.1	100	22.3
Alaska	13	2	15.4	3	23.1	7	53.8	1	7.7	0	0.0	0	0.0	6	46.2	6	46.2	5	38.5	6	46.2	3	23.1
California	284	41	14.4	52	18.3	189	66.5	43	15.1	5	1.8	55	19.4	47	16.5	85	29.9	55	19.4	80	28.2	67	23.6
Hawaii	20	2	10.0	1	5.0	13	65.0	4	20.0	2	10.0	5	25.0	3	15.0	4	20.0	5	25.0	5	25.0	6	30.0
Oregon	61	14	23.0	15	24.6	50	82.0	9	14.8	3	4.9	7	11.5	9	14.8	22	36.1	14	23.0	26	42.6	9	14.8
Washington	70	12	17.1	21	30.0	53	75.7	22	31.4	2	2.9	17	24.3	15	21.4	22	31.4	19	27.1	27	38.6	15	21.4

Table 7 (Continued)

These data include only hospital-based facilities and services as reported by responding hospitals in Section C of the 2009 AHA Annual Survey, beginning on page 215. All hospitals are represented with Community Hospitals listed separately under United States. No estimates have been made for nonresponding hospitals. Definitions of facilities and services are listed in the Glossary, page 201.

| | | PSYCHIATRIC SERVICES | | | | RADIOLOGY, DIAGNOSTIC | | | | | | | | | | | | | |
CLASSIFICATION	HOSPITALS REPORTING	OUTPATIENT SERVICES Number	OUTPATIENT SERVICES Percent	PARTIAL HOSPITALIZATION PROGRAM Number	PARTIAL HOSPITALIZATION PROGRAM Percent	CT SCANNER Number	CT SCANNER Percent	DIAGNOSTIC RADIOISOTOPE FACILITY Number	DIAGNOSTIC RADIOISOTOPE FACILITY Percent	ELECTRON BEAM COMPUTED TOMOGRAPHY (EBCT) Number	ELECTRON BEAM COMPUTED TOMOGRAPHY (EBCT) Percent	FULL-FIELD DIGITAL MAMMOGRAPHY (FFDM) Number	FULL-FIELD DIGITAL MAMMOGRAPHY (FFDM) Percent	MAGNETIC RESONANCE IMAGING (MRI) Number	MAGNETIC RESONANCE IMAGING (MRI) Percent	INTRAOPERATIVE MAGNETIC IMAGING Number	INTRAOPERATIVE MAGNETIC IMAGING Percent	MULTI-SLICE SPIRAL COMPUTED TOMOGRAPHY (<64 SLICE CT) Number	MULTI-SLICE SPIRAL COMPUTED TOMOGRAPHY (<64 SLICE CT) Percent
UNITED STATES	4,782	1,300	27.2	740	15.5	3,933	82.2	2,620	54.8	311	6.5	2,072	43.3	3,012	63.0	209	4.4	2,736	57.2
COMMUNITY HOSPITALS	4,079	1,050	25.7	572	14.0	3,696	90.6	2,526	61.9	297	7.3	2,009	49.3	2,851	69.9	195	4.8	2,624	64.3
CENSUS DIVISION 1. NEW ENGLAND	198	103	52.0	68	34.3	169	85.4	134	67.7	12	6.1	123	62.1	131	66.2	12	6.1	124	62.6
Connecticut	32	22	68.8	17	53.1	27	84.4	22	68.8	7	21.9	18	56.3	24	75.0	6	18.8	23	71.9
Maine	40	17	42.5	7	17.5	35	87.5	29	72.5	0	0.0	21	52.5	25	62.5	2	5.0	22	55.0
Massachusetts	74	38	51.4	27	36.5	60	81.1	53	71.6	4	5.4	49	66.2	47	63.5	4	5.4	45	60.8
New Hampshire	28	11	39.3	8	28.6	24	85.7	13	46.4	0	0.0	18	64.3	14	50.0	0	0.0	17	60.7
Rhode Island	12	9	75.0	7	58.3	11	91.7	9	75.0	1	8.3	9	75.0	11	91.7	0	0.0	10	83.3
Vermont	12	6	50.0	2	16.7	12	100.0	8	66.7	0	0.0	8	66.7	10	83.3	0	0.0	7	58.3
CENSUS DIVISION 2. MIDDLE ATLANTIC	414	173	41.8	94	22.7	350	84.5	292	70.5	52	12.6	228	55.1	304	73.4	29	7.0	264	63.8
New Jersey	73	34	46.6	28	38.4	58	79.5	53	72.6	11	15.1	41	56.2	53	72.6	6	8.2	51	69.9
New York	168	87	51.8	36	21.4	152	90.5	120	71.4	22	13.1	102	60.7	127	75.6	13	7.7	108	64.3
Pennsylvania	173	52	30.1	30	17.3	140	80.9	119	68.8	19	11.0	85	49.1	124	71.7	10	5.8	105	60.7
CENSUS DIVISION 3. SOUTH ATLANTIC	715	184	25.7	123	17.2	589	82.4	455	63.6	56	7.8	346	48.4	495	69.2	18	2.5	464	64.9
Delaware	11	5	45.5	4	36.4	7	63.6	7	63.6	1	9.1	5	45.5	7	63.6	0	0.0	5	45.5
District of Columbia	12	5	41.7	4	33.3	7	58.3	7	58.3	1	8.3	4	33.0	7	58.3	1	8.3	7	58.3
Florida	160	35	21.9	21	13.1	133	83.1	108	67.5	16	10.0	88	55.0	122	76.3	6	3.8	115	71.9
Georgia	128	26	20.3	21	16.4	116	90.6	75	58.6	6	4.7	63	49.2	96	75.0	6	4.7	80	62.5
Maryland	58	29	50.0	26	44.8	46	79.3	41	70.7	4	6.9	21	36.2	38	65.5	2	3.4	41	70.7
North Carolina	115	32	27.8	13	11.3	99	86.1	73	63.5	9	7.8	59	51.3	84	73.0	1	0.9	77	67.0
South Carolina	79	17	21.5	10	12.7	57	72.2	47	59.5	5	6.3	36	45.6	45	57.0	1	1.3	47	59.5
Virginia	89	25	28.1	17	19.1	74	83.1	62	69.7	12	13.5	49	55.1	64	71.9	1	1.1	59	66.3
West Virginia	63	10	15.9	7	11.1	50	79.4	35	55.6	2	3.2	21	33.3	32	50.8	0	0.0	33	52.4
CENSUS DIVISION 4. EAST NORTH CENTRAL	721	257	35.6	157	21.8	643	89.2	485	67.3	58	8.0	393	54.5	513	71.2	47	6.5	451	62.6
Illinois	173	72	41.6	48	27.7	160	92.5	116	67.1	10	5.8	106	61.3	125	72.3	5	2.9	116	67.1
Indiana	108	27	25.0	19	17.6	95	88.0	69	63.9	7	6.5	60	55.6	86	79.6	6	5.6	70	64.8
Michigan	147	53	36.1	28	19.0	128	87.1	107	72.8	12	8.2	84	57.1	88	59.9	8	5.4	94	63.9
Ohio	152	58	38.2	38	25.0	141	92.8	114	75.0	20	13.2	89	58.6	130	85.5	12	7.9	113	74.3
Wisconsin	141	47	33.3	24	17.0	119	84.4	79	56.0	9	6.4	54	38.3	84	59.6	16	11.3	58	41.1
CENSUS DIVISION 5. EAST SOUTH CENTRAL	419	71	16.9	39	9.3	332	79.2	212	50.6	17	4.1	135	32.2	250	59.7	13	3.1	197	47.0
Alabama	120	21	17.5	9	7.5	91	75.8	64	53.3	3	2.5	34	28.3	69	57.5	1	0.8	55	45.8
Kentucky	98	18	18.4	12	12.2	81	82.7	53	54.1	3	3.1	43	43.9	68	69.4	7	7.1	62	63.3
Mississippi	110	13	11.8	5	4.5	84	76.4	51	46.4	8	7.3	13	11.8	50	45.5	2	1.8	25	22.7
Tennessee	91	19	20.9	13	14.3	76	83.5	44	48.4	3	3.3	45	49.5	63	69.2	3	3.3	55	60.4
CENSUS DIVISION 6. WEST NORTH CENTRAL	649	159	24.5	67	10.3	550	84.7	247	38.1	23	3.5	230	35.4	358	55.2	18	2.8	365	56.2
Iowa	125	33	26.4	15	12.0	116	92.8	46	36.8	4	3.2	50	40.0	66	52.8	2	1.6	86	68.8
Kansas	153	15	9.8	8	5.2	117	76.5	50	32.7	2	1.3	29	19.0	55	35.9	3	2.0	63	41.2
Minnesota	102	35	34.3	14	13.7	94	92.2	43	42.2	7	6.9	51	50.0	68	66.7	5	4.9	60	58.8
Missouri	149	50	33.6	16	10.7	120	80.5	68	45.6	5	3.4	50	33.6	110	73.8	4	2.7	85	57.0
Nebraska	52	14	26.9	8	15.4	44	84.6	20	38.5	4	7.7	26	50.0	32	61.5	2	3.8	33	63.5
North Dakota	24	7	29.2	4	16.7	22	91.7	8	33.3	1	4.2	8	33.3	12	50.0	1	4.2	16	66.7
South Dakota	44	5	11.4	2	4.5	37	84.1	12	27.3	0	0.0	16	36.4	15	34.1	1	2.3	22	50.0
CENSUS DIVISION 7. WEST SOUTH CENTRAL	883	151	17.1	75	8.5	635	71.9	354	40.1	32	3.6	268	30.4	455	51.5	30	3.4	414	46.9
Arkansas	91	21	23.1	8	8.8	68	74.7	34	37.4	4	4.4	29	31.9	52	57.1	2	2.2	48	52.7
Louisiana	102	26	25.5	15	14.7	73	71.6	48	47.1	9	8.8	46	45.1	55	53.9	2	2.0	50	49.0
Oklahoma	123	25	20.3	4	3.3	97	78.9	42	34.1	2	1.6	44	35.8	73	59.3	3	2.4	56	45.5
Texas	567	79	13.9	48	8.5	397	70.0	230	40.6	17	3.0	149	26.3	275	48.5	23	4.1	260	45.9
CENSUS DIVISION 8. MOUNTAIN	335	76	22.7	44	13.1	280	83.6	162	48.4	24	7.2	136	40.6	211	63.0	17	5.1	188	56.1
Arizona	59	15	25.4	10	16.9	47	79.7	37	62.7	7	11.9	26	44.1	45	76.3	6	10.2	38	64.4
Colorado	71	14	19.7	7	9.9	64	90.1	38	53.5	4	5.6	30	42.3	52	73.2	4	5.6	45	63.4
Idaho	30	8	26.7	3	10.0	27	90.0	13	43.3	2	6.7	8	26.7	19	63.3	2	6.7	20	66.7
Montana	53	7	13.2	8	15.1	40	75.5	17	32.1	0	0.0	22	41.5	20	37.7	0	0.0	25	47.2
Nevada	27	6	22.2	4	14.8	21	77.8	17	63.0	3	11.1	9	33.3	20	74.1	1	3.7	12	44.4
New Mexico	36	12	33.3	2	5.6	29	80.6	12	33.3	2	5.6	10	27.8	18	50.0	2	5.6	19	52.8
Utah	32	7	21.9	6	18.8	28	87.5	17	53.1	5	15.6	23	71.9	23	71.9	2	6.3	18	56.3
Wyoming	27	7	25.9	4	14.8	24	88.9	11	40.7	1	3.7	8	29.6	14	51.9	0	0.0	11	40.7
CENSUS DIVISION 9. PACIFIC	448	126	28.1	73	16.3	385	85.9	279	62.3	37	8.3	213	47.5	295	65.8	25	5.6	269	60.0
Alaska	13	5	38.5	3	23.1	8	61.5	5	38.5	0	0.0	5	38.5	8	61.5	0	0.0	6	46.2
California	284	80	28.2	48	16.9	241	84.9	182	64.1	26	9.2	126	44.4	184	64.8	16	5.6	160	56.3
Hawaii	20	4	20.0	3	15.0	12	60.0	5	25.0	1	5.0	8	40.0	10	50.0	0	0.0	9	45.0
Oregon	61	14	23.0	8	13.1	59	96.7	39	63.9	3	4.9	38	62.3	43	70.5	5	8.2	46	75.4
Washington	70	23	32.9	11	15.7	65	92.9	43	61.4	7	10.0	36	51.4	50	71.4	4	5.7	48	68.6

Table 7 (Continued)

These data include only hospital-based facilities and services as reported by responding hospitals in Section C of the 2009 AHA Annual Survey, beginning on page 215. All hospitals are represented with Community Hospitals listed separately under United States. No estimates have been made for nonresponding hospitals. Definitions of facilities and services are listed in the Glossary, page 201.

CLASSIFICATION	HOSPITALS REPORTING	MULTI-SLICE CT (64+ SLICE CT) No.	%	PET No.	%	PET/CT No.	%	SPECT No.	%	ULTRASOUND No.	%	IGRT No.	%	IMRT No.	%	PROTON BEAM No.	%	SHAPED BEAM No.	%	STEREOTACTIC RADIOSURGERY No.	%
UNITED STATES	4,782	1,845	38.6	723	15.1	891	18.6	1,760	36.8	3,840	80.3	863	18.0	1,067	22.3	103	2.2	827	17.3	812	17.0
COMMUNITY HOSPITALS	4,079	1,756	43.0	693	17.0	859	21.1	1,713	42.0	3,609	88.5	838	20.5	1,040	25.5	96	2.4	810	19.9	792	19.4
CENSUS DIVISION 1, NEW ENGLAND	198	101	51.0	41	20.7	54	27.3	105	53.0	173	87.4	50	25.3	58	29.3	3	1.5	49	24.7	48	24.2
Connecticut	32	19	59.4	15	46.9	21	65.6	22	68.8	27	84.4	16	50.0	16	50.0	1	3.1	12	37.5	12	37.5
Maine	40	16	40.0	3	7.5	5	12.5	19	47.5	34	85.0	3	7.5	6	15.0	0	0.0	5	12.5	5	12.5
Massachusetts	74	42	56.8	14	18.9	19	25.7	39	52.7	65	87.8	23	31.1	27	36.5	2	2.7	26	35.1	23	31.1
New Hampshire	28	13	46.4	6	21.4	6	21.4	14	50.0	24	85.7	5	17.9	6	21.4	0	0.0	4	14.3	4	14.3
Rhode Island	12	6	50.0	1	8.3	1	8.3	6	50.0	11	91.7	1	8.3	1	8.3	0	0.0	1	8.3	3	25.0
Vermont	12	5	41.7	2	16.7	2	16.7	5	41.7	12	100.0	2	16.7	2	16.7	0	0.0	1	8.3	1	8.3
CENSUS DIVISION 2, MIDDLE ATLANTIC	414	223	53.9	100	24.2	119	28.7	219	52.9	355	85.7	124	30.0	164	39.6	16	3.9	124	30.0	113	27.3
New Jersey	73	35	47.9	20	27.4	28	38.4	37	50.7	58	79.5	30	41.1	40	54.8	2	2.7	35	47.9	23	31.5
New York	168	94	56.0	38	22.6	40	23.8	82	48.8	155	92.3	48	28.6	62	36.9	9	5.4	41	24.4	42	25.0
Pennsylvania	173	94	54.3	42	24.3	51	29.5	100	57.8	142	82.1	46	26.6	62	35.8	5	2.9	48	27.7	48	27.7
CENSUS DIVISION 3, SOUTH ATLANTIC	715	299	41.8	122	17.1	153	21.4	311	43.5	593	82.9	158	22.1	194	27.1	10	1.4	153	21.4	143	20.0
Delaware	11	5	45.5	2	18.2	4	36.4	6	54.5	7	63.6	2	18.2	4	36.4	0	0.0	4	27.3	3	27.3
District of Columbia	12	4	33.3	3	25.0	4	33.3	5	41.7	8	66.7	4	33.3	4	33.3	0	0.0	4	33.3	3	25.0
Florida	160	71	44.4	35	21.9	41	25.6	62	38.8	134	83.8	43	26.9	46	28.8	4	2.5	38	23.8	50	31.3
Georgia	128	43	33.6	25	19.5	28	21.9	39	30.5	114	89.1	20	15.6	23	18.0	0	0.0	19	14.8	22	17.2
Maryland	58	35	60.3	10	17.2	11	19.0	35	60.3	47	81.0	17	29.3	21	36.2	0	0.0	16	27.6	11	19.0
North Carolina	115	52	45.2	18	15.7	25	21.7	64	55.7	98	85.2	30	26.1	39	33.9	4	3.5	31	27.0	22	19.1
South Carolina	79	25	31.6	4	5.1	8	10.1	23	29.1	59	74.7	8	10.1	14	17.7	0	0.0	9	11.4	6	7.6
Virginia	89	40	44.9	15	16.9	22	24.7	51	57.3	75	84.3	28	31.5	33	37.1	1	1.1	24	27.0	19	21.3
West Virginia	63	24	38.1	10	15.9	10	15.9	26	41.3	51	81.0	6	9.5	10	15.9	0	0.0	9	14.3	7	11.1
CENSUS DIVISION 4, EAST NORTH CENTRAL	721	348	48.3	162	22.5	197	27.3	362	50.2	628	87.1	179	24.8	212	29.4	19	2.6	169	23.4	149	20.7
Illinois	173	106	61.3	32	18.5	38	22.0	78	45.1	156	90.2	44	25.4	57	32.9	4	2.3	44	25.4	37	21.4
Indiana	108	46	42.6	18	16.7	27	25.0	44	40.7	94	87.0	28	25.9	37	34.3	4	3.7	26	24.1	20	18.5
Michigan	147	83	56.5	31	21.1	47	32.0	78	53.1	129	87.8	37	25.2	42	28.6	3	1.4	35	23.8	37	25.2
Ohio	152	72	47.4	51	33.6	55	36.2	101	66.4	138	90.8	42	27.6	45	29.6	6	4.0	38	25.0	34	22.4
Wisconsin	141	41	29.1	30	21.3	30	21.3	61	43.3	111	78.7	28	19.9	31	22.0	6	4.3	26	18.4	21	14.9
CENSUS DIVISION 5, EAST SOUTH CENTRAL	419	115	27.4	57	13.6	55	13.1	132	31.5	325	77.6	44	10.5	63	15.0	9	2.1	44	10.5	53	12.6
Alabama	120	34	28.3	16	13.3	17	14.2	33	27.5	89	74.2	14	11.7	16	13.3	2	1.7	12	10.0	11	9.2
Kentucky	98	38	38.8	10	10.2	17	17.3	34	34.7	80	81.6	10	10.2	16	16.3	2	2.0	10	10.2	19	19.4
Mississippi	110	15	13.6	16	14.5	6	5.5	32	29.1	82	74.5	7	6.4	9	8.2	1	0.9	7	6.4	6	5.5
Tennessee	91	28	30.8	15	16.5	15	16.5	33	36.3	74	81.3	13	14.3	22	24.2	4	4.4	15	16.5	17	18.7
CENSUS DIVISION 6, WEST NORTH CENTRAL	649	166	25.6	60	9.2	88	13.6	170	26.2	510	78.6	84	12.9	103	15.9	14	2.2	74	11.4	69	10.6
Iowa	125	32	25.6	12	9.6	15	12.0	37	29.6	114	91.2	10	8.0	13	10.4	0	0.0	11	8.8	13	10.4
Kansas	153	25	16.3	6	3.9	10	6.5	25	16.3	97	63.4	9	5.9	14	9.2	4	2.6	12	7.8	10	4.6
Minnesota	102	37	36.3	8	7.8	13	12.7	26	25.5	89	87.3	16	15.7	18	17.6	4	2.9	11	10.8	10	9.8
Missouri	149	46	30.9	21	14.1	30	20.1	53	35.6	119	79.9	28	18.8	35	23.5	4	2.7	20	13.4	24	16.1
Nebraska	52	15	28.8	7	13.5	14	26.9	17	32.7	41	78.8	13	25.0	13	25.0	2	3.8	13	25.0	10	19.2
North Dakota	24	4	16.7	2	8.3	3	12.5	5	20.8	18	75.0	3	12.5	3	12.5	1	4.2	1	4.2	3	12.5
South Dakota	44	8	18.2	4	9.1	3	6.8	7	15.9	32	72.7	5	11.4	7	15.9	0	0.0	6	13.6	2	4.5
CENSUS DIVISION 7, WEST SOUTH CENTRAL	883	255	28.9	58	6.6	84	9.5	194	22.0	594	67.3	72	8.2	91	10.3	9	1.0	67	7.6	94	10.6
Arkansas	91	22	24.2	7	7.7	9	9.9	20	22.0	68	74.7	7	7.7	6	6.6	1	1.1	4	4.4	10	11.0
Louisiana	102	37	36.3	6	5.9	14	13.7	24	23.5	78	76.5	17	16.7	16	15.7	2	2.0	12	11.8	17	16.7
Oklahoma	123	37	30.1	12	9.8	15	12.2	24	19.5	88	71.5	17	13.8	18	14.6	1	0.8	16	13.0	14	11.4
Texas	567	159	28.0	33	5.8	46	8.1	126	22.2	360	63.5	31	5.5	51	9.0	5	0.9	35	6.2	53	9.3
CENSUS DIVISION 8, MOUNTAIN	335	143	42.7	48	14.3	50	14.9	93	27.8	277	82.7	52	15.5	62	18.5	9	2.7	50	14.9	51	15.2
Arizona	59	33	55.9	17	28.8	16	27.1	28	47.5	48	81.4	12	20.3	15	25.4	2	3.4	11	18.6	14	23.7
Colorado	71	37	52.1	11	15.5	10	14.1	21	29.6	62	87.3	12	16.9	15	21.1	1	1.4	13	18.3	14	19.7
Idaho	30	11	36.7	4	13.3	4	13.3	7	23.3	27	90.0	6	20.0	6	20.0	2	6.7	5	16.7	2	6.7
Montana	53	16	30.2	3	5.7	4	7.5	11	20.8	39	73.6	5	9.4	7	13.2	2	3.8	5	9.4	5	9.4
Nevada	27	9	33.3	2	7.4	2	7.4	5	18.5	21	77.8	5	18.5	3	11.1	0	0.0	3	11.1	3	11.1
New Mexico	36	14	38.9	4	11.1	5	13.9	8	22.2	28	77.8	4	11.1	5	13.9	1	2.8	4	11.1	5	13.9
Utah	32	15	46.9	6	18.8	9	28.1	9	28.1	28	87.5	6	18.8	7	21.9	1	3.1	6	18.8	6	18.8
Wyoming	27	8	29.6	1	3.7	0	0.0	4	14.8	24	88.9	4	14.8	4	14.8	0	0.0	2	7.4	2	7.4
CENSUS DIVISION 9, PACIFIC	448	195	43.5	75	16.7	91	20.3	174	38.8	385	85.9	100	22.3	120	26.8	14	3.1	97	21.7	92	20.5
Alaska	13	4	30.8	0	0.0	0	0.0	2	15.4	10	76.9	1	7.7	2	15.4	0	0.0	1	7.7	2	15.4
California	284	131	46.1	49	17.3	58	20.4	114	40.1	243	85.6	64	22.5	76	26.8	11	3.9	60	21.1	62	21.8
Hawaii	20	6	30.0	2	10.0	3	15.0	3	15.0	13	65.0	4	20.0	4	20.0	0	0.0	3	15.0	2	10.0
Oregon	61	27	44.3	8	13.1	9	14.8	29	47.5	59	96.7	14	23.0	16	26.2	2	3.3	13	21.3	10	16.4
Washington	70	27	38.6	16	22.9	21	30.0	26	37.1	60	85.7	20	28.6	22	31.4	1	1.4	20	28.6	16	22.9

Table 7 (Continued)

These data include only hospital-based facilities and services as reported by responding hospitals in Section C of the 2009 AHA Annual Survey, beginning on page 215. All hospitals are represented with Community Hospitals listed separately under United States. No estimates have been made for nonresponding hospitals. Definitions of facilities and services are listed in the Glossary, page 201.

CLASSIFICATION	HOSPITALS REPORTING	TRANSPLANT BONE MARROW		HEART		KIDNEY		LIVER		LUNG		TISSUE		OTHER	
		Number	Percent	Number	Percent	Number	Percent	Number	Percent	Number	Percent	Number	Percent	Number	Percent
UNITED STATES	4,782	207	4.3	132	2.8	228	4.8	127	2.7	76	1.6	321	6.7	232	4.9
COMMUNITY HOSPITALS	4,079	201	4.9	127	3.1	222	5.4	123	3.0	74	1.8	308	7.6	227	5.6
CENSUS DIVISION 1, NEW ENGLAND	198	16	8.1	7	3.5	17	8.6	8	4.0	5	2.5	17	8.6	14	7.1
Connecticut	32	1	3.1	2	6.3	3	9.4	2	6.3	1	3.1	2	6.3	2	6.3
Maine	40	1	2.5	0	0.0	1	2.5	0	0.0	0	0.0	0	0.0	1	2.5
Massachusetts	74	10	13.5	4	5.4	9	12.2	5	6.8	3	4.1	10	13.5	7	9.5
New Hampshire	28	1	3.6	0	0.0	1	3.6	0	0.0	0	0.0	1	3.6	1	3.6
Rhode Island	12	2	16.7	1	8.3	2	16.7	1	8.3	1	8.3	2	16.7	2	16.7
Vermont	12	1	8.3	0	0.0	1	8.3	0	0.0	0	0.0	2	16.7	1	8.3
CENSUS DIVISION 2, MIDDLE ATLANTIC	414	26	6.3	16	3.9	34	8.2	19	4.6	9	2.2	36	8.7	39	9.4
New Jersey	73	2	2.7	2	2.7	5	6.8	2	2.7	1	1.4	4	5.5	5	6.8
New York	168	12	7.1	5	3.0	14	8.3	6	3.6	2	1.2	15	8.9	16	9.5
Pennsylvania	173	12	6.9	9	5.2	15	8.7	11	6.4	6	3.5	17	9.8	18	10.4
CENSUS DIVISION 3, SOUTH ATLANTIC	715	39	5.5	24	3.4	32	4.5	20	2.8	12	1.7	59	8.3	42	5.9
Delaware	11	2	18.2	1	9.1	2	18.2	1	9.1	0	0.0	0	0.0	0	0.0
District of Columbia	12	3	25.0	2	16.7	2	16.7	1	8.3	0	0.0	4	33.3	3	25.0
Florida	160	9	5.6	6	3.8	8	5.0	6	3.8	4	2.5	14	8.8	6	3.8
Georgia	128	6	4.7	4	3.1	5	3.9	4	3.1	2	1.6	8	6.3	7	5.5
Maryland	58	3	5.2	2	3.4	2	3.4	2	3.4	2	3.4	5	8.6	5	8.6
North Carolina	115	5	4.3	4	3.5	5	4.3	3	2.6	2	1.7	6	5.2	9	7.8
South Carolina	79	4	5.1	1	1.3	1	1.3	1	1.3	0	0.0	7	8.9	4	5.1
Virginia	89	5	5.6	4	4.5	6	6.7	2	2.2	2	2.2	11	12.4	7	7.9
West Virginia	63	2	3.2	0	0.0	1	1.6	0	0.0	0	0.0	4	6.3	1	1.6
CENSUS DIVISION 4, EAST NORTH CENTRAL	721	35	4.9	24	3.3	34	4.7	21	2.9	14	1.9	72	10.0	32	4.4
Illinois	173	11	6.4	6	3.5	8	4.6	6	3.5	2	1.2	18	10.4	11	6.4
Indiana	108	3	2.8	3	2.8	3	2.8	1	0.9	1	0.9	8	7.4	0	0.0
Michigan	147	8	5.4	6	4.1	10	6.8	5	3.4	4	2.7	22	15.0	11	7.5
Ohio	152	8	5.3	5	3.3	9	5.9	5	3.3	3	2.0	19	12.5	6	3.9
Wisconsin	141	5	3.5	4	2.8	4	2.8	4	2.8	4	2.8	5	3.5	4	2.8
CENSUS DIVISION 5, EAST SOUTH CENTRAL	419	14	3.3	8	1.9	13	3.1	5	1.2	5	1.2	19	4.5	12	2.9
Alabama	120	3	2.5	1	0.8	1	0.8	1	0.8	1	0.8	4	3.3	2	1.7
Kentucky	98	4	4.1	3	3.1	3	3.1	2	2.0	2	2.0	4	4.1	3	3.1
Mississippi	110	1	0.9	1	0.9	1	0.9	0	0.0	0	0.0	1	0.9	0	0.0
Tennessee	91	6	6.6	3	3.3	8	8.8	2	2.2	2	2.2	10	11.0	7	7.7
CENSUS DIVISION 6, WEST NORTH CENTRAL	649	16	2.5	8	1.2	22	3.4	10	1.5	5	0.8	26	4.0	22	3.4
Iowa	125	1	0.8	1	0.8	4	3.2	1	0.8	1	0.8	3	2.4	5	4.0
Kansas	153	2	1.3	0	0.0	2	1.3	1	0.7	0	0.0	1	0.7	2	1.3
Minnesota	102	4	3.9	2	2.0	3	2.9	2	2.0	2	2.0	6	5.9	2	2.0
Missouri	149	6	4.0	4	2.7	8	5.4	5	3.4	2	1.3	11	7.4	9	6.0
Nebraska	52	2	3.8	1	1.9	1	1.9	1	1.9	0	0.0	2	3.8	2	3.8
North Dakota	24	0	0.0	0	0.0	2	8.3	0	0.0	0	0.0	0	0.0	1	4.2
South Dakota	44	1	2.3	0	0.0	2	4.5	0	0.0	0	0.0	3	6.8	1	2.3
CENSUS DIVISION 7, WEST SOUTH CENTRAL	883	20	2.3	19	2.2	35	4.0	18	2.0	11	1.2	35	4.0	27	3.1
Arkansas	91	3	3.3	2	2.2	3	3.3	1	1.1	0	0.0	2	2.2	0	0.0
Louisiana	102	3	2.9	2	2.0	3	2.9	2	2.0	1	1.0	7	6.9	5	4.9
Oklahoma	123	2	1.6	2	1.6	5	4.1	2	1.6	1	0.8	4	3.3	1	0.8
Texas	567	12	2.1	13	2.3	24	4.2	13	2.3	9	1.6	22	3.9	21	3.7
CENSUS DIVISION 8, MOUNTAIN	335	15	4.5	10	3.0	15	4.5	10	3.0	6	1.8	20	6.0	14	4.2
Arizona	59	4	6.8	3	5.1	4	6.8	3	5.1	3	5.1	6	10.2	4	6.8
Colorado	71	4	5.6	2	2.8	4	5.6	3	4.2	1	1.4	5	7.0	3	4.2
Idaho	30	1	3.3	0	0.0	0	0.0	0	0.0	0	0.0	1	3.3	1	3.3
Montana	53	2	3.8	1	1.9	1	1.9	1	1.9	1	1.9	3	5.7	1	1.9
Nevada	27	0	0.0	0	0.0	1	3.7	0	0.0	0	0.0	0	0.0	0	0.0
New Mexico	36	1	2.8	0	0.0	2	5.6	0	0.0	0	0.0	0	0.0	2	5.6
Utah	32	3	9.4	4	12.5	3	9.4	3	9.4	1	3.1	5	15.6	3	9.4
Wyoming	27	0	0.0	0	0.0	0	0.0	0	0.0	0	0.0	0	0.0	0	0.0
CENSUS DIVISION 9, PACIFIC	448	26	5.8	16	3.6	26	5.8	16	3.6	9	2.0	37	8.3	30	6.7
Alaska	13	0	0.0	0	0.0	0	0.0	0	0.0	0	0.0	0	0.0	1	7.7
California	284	17	6.0	11	3.9	19	6.7	12	4.2	8	2.8	29	10.2	23	8.1
Hawaii	20	1	5.0	0	0.0	0	0.0	0	0.0	0	0.0	0	0.0	1	5.0
Oregon	61	3	4.9	3	4.9	3	4.9	2	3.3	0	0.0	4	6.6	2	3.3
Washington	70	5	7.1	2	2.9	4	5.7	2	2.9	1	1.4	4	5.7	3	4.3

Table 8

Table		Page

MSAs

Metropolitan Statistical Areas

Metropolitan Statistical Areas (MSAs) definitions announced by the U.S. Office of Management and Budget (OMB) effective June 6, 2003 were added with the 2006 edition.

According to the OMB, an MSA is a geographical designation that represents an integrated social and economic unit with a large population nucleus. Under these standards, an area qualifies for recognition as an MSA if there is a city within the area of at least 50,000 with a total metropolitan population of at least 100,000. MSAs are defined as entire counties. In addition to the county containing the main city, an MSA also includes additional counties having strong economic and social ties to the central county. Such counties must have a specified level of commuting to the central counties and must meet certain standards regarding metropolitan character, such as population density.

When an MSA encompasses two or more central cities, up to three cities may be specified in the MSA title. They will be listed in order of population size. When a single central city exists, the MSA is named for that particular city. A MSA may extend beyond a single state.

An MSA containing a single core with a population of 2.5 million or more may be subdivided to form smaller groupings of counties referred to as Metropolitan Divisions. Where they exist the Metropolitan Divisions are shown in this table rather than the entire MSA.

MSAs

CLASSIFICATION	Hospitals	Beds	Admissions	Inpatient Days	Adjusted Patient Days	Average Daily Census	Adjusted Average Daily Census	Average Stay (days)	Surgical Operations	NEWBORNS Bassinets	Births	OUTPATIENT VISITS Emergency	Total
UNITED STATES	4,985	804,943	35,149,427	189,593,349	355,023,656	519,540	972,930	5.4	27,311,998	56,610	3,818,399	127,249,317	651,423,717
Nonmetropolitan	1,987	137,779	4,307,936	27,147,315	70,298,276	74,403	192,723	6.3	4,153,393	10,938	451,316	23,425,674	123,164,591
Metropolitan	2,998	667,164	30,841,491	162,446,034	284,725,380	445,137	780,207	5.3	23,158,605	45,672	3,367,083	103,823,643	528,259,126
CENSUS DIVISION 1, NEW ENGLAND	203	33,974	1,668,378	8,813,799	19,643,552	24,164	53,844	5.3	1,458,312	2,481	152,389	7,120,183	46,735,546
Nonmetropolitan	58	3,905	150,242	880,910	2,719,025	2,414	7,452	5.9	192,931	400	14,174	1,055,702	7,898,865
Metropolitan	145	30,069	1,518,136	7,932,889	16,924,527	21,750	46,392	5.2	1,265,381	2,081	138,215	6,064,481	38,836,681
Connecticut	34	8,091	406,718	2,290,323	4,145,379	6,273	11,359	5.6	309,550	532	37,483	1,661,088	8,266,802
Nonmetropolitan	5	387	21,191	90,519	220,708	248	605	4.3	20,511	51	1,850	148,030	838,304
Metropolitan	29	7,704	385,527	2,199,804	3,924,671	6,025	10,754	5.7	289,039	481	35,633	1,513,058	7,428,498
Bridgeport-Stamford-Norwalk	6	1,845	94,145	490,923	896,649	1,344	2,457	5.2	65,084	154	11,531	352,544	1,970,182
Hartford-West Hartford-East Hartford.	12	2,858	135,649	839,092	1,487,303	2,298	4,075	6.2	111,617	163	12,447	567,821	3,366,100
New Haven-Milford	9	2,565	130,554	756,286	1,275,525	2,072	3,496	5.8	88,913	132	9,221	443,060	1,411,703
Norwich-New London	2	436	25,179	113,503	265,194	311	726	4.5	23,425	32	2,434	149,633	680,513
Maine	37	3,571	145,806	808,166	2,040,925	2,213	5,595	5.5	179,952	310	12,874	790,243	5,965,149
Nonmetropolitan	22	1,303	44,924	281,440	862,788	771	2,365	6.3	68,081	143	4,293	388,320	2,614,849
Metropolitan	15	2,268	100,882	526,726	1,178,137	1,442	3,230	5.2	111,871	167	8,581	401,923	3,350,300
Bangor	4	483	26,972	121,102	253,363	331	696	4.5	29,470	26	1,799	79,232	619,066
Lewiston-Auburn	2	361	16,136	79,286	184,005	217	504	4.9	11,599	35	1,438	77,658	984,689
Portland-South Portland-Biddeford.	9	1,424	57,774	326,338	740,769	894	2,030	5.6	70,802	106	5,344	245,033	1,746,545
Massachusetts	79	15,694	823,246	4,164,008	9,434,262	11,427	25,866	5.1	681,088	1,115	72,306	3,153,290	21,751,045
Nonmetropolitan	2	44	1,613	6,190	42,431	17	116	3.8	2,364	10	251	25,290	119,668
Metropolitan	77	15,650	821,633	4,157,818	9,391,831	11,410	25,750	5.1	678,724	1,105	72,055	3,128,000	21,631,377
Barnstable Town	3	414	23,178	102,916	234,616	283	643	4.4	13,971	18	1,426	125,964	892,079
Boston-Cambridge-Quincy.	48	10,406	557,853	2,856,042	6,427,467	7,842	17,626	5.1	472,600	738	49,401	1,824,832	13,657,154
Pittsfield.	3	334	15,350	77,945	211,525	213	579	5.1	16,178	27	1,077	86,577	590,375
Providence-New Bedford-Fall River	4	1,178	59,169	282,612	654,800	774	1,794	4.8	42,075	74	4,867	321,058	1,479,371
Springfield	10	1,694	78,932	408,517	873,010	1,120	2,393	5.2	59,427	107	6,631	389,055	2,478,572
Worcester.	9	1,624	87,151	429,786	990,413	1,178	2,715	4.9	74,473	141	8,653	380,514	2,533,826
New Hampshire	28	2,851	119,971	624,399	1,747,331	1,711	4,788	5.2	126,072	272	12,630	667,605	4,777,515
Nonmetropolitan	17	1,357	55,485	318,041	972,508	871	2,665	5.7	65,062	117	4,690	271,558	2,637,310
Metropolitan	11	1,494	64,486	306,358	774,823	840	2,123	4.8	61,010	155	7,940	396,047	2,140,205
Manchester-Nashua	5	832	36,292	172,193	458,645	471	1,257	4.7	28,741	96	5,170	183,893	1,198,297
Rockingham County-Strafford County	6	662	28,194	134,165	316,178	369	866	4.8	32,269	59	2,770	212,154	941,908
Rhode Island	11	2,479	123,188	621,614	1,240,239	1,703	3,399	5.0	99,542	142	11,492	495,149	2,622,415
Metropolitan	11	2,479	123,188	621,614	1,240,239	1,703	3,399	5.0	99,542	142	11,492	495,149	2,622,415
Providence-New Bedford-Fall River	11	2,479	123,188	621,614	1,240,239	1,703	3,399	5.0	99,542	142	11,492	495,149	2,622,415
Vermont	14	1,288	49,449	305,289	1,035,416	837	2,837	6.2	62,108	110	5,604	352,808	3,352,620
Nonmetropolitan	12	814	27,029	184,720	620,590	507	1,701	6.8	36,913	79	3,090	222,504	1,688,734
Metropolitan	2	474	22,420	120,569	414,826	330	1,136	5.4	25,195	31	2,514	130,304	1,663,886
Burlington-South Burlington	2	474	22,420	120,569	414,826	330	1,136	5.4	25,195	31	2,514	130,304	1,663,886

TABLE 8

U.S. CENSUS DIVISION 1, NEW ENGLAND

U.S. Community Hospitals
(Nonfederal, short-term general and other special hospitals)

2010 Utilization, Personnel and Finances

FULL-TIME EQUIVALENT PERSONNEL					FULL-TIME EQUIV. TRAINEES			EXPENSES						
								LABOR				TOTAL		
Physicians and Dentists	Registered Nurses	Licensed Practical Nurses	Other Salaried Personnel	Total Personnel	Medical and Dental Residents	Other Trainees	Total Trainees	Payroll (in thousands)	Employee Benefits (in thousands)	Total (in thousands)	Percent of Total	Amount (in thousands)	Adjusted per Admission	Adjusted per Inpatient Day
103,332	1,293,945	91,057	3,111,418	4,599,752	95,270	8,153	103,423	$274,300,010	$73,831,160	$348,131,210	51.3	$677,968,038	$10,313.44	$1,909.64
13,050	155,574	26,968	467,595	663,187	1,715	434	2,149	32,684,219	9,001,043	41,685,291	53.4	78,085,310	7,010.73	1,110.77
90,282	1,138,371	64,089	2,643,823	3,936,565	93,555	7,719	101,274	241,615,791	64,830,116	306,445,919	51.1	599,882,728	10,987.18	2,106.88
12,127	64,103	2,486	196,752	275,468	8,443	1,293	9,736	18,325,244	4,954,893	23,280,140	52.5	44,366,269	11,633.48	2,258.57
1,627	7,315	590	25,185	34,717	422	25	447	2,116,492	624,711	2,741,204	56.4	4,859,027	10,303.54	1,787.05
10,500	56,788	1,896	171,567	240,751	8,021	1,268	9,289	16,208,752	4,330,182	20,538,936	52.0	39,507,242	11,821.15	2,334.32
1,070	13,788	362	37,524	52,744	1,478	219	1,697	3,794,998	1,089,838	4,884,837	54.7	8,928,296	11,730.56	2,153.79
53	605	52	1,783	2,493	4	1	5	195,320	57,551	252,871	56.1	450,921	8,494.80	2,043.07
1,017	13,183	310	35,741	50,251	1,474	218	1,692	3,599,678	1,032,287	4,631,966	54.6	8,477,375	11,973.15	2,160.02
275	2,853	47	8,084	11,259	368	12	380	884,837	269,903	1,154,741	55.4	2,084,732	11,962.38	2,325.03
517	4,573	115	14,721	19,926	132	166	298	1,349,720	374,793	1,724,514	56.1	3,075,232	12,103.97	2,067.66
172	5,207	114	10,656	16,149	974	40	1,014	1,111,942	320,085	1,432,027	51.7	2,772,516	12,566.64	2,173.63
53	550	34	2,280	2,917	0	0	0	253,178	67,506	320,684	58.9	544,896	9,225.35	2,054.71
1,498	6,640	304	20,340	28,782	291	2	293	1,686,529	437,984	2,124,514	50.1	4,238,756	11,389.24	2,076.88
461	2,324	136	8,659	11,580	4	2	6	598,622	151,280	749,902	54.4	1,379,181	9,434.23	1,598.52
1,037	4,316	168	11,681	17,202	287	0	287	1,087,907	286,704	1,374,612	48.1	2,859,575	12,653.94	2,427.20
263	1,197	32	2,556	4,048	28	0	28	282,291	75,906	358,198	54.2	683,685	11,709.94	2,698.44
267	762	91	2,148	3,268	21	0	21	172,807	39,381	212,188	48.7	435,862	11,659.37	2,368.75
507	2,357	45	6,977	9,886	238	0	238	632,809	171,417	804,226	46.2	1,740,028	13,362.73	2,348.95
7,001	31,829	1,148	100,084	140,062	5,108	1,019	6,127	9,111,755	2,339,882	11,451,637	50.2	22,819,003	11,832.00	2,418.74
27	82	11	340	460	0	0	0	40,873	9,231	50,104	61.8	81,116	6,660.86	1,911.71
6,974	31,747	1,137	99,744	139,602	5,108	1,019	6,127	9,070,882	2,330,651	11,401,533	50.1	22,737,887	11,864.86	2,421.03
55	568	16	1,683	2,322	0	0	0	211,802	65,044	276,846	54.2	510,652	9,397.51	2,176.54
5,251	23,492	774	71,506	101,023	4,094	944	5,038	6,641,704	1,694,186	8,335,890	49.0	16,996,409	13,082.07	2,644.34
83	606	52	1,883	2,624	80	3	83	186,665	50,862	237,527	58.8	404,103	9,471.97	1,910.43
61	1,811	42	5,192	7,106	0	0	0	476,049	129,112	605,160	59.7	1,014,147	7,341.98	1,548.79
522	2,461	117	9,162	12,262	333	5	338	696,600	167,320	863,922	52.7	1,638,798	9,448.35	1,877.18
1,002	2,809	136	10,318	14,265	601	67	668	858,060	224,127	1,082,188	49.8	2,173,778	10,420.20	2,194.82
1,156	5,802	347	19,404	26,709	415	19	434	1,669,603	497,568	2,167,172	57.3	3,781,620	11,242.11	2,164.23
810	3,116	216	10,198	14,340	409	19	428	963,566	302,732	1,266,299	59.5	2,126,482	12,609.89	2,186.60
346	2,686	131	9,206	12,369	6	0	6	706,037	194,836	900,873	54.4	1,655,139	9,867.05	2,136.15
271	1,517	60	5,509	7,357	2	0	2	393,202	110,384	503,586	55.9	901,298	9,188.76	1,965.13
75	1,169	71	3,697	5,012	4	0	4	312,835	84,452	397,287	52.7	753,841	10,822.18	2,384.23
668	3,638	83	11,442	15,831	857	1	858	1,302,114	368,793	1,670,907	57.9	2,883,694	11,658.07	2,325.11
668	3,638	83	11,442	15,831	857	1	858	1,302,114	368,793	1,670,907	57.9	2,883,694	11,658.07	2,325.11
668	3,638	83	11,442	15,831	857	1	858	1,302,114	368,793	1,670,907	57.9	2,883,694	11,658.07	2,325.11
734	2,406	242	7,958	11,340	294	33	327	760,245	220,828	981,073	57.2	1,714,900	10,203.85	1,656.24
276	1,188	175	4,205	5,844	5	3	8	318,111	103,917	422,028	51.4	821,327	8,975.96	1,323.46
458	1,218	67	3,753	5,496	289	30	319	442,134	116,911	559,045	62.6	893,572	11,671.38	2,154.09
458	1,218	67	3,753	5,496	289	30	319	442,134	116,911	559,045	62.6	893,572	11,671.38	2,154.09

MSAs

TABLE 8

U.S. CENSUS DIVISION 2, MIDDLE ATLANTIC

U.S. Community Hospitals
(Nonfederal, short-term general and other special hospitals)

2010 Utilization, Personnel and Finances

CLASSIFICATION	Hospitals	Beds	Admissions	Inpatient Days	Adjusted Patient Days	Average Daily Census	Adjusted Average Daily Census	Average Stay (days)	Surgical Operations	NEWBORNS Bassinets	NEWBORNS Births	OUTPATIENT VISITS Emergency	OUTPATIENT VISITS Total
UNITED STATES	4,985	804,943	35,149,427	189,593,349	355,023,656	519,540	972,930	5.4	27,311,998	56,610	3,818,399	127,249,317	651,423,717
Nonmetropolitan	1,987	137,779	4,307,936	27,147,315	70,298,276	74,403	192,723	6.3	4,153,393	10,938	451,316	23,425,674	123,164,591
Metropolitan	2,998	667,164	30,841,491	162,446,034	284,725,380	445,137	780,207	5.3	23,158,605	45,672	3,367,083	103,823,643	528,259,126
CENSUS DIVISION 2, MIDDLE ATLANTIC	454	120,495	5,387,182	32,429,928	55,816,121	88,843	152,923	6.0	4,134,871	6,483	473,143	17,544,922	108,183,355
Nonmetropolitan	87	11,145	352,446	2,552,335	6,263,142	6,990	17,160	7.2	387,171	678	28,790	1,827,087	13,386,168
Metropolitan	367	109,350	5,034,736	29,877,593	49,552,979	81,853	135,763	5.9	3,747,700	5,805	444,353	15,717,835	94,797,187
New Jersey	73	21,096	1,067,267	5,433,359	8,237,849	14,885	22,570	5.1	632,698	1,434	100,677	3,360,970	15,980,614
Metropolitan	73	21,096	1,067,267	5,433,359	8,237,849	14,885	22,570	5.1	632,698	1,434	100,677	3,360,970	15,980,614
Allentown-Bethlehem-Easton	2	241	11,301	45,192	91,057	124	249	4.0	16,606	12	742	51,804	199,174
Atlantic City	3	824	43,275	207,803	336,092	570	921	4.8	16,426	56	3,558	144,587	432,589
Camden	10	2,882	146,504	706,563	1,035,722	1,935	2,837	4.8	85,503	141	13,424	550,424	1,499,807
Edison	17	5,122	262,317	1,367,548	1,961,195	3,748	5,373	5.2	143,948	382	25,917	798,460	2,663,169
New York-White Plains-Wayne	12	4,084	237,927	1,099,452	1,673,128	3,012	4,586	4.6	124,960	324	22,934	620,111	4,904,483
Newark-Union	18	5,774	265,305	1,470,815	2,227,175	4,028	6,103	5.5	169,771	351	25,006	829,439	4,373,626
Ocean City	1	208	10,355	38,479	61,332	105	168	3.7	4,285	16	549	45,694	141,741
Trenton-Ewing	6	1,368	62,168	359,944	613,168	986	1,679	5.8	49,378	104	5,495	197,717	1,345,200
Vineland-Millville-Bridgeton	2	365	18,363	96,704	166,859	265	457	5.3	14,171	24	2,165	81,129	300,118
Wilmington	2	228	9,752	40,859	72,121	112	197	4.2	7,650	24	887	41,605	120,707
New York	185	59,510	2,509,980	17,226,868	29,779,209	47,192	81,589	6.9	2,052,696	3,135	238,062	8,063,821	53,650,212
Nonmetropolitan	38	5,318	141,183	1,337,201	3,270,452	3,664	8,963	9.5	171,916	300	13,763	704,049	6,206,590
Metropolitan	147	54,192	2,368,797	15,889,667	26,508,757	43,528	72,626	6.7	1,880,780	2,835	224,299	7,359,772	47,443,622
Albany-Schenectady-Troy	9	2,562	108,690	699,344	1,307,010	1,916	3,581	6.4	92,138	65	8,618	347,221	2,253,603
Binghamton	2	608	26,831	143,108	385,638	392	1,057	5.3	35,752	40	2,759	98,430	1,792,588
Buffalo-Niagara Falls	11	5,259	157,989	1,492,305	2,393,627	4,087	6,559	9.4	159,176	219	12,619	505,926	3,048,893
Elmira	2	496	17,667	127,836	225,625	350	618	7.2	17,824	20	1,441	75,770	498,357
Glens Falls	1	260	17,320	82,120	144,938	225	397	4.7	13,603	20	1,560	154,725	771,313
Ithaca	1	209	6,080	28,706	82,099	79	225	4.7	6,440	19	787	30,031	234,671
Kingston	3	295	14,212	79,532	124,348	218	340	5.6	7,019	20	592	46,958	309,411
Nassau-Suffolk	24	8,878	419,135	2,766,071	4,268,069	7,577	11,694	6.6	325,543	476	34,654	1,088,707	5,785,593
New York-White Plains-Wayne	64	28,030	1,284,317	8,373,374	13,469,577	22,940	36,904	6.5	958,761	1,456	128,862	3,987,572	22,866,564
Poughkeepsie-Newburgh-Middletown	7	1,576	72,130	375,855	615,358	1,029	1,685	5.2	54,169	87	6,985	257,637	966,453
Rochester	11	3,070	123,379	918,665	1,928,279	2,517	5,282	7.4	115,619	209	12,821	432,807	6,245,547
Syracuse	7	1,984	82,516	528,340	958,925	1,447	2,626	6.4	63,594	132	8,954	211,343	1,557,809
Utica-Rome	5	965	38,531	274,411	605,264	751	1,658	7.1	31,142	72	3,647	122,645	1,112,820
Pennsylvania	196	39,889	1,809,935	9,769,701	17,799,063	26,766	48,764	5.4	1,449,477	1,914	134,404	6,120,131	38,552,529
Nonmetropolitan	49	5,827	211,263	1,215,134	2,992,690	3,326	8,197	5.8	215,255	378	15,027	1,123,038	7,179,578
Metropolitan	147	34,062	1,598,672	8,554,567	14,806,373	23,440	40,567	5.4	1,234,222	1,536	119,377	4,997,093	31,372,951
Allentown-Bethlehem-Easton	9	2,319	114,147	612,669	1,095,113	1,679	3,000	5.4	71,930	86	8,551	382,041	1,863,655
Altoona	4	580	24,073	122,081	249,584	335	684	5.1	23,145	30	1,746	88,011	555,508
Erie	7	1,169	43,721	243,218	409,148	665	1,122	5.6	32,307	57	3,511	152,622	612,873
Harrisburg-Carlisle	9	1,789	81,098	421,618	708,391	1,154	1,940	5.2	72,638	74	7,368	286,304	1,545,793
Johnstown	3	594	26,035	146,886	274,005	402	751	5.6	26,340	14	1,365	84,303	552,634
Lancaster	4	1,063	49,942	246,450	446,582	675	1,224	4.9	52,446	63	5,311	187,578	1,925,594
Lebanon	1	158	8,421	40,711	90,963	112	249	4.8	9,335	19	930	51,112	271,746
Philadelphia	46	12,712	643,604	3,315,209	5,327,274	9,086	14,597	5.2	447,084	634	48,111	1,778,939	9,902,873
Pittsburgh	36	8,832	400,541	2,275,537	3,896,913	6,235	10,675	5.7	351,666	304	23,993	1,180,384	8,191,630
Reading	3	1,018	39,694	224,151	408,609	614	1,120	5.6	24,353	56	4,304	156,621	1,309,057
Scranton--Wilkes-Barre	13	1,791	78,677	419,609	796,115	1,150	2,180	5.3	46,965	70	6,063	287,209	2,001,734
State College	2	280	12,354	60,360	104,950	165	288	4.9	9,720	5	1,373	50,232	239,973
Williamsport	3	405	14,008	105,954	275,983	291	756	7.6	21,853	22	1,152	83,066	473,156
York-Hanover	4	831	41,202	209,109	444,999	573	1,219	5.1	23,860	73	4,339	145,624	1,281,295
Youngstown-Warren-Boardman	3	521	21,155	111,005	277,744	304	762	5.2	20,580	29	1,260	83,047	645,430

TABLE **8**

U.S. CENSUS DIVISION 2, MIDDLE ATLANTIC

U.S. Community Hospitals
(Nonfederal, short-term general and other special hospitals)

2010 Utilization, Personnel and Finances

FULL-TIME EQUIVALENT PERSONNEL					FULL-TIME EQUIV. TRAINEES			EXPENSES						
								LABOR				TOTAL		
Physicians and Dentists	Registered Nurses	Licensed Practical Nurses	Other Salaried Personnel	Total Personnel	Medical and Dental Residents	Other Trainees	Total Trainees	Payroll (in thousands)	Employee Benefits (in thousands)	Total (in thousands)	Percent of Total	Amount (in thousands)	Adjusted per Admission	Adjusted per Inpatient Day
103,332	1,293,945	91,057	3,111,418	4,599,752	95,270	8,153	103,423	$274,300,010	$73,831,160	$348,131,210	51.3	$677,968,038	$10,313.44	$1,909.64
13,050	155,574	26,968	467,595	663,187	1,715	434	2,149	32,684,219	9,001,043	41,685,291	53.4	78,085,310	7,010.73	1,110.77
90,282	1,138,371	64,089	2,643,823	3,936,565	93,555	7,719	101,274	241,615,791	64,830,116	306,445,919	51.1	599,882,728	10,987.18	2,106.88
22,397	190,323	11,187	487,537	711,444	25,906	1,012	26,918	45,579,954	12,954,560	58,534,517	54.2	107,964,478	11,652.19	1,934.29
1,231	12,079	2,125	38,132	53,567	483	15	498	2,645,509	762,867	3,408,374	53.0	6,433,344	7,300.21	1,027.18
21,166	178,244	9,062	449,405	657,877	25,423	997	26,420	42,934,444	12,191,694	55,126,143	54.3	101,531,134	12,109.61	2,048.94
2,339	33,314	1,146	82,253	119,052	2,381	57	2,438	7,771,588	1,972,899	9,744,488	54.3	17,953,894	11,080.71	2,179.44
2,339	33,314	1,146	82,253	119,052	2,381	57	2,438	7,771,588	1,972,899	9,744,488	54.3	17,953,894	11,080.71	2,179.44
7	400	20	1,451	1,878	19	0	19	85,079	22,226	107,305	52.6	204,175	9,095.05	2,242.28
113	1,502	56	3,666	5,337	51	2	53	346,880	115,811	462,691	56.4	819,722	11,876.76	2,438.98
530	4,385	124	10,265	15,304	323	0	323	964,934	244,140	1,209,074	47.7	2,532,366	11,854.65	2,445.02
271	7,943	261	18,522	26,997	353	10	363	1,733,126	429,713	2,162,840	52.2	4,142,870	10,991.55	2,112.42
596	7,152	180	18,418	26,346	461	23	484	1,750,922	422,797	2,173,718	55.9	3,891,997	10,758.39	2,326.18
645	9,005	287	22,044	31,981	1,064	16	1,080	2,161,565	542,780	2,704,345	57.0	4,747,008	11,773.89	2,131.40
0	233	3	630	866	0	4	4	48,146	17,232	65,378	61.1	106,931	6,478.69	1,743.48
175	1,973	112	5,240	7,500	103	2	105	502,701	124,850	627,550	57.1	1,098,575	10,277.62	1,791.64
0	485	71	1,516	2,072	5	0	5	128,685	40,037	168,722	58.0	291,051	8,894.38	1,744.29
2	236	32	501	771	2	0	2	49,550	13,314	62,865	52.7	119,199	6,922.14	1,652.77
12,636	91,314	5,851	247,470	357,271	15,761	436	16,197	24,765,608	7,440,576	32,206,186	57.4	56,081,001	12,929.60	1,883.23
513	4,995	953	17,108	23,569	46	4	50	1,206,387	333,667	1,540,054	57.5	2,678,106	7,386.53	818.88
12,123	86,319	4,898	230,362	333,702	15,715	432	16,147	23,559,221	7,106,909	30,666,132	57.4	53,402,895	13,435.21	2,014.54
340	3,739	240	10,425	14,744	210	17	227	786,699	176,046	962,745	49.5	1,943,527	9,829.59	1,487.00
99	1,015	100	3,266	4,480	81	0	81	258,536	84,263	342,799	52.4	653,969	8,602.70	1,695.81
417	6,545	331	16,678	23,971	315	78	393	1,355,166	475,085	1,830,252	56.7	3,228,959	12,611.20	1,348.98
62	820	53	2,030	2,965	32	3	35	113,826	16,219	130,044	46.4	280,013	8,979.97	1,241.06
53	685	43	1,731	2,512	30	3	33	111,028	30,291	141,319	51.3	275,263	9,004.66	1,899.18
6	280	3	699	988	0	0	0	48,273	17,892	66,165	53.4	123,843	7,121.91	1,508.46
4	407	33	1,153	1,597	6	1	7	77,238	18,460	95,698	49.0	195,240	8,734.40	1,570.11
3,165	16,087	538	36,763	56,553	3,406	39	3,445	4,059,880	1,189,737	5,249,618	59.2	8,873,355	13,500.87	2,079.01
6,845	44,202	2,155	126,310	179,512	10,638	272	10,910	14,067,745	4,310,517	18,378,263	58.1	31,604,984	15,143.87	2,346.40
59	2,257	81	5,264	7,661	4	0	4	471,227	153,995	625,222	52.5	1,190,612	10,086.09	1,934.83
870	5,716	572	14,056	21,214	602	4	606	1,187,409	322,433	1,509,842	56.8	2,660,306	10,326.19	1,379.63
110	2,987	499	7,962	11,558	358	15	373	735,874	227,014	962,888	56.0	1,718,470	11,906.37	1,792.08
93	1,579	250	4,025	5,947	33	0	33	286,321	84,957	371,277	56.7	654,354	8,246.95	1,081.11
7,422	65,695	4,190	157,814	235,121	7,764	519	8,283	13,042,758	3,541,086	16,583,843	48.9	33,929,583	10,257.13	1,906.26
718	7,084	1,172	21,024	29,998	437	11	448	1,439,122	429,200	1,868,320	49.8	3,755,238	7,239.86	1,254.80
6,704	58,611	3,018	136,790	205,123	7,327	508	7,835	11,603,635	3,111,886	14,715,523	48.8	30,174,346	10,818.23	2,037.93
552	4,464	151	9,471	14,638	421	70	491	739,214	210,900	950,115	47.8	1,989,242	10,283.94	1,816.47
31	858	84	1,723	2,696	20	0	20	150,768	46,368	197,137	53.4	368,988	7,032.77	1,478.41
113	1,581	86	3,651	5,431	65	5	70	254,882	72,936	327,818	47.4	691,613	9,349.91	1,690.37
733	3,107	301	9,284	13,425	643	136	779	681,548	198,291	879,839	51.9	1,694,449	12,418.46	2,391.97
17	1,075	97	2,368	3,557	79	0	79	148,741	42,466	191,207	50.1	381,833	7,761.15	1,393.53
162	1,914	197	5,471	7,744	50	3	53	433,783	149,289	583,073	54.3	1,072,985	11,656.55	2,402.66
23	237	29	892	1,181	0	0	0	52,644	20,950	73,594	48.1	153,029	8,132.93	1,682.32
3,045	23,499	663	51,203	78,410	4,303	226	4,529	5,346,318	1,360,458	6,706,776	50.4	13,312,380	12,750.93	2,498.91
1,660	14,847	496	34,338	51,341	1,385	53	1,438	2,370,786	591,063	2,961,849	43.7	6,773,964	9,557.43	1,738.29
88	1,462	187	4,386	6,123	96	7	103	337,837	103,903	441,739	53.2	830,193	11,345.63	2,031.76
188	2,473	339	5,909	8,909	51	3	54	447,370	113,377	560,746	45.3	1,236,538	8,127.90	1,553.21
0	333	43	961	1,337	0	0	0	79,604	21,820	101,424	52.2	194,187	8,664.04	1,850.28
8	534	102	1,248	1,892	26	0	26	96,789	27,657	124,446	50.5	246,538	8,499.26	893.31
56	1,540	164	4,018	5,778	180	0	180	344,978	113,617	458,595	50.9	900,782	9,966.72	2,024.23
28	687	79	1,867	2,661	8	5	13	118,374	38,791	157,165	48.0	327,622	6,189.60	1,179.58

MSAs

TABLE 8

U.S. CENSUS DIVISION 3, SOUTH ATLANTIC

U.S. Community Hospitals
(Nonfederal, short-term general and other special hospitals)

2010 Utilization, Personnel and Finances

CLASSIFICATION	Hospitals	Beds	Admissions	Inpatient Days	Adjusted Patient Days	Average Daily Census	Adjusted Average Daily Census	Average Stay (days)	Surgical Operations	NEWBORNS Bassinets	NEWBORNS Births	OUTPATIENT VISITS Emergency	OUTPATIENT VISITS Total
UNITED STATES	4,985	804,943	35,149,427	189,593,349	355,023,656	519,540	972,930	5.4	27,311,998	56,610	3,818,399	127,249,317	651,423,717
Nonmetropolitan	1,987	137,779	4,307,936	27,147,315	70,298,276	74,403	192,723	6.3	4,153,393	10,938	451,316	23,425,674	123,164,591
Metropolitan	2,998	667,164	30,841,491	162,446,034	284,725,380	445,137	780,207	5.3	23,158,605	45,672	3,367,083	103,823,643	528,259,126
CENSUS DIVISION 3, SOUTH ATLANTIC.	758	156,678	6,970,769	37,775,346	68,291,604	103,485	187,099	5.4	5,253,140	10,270	718,161	25,132,194	96,113,038
Nonmetropolitan	244	24,444	836,582	5,277,164	12,065,788	14,453	33,060	6.3	729,472	1,730	76,960	4,430,609	16,968,591
Metropolitan	514	132,234	6,134,187	32,498,182	56,225,816	89,032	154,039	5.3	4,523,668	8,540	641,201	20,701,585	79,144,447
Delaware	7	2,155	101,735	580,261	1,052,393	1,590	2,884	5.7	96,680	88	11,486	406,652	1,787,310
Nonmetropolitan	2	404	14,383	95,367	214,785	261	589	6.6	15,611	28	1,763	84,679	539,061
Metropolitan	5	1,751	87,352	484,894	837,608	1,329	2,295	5.6	81,069	60	9,723	321,973	1,248,249
Dover	1	317	18,053	93,644	182,467	257	500	5.2	13,147	11	2,362	78,601	436,125
Wilmington	4	1,434	69,299	391,250	655,141	1,072	1,795	5.6	67,922	49	7,361	243,372	812,124
District of Columbia	11	3,458	131,976	926,254	1,471,515	2,538	4,031	7.0	100,643	196	13,814	430,637	2,318,882
Metropolitan	11	3,458	131,976	926,254	1,471,515	2,538	4,031	7.0	100,643	196	13,814	430,637	2,318,882
Washington-Arlington-Alexandria. .	11	3,458	131,976	926,254	1,471,515	2,538	4,031	7.0	100,643	196	13,814	430,637	2,318,882
Florida	210	53,318	2,452,089	12,191,209	19,774,808	33,402	54,172	5.0	1,448,746	2,793	202,862	7,559,853	24,243,101
Nonmetropolitan	29	1,956	93,254	396,338	859,872	1,085	2,354	4.3	62,243	93	5,241	418,461	1,634,777
Metropolitan	181	51,362	2,358,835	11,794,871	18,914,936	32,317	51,818	5.0	1,386,503	2,700	197,621	7,141,392	22,608,324
Cape Coral-Fort Myers	4	2,068	77,478	397,764	680,949	1,089	1,866	5.1	42,061	147	6,480	158,650	1,297,023
Deltona-Daytona Beach-Ormond Beach	5	1,435	59,213	274,727	490,029	753	1,341	4.6	36,249	59	4,262	304,291	747,032
Fort Lauderdale-Pompano Beach-Deerfield Beach	18	5,448	244,318	1,175,739	1,966,907	3,222	5,387	4.8	131,019	246	22,194	810,849	2,183,059
Fort Walton Beach-Crestview-Destin	3	424	21,654	93,543	146,445	256	401	4.3	12,888	32	1,698	75,016	200,831
Gainesville	3	1,322	62,919	354,837	517,281	973	1,417	5.6	53,590	38	5,660	120,010	844,545
Jacksonville	13	3,773	176,808	950,787	1,519,651	2,606	4,164	5.4	130,403	281	15,653	617,335	1,704,654
Lakeland	5	1,744	76,783	342,701	568,078	939	1,556	4.5	39,121	51	5,292	287,505	604,409
Miami-Miami Beach-Kendall	26	7,998	336,546	1,827,406	2,776,052	5,006	7,605	5.4	174,289	295	25,477	907,235	3,156,328
Naples-Marco Island	2	751	32,992	154,075	234,106	422	642	4.7	14,299	36	3,149	104,134	333,733
North Port-Bradenton-Sarasota. . .	8	1,845	78,114	365,243	588,400	1,000	1,611	4.7	41,796	59	5,135	260,200	941,361
Ocala	3	722	37,747	172,125	282,737	472	775	4.6	21,162	26	2,624	122,878	252,673
Orlando-Kissimmee.	11	5,396	297,540	1,468,861	2,300,932	4,024	6,304	4.9	170,901	459	29,690	918,934	2,191,683
Palm Bay-Melbourne-Titusville . . .	6	1,320	58,565	304,743	567,171	834	1,553	5.2	34,739	100	5,356	196,201	717,584
Palm Coast.	1	99	6,276	25,110	61,997	69	170	4.0	4,754	0	0	38,229	99,537
Panama City-Lynn Haven.	4	567	28,733	140,832	251,581	387	689	4.9	19,083	28	2,686	111,257	354,694
Pensacola-Ferry Pass-Brent	7	1,418	64,072	305,987	558,998	838	1,532	4.8	46,666	69	6,364	289,831	1,091,264
Port St. Lucie-Fort Pierce	3	876	45,193	208,501	330,020	571	904	4.6	26,104	50	4,097	134,198	228,184
Punta Gorda	3	742	30,384	145,312	214,190	398	586	4.8	21,365	10	932	81,355	206,166
Sebastian-Vero Beach	3	429	20,695	104,793	164,770	287	451	5.1	10,185	22	1,114	63,896	198,766
Tallahassee	4	827	39,598	202,651	348,600	555	956	5.1	24,918	72	4,808	102,957	505,282
Tampa-St. Petersburg-Clearwater .	35	8,559	387,229	1,948,547	3,016,138	5,339	8,263	5.0	239,170	450	31,086	1,007,664	3,305,119
West Palm Beach-Boca Raton-Boynton Beach	14	3,599	175,978	830,587	1,329,904	2,277	3,645	4.7	91,741	170	13,864	428,767	1,444,397
Georgia	154	25,513	961,391	6,138,828	12,017,900	16,812	32,931	6.4	763,718	1,932	128,531	4,095,951	14,291,580
Nonmetropolitan	65	6,460	149,281	1,456,314	3,426,849	3,987	9,393	9.8	150,229	381	17,423	929,752	2,980,319
Metropolitan	89	19,053	812,110	4,682,514	8,591,051	12,825	23,538	5.8	613,489	1,551	111,108	3,166,199	11,311,261
Albany.	3	566	22,073	119,600	265,273	328	726	5.4	17,355	42	2,962	98,457	729,257
Athens-Clarke County	2	540	27,116	122,545	245,848	335	673	4.5	24,810	44	3,977	104,916	353,885
Atlanta-Sandy Springs-Marietta . .	45	9,898	448,900	2,586,970	4,780,971	7,087	13,101	5.8	326,801	867	70,639	1,727,982	5,899,058
Augusta-Richmond County	8	1,664	63,192	370,709	615,639	1,015	1,687	5.9	50,764	128	5,866	276,906	1,121,124
Brunswick.	1	538	11,123	125,965	223,544	345	612	11.3	10,306	20	1,318	51,353	62,751
Chattanooga	2	307	6,682	70,585	130,585	193	358	10.6	6,929	15	707	22,422	97,115
Columbus.	5	1,131	35,307	213,405	398,852	584	1,092	6.0	26,301	31	4,416	138,922	361,416
Dalton	2	285	11,226	44,342	85,015	121	233	3.9	7,376	44	1,973	73,744	260,406
Gainesville	1	513	28,208	121,676	200,864	333	550	4.3	18,555	64	3,553	98,701	251,740
Hinesville-Fort Stewart	1	25	1,631	2,836	9,658	8	26	1.7	904	0	0	4,611	26,771
Macon.	6	1,050	45,351	270,131	417,993	740	1,146	6.0	32,900	96	3,488	112,575	518,850
Rome	2	553	25,911	124,564	237,128	341	650	4.8	20,866	31	2,404	108,431	305,840
Savannah.	5	1,219	50,347	323,750	610,381	887	1,672	6.4	44,648	71	5,538	192,337	788,372
Valdosta	4	488	19,157	113,863	215,000	312	589	5.9	14,765	64	2,161	74,010	266,658
Warner Robins	2	276	15,886	71,573	154,300	196	423	4.5	10,209	34	2,106	80,832	268,018

TABLE **8**

U.S. CENSUS DIVISION 3, SOUTH ATLANTIC

U.S. Community Hospitals
(Nonfederal, short-term general and other special hospitals)

2010 Utilization, Personnel and Finances

	FULL-TIME EQUIVALENT PERSONNEL				FULL-TIME EQUIV. TRAINEES			EXPENSES						
								LABOR				TOTAL		
Physicians and Dentists	Registered Nurses	Licensed Practical Nurses	Other Salaried Personnel	Total Personnel	Medical and Dental Residents	Other Trainees	Total Trainees	Payroll (in thousands)	Employee Benefits (in thousands)	Total (in thousands)	Percent of Total	Amount (in thousands)	Adjusted per Admission	Adjusted per Inpatient Day
103,332	1,293,945	91,057	3,111,418	4,599,752	95,270	8,153	103,423	$274,300,010	$73,831,160	$348,131,210	51.3	$677,968,038	$10,313.44	$1,909.64
13,050	155,574	26,968	467,595	663,187	1,715	434	2,149	32,684,219	9,001,043	41,685,291	53.4	78,085,310	7,010.73	1,110.77
90,282	1,138,371	64,089	2,643,823	3,936,565	93,555	7,719	101,274	241,615,791	64,830,116	306,445,919	51.1	599,882,728	10,987.18	2,106.88
13,137	250,884	16,330	560,481	840,832	14,453	723	15,176	46,959,848	11,836,368	58,796,222	49.8	118,053,521	9,417.69	1,728.67
1,450	27,729	4,546	75,470	109,195	170	31	201	5,090,029	1,351,981	6,442,010	52.5	12,280,725	6,442.81	1,017.81
11,687	223,155	11,784	485,011	731,637	14,283	692	14,975	41,869,819	10,484,388	52,354,212	49.5	105,772,796	9,951.17	1,881.21
531	4,787	188	10,976	16,482	325	1	326	996,087	324,483	1,320,571	56.3	2,344,087	13,022.06	2,227.39
33	643	18	1,530	2,224	0	0	0	126,935	45,861	172,796	51.5	335,232	10,962.45	1,560.78
498	4,144	170	9,446	14,258	325	1	326	869,152	278,622	1,147,775	57.1	2,008,855	13,443.54	2,398.32
27	690	43	1,776	2,536	0	0	0	144,552	47,599	192,151	52.6	365,366	10,386.50	2,002.37
471	3,454	127	7,670	11,722	325	1	326	724,600	231,024	955,624	58.1	1,643,489	14,384.78	2,508.60
1,176	6,440	290	16,731	24,637	614	32	646	1,643,345	327,866	1,971,212	55.0	3,582,285	16,918.00	2,434.42
1,176	6,440	290	16,731	24,637	614	32	646	1,643,345	327,866	1,971,212	55.0	3,582,285	16,918.00	2,434.42
1,176	6,440	290	16,731	24,637	614	32	646	1,643,345	327,866	1,971,212	55.0	3,582,285	16,918.00	2,434.42
3,326	78,259	4,554	165,026	251,165	4,785	198	4,983	14,297,797	3,613,439	17,911,238	49.3	36,318,160	9,057.42	1,836.59
151	2,434	398	6,285	9,268	12	4	16	471,288	113,699	584,988	50.8	1,152,388	5,960.70	1,340.19
3,175	75,825	4,156	158,741	241,897	4,773	194	4,967	13,826,509	3,499,740	17,326,250	49.3	35,165,772	9,214.30	1,859.15
258	2,804	194	6,831	10,087	525	34	559	605,806	178,009	783,815	56.2	1,394,752	10,473.94	2,048.25
131	1,926	150	4,739	6,946	30	0	30	367,634	99,123	466,757	56.4	827,836	7,786.27	1,689.36
386	6,715	362	13,848	21,311	393	29	422	1,372,162	312,449	1,684,611	48.4	3,480,397	8,417.72	1,769.48
7	521	43	891	1,462	8	0	8	75,988	14,709	90,697	47.9	189,472	5,499.90	1,293.81
5	2,505	93	5,784	8,387	570	6	576	426,182	107,256	533,438	46.5	1,146,092	12,434.81	2,215.61
364	6,435	148	11,936	18,883	500	1	501	939,057	295,314	1,234,371	45.4	2,719,338	9,477.39	1,789.45
57	2,359	220	5,281	7,917	3	19	22	385,047	88,106	473,153	53.1	891,572	6,993.87	1,569.45
371	12,011	662	25,568	38,612	1,365	12	1,377	2,362,897	614,512	2,977,410	51.7	5,755,248	11,162.71	2,073.18
6	1,048	67	2,030	3,151	0	0	0	177,110	38,360	215,472	55.6	387,833	7,735.78	1,656.66
19	2,386	195	4,723	7,323	21	1	22	388,702	93,841	482,543	51.1	944,503	7,452.87	1,605.21
28	1,111	60	2,317	3,516	12	0	12	189,505	50,209	239,714	56.4	425,187	6,818.16	1,503.83
378	11,674	421	22,630	35,103	431	23	454	1,811,984	484,115	2,296,097	45.4	5,009,264	10,814.33	2,177.06
89	1,686	51	3,870	5,696	15	17	32	363,399	81,769	445,169	50.4	882,442	7,851.39	1,555.87
14	155	18	477	664	1	0	1	48,494	12,430	60,923	50.7	110,695	7,143.90	1,785.49
30	679	97	1,546	2,352	0	0	0	135,233	27,506	162,739	46.4	351,071	6,634.24	1,395.46
13	2,113	126	3,477	5,729	10	3	13	305,356	68,592	373,947	42.4	882,292	7,450.91	1,578.35
19	1,105	46	1,959	3,129	12	0	12	221,316	56,389	277,706	49.7	558,342	7,802.76	1,691.84
10	796	70	1,462	2,338	7	0	7	140,985	33,171	174,155	46.6	373,324	8,333.11	1,742.95
34	524	36	1,337	1,931	2	0	2	105,209	24,086	129,296	51.9	249,052	7,320.11	1,511.51
71	1,126	121	2,758	4,076	35	0	35	220,607	53,652	274,258	52.0	527,823	7,643.08	1,514.12
812	11,702	649	26,675	39,838	773	46	819	2,315,271	569,293	2,884,564	49.2	5,865,051	9,713.98	1,944.56
73	4,444	327	8,602	13,446	60	3	63	868,565	196,849	1,065,415	48.6	2,194,186	7,780.20	1,649.88
1,229	35,631	3,703	85,074	125,637	877	85	962	6,489,753	1,629,184	8,118,932	50.5	16,079,597	8,847.73	1,337.97
275	5,182	1,542	16,299	23,298	30	3	33	985,130	262,873	1,248,002	53.3	2,340,443	6,583.82	682.97
954	30,449	2,161	68,775	102,339	847	82	929	5,504,623	1,366,310	6,870,930	50.0	13,739,154	9,398.25	1,599.24
87	991	147	2,659	3,884	18	0	18	159,297	58,543	217,840	44.4	490,961	9,980.29	1,850.77
11	1,008	43	2,544	3,606	0	0	0	189,488	53,953	243,441	49.4	493,175	9,068.05	2,006.02
496	16,936	890	37,144	55,466	306	18	324	3,055,849	727,511	3,783,357	51.1	7,404,001	9,196.19	1,548.64
23	2,643	254	5,284	8,204	14	0	14	457,488	112,054	569,541	50.0	1,139,634	10,845.29	1,851.14
43	406	21	937	1,407	87	8	95	71,105	25,036	96,141	43.8	219,440	11,117.08	981.64
15	272	26	725	1,038	10	1	11	45,476	13,374	58,850	55.2	106,694	8,679.93	817.04
76	1,206	129	3,030	4,441	49	0	49	223,822	48,869	272,689	45.0	605,846	9,125.70	1,518.97
5	358	60	916	1,339	0	0	0	81,232	21,864	103,097	52.1	197,730	9,082.70	2,325.83
93	713	25	1,673	2,504	114	7	121	179,182	47,315	226,496	46.3	489,415	10,510.15	2,436.55
4	46	13	168	231	0	0	0	11,315	2,926	14,241	57.1	24,931	4,488.87	2,581.40
22	1,787	118	3,913	5,840	113	1	114	317,401	78,721	396,123	50.4	786,118	11,140.81	1,880.70
66	908	136	2,027	3,137	18	43	61	169,232	34,797	204,029	52.1	391,528	7,962.75	1,651.13
4	1,866	81	4,592	6,543	118	4	122	355,676	78,682	434,358	49.6	875,801	10,170.96	1,434.84
9	754	125	1,835	2,723	0	0	0	105,241	41,821	147,062	48.2	304,932	8,546.53	1,418.29
0	555	93	1,328	1,976	0	0	0	82,820	20,845	103,665	49.6	208,948	6,095.34	1,354.17

Table continues

MSAs

2010 Utilization, Personnel and Finances

MSAs

CLASSIFICATION	Hospitals	Beds	Admissions	Inpatient Days	Adjusted Patient Days	Average Daily Census	Adjusted Average Daily Census	Average Stay (days)	Surgical Operations	NEWBORNS Bassinets	NEWBORNS Births	OUTPATIENT VISITS Emergency	OUTPATIENT VISITS Total
Maryland	47	11,682	707,549	3,160,045	5,188,839	8,656	14,217	4.5	548,347	945	69,042	2,460,678	8,373,605
Nonmetropolitan	6	427	32,221	107,508	219,806	294	603	3.3	36,844	50	2,798	178,575	855,498
Metropolitan	41	11,255	675,328	3,052,537	4,969,033	8,362	13,614	4.5	511,503	895	66,244	2,282,103	7,518,107
Baltimore-Towson	21	6,918	423,334	1,897,262	3,076,081	5,198	8,427	4.5	343,564	450	35,076	1,332,629	4,602,396
Bethesda-Gaithersburg-Frederick	7	1,729	115,649	494,668	771,440	1,356	2,114	4.3	69,383	224	18,759	358,778	1,019,444
Cumberland	1	363	16,414	98,889	177,733	271	487	6.0	8,855	20	1,104	51,812	429,186
Hagerstown-Martinsburg	1	286	16,166	70,923	129,232	194	354	4.4	8,274	41	1,950	70,314	203,752
Salisbury	3	531	26,528	146,638	251,572	402	689	5.5	17,402	28	2,089	92,289	537,309
Washington-Arlington-Alexandria	7	1,313	69,251	315,061	506,425	861	1,388	4.5	56,590	120	6,544	330,117	561,732
Wilmington	1	115	7,986	29,096	56,550	80	155	3.6	7,435	12	722	46,164	164,288
North Carolina	117	23,012	1,038,337	5,852,967	11,538,499	16,034	31,614	5.6	851,391	1,682	117,422	4,259,853	18,285,895
Nonmetropolitan	58	6,532	262,130	1,428,221	3,169,990	3,914	8,684	5.4	213,031	583	25,901	1,470,801	5,108,125
Metropolitan	59	16,480	776,207	4,424,746	8,368,509	12,120	22,930	5.7	638,360	1,099	91,521	2,789,052	13,177,770
Asheville	6	1,221	60,220	298,823	541,788	818	1,485	5.0	58,389	58	4,976	178,352	1,129,277
Burlington	1	210	11,493	49,242	86,910	135	238	4.3	6,992	20	1,046	23,763	118,460
Charlotte-Gastonia-Concord	13	3,400	180,370	952,433	1,840,218	2,609	5,043	5.3	136,045	295	24,234	695,800	2,930,869
Durham	6	1,979	94,691	596,446	1,148,670	1,634	3,147	6.3	83,143	63	8,933	232,225	2,357,652
Fayetteville	1	666	31,595	197,318	325,991	541	893	6.2	16,198	48	4,663	122,758	555,831
Goldsboro	1	267	12,935	60,245	115,429	165	316	4.7	13,180	30	1,366	52,737	145,507
Greensboro-High Point	5	1,736	73,629	450,628	896,242	1,233	2,456	6.1	47,357	105	9,078	313,605	1,195,220
Greenville	1	861	39,193	248,987	346,774	682	950	6.4	19,866	42	3,688	108,343	371,891
Hickory-Lenoir-Morganton	5	994	35,025	242,585	515,841	665	1,413	6.9	30,919	62	3,986	153,197	651,400
Jacksonville	1	144	8,438	32,564	81,598	89	224	3.9	5,738	23	1,976	56,076	230,457
Raleigh-Cary	6	1,869	95,567	510,975	1,026,933	1,400	2,814	5.3	100,542	144	14,949	384,169	2,045,539
Rocky Mount	2	403	17,467	80,844	159,388	221	437	4.6	11,502	34	1,836	85,535	238,809
Wilmington	4	915	38,429	214,625	452,547	588	1,240	5.6	33,885	50	4,364	167,468	498,486
Winston-Salem	7	1,815	77,155	489,031	830,180	1,340	2,274	6.3	74,604	125	6,426	215,024	708,372
South Carolina	67	12,495	522,793	3,002,541	5,230,523	8,226	14,329	5.7	484,689	886	54,894	1,453,696	6,376,329
Nonmetropolitan	25	2,986	105,695	629,908	1,260,802	1,725	3,456	6.0	87,429	235	10,442	296,263	1,132,272
Metropolitan	42	9,509	417,098	2,372,633	3,969,721	6,501	10,873	5.7	397,260	651	44,452	1,157,433	5,244,057
Anderson	2	435	20,853	106,574	167,018	292	457	5.1	15,867	28	1,991	59,549	588,152
Augusta-Richmond County	2	281	12,436	61,908	103,148	170	282	5.0	10,115	18	1,140	57,835	155,182
Charleston-North Charleston	6	1,809	84,762	447,498	764,864	1,226	2,095	5.3	78,285	125	9,884	235,524	1,501,797
Charlotte-Gastonia-Concord	2	321	15,289	76,146	115,408	209	316	5.0	15,607	37	2,019	62,944	162,120
Columbia	7	2,102	88,291	544,943	901,530	1,493	2,470	6.2	71,102	131	9,975	215,147	757,147
Florence	6	1,290	45,981	292,700	464,563	802	1,273	6.4	55,990	60	3,355	50,877	192,720
Greenville	11	1,556	77,826	407,361	685,297	1,115	1,877	5.2	73,760	117	8,341	229,946	921,927
Myrtle Beach-Conway-North Myrtle Beach	3	701	27,710	182,247	358,325	499	981	6.6	22,577	54	2,628	98,326	336,634
Spartanburg	2	711	34,568	181,512	290,260	498	795	5.3	38,183	57	3,864	92,706	488,223
Sumter	1	303	9,382	71,744	119,308	197	327	7.6	15,774	24	1,255	54,579	140,155
Virginia	89	17,747	776,678	4,310,430	8,472,597	11,809	23,206	5.5	662,500	1,335	99,623	3,256,956	13,781,936
Nonmetropolitan	30	2,927	89,314	588,049	1,353,164	1,612	3,704	6.6	81,634	199	6,556	520,712	2,178,522
Metropolitan	59	14,820	687,364	3,722,381	7,119,433	10,197	19,502	5.4	580,866	1,136	93,067	2,736,244	11,603,414
Blacksburg-Christiansburg-Radford	4	328	14,992	59,821	132,212	165	362	4.0	18,641	34	1,563	88,611	238,250
Charlottesville	3	776	39,119	215,403	404,739	590	1,109	5.5	74,952	45	3,437	106,960	2,081,804
Danville	1	290	8,981	41,065	77,884	113	213	4.6	6,082	20	798	39,378	95,297
Harrisonburg	1	238	14,653	54,635	138,038	150	378	3.7	18,650	28	1,742	70,301	295,493
Kingsport-Bristol-Bristol	1	100	5,945	22,427	68,069	61	186	3.8	7,713	12	637	36,675	154,021
Lynchburg	2	1,235	33,212	330,386	572,979	905	1,570	9.9	17,096	51	2,697	107,729	460,703
Richmond	14	3,438	151,996	836,568	1,443,470	2,292	3,954	5.5	110,769	197	20,078	476,079	1,711,055
Roanoke	3	1,207	56,905	326,370	548,917	894	1,504	5.7	41,252	57	4,889	220,574	570,659
Virginia Beach-Norfolk-Newport News	15	3,296	156,077	845,901	1,829,218	2,316	5,010	5.4	133,505	259	18,381	815,910	3,389,237
Washington-Arlington-Alexandria	14	3,491	181,436	878,093	1,709,355	2,405	4,683	4.8	140,935	417	36,534	708,718	2,287,583
Winchester	1	421	24,048	111,712	194,552	306	533	4.6	11,271	16	2,311	65,309	319,312
West Virginia	56	7,298	278,221	1,612,811	3,544,530	4,418	9,715	5.8	296,426	413	20,487	1,207,918	6,654,400
Nonmetropolitan	29	2,752	90,304	575,459	1,560,520	1,575	4,277	6.4	82,451	161	6,836	531,366	2,540,017
Metropolitan	27	4,546	187,917	1,037,352	1,984,010	2,843	5,438	5.5	213,975	252	13,651	676,552	4,114,383
Charleston	7	1,315	53,490	302,799	576,352	829	1,579	5.7	90,848	68	3,859	171,907	969,027
Cumberland	1	25	895	3,121	14,216	9	39	3.5	1,705	0	0	13,090	51,940
Hagerstown-Martinsburg	2	169	7,495	39,932	104,473	109	287	5.3	8,659	21	856	51,944	219,420
Huntington-Ashland	3	722	42,710	182,958	339,735	501	931	4.3	28,618	55	2,889	125,745	729,204
Morgantown	4	789	36,703	213,861	327,079	587	897	5.8	32,827	14	2,281	82,202	783,064
Parkersburg-Marietta-Vienna	3	485	17,521	87,278	154,168	240	423	5.0	16,653	43	1,650	75,257	374,830
Washington-Arlington-Alexandria	1	25	1,611	5,073	19,817	14	54	3.1	3,161	10	283	23,410	68,131
Weirton-Steubenville	1	238	6,427	36,514	90,770	100	249	5.7	6,594	21	376	40,037	191,293
Wheeling	4	734	20,697	153,370	300,001	420	822	7.4	24,702	20	1,457	84,882	696,977
Winchester	1	44	368	12,446	57,399	34	157	33.8	208	0	0	8,078	30,497

TABLE 8

U.S. CENSUS DIVISION 3, SOUTH ATLANTIC CONTINUED

U.S. Community Hospitals
(Nonfederal, short-term general and other special hospitals)

2010 Utilization, Personnel and Finances

FULL-TIME EQUIVALENT PERSONNEL					FULL-TIME EQUIV. TRAINEES			EXPENSES						
								LABOR				TOTAL		
Physicians and Dentists	Registered Nurses	Licensed Practical Nurses	Other Salaried Personnel	Total Personnel	Medical and Dental Residents	Other Trainees	Total Trainees	Payroll (in thousands)	Employee Benefits (in thousands)	Total (in thousands)	Percent of Total	Amount (in thousands)	Adjusted per Admission	Adjusted per Inpatient Day
2,303	21,562	521	55,430	79,816	1,431	67	1,498	4,865,313	1,153,071	6,018,386	49.6	12,132,498	10,321.69	2,338.19
53	929	28	2,584	3,594	0	8	8	203,342	51,608	254,950	54.0	471,953	7,166.43	2,147.13
2,250	20,633	493	52,846	76,222	1,431	59	1,490	4,661,971	1,101,464	5,763,436	49.4	11,660,545	10,508.96	2,346.64
1,998	14,195	271	36,676	53,140	1,387	47	1,434	3,186,392	750,695	3,937,086	48.6	8,105,938	11,663.82	2,635.15
44	2,700	23	6,854	9,621	0	7	7	647,515	143,501	791,016	50.5	1,565,248	8,614.56	2,028.99
33	482	22	1,327	1,864	0	0	0	100,743	36,880	137,623	49.9	275,862	9,350.95	1,552.12
7	550	21	1,142	1,720	0	0	0	110,590	30,595	141,185	58.5	241,204	8,188.36	1,866.45
41	740	70	2,077	2,928	0	0	0	158,896	42,107	201,003	50.2	400,230	9,007.10	1,590.92
100	1,744	82	4,140	6,066	44	1	45	406,560	87,604	494,164	52.0	950,172	8,334.48	1,876.24
27	222	4	630	883	0	4	4	51,276	10,083	61,359	50.3	121,889	7,853.19	2,155.43
1,552	44,352	1,832	97,700	145,436	2,751	159	2,910	7,772,548	1,994,782	9,767,332	51.8	18,847,920	9,151.10	1,633.48
368	9,166	808	24,279	34,621	26	6	32	1,551,441	401,455	1,952,907	54.0	3,615,244	6,061.41	1,140.46
1,184	35,186	1,024	73,421	110,815	2,725	153	2,878	6,221,097	1,593,326	7,814,425	51.3	15,232,676	10,410.53	1,820.24
89	2,601	91	5,711	8,492	6	6	12	447,738	112,188	559,926	52.2	1,071,630	9,662.86	1,977.95
36	468	30	1,169	1,703	19	2	21	76,361	20,833	97,194	51.3	189,317	9,332.84	2,178.31
347	7,636	141	15,377	23,501	291	11	302	1,393,205	346,451	1,739,657	46.7	3,729,129	10,476.38	2,026.46
43	5,855	95	12,080	18,073	1,298	45	1,343	1,068,232	237,592	1,305,824	52.4	2,492,349	13,922.72	2,169.77
129	1,210	157	3,027	4,523	2	0	2	264,864	59,716	324,580	65.0	499,285	9,565.21	1,531.59
4	526	11	910	1,451	0	0	0	72,995	19,787	92,782	54.3	170,984	6,899.26	1,481.30
246	2,934	137	6,891	10,208	61	0	61	497,599	170,969	668,568	55.5	1,204,054	8,396.41	1,343.45
0	1,715	13	3,789	5,517	343	25	368	315,446	105,624	421,071	47.9	879,233	16,107.30	2,535.46
90	1,239	58	3,149	4,536	5	1	6	259,665	68,097	327,762	54.6	600,278	8,336.96	1,163.69
0	355	20	715	1,090	0	0	0	49,004	15,075	64,079	71.3	89,865	4,250.13	1,101.31
180	4,493	76	8,543	13,292	0	10	10	789,196	181,072	970,268	54.0	1,797,814	9,363.47	1,750.66
3	760	15	1,465	2,243	0	0	0	109,412	32,360	141,772	55.6	255,070	7,389.28	1,600.31
4	1,378	47	3,257	4,686	63	0	63	260,750	72,387	333,136	48.8	683,197	9,343.76	1,509.67
13	4,016	133	7,338	11,500	637	53	690	616,629	151,177	767,806	48.9	1,570,470	12,146.98	1,891.72
1,141	20,068	1,234	42,062	64,505	1,235	1	1,236	3,415,562	890,609	4,306,173	46.1	9,349,824	10,192.52	1,787.55
133	3,495	366	8,590	12,584	37	0	37	640,518	176,288	816,808	49.2	1,659,613	7,783.02	1,316.32
1,008	16,573	868	33,472	51,921	1,198	1	1,199	2,775,043	714,321	3,489,365	45.4	7,690,211	10,922.25	1,937.22
70	625	45	2,213	2,953	30	0	30	147,378	39,174	186,553	47.4	393,317	11,669.76	2,354.94
14	333	18	607	972	0	0	0	56,223	10,886	67,109	44.8	149,933	7,292.09	1,453.57
15	3,834	127	7,062	11,038	653	0	653	653,736	163,308	817,045	44.5	1,837,341	12,558.38	2,402.18
0	320	16	789	1,125	0	0	0	69,497	15,466	84,963	40.0	212,171	8,804.89	1,838.45
65	3,930	200	7,950	12,145	236	0	236	643,930	158,188	802,090	47.1	1,704,635	11,732.31	1,890.82
46	1,741	161	3,660	5,608	26	0	26	268,717	66,361	335,079	44.6	750,855	9,606.64	1,616.26
545	2,982	79	4,914	8,520	177	0	177	473,832	132,905	606,737	43.3	1,401,374	10,403.75	2,044.92
17	910	88	1,851	2,866	0	0	0	141,254	40,640	181,894	49.0	371,590	7,387.03	1,037.02
215	1,555	118	3,587	5,475	60	0	60	244,887	66,818	311,705	45.9	679,457	12,272.76	2,340.86
21	343	16	839	1,219	16	1	17	75,616	20,573	96,190	50.7	189,538	12,148.33	1,588.65
1,329	29,549	2,576	61,942	95,396	1,822	137	1,959	5,708,163	1,353,746	7,061,909	48.0	14,709,796	9,447.46	1,736.16
172	2,978	665	7,709	11,524	25	8	33	570,524	138,991	709,515	50.5	1,405,653	6,426.11	1,038.79
1,157	26,571	1,911	54,233	83,872	1,797	129	1,926	5,137,639	1,214,754	6,352,394	47.7	13,304,143	9,941.31	1,868.71
5	582	54	991	1,632	27	0	27	96,504	22,023	118,528	46.0	257,713	7,724.53	1,949.24
57	2,089	147	4,347	6,640	736	5	741	424,360	114,498	538,858	46.7	1,152,843	14,822.79	2,848.36
10	213	28	793	1,044	12	0	12	45,491	11,890	57,381	45.0	127,621	7,492.54	1,638.60
68	587	59	1,458	2,172	0	0	0	124,225	30,550	154,775	48.7	317,696	8,581.51	2,301.51
15	193	41	492	741	0	0	0	37,562	7,540	45,102	53.0	85,036	4,712.72	1,249.27
87	929	176	3,319	4,511	18	5	23	257,191	62,915	320,105	56.7	564,688	10,055.52	985.53
144	6,372	540	11,414	18,470	702	96	798	1,111,445	283,090	1,394,536	47.8	2,917,476	10,936.13	2,021.15
377	2,385	165	4,332	7,259	195	3	198	495,920	106,113	602,033	49.6	1,214,191	12,305.95	2,211.98
104	5,643	456	12,626	18,829	2	11	13	1,108,875	250,325	1,359,201	45.9	2,961,796	8,690.77	1,619.16
257	6,862	175	12,606	19,900	105	9	114	1,298,903	293,814	1,592,717	48.3	3,299,134	9,405.78	1,930.05
33	716	70	1,855	2,674	0	0	0	137,162	31,996	169,158	41.7	405,949	9,692.92	2,086.59
550	10,236	1,432	25,540	37,758	613	43	656	1,771,280	549,189	2,320,469	49.5	4,689,353	7,725.38	1,322.98
265	2,902	721	8,194	12,082	40	2	42	540,840	161,205	702,044	54.0	1,300,199	5,593.48	833.18
285	7,334	711	17,346	25,676	573	41	614	1,230,440	387,984	1,618,425	47.8	3,389,154	9,048.43	1,708.23
110	2,470	224	5,048	7,852	168	17	185	375,035	115,589	490,624	45.7	1,074,207	10,190.75	1,863.80
0	42	8	146	196	0	0	0	6,802	1,447	8,249	41.7	19,794	4,855.15	1,392.41
5	271	19	593	888	0	0	0	51,960	17,592	69,552	56.4	123,267	6,942.66	1,179.89
35	1,277	136	2,787	4,235	0	0	0	227,917	100,994	328,909	49.8	660,328	8,127.91	1,943.66
31	1,545	93	3,656	5,325	329	19	348	271,979	75,667	347,647	45.8	759,272	12,811.69	2,321.37
20	501	68	1,823	2,412	13	4	17	85,822	24,899	110,720	41.5	266,894	8,268.61	1,731.19
0	71	8	164	243	0	0	0	15,435	5,210	20,645	57.7	35,772	5,684.46	1,805.13
8	218	26	559	811	0	0	0	38,391	12,357	50,748	57.1	88,851	5,561.21	978.86
74	923	120	2,465	3,582	63	1	64	151,954	32,915	184,870	53.1	348,145	6,885.24	1,160.48
2	16	9	105	132	0	0	0	5,147	1,314	6,461	51.2	12,622	7,437.94	219.90

MSAs

TABLE 8

U.S. CENSUS DIVISION 4, EAST NORTH CENTRAL

U.S. Community Hospitals
(Nonfederal, short-term general and other special hospitals)

2010 Utilization, Personnel and Finances

CLASSIFICATION	Hospitals	Beds	Admissions	Inpatient Days	Adjusted Patient Days	Average Daily Census	Adjusted Average Daily Census	Average Stay (days)	Surgical Operations	NEWBORNS		OUTPATIENT VISITS	
										Bassinets	Births	Emergency	Total
UNITED STATES	4,985	804,943	35,149,427	189,593,349	355,023,656	519,540	972,930	5.4	27,311,998	56,610	3,818,399	127,249,317	651,423,717
Nonmetropolitan	1,987	137,779	4,307,936	27,147,315	70,298,276	74,403	192,723	6.3	4,153,393	10,938	451,316	23,425,674	123,164,591
Metropolitan	2,998	667,164	30,841,491	162,446,034	284,725,380	445,137	780,207	5.3	23,158,605	45,672	3,367,083	103,823,643	528,259,126
CENSUS DIVISION 4, EAST NORTH CENTRAL	777	124,528	5,573,945	28,088,741	57,656,743	76,973	157,990	5.0	4,806,580	9,655	549,668	21,645,563	131,901,411
Nonmetropolitan	274	18,724	670,246	3,577,523	11,161,422	9,809	30,585	5.3	724,120	1,856	70,446	4,067,963	24,036,408
Metropolitan	503	105,804	4,903,699	24,511,218	46,495,321	67,164	127,405	5.0	4,082,460	7,799	479,222	17,577,600	107,865,003
Illinois	189	33,310	1,542,958	7,552,956	14,718,871	20,699	40,328	4.9	1,142,009	2,624	159,563	5,366,010	32,558,096
Nonmetropolitan	64	4,291	157,416	791,549	2,342,386	2,170	6,419	5.0	161,463	311	12,889	870,125	4,990,993
Metropolitan	125	29,019	1,385,542	6,761,407	12,376,485	18,529	33,909	4.9	980,546	2,313	146,674	4,495,885	27,567,103
Bloomington-Normal	2	355	17,070	62,829	114,077	172	312	3.7	11,481	33	2,376	67,099	489,781
Champaign-Urbana	4	563	28,320	137,365	275,150	376	754	4.9	22,509	66	3,495	105,975	617,681
Chicago-Naperville-Joliet	78	20,509	1,003,129	4,937,265	8,623,965	13,531	23,629	4.9	642,242	1,585	107,280	3,045,575	18,904,556
Danville	2	226	7,101	51,873	158,091	143	433	7.3	4,061	26	740	42,423	231,536
Davenport-Moline-Rock Island	5	544	22,997	109,957	277,596	301	760	4.8	18,513	73	2,395	103,243	637,082
Decatur	2	446	18,852	83,537	228,220	229	625	4.4	15,267	36	1,738	82,899	443,890
Kankakee-Bradley	2	468	19,099	83,975	182,838	230	501	4.4	17,771	34	1,472	71,406	543,948
Lake County-Kenosha County	5	916	55,956	199,595	379,501	547	1,040	3.6	42,575	113	7,114	162,558	748,327
Peoria	6	1,203	57,081	290,699	550,171	796	1,508	5.1	69,686	81	4,662	249,090	1,692,123
Rockford	4	910	42,800	214,731	360,122	588	986	5.0	40,888	68	4,787	144,256	1,094,624
Springfield	2	898	44,958	226,951	389,333	622	1,067	5.0	34,340	56	3,584	125,387	764,855
St. Louis	13	1,981	68,179	362,630	837,421	994	2,294	5.3	61,213	142	7,031	295,974	1,398,700
Indiana	125	17,759	718,348	3,756,021	7,817,448	10,294	21,437	5.2	629,951	1,401	77,124	3,185,166	18,728,772
Nonmetropolitan	40	2,294	88,796	421,853	1,365,063	1,154	3,740	4.8	108,604	290	11,847	659,232	3,585,510
Metropolitan	85	15,465	629,552	3,334,168	6,452,385	9,140	17,697	5.3	521,347	1,111	65,277	2,525,934	15,143,262
Anderson	2	225	8,341	43,785	130,909	120	358	5.2	14,403	12	397	51,791	288,401
Bloomington	2	318	14,212	61,578	125,538	169	344	4.3	8,780	19	2,055	67,363	790,609
Cincinnati-Middletown	1	78	4,355	17,683	44,828	48	123	4.1	6,107	11	510	18,900	138,815
Columbus	1	234	8,519	33,116	79,229	91	217	3.9	10,967	20	1,165	40,443	233,255
Elkhart-Goshen	2	419	18,627	74,146	138,452	203	379	4.0	14,094	51	2,380	86,710	611,480
Evansville	7	1,217	47,556	280,486	561,231	770	1,537	5.9	39,358	62	4,650	166,309	972,843
Fort Wayne	9	1,630	63,226	346,930	639,263	951	1,751	5.5	65,497	130	7,194	203,538	1,003,013
Gary	11	2,522	103,477	569,345	1,031,765	1,559	2,828	5.5	68,033	199	8,409	394,460	1,874,524
Indianapolis	26	5,444	204,999	1,173,931	2,252,299	3,217	6,171	5.7	169,426	322	22,700	900,191	6,315,238
Kokomo	4	308	12,676	62,771	169,110	172	464	5.0	14,509	35	1,221	57,309	344,081
Lafayette	3	473	19,811	94,182	195,360	258	535	4.8	14,448	35	2,431	107,493	440,141
Louisville	6	626	32,176	147,051	289,080	407	811	4.6	27,260	48	2,809	111,633	626,301
Michigan City-La Porte	2	375	12,865	73,399	150,442	201	412	5.7	11,373	35	1,387	51,690	256,048
Muncie	1	347	18,558	82,706	147,805	227	405	4.5	6,371	24	1,677	55,261	314,341
South Bend-Mishawaka	3	624	33,019	148,577	233,503	407	640	4.5	21,664	59	4,004	106,556	345,643
Terre Haute	5	625	27,135	124,482	263,571	340	722	4.6	29,057	49	2,288	106,287	588,529
Michigan	156	25,623	1,207,546	6,214,588	12,693,806	17,026	34,772	5.1	1,060,224	1,727	111,192	4,550,617	30,250,337
Nonmetropolitan	59	4,438	151,225	882,240	2,779,464	2,419	7,613	5.8	173,443	372	14,249	840,515	5,818,655
Metropolitan	97	21,185	1,056,321	5,332,348	9,914,342	14,607	27,159	5.0	886,781	1,355	96,943	3,710,102	24,431,682
Ann Arbor	6	1,596	82,752	449,177	836,965	1,231	2,293	5.4	76,108	52	6,809	194,908	2,889,134
Battle Creek	3	315	16,158	69,865	179,635	192	493	4.3	10,907	26	1,709	65,031	352,755
Bay City	2	364	17,518	87,734	136,885	240	375	5.0	11,109	14	913	44,489	346,676
Detroit-Livonia-Dearborn	20	5,420	257,383	1,353,092	2,496,661	3,707	6,838	5.3	192,689	306	22,642	994,687	5,503,092
Flint	4	1,189	70,531	310,792	533,810	851	1,463	4.4	46,043	89	5,638	225,664	1,530,785
Grand Rapids-Wyoming	8	1,810	92,476	440,769	827,903	1,207	2,268	4.8	114,748	162	11,955	336,296	2,336,363
Holland-Grand Haven	3	226	11,045	38,910	92,277	106	253	3.5	12,933	52	1,105	111,363	565,316
Jackson	2	349	20,705	87,580	186,591	240	512	4.2	11,332	17	1,813	70,392	606,521
Kalamazoo-Portage	5	848	46,255	208,623	381,021	571	1,043	4.5	33,810	70	5,194	177,314	1,176,939
Lansing-East Lansing	5	1,026	52,223	247,069	505,120	677	1,384	4.7	45,717	41	5,421	199,943	1,175,799
Monroe	1	169	9,795	40,015	90,925	110	249	4.1	9,231	13	857	43,857	177,712
Muskegon-Norton Shores	4	448	19,936	82,143	227,457	225	623	4.1	25,576	46	2,212	108,333	866,848
Niles-Benton Harbor	3	509	17,063	126,414	207,431	346	568	7.4	13,555	35	1,831	80,359	365,133
Saginaw-Saginaw Township North	4	1,129	43,270	304,481	462,268	835	1,267	7.0	22,978	31	3,155	127,117	657,623
South Bend-Mishawaka	1	25	866	2,813	12,935	8	35	3.2	942	0	0	9,042	109,048
Warren-Farmington Hills-Troy	26	5,762	298,345	1,482,871	2,736,458	4,061	7,495	5.0	259,103	401	25,689	921,307	5,771,938

TABLE 8

U.S. CENSUS DIVISION 4, EAST NORTH CENTRAL

U.S. Community Hospitals
(Nonfederal, short-term general and other special hospitals)

2010 Utilization, Personnel and Finances

FULL-TIME EQUIVALENT PERSONNEL					FULL-TIME EQUIV. TRAINEES			EXPENSES						
								LABOR				TOTAL		
Physicians and Dentists	Registered Nurses	Licensed Practical Nurses	Other Salaried Personnel	Total Personnel	Medical and Dental Residents	Other Trainees	Total Trainees	Payroll (in thousands)	Employee Benefits (in thousands)	Total (in thousands)	Percent of Total	Amount (in thousands)	Adjusted per Admission	Adjusted per Inpatient Day
103,332	1,293,945	91,057	3,111,418	4,599,752	95,270	8,153	103,423	$274,300,010	$73,831,160	$348,131,210	51.3	$677,968,038	$10,313.44	$1,909.64
13,050	155,574	26,968	467,595	663,187	1,715	434	2,149	32,684,219	9,001,043	41,685,291	53.4	78,085,310	7,010.73	1,110.77
90,282	1,138,371	64,089	2,643,823	3,936,565	93,555	7,719	101,274	241,615,791	64,830,116	306,445,919	51.1	599,882,728	10,987.18	2,106.88
20,653	214,841	11,400	539,440	786,334	20,435	2,523	22,958	45,868,374	12,387,578	58,255,973	50.2	116,021,100	10,189.06	2,012.27
2,456	26,167	3,169	81,347	113,139	170	109	279	5,938,176	1,774,961	7,713,154	53.1	14,513,014	7,149.01	1,300.28
18,197	188,674	8,231	458,093	673,195	20,265	2,414	22,679	39,930,198	10,612,616	50,542,819	49.8	101,508,086	10,848.65	2,183.19
4,611	53,689	2,178	134,041	194,519	5,991	225	6,216	11,515,744	3,180,610	14,696,357	50.3	29,193,599	9,781.95	1,983.41
471	5,761	842	17,366	24,440	40	6	46	1,203,027	365,558	1,568,589	53.4	2,937,099	6,539.14	1,253.89
4,140	47,928	1,336	116,675	170,079	5,951	219	6,170	10,312,717	2,815,052	13,127,768	50.0	26,256,500	10,356.46	2,121.48
96	551	15	1,422	2,084	16	0	16	123,721	32,381	156,101	52.6	296,997	9,577.76	2,603.48
15	1,164	32	2,546	3,757	28	4	32	189,758	54,186	243,944	44.7	545,347	10,808.36	1,982.00
3,425	35,100	764	83,245	122,534	5,433	164	5,597	7,650,464	2,058,699	9,709,162	50.6	19,193,524	10,852.40	2,225.60
5	204	23	641	873	0	1	1	41,635	13,164	54,798	46.7	117,313	6,580.28	742.06
28	758	32	1,885	2,703	0	0	0	137,545	37,715	175,260	44.1	397,011	7,142.28	1,430.17
66	569	99	2,169	2,903	15	0	15	148,961	37,589	186,549	49.0	381,096	7,356.93	1,669.86
40	738	23	1,476	2,277	5	0	5	122,213	30,109	152,322	46.0	330,807	7,970.68	1,809.29
34	1,571	48	3,690	5,343	0	0	0	339,861	92,453	432,314	47.0	918,910	8,709.39	2,421.36
290	2,360	71	5,857	8,578	224	22	246	509,018	138,013	647,032	50.2	1,288,341	11,946.34	2,341.71
106	1,639	37	4,077	5,859	0	26	26	349,928	105,073	455,002	52.8	861,980	11,829.99	2,393.58
1	1,259	85	3,925	5,270	230	1	231	300,273	97,182	397,456	43.3	917,297	11,886.40	2,356.07
34	2,015	107	5,742	7,898	0	1	1	399,338	118,488	517,828	51.4	1,007,878	6,497.83	1,203.55
1,997	29,420	2,104	71,700	105,221	1,301	251	1,552	5,900,489	1,605,755	7,506,246	48.9	15,349,923	9,948.75	1,963.55
450	3,759	540	11,669	16,418	1	38	39	838,161	243,617	1,081,780	53.6	2,016,473	6,587.61	1,477.20
1,547	25,661	1,564	60,031	88,803	1,300	213	1,513	5,062,328	1,362,138	6,424,466	48.2	13,333,449	10,780.61	2,066.44
24	266	39	1,102	1,431	0	0	0	81,773	24,152	105,925	54.6	193,958	7,801.69	1,481.62
21	679	49	1,815	2,564	0	0	0	133,433	43,702	177,135	57.5	308,249	10,524.03	2,455.42
5	129	27	506	667	0	0	0	32,230	10,766	42,996	65.7	65,413	5,925.06	1,459.19
0	257	25	1,069	1,351	0	0	0	68,974	26,471	95,445	51.0	187,134	9,181.32	2,361.93
54	727	40	1,756	2,577	5	1	6	141,287	19,710	160,997	41.6	386,891	11,098.11	2,794.41
128	1,673	100	4,795	6,696	20	7	27	347,361	103,734	451,094	48.5	929,439	10,061.58	1,656.07
42	2,298	131	4,941	7,412	0	0	0	365,104	98,299	463,403	43.2	1,073,694	9,523.46	1,679.58
198	3,501	197	8,156	12,052	94	14	108	686,959	174,636	861,594	49.0	1,758,842	9,396.73	1,704.69
584	10,623	525	21,883	33,615	1,020	184	1,204	2,073,944	564,906	2,638,851	48.0	5,501,542	13,394.12	2,442.63
52	475	29	1,611	2,167	0	0	0	116,877	29,920	146,798	52.7	278,418	7,982.41	1,646.37
182	977	73	2,279	3,511	21	6	27	249,959	62,172	312,130	52.2	597,423	15,046.17	3,058.06
70	901	81	2,845	3,897	0	0	0	175,973	42,243	218,216	54.8	398,231	6,024.30	1,377.58
78	456	26	1,582	2,142	4	0	4	122,799	33,989	156,787	51.8	302,610	11,505.20	2,011.47
51	610	38	1,398	2,097	54	0	54	99,439	26,970	126,409	44.7	282,837	8,528.18	1,913.58
16	1,140	19	2,185	3,360	56	0	56	195,216	56,787	252,003	44.7	564,281	10,634.57	2,416.59
42	949	165	2,108	3,264	26	1	27	171,001	43,681	214,683	42.6	504,488	8,392.47	1,914.05
5,601	45,561	1,833	118,215	171,210	5,715	108	5,823	10,101,837	2,566,134	12,667,982	50.9	24,872,817	10,101.43	1,959.45
617	5,631	727	19,323	26,298	70	13	83	1,383,597	403,039	1,786,643	52.2	3,421,185	7,662.61	1,230.88
4,984	39,930	1,106	98,892	144,912	5,645	95	5,740	8,718,240	2,163,096	10,881,339	50.7	21,451,633	10,641.59	2,163.70
1,467	5,429	104	12,217	19,217	1,381	0	1,381	1,047,280	329,872	1,377,152	53.3	2,582,939	16,357.86	3,086.08
37	599	22	1,392	2,050	0	1	1	125,119	33,568	158,687	50.2	315,972	7,723.03	1,758.97
17	415	51	1,168	1,651	10	15	25	103,256	26,060	129,316	55.6	232,539	8,238.47	1,698.79
1,200	9,317	137	22,864	33,518	2,189	26	2,215	2,263,231	508,435	2,771,667	48.8	5,681,279	11,964.37	2,275.55
104	2,568	56	4,383	7,111	278	0	278	463,605	153,442	617,047	55.8	1,106,117	9,144.41	2,072.12
251	3,248	141	10,087	13,727	74	1	75	787,145	219,097	1,006,241	48.2	2,088,949	11,938.96	2,523.18
48	498	44	1,552	2,142	8	0	8	101,823	25,854	127,678	54.5	234,414	8,798.35	2,540.33
58	663	62	2,463	3,246	0	0	0	165,658	36,900	202,559	54.1	374,411	8,040.62	2,006.59
165	1,610	19	4,173	5,967	0	0	0	406,552	103,343	509,895	51.3	994,039	11,471.36	2,608.88
199	2,063	31	5,169	7,462	227	0	227	478,008	142,203	620,212	55.5	1,117,828	10,028.33	2,213.00
14	320	22	945	1,301	0	0	0	62,528	15,076	77,604	53.4	145,236	6,525.42	1,597.32
115	628	13	2,143	2,899	22	0	22	173,713	56,878	230,591	46.2	498,777	8,865.73	2,192.84
147	560	77	2,364	3,148	0	0	0	123,884	38,654	162,538	51.2	317,534	8,863.98	1,530.80
128	1,526	143	4,476	6,273	0	18	18	302,055	80,670	382,725	51.7	739,659	10,115.69	1,600.07
9	43	0	170	222	0	0	0	13,319	4,099	17,418	60.7	28,677	7,201.66	2,217.01
1,025	10,443	184	23,326	34,978	1,456	34	1,490	2,101,063	388,946	2,490,009	49.9	4,993,259	8,993.01	1,824.72

Table continues

MSAs

2010 Utilization, Personnel and Finances

CLASSIFICATION	Hospitals	Beds	Admissions	Inpatient Days	Adjusted Patient Days	Average Daily Census	Adjusted Average Daily Census	Average Stay (days)	Surgical Operations	NEWBORNS Bassinets	Births	OUTPATIENT VISITS Emergency	Total
Ohio	183	34,316	1,516,501	7,598,267	15,139,402	20,825	41,489	5.0	1,223,063	2,636	133,946	6,383,429	35,759,248
Nonmetropolitan	55	4,423	168,782	719,581	1,997,969	1,975	5,482	4.3	165,668	575	19,429	1,141,004	6,101,061
Metropolitan	128	29,893	1,347,719	6,878,686	13,141,433	18,850	36,007	5.1	1,057,395	2,061	114,517	5,242,425	29,658,187
Akron	8	1,978	91,737	475,246	953,406	1,303	2,613	5.2	63,757	108	7,559	385,199	2,260,535
Canton-Massillon	5	1,436	50,884	296,072	593,070	812	1,626	5.8	45,181	111	4,270	221,724	1,374,926
Cincinnati-Middletown	20	4,523	215,087	1,056,531	1,844,723	2,895	5,053	4.9	158,920	419	22,704	806,128	3,531,651
Cleveland-Elyria-Mentor	31	7,889	350,508	1,933,551	3,875,791	5,297	10,616	5.5	311,655	409	22,575	1,106,336	8,998,747
Columbus	19	5,143	250,382	1,156,861	2,141,788	3,171	5,869	4.6	180,114	380	28,321	1,012,594	5,304,877
Dayton	10	2,682	113,109	578,381	1,064,488	1,586	2,918	5.1	104,692	171	10,519	470,606	1,984,859
Lima	4	681	28,838	126,663	243,774	347	668	4.4	18,732	49	2,288	104,415	656,523
Mansfield	2	314	15,013	68,665	122,928	188	337	4.6	7,916	38	1,174	67,435	373,517
Parkersburg-Marietta-Vienna	2	177	8,845	39,218	79,578	107	218	4.4	10,303	16	305	51,287	239,006
Sandusky	1	227	9,678	52,447	110,751	144	303	5.4	10,866	15	687	47,218	259,440
Springfield	1	284	14,557	66,876	126,346	183	346	4.6	9,688	31	1,314	72,376	321,394
Toledo	13	2,455	108,577	544,818	1,100,972	1,492	3,017	5.0	83,693	167	8,766	418,102	2,687,162
Weirton-Steubenville	1	319	11,402	68,628	149,239	188	409	6.0	5,803	18	557	49,500	233,076
Wheeling	3	263	7,443	59,217	143,530	163	394	8.0	7,257	10	409	44,111	256,972
Youngstown-Warren-Boardman	8	1,522	71,659	355,512	591,049	974	1,620	5.0	38,818	119	3,069	385,394	1,175,502
Wisconsin	124	13,520	588,592	2,966,909	7,287,216	8,129	19,964	5.0	751,333	1,267	67,843	2,160,341	14,604,958
Nonmetropolitan	56	3,278	104,027	762,300	2,676,540	2,091	7,331	7.3	114,942	308	12,032	557,087	3,540,189
Metropolitan	68	10,242	484,565	2,204,609	4,610,676	6,038	12,633	4.5	636,391	959	55,811	1,603,254	11,064,769
Appleton	4	396	18,856	76,314	182,575	209	500	4.0	32,465	58	2,236	71,725	349,934
Duluth	1	25	541	5,091	46,741	14	128	9.4	2,199	0	0	14,427	46,465
Eau Claire	5	555	23,823	113,733	259,346	311	712	4.8	18,661	40	2,308	69,595	422,689
Fond du Lac	3	217	8,554	34,144	127,191	94	348	4.0	14,224	21	1,056	43,228	688,361
Green Bay	5	754	32,657	134,042	308,936	367	846	4.1	55,387	97	4,609	142,317	1,029,833
Janesville	3	352	15,224	64,350	137,821	177	377	4.2	12,867	20	1,757	66,927	1,143,263
La Crosse	2	413	21,510	83,359	161,839	229	443	3.9	23,619	42	2,410	35,908	294,709
Lake County-Kenosha County	3	488	24,262	97,747	224,282	267	614	4.0	22,846	66	3,140	152,085	899,017
Madison	7	1,485	72,477	370,938	777,570	1,017	2,131	5.1	120,872	96	7,820	178,679	1,384,255
Milwaukee-Waukesha-West Allis	21	4,090	198,413	935,957	1,733,777	2,563	4,752	4.7	240,874	328	21,232	617,465	3,621,132
Minneapolis-St. Paul-Bloomington	4	92	5,305	16,033	51,783	44	142	3.0	6,756	25	880	24,416	104,067
Oshkosh-Neenah	4	452	18,929	75,910	160,387	207	440	4.0	29,549	66	2,808	55,689	273,393
Racine	2	433	17,689	96,304	239,282	264	655	5.4	27,522	47	2,201	60,242	536,525
Sheboygan	2	162	8,534	30,896	73,076	84	200	3.6	15,869	28	1,397	29,809	148,658
Wausau	2	328	17,791	69,791	126,070	191	345	3.9	12,681	25	1,957	40,742	122,468

MSAs

TABLE **8**

U.S. CENSUS DIVISION 4, EAST NORTH CENTRAL CONTINUED

U.S. Community Hospitals
(Nonfederal, short-term general and other special hospitals)

2010 Utilization, Personnel and Finances

FULL-TIME EQUIVALENT PERSONNEL					FULL-TIME EQUIV. TRAINEES			EXPENSES						
								LABOR				TOTAL		
Physicians and Dentists	Registered Nurses	Licensed Practical Nurses	Other Salaried Personnel	Total Personnel	Medical and Dental Residents	Other Trainees	Total Trainees	Payroll (in thousands)	Employee Benefits (in thousands)	Total (in thousands)	Percent of Total	Amount (in thousands)	Adjusted per Admission	Adjusted per Inpatient Day
7,493	63,916	4,210	154,276	229,895	6,668	702	7,370	13,201,068	3,452,399	16,653,472	51.4	32,374,140	10,560.22	2,138.40
548	7,008	768	19,136	27,460	58	6	64	1,362,152	409,415	1,771,569	51.9	3,415,713	6,996.50	1,709.59
6,945	56,908	3,442	135,140	202,435	6,610	696	7,306	11,838,916	3,042,984	14,881,903	51.4	28,958,427	11,235.23	2,203.60
519	3,847	401	9,549	14,316	443	60	503	786,795	196,540	983,335	53.0	1,855,696	10,025.53	1,946.39
114	2,136	172	5,301	7,723	73	6	79	351,213	100,056	451,269	53.7	840,513	8,199.73	1,417.22
751	9,4C4	354	24,067	34,576	948	302	1,250	2,002,462	522,492	2,524,954	50.7	4,983,341	12,996.64	2,701.40
2,735	15,091	1,271	40,210	59,307	2,591	273	2,864	3,899,360	985,073	4,884,432	56.5	8,648,609	12,370.00	2,231.44
2,451	10,225	181	21,155	34,012	1,491	10	1,501	1,944,167	500,857	2,445,025	46.9	5,217,339	10,947.85	2,435.97
79	4,961	161	11,732	16,933	426	1	427	906,936	218,070	1,125,008	49.2	2,286,201	10,785.65	2,147.70
1	1,069	89	2,321	3,480	0	0	0	176,595	52,569	229,163	48.1	476,920	8,549.24	1,956.40
38	580	38	1,373	2,029	19	3	22	113,095	30,469	143,565	50.2	285,780	10,574.67	2,324.78
25	322	45	897	1,289	6	1	7	86,215	23,495	109,709	52.7	208,363	11,580.89	2,618.35
3	243	48	1,053	1,347	15	0	15	72,733	19,618	92,351	49.7	185,971	9,099.72	1,679.18
0	543	65	1,005	1,613	0	0	0	74,056	20,135	94,190	46.6	202,094	7,348.32	1,599.53
117	4,964	283	9,413	14,777	484	33	517	881,376	237,332	1,118,709	48.3	2,317,316	11,190.82	2,104.79
15	441	29	1,057	1,542	0	0	0	67,554	22,624	90,178	53.0	170,035	6,857.63	1,139.35
20	271	53	726	1,070	0	0	0	45,900	14,291	60,192	57.1	105,473	5,737.22	734.85
77	2,811	252	5,281	8,421	114	7	121	430,460	99,364	529,823	45.1	1,174,775	9,810.31	1,987.61
951	22,255	1,075	61,208	85,489	760	1,237	1,997	5,149,235	1,582,680	6,731,916	47.3	14,230,621	10,687.56	1,952.82
370	4,008	292	13,853	18,523	1	46	47	1,151,239	353,333	1,504,573	55.3	2,722,544	8,004.30	1,017.19
581	18,247	783	47,355	66,966	759	1,191	1,950	3,997,996	1,229,347	5,227,343	45.4	11,508,076	11,608.16	2,495.96
5	616	53	1,506	2,180	0	25	25	138,121	43,310	181,432	51.1	355,081	7,814.10	1,944.85
0	37	9	143	189	0	0	0	16,092	4,621	20,713	64.7	32,035	6,449.60	685.38
10	929	18	2,348	3,305	0	5	5	183,320	57,691	241,010	52.1	462,221	9,886.46	1,782.26
35	371	114	1,187	1,707	0	0	0	106,730	26,480	133,210	43.6	305,194	9,598.21	2,399.50
78	1,314	107	3,747	5,246	0	17	17	313,188	97,180	410,367	46.4	884,773	11,599.32	2,863.94
228	654	42	2,497	3,421	20	1	21	136,677	47,009	183,686	37.4	490,507	15,309.69	3,559.02
28	828	37	2,027	2,920	20	0	20	163,007	65,121	228,127	52.9	431,614	10,330.63	2,666.93
84	974	52	2,670	3,780	15	21	36	219,541	60,904	280,444	51.4	546,035	9,665.70	2,434.59
56	2,843	70	7,846	10,815	515	78	593	704,712	250,491	955,204	53.3	1,792,234	13,966.26	2,304.92
49	7,311	157	16,850	24,367	189	925	1,114	1,523,530	420,312	1,943,842	40.8	4,764,921	12,764.66	2,748.29
1	188	5	627	821	0	0	0	47,615	12,542	60,158	64.7	126,142	7,324.03	2,435.97
6	619	32	1,474	2,131	0	34	34	132,164	42,288	174,452	48.3	361,324	8,829.79	2,252.83
0	692	65	2,073	2,830	0	22	22	136,359	45,629	181,988	45.5	399,788	9,071.87	1,670.78
0	217	5	651	873	0	53	53	49,818	18,564	68,381	40.9	167,028	8,291.69	2,285.67
1	654	17	1,709	2,381	0	10	10	127,123	37,206	164,329	42.2	389,180	12,216.07	3,087.01

MSAs

TABLE **8**

U.S. CENSUS DIVISION 5, EAST SOUTH CENTRAL

U.S. Community Hospitals
(Nonfederal, short-term general and other special hospitals)

2010 Utilization, Personnel and Finances

CLASSIFICATION	Hospitals	Beds	Admissions	Inpatient Days	Adjusted Patient Days	Average Daily Census	Adjusted Average Daily Census	Average Stay (days)	Surgical Operations	NEWBORNS Bassinets	Births	OUTPATIENT VISITS Emergency	Total
UNITED STATES	4,985	804,943	35,149,427	189,593,349	355,023,656	519,540	972,930	5.4	27,311,998	56,610	3,818,399	127,249,317	651,423,717
Nonmetropolitan	1,987	137,779	4,307,936	27,147,315	70,298,276	74,403	192,723	6.3	4,153,393	10,938	451,316	23,425,674	123,164,591
Metropolitan	2,998	667,164	30,841,491	162,446,034	284,725,380	445,137	780,207	5.3	23,158,605	45,672	3,367,083	103,823,643	528,259,126
CENSUS DIVISION 5, EAST SOUTH CENTRAL	441	63,079	2,486,454	13,614,893	25,988,300	37,337	71,304	5.5	2,073,101	4,345	221,646	9,527,974	35,254,725
Nonmetropolitan	233	21,114	670,531	4,028,124	9,265,577	11,034	25,406	6.0	574,397	1,436	58,613	3,396,776	11,458,214
Metropolitan	208	41,965	1,815,923	9,586,769	16,722,723	26,303	45,898	5.3	1,498,704	2,909	163,033	6,131,198	23,796,511
Alabama	105	15,086	642,309	3,336,285	6,076,423	9,180	16,736	5.2	569,964	1,419	58,287	2,304,682	8,800,721
Nonmetropolitan	47	3,246	120,898	569,020	1,322,972	1,558	3,626	4.7	113,908	275	10,397	642,486	2,284,634
Metropolitan	58	11,840	521,411	2,767,265	4,753,451	7,622	13,110	5.3	456,056	1,144	47,890	1,662,196	6,516,087
Anniston-Oxford	3	427	20,696	94,201	171,005	258	469	4.6	11,220	38	1,737	79,188	205,699
Auburn-Opelika	1	373	15,051	103,540	216,329	284	593	6.9	12,891	38	1,693	44,065	112,517
Birmingham-Hoover	17	4,361	184,642	1,036,818	1,672,080	2,842	4,582	5.6	171,942	449	16,097	517,797	2,704,257
Columbus	1	48	896	13,420	14,007	37	38	15.0	0	0	0	0	4,363
Decatur	4	432	14,028	61,452	128,091	204	437	4.4	11,418	23	727	76,736	229,149
Dothan	4	861	33,620	170,784	332,076	469	910	5.1	29,495	62	2,935	102,205	295,491
Florence-Muscle Shoals	3	568	20,047	94,402	188,628	259	517	4.7	18,645	46	1,425	93,014	220,532
Gadsden	3	522	20,950	121,141	196,789	332	538	5.8	26,022	32	1,169	55,359	188,374
Huntsville	4	1,141	57,386	277,926	528,417	762	1,447	4.8	66,655	100	6,542	196,215	922,960
Mobile	6	1,414	66,268	365,832	606,858	1,003	1,663	5.5	52,703	187	6,522	180,513	669,624
Montgomery	8	1,093	51,380	244,233	410,073	669	1,124	4.8	36,011	112	5,713	190,786	412,559
Tuscaloosa	4	600	36,447	183,516	289,098	503	792	5.0	19,054	57	3,330	126,318	550,562
Kentucky	106	14,238	608,644	3,141,502	6,338,336	8,604	17,363	5.2	559,616	934	53,630	2,386,673	10,437,539
Nonmetropolitan	63	5,801	223,608	1,132,713	2,583,859	3,101	7,079	5.1	182,984	414	17,963	1,078,198	4,118,980
Metropolitan	43	8,437	385,036	2,008,789	3,754,477	5,503	10,284	5.2	376,632	520	35,667	1,308,475	6,318,559
Bowling Green	3	549	21,673	110,691	192,819	303	528	5.1	18,302	19	2,378	66,439	148,741
Cincinnati-Middletown	5	907	47,896	218,108	422,636	597	1,156	4.6	29,673	50	4,555	201,095	937,175
Clarksville	2	164	7,466	34,231	76,703	94	210	4.6	4,215	18	591	31,921	176,395
Elizabethtown	2	308	13,523	67,889	153,541	186	421	5.0	8,611	26	1,586	51,869	271,596
Evansville	1	192	5,296	25,071	69,768	69	191	4.7	3,894	12	700	28,466	229,961
Huntington-Ashland	2	767	31,905	201,942	449,097	553	1,230	6.3	63,233	34	1,582	102,099	976,198
Lexington-Fayette	14	2,051	90,907	490,168	844,375	1,341	2,313	5.4	78,298	161	8,512	271,826	1,312,875
Louisville	13	3,128	148,015	779,473	1,372,187	2,137	3,760	5.3	151,052	170	14,032	491,168	1,783,396
Owensboro	1	371	18,355	81,216	173,351	223	475	4.4	19,354	30	1,731	63,592	482,222
Mississippi	96	12,925	402,947	2,557,704	4,885,435	7,008	13,388	6.3	282,466	781	39,044	1,705,959	4,586,136
Nonmetropolitan	67	7,478	189,193	1,439,541	2,975,032	3,945	8,155	7.6	144,766	456	18,598	934,114	2,422,600
Metropolitan	29	5,447	213,754	1,118,163	1,910,403	3,063	5,233	5.2	137,700	325	20,446	771,845	2,163,536
Gulfport-Biloxi	6	906	29,629	155,528	266,168	426	728	5.2	26,306	66	2,823	154,822	573,817
Hattiesburg	3	756	36,646	183,731	288,617	504	791	5.0	18,665	35	3,983	108,737	212,580
Jackson	15	3,018	108,923	604,400	1,054,719	1,654	2,889	5.5	75,184	168	9,951	314,967	806,677
Memphis	3	338	18,463	84,449	136,856	232	375	4.6	5,937	24	2,020	71,086	124,358
Pascagoula	2	429	20,093	90,055	164,043	247	450	4.5	11,608	32	1,669	122,233	446,104
Tennessee	134	20,830	832,554	4,579,402	8,688,106	12,545	23,817	5.5	661,055	1,211	70,685	3,130,660	11,430,329
Nonmetropolitan	56	4,589	136,832	886,850	2,383,714	2,430	6,546	6.5	132,739	291	11,655	741,978	2,632,000
Metropolitan	78	16,241	695,722	3,692,552	6,304,392	10,115	17,271	5.3	528,316	920	59,030	2,388,682	8,798,329
Chattanooga	6	1,599	69,067	373,670	624,675	1,023	1,712	5.4	61,612	63	7,134	246,306	820,756
Clarksville	1	247	11,908	44,152	78,236	121	214	3.7	9,105	30	1,952	57,392	155,578
Cleveland	2	245	11,463	44,967	97,694	123	268	3.9	13,372	22	972	54,160	122,869
Jackson	2	773	32,534	170,029	333,286	466	913	5.2	28,547	47	3,480	101,296	215,773
Johnson City	5	795	34,497	200,890	351,929	551	964	5.8	20,654	32	1,720	115,544	418,769
Kingsport-Bristol-Bristol	6	1,017	43,865	205,827	368,671	563	1,009	4.7	27,151	66	2,791	187,789	514,099
Knoxville	11	2,627	115,465	626,836	1,116,558	1,717	3,061	5.4	85,519	163	8,617	377,692	1,644,595
Memphis	15	3,632	145,612	865,674	1,338,458	2,372	3,667	5.9	89,332	189	15,227	498,947	1,188,732
Morristown	3	332	10,353	43,261	84,882	119	232	4.2	13,861	29	958	47,501	210,974
Nashville-Davidson--Murfreesboro	27	4,974	220,958	1,117,246	1,910,003	3,060	5,231	5.1	179,163	279	16,179	702,055	3,506,184

TABLE 8

U.S. CENSUS DIVISION 5, EAST SOUTH CENTRAL

U.S. Community Hospitals
(Nonfederal, short-term general and other special hospitals)

2010 Utilization, Personnel and Finances

FULL-TIME EQUIVALENT PERSONNEL					FULL-TIME EQUIV. TRAINEES			EXPENSES						
								LABOR				TOTAL		
Physicians and Dentists	Registered Nurses	Licensed Practical Nurses	Other Salaried Personnel	Total Personnel	Medical and Dental Residents	Other Trainees	Total Trainees	Payroll (in thousands)	Employee Benefits (in thousands)	Total (in thousands)	Percent of Total	Amount (in thousands)	Adjusted per Admission	Adjusted per Inpatient Day
103,332	1,293,945	91,057	3,111,418	4,599,752	95,270	8,153	103,423	$274,300,010	$73,831,160	$348,131,210	51.3	$677,968,038	$10,313.44	$1,909.64
13,050	155,574	26,968	467,595	663,187	1,715	434	2,149	32,684,219	9,001,043	41,685,291	53.4	78,085,310	7,010.73	1,110.77
90,282	1,138,371	64,089	2,643,823	3,936,565	93,555	7,719	101,274	241,615,791	64,830,116	306,445,919	51.1	599,882,728	10,987.18	2,106.88
5,172	85,999	8,473	194,705	294,349	3,841	224	4,065	14,220,878	3,732,797	17,953,675	49.2	36,471,494	7,680.56	1,403.38
1,147	21,383	3,770	57,854	84,154	171	42	213	3,480,806	940,288	4,421,090	52.3	8,453,502	5,507.91	912.36
4,025	64,616	4,703	136,851	210,195	3,670	182	3,852	10,740,072	2,792,509	13,532,585	48.3	28,017,992	8,718.15	1,675.44
694	22,290	1,797	46,320	71,101	1,174	38	1,212	3,274,894	833,751	4,108,643	49.3	8,334,445	6,962.10	1,371.60
161	3,447	546	8,859	13,013	14	4	18	466,268	121,784	588,049	52.1	1,128,899	4,012.24	853.31
533	18,843	1,251	37,461	58,088	1,160	34	1,194	2,808,626	711,967	3,520,594	48.9	7,205,546	7,868.45	1,515.86
9	563	69	1,114	1,755	0	0	0	84,542	22,732	107,273	58.6	183,015	4,888.87	1,070.23
17	549	52	1,775	2,393	0	0	0	87,683	21,382	109,064	48.6	224,243	7,130.83	1,036.58
180	7,256	300	13,538	21,274	828	1	829	1,144,369	281,589	1,425,960	45.4	3,142,516	10,323.23	1,879.41
0	23	5	105	133	0	0	0	5,780	1,162	6,942	63.8	10,879	11,635.41	776.69
18	464	33	1,005	1,520	1	0	1	70,213	15,144	85,358	59.0	144,635	5,003.11	1,129.16
49	1,121	151	2,671	3,992	4	0	4	182,221	37,141	219,363	58.0	378,308	5,630.84	1,139.22
19	585	47	1,366	2,017	13	0	13	85,888	28,050	113,938	55.5	205,118	5,114.02	1,087.42
9	691	40	1,013	1,753	0	0	0	75,990	20,948	96,938	42.0	230,843	6,824.02	1,173.05
105	2,459	149	4,443	7,156	0	6	6	323,014	107,169	430,183	51.2	840,702	7,440.43	1,590.98
68	2,321	105	4,957	7,451	294	4	298	355,154	95,306	450,460	49.1	917,226	8,235.77	1,511.43
42	1,625	145	2,942	4,754	20	1	21	202,718	41,261	243,979	43.5	561,126	6,301.82	1,368.36
17	1,186	155	2,532	3,890	0	22	22	191,055	40,082	231,136	63.0	366,934	6,316.86	1,269.24
810	20,702	1,843	48,681	72,036	579	32	611	3,596,514	1,018,345	4,614,858	47.1	9,801,871	7,757.38	1,546.44
445	6,769	1,061	18,296	26,571	87	15	102	1,183,626	340,060	1,523,684	51.1	2,981,144	5,634.51	1,153.76
365	13,933	782	30,385	45,465	492	17	509	2,412,889	678,286	3,091,174	45.3	6,820,727	9,286.62	1,816.69
0	706	34	1,452	2,192	0	0	0	115,005	31,275	146,280	47.7	306,486	8,102.31	1,589.50
67	1,104	73	3,471	4,715	23	0	23	297,156	99,188	396,343	56.1	706,412	7,357.54	1,671.44
18	230	25	700	973	5	0	5	43,179	11,300	54,479	52.5	103,716	6,247.19	1,352.17
18	394	12	1,075	1,499	0	0	0	72,866	23,421	96,287	51.9	185,644	5,831.82	1,209.09
25	227	28	653	933	6	9	15	46,233	17,654	63,887	58.6	109,017	7,397.02	1,562.57
139	1,120	266	3,047	4,572	6	0	6	223,353	75,610	298,962	47.6	627,811	8,449.22	1,397.94
30	3,457	155	8,101	11,743	441	4	445	600,150	156,079	756,231	41.9	1,804,849	11,289.05	2,137.50
64	6,054	158	10,026	16,302	11	4	15	905,454	228,095	1,133,549	42.4	2,673,633	10,123.64	1,948.45
4	641	31	1,860	2,536	0	0	0	109,493	35,663	145,156	47.9	303,160	7,738.00	1,748.82
925	13,919	1,739	35,369	51,952	546	47	593	2,426,730	609,683	3,036,417	53.9	5,635,913	7,478.82	1,153.62
377	6,476	1,219	18,091	26,163	32	16	48	1,106,042	287,439	1,393,482	52.9	2,636,445	6,818.12	886.19
548	7,443	520	17,278	25,789	514	31	545	1,320,688	322,244	1,642,935	54.8	2,999,468	8,175.14	1,570.07
128	1,301	85	2,683	4,197	0	0	0	209,183	59,706	268,889	54.5	493,755	9,536.73	1,855.05
37	961	104	2,477	3,579	0	0	0	178,811	31,084	209,894	45.8	458,206	8,011.02	1,587.59
309	3,861	245	8,952	13,367	514	19	533	712,978	168,949	881,930	57.5	1,534,244	8,010.59	1,454.65
0	632	48	1,123	1,803	0	12	12	83,461	19,483	102,944	54.8	187,733	6,280.57	1,371.75
74	688	38	2,043	2,843	0	0	0	136,257	43,021	179,278	55.1	325,530	8,915.70	1,984.42
2,743	29,088	3,094	64,335	99,260	1,542	107	1,649	4,922,739	1,271,017	6,193,757	48.8	12,699,266	8,276.94	1,461.68
164	4,691	944	12,608	18,407	38	7	45	724,871	191,005	915,875	53.7	1,707,014	5,055.41	716.12
2,579	24,397	2,150	51,727	80,853	1,504	100	1,604	4,197,868	1,080,013	5,277,882	48.0	10,992,252	9,185.98	1,743.59
140	2,623	254	5,220	8,237	217	4	221	457,769	117,755	575,524	51.9	1,109,291	9,623.00	1,775.79
30	349	33	639	1,051	0	0	0	45,771	10,030	55,801	45.3	123,305	5,843.57	1,576.07
3	383	38	654	1,078	0	1	1	45,926	9,775	55,700	47.8	116,435	4,691.19	1,191.84
21	1,111	156	3,163	4,451	3	0	3	204,284	51,185	255,470	53.9	473,574	7,497.17	1,420.92
1	1,041	129	2,307	3,478	0	0	0	163,093	36,390	199,483	47.5	420,407	7,267.94	1,194.58
7	1,119	95	3,037	4,258	0	0	0	191,584	69,445	261,029	44.4	588,215	7,431.00	1,595.50
192	3,887	392	8,625	13,096	61	21	82	705,261	183,208	888,469	49.8	1,783,223	8,635.88	1,597.07
83	5,626	249	10,490	16,448	311	65	376	885,185	214,210	1,099,395	49.1	2,240,864	9,744.41	1,674.21
19	329	31	820	1,199	4	0	4	51,412	13,363	64,775	50.5	128,220	6,256.77	1,510.57
2,083	7,929	773	16,772	27,557	908	9	917	1,447,582	374,652	1,822,236	45.5	4,008,717	10,596.02	2,098.80

MSAs

TABLE 8

U.S. CENSUS DIVISION 6, WEST NORTH CENTRAL

U.S. Community Hospitals
(Nonfederal, short-term general and other special hospitals)

2010 Utilization, Personnel and Finances

MSAs

CLASSIFICATION	Hospitals	Beds	Admissions	Inpatient Days	Adjusted Patient Days	Average Daily Census	Adjusted Average Daily Census	Average Stay (days)	Surgical Operations	NEWBORNS Bassinets	NEWBORNS Births	OUTPATIENT VISITS Emergency	OUTPATIENT VISITS Total
UNITED STATES	4,985	804,943	35,149,427	189,593,349	355,023,656	519,540	972,930	5.4	27,311,998	56,610	3,818,399	127,249,317	651,423,717
Nonmetropolitan	1,987	137,779	4,307,936	27,147,315	70,298,276	74,403	192,723	6.3	4,153,393	10,938	451,316	23,425,674	123,164,591
Metropolitan	2,998	667,164	30,841,491	162,446,034	284,725,380	445,137	780,207	5.3	23,158,605	45,672	3,367,083	103,823,643	528,259,126
CENSUS DIVISION 6, WEST NORTH CENTRAL	685	68,830	2,464,267	14,928,227	32,619,893	40,923	89,439	6.1	2,006,144	4,757	264,621	8,260,672	58,263,936
Nonmetropolitan	462	26,375	588,233	5,188,960	14,253,836	14,232	39,109	8.8	596,374	1,953	70,466	2,802,947	21,888,834
Metropolitan	223	42,455	1,876,034	9,739,267	18,366,057	26,691	50,330	5.2	1,409,770	2,804	194,155	5,457,725	36,375,102
Iowa	118	10,075	341,744	2,058,304	5,384,421	5,659	14,815	6.0	340,491	727	38,193	1,223,271	11,028,579
Nonmetropolitan	84	4,387	104,732	831,339	2,758,486	2,295	7,618	7.9	131,805	331	10,802	492,108	4,764,775
Metropolitan	34	5,688	237,012	1,226,965	2,625,935	3,364	7,197	5.2	208,686	396	27,391	731,163	6,263,804
Ames	2	274	9,736	63,932	146,987	176	403	6.6	9,480	17	1,093	27,931	170,147
Cedar Rapids	4	772	28,303	163,272	450,706	448	1,235	5.8	31,237	54	3,474	108,895	950,592
Davenport-Moline-Rock Island	3	501	23,345	101,458	178,243	278	489	4.3	12,699	33	2,787	90,085	213,954
Des Moines	8	1,414	66,296	331,476	648,069	908	1,776	5.0	46,158	118	9,081	183,829	1,680,398
Dubuque	3	416	12,860	69,703	136,535	192	375	5.4	13,853	34	1,576	51,527	137,545
Iowa City	3	1,001	38,732	237,342	469,661	651	1,287	6.1	31,535	48	3,079	81,088	1,445,597
Omaha-Council Bluffs	3	297	13,921	57,347	118,222	158	324	4.1	11,709	22	1,129	55,726	240,959
Sioux City	2	392	20,045	90,287	145,042	247	398	4.5	11,927	32	2,469	58,178	325,554
Waterloo-Cedar Falls	6	621	23,774	112,148	332,530	306	910	4.7	40,088	38	2,703	73,904	1,099,058
Kansas	130	9,965	304,769	1,960,261	4,415,198	5,371	12,101	6.4	237,051	703	39,777	1,019,521	6,679,814
Nonmetropolitan	97	4,797	99,653	922,868	2,577,191	2,528	7,063	9.3	96,056	346	11,704	387,870	3,235,634
Metropolitan	33	5,168	205,116	1,037,393	1,838,007	2,843	5,038	5.1	140,995	357	28,073	631,651	3,444,180
Kansas City	15	2,402	98,753	495,860	866,140	1,359	2,374	5.0	74,803	188	13,565	272,000	1,706,533
Lawrence	1	152	6,551	23,435	86,530	64	237	3.6	4,530	13	1,148	35,627	216,652
Topeka	6	834	30,743	162,292	327,670	444	898	5.3	18,541	40	3,074	94,787	634,212
Wichita	11	1,780	69,069	355,806	557,667	976	1,529	5.2	43,121	116	10,286	229,237	886,783
Minnesota	133	15,346	591,919	3,596,879	7,802,827	9,853	21,375	6.1	481,439	1,260	62,885	1,832,257	11,064,883
Nonmetropolitan	82	5,365	112,016	1,150,031	3,214,225	3,148	8,802	10.3	126,713	409	15,394	571,810	3,880,609
Metropolitan	51	9,981	479,903	2,446,848	4,588,602	6,705	12,573	5.1	354,726	851	47,491	1,260,447	7,184,274
Duluth	10	1,381	42,005	316,640	823,335	869	2,254	7.5	46,517	94	3,396	123,302	675,966
Grand Forks	2	124	1,783	21,412	53,524	59	146	12.0	4,666	8	434	15,783	82,379
Minneapolis-St. Paul-Bloomington	31	6,447	337,562	1,540,872	2,672,789	4,220	7,326	4.6	257,124	667	38,999	944,625	4,991,633
Rochester	4	1,338	69,952	392,572	684,227	1,076	1,875	5.6	30,986	51	1,736	115,063	923,721
St. Cloud	4	691	28,601	175,352	354,727	481	972	6.1	15,433	31	2,926	61,674	510,575
Missouri	122	18,745	821,322	4,196,865	8,341,254	11,500	22,855	5.1	587,805	1,142	74,903	2,871,884	19,800,925
Nonmetropolitan	53	3,775	136,692	631,303	1,717,372	1,729	4,703	4.6	112,746	344	14,300	705,473	5,065,393
Metropolitan	69	14,970	684,630	3,565,562	6,623,882	9,771	18,152	5.2	475,059	798	60,603	2,166,411	14,735,532
Columbia	4	895	39,265	205,622	321,694	564	882	5.2	31,534	41	3,857	81,168	861,520
Jefferson City	3	284	17,454	64,890	138,509	179	380	3.7	11,546	30	1,560	73,261	672,433
Joplin	4	749	36,587	178,029	348,034	488	954	4.9	23,879	57	3,342	173,227	1,026,637
Kansas City	22	3,485	151,797	806,737	1,603,847	2,210	4,395	5.3	106,495	190	14,591	600,760	3,653,924
Springfield	5	1,415	69,655	343,703	698,362	942	1,914	4.9	61,102	83	6,723	239,696	2,509,674
St. Joseph	2	393	18,469	84,379	156,896	231	430	4.6	10,136	20	1,769	54,251	709,432
St. Louis	29	7,749	351,403	1,882,202	3,356,540	5,157	9,197	5.4	230,367	377	28,761	944,048	5,301,912
Nebraska	88	7,246	208,949	1,461,558	3,108,327	4,007	8,517	7.0	177,529	523	24,575	700,818	4,571,641
Nonmetropolitan	71	3,672	74,053	694,607	1,840,683	1,905	5,043	9.4	67,887	315	8,278	309,962	2,489,469
Metropolitan	17	3,574	134,896	766,951	1,267,644	2,102	3,474	5.7	109,642	208	16,297	390,856	2,082,172
Lincoln	4	969	37,244	242,312	363,118	664	995	6.5	22,828	63	5,018	102,180	407,878
Omaha-Council Bluffs	13	2,605	97,652	524,639	904,526	1,438	2,479	5.4	86,814	145	11,279	288,676	1,674,294
North Dakota	41	3,345	94,436	718,950	1,596,362	1,971	4,374	7.6	83,723	168	12,851	353,557	3,075,737
Nonmetropolitan	33	1,874	26,295	398,063	850,940	1,092	2,332	15.1	28,289	65	5,741	208,187	1,284,546
Metropolitan	8	1,471	68,141	320,887	745,422	879	2,042	4.7	55,434	103	7,110	145,370	1,791,191
Bismarck	3	543	22,142	98,456	224,240	269	613	4.4	17,696	27	2,041	53,206	665,025
Fargo	3	591	32,321	143,296	299,279	393	821	4.4	27,316	53	3,493	62,714	553,505
Grand Forks	2	337	13,678	79,135	221,903	217	608	5.8	10,422	23	1,576	29,450	572,661
South Dakota	53	4,108	101,128	935,410	1,971,504	2,562	5,402	9.2	98,106	234	11,437	259,364	2,042,357
Nonmetropolitan	42	2,505	34,792	560,749	1,294,939	1,535	3,548	16.1	32,878	143	4,247	127,537	1,168,408
Metropolitan	11	1,603	66,336	374,661	676,565	1,027	1,854	5.6	65,228	91	7,190	131,827	873,949
Rapid City	3	509	17,451	123,390	205,032	338	562	7.1	10,752	52	2,218	57,384	197,393
Sioux Falls	8	1,094	48,885	251,271	471,533	689	1,292	5.1	54,476	39	4,972	74,443	676,556

TABLE 8

U.S. CENSUS DIVISION 6, WEST NORTH CENTRAL

U.S. Community Hospitals
(Nonfederal, short-term general and other special hospitals)

2010 Utilization, Personnel and Finances

FULL-TIME EQUIVALENT PERSONNEL					FULL-TIME EQUIV. TRAINEES			EXPENSES						
								LABOR				TOTAL		
Physicians and Dentists	Registered Nurses	Licensed Practical Nurses	Other Salaried Personnel	Total Personnel	Medical and Dental Residents	Other Trainees	Total Trainees	Payroll (in thousands)	Employee Benefits (in thousands)	Total (in thousands)	Percent of Total	Amount (in thousands)	Adjusted per Admission	Adjusted per Inpatient Day
103,332	1,293,945	91,057	3,111,418	4,599,752	95,270	8,153	103,423	$274,300,010	$73,831,160	$348,131,210	51.3	$677,968,038	$10,313.44	$1,909.64
13,050	155,574	26,968	467,595	663,187	1,715	434	2,149	32,684,219	9,001,043	41,685,291	53.4	78,085,310	7,010.73	1,110.77
90,282	1,138,371	64,089	2,643,823	3,936,565	93,555	7,719	101,274	241,615,791	64,830,116	306,445,919	51.1	599,882,728	10,987.18	2,106.88
8,837	99,727	9,517	256,924	375,005	4,000	550	4,550	20,967,611	5,473,899	26,441,520	51.1	51,771,368	9,981.94	1,587.11
2,422	25,808	4,956	80,271	113,457	190	148	338	5,457,050	1,422,770	6,879,832	54.0	12,741,572	7,699.66	893.90
6,415	73,919	4,561	176,653	261,548	3,810	402	4,212	15,510,561	4,051,128	19,561,688	50.1	39,029,795	11,051.33	2,125.10
1,121	14,007	1,045	38,417	54,590	680	13	693	2,790,998	790,478	3,581,479	51.6	6,934,528	8,197.93	1,287.89
406	5,044	648	15,253	21,351	28	0	28	990,619	264,099	1,254,724	53.8	2,332,301	6,693.72	845.50
715	8,963	397	23,164	33,239	652	13	665	1,800,378	526,379	2,326,755	50.6	4,602,227	9,251.51	1,752.60
3	337	8	894	1,242	0	0	0	64,167	18,786	82,952	50.6	163,986	7,906.73	1,115.65
39	1,155	82	3,000	4,276	0	2	2	204,062	66,140	270,202	51.4	525,365	7,520.90	1,165.65
3	754	7	1,393	2,157	8	0	8	110,981	29,377	140,357	37.4	375,121	8,776.41	2,104.55
318	2,476	31	6,777	9,602	158	2	160	527,204	131,094	658,296	53.3	1,236,076	9,385.69	1,907.32
8	505	9	1,189	1,711	0	0	0	74,411	19,809	94,220	42.6	221,299	8,551.30	1,620.82
115	1,897	29	4,881	6,922	483	8	491	405,381	154,426	559,807	52.8	1,060,442	14,213.90	2,258.18
25	445	14	944	1,428	0	0	0	74,199	20,514	94,713	46.3	204,430	7,080.82	1,729.21
69	634	32	1,502	2,237	0	0	0	123,843	33,787	157,630	51.6	305,427	9,489.73	2,105.78
135	760	185	2,584	3,664	3	1	4	216,131	52,447	268,578	52.7	510,080	7,196.19	1,533.94
910	13,115	1,277	30,455	45,757	5	205	210	2,439,570	587,393	3,026,967	52.6	5,759,373	8,869.73	1,304.44
329	4,377	735	13,469	18,910	0	87	87	853,584	198,617	1,052,206	56.2	1,871,636	7,186.85	726.23
581	8,738	542	16,986	26,847	5	118	123	1,585,986	388,776	1,974,761	50.8	3,887,737	9,996.65	2,115.19
206	4,506	104	8,086	12,902	0	96	96	767,872	194,356	962,228	47.7	2,016,069	10,682.46	2,327.65
30	289	18	763	1,100	0	0	0	61,569	12,732	74,302	50.1	148,294	6,130.90	1,713.79
246	1,266	321	3,285	5,118	0	3	3	336,592	79,310	415,902	59.5	698,961	10,603.33	2,133.12
99	2,677	99	4,852	7,727	5	19	24	419,952	102,378	522,329	51.0	1,024,413	9,306.92	1,836.96
2,787	21,754	2,349	59,788	86,678	1,118	163	1,281	5,723,799	1,585,006	7,308,808	54.1	13,507,569	11,213.85	1,731.11
551	4,790	1,277	16,320	22,938	18	13	31	1,227,421	322,399	1,549,821	54.8	2,825,658	8,490.66	879.11
2,236	16,964	1,072	43,468	63,740	1,100	150	1,250	4,496,378	1,262,606	5,758,987	53.9	10,681,911	12,253.45	2,327.92
575	1,630	241	6,650	9,096	1	1	2	582,557	163,266	745,823	62.7	1,189,197	11,363.24	1,444.37
13	178	21	514	726	1	0	1	21,460	6,052	27,513	52.0	52,915	11,872.31	988.62
1,381	12,139	500	28,943	42,963	960	129	1,089	3,116,672	870,981	3,987,655	52.6	7,574,367	12,866.74	2,833.88
240	1,863	141	4,290	6,534	125	20	145	539,411	147,013	686,425	52.5	1,306,650	10,490.29	1,909.67
27	1,154	169	3,071	4,421	13	0	13	236,277	75,294	311,571	55.8	558,782	11,311.15	1,575.25
2,351	32,057	2,753	79,036	116,197	2,034	146	2,180	6,263,850	1,584,782	7,848,632	47.5	16,521,829	10,120.93	1,980.74
591	5,062	1,164	15,350	22,167	52	27	79	1,073,333	288,318	1,361,652	51.2	2,660,579	7,297.44	1,549.22
1,760	26,995	1,589	63,686	94,030	1,982	119	2,101	5,190,517	1,296,464	6,486,980	46.8	13,861,250	10,932.88	2,092.62
30	1,500	236	4,733	6,499	362	1	363	284,001	84,865	368,866	43.4	849,379	13,572.91	2,640.33
97	560	121	1,462	2,240	10	0	10	121,413	31,506	152,920	48.8	313,405	8,272.54	2,262.71
146	1,281	74	3,292	4,793	23	0	23	257,939	47,769	305,708	51.3	595,482	8,211.73	1,710.99
450	6,734	344	15,011	22,539	211	117	328	1,308,713	306,238	1,614,949	49.1	3,290,390	11,722.13	2,051.56
244	2,864	287	9,702	13,097	25	0	25	674,556	171,339	845,895	48.4	1,747,575	12,140.75	2,502.39
110	657	145	1,953	2,865	0	0	0	189,894	47,935	237,829	56.1	424,181	11,982.52	2,703.58
683	13,399	382	27,533	41,997	1,351	1	1,352	2,354,001	606,812	2,960,813	44.6	6,640,837	10,460.85	1,978.48
480	10,178	1,101	24,464	36,223	38	12	50	1,817,994	495,748	2,313,740	49.1	4,710,906	11,142.74	1,515.58
256	3,545	743	10,876	15,420	6	10	16	705,279	194,961	900,240	53.6	1,678,112	8,670.26	911.68
224	6,633	358	13,588	20,803	32	2	34	1,112,715	300,787	1,413,500	46.6	3,032,795	13,230.36	2,392.47
19	1,505	186	3,681	5,391	0	0	0	277,106	91,921	369,026	50.8	726,483	11,864.44	2,000.68
205	5,128	172	9,907	15,412	32	2	34	835,609	208,866	1,044,474	45.3	2,306,311	13,728.21	2,549.75
703	4,116	712	12,406	17,937	104	11	115	954,923	206,096	1,161,018	54.2	2,142,846	9,423.08	1,342.33
156	1,511	223	4,288	6,178	84	11	95	259,117	65,736	324,851	51.8	626,724	9,292.10	736.51
547	2,605	489	8,118	11,759	20	0	20	695,806	140,360	836,167	55.2	1,516,122	9,478.31	2,033.91
199	917	167	2,911	4,194	0	0	0	254,297	38,640	292,937	58.8	498,122	9,818.51	2,221.38
166	1,197	283	2,633	4,279	0	0	0	238,894	57,597	296,491	46.6	635,942	9,128.58	2,124.91
182	491	39	2,574	3,286	20	0	20	202,616	44,123	246,739	64.6	382,057	9,657.91	1,721.73
485	4,500	280	12,358	17,623	21	0	21	976,478	224,396	1,200,876	54.7	2,194,316	10,749.97	1,113.02
133	1,479	166	4,715	6,493	2	0	2	347,696	88,639	436,338	58.4	746,562	8,523.85	576.52
352	3,021	114	7,643	11,130	19	0	19	628,782	135,757	764,538	52.8	1,447,754	12,423.02	2,139.86
49	734	50	1,816	2,649	19	0	19	140,238	19,854	160,091	48.4	330,443	11,480.08	1,611.66
303	2,287	64	5,827	8,481	0	0	0	488,544	115,903	604,447	54.1	1,117,312	12,732.32	2,369.53

MSAs

TABLE 8

U.S. CENSUS DIVISION 7, WEST SOUTH CENTRAL

U.S. Community Hospitals
(Nonfederal, short-term general and other special hospitals)

2010 Utilization, Personnel and Finances

CLASSIFICATION	Hospitals	Beds	Admissions	Inpatient Days	Adjusted Patient Days	Average Daily Census	Adjusted Average Daily Census	Average Stay (days)	Surgical Operations	NEWBORNS Bassinets	Births	OUTPATIENT VISITS Emergency	Total
UNITED STATES	4,985	804,943	35,149,427	189,593,349	355,023,656	519,540	972,930	5.4	27,311,998	56,610	3,818,399	127,249,317	651,423,717
Nonmetropolitan	1,987	137,779	4,307,936	27,147,315	70,298,276	74,403	192,723	6.3	4,153,393	10,938	451,316	23,425,674	123,164,591
Metropolitan	2,998	667,164	30,841,491	162,446,034	284,725,380	445,137	780,207	5.3	23,158,605	45,672	3,367,083	103,823,643	528,259,126
CENSUS DIVISION 7, WEST SOUTH CENTRAL	750	97,399	4,005,387	20,922,699	36,790,236	57,343	100,842	5.2	2,857,811	7,432	528,045	15,392,542	61,316,690
Nonmetropolitan	314	16,600	573,498	2,647,673	6,319,465	7,264	17,345	4.6	429,308	1,408	59,250	3,056,396	12,331,077
Metropolitan	436	80,799	3,431,889	18,275,026	30,470,771	50,079	83,497	5.3	2,428,503	6,024	468,795	12,336,146	48,985,613
Arkansas	85	9,451	370,401	1,908,843	3,550,896	5,230	9,733	5.2	260,696	642	36,913	1,376,649	5,022,211
Nonmetropolitan	48	3,254	109,361	556,465	1,281,593	1,525	3,515	5.1	73,115	241	9,834	508,447	1,901,232
Metropolitan	37	6,197	261,040	1,352,378	2,269,303	3,705	6,218	5.2	187,581	401	27,079	868,202	3,120,979
Fayetteville-Springdale-Rogers . . .	8	886	43,775	183,525	302,497	502	829	4.2	37,246	92	6,970	165,420	371,516
Fort Smith	7	895	34,729	191,496	310,365	524	850	5.5	25,967	54	3,485	132,582	360,200
Hot Springs	3	489	17,414	96,071	159,334	263	437	5.5	12,752	24	1,701	58,721	319,122
Jonesboro	3	542	26,801	130,563	231,481	357	635	4.9	17,441	32	2,064	71,616	275,816
Little Rock-North Little Rock	14	2,870	122,423	672,576	1,123,354	1,844	3,078	5.5	85,483	151	10,936	361,586	1,612,021
Memphis	1	142	4,030	18,098	34,083	50	93	4.5	3,454	12	679	23,277	28,860
Pine Bluff	1	373	11,868	60,049	108,189	165	296	5.1	5,238	36	1,244	55,000	153,444
Louisiana	126	15,421	625,489	3,341,419	6,147,249	9,162	16,852	5.3	458,840	1,020	61,525	2,514,006	12,354,940
Nonmetropolitan	50	3,120	111,613	559,661	1,228,037	1,531	3,360	5.0	94,382	223	8,739	530,613	1,978,352
Metropolitan	76	12,301	513,876	2,781,758	4,919,212	7,631	13,492	5.4	364,458	797	52,786	1,983,393	10,376,588
Alexandria	6	791	32,548	181,412	328,297	498	900	5.6	20,224	64	2,725	133,059	406,896
Baton Rouge.	13	2,322	90,934	564,390	1,046,487	1,556	2,879	6.2	61,621	130	11,364	332,123	1,260,594
Houma-Bayou Cane-Thibodaux . . .	5	558	25,272	115,827	231,700	317	634	4.6	20,939	64	3,946	139,704	508,459
Lafayette	8	873	36,652	204,165	339,885	560	931	5.6	22,156	56	2,558	157,877	552,731
Lake Charles.	8	799	30,126	146,119	298,421	401	819	4.9	26,026	54	3,388	116,293	422,334
Monroe	9	855	36,493	198,821	354,256	544	972	5.4	26,813	62	3,771	124,533	511,215
New Orleans-Metairie-Kenner	18	3,919	162,094	864,376	1,495,072	2,367	4,097	5.3	110,734	269	17,733	659,285	5,398,728
Shreveport-Bossier City	9	2,184	99,757	506,648	825,094	1,388	2,260	5.1	75,945	98	7,301	320,519	1,315,631
Oklahoma	113	11,170	429,096	2,340,946	4,326,931	6,414	11,858	5.5	315,785	762	48,569	1,762,821	5,658,712
Nonmetropolitan	65	3,758	129,116	630,318	1,442,491	1,728	3,952	4.9	97,555	343	13,648	654,001	2,279,019
Metropolitan	48	7,412	299,980	1,710,628	2,884,440	4,686	7,906	5.7	218,230	419	34,921	1,108,820	3,379,693
Fort Smith	2	110	3,687	13,556	33,084	37	91	3.7	1,556	11	476	31,530	50,099
Lawton	2	530	15,794	130,641	246,322	358	675	8.3	11,064	32	1,816	66,504	190,356
Oklahoma City.	21	3,807	150,619	911,093	1,496,975	2,494	4,100	6.0	111,763	210	18,864	617,911	1,806,521
Tulsa	23	2,965	129,880	655,338	1,108,059	1,797	3,040	5.0	93,847	166	13,765	392,875	1,332,717
Texas	426	61,357	2,580,401	13,331,491	22,765,160	36,537	62,399	5.2	1,822,490	5,008	381,038	9,739,066	38,280,827
Nonmetropolitan	151	6,468	223,408	901,229	2,367,344	2,480	6,518	4.0	164,256	601	27,029	1,363,335	6,172,474
Metropolitan	275	54,889	2,356,993	12,430,262	20,397,816	34,057	55,881	5.3	1,658,234	4,407	354,009	8,375,731	32,108,353
Metropolitan	1	44	461	5,814	5,814	16	16	12.6	0	0	0	0	0
Abilene	5	637	24,477	126,116	219,230	345	601	5.2	20,088	46	2,726	91,979	388,118
Amarillo	5	1,035	40,662	212,359	315,286	581	863	5.2	22,582	54	4,624	104,390	388,270
Austin-Round Rock	22	2,907	126,451	624,546	1,047,242	1,711	2,867	4.9	102,691	284	22,648	584,432	1,704,593
Beaumont-Port Arthur	9	1,454	60,331	303,532	526,375	830	1,441	5.0	35,426	90	6,757	246,898	725,630
Brownsville-Harlingen	3	976	39,373	195,211	287,011	535	787	5.0	21,784	92	7,258	112,778	199,795
College Station-Bryan	4	434	23,958	98,196	179,195	269	490	4.1	18,331	52	3,751	96,485	423,634
Corpus Christi	6	1,455	58,978	328,087	505,311	899	1,385	5.6	40,404	100	6,835	205,171	556,565
Dallas-Plano-Irving	50	8,928	385,105	2,053,984	3,282,466	5,630	8,992	5.3	253,913	763	62,070	1,507,822	4,861,077
El Paso	6	1,711	81,089	381,441	604,427	1,045	1,655	4.7	55,349	168	15,448	287,081	1,157,927
Fort Worth-Arlington	26	4,852	219,266	1,142,892	1,802,177	3,132	4,937	5.2	129,417	401	33,832	893,756	2,672,470
Houston-Sugar Land-Baytown . . .	59	13,827	565,696	3,228,590	5,437,040	8,846	14,898	5.7	389,221	1,199	93,935	1,724,018	8,959,544
Killeen-Temple-Fort Hood	4	873	40,943	193,893	475,451	533	1,303	4.7	40,150	56	5,036	173,140	1,494,647
Laredo	2	509	26,202	122,398	201,327	335	552	4.7	23,022	63	6,041	77,382	265,089
Longview	5	636	27,440	135,469	236,585	371	648	4.9	23,279	59	3,920	134,844	289,406
Lubbock.	6	1,238	54,680	256,913	411,952	703	1,129	4.7	38,233	59	5,206	167,972	714,642
McAllen-Edinburg-Mission	7	2,198	96,356	450,206	683,494	1,233	1,871	4.7	94,227	191	17,140	195,401	483,154
Midland	4	399	14,002	76,403	134,330	210	368	5.5	13,348	34	2,467	62,856	172,665
Odessa	3	536	21,097	112,279	171,871	308	471	5.3	13,119	39	3,798	69,589	244,626
San Angelo	2	409	18,630	86,188	165,520	236	453	4.6	19,363	36	2,004	78,099	188,119
San Antonio	22	5,760	267,221	1,344,126	2,114,330	3,682	5,791	5.0	189,620	426	32,480	936,613	4,115,580
Sherman-Denison	2	466	17,187	91,457	155,438	251	426	5.3	16,540	35	1,282	61,789	118,901
Texarkana TX-Texarkana AR	5	628	26,228	138,396	218,471	380	599	5.3	12,522	24	2,717	102,556	309,332
Tyler	6	1,109	50,190	287,546	458,446	787	1,257	5.7	32,743	41	3,393	151,316	774,711
Victoria	4	571	21,451	105,559	176,796	289	485	4.9	19,212	34	2,276	78,150	210,245
Waco	2	849	30,714	239,477	438,169	656	1,201	7.8	16,355	41	4,130	140,567	497,150
Wichita Falls	5	448	18,805	89,184	144,062	244	395	4.7	17,295	20	2,235	90,647	192,463

TABLE **8**

U.S. CENSUS DIVISION 7, WEST SOUTH CENTRAL

U.S. Community Hospitals
(Nonfederal, short-term general and other special hospitals)

2010 Utilization, Personnel and Finances

| | FULL-TIME EQUIVALENT PERSONNEL | | | | FULL-TIME EQUIV. TRAINEES | | | EXPENSES | | | | | | |
| | | | | | | | | LABOR | | | | TOTAL | | |
Physicians and Dentists	Registered Nurses	Licensed Practical Nurses	Other Salaried Personnel	Total Personnel	Medical and Dental Residents	Other Trainees	Total Trainees	Payroll (in thousands)	Employee Benefits (in thousands)	Total (in thousands)	Percent of Total	Amount (in thousands)	Adjusted per Admission	Adjusted per Inpatient Day
103,332	1,293,945	91,057	3,111,418	4,599,752	95,270	8,153	103,423	$274,300,010	$73,831,160	$348,131,210	51.3	$677,968,038	$10,313.44	$1,909.64
13,050	155,574	26,968	467,595	663,187	1,715	434	2,149	32,684,219	9,001,043	41,685,291	53.4	78,085,310	7,010.73	1,110.77
90,282	1,138,371	64,089	2,643,823	3,936,565	93,555	7,719	101,274	241,615,791	64,830,116	306,445,919	51.1	599,882,728	10,987.18	2,106.88
5,250	139,634	17,553	315,818	478,255	4,847	1,006	5,853	26,104,689	6,117,543	32,222,238	49.2	65,549,934	8,985.15	1,781.72
737	16,621	5,553	50,011	72,922	48	31	79	3,264,265	794,036	4,058,307	52.1	7,795,688	5,544.24	1,233.60
4,513	123,013	12,000	265,807	405,333	4,799	975	5,774	22,840,424	5,323,507	28,163,931	48.8	57,754,246	9,806.68	1,895.40
509	13,093	2,223	28,675	44,500	6	8	14	2,034,628	478,392	2,513,024	47.9	5,246,235	7,379.85	1,477.44
137	3,301	1,014	8,769	13,221	4	1	5	558,232	129,485	687,720	52.3	1,316,040	5,002.70	1,026.88
372	9,792	1,209	19,906	31,279	2	7	9	1,476,396	348,907	1,825,304	46.4	3,930,195	8,776.28	1,731.90
101	1,407	142	2,779	4,429	0	0	0	197,873	41,685	239,559	44.8	534,904	7,018.26	1,768.30
89	914	227	2,393	3,623	0	0	0	159,727	42,906	202,633	45.4	446,532	7,641.12	1,438.73
84	617	164	1,451	2,316	0	0	0	88,339	23,791	112,131	49.1	228,290	7,773.44	1,432.78
16	847	154	1,626	2,643	0	0	0	106,432	25,321	131,752	42.1	312,695	6,562.61	1,350.85
58	5,410	409	10,283	16,160	2	5	7	831,078	195,774	1,026,852	47.0	2,184,002	10,541.67	1,944.18
11	151	36	403	601	0	0	0	22,154	5,919	28,073	51.6	54,426	7,170.79	1,596.87
13	446	77	971	1,507	0	2	2	70,793	13,510	84,304	49.8	169,346	7,920.01	1,565.28
1,544	20,908	3,194	52,599	78,245	910	31	941	3,842,967	927,470	4,770,435	49.7	9,593,367	8,158.92	1,560.60
226	3,304	852	9,688	14,070	23	7	30	641,794	172,135	813,930	56.5	1,440,601	5,590.96	1,173.09
1,318	17,604	2,342	42,911	64,175	887	24	911	3,201,172	755,335	3,956,505	48.5	8,152,765	8,879.59	1,657.33
39	1,041	152	2,772	4,004	6	0	6	179,389	40,652	220,041	48.6	452,929	8,014.18	1,379.63
203	3,156	382	8,629	12,370	42	2	44	625,258	145,510	770,767	48.4	1,592,975	8,955.24	1,522.21
55	842	94	2,488	3,479	8	7	15	170,762	42,687	213,448	50.5	422,599	8,250.82	1,823.90
68	1,362	229	3,197	4,856	12	1	13	213,194	56,939	270,132	44.7	603,934	9,724.87	1,776.88
15	864	196	2,602	3,677	1	0	1	168,771	48,009	216,780	45.0	481,894	7,902.76	1,614.81
36	1,048	186	2,719	3,989	4	2	6	193,526	51,832	245,358	47.2	519,930	7,984.79	1,467.67
250	6,510	628	13,485	20,873	320	11	331	1,220,026	273,838	1,493,863	47.9	3,115,901	11,076.59	2,084.11
652	2,781	475	7,019	10,927	494	1	495	430,247	95,869	526,116	54.7	962,603	5,904.46	1,166.66
609	13,094	1,974	34,170	49,847	246	58	304	2,498,095	593,131	3,091,229	47.7	6,484,582	7,833.00	1,498.66
266	3,601	1,004	11,199	16,070	21	13	34	740,287	172,551	912,839	51.9	1,757,671	5,806.13	1,218.50
343	9,493	970	22,971	33,777	225	45	270	1,757,807	420,580	2,178,390	46.1	4,726,911	9,001.46	1,638.76
8	80	43	326	457	0	0	0	15,207	3,449	18,656	69.5	26,829	2,863.95	810.95
73	258	104	950	1,385	0	4	4	104,766	21,979	126,745	48.7	260,298	8,842.55	1,056.74
235	5,235	424	11,207	17,101	82	40	122	960,109	232,299	1,192,409	45.5	2,619,256	10,186.62	1,749.70
27	3,920	399	10,488	14,834	143	1	144	677,726	162,853	840,580	46.2	1,820,527	7,943.14	1,642.99
2,588	92,539	10,162	200,374	305,663	3,685	909	4,594	17,728,999	4,118,550	21,847,550	49.4	44,225,750	9,654.57	1,942.69
108	6,415	2,683	20,355	29,561	0	10	10	1,323,951	319,865	1,643,818	50.1	3,281,376	5,632.03	1,386.10
2,480	86,124	7,479	180,019	276,102	3,685	899	4,584	16,405,048	3,798,685	20,203,732	49.3	40,944,374	10,240.75	2,007.29
0	23	5	46	74	0	0	0	4,711	643	5,355	57.9	9,243	20,050.24	1,589.81
2	876	253	1,955	3,086	0	27	27	137,430	28,107	165,536	46.7	354,540	8,294.88	1,617.20
34	1,318	141	2,945	4,438	0	1	1	194,396	39,310	233,705	42.8	546,190	8,753.88	1,732.36
179	5,092	283	8,521	14,075	243	36	279	830,637	165,981	996,614	45.9	2,172,234	9,701.50	2,074.24
22	1,850	236	3,236	5,344	11	1	12	305,985	73,053	379,039	45.2	839,406	7,704.72	1,594.69
0	1,012	175	1,663	2,850	0	0	0	158,789	42,033	200,822	45.9	437,569	7,561.38	1,524.57
38	764	100	1,626	2,528	0	0	0	142,365	36,164	178,529	53.1	336,085	7,577.86	1,875.53
0	2,036	197	4,671	6,904	128	0	128	356,782	85,505	442,288	46.0	962,397	10,388.01	1,904.56
266	16,507	614	30,185	47,572	1,453	0	1,453	3,045,817	695,179	3,740,996	50.8	7,366,252	11,531.06	2,244.12
10	2,329	136	4,670	7,145	0	0	0	392,522	80,899	473,421	48.0	986,149	7,559.19	1,631.54
23	8,026	719	15,239	24,007	226	0	226	1,475,490	314,495	1,789,988	45.6	3,922,006	10,983.00	2,176.26
1,200	22,778	1,425	53,548	78,951	823	746	1,569	5,344,838	1,329,401	6,674,241	57.9	12,357,281	12,400.82	2,272.80
469	1,507	227	4,317	6,520	384	0	384	308,653	68,303	376,955	49.2	766,926	7,655.02	1,613.05
0	627	40	1,342	2,009	0	0	0	90,449	19,372	109,821	43.5	252,469	5,842.30	1,254.03
0	942	52	1,716	2,710	0	0	0	141,526	29,061	170,586	43.9	388,370	7,796.40	1,641.57
0	2,092	210	3,755	6,057	0	0	0	309,850	85,288	395,138	47.1	839,158	9,374.81	2,037.03
0	2,737	218	5,370	8,325	0	2	2	404,787	84,649	489,437	51.1	958,328	6,359.31	1,402.10
2	465	63	1,300	1,830	0	0	0	102,499	25,160	127,659	52.5	243,163	8,905.12	1,810.19
6	731	101	1,456	2,294	0	0	0	124,569	35,615	160,183	54.9	292,011	8,854.99	1,699.01
0	551	135	1,426	2,112	0	0	0	99,026	25,252	124,278	49.2	252,668	7,073.76	1,526.51
95	8,709	1,109	17,523	27,436	389	25	414	1,482,239	308,359	1,790,596	43.1	4,152,895	9,678.47	1,964.17
0	575	84	1,160	1,819	0	0	0	92,461	23,225	115,686	48.2	239,865	8,257.25	1,543.15
0	884	210	1,808	2,902	0	0	0	119,498	29,480	148,979	43.4	343,543	7,825.95	1,572.49
88	1,658	287	5,376	7,409	28	53	81	336,297	85,734	422,031	45.5	927,010	11,035.04	2,022.07
12	687	133	1,516	2,348	0	8	8	115,098	26,923	142,021	52.3	271,292	7,343.93	1,534.49
31	760	169	2,171	3,131	0	0	0	163,311	37,351	200,662	47.2	424,925	7,415.80	969.78
3	588	157	1,478	2,226	0	0	0	125,024	24,142	149,166	49.3	302,398	9,362.44	2,099.08

MSAs

TABLE 8

U.S. CENSUS DIVISION 8, MOUNTAIN

U.S. Community Hospitals
(Nonfederal, short-term general and other special hospitals)

2010 Utilization, Personnel and Finances

CLASSIFICATION	Hospitals	Beds	Admissions	Inpatient Days	Adjusted Patient Days	Average Daily Census	Adjusted Average Daily Census	Average Stay (days)	Surgical Operations	NEWBORNS Bassinets	NEWBORNS Births	OUTPATIENT VISITS Emergency	OUTPATIENT VISITS Total
UNITED STATES	4,985	804,943	35,149,427	189,593,349	355,023,656	519,540	972,930	5.4	27,311,998	56,610	3,818,399	127,249,317	651,423,717
Nonmetropolitan	1,987	137,779	4,307,936	27,147,315	70,298,276	74,403	192,723	6.3	4,153,393	10,938	451,316	23,425,674	123,164,591
Metropolitan	2,998	667,164	30,841,491	162,446,034	284,725,380	445,137	780,207	5.3	23,158,605	45,672	3,367,083	103,823,643	528,259,126
CENSUS DIVISION 8, MOUNTAIN . . .	382	46,872	2,091,454	10,379,491	19,768,000	28,434	54,156	5.0	1,644,739	4,160	278,694	7,497,043	36,929,846
Nonmetropolitan	193	9,658	264,082	1,822,076	5,094,018	4,991	13,957	6.9	275,488	897	41,073	1,518,066	7,856,994
Metropolitan	189	37,214	1,827,372	8,557,415	14,673,982	23,443	40,199	4.7	1,369,251	3,263	237,621	5,978,977	29,072,852
Arizona.	73	13,385	711,901	3,160,244	5,186,031	8,658	14,206	4.4	505,416	1,099	80,960	2,240,946	8,127,466
Nonmetropolitan	15	643	31,977	130,455	395,954	358	1,084	4.1	25,894	65	4,799	155,599	588,575
Metropolitan	58	12,742	679,924	3,029,789	4,790,077	8,300	13,122	4.5	479,522	1,034	76,161	2,085,347	7,538,891
Flagstaff.	3	370	17,462	76,762	160,614	211	440	4.4	12,569	43	2,075	77,031	533,418
Lake Havasu City-Kingman	4	527	27,065	118,448	222,606	325	609	4.4	17,344	33	2,626	123,423	482,329
Phoenix-Mesa-Scottsdale	35	8,532	471,976	2,083,030	3,193,508	5,704	8,748	4.4	339,271	776	54,353	1,332,481	4,696,225
Prescott.	3	316	15,963	56,682	108,729	156	298	3.6	9,309	11	586	97,418	274,551
Tucson	11	2,623	129,036	618,773	940,499	1,695	2,577	4.8	90,182	152	13,125	381,823	1,381,091
Yuma	2	374	18,422	76,094	164,121	209	450	4.1	10,847	19	3,396	73,171	171,277
Colorado.	80	10,208	449,369	2,234,925	4,379,027	6,124	11,997	5.0	353,481	997	63,653	1,677,353	8,250,144
Nonmetropolitan	37	1,556	41,331	258,650	833,613	708	2,286	6.3	48,056	151	7,259	248,025	1,515,676
Metropolitan	43	8,652	408,038	1,976,275	3,545,414	5,416	9,711	4.8	305,425	846	56,394	1,429,328	6,734,468
Boulder	4	644	34,233	136,668	257,781	374	706	4.0	24,696	98	7,182	113,965	676,404
Colorado Springs	5	1,044	68,262	303,548	562,787	832	1,542	4.4	36,585	82	7,202	216,782	720,090
Denver-Aurora	23	5,051	221,973	1,127,647	1,939,984	3,090	5,315	5.1	180,389	506	31,581	800,882	3,220,241
Fort Collins-Loveland.	4	563	29,446	119,649	231,415	328	634	4.1	21,326	53	3,845	102,384	819,985
Grand Junction	3	490	14,690	101,649	225,548	279	617	6.9	12,442	32	2,285	57,624	533,852
Greeley	2	313	17,085	73,534	125,783	202	344	4.3	13,260	38	2,026	51,251	505,527
Pueblo.	2	547	22,349	113,580	202,116	311	553	5.1	16,727	37	2,273	86,440	258,369
Idaho	41	3,376	131,375	628,840	1,456,700	1,720	3,991	4.8	113,023	276	18,941	489,718	3,161,958
Nonmetropolitan	26	1,117	34,245	216,548	622,166	593	1,705	6.3	31,035	108	5,622	166,185	900,698
Metropolitan	15	2,259	97,130	412,292	834,534	1,127	2,286	4.2	81,988	168	13,319	323,533	2,261,260
Boise City-Nampa	8	1,305	58,336	225,594	463,434	616	1,270	3.9	48,577	103	8,027	185,089	1,670,738
Coeur d'Alene	1	246	13,966	52,326	100,849	143	276	3.7	6,467	18	1,379	49,576	110,555
Idaho Falls	2	310	10,909	61,607	99,137	169	271	5.6	12,222	10	1,550	36,331	166,930
Lewiston	1	136	4,911	21,464	42,587	59	117	4.4	4,273	15	662	13,662	103,169
Logan	1	65	918	15,827	43,101	43	118	17.2	617	5	107	723	3,647
Pocatello	2	197	8,090	35,474	85,426	97	234	4.4	9,832	17	1,594	38,152	206,221
Montana	48	3,692	97,453	848,356	1,998,685	2,322	5,477	8.7	77,179	220	10,217	357,543	3,504,384
Nonmetropolitan	42	2,311	43,989	517,100	1,295,132	1,415	3,550	11.8	38,013	141	4,638	209,265	1,454,121
Metropolitan	6	1,381	53,464	331,256	703,553	907	1,927	6.2	39,166	79	5,579	148,278	2,050,263
Billings	3	606	27,286	156,432	384,961	428	1,054	5.7	19,996	34	2,600	67,314	1,478,147
Great Falls	1	438	12,563	111,569	200,664	306	550	8.9	8,523	24	1,480	36,570	277,023
Missoula	2	337	13,615	63,255	117,928	173	323	4.6	10,647	21	1,499	44,394	295,093
Nevada	36	5,192	241,296	1,296,929	2,090,504	3,555	5,724	5.4	173,334	305	24,844	820,675	2,669,938
Nonmetropolitan	11	404	10,506	70,619	194,920	193	533	6.7	16,265	35	1,689	99,048	558,160
Metropolitan	25	4,788	230,790	1,226,310	1,895,584	3,362	5,191	5.3	157,069	270	23,155	721,627	2,111,778
Carson City	1	184	9,944	42,831	68,513	117	188	4.3	2,741	12	918	32,081	158,041
Las Vegas-Paradise	17	3,456	177,178	932,818	1,402,475	2,556	3,841	5.3	114,080	191	16,454	525,854	1,475,105
Reno-Sparks	7	1,148	43,668	250,661	424,596	689	1,162	5.7	40,248	67	5,783	163,692	478,632
New Mexico	36	3,975	186,092	831,384	1,720,091	2,277	4,714	4.5	141,514	464	23,767	844,650	4,639,987
Nonmetropolitan	22	1,478	56,683	212,055	516,646	582	1,416	3.7	53,654	160	6,763	365,338	1,390,450
Metropolitan	14	2,497	129,409	619,329	1,203,445	1,695	3,298	4.8	87,860	304	17,004	479,312	3,249,537
Albuquerque	9	1,707	89,007	448,546	887,315	1,228	2,431	5.0	60,048	212	12,085	269,635	2,300,370
Farmington	1	198	10,392	41,410	77,209	113	212	4.0	5,763	22	1,281	46,593	209,713
Las Cruces	3	397	19,544	87,607	156,215	240	428	4.5	17,245	46	2,516	68,854	264,856
Santa Fe	1	195	10,466	41,766	82,706	114	227	4.0	4,804	24	1,122	94,230	474,598

MSAs

TABLE **8**

U.S. CENSUS DIVISION 8, MOUNTAIN

U.S. Community Hospitals
(Nonfederal, short-term general and other special hospitals)

2010 Utilization, Personnel and Finances

FULL-TIME EQUIVALENT PERSONNEL					FULL-TIME EQUIV. TRAINEES			EXPENSES						
								LABOR				TOTAL		
Physicians and Dentists	Registered Nurses	Licensed Practical Nurses	Other Salaried Personnel	Total Personnel	Medical and Dental Residents	Other Trainees	Total Trainees	Payroll (in thousands)	Employee Benefits (in thousands)	Total (in thousands)	Percent of Total	Amount (in thousands)	Adjusted per Admission	Adjusted per Inpatient Day
103,332	1,293,945	91,057	3,111,418	4,599,752	95,270	8,153	103,423	$274,300,010	$73,831,160	$348,131,210	51.3	$677,968,038	$10,313.44	$1,909.64
13,050	155,574	26,968	467,595	663,187	1,715	434	2,149	32,684,219	9,001,043	41,685,291	53.4	78,085,310	7,010.73	1,110.77
90,282	1,138,371	64,089	2,643,823	3,936,565	93,555	7,719	101,274	241,615,791	64,830,116	306,445,919	51.1	599,882,728	10,987.18	2,106.88
5,209	78,284	4,095	178,120	265,708	2,325	279	2,604	15,777,960	3,962,551	19,740,505	50.9	38,771,182	10,044.99	1,961.31
1,172	9,712	1,308	32,751	44,943	34	12	46	2,401,884	605,608	3,007,489	53.2	5,649,786	7,785.96	1,109.10
4,037	68,572	2,787	145,369	220,765	2,291	267	2,558	13,376,076	3,356,944	16,733,016	50.5	33,121,396	10,568.02	2,257.15
1,358	25,147	873	49,856	77,234	1,020	101	1,121	4,543,648	1,071,000	5,614,647	49.8	11,271,575	9,563.80	2,173.45
86	830	102	2,851	3,869	1	3	4	210,404	51,065	261,469	50.6	516,802	5,540.03	1,305.21
1,272	24,317	771	47,005	73,365	1,019	98	1,117	4,333,244	1,019,934	5,353,178	49.8	10,754,773	9,909.66	2,245.22
88	815	11	1,668	2,582	0	19	19	180,542	53,031	233,573	50.6	417,131	10,378.20	2,597.10
56	890	66	2,222	3,234	7	8	15	166,121	44,479	210,601	50.4	417,460	8,216.91	1,875.33
1,000	16,532	532	30,781	48,845	952	65	1,017	2,971,782	700,883	3,672,662	49.5	7,425,319	10,188.25	2,325.13
19	796	3	1,750	2,568	0	6	6	141,527	37,944	179,471	57.0	315,133	10,263.58	2,898.33
106	4,671	140	9,228	14,145	60	0	60	756,683	147,990	904,675	48.0	1,884,791	9,520.59	2,004.03
3	613	19	1,356	1,991	0	0	0	116,589	35,607	152,196	51.6	294,939	8,015.08	1,797.08
1,197	18,403	640	41,919	62,159	489	61	550	3,858,383	932,726	4,791,106	50.0	9,590,947	11,409.25	2,190.20
258	1,841	230	6,624	8,953	1	0	1	497,199	126,625	623,823	51.7	1,206,408	10,505.94	1,447.20
939	16,562	410	35,295	53,206	488	61	549	3,361,183	806,100	4,167,283	49.7	8,384,539	11,552.17	2,364.90
49	1,251	50	3,470	4,820	1	0	1	275,167	68,424	343,591	50.6	679,397	10,513.73	2,635.56
38	1,901	24	4,126	6,089	7	0	7	363,347	93,410	456,757	48.4	943,129	7,434.94	1,675.82
658	10,076	213	20,054	31,001	403	61	464	2,067,471	482,722	2,550,193	50.2	5,079,372	13,196.77	2,618.25
47	1,282	30	2,210	3,569	18	0	18	230,345	62,988	293,333	48.7	601,935	11,241.45	2,601.11
59	579	21	1,789	2,448	23	0	23	147,635	34,873	182,509	46.1	396,033	14,702.19	1,755.87
36	579	18	1,372	2,005	28	0	28	127,950	27,285	155,235	45.4	341,862	11,772.11	2,717.87
52	894	54	2,274	3,274	8	0	8	149,267	36,398	185,665	54.2	342,810	8,589.79	1,696.11
562	5,224	484	15,311	21,581	10	6	16	1,106,740	276,770	1,383,512	54.3	2,546,624	8,750.47	1,748.21
138	1,286	227	4,384	6,035	6	2	8	298,291	77,195	375,487	54.3	692,017	7,140.45	1,112.27
424	3,938	257	10,927	15,546	4	4	8	808,450	199,575	1,008,025	54.4	1,854,607	9,554.32	2,222.33
363	2,462	128	7,871	10,824	4	4	8	540,045	129,696	669,741	55.1	1,214,569	10,186.26	2,620.80
1	404	4	1,024	1,433	0	0	0	87,925	23,534	111,459	54.5	204,651	7,603.04	2,029.28
4	511	53	624	1,192	0	0	0	63,050	17,152	80,202	52.4	153,045	8,439.68	1,543.77
18	214	7	522	761	0	0	0	43,850	11,959	55,809	50.6	110,201	11,309.64	2,587.67
4	38	7	125	174	0	0	0	6,547	1,840	8,387	64.9	12,924	5,169.62	299.86
34	309	58	761	1,162	0	0	0	67,032	15,395	82,427	51.8	159,216	9,056.16	1,863.79
721	3,911	606	13,139	18,377	1	5	6	1,026,226	233,517	1,259,742	52.9	2,379,151	10,398.98	1,190.36
260	1,850	242	6,713	9,065	1	0	1	446,283	108,847	555,129	54.7	1,014,511	8,688.56	783.33
461	2,061	364	6,426	9,312	0	5	5	579,943	124,670	704,613	51.6	1,364,640	12,181.79	1,939.64
311	998	207	3,416	4,932	0	0	0	343,515	72,654	416,169	55.9	744,859	11,636.06	1,934.89
50	511	73	1,392	2,026	0	0	0	122,179	22,933	145,112	50.7	286,380	12,674.48	1,427.16
100	552	84	1,618	2,354	0	5	5	114,249	29,083	143,332	43.0	333,401	13,118.29	2,827.16
125	7,156	439	15,082	22,802	35	2	37	1,537,343	413,289	1,950,632	49.5	3,940,182	10,165.96	1,884.80
25	410	47	1,351	1,833	1	0	1	101,707	27,031	128,738	54.1	238,053	8,304.08	1,221.29
100	6,746	392	13,731	20,969	34	2	36	1,435,637	386,258	1,821,894	49.2	3,702,129	10,314.66	1,953.03
0	321	6	749	1,076	0	1	1	63,575	14,633	78,208	48.2	162,229	10,198.60	2,367.86
96	5,004	336	9,816	15,252	34	1	35	1,049,561	290,915	1,340,475	51.1	2,620,693	9,815.88	1,868.62
4	1,421	50	3,166	4,641	0	0	0	322,500	80,711	403,211	43.9	919,207	12,090.53	2,164.90
720	7,055	453	14,967	23,195	45	33	78	1,570,508	372,355	1,942,863	54.9	3,540,766	9,053.42	2,058.48
192	1,664	181	4,791	6,828	11	4	15	407,250	100,063	507,314	50.9	996,600	6,990.20	1,928.98
528	5,391	272	10,176	16,367	34	29	63	1,163,258	272,291	1,435,549	56.4	2,544,167	10,237.02	2,114.07
417	4,052	215	7,193	11,877	7	29	36	869,932	197,864	1,067,796	58.4	1,829,732	10,536.84	2,062.10
60	432	2	1,026	1,520	0	0	0	98,537	28,149	126,686	59.5	212,748	10,979.95	2,755.48
25	578	28	1,070	1,701	20	0	20	97,424	20,265	117,688	44.8	262,484	7,548.30	1,680.28
26	329	27	887	1,269	7	0	7	97,366	26,013	123,379	51.6	239,202	11,541.73	2,892.20

Table continues

MSAs

U.S. CENSUS DIVISION 8, MOUNTAIN CONTINUED

U.S. Community Hospitals
(Nonfederal, short-term general and other special hospitals)

2010 Utilization, Personnel and Finances

CLASSIFICATION	Hospitals	Beds	Admissions	Inpatient Days	Adjusted Patient Days	Average Daily Census	Adjusted Average Daily Census	Average Stay (days)	Surgical Operations	NEWBORNS		OUTPATIENT VISITS	
										Bassinets	Births	Emergency	Total
Utah	44	5,086	224,264	979,963	2,001,937	2,685	5,487	4.4	237,373	629	49,392	834,897	5,477,724
Nonmetropolitan	18	620	15,756	104,764	439,543	287	1,204	6.6	30,451	107	5,657	116,604	581,199
Metropolitan	26	4,466	208,508	875,199	1,562,394	2,398	4,283	4.2	206,922	522	43,735	718,293	4,896,525
Logan	2	150	7,757	23,496	53,938	65	148	3.0	8,868	34	2,618	31,152	335,392
Ogden-Clearfield	4	794	34,922	135,716	236,954	371	650	3.9	26,061	103	7,031	162,891	516,152
Provo-Orem	6	722	34,625	138,042	244,076	377	670	4.0	33,521	133	11,433	111,843	676,194
Salt Lake City	13	2,539	117,176	526,960	933,082	1,445	2,557	4.5	126,588	236	20,107	373,411	2,929,434
St. George	1	261	14,028	50,985	94,344	140	258	3.6	11,884	16	2,546	38,996	439,353
Wyoming	24	1,958	49,704	398,850	935,025	1,093	2,560	8.0	43,419	170	6,920	231,261	1,098,245
Nonmetropolitan	22	1,529	29,595	311,885	796,044	855	2,179	10.5	32,120	130	4,646	158,002	868,115
Metropolitan	2	429	20,109	86,965	138,981	238	381	4.3	11,299	40	2,274	73,259	230,130
Casper	1	207	8,622	35,859	54,222	98	149	4.2	5,364	24	1,104	34,907	84,689
Cheyenne.	1	222	11,487	51,106	84,759	140	232	4.4	5,935	16	1,170	38,352	145,441

MSAs

2010 Utilization, Personnel and Finances

FULL-TIME EQUIVALENT PERSONNEL					FULL-TIME EQUIV. TRAINEES			EXPENSES						
								LABOR				TOTAL		
Physicians and Dentists	Registered Nurses	Licensed Practical Nurses	Other Salaried Personnel	Total Personnel	Medical and Dental Residents	Other Trainees	Total Trainees	Payroll (in thousands)	Employee Benefits (in thousands)	Total (in thousands)	Percent of Total	Amount (in thousands)	Adjusted per Admission	Adjusted per Inpatient Day
349	9,480	453	21,756	32,038	713	68	781	1,664,817	533,406	2,198,223	49.2	4,470,511	10,311.60	2,233.09
45	594	149	2,048	2,836	1	2	3	129,005	34,432	163,437	51.5	317,213	5,647.08	721.69
304	8,886	304	19,708	29,202	712	66	778	1,535,813	498,974	2,034,786	49.0	4,153,297	11,005.93	2,658.29
5	296	13	619	933	0	0	0	41,338	16,318	57,657	49.7	115,915	6,484.03	2,149.04
32	1,280	87	2,572	3,971	27	1	28	206,784	64,112	270,895	48.8	554,563	9,127.25	2,340.38
33	1,315	58	3,095	4,501	41	5	46	229,187	78,004	307,191	51.2	599,435	9,426.71	2,455.94
220	5,485	144	12,126	17,975	644	60	704	967,253	305,653	1,272,906	48.9	2,602,046	12,438.91	2,788.66
14	510	2	1,296	1,822	0	0	0	91,250	34,887	126,137	44.8	281,338	10,838.21	2,982.05
177	1,908	147	6,090	8,322	12	3	15	470,294	129,489	599,780	58.2	1,031,426	9,504.48	1,103.10
168	1,237	130	3,989	5,524	12	1	13	311,745	80,350	392,092	58.7	668,182	8,742.18	839.38
9	671	17	2,101	2,798	0	2	2	158,549	49,139	207,688	57.2	363,243	11,320.22	2,613.62
0	305	3	841	1,149	0	2	2	65,361	22,096	87,457	50.5	173,262	13,290.04	3,195.42
9	366	14	1,260	1,649	0	0	0	93,187	27,044	120,231	63.3	189,981	9,972.23	2,241.42

MSAs

TABLE 8

U.S. CENSUS DIVISION 9, PACIFIC

U.S. Community Hospitals
(Nonfederal, short-term general and other special hospitals)

2010 Utilization, Personnel and Finances

CLASSIFICATION	Hospitals	Beds	Admissions	Inpatient Days	Adjusted Patient Days	Average Daily Census	Adjusted Average Daily Census	Average Stay (days)	Surgical Operations	NEWBORNS Bassinets	Births	OUTPATIENT VISITS Emergency	Total
UNITED STATES	4,985	804,943	35,149,427	189,593,349	355,023,656	519,540	972,930	5.4	27,311,998	56,610	3,818,399	127,249,317	651,423,717
Nonmetropolitan	1,987	137,779	4,307,936	27,147,315	70,298,276	74,403	192,723	6.3	4,153,393	10,938	451,316	23,425,674	123,164,591
Metropolitan	2,998	667,164	30,841,491	162,446,034	284,725,380	445,137	780,207	5.3	23,158,605	45,672	3,367,083	103,823,643	528,259,126
CENSUS DIVISION 9, PACIFIC	535	93,088	4,501,591	22,640,225	38,449,207	62,038	105,333	5.0	3,077,300	7,027	632,032	15,128,224	76,725,170
Nonmetropolitan	122	5,814	202,076	1,172,550	3,156,003	3,216	8,649	5.8	244,132	580	31,544	1,270,128	7,339,440
Metropolitan	413	87,274	4,299,515	21,467,675	35,293,204	58,822	96,684	5.0	2,833,168	6,447	600,488	13,858,096	69,385,730
Alaska	22	1,543	57,005	342,960	787,190	940	2,157	6.0	65,416	160	8,919	296,573	1,782,942
Nonmetropolitan	17	613	15,119	129,722	384,659	356	1,053	8.6	24,428	59	2,839	89,087	522,459
Metropolitan	5	930	41,886	213,238	402,531	584	1,104	5.1	40,988	101	6,080	207,486	1,260,483
Anchorage	4	723	36,461	164,882	299,295	452	821	4.5	35,244	85	4,893	174,063	880,414
Fairbanks	1	207	5,425	48,356	103,236	132	283	8.9	5,744	16	1,187	33,423	380,069
California	343	70,440	3,423,820	17,443,427	28,168,218	47,793	77,162	5.1	2,169,539	5,090	493,712	10,945,256	51,729,263
Nonmetropolitan	31	1,473	54,506	314,228	805,903	860	2,207	5.8	65,500	127	8,256	421,280	2,393,312
Metropolitan	312	68,967	3,369,314	17,129,199	27,362,315	46,933	74,955	5.1	2,104,039	4,963	485,456	10,523,976	49,335,951
Bakersfield	8	1,422	70,373	349,762	543,411	958	1,489	5.0	39,948	91	14,209	223,267	646,057
Chico	4	529	30,175	136,734	241,186	375	661	4.5	17,293	43	2,919	96,783	871,947
El Centro	2	272	12,864	46,244	95,627	127	261	3.6	8,864	25	3,004	88,050	207,437
Fresno	8	1,614	92,706	449,472	745,470	1,231	2,043	4.8	44,154	184	13,969	196,159	1,590,170
Hanford-Corcoran	3	234	12,174	53,100	126,166	146	346	4.4	9,950	20	1,035	66,235	340,739
Los Angeles-Long Beach-Glendale	90	21,083	1,028,045	5,251,556	8,000,736	14,391	21,918	5.1	579,163	1,516	136,988	2,588,956	12,623,043
Madera	3	470	18,885	105,845	173,250	290	475	5.6	17,230	10	1,752	114,603	385,687
Merced	2	232	12,614	53,672	99,823	147	273	4.3	7,539	20	2,552	69,104	218,532
Modesto	4	1,368	54,231	334,409	496,496	915	1,360	6.2	35,157	74	8,446	208,820	376,393
Napa	2	351	15,990	84,872	135,096	233	370	5.3	12,703	12	1,167	33,264	313,384
Oakland-Fremont-Hayward	18	4,399	216,277	1,093,461	1,750,797	2,994	4,794	5.1	116,997	287	26,315	737,871	3,586,890
Oxnard-Thousand Oaks-Ventura	6	1,045	62,670	286,201	515,858	784	1,413	4.6	34,167	100	9,118	214,573	1,039,334
Redding	3	503	23,235	117,498	203,013	322	556	5.1	10,868	13	2,136	73,420	208,065
Riverside-San Bernardino-Ontario	33	6,746	357,026	1,692,329	2,733,248	4,639	7,485	4.7	221,362	479	55,670	1,253,916	3,624,184
Sacramento—Arden-Arcade—Roseville	15	3,821	196,178	1,003,800	1,646,320	2,749	4,510	5.1	141,544	335	23,903	555,185	3,234,830
Salinas	4	758	33,601	173,506	256,535	476	704	5.2	28,299	81	6,903	158,192	580,817
San Diego-Carlsbad-San Marcos	21	5,481	283,444	1,436,743	2,195,157	3,935	6,013	5.1	194,151	380	42,616	754,529	3,021,283
San Francisco-San Mateo-Redwood City	18	4,834	172,005	1,162,716	2,051,245	3,185	5,619	6.8	136,460	184	18,330	642,488	4,828,844
San Jose-Sunnyvale-Santa Clara	11	3,260	160,896	831,065	1,351,918	2,276	3,703	5.2	101,978	346	28,997	664,258	4,433,893
San Luis Obispo-Paso Robles	4	457	19,780	81,962	117,653	225	322	4.1	12,315	37	2,907	85,967	275,954
Santa Ana-Anaheim-Irvine	24	5,617	266,309	1,276,065	1,968,654	3,495	5,396	4.8	194,613	345	41,798	724,270	3,113,709
Santa Barbara-Santa Maria	5	865	34,232	212,270	343,100	581	940	6.2	25,511	76	6,437	135,703	439,150
Santa Cruz-Watsonville	3	410	20,710	94,470	175,028	260	479	4.6	16,483	47	3,851	59,620	306,574
Santa Rosa-Petaluma	7	659	36,892	153,066	285,130	420	781	4.1	28,331	43	5,462	110,998	486,391
Stockton	7	1,186	62,889	272,422	494,711	748	1,356	4.3	34,927	101	10,985	293,668	1,294,975
Vallejo-Fairfield	3	503	25,709	117,741	208,310	323	570	4.6	13,761	45	4,308	135,093	352,957
Visalia-Porterville	3	679	37,137	206,057	322,790	565	884	5.5	16,443	53	7,587	192,751	761,076
Yuba City	1	169	12,267	52,161	85,587	143	234	4.3	3,828	16	2,092	46,233	173,636
Hawaii	26	3,148	110,577	827,977	1,487,959	2,269	4,077	7.5	89,228	202	9,271	365,903	2,194,082
Nonmetropolitan	12	889	28,789	219,786	461,364	603	1,264	7.6	27,085	72	4,082	104,096	356,109
Metropolitan	14	2,259	81,788	608,191	1,026,595	1,666	2,813	7.4	62,143	130	5,189	261,807	1,837,973
Honolulu	14	2,259	81,788	608,191	1,026,595	1,666	2,813	7.4	62,143	130	5,189	261,807	1,837,973
Oregon	58	6,420	321,334	1,387,082	2,795,289	3,802	7,663	4.3	320,225	655	41,914	1,229,539	9,212,253
Nonmetropolitan	29	1,338	59,164	243,666	704,660	668	1,933	4.1	63,061	169	8,153	360,230	2,290,552
Metropolitan	29	5,082	262,170	1,143,416	2,090,629	3,134	5,730	4.4	257,164	486	33,761	869,309	6,921,701
Bend	2	309	16,810	64,886	109,371	178	300	3.9	18,273	33	1,955	52,679	228,577
Corvallis	1	178	9,335	40,835	74,336	112	204	4.4	9,689	20	1,074	21,942	173,673
Eugene-Springfield	4	240	10,759	44,120	93,261	120	255	4.1	7,617	20	658	71,255	208,879
Medford	3	477	21,621	95,212	159,501	261	438	4.4	21,562	40	2,392	73,143	711,100
Portland-Vancouver-Beaverton	15	3,332	175,986	781,686	1,440,316	2,143	3,948	4.4	181,838	314	22,465	508,977	4,853,607
Salem	4	546	27,659	116,677	213,844	320	585	4.2	18,185	59	5,217	141,313	745,865

TABLE **8**

U.S. CENSUS DIVISION 9, PACIFIC

U.S. Community Hospitals
(Nonfederal, short-term general and other special hospitals)

2010 Utilization, Personnel and Finances

FULL-TIME EQUIVALENT PERSONNEL					FULL-TIME EQUIV. TRAINEES			EXPENSES						
								LABOR				TOTAL		
Physicians and Dentists	Registered Nurses	Licensed Practical Nurses	Other Salaried Personnel	Total Personnel	Medical and Dental Residents	Other Trainees	Total Trainees	Payroll (in thousands)	Employee Benefits (in thousands)	Total (in thousands)	Percent of Total	Amount (in thousands)	Adjusted per Admission	Adjusted per Inpatient Day
103,332	1,293,945	91,057	3,111,418	4,599,752	95,270	8,153	103,423	$274,300,010	$73,831,160	$348,131,210	51.3	$677,968,038	$10,313.44	$1,909.64
13,050	155,574	26,968	467,595	663,187	1,715	434	2,149	32,684,219	9,001,043	41,685,291	53.4	78,085,310	7,010.73	1,110.77
90,282	1,138,371	64,089	2,643,823	3,936,565	93,555	7,719	101,274	241,615,791	64,830,116	306,445,919	51.1	599,882,728	10,987.18	2,106.88
10,550	170,150	10,016	381,641	572,357	11,020	543	11,563	40,495,452	12,410,971	52,906,420	53.4	98,998,693	12,949.79	2,574.79
808	8,760	951	26,574	37,093	27	21	48	2,290,007	723,822	3,013,831	56.2	5,358,651	10,156.77	1,697.92
9,742	161,390	9,065	355,067	535,264	10,993	522	11,515	38,205,445	11,687,149	49,892,589	53.3	93,640,041	13,156.84	2,653.20
222	2,692	193	7,738	10,845	42	12	54	677,354	194,911	872,268	54.9	1,590,215	12,904.24	2,020.12
100	932	122	3,078	4,232	3	8	11	234,840	74,104	308,946	56.0	552,149	12,048.04	1,435.43
122	1,760	71	4,660	6,613	39	4	43	442,514	120,808	563,322	54.3	1,038,065	13,411.18	2,578.85
117	1,450	64	3,822	5,453	39	4	43	362,528	97,223	459,751	55.2	832,155	12,642.69	2,780.38
5	310	7	838	1,160	0	0	0	79,986	23,584	103,571	50.3	205,911	17,778.51	1,994.56
4,898	127,285	8,119	274,370	414,672	8,463	384	8,847	29,419,150	9,202,045	38,621,190	53.4	72,279,547	13,096.14	2,566.00
57	2,390	300	6,412	9,159	3	2	5	591,774	220,588	812,361	54.7	1,485,055	11,322.38	1,842.72
4,841	124,895	7,819	267,958	405,513	8,460	382	8,842	28,827,376	8,981,457	37,808,829	53.4	70,794,491	13,139.31	2,587.30
123	2,142	164	4,894	7,323	130	2	132	475,418	153,993	629,410	56.3	1,118,334	10,618.14	2,057.99
5	1,071	125	2,850	4,051	0	1	1	246,971	107,667	354,638	56.5	627,299	12,347.67	2,600.89
0	398	21	1,064	1,483	0	0	0	73,504	21,638	95,142	55.4	171,807	6,457.93	1,796.64
203	2,585	158	6,696	9,642	188	12	200	544,767	144,741	689,509	50.6	1,361,769	8,627.48	1,826.73
34	405	47	1,147	1,633	6	2	8	108,256	28,864	137,120	52.0	263,678	8,563.49	2,089.93
1,472	37,676	2,715	81,354	123,217	3,281	151	3,432	8,276,660	2,439,154	10,715,812	52.7	20,346,632	12,924.03	2,543.10
1	756	67	2,138	2,962	0	0	0	184,758	78,255	263,012	63.3	415,397	13,822.16	2,397.68
9	411	45	1,014	1,479	1	2	3	99,755	27,371	127,126	56.7	224,104	9,589.37	2,245.01
12	2,315	97	3,567	5,991	3	1	4	427,549	123,893	551,443	65.3	844,651	10,856.41	1,701.22
16	593	23	1,329	1,961	3	1	4	156,286	66,722	223,009	55.2	403,638	15,752.33	2,987.78
425	7,062	566	16,742	24,795	258	16	274	2,224,153	750,254	2,974,407	57.0	5,220,954	14,985.86	2,982.04
74	1,824	150	4,163	6,211	27	4	31	478,366	150,844	629,211	52.0	1,210,912	10,603.62	2,347.37
4	862	26	1,335	2,227	24	0	24	161,819	64,500	226,319	51.8	436,985	12,997.00	2,152.50
868	12,534	1,195	25,523	40,120	998	55	1,053	2,247,763	661,889	2,909,651	50.9	5,721,568	9,839.55	2,093.32
424	7,426	303	17,055	25,208	776	24	800	2,058,014	574,726	2,632,741	56.8	4,636,461	14,210.24	2,816.26
41	1,154	43	3,098	4,336	27	0	27	395,122	189,786	584,907	62.4	937,615	19,889.58	3,654.92
148	11,484	485	20,023	32,140	851	24	875	2,195,233	591,146	2,786,379	51.6	5,403,343	12,650.52	2,461.48
407	6,973	393	16,767	24,540	236	27	263	2,455,729	720,360	3,176,090	53.6	5,923,226	19,558.28	2,887.62
213	7,108	218	15,525	23,064	1,286	35	1,321	2,144,826	803,485	2,948,310	51.9	5,678,915	21,680.87	4,200.64
3	675	19	1,040	1,737	2	0	2	143,693	30,673	174,366	52.6	331,239	11,592.32	2,815.39
88	10,260	377	21,592	32,317	126	8	134	1,945,360	658,996	2,604,356	50.7	5,140,232	12,364.77	2,611.04
18	1,360	99	2,995	4,472	55	0	55	305,319	89,927	395,246	56.1	705,143	13,545.60	2,055.21
54	689	50	1,761	2,554	24	2	26	181,431	49,174	230,605	51.5	447,900	11,445.87	2,559.02
30	1,148	74	2,745	3,997	41	1	42	283,985	126,781	410,766	52.3	785,364	11,614.38	2,754.41
169	2,229	133	5,201	7,732	107	7	114	453,857	147,669	601,525	56.6	1,062,679	9,254.29	2,148.08
0	2,058	75	2,383	4,516	0	5	5	228,083	66,406	294,491	49.1	599,435	13,182.79	2,877.61
0	1,237	124	2,917	4,278	0	2	2	247,327	70,972	318,299	58.0	548,876	9,318.46	1,700.41
0	460	27	1,040	1,527	10	0	10	83,370	41,570	124,939	55.2	226,335	11,244.80	2,644.51
392	4,342	318	11,144	16,196	70	31	101	1,100,346	292,953	1,393,297	53.4	2,611,062	12,906.05	1,754.79
81	963	131	2,657	3,832	15	0	15	242,317	74,379	316,697	56.7	558,134	9,490.13	1,209.75
311	3,379	187	8,487	12,364	55	31	86	858,028	218,573	1,076,600	52.4	2,052,928	14,306.02	1,999.75
311	3,379	187	8,487	12,364	55	31	86	858,028	218,573	1,076,600	52.4	2,052,928	14,306.02	1,999.75
1,814	12,795	253	29,565	44,427	989	30	1,019	3,109,155	1,001,088	4,110,247	52.2	7,875,937	12,101.26	2,817.58
334	2,371	100	7,454	10,259	0	5	5	638,634	199,864	838,501	57.5	1,457,064	9,114.91	2,067.75
1,480	10,424	153	22,111	34,168	989	25	1,014	2,470,521	801,224	3,271,746	51.0	6,418,873	13,073.57	3,070.31
24	673	0	1,683	2,380	1	0	1	161,269	58,018	219,287	50.3	435,635	15,083.29	3,983.10
88	336	18	1,004	1,446	25	5	30	122,285	38,030	160,315	54.4	294,569	17,334.71	3,962.67
75	440	15	1,639	2,169	0	0	0	100,674	31,217	131,891	54.8	240,774	10,365.67	2,581.72
38	784	17	1,911	2,750	0	3	3	177,775	72,424	250,199	49.5	505,642	13,804.41	3,170.15
1,175	7,023	80	13,202	21,480	963	17	980	1,637,563	529,384	2,166,947	50.1	4,328,451	13,114.45	3,005.21
80	1,168	23	2,672	3,943	0	0	0	270,956	72,151	343,107	55.9	613,802	11,120.21	2,870.33

Table continues

TABLE 8

U.S. CENSUS DIVISION 9, PACIFIC CONTINUED

U.S. Community Hospitals
(Nonfederal, short-term general and other special hospitals)

2010 Utilization, Personnel and Finances

CLASSIFICATION	Hospitals	Beds	Admissions	Inpatient Days	Adjusted Patient Days	Average Daily Census	Adjusted Average Daily Census	Average Stay (days)	Surgical Operations	NEWBORNS		OUTPATIENT VISITS	
										Bassinets	Births	Emergency	Total
Washington	86	11,537	588,855	2,638,779	5,210,551	7,234	14,274	4.5	432,892	920	78,216	2,290,953	11,806,630
Nonmetropolitan	33	1,501	44,498	265,148	799,417	729	2,192	6.0	64,058	153	8,214	295,435	1,777,008
Metropolitan	53	10,036	544,357	2,373,631	4,411,134	6,505	12,082	4.4	368,834	767	70,002	1,995,518	10,029,622
Bellingham	1	233	14,883	60,100	106,074	165	291	4.0	5,867	20	1,678	20,897	104,173
Bremerton-Silverdale	1	262	15,376	59,815	99,368	164	272	3.9	12,461	24	1,889	74,050	234,663
Kennewick-Richland-Pasco	4	419	22,552	93,783	197,247	257	540	4.2	14,580	37	4,793	100,059	342,805
Lewiston	1	25	1,615	6,370	21,134	17	58	3.9	2,347	0	0	13,813	70,308
Longview	1	202	10,066	41,197	72,711	113	199	4.1	3,483	27	1,102	57,188	285,088
Mount Vernon-Anacortes	3	205	12,699	43,827	115,003	120	314	3.5	11,949	32	1,611	60,723	509,518
Olympia	2	461	23,757	102,634	151,301	281	414	4.3	11,701	24	2,737	83,144	320,737
Portland-Vancouver-Beaverton	2	646	35,242	133,874	236,120	367	646	3.8	19,074	60	5,290	129,071	502,795
Seattle-Bellevue-Everett	19	4,233	238,262	1,091,694	2,143,410	2,989	5,873	4.6	172,464	320	29,759	822,900	5,522,025
Spokane	6	1,469	60,047	315,407	496,467	865	1,359	5.3	40,139	70	6,371	203,841	637,103
Tacoma	6	1,197	74,743	291,976	508,352	802	1,393	3.9	51,055	77	8,878	263,692	817,224
Wenatchee	3	160	10,056	39,451	73,455	108	201	3.9	6,393	25	1,748	13,660	103,037
Yakima	4	524	25,059	93,503	190,492	257	522	3.7	17,321	51	4,146	152,480	580,146

FULL-TIME EQUIVALENT PERSONNEL					FULL-TIME EQUIV. TRAINEES			EXPENSES							
								LABOR				TOTAL			
Physicians and Dentists	Registered Nurses	Licensed Practical Nurses	Other Salaried Personnel	Total Personnel	Medical and Dental Residents	Other Trainees	Total Trainees	Payroll (in thousands)	Employee Benefits (in thousands)	Total (in thousands)	Percent of Total	Amount (in thousands)	Adjusted per Admission	Adjusted per Inpatient Day
3,224	23,036	1,133	58,824	86,217	1,456	86	1,542	6,189,447	1,719,973	7,909,418	54.0	14,641,932	12,740.11	2,810.05
236	2,104	298	6,973	9,611	6	6	12	582,442	154,886	737,326	56.4	1,306,249	9,900.55	1,634.00
2,988	20,932	835	51,851	76,606	1,450	80	1,530	5,607,005	1,565,087	7,172,092	53.8	13,335,683	13,108.37	3,023.19
51	673	43	1,683	2,450	28	3	31	146,953	40,092	187,044	51.3	364,328	13,869.66	3,434.66
35	534	28	1,256	1,853	0	8	8	129,522	37,012	166,535	55.4	300,427	11,761.61	3,023.38
40	869	52	2,219	3,180	9	3	12	205,433	53,307	258,740	53.0	488,211	10,404.50	2,475.12
10	80	13	264	367	1	2	3	23,376	6,285	29,661	52.2	56,821	10,604.90	2,688.61
27	368	24	915	1,334	15	1	16	94,631	25,817	120,448	51.3	234,610	13,205.56	3,226.61
88	400	11	1,408	1,907	0	0	0	123,880	29,496	153,377	52.7	290,816	8,657.55	2,528.77
10	822	41	1,631	2,504	2	0	2	165,041	46,913	211,954	49.9	424,561	12,024.49	2,806.07
68	1,216	19	2,267	3,570	27	0	27	270,103	86,968	357,070	55.2	647,037	10,418.43	2,740.29
2,273	10,345	350	26,620	39,588	1,296	46	1,342	3,013,436	842,355	3,855,791	55.1	6,992,391	14,965.66	3,262.27
53	1,902	41	4,464	6,460	45	14	59	511,446	147,680	659,127	50.0	1,318,033	13,607.47	2,654.82
264	2,311	105	5,853	8,533	14	0	14	650,420	177,756	828,176	50.8	1,631,152	12,543.95	3,208.71
35	388	29	1,051	1,503	6	1	7	97,060	24,126	121,185	59.0	205,407	11,187.75	2,796.37
34	1,024	79	2,220	3,357	7	2	9	175,705	47,279	222,984	58.4	381,891	7,344.90	2,004.76

MSAs

Statistics for Multihospital Health Care Systems and their Hospitals

The following tables describing multihospital health care systems refers to information in section B of the 2012 *AHA Guide*.

Table 1 shows the number of multihospital health care systems by type of control. Table 2 provides a breakdown of the number of systems that own, lease, sponsor or contract manage hospitals within each control category. Table 3 gives the number of hospitals and beds in each control category as well as total hospitals and beds. Finally, Table 4 shows the percentage of hospitals and beds in each control category.

For more information on multihospital health care systems, please write to the Section for Health Care Systems, 155 N. Wacker Drive, Chicago, Illinois 60606 or call 312/422–3000.

Table 1. Multihospital Health Care Systems, by Type of Organizaton Control

Type of Control	Code	Number of Systems
Catholic (Roman) church–related	CC	39
Other church–related	CO	13
Subtotal, church–related		52
Other not–for–profit	NP	267
Subtotal, not–for–profit		319
Investor Owned	IO	90
Federal Government	FG	5
Total		414

Table 2. Multihospital Health Care Systems, by Type of Ownership and Control

Type of Ownership	Catholic Church–Related (CC)	Other Church–Related (CO)	Total Church–Related (CC + CO)	Other Not–for–Profit (NP)	Total Not–for–Profit (CC, CO, + NP)	Investor–Owned (IO)	Federal Govern–ment (FG)	All Systems
Systems that only own, lease or sponsor	33	9	42	238	280	82	5	367
Systems that only contract–manage	0	0	0	0	0	3	0	3
Systems that manage, own, lease, or sponsor	6	4	10	29	39	5	0	44
Total	39	13	52	267	319	90	5	414

Table 3. Hospitals and Beds in Multihospital Health Care Systems, by Type of Ownership and Control

Type of Ownership	Catholic Church–Related (CC)		Other Church–Related (CO)		Total Church–Related (CC + CO)		Other Not–for–Profit (NP)		Total Not–for–Profit (CC, CO, + NP)		Investor–Owned (IO)		Federal Govern–ment (FG)		All Systems	
	H	B	H	B	H	B	H	B	H	B	H	B	H	B	H	B
Owned, leased or sponsored	547	104,424	108	23,065	655	127,489	1,331	289,931	1,986	417,420	1,261	149,746	214	47,290	3,461	614,456
Contract–managed	39	1,614	6	546	45	2,160	78	6,220	123	8,380	153	10,344	0	0	276	18,724
Total	586	106,038	114	23,611	700	129,649	1,409	296,151	2,109	425,800	1,414	160,090	214	47,290	3,737	633,180

H = hospitals; B = beds.

Table 4. Hospitals and Beds in Multihospital Health Care Systems, by Type of Ownership and Control as a Percentage of All Systems

Type of Ownership	Catholic Church–Related (CC)		Other Church–Related (CO)		Total Church–Related (CC + CO)		Other Not–for–Profit (NP)		Total Not–for–Profit (CC, CO, + NP)		Investor–Owned (IO)		Federal Govern–ment (FG)		All Systems	
	H	B	H	B	H	B	H	B	H	B	H	B	H	B	H	B
Owned, leased or sponsored	15.8	17.0	3.1	3.8	18.9	20.7	38.5	47.2	57.4	67.9	36.4	24.4	6.2	7.7	100.0	100.0
Contract–managed	14.1	8.6	2.2	2.9	16.3	11.5	28.3	33.2	44.6	44.8	55.4	55.2	0.0	0.0	100.0	100.0
Total	15.7	16.7	3.1	3.7	18.7	20.5	37.7	46.8	56.4	67.2	37.8	25.3	5.7	7.5	100.0	100.0

H = hospitals; B = beds.
*Please note that figures may not always equal the provided subtotal or total percentages due to rounding.

Glossary

This glossary explains specific terms as they are used in the tables and text of AHA Hospital Statistics

Ablation of Barrett's esophagus:
Premalignant condition that can lead to adenocarcinoma of the esophagus. The non surgical ablation of the premalignant tissue in Barrett's esophagus by the application of thermal energy or light through an endoscope passed from the mouth into the esophagus.

Acute long term care: Providers specialized acute hospital care to medically complex patients who are critically ill, have multisystem complications and/or failure, and require hospitalization averaging 25 days, in a facility offering specialized treatment programs and therapeutic intervention on a 24 hour/7day a week basis.

Adjusted average daily census: An estimate of the average number of patients (both inpatients and outpatients) receiving care each day during the reporting period, which is usually 12 months. The figure is derived by dividing the number of inpatient day equivalents (also called adjusted inpatient days) by the number of days in the reporting period.

Adjusted inpatient days: An aggregate figure reflecting the number of days of inpatient care, plus an estimate of the volume of outpatient services, expressed in units equivalent to an inpatient day in terms of level of effort. The figure is derived by first multiplying the number of outpatient visits by the ratio of outpatient revenue per outpatient visit to inpatient revenue per inpatient day. The product (which represents the number of patient days attributable to outpatient services) is then added to the number of *inpatient days*. Originally, the purpose of this calculation was to summarize overall productivity and calculate a unit cost that would include both inpatient and outpatient activities.

Formula 1:

$$\frac{\text{total expenses}}{\text{inpatient days} + \text{outpatient visits}\left(\frac{\frac{\text{outpatient revenue}}{\text{per outpatient visit}}}{\frac{\text{inpatient revenue}}{\text{per inpatient day}}}\right)}$$

However, the value of this calculation has changed over the years as the outpatient share of total revenue has grown and third-party payers have exerted a greater influence on pricing.

Admissions: The number of patients, excluding newborns, accepted for inpatient service during the reporting period; the number includes patients who visit the emergency room and are later admitted for inpatient service.

Adult Cardiac Surgery: Includes minimally invasive procedures that include surgery done with only a small incision or no incision at all, such as through a laparoscope or an endoscope and more invasive major surgical procedures that include open chest and open heart surgery.

Adult Cardiology Services: An organized clinical service offering diagnostic and interventional procedures to manage the full range of adult heart conditions.

Adult day care program: Program providing supervision, medical and psychological care, and social activities for older adults who live at home or in another family setting, but cannot be alone or prefer to be with others during the day. May include intake assessment, health monitoring, occupational therapy, personal care, noon meal, and transportation services.

Adult Diagnostic/invasive catheterization: (also called coronary angiography or coronary arteriography) is used to assist in diagnosing complex heart conditions. Cardiac angiography involves the insertion of a tiny catheter into the artery in the groin then carefully threading the catheter up into the aorta where the coronary arteries originate. Once the catheter is in place, a dye is injected which allows the cardiologist to see the size, shape, and distribution of the coronary arteries. These images are used to diagnose heart disease and to determine, among other things, whether or not surgery is indicated.

Adult Interventional cardiac catheterization: Non surgical procedure that utilizes the same basic principles as diagnostic catheterization and then uses advanced techniques to improve the heart's function. It can be a less-invasive alternative to heart surgery.

Airborne infection isolation room: A single-occupancy room for patient care where environmental factors are controlled in an effort to minimize the transmission of those infectious agents, usually spread person to person by droplet nuclei associated with coughing and inhalation. Such rooms typically have specific ventilation requirements for controlled ventilation, air pressure and filtration.

Alcoholism-drug abuse or dependency inpatient care: Provides diagnosis and therapeutic services to patients with alcoholism or other drug dependencies. Includes care for inpatient/residential treatment for patients whose course of treatment involves more intensive care than provided in an outpatient setting or where patient requires supervised withdrawal.

Alcoholism-drug abuse or dependency outpatient services: Organized hospital services that provide medical care and/or rehabilitative treatment services to outpatients for whom the primary diagnosis is alcoholism or other chemical dependency.

Alzheimer Center: Facility that offers care to persons with Alzheimer's disease and their families through an integrated program of clinical services, research, and education.

Ambulance services: Provision of ambulance services to the ill and injured who require medical attention on a scheduled or unscheduled basis.

Ambulatory Surgery Center: Facility that provides care to patients requiring surgery who are admitted and discharged on the same day. Ambulatory surgery centers are distinct from same day surgical units within the hospital outpatient departments for purposes of Medicare payments.

Arthritis treatment center: Specifically equipped and staffed center for the diagnosis and treatment of arthritis and other joint disorders.

Assisted living: A special combination of housing, supportive services, personalized assistance and health care designed to respond to the individual needs of those who need help in activities of daily living and instrumental activities of daily living. Supportive services are available, 24 hours a day, to meet scheduled and unscheduled needs, in a way that promotes maximum independence and dignity for each resident and encourages the involvement of a resident's family, neighbor and friends.

Assistive Technology Center: A program providing access to specialized hardware and software with adaptations allowing individuals greater independence with mobility, dexterity, or increased communication options.

Auxiliary: A volunteer community organization formed to assist the hospital in carrying out its purpose and to serve as a link between the institution and the community.

Average daily census: The average number of people served on an inpatient basis on a single day during the reporting period; the figure is calculated by dividing the number of inpatient days by the number of days in the reporting period.

Bariatric/weight control services: Bariatrics is the medical practice of weight reduction.

Beds: Number of beds regularly maintained (set up and staffed for use) for inpatients as of the close of the reporting period. Excludes newborn bassinets.

Bed-size category: Hospitals are categorized by the number of beds set up and staffed for use at the end of the reporting period. The eight categories in Hospital Statistics are: 6 to 24 beds; 25 to 49; 50 to 99; 100 to 199; 200 to 299; 300 to 399; 400 to 499; and 500 or more.

Birthing room-LDR room-LDRP room: A single-room type of maternity care with a more homelike setting for families than the traditional three-room unit (labor/delivery/recovery) with a separate postpartum area. A birthing room combines labor and delivery in one room. An LDR room accommodates three stages in the birthing process—labor, delivery, and recovery. An LDRP room accommodates all four stages of the birth process—labor, delivery, recovery, and postpartum.

Births: Total number of infants born in the hospital during the reporting period. Births do not include infants transferred from other institutions, and are excluded from admission and discharge figures.

Blood Donor Center: A facility that performs, or is responsible for the collection, processing, testing or distribution of blood and components.

Bone marrow transplant: See definition for Transplant service on page 213.

Breast cancer screening/mammograms: Mammography screening – The use of breast x-ray to detect unsuspected breast cancer in asymptomatic women. Diagnostic mammography – The x-ray imaging of breast tissue in symptomatic women who are considered to have a substantial likelihood of having breast cancer already.

Burn care: Provides care to severely burned patients. Severely burned patients are those with any of the following: (1) second-degree burns of more than 25% total body surface area for adults or 20% total body surface area for children: (2) third-degree burns of more than 10% total body surface area; (3) any severe burns of the hands, face, eyes, ears, or feet; or (4) all inhalation injuries, electrical burns, complicated burn injuries involving fractures and other major traumas, and all other poor risk factors.

Cardiac electrophysiology: Evaluation and management of patients with complex rhythm or conduction abnormalities, including diagnostic testing, treatment of arrhythmias by catheter ablation or drug therapy, and pacemaker/defibrillator implantation and follow-up.

Cardiac intensive care: Provides patient care of a more specialized nature than the usual medical and surgical care, on the basis of physicians' orders and approved nursing care plans. The unit is staffed with specially trained nursing personnel and contains monitoring and specialized support or treatment equipment for patients who, because of heart seizure, open-heart surgery, or other life-threatening conditions, require intensified, comprehensive observation and care. May include myocardial infarction, pulmonary care, and heart transplant units.

Cardiac Rehabilitation: A medically supervised program to help heart patients recover quickly and improve their overall physical and mental functioning. The goal is to reduce risk of another cardiac event or to keep an already present heart condition from getting worse. Cardiac rehabilitation programs include: counseling to patients, an exercise program, helping patients modify risk factors such as smoking and high blood pressure, providing vocational guidance to enable the patient to return to work, supplying information on physical limitations and lending emotional support.

Case management: A system of assessment, treatment planning, referral and follow-up that ensures the provision of comprehensive and continuous services and the coordination of payment and reimbursement for care.

Chaplaincy/pastoral care services: A service ministering religious activities and providing pastoral counseling to patients, their families, and staff of a health care organization.

Chemotherapy: An organized program for the treatment of cancer by the use of drugs or chemicals.

Children's wellness program: A program that encourages improved health status and a healthful lifestyle of children through health education, exercise, nutrition and health promotion.

Chiropractic services: An organized clinical service including spinal manipulation or adjustment and related diagnostic and therapeutic services.

Closed physician-hospital organization (Closed PHO): A joint venture between the hospital and physicians who have been selected on the basis of cost-effectiveness and/or high quality. The PHO can act as a unified agent in managed care contracting, own a managed care plan, own and operate ambulatory care centers or ancillary services projects, or provide administrative services to physician members.

Community health education: Education that provides health information to individuals and populations, as well as support for personal, family and community health decisions with the objective of improving health status.

Community hospitals: All nonfederal, short-term general, and special hospitals whose facilities and services are available to the public. (Special hospitals include obstetrics and gynecology; eye, ear, nose, and throat; rehabilitation; orthopedic; and other individually described specialty services.) Short-term general and special childrens hospitals are also considered to be community hospitals.

A hospital may include a nursing-home-type unit and still be classified as short-term, provided that the majority of its patients are admitted to units where the average length of stay is less than 30 days. Therefore, statistics for community hospitals often include some data about such nursing-home-type units. An example is furnished by Montana, where in 1995 63.6 percent of all hospitals classified as community hospitals include nursing-home-type units. Expense, revenue, utilization, and personnel data for these hospitals include data about their nursing-home-type units. Thus, total admissions to Montana community hospitals in 1995 were 96,154; total inpatient days, 997,759; total expenses, $791,806,393; and total payroll expenses, $352,583,331. If nursing-home-type unit data were excluded, these same items would be 94,034; 457,340; 752,567,865; and $328,911841, respectively.

Note that before 1972, hospital units of institutions such as prison and college infirmaries were included in the category of community hospitals. Including these units made this category equivalent to the short-term general and other special hospitals category. Although these hospital units are few in number and small in size, this change in definition should be taken into consideration when comparing data.

Community outreach: A program that systematically interacts with the community to identify those in need of services, alerting persons and their families to the availability of services, locating needed services, and enabling persons to enter the service delivery system.

Complementary and alternative medicine services: Organized hospital services or formal arrangements to providers that provide care or treatment not based solely on traditional western allopathic medical teachings as instructed in most U.S. medical schools. Includes any of the following: acupuncture, chiropractic, homeopathy, osteopathy, diet and lifestyle changes, herbal medicine, message therapy, etc.

Computer assisted orthopedic surgery (CAOS): Orthopedic surgery using computer technology, enabling three-dimensional graphic models to visualize a patient's anatomy.

Control: The type of organization responsible for establishing policy concerning the overall operation of hospitals. The three major categories are government (including federal, state, and local); nongovernment (nonprofit); and investor-owned (for-profit).

Crisis prevention: Services provided in order to promote physical and mental well being and the early identification of disease and ill health prior to the onset and recognition of symptoms so as to permit early treatment.

CT scanner: Computed tomographic scanner for head or whole body scans.

Deduction from revenue: The difference between revenue at full established rates (gross) and the payment actually received from payers (net).

Dental Services: An organized dental service or dentists on staff, not necessarily involving special facilities, providing dental or oral services to inpatients or outpatients.

Diagnostic radioisotope facility: The use of radioactive isotopes (Radiopharmaceuticals) as tracers or indicators to detect an abnormal condition or disease.

Electrodiagnostic Services: Diagnostic testing services for nerve and muscle function including services such as nerve conduction studies and needle electromyography.

Electron beam computed tomography (EBCT): A high tech computed tomography scan used to detect coronary artery disease by measuring coronary calcifications. This imaging procedure uses electron beams which are magnetically steered to produce a visual of the coronary artery and the images are produced faster than conventional CT scans.

Emergency department: Hospital facilities for the provision of unscheduled outpatient services to patients whose conditions require immediate care.

Emergency room visits: The number of visits to the emergency unit. When emergency outpatients are admitted to the inpatient areas of the hospital, they are counted as emergency room visits and subsequently, as inpatient admissions.

Enabling services: A program that is designed to help the patient access health care services by offering any of the following: linguistic services, transportation services, and/or referrals to local social services agencies.

End of Life: Services offered to patients suffering from chronic, severe, and life-threatening diseases including comprehensive services that give patients and caregivers the resources and the confidence to manage symptoms, avoid emergency room admissions and frequent hospitalization, and remain in familiar and comfortable settings.

Endoscopic retrograde cholangiopancreatography (ERCP):
A procedure in which a catheter is introduced through an endoscope into the bile ducts and pancreatic ducts. Injection of contrast materials permits detailed x-ray of these structures. The procedure is used diagnostically as well as therapeutically to relieve obstruction or remove stones.

Endoscopic ultrasound:
Specially designed endoscope that incorporates an ultrasound transductor used to obtain detailed images of organs in the chest and abdomen. The endoscope can be passed through the mouth or the anus. When combined with needle biopsy the procedure can assist in diagnosis and staging of cancer.

Enrollment assistance services:
A program that provides enrollment assistance for patients who are potentially eligible for public health insurance programs such as Medicaid, State Children's Health Insurance, or local/state indigent care programs. The specific services offered could include explanation of benefits, assist applicants in completing the application and locating all relevant documents, conduct eligibility interviews, and/or forward applications and documentation to state/local social service or health agency.

Equity model:
An arrangement that allows established practitioners to become shareholders in a professional corporation in exchange for tangible and intangible assets of their existing practices.

Esophageal impedance study:
A test in which a catheter is placed through the nose into the esophagus to measure whether gas or liquids are passing from the stomach into the esophagus and causing symptoms.

Expenses:
Includes all expenses for the reporting period including payroll, non-payroll, and all nonoperating expenses. *Payroll expenses* include all salaries and wages. *Non-payroll expenses* are all professional fees and those salary expenditures excluded from payroll. *Labor related expenses* are defined as payroll expenses plus employee benefits. *Non-labor related expenses* are all other non-payroll expenses. *Bad debt* has been reclassified from a "reduction in revenue" to an expense in accordance with the revised AICPA Audit Guide. However, for purposes of historical consistency, the expense total that appears throughout *AHA Hospital Statistics* *does not include "bad debt" as an expense item.* Note: Financial data may not add due to rounding.

Extracorporeal shock wave lithotripter (ESWL):
A medical device used for treating stones in the kidney or urethra. The device disintegrates kidney stones noninvasively through the transmission of acoustic shock waves directed at the stones.

Fertility Clinic:
A specialized program set in an infertility center that provides counseling and education as well as advanced reproductive techniques such as: injectable therapy, reproductive surgeries, treatment for endometriosis, male factor infertility, tubal reversals, in vitro fertilization (IVF), donor eggs, and other such services to help patients achieve successful pregnancies.

Fitness center:
Provides exercise, testing, or evaluation programs and fitness activities to the community and hospital employees.

Foundation:
A corporation, organized as a hospital affiliate or subsidiary, that purchases both tangible and intangible assets of one or more medical group practices. Physicians remain in a separate corporate entity but sign a professional services agreement with the foundation.

Freestanding/Satellite Emergency Department:
A facility owned an operated by the hospital but physically separate from the hospital for the provision of unscheduled outpatient services to patients whose conditions require immediate care.

Full-field digital mammography (FFDM):
Combines the x-ray generators and tubes used in analog screen-film mammography (SFM) with a detector plate that converts the x-rays into a digital signal.

Full time equivalent employees (FTE):
Full time personnel on payroll plus one half of the part time personnel on payroll. For purposes of *AHA Hospital Statistics*, full time and part time medical and dental residents/interns and other trainees are excluded from the calculation.

General medical-surgical care:
Provides acute care to patients in medical and surgical units on the basis of physicians' orders and approved nursing care plans.

Genetic testing/counseling: A service equipped with adequate laboratory facilities and directed by a qualified physician to advise parents and prospective parents on potential problems in cases of genetic defects. A genetic test is the analysis of human DNA, RNA, chromosomes, proteins, and certain metabolites in order to detect heritable disease-related genotypes, mutations, phenotypes, or karyotypes for clinical purposes. Genetic tests can have diverse purposes, including the diagnosis of genetic diseases in newborns, children, and adults; the identification of future health risks; the prediction of drug responses; and the assessment of risks to future children.

Geriatric services: The branch of medicine dealing with the physiology of aging and the diagnosis and treatment of disease affecting the aged. Services could include: Adult day care; Alzheimer's diagnostic-assessment services; Comprehensive geriatric assessment; Emergency response system; Geriatric acute care unit; and/or Geriatric clinics.

Government, nonfederal, state, local: Controlled by an agency of state, county, or city government.

Gross inpatient revenue: Revenue from services rendered to inpatients at full established rates (also known as "charges").

Gross outpatient revenue: Revenue from services rendered to outpatients at full established rates.

Group practice without walls: In this organization, the hospital sponsors the formation of a physician group or provides capital to physicians to establish one. The group shares administrative expenses, although the physicians remain independent practitioners.

Group Purchasing Organization: An organization whose primary function is to negotiate contracts for the purpose of purchasing for members of the group or has a central supply site for its members.

Health fair: Community health education events that focus on the prevention of disease and promotion of health through such activities as audiovisual exhibits and free diagnostic services.

Health maintenance organization (HMO): A health care organization that acts as both insurer and provider of comprehensive but specified medical services in return for prospective per capita (capitation) payments.

Health Research: Organized hospital research program in any of the following areas: basic research, clinical research, community health research, and/or research on innovative health care delivery.

Health screening: A preliminary procedure such as a test or examination to detect the most characteristic sign or signs of a disorder that may require further investigation.

Heart transplant: See definition for Transplant services on page 213.

Hemodialysis: Provision of equipment and personnel for the treatment of renal insufficiency on an inpatient or outpatient basis.

HIV-AIDS services: (could include). *HIV-AIDS unit* – Special unit or team designated and equipped specifically for diagnosis, treatment, continuing care planning, and counseling services for HIV-AIDS patients and their families. *General inpatient care for HIV-AIDS* – Inpatient diagnosis and treatment for human immunodeficiency virus and acquired immunodeficiency syndrome patients, but dedicated unit is not available. *Specialized outpatient program for HIV-AIDS* – Special outpatient program providing diagnostic, treatment, continuing care planning, and counseling for HIV-AIDS patients and their families.

Home health services: Service providing nursing, therapy, and health-related homemaker or social services in the patient's home.

Hospice: A program providing palliative care, chiefly medical relief of pain and supportive services, addressing the emotional, social, financial, and legal needs of terminally ill patients and their families. Care can be provided in a variety of settings, both inpatient and at home.

Hospital unit: The hospital operation, excluding activity pertaining to nursing-home-type unit (as described below), for the following items: Admissions, Beds, FTEs (full-time, part-time, and total), Inpatient Days, Length of Stay, Net Revenue, and Total Expense.

Hospital unit of institutions: A hospital unit that is not open to the public and is contained within a nonhospital unit. An example is an infirmary that is contained within a college.

Hospitals in a network: Hospitals participating in a group that may include other hospitals, physicians, other providers, insurers, and/or community agencies that work together to coordinate and deliver a broad spectrum of services to the community.

Hospitals in a system: Hospitals belonging to a corporate body that owns and/or manages health provider facilities or health-related subsidiaries; the system may also own non-health-related facilities.

Image-guided radiation therapy (IGRT): Automated system for image-guided radiation therapy that enables clinicians to obtain high-resolution x-ray images to pinpoint tumor sites, adjust patient positioning when necessary, and complete a treatment, all within the standard treatment time slot, allowing for more effective cancer treatments.

Immunization program: Program that plans, coordinates and conducts immunization services in the community.

Indemnity fee for service: The traditional type of health insurance, in which the insured is reimbursed for covered expenses without regard to choice of provider. Payment up to a stated limit may be made either to the individual incurring and claiming the expense, or directly to providers.

Independent practice association (IPA): An IPA is a legal entity that holds managed care contracts and contracts with physicians, usually in solo practice, to provide care either on a fee-for-services or capitated basis. The purpose of an IPA is to assist solo physicians in obtaining managed care contracts.

Indigent care clinic: Health care services for uninsured and underinsured persons where care is free of charge or charged on a sliding scale. This would include "free clinics" staffed by volunteer practitioners, but could also be staffed by employees with sponsoring health care organizations subsidizing the cost of service.

Inpatient days: The number of adult and pediatric days of care, excluding newborn days of care, rendered during the entire reporting period.

Inpatient palliative care unit: An inpatient palliative care ward is a physically discreet, inpatient nursing unit where the focus is palliative care. The patient care focus is on symptom relief for complex patients who may be continuing to undergo primary treatment. Care is delivered by palliative medicine specialists.

Inpatient surgeries: Surgical services provided to patients who remain in the hospital overnight.

Insurance product: In tables 3 through 6, insurance product refers to a hospital-owned insurance product.

Integrated salary model: In this arrangement, physicians are salaried by the hospital or other entity of a health system to provide medical services for primary care and specialty care.

Intensity-Modulated Radiation Therapy (IMRT): A type of three-dimensional radiation therapy, which improves the targeting of treatment delivery in a way that is likely to decrease damage to normal tissues and allows varying intensities.

Intermediate nursing care: Provides health-related services (skilled nursing care and social services) to residents with a variety of physical conditions or functional disabilities. These residents do not require the care provided by a hospital or skilled nursing facility, but do need supervision and support services.

Intraoperative magnetic resonance imaging. An integrated surgery system which provides an MRI system in an operating room. The system allows for immediate evaluation of the degree to tumor resection while the patient is undergoing a surgical resection. Intraoperative MRI exists when a MRI (low-field or high-field) is placed in the operating theater and is used during surgical resection without moving the patient from the operating room to the diagnostic imaging suite.

Investor-owned, for-profit: Investor-owned, for-profit hospitals are those controlled on a for-profit basis by an individual, partnership, or profit-making corporation.

Kidney transplant: See definition for Transplant sevices on page 213.

Labor-related expenses: Payroll expenses plus employee benefits. *Non-labor-related expenses refers* to all other nonpayroll expenses, such as interest depreciation, supplies, purchased services, professional fees, and others.

Length of stay (LOS): LOS refers to the average number of days a patient stays at the facility. Short-term hospitals are those where the average LOS is less than 30 days. Long-term hospitals are those where the average LOS is 30 days or more. The figure is derived by dividing the number of inpatient days by the number of admissions.

Note that this publication carries two LOS variables: *total facility length of stay and hospital unit length of stay*. *Total facility* includes admissions and inpatient days from nursing-home-type units under control of the hospital. In *hospital unit length of stay*, nursing home utilization is subtracted.

Licensed practical nurse (LPN): A nurse who has graduated from an approved school of practical (vocational) nursing and works under the supervision of registered nurses and/or physicians.

Linguistic/Translation services: Services provided by the hospital designed to make health care more accessible to non-English speaking patients and their physicians.

Liver transplant: See definition for Transplant on page 213.

Long-term: Hospitals are classified either short-term or long-term according to the average length of stay (LOS). A long-term hospital is one in which the average LOS is 30 days or more.

Lung transplant: See definition for Transplant services on page 213.

Magnetic resonance imaging (MRI): The use of a uniform magnetic field and radio frequencies to study tissue and structure of the body. This procedure enables the visualization of biochemical activity of the cell in vivo without the use of ionizing radiation, radio-isotopic substances, or high-frequency sound.

Managed care: A term covering a broad spectrum of arrangements for health care delivery and financing, including managed indemnity plans (MIP), health maintenance organizations (HMO), preferred provider organizations (PPO), point-of-service plans (POS), and direct contracting arrangements between employers and providers.

Managed care contract: A contract between the hospital and a managed care organization.

Management services organization (MSO): A corporation owned by the hospital or a physician/hospital joint venture that provides management services to one or more medical group practices. As part of a full-service management agreement, the MSO purchases the tangible assets of the practices and leases them back, employs all non-physician staff, and provides all supplies/administrative systems for a fee.

Meals on wheels: A hospital sponsored program which delivers meals to people, usually the elderly, who are unable to prepare their own meals. Low cost, nutritional meals are delivered to individuals' homes on a regular basis.

Medical surgical intensive care: Provides patient care of a more intensive nature than the usual medical and surgical care, on the basis of physicians' orders and approved nursing care plans. These units are staffed with specially trained nursing personnel and contain monitoring and specialized support equipment for patients who, because of shock, trauma, or other life-threatening conditions, require intensified, comprehensive observation and care. Includes mixed intensive care units.

Mobile health services: Vans and other vehicles used to deliver primary care services.

Multi-slice spiral computed tomography (<64 slice CT): A specialized computed tomography procedure that provides three-dimensional processing and allows narrower and multiple slices with increased spatial resolution and faster scanning times as compared to a regular computed tomography scan.

Multi-slice spiral computed tomography (64+ slice CT): Involves the acquisition of volumetric tomographic x-ray absorption data expressed in Hounsfield units using multiple rows of detectors. 64+ systems reconstruct the equivalent of 64 or greater slices to cover the imaged volume.

Neonatal intensive care: A unit that must be separate from the newborn nursery providing intensive care to all sick infants including those with the very lowest birth weights (less than 1500 grams). NICU has potential for providing mechanical ventilation, neonatal surgery, and special care for the sickest infants born in the hospital or transferred from another institution. A full-time neonatologist serves as director of the NICU.

Neonatal intermediate care: A unit that must be separate from the normal newborn nursery and that provides intermediate and/or recovery care and some specialized services, including immediate resuscitation, intravenous therapy, and capacity for prolonged oxygen therapy and monitoring.

Net patient revenue: The estimated net realizable amounts from patients, third-party payers, and others for services rendered. The number includes estimated retroactive adjustments called for by agreements with third-party payers; retroactive adjustments are accrued on an estimated basis in the period the related services are rendered and then adjusted later as final settlements are determined.

Net total revenue: Net patient revenue plus all other revenue, including contributions, endowment revenue, governmental grants, and all other payments not made on behalf of individual patients.

Neurological services: Services provided by the hospital dealing with the operative and nonoperative management of disorders of the central, peripheral, and autonomic nervous system.

Nongovernment, nonprofit: Hospitals that are nongovernment, nonprofit are controlled by not-for-profit organizations, including religious organizations (Catholic hospitals, for example), fraternal societies, and others.

Nursing-home-type unit/facility: A unit/facility that primarily offers the following type of services to a majority of all admissions:

- *Skilled nursing*: The provision of medical and nursing care services, health-related services, and social services under the supervision of a registered nurse on a 24-hour basis.

- *Intermediate care*: The provision, on a regular basis, of health-related care and services to individuals who do not require the degree of care or treatment that a skilled nursing unit is designed to provide.

- *Personal care*: The provision of general supervision and direct personal care services for residents who require assistance in activities of daily living but who do not need nursing services or inpatient care. Medical and nursing services are available as needed.

- *Sheltered/residential care*: The provision of general supervision and protective services for residents who do not need nursing services or continuous personal care services in the conduct of daily life. Medical and nursing services are available as needed.

Nutrition programs: Those services within a health care facility which are designed to provide inexpensive, nutritionally sound meals to patients.

Obstetrics: Levels should be designated: (1) unit provides services for uncomplicated maternity and newborn cases; (2) unit provides services for uncomplicated cases, the majority of complicated problems, and special neonatal services; and (3) unit provides services for all serious illnesses and abnormalities and is supervised by a full-time maternal/fetal specialist.

Occupational health services: Includes services designed to protect the safety of employees from hazards in the work environment.

Oncology services: An organized program for the treatment of cancer by the use of drugs or chemicals.

Open physician hospital organization (Open PHO): A joint venture between the hospital and all members of the medical staff who wish to participate. The open PHO can act as a unified agent in managed care contracting, own a managed care plan, own and operate ambulatory care centers or ancillary services projects, or provide administrative services to physician members.

Optical colonoscopy: An examination of the interior of the colon using a long, flexible, lighted tube with a small built-in camera.

Orthopedic services: Services provided for the prevention or correction of injuries or disorders of the skeletal system and associated muscles, joints and ligaments.

Osteopathic hospitals: Osteopathic medicine is a medical practice based on a theory that diseases are due chiefly to a loss of structural integrity, which can be restored by manipulation of the neuro-muscular and skeletal systems, supplemented by therapeutic measures (such as medicine or surgery).

Other Intensive Care: A distinct intensive care unit that is not one of the following types: medical/surgical, cardiac, pediatric and neonatal.

Other long term care: Provision of long term care other than skilled nursing care or intermediate care. This can include residential care-elderly housing services for those who do not require daily medical or nursing services, but may require some assistance in the activities of daily living, or sheltered care facilities for developmentally disabled.

Other special care: Provides care to patients requiring care more intensive than that provided in the acute area, yet not sufficiently intensive to require admission to an intensive care unit. Patients admitted to this area are usually transferred here from an intensive care unit once their condition has improved. These units are sometimes referred to as definitive observation, step-down, or progressive care units.

Other transplant: See definition for Transplant services on page 213.

Outpatient care: Treatment provided to patients who do not remain in the hospital for overnight care. Hospitals may deliver outpatient care on site or through a facility owned and operated by the hospital, but physically separate from the hospital. In addition to treating minor illnesses or injuries, a free-standing center will stabilize seriously ill or injured patients before transporting them to a hospital. Laboratory and radiology services are usually available.

Outpatient care center (Freestanding): A facility owned and operated by the hospital, but physically separate from the hospital, that provides various medical treatments on an outpatient basis only. In addition to treating minor illnesses or injuries, the center will stabilize seriously ill or injured patients before transporting them to a hospital. Laboratory and radiology services are usually available.

Outpatient care center-services (Hospital-based): Organized hospital health care services offered by appointment on an ambulatory basis. Services may include outpatient surgery, examination, diagnosis, and treatment of a variety of medical conditions on a nonemergency basis, and laboratory and other diagnostic testing as ordered by staff or outside physician referral.

Outpatient surgeries: Scheduled surgical services provided to patients who do not remain in the hospital overnight. In the AHA Annual Survey, outpatient surgery may be performed in operating suites also used for inpatient surgery, specially designated surgical suites for outpatient surgery, or procedure rooms within an outpatient care facility.

Outpatient visit: A visit by a patient who is not lodged in the hospital while receiving medical, dental, or other services. Each visit an outpatient makes to a discrete unit constitutes one visit regardless of the number of diagnostic and/or therapeutic treatments that the patient receives. Total outpatient visits should include all clinic visits, referred visits, observation services, outpatient surgeries, and emergency room visits.

Pain Management Program: A recognized clinical service or program providing specialized medical care, drugs or therapies for the management of acute or chronic pain or other distressing symptom, administered by specially trained physicians and other clinicians, to patients suffering from acute illness of diverse causes.

Palliative Care Inpatient Unit: An inpatient palliative care ward is a physically discreet, inpatient nursing unit where the focus is palliative care. The patient care focus is on symptom relief for complex patients who may be continuing to undergo primary treatment. Care is delivered by palliative medicine specialists.

Palliative care program: An organized program providing specialized medical care, drugs or therapies for the management of acute or chronic pain and/or the control of symptoms administered by specially trained physicians and other clinicians; and supportive care services, such as counseling on advanced directives, spiritual care, and social services, to patients with advanced disease and their families.

Patient Controlled Analgesia (PCA). Patient-controlled Analgesia (PCA) is intravenously administered pain medicine under the patient's control. The patient has a button on the end of a cord than can be pushed at will, whenever more pain medicine is desired. This button will only deliver more pain medicine at pre-determined intervals, as programmed by the doctor's order.

Patient education center: Written goals and objectives for the patient and/or family related to therapeutic regimens, medical procedures, and self care.

Patient representative services: Organized hospital services providing personnel through whom patients and staff can seek solutions to institutional problems affecting the delivery of high-quality care and services.

Payroll expenses: Includes all salaries and wages. All professional fees and salary expenditures excluded from payroll, such as employee benefits, are defined as nonpayroll expenses and are included in total expenses.

Pediatric Cardiac Surgery: Includes minimally invasive procedures that include surgery done with only a small incision or no incision at all, such as through a laparoscope or an endoscope and more invasive major surgical procedures that include open chest and open heart surgery.

Pediatric Cardiology Services: An organized clinical service offering diagnostic and interventional procedures to manage the full range of pediatric heart conditions.

Pediatric Diagnostic/invasive catheterization: (also called coronary angiography or coronary arteriography) is used to assist in diagnosing complex heart conditions. Cardiac angiography involves the insertion of a tiny catheter into the artery in the groin then carefully threading the catheter up into the aorta where the coronary arteries originate. Once the catheter is in place, a dye is injected which allows the cardiologist to see the size, shape, and distribution of the coronary arteries. These images are used to diagnose heart disease and to determine, among other things, whether or not surgery is indicated.

Pediatric intensive care: Provides care to pediatric patients that is of a more intensive nature than that usually provided to pediatric patients. The unit is staffed with specially trained personnel and contains monitoring and specialized support equipment for treatment of patients who, because of shock, trauma, or other life-threatening conditions, require intensified, comprehensive observation and care.

Pediatric Interventional cardiac catheterization: Non surgical procedure that utilizes the same basic principles as diagnostic catheterization and then uses advanced techniques to improve the heart's function. It can be a less-invasive alternative to heart surgery.

Pediatric medical-surgical care: Provides acute care to pediatric patients on the basis of physicians' orders and approved nursing care plans.

Personnel: Number of persons on the hospital payroll at the end of the reporting period. Personnel are recorded in *Hospital Statistics* as full-time equivalents (FTEs), which are calculated by adding the number of full-time personnel to one-half the number of part-time personnel, excluding medical and dental residents, interns, and other trainees. *Per 100 adjusted census* indicates the ratio of personnel to adjusted average daily census, calculated on a per-100 basis.

Physical rehabilitation inpatient care: Provides care encompassing a comprehensive array of restoration services for the disabled and all support services necessary to help patients attain their maximum functional capacity.

Physical rehabilitation outpatient services: Outpatient program providing medical, health-related, therapy, social, and/or vocational services to help disabled persons attain or retain their maximum functional capacity.

Population: Population refers to the residential population of the United States. This includes both civilian and military personnel. Note that population is being used to calculate the values *for community health indicators per 1000 population.*

Positron emission tomography/CT (PET/CT): Provides metabolic functional information for the monitoring of chemotherapy, radiotherapy and surgical planning.

Positron emission tomography scanner (PET): A nuclear medicine imaging technology which uses radioactive (positron emitting) isotopes created in a cyclotron or generator and computers to produce composite pictures of the brain and heart at work. PET scanning produces sectional images depicting metabolic activity or blood flow rather than anatomy.

Preferred provider organization (PPO): A pre-set arrangement in which purchasers and providers agree to furnish specified health services to a group of employees/patients.

Primary care department: A unit or clinic within the hospital that provides primary care services (e.g. general pediatric care, general internal medicine, family practice, gynecology) through hospital-salaried medical and/or nursing staff, focusing on evaluating and diagnosing medical problems and providing medical treatment on an outpatient basis.

Prosthetic and Orthotic Services:
Services providing comprehensive prosthetic and orthotic evaluation, fitting, and training.

Proton beam therapy:
A form of radiation therapy which administers proton beams. While producing the same biologic effects as x-ray beams, the energy distribution of protons differs from conventional x-ray beams in that they can be more precisely focused in tissue volumes in a three-dimensional pattern resulting in less surrounding tissue damage than conventional radiation therapy permitting administration of higher doses.

Psychiatric child-adolescent services:
Provides care to emotionally disturbed children and adolescents, including those admitted for diagnosis and those admitted for treatment.

Psychiatric consultation-liaison services:
Provides organized psychiatric consultation/liaison services to nonpsychiatric hospital staff and/or departments on psychological aspects of medical care that may be generic or specific to individual patients.

Psychiatric education services:
Provides psychiatric educational services to community agencies and workers such as schools, police, courts, public health nurses, welfare agencies, clergy, and so forth. The purpose is to expand the mental health knowledge and competence of personnel not working in the mental health field and to promote good mental health through improved understanding, attitudes, and behavioral patterns.

Psychiatric emergency services:
Services of facilities available on a 24-hour basis to provide immediate unscheduled out-patient care, diagnosis, evaluation, crisis intervention, and assistance to persons suffering acute emotional or mental distress.

Psychiatric geriatric services:
Provides care to emotionally disturbed elderly patients, including those admitted for diagnosis and those admitted for treatment.

Psychiatric inpatient care:
Provides acute or long-term care to emotionally disturbed patients, including patients admitted for diagnosis and those admitted for treatment of psychiatric problems, on the basis of physicians' orders and approved nursing care plans. Long-term care may include intensive supervision to the chronically mentally ill, mentally disordered, or other mentally incompetent persons.

Psychiatric outpatient services:
Provides medical care, including diagnosis and treatment, of psychiatric outpatients.

Psychiatric partial hospitalization program:
Organized hospital services of intensive day/evening outpatient services of three hours of more duration, distinguished from other outpatient visits of one hour.

Radiology, diagnostic:
The branch of radiology that deals with the utilization of all modalities of radiant energy in medical diagnoses and therapeutic procedures using radiologic guidance. This includes, but is not restricted to, imaging techniques and methodologies utilizing radiation emitted by x-ray tubes, radionnuclides, and ultrasonographic devices and the radiofrequency electromagnetic radiation emitted by atoms.

Radiology, therapeutic:
The branch of medicine concerned with radioactive substances and using various techniques of visualization, with the diagnosis and treatment of disease using any of the various sources of radiant energy. Services could include: megavoltage radiation therapy; radioactive implants; stereotactic radiosurgery; therapeutic radioisotope facility; X-ray radiation therapy.

Registered nurse (RN):
A nurse who has graduated from an approved school of nursing and who is currently registered by the state. RNs are responsible for the nature and quality of all nursing care that patients receive. In these tables, the number of RNs does not include those registered nurses more appropriately reported in other occupational categories, such as facility administrators, which are listed under *all other personnel* (Tables 1 and 2).

Rehabilitation services:
A wide array of restoration services for disabled and recuperating patients, including all support services necessary to help them attain their maximum functional capacity.

Retirement housing:
A facility which provides social activities to senior citizens, usually retired persons, who do not require health care but some short-term skilled nursing care may be provided. A retirement center may furnish housing and may also have acute hospital and long-term care facilities, or it may arrange for acute and long term care through affiliated institutions.

Robot-assisted walking therapy:
A form of physical therapy that uses a robotic device to assist patients who are relearning how to walk.

Robotic surgery: The use of mechanical guidance devices to remotely manipulate surgical instrumentation.

Rural: A rural hospital is located outside a Metropolitan Statistical Area (MSA), as designated by the U.S. Office of Management and Budget (OMB) effective June 6, 2003. An urban area is a geographically defined, integrated social and economic unit with a large population nucleus. Micropolitan areas, which are new to the OMB June 6, 2003 definitions, continue to be classified as rural for purposes of this publication.

Rural Health Clinic: A clinic located in a rural, medically under-served area in the United States that has a separate reimbursement structure from the standard medical office under the Medicare and Medicaid programs.

Shaped beam radiation system: A precise, non-invasive treatment that involves targeting beams of radiation that mirror the exact size and shape of a tumor at a specific area of a tumor to shrink or destroy cancerous cells. This procedure delivers a therapeutic dose of radiation that conforms precisely to the shape of the tumor, thus minimizing the risk to nearby tissues.

Simulated rehabilitation environment: Rehabilitation focused on retraining functional skills in a contextually appropriate environment (simulated home and community settings) or in a traditional setting (gymnasium) using motor learning principles.

Single photon emission computerized tomography (SPECT): A nuclear medicine imaging technology that combines existing technology of gamma camera imaging with computed tomographic imaging technology to provide a more precise and clear image.

Skilled nursing care: Provides non-acute medical and skilled nursing care services, therapy, and social services under the supervision of a licensed registered nurse on a 24-hour basis.

Sleep Center: Specially equipped and staffed center for the diagnosis and treatment of sleep disorders.

Social work services (could include): Organized services that are properly directed and sufficiently staffed by qualified individuals who provide assistance and counseling to patients and their families in dealing with social, emotional, and environmental problems associated with illness or disability, often in the context of financial or discharge planning coordination.

Sports medicine: Provision of diagnostic screening and assessment and clinical and rehabilitation services for the prevention and treatment of sports-related injuries.

Stereotactic radiosurgery: Stereotactic radiosurgery (SRS) is a radiotherapy modality that delivers a high dosage of radiation to a discrete treatment area in as few as one treatment session. Includes gamma knife, cyberknife, etc.

Support groups: A hospital sponsored program which allows a group of individuals with the same or similar problems who meet periodically to share experiences, problems, and solutions in order to support each other.

Surgical operations: Those surgical operations, whether major or minor, performed in the operating room(s). A surgical operation involving more than one surgical procedure is still considered only one surgical operation.

Swing bed services: A hospital bed that can be used to provide either acute or long-term care depending on community or patient needs. To be eligible a hospital must have a Medicare provider agreement in place, have fewer than 100 beds, be located in a rural area, do not have a 24 hour nursing service waiver in effect, have not been terminated from the program in the prior two years, and meet various service conditions.

Teen outreach services: A program focusing on the teenager which encourages an improved health status and a healthful lifestyle including physical, emotional, mental, social, spiritual and economic health through education, exercise, nutrition and health promotion.

Tissue transplant: See definition for Transplant sevices on page 213.

Tobacco treatment/cessation program: Organized hospital services with the purpose of ending tobacco-use habits of patients addicted to tobacco/nicotine.

Transplant services. The branch of medicine that transfers an organ or tissue from one person to another or from one body part to another to replace a diseased structure or to restore function or to change appearance. Services could include: Bone marrow transplant program; heart, lung, kidney, intestine, or tissue transplant. The other transplant services include transplant services other than bone marrow, heart, kidney, liver, lung, tissue and heart/lung or other multi-transplant surgeries.

Transportation to health facilities:
A long-term care support service designed to assist the mobility of the elderly. Some programs offer improved financial access by offering reduced rates and barrier-free buses or vans with ramps and lifts to assist the elderly or handicapped; others offer subsidies for public transport systems or operate mini-bus services exclusively for use by senior citizens.

Trauma center (certified): A facility to provide emergency and specialized intensive care to critically ill and injured patients. **Level 1:** A regional resource trauma center, which is capable of providing total care for every aspect of injury and plays a leadership role in trauma research and education. **Level 2:** A community trauma center, which is capable of providing trauma care to all but the most severely injured patients who require highly specialized care. **Level 3:** A rural trauma hospital, which is capable of providing care to a large number of injury victims and can resuscitate and stabilize more severely injured patients so that they can be transported to Level 1 or 2 facilities.

Ultrasound: The use of acoustic waves above the range of 20,000 cycles per second to visualize internal body structures.

Urban: An urban hospital is located inside a Metropolitan Statistical Area (MSA), designated by the U.S. Office of Management and Budget effective June 6, 2003. An urban areas is a geographically defined, integrated social and economic unit with a large population base. Micropolitan areas, which are new to the OMB June 6, 2003 definitions, are not considered to be urban for purposes of this publication.

Urgent care center: A facility that provides care and treatment for problems that are not life-threatening but require attention over the short term. These units function like emergency rooms but are separate from hospitals with which they may have backup affiliation arrangements.

Virtual colonoscopy: Noninvasive screening procedure used to visualize, analyze and detect cancerous or potentially cancerous polyps in the colon.

Volunteer services department: An organized hospital department responsible for coordinating the services of volunteers working within the institution.

Women's health center/services: An area set aside for coordinated education and treatment services specifically for and promoted to women as provided by this special unit. Services may or may not include obstetrics but include a range of services other than OB.

Wound Management Services: Services for patients with chronic wounds and nonhealing wounds often resulting from diabetes, poor circulation, improper seating and immunocompromising conditions. The goals are to progress chronic wounds through stages of healing, reduce and eliminate infections, increase physical function to minimize complications from current wounds and prevent future chronic wounds. Wound management services are provided on an inpatient or outpatient basis, depending on the intensity of service needed.

2010 AHA Annual Survey
Health Forum, L.L.C.

Please return to:
AHA Annual Survey
155 N. Wacker Drive
Chicago, IL 60606

A. REPORTING PERIOD (please refer to the instructions and definitions at the end of this questionnaire)

Report data for a full 12-month period, preferably your last completed fiscal year (365 days). (Be consistent in using the same reporting period for responses throughout various sections of this survey.)

1. Reporting Period used (beginning and ending date) ...... ___ / ___ / __ __ __ __ to ___ / ___ / __ __ __ __
   Month   Day   Year   Month   Day   Year

2. a. Were you in operation 12 full months
   at the end of your reporting period .... YES ☐   NO ☐

   b. Number of days open
      during reporting period .... _____

3. Indicate the beginning of your current fiscal year .... ___ / ___ / __ __ __ __
   Month   Day   Year

B. ORGANIZATIONAL STRUCTURE

1. CONTROL

Indicate the type of organization that is responsible for establishing policy for overall operation of your hospital. CHECK ONLY ONE:

Government, nonfederal
- ☐ 12 State
- ☐ 13 County
- ☐ 14 City
- ☐ 15 City-County
- ☐ 16 Hospital district or authority

Nongovernment, not-for profit (NFP)
- ☐ 21 Church-operated
- ☐ 23 Other not-for-profit (including NFP Corporation)

Investor-owned, for-profit
- ☐ 31 Individual
- ☐ 32 Partnership
- ☐ 33 Corporation

Government, federal
- ☐ 41 Air Force
- ☐ 42 Army
- ☐ 43 Navy
- ☐ 44 Public Health Service
- ☐ 45 Veterans' Affairs
- ☐ 46 Federal other than 41-45 or 47-48
- ☐ 47 PHS Indian Service
- ☐ 48 Department of Justice

2. SERVICE

Indicate the ONE category that BEST describes your hospital or the type of service it provides to the MAJORITY of patients:

- ☐ 10 General medical and surgical
- ☐ 11 Hospital unit of an institution (prison hospital, college infirmary)
- ☐ 12 Hospital unit within an institution for the mentally retarded
- ☐ 13 Surgical
- ☐ 22 Psychiatric
- ☐ 33 Tuberculosis and other respiratory diseases
- ☐ 41 Cancer
- ☐ 42 Heart
- ☐ 44 Obstetrics and gynecology
- ☐ 45 Eye, ear, nose, and throat

- ☐ 46 Rehabilitation
- ☐ 47 Orthopedic
- ☐ 48 Chronic disease
- ☐ 62 Institution for the mentally retarded
- ☐ 80 Acute long-term care hospital
- ☐ 82 Alcoholism and other chemical dependency
- ☐ 49 Other-specify treatment area: _____

3. OTHER

a. Does your hospital restrict admissions primarily to children? .... YES ☐   NO ☐

1

B. ORGANIZATIONAL STRUCTURE (continued)

b. Does the hospital itself operate subsidiary corporations? .... YES ☐   NO ☐

c. Is the hospital contract managed? If yes, please provide the name, city, and state of the organization .. YES ☐   NO ☐

   Name: _____   City: _____   State: _____

d. Is the hospital a participant in a network?

   If yes, please provide the name, city and state and telephone number........ YES ☐   NO ☐
   of the network. If the hospital participates in more than one network, please provide the name, city, and state and telephone number of the network on page 13, under supplemental information.
   Name: _____   City: _____   State: _____ Telephone_____

e. Is your hospital owned in whole or in part by physicians or a physician group?... YES ☐   NO ☐

f. If you checked 80 Acute long-term care hospital (LTCH) in the Section B2 (Service), please indicate if you are a freestanding LTCH or a LTCH collocated within a general acute care hospital.
   ☐ Free standing LTCH   ☐ LTCH collocated in a general acute care hospital

   If you are collocated in a general acute care hospital, what is your host hospital's name?
   Name_____   City_____   State_____

4.   NATIONAL PROVIDER IDENTIFIER (NPI)

a. Does your hospital have its new National Provider Identifier (NPI) from the National Plan and Provider Enumeration System?
   Yes ☐   No ☐

If yes, please report the ten digit NPI _ _ _ _ _ _ _ _ _ _

Does your hospital also have a Subpart NPI? Yes_____   No____

If yes, please report the Subpart NPI and provide the relevant taxonomy code to indicate the type of service provided. If you have multiple Subpart NPIs please report them all (in the supplemental section on page 12, at the end of this questionnaire or on a separate sheet).

Subpart NPI 1 _ _ _ _ _ _ _ _ _ _   Taxonomy Code _ _

Subpart NPI 2 _ _ _ _ _ _ _ _ _ _   Taxonomy Code _ _

Subpart NPI 3 _ _ _ _ _ _ _ _ _ _   Taxonomy Code _ _

Taxonomy Codes
Ambulatory Health Care Facility   01
Medicare Defined Swing Bed Unit 02
Psychiatric Unit   03
Rehabilitation Unit   04
Rehabilitation, Substance Use Disorder Unit 05
Laboratory   06
Nursing and Custodial Care Facility   07
Residential Treatment Facility   08
Respite Care Facility   09
Other 10

2

C. FACILITIES AND SERVICES

For each service or facility listed below, please check all the categories that describe how each item is provided **as of the last day of the reporting period**. Check all categories that apply for an item. Leave all categories blank for a facility or service that is not provided. Column 3 refers to the networks that were identified in section B, question 3d. If you checked column (1) C1-19, please include the number of beds.
The sum of the beds reported in 1-19 should equal Section D(1b), beds set up and staffed on page 8.

	(1) Owned or provided by my hospital or its subsidiary	(2) Provided by my Health System (in my local community)	(3) Provided by my network (in my local community)	(4) Provided through a formal contractual arrangement or joint venture with another provider that is not in my system or network
1. General medical-surgical care.....................(# Beds: _____)	☐	☐	☐	☐
2. Pediatric medical-surgical care ....(# Beds: _____)	☐	☐	☐	☐
3. Obstetrics [Level of unit (1-3): (___)]................(# Beds: _____)	☐	☐	☐	☐
4. Medical- surgical intensive care.....................(# Beds: _____)	☐	☐	☐	☐
5. Cardiac intensive care.................................(# Beds: _____)	☐	☐	☐	☐
6. Neonatal intensive care............................. (# Beds: _____)	☐	☐	☐	☐
7. Neonatal intermediate care...........................(# Beds: _____)	☐	☐	☐	☐
8. Pediatric intensive care................................ (# Beds:_____)	☐	☐	☐	☐
9. Burn care.. (# Beds: _____)	☐	☐	☐	☐
10. Other special care _____..... (# Beds: _____)	☐	☐	☐	☐
11. Other intensive care_____......(# Beds: _____)	☐	☐	☐	☐
12. Physical rehabilitation................................(# Beds: _____)	☐	☐	☐	☐
13. Alcoholism-drug abuse or dependency care.......(# Beds: _____)	☐	☐	☐	☐
14. Psychiatric care...(# Beds: _____)	☐	☐	☐	☐
15. Skilled nursing care.................................. (# Beds: _____)	☐	☐	☐	☐
16. Intermediate nursing care.............................(# Beds: _____)	☐	☐	☐	☐
17. Acute long-term care.................................. (# Beds: _____)	☐	☐	☐	☐
18. Other long-term care................................ (# Beds: _____)	☐	☐	☐	☐
19. Other care (specify): _____......(# Beds: _____)	☐	☐	☐	☐
20. Adult day care program....................................	☐	☐	☐	☐
21. Airborne infection isolation room (# rooms _____).....................	☐	☐	☐	☐
22. Alcoholism-drug abuse or dependency outpatient services..........	☐	☐	☐	☐
23. Alzheimer Center..	☐	☐	☐	☐
24. Ambulance services...	☐	☐	☐	☐
25. Ambulatory surgery center....................................	☐	☐	☐	☐
26. Arthritis treatment center.....................................	☐	☐	☐	☐
27. Assisted living...	☐	☐	☐	☐
28. Auxiliary...	☐	☐	☐	☐
29. Bariatric/weight control services.............................	☐	☐	☐	☐
30. Birthing room/LDR room/LDRP room..............................	☐	☐	☐	☐
31. Blood Donor Center..	☐	☐	☐	☐
32. Breast cancer screening/mammograms..............................	☐	☐	☐	☐

C. FACILITIES AND SERVICES (continued)

	(1) Owned or provided by my hospital or its subsidiary	(2) Provided by my Health System (in my local community)	(3) Provided by my network (in my local community)	(4) Provided through formal contractual arrangement or joint venture with another provider that is not in my system or network (in local community)
33. Cardiology and cardiac surgery services				
a. Adult cardiology services	☐	☐	☐	☐
b. Pediatric cardiology services	☐	☐	☐	☐
c. Adult diagnostic catheterization	☐	☐	☐	☐
d. Pediatric diagnostic catheterization	☐	☐	☐	☐
e. Adult interventional cardiac catheterization	☐	☐	☐	☐
f. Pediatric interventional cardiac catheterization	☐	☐	☐	☐
g. Adult cardiac surgery	☐	☐	☐	☐
h. Pediatric cardiac surgery	☐	☐	☐	☐
i. Adult cardiac electrophysiology	☐	☐	☐	☐
j. Pediatric cardiac electrophysiology	☐	☐	☐	☐
k. Cardiac rehabilitation	☐	☐	☐	☐
34. Case management	☐	☐	☐	☐
35. Chaplaincy/pastoral care services	☐	☐	☐	☐
36. Chemotherapy	☐	☐	☐	☐
37. Children's wellness program	☐	☐	☐	☐
38. Chiropractic services	☐	☐	☐	☐
39. Community outreach	☐	☐	☐	☐
40. Complementary and alternative medicine services	☐	☐	☐	☐
41. Computer assisted orthopedic surgery (CAOS)	☐	☐	☐	☐
42. Crisis prevention	☐	☐	☐	☐
43. Dental services	☐	☐	☐	☐
44. Emergency services				
a. Emergency department	☐	☐	☐	☐
b. Satellite emergency department	☐	☐	☐	☐
c. If you checked column 1 (44b), is the department open 24 hours a day, 7 days a week?	Yes ☐	No ☐		
d. Trauma center (certified) [Level of unit (1-3) ____]	☐	☐	☐	☐
45. Enabling services	☐	☐	☐	☐
46. Endoscopic services				
a. Optical colonoscopy	☐	☐	☐	☐
b. Endoscopic ultrasound	☐	☐	☐	☐
c. Ablation of Barrett's esophagus	☐	☐	☐	☐
d. Esophageal impedance study	☐	☐	☐	☐
e. Endoscopic retrograde cholangiopancreatography (ERCP)	☐	☐	☐	☐
47. Enrollment assistance services	☐	☐	☐	☐
48. Extracorporeal shock wave lithotripter (ESWL)	☐	☐	☐	☐
49. Fertility clinic	☐	☐	☐	☐
50. Fitness center	☐	☐	☐	☐
51. Freestanding outpatient care center	☐	☐	☐	☐
52. Geriatric services	☐	☐	☐	☐
53. Health fair	☐	☐	☐	☐

C. FACILITIES AND SERVICES (continued)

	(1) Owned or provided by my hospital or its subsidiary	(2) Provided by my Health System (in my local community)	(3) Provided by my network (in my local community)	(4) Provided through a formal contractual arrangement or joint venture with another provider that is not in my system or network (in local community)
4. Community health education	☐	☐	☐	☐
5. Genetic testing/counseling	☐	☐	☐	☐
6. Health screenings	☐	☐	☐	☐
7. Health research	☐	☐	☐	☐
8. Hemodialysis	☐	☐	☐	☐
9. HIV/AIDS services	☐	☐	☐	☐
0. Home health services	☐	☐	☐	☐
1. Hospice program	☐	☐	☐	☐
2. Hospital-based outpatient care center services	☐	☐	☐	☐
3. Immunization program	☐	☐	☐	☐
4. Indigent care clinic	☐	☐	☐	☐
5. Linguistic/translation services	☐	☐	☐	☐
6. Meal on wheels	☐	☐	☐	☐
7. Mobile health services	☐	☐	☐	☐
8. Neurological services	☐	☐	☐	☐
9. Nutrition program	☐	☐	☐	☐
0. Occupational health services	☐	☐	☐	☐
1. Oncology services	☐	☐	☐	☐
2. Orthopedic services	☐	☐	☐	☐
3. Outpatient surgery	☐	☐	☐	☐
4. Pain management program	☐	☐	☐	☐
5. Palliative care program	☐	☐	☐	☐
6. Palliative care inpatient unit	☐	☐	☐	☐
7. Patient controlled analgesia (PCA)	☐	☐	☐	☐
8. Patient education center	☐	☐	☐	☐
9. Patient representative services	☐	☐	☐	☐
0. Physical rehabilitation services				
a. Assistive technology center	☐	☐	☐	☐
b. Electrodiagnostic services	☐	☐	☐	☐
c. Physical rehabilitation outpatient services	☐	☐	☐	☐
d. Prosthetic and orthotic services	☐	☐	☐	☐
e. Robot-assisted walking therapy	☐	☐	☐	☐
f. Simulated rehabilitation environment	☐	☐	☐	☐
1. Primary care department	☐	☐	☐	☐
2. Psychiatric services				
a. Psychiatric child-adolescent services	☐	☐	☐	☐
b. Psychiatric consultation-liaison services	☐	☐	☐	☐
c. Psychiatric education services	☐	☐	☐	☐
d. Psychiatric emergency services	☐	☐	☐	☐
e. Psychiatric geriatric services	☐	☐	☐	☐
f. Psychiatric outpatient services	☐	☐	☐	☐
g. Psychiatric partial hospitalization services	☐	☐	☐	☐

C. FACILITIES AND SERVICES (continued)

	(1) Owned or provided by my hospital or its subsidiary	(2) Provided by my Health System (in my local community)	(3) Provided by my network (in my local community)	(4) Provided through formal contractual arrangement or joint venture with another provider that is not in my system or network (in local community)
83. Radiology, diagnostic				
a. CT Scanner	☐	☐	☐	☐
b. Diagnostic radioisotope facility	☐	☐	☐	☐
c. Electron beam computed tomography (EBCT)	☐	☐	☐	☐
d. Full-field digital mammography (FFDM)	☐	☐	☐	☐
e. Magnetic resonance imaging (MRI)	☐	☐	☐	☐
f. Intraoperative magnetic resonance imaging	☐	☐	☐	☐
g. Multi-slice spiral computed tomography (<64+ slice CT)	☐	☐	☐	☐
h. Multi-slice spiral computed tomography (64+ slice CT)	☐	☐	☐	☐
i. Positron emission tomography (PET)	☐	☐	☐	☐
j. Positron emission tomography/CT (PET/CT)	☐	☐	☐	☐
k. Single photon emission computerized tomography (SPECT)	☐	☐	☐	☐
l. Ultrasound	☐	☐	☐	☐
84. Radiology, therapeutic				
a. Image-guided radiation therapy (IGRT)	☐	☐	☐	☐
b. Intensity-modulated radiation therapy (IMRT)	☐	☐	☐	☐
c. Proton beam therapy	☐	☐	☐	☐
d. Shaped beam radiation system	☐	☐	☐	☐
e. Stereotactic radiosurgery	☐	☐	☐	☐
85. Retirement housing	☐	☐	☐	☐
86. Robotic surgery	☐	☐	☐	☐
87. Rural health clinic	☐	☐	☐	☐
88. Sleep center	☐	☐	☐	☐
89. Social work services	☐	☐	☐	☐
90. Sports medicine	☐	☐	☐	☐
91. Support groups	☐	☐	☐	☐
92. Swing bed services	☐	☐	☐	☐
93. Teen outreach services	☐	☐	☐	☐
94. Tobacco treatment/cessation program	☐	☐	☐	☐
95. Transplant services				
a. Bone marrow	☐	☐	☐	☐
b. Heart	☐	☐	☐	☐
c. Kidney	☐	☐	☐	☐
d. Liver	☐	☐	☐	☐
e. Lung	☐	☐	☐	☐
f. Tissue	☐	☐	☐	☐
g. Other	☐	☐	☐	☐
96. Transportation to health services	☐	☐	☐	☐
97. Urgent care center	☐	☐	☐	☐
98. Virtual colonoscopy	☐	☐	☐	☐
99. Volunteer services department	☐	☐	☐	☐
100. Women's health center/services	☐	☐	☐	☐
101. Wound management services	☐	☐	☐	☐

C. FACILITIES AND SERVICES (continued)

102a. In which of the following physician arrangements does your hospital or system/network participate? Column 3 refers to the networks that were identified in section B, question 3d. For hospital level physician arrangements that are reported in column 1, please report the number of physicians involved.

	(1) My Hospital		(2) My Health System	(3) My Health Network
a. Independent Practice Association	☐	(# of physicians _____)	☐	☐
b. Group practice without walls	☐	(# of physicians _____)	☐	☐
c. Open Physician-Hospital Organization (PHO)	☐	(# of physicians _____)	☐	☐
d. Closed Physician-Hospital Organization (PHO)	☐	(# of physicians _____)	☐	☐
e. Management Service Organization (MSO)	☐	(# of physicians _____)	☐	☐
f. Integrated Salary Model	☐	(# of physicians _____)	☐	☐
g. Equity Model	☐	(# of physicians _____)	☐	☐
h. Foundation	☐	(# of physicians _____)	☐	☐
i. Other, please specify _____	☐	(# of physicians _____)	☐	☐

102b. Looking across all the relationships identified in question 102a, what is the total number of physicians (count each physician only once) that are engaged in an arrangement with your hospital that allows for joint contracting with payers or shared responsibility for financial risk or clinical performance between the hospital and physician (arrangement may be at the hospital, system or network level)?   # of physicians _____

103a. Does your hospital participate in any joint venture arrangements with physicians or physician groups?   YES ☐   NO ☐

103b. If your hospital participates in any joint ventures with physicians or physician groups, please indicate which types of services are involved in those joint ventures (Check all that apply)

- a. ☐ Limited service hospital
- b. ☐ Ambulatory surgical centers
- c. ☐ Imaging centers
- d. ☐ Other _____

103c. If you selected 'a. Limited Service Hospital', please tell us what type(s) of services are provided. (Check all that apply.)

- a. ☐ Cardiac
- b. ☐ Orthopedic
- c. ☐ Surgical
- d. ☐ Other _____

103d. Does your hospital participate in joint venture arrangements with organizations other than physician groups?   YES ☐   NO ☐

104. Does your hospital, health system or health network have an equity interest in any of the following insurance products? (Check all that apply) Contractual relationships with HMOs and PPOs should not be reported here but in Question 105. Column 3 refers to the networks that were identified in section B, question 3d.

	(1) My Hospital	(2) My Health System	(3) My Health Network	(4) Joint Venture with Insurer
a. Health Maintenance Organization	☐	☐	☐	☐
b. Preferred Provider Organization	☐	☐	☐	☐
c. Indemnity Fee for Service Plan	☐	☐	☐	☐

105. Does your hospital have a formal written contract that specifies the obligations of each party with:

- a. Health maintenance organization (HMO) .... YES ☐   NO ☐   b. If YES, how many contracts? _____
- c. Preferred provider organization (PPO) .... YES ☐   NO ☐   d. If YES, how many contracts? _____

106a. What percentage of the hospital's net patient revenue is paid on a capitated basis? If the hospital does not participate in capitated arrangements, please enter "0")   _____ %

106b. What percentage of the hospital's net patient revenue is paid on a shared risk basis?   _____ %

107. Does your hospital contract directly with employers or a coalition of employers to provide care on a capitated, predetermined, or shared risk basis? .... YES ☐   NO ☐

108. If your hospital has arrangements to care for a specific group of enrollees in exchange for a capitated payment, how many lives are covered?   _____

D. TOTAL FACILITY BEDS, UTILIZATION, FINANCES, AND STAFFING

Please report beds, utilization, financial, and staffing data for a 12-month period that is consistent with the period reported on page 1. Report financial data for reporting period only. Include within your operations all activities that are wholly owned by the hospital, including subsidiary corporations regardless of where the activity is physically located. Please do not include within your operations distinct and separate divisions that may be owned by your hospital's parent corporation. If final figures are not available, please estimate. Round to the nearest dollar. Report all personnel who were on the payroll and whose payroll expenses are reported in D3f. (Please refer to specific definitions on pages 21-23.)

	(1) Total Facility	(2) Nursing Home Unit/Facility
Fill out column (2) if hospital owns and operates a nursing home type unit/facility. Column (1) should be the combined total of hospital plus Nursing Home Unit/Facility.		

1. BEDS AND UTILIZATION

	(1) Total Facility	(2) Nursing Home Unit/Facility
a. Total licensed beds	_____	_____
b. Beds set up and staffed for use at the end of the reporting period	_____	_____
c. Bassinets set up and staffed for use at the end of the reporting period	_____	
d. Births (exclude fetal deaths)	_____	
e. Admissions (exclude newborns, include neonatal & swing admissions)	_____	_____
f. Inpatient days (exclude newborns, include neonatal & swing days)	_____	_____
g. Emergency department visits	_____	
h. Total outpatient visits (include emergency department visits & outpatient surgeries)	_____	
i. Inpatient surgical operations	_____	
j. Number of operating rooms	_____	
k. Outpatient surgical operations	_____	

2. MEDICARE/MEDICAID UTILIZATION (exclude newborns, include neonatal & swing days and deaths)

	(1) Total Facility	(2) Nursing Home Unit/Facility
a1. Total Medicare (Title XVIII) inpatient discharges (including Medicare Managed Care)	_____	_____
a2. How many Medicare inpatient discharges were Medicare Managed Care	_____	_____
b1. Total Medicare (Title XVIII) inpatient days (including Medicare Managed Care)	_____	_____
b2. How many Medicare inpatient days were Medicare Managed Care	_____	_____
c1. Total Medicaid (Title XIX) inpatient discharges (including Medicaid Managed Care)	_____	_____
c2. How many Medicaid inpatient discharges were Medicaid Managed Care	_____	_____
d1. Total Medicaid (Title XIX) inpatient days (including Medicaid Managed Care)	_____	_____
d2. How many Medicaid inpatient days were Medicaid Managed Care	_____	_____

3. FINANCIAL

	(1) Total Facility	(2) Nursing Home Unit/Facility
*a. Net patient revenue	_____.00	_____.00
*b. Tax appropriations	_____.00	
*c. Other operating revenue	_____.00	
*d. Nonoperating revenue	_____.00	
*e. TOTAL REVENUE (add 3a thru 3d)	_____.00	_____.00
f. Payroll expenses (only)	_____.00	_____.00
g. Employee benefits	_____.00	_____.00
h. Depreciation expense (for reporting period only)	_____.00	
i. Interest expense	_____.00	
j. Supply expense	_____.00	
k. TOTAL EXPENSES (Payroll plus all non-payroll expenses, including bad debt)	_____.00	_____.00

l. Due to differing accounting standards in use, please indicate whether or not bad debt is included in:

Total Expenses	YES ☐	NO ☐
Net Patient Revenue	YES ☐	NO ☐

4. REVENUE BY TYPE

	(1) Total Facility
a. Total gross inpatient revenue	_____.00
b. Total gross outpatient revenue	_____.00
c. Total gross patient revenue	_____.00

5. UNCOMPENSATED CARE

a. Bad debt expense .... _____ .00

b. Charity (Revenue forgone at full-established rates. Include in gross revenue.)......... _____ .00

c. Is your bad debt reported here (5a) reported on the basis of full charges?   YES ☐   NO ☐

6. REVENUE BY PAYOR (report total facility gross and net figures)

	(1) Gross	(2) Net
*a. GOVERNMENT (1) Medicare:		
a) Fee for service patient revenue	.00	.00
b) Managed care revenue	.00	.00
c) Total (a + b)	**.00**	**.00**
(2) Medicaid:		
a) Fee for service patient revenue................................	.00	.00
b) Managed care revenue	.00	.00
c) Medicaid Disproportionate Share Hospital Payments (DSH)	.00	.00
d) Medicaid supplemental payments: not including Medicaid Disproportionate Share Hospital Payments (DSH)	.00	.00
e) Total (a + b + c + d)	**.00**	**.00**
(3) Other government:	.00	.00
*b. NONGOVERNMENT (1) Self-pay....................................	.00	.00
(2) Third-party payors:		
a) Managed care (includes HMO and PPO)	.00	.00
b) Other third-party payors	.00	.00
c) Total third-party payors (a + b)	**.00**	**.00**
(3) All Other nongovernment:	.00	.00
*c. TOTAL	**.00**	**.00**

(Total gross should equal 4c on page 8. Total net should equal 3a on page 8.)

Are the financial data on pages 8 and 9 from your audited financial statement? .... YES ☐   No ☐

---

7. FIXED ASSETS

a. Property, plant and equipment at <u>cost</u> .... _____ .00

b. Accumulated <u>depreciation</u> .... _____ .00

c. Net property, plant and equipment (a-b) .... _____ .00

d. Total gross square feet of your physical plant used for or in support of your healthcare activities .... _____

8. TOTAL CAPITAL EXPENSES

Include all expenses used to acquire assets, including buildings, remodeling projects, equipment, or property. _____ .00

9. ENERGY CONSUMPTION

a. Total energy usage (in MMBTU) for total gross square footage identified in 7 (d) _____ (MMBTU)

b. If you have obtained an Energy Star rating from the EPA, what is your rating? _____

D. TOTAL FACILITY BEDS, UTILIZATION, FINANCES, AND STAFFING (continued)

10. INFORMATION TECHNOLOGY

*a. IT operating expense.._____.00

*b. IT Capital expense..._____.00

*c. Number of employed IT staff (in FTEs) ...._____

*d. Number of outsourced IT staff (in FTEs)..._____

e. Does your hospital have an electronic health record (see definition)?

☐ Yes, fully implemented ☐ Yes, partially implemented ☐ No

For additional questions regarding use of an electronic health record, please respond to the 2010 AHA Annual Survey Information Technology Supplement sent under separate cover.

11. STAFFING

Report full-time (35 hours or more) and part-time (less than 35 hours) personnel who were on the hospital/facility **payroll at the end of your reporting period.** Include members of religious orders for whom dollar equivalents were reported. Exclude private-duty nurses, volunteers, and all personnel whose salary is financed entirely by outside research grants. Exclude physicians and dentists who are paid on a fee basis. FTE is the total number of hours worked by all employees over the full (12 month) reporting period divided by the normal number of hours worked by a full-time employee for that same time period. For example, if your hospital considers a normal workweek for a full-time employee to be 40 hours, a total of 2,080 would be worked over a full year (52 weeks). If the total number of hours worked by all employees on the payroll is 208,000, then the number of Full-Time Equivalents (FTE) is 100 (employees). The FTE calculation for a specific occupational category such as Registered nurses is exactly the same. The calculation for each occupational category should be based on the number of hours worked by staff employed in that specific category.

For each occupational category, please report the number of staff vacancies as of the last day of your reporting period. A vacancy is defined as a budgeted staff position which is unfilled as of the last day of the reporting period and for which the hospital is actively seeking either a full-time or part-time permanent replacement. Personnel who work in more than one area should be included only in the category of their primary responsibility and should be counted only once.

	(1) Full-Time (35 hr/wk or more) On Payroll	(2) Part-Time (Less than 35hr/wk) On Payroll	(3) FTE	(4) Vacancies
a. Physicians and dentists................................	_____	_____	_____	_____
b. Medical and dental residents/interns............................	_____	_____	_____	_____
c. Other trainees..	_____	_____	_____	_____
d. Registered nurses......................................	_____	_____	_____	_____
e. Licensed practical (vocational) nurses........................	_____	_____	_____	_____
f. Nursing assistive personnel.....................................	_____	_____	_____	_____
g. Radiology technicians..............................	_____	_____	_____	_____
h. Laboratory technicians...	_____	_____	_____	_____
i. Pharmacists, licensed..	_____	_____	_____	_____
j. Pharmacy technicians...	_____	_____	_____	_____
k. Respiratory therapists............................	_____	_____	_____	_____
l. All other personnel....................................	_____	_____	_____	_____
m. Total facility personnel (add 11a through 11l)................	_____	_____	_____	_____

(Total facility personnel should include hospital plus nursing home type unit/facility personnel reported in 11n and 11o.)

n. Nursing home type unit/facility registered nurses.............	_____	_____	_____	_____
o. Total nursing home type unit/facility personnel.................	_____	_____	_____	_____

12. PRIVILEGED PHYSICIANS

Report the total number of physicians with privileges at your hospital by type of relationship with the hospital. <u>The sum of the physicians reported in 12a-12f should equal the total number of privileged physicians (12g) in the hospital.</u>

	(1) Total Employed	(2) Total Individual Contract	(3) Total Group Contract	(4) Not Employed or Under Contract	(5) Total Privileged
a. Primary care (general practitioner, general internal medicine, family practice, general pediatrics, obstetrics/gynecology, geriatrics)	_____	_____	_____	_____	_____
b. Emergency medicine	_____	_____	_____	_____	_____
c. Hospitalist	_____	_____	_____	_____	_____
d. Intensivist	_____	_____	_____	_____	_____
e. Radiologist/pathologist/anesthesiologist	_____	_____	_____	_____	_____
f. Other specialist	_____	_____	_____	_____	_____
g. Total (add 12a-12f)	_____	_____	_____	_____	_____

13. HOSPITALISTS

13a. Do hospitalists provide care for patients in your hospital? .... YES ☐ NO ☐ **(if yes, please report in D.12c.)**

13b. If yes, please report the total number of full-time equivalents (FTE) hospitalists......................FTE _____

14. INTENSIVISTS

a. Do intensivists provide care for patients in your hospital? (If no, please skip to 15.) YES ☐ NO ☐ **(if yes, please report in D.12d.)**

b. If yes, please report the total number of FTE intensivists and assign them to the following areas. Please indicate whether the intensive care area is closed to intensivists. (Meaning that only intensivists are authorized to care for ICU patients.)

		FTE	Closed
1.	Medical-surgical intensive care	_____	☐
2.	Cardiac intensive care	_____	☐
3.	Neonatal intensive care	_____	☐
4.	Pediatric intensive care	_____	☐
5.	Other intensive care	_____	☐
6.	**Total**	_____	☐

15. ADVANCED PRACTICE REGISTERED NURSES

a. Do advanced practice nurses provide care for patients in your hospital? .... YES ☐ NO ☐ (if no, please skip to 16.)

b. If yes, please report the number of full time, part time and FTE advanced practice nurses employed or contracted to provide care for patients in your hospital.

_____ Full-time _____ Part-time _____ FTE

c. If yes, please indicate the type of service the nurses provide (Please check all that apply).

☐ Primary care ☐ Anesthesia services ☐ Emergency department care

☐ Other specialty care ☐ Patient education ☐ Case management ☐ Other

16. FOREIGN EDUCATED NURSES

a. Did your facility hire more foreign-educated nurses (including contract or agency nurses) to help fill RN vacancies in 2010 vs. 2009?

More ☐ Less ☐ Same ☐ Did not hire foreign nurses ☐

b. From which countries/continents are you recruiting foreign-educated nurses? <u>Check all that apply</u>.

Africa ☐ Korea ☐ Canada ☐ Philippines ☐ China ☐ India ☐ Other ☐

E. SUPPLEMENTAL INFORMATION

1. COMMUNITY BENEFIT

		YES	NO
a.	Does your hospital's mission statement include a focus on community benefit?	☐	☐
b.	Does your hospital have long-term plan for improving the health of its community?	☐	☐
c.	Does your hospital have a specific budget for its community benefit activities?	☐	☐
d.	Does your hospital have dedicated staff to manage community benefit activities?	☐	☐
e.	Does your hospital provide support for community building activities (e.g. economic development, housing, environmental improvements, coalition building)?	☐	☐
f.	Does your hospital make financial contributions (grants, donations, scholarships), provide in-kind support or participate in fundraising for community programs not directly affiliated with the hospital?	☐	☐
g.	Does your hospital partner with your local school system to offer health or wellness programs to help your community?	☐	☐
h.	Does your hospital work with other providers, public agencies, or community representatives to conduct a health status assessment of the community?	☐	☐
i.	Does your hospital use health status indicators (such as rates of health problems or surveys of self reported health for defined populations) to design new services or modify existing services?	☐	☐
j1.	Does your hospital work with other local providers, public agencies, or community representatives to develop a written assessment of the appropriate capacity for health services in the community?	☐	☐
j2.	If yes, have you used the assessment to identify unmet health needs, excess capacity, or duplicative services in the community?	☐	☐
k.	Does your hospital work with other providers to collect, track and communicate clinical and health information across cooperating organizations?	☐	☐
l.	Does your hospital either by itself or in conjunction with others disseminate reports to the community on the quality and costs of health care services?	☐	☐

2. DIVERSITY, LANGUAGE AND LEADERSHIP

		YES	NO
a.	Does your hospital gather information on a patient's race/ethnicity at any point during their stay?	☐	☐
b.	Does your hospital gather information on a patient's primary language at any point during their stay?	☐	☐
c.	Does your hospital or health system currently have or plan to develop, implement, or evaluate a leadership development program?	☐	☐
d.	Does your hospital or health system currently have or plan to develop, execute, or evaluate a diversity strategy or plan?	☐	☐
e.	Does your hospital or health system engage in leadership succession planning?	☐	☐
f.	Does your hospital or health system currently provide career development resources to administrators?	☐	☐

3. OTHER

a. Does your hospital provide services through one or more satellite facilities?　　　　YES ☐　　　NO ☐

b. Does the hospital participate in a group purchasing arrangement? If yes, please provide the name, city, and state of the group purchasing organization. If the hospital participates in more than one group purchasing organization, please provide the name, city, state and telephone number of the group purchasing organization(s) on page 13 (3f), under supplemental information　　YES ☐　　　NO ☐

Name: _____　City: _____　State: _____

c. Does the hospital purchase medical/surgical supplies directly through a distributor? If yes, please provide the name of the distributor.

　　　　　　　　　　　　　　　　　　　　　　　　　　　　　YES ☐　　　NO ☐

Name: _____

d. Which of the following best describes the type of triage system your emergency department uses on a daily basis to determine which patients can wait to be seen and which need to be seen immediately.

1.	Three (3) level system (emergent, urgent, non urgent, red, yellow, green)	☐
2.	Four (4) level system (emergent, unstable urgent, stable urgent, non-urgent)	☐
3.	Five (5) level Emergency Severity Index (ESI)	☐
4.	Five (5) level system (Australasian, Manchester or Acuity Scale)	☐
5.	Other (please specify) _____	☐
6.	Don't know	☐

e.Does your hospital outsource the HIM coding function under any of the following conditions?

	YES	NO
1.To handle backlog due to staff vacations or shortages.	☐	☐
2.Partially outsource during normal operations.	☐	☐
3.Completely outsourced during normal operations	☐	☐

f. Use this space to describe your community benefit activities as well as any partners you are currently working with on such activities. Also use this space or additional sheets if more space is required for comments or to elaborate on any information supplied on this survey. Refer to the response by page, section and item name.

_____

_____

_____

_____

_____

_____

_____

_____

_____

_____

_____

_____

_____

_____

_____

_____

_____

_____

_____

_____

_____

_____

_____

_____

_____

_____

_____

_____

_____

_____

_____

_____

As declared previously, hospital specific revenue data are treated as confidential. AHA's policy is not to release these data without written permission from your institution. The AHA will however, share these data with your respective state hospital association and if requested with your appropriate metropolitan/regional association.

On occasion, the AHA is asked to provide these data to external organizations, both public and private, for their use in analyzing crucial health care policy or research issues. The AHA is requesting your permission to allow us to release your confidential data to those requests that we consider legitimate and worthwhile. In every instance of disclosure, the receiving organization will be prohibited from releasing hospital specific information.

Please indicate below whether or not you agree to these types of disclosure:

[ ] I hereby grant AHA permission to release my hospital's revenue data to external users that the AHA determines have a legitimate and worthwhile need to gain access to these data subject to the user's agreement with the AHA not to release hospital specific information.

_____

Chief Executive Officer   Date

[ ] I do not grant AHA permission to release my confidential data.

_____

Chief Executive Officer   Date

Does your hospital or health system have an Internet or Homepage address? Yes ☐ No ☐
If yes, please provide the address: http:// _____

Thank you for your cooperation in completing this survey. If there are any questions about your responses to this survey, who should be contacted?

_____   _____   ( )_____
Name (please print)   Title   (Area Code) Telephone Number

____/____/____   _____   ( )_____
Date of Completion   Chief Executive Officer   Hospital's Main Fax Number

Contact Email address: _____

NOTE: PLEASE PHOTOCOPY THE INFORMATION FOR YOUR HOSPITAL FILE BEFORE RETURNING THE ORIGINAL FORM TO THE AMERICAN HOSPITAL ASSOCIATION. ALSO, PLEASE FORWARD A PHOTOCOPY OF THE COMPLETED QUESTIONNAIRE TO YOUR STATE HOSPITAL ASSOCIATION.

THANK YOU

SECTION A
REPORTING PERIOD
Instructions

INSTRUCTIONS AND DEFINITIONS FOR THE 2010 ANNUAL SURVEY OF HOSPITALS.
For purposes of this survey, a hospital is defined as the organization or corporate entity licensed or registered as a hospital by a state to provide diagnostic and therapeutic patient services for a variety of medical conditions, both surgical and nonsurgical.

1. Reporting period used (beginning and ending date): Record the beginning and ending dates of the reporting period in an eight-digit number: for example, January 1, 2009 should be shown as 01/01/2009. Number of days should equal the time span between the two dates that the hospital was open. If you are reporting for less than 365 days, utilization and finances should be presented for days reported only.
2. Were you in operation 12 full months at the end of your reporting period? If you are reporting for less than 365 days, utilization and finances should be presented for days reported only.
3. Number of days open during reporting period: Number of days should equal the time span between the two dates that the hospital was open.

SECTION B
ORGANIZATIONAL STRUCTURE
Instructions and Definitions

1. CONTROL
Check the box to the left of the type of organization that is responsible for establishing policy for overall operation of the hospital.
> **Government, nonfederal.**
>> **State.** Controlled by an agency of state government.
>> **County.** Controlled by an agency of county government.
>> **City.** Controlled by an agency of municipal government.
>> **City-County.** Controlled jointly by agencies of municipal and county governments.
>> **Hospital district or authority.** Controlled by a political subdivision of a state, county, or city created solely for the purpose of establishing and maintaining medical care or health-related care institutions.
> **Nongovernment, not for profit.** Controlled by not-for-profit organizations, including religious organizations (Catholic hospitals, for example), community hospitals, cooperative hospitals, hospitals operated by fraternal societies, and so forth.
> **Investor owned, for profit.** Controlled on a for profit basis by an individual, partnership, or a profit making corporation.
> **Government, federal.** Controlled by an agency or department of the federal government.

2. SERVICE
Indicate the ONE category that best describes the type of service that your hospital provides to the majority of patients.
> **General medical and surgical.** Provides diagnostic and therapeutic services to patients for a variety of medical conditions, both surgical and nonsurgical.
> **Hospital unit of an institution.** Provides diagnostic and therapeutic services to patients in an institution.
> **Hospital unit within an institution for the mentally retarded.** Provides diagnostic and therapeutic services to patients in an institution for the mentally retarded.
> **Surgical.** An acute care specialty hospital where 2/3 or more of its inpatient claims are for surgical/diagnosis related groups.
> **Psychiatric.** Provides diagnostic and therapeutic services to patients with mental or emotional disorders.
> **Tuberculosis and other respiratory diseases.** Provides medical care and rehabilitative services to patients for whom the primary diagnosis is tuberculosis or other respiratory diseases.
> **Cancer.** Provides medical care to patients for whom the primary diagnosis is cancer.
> **Heart.** Provides diagnosis and treatment of heart disease.
> **Obstetrics and gynecology.** Provides medical and surgical treatment to pregnant women and to mothers following delivery. Also provides diagnostic and therapeutic services to women with diseases or disorders of the reproductive organs.
> **Eye, ear, nose, and throat.** Provides diagnosis and treatment of diseases and injuries of the eyes, ears, nose, and throat.
> **Rehabilitation.** Provides a comprehensive array of restoration services for the disabled and all support services necessary to help them attain their maximum functional capacity.
> **Orthopedic.** Provides corrective treatment of deformities, diseases, and ailments of the locomotive apparatus, especially affecting the limbs, bones, muscles, and joints.
> **Chronic disease.** Provides medical and skilled nursing services to patients with long-term illnesses who are not in an acute phase, but who require an intensity of services not available in nursing homes.
> **Institution for the mentally retarded.** Provides health-related care on a regular basis to patients with psychiatric or developmental impairment who cannot be treated in a skilled nursing unit.
> **Acute long term care hospital.** Provides high acuity interdisciplinary services to medically complex patients that require more intensive recuperation and care than can be provided in a typical nursing facility.
> **Alcoholism and other chemical dependency.** Provides diagnostic and therapeutic services to patients with alcoholism or other drug dependencies.

3. OTHER
> a. **Children admissions.** A hospital whose primary focus is the health and treatment of children and adolescents.
> b. **Subsidiary.** A company that is wholly controlled by another or one that is more than 50% owned by another organization.
> c. **Contract managed.** General day-to-day management of an entire organization by another organization under a formal contract. Managing organization reports directly to the board of trustees or owners of the managed organization; managed organization retains total legal responsibility and ownership of the facility's assets and liabilities.
> d. **Network.** A group of hospitals, physicians, other providers, insurers and/or community agencies that voluntarily work together to coordinate and deliver health services
> e. **Group Purchasing Organization.** An organization whose primary function is to negotiate contracts for the purpose of purchasing for members of the group or has a central supply site for its members.

4. National Provider Identifier (NPI) is a unique identification number for covered health care providers. Covered health care providers and all health plans and health care clearinghouses must use the NPIs in the administrative and financial transactions adopted under HIPAA. The NPI is a 10-position, intelligence-free numeric identifier (10-digit number).

Owned/provided by the hospital or its subsidiary. All patient revenues, expenses and utilization related to the provision of the service are reflected in the hospital's statistics reported elsewhere in this survey.

Provided by my Health System (in my local community). Another health care provider in the same system as your hospital provides the service and patient revenue, expenses, and utilization related to the provision of the service are recorded at the point where the service was provided and would not be reflected in your hospital's statistics reported elsewhere in this survey. (A system is a corporate body that owns, leases, religiously sponsors and/or manages health provider)

Provided by my network (in my local community). Another health care provider in the same network as your hospital provides the service and patient revenue, expenses and utilization related to the provision of the service are recorded at the point where the service was provided and would not be reflected in your hospital's statistics reported elsewhere in this survey. (A network is a group of hospitals, physicians, other providers, insurers and/or community agencies that voluntarily work together to coordinate and deliver health services. When reporting a service for a network, please indicate the name of the network in Section B, question d.)

Provided through a formal contractual arrangement or joint venture with another provider that is not in my system or network. All patient revenues and utilization related to the provision of the service are recorded at the site where the service was provided and would not be reflected in your hospital statistics reported elsewhere in this survey. (A joint venture is a contractual arrangement between two or more parties forming an unincorporated business. The participants in the arrangement remain independent and separate outside of the venture's purpose.)

1. **General medical-surgical care.** Provides acute care to patients in medical and surgical units on the basis of physicians' orders and approved nursing care plans.
2. **Pediatric medical-surgical care.** Provides acute care to pediatric patients on the basis of physicians' orders and approved nursing care plans.
3. **Obstetrics.** Levels should be designated: (1) unit provides services for uncomplicated maternity and newborn cases; (2) unit provides services for uncomplicated cases, the majority of complicated problems, and special neonatal services; and (3) unit provides services for all serious illnesses and abnormalities and is supervised by a full-time maternal/fetal specialist.
4. **Medical surgical intensive care.** Provides patient care of a more intensive nature than the usual medical and surgical care, on the basis of physicians' orders and approved nursing care plans. These units are staffed with specially trained nursing personnel and contain monitoring and specialized support equipment for patients who because of shock, trauma or other life-threatening conditions require intensified comprehensive observation and care. Includes mixed intensive care units.
5. **Cardiac intensive care.** Provides patient care of a more specialized nature than the usual medical and surgical care, on the basis of physicians' orders and approved nursing care plans. The unit is staffed with specially trained nursing personnel and contains monitoring and specialized support or treatment equipment for patients who, because of heart seizure, open-heart surgery, or other life-threatening conditions, require intensified, comprehensive observation and care. May include myocardial infarction, pulmonary care, and heart transplant units.
6. **Neonatal intensive care.** A unit that must be separate from the newborn nursery providing intensive care to all sick infants including those with the very lowest birth weights (less than 1500 grams). NICU has potential for providing mechanical ventilation, neonatal surgery, and special care for the sickest infants born in the hospital or transferred from another institution. A full-time neonatologist serves as director of the NICU.
7. **Neonatal intermediate care.** A unit that must be separate from the normal newborn nursery and that provides intermediate and/or recovery care and some specialized services, including immediate resuscitation, intravenous therapy, and capacity for prolonged oxygen therapy and monitoring.
8. **Pediatric intensive care.** Provides care to pediatric patients that is of a more intensive nature than that usually provided to pediatric patients. The unit is staffed with specially trained personnel and contains monitoring and specialized support equipment for treatment of patients who, because of shock, trauma, or other life-threatening conditions, require intensified, comprehensive observation and care.
9. **Burn care.** Provides care to severely burned patients. Severely burned patients are those with any of the following: (1) second-degree burns of more than 25% total body surface area for adults or 20% total body surface area for children: (2) third-degree burns of more than 10% total body surface area; (3) any severe burns of the hands, face, eyes, ears, or feet; or (4) all inhalation injuries, electrical burns, complicated burn injuries involving fractures and other major traumas, and all other poor risk factors.
10. **Other special care.** Provides care to patients requiring care more intensive than that provided in the acute area, yet not sufficiently intensive to require admission to an intensive care unit. Patients admitted to this area are usually transferred here from an intensive care unit once their condition has improved. These units are sometimes referred to as definitive observation, step-down or progressive care units.
11. **Other intensive care.** A specially staffed, specialty equipped, separate section of a hospital dedicated to the observation, care, and treatment of patients with life threatening illnesses, injuries, or complications from which recovery is possible. It provides special expertise and facilities for the support of vital function and utilizes the skill of medical nursing and other staff experienced in the management of these problems.
12. **Physical rehabilitation.** Provides care encompassing a comprehensive array of restoration services for the disabled and all support services necessary to help patients attain their maximum functional capacity.
13. **Alcoholism-drug abuse or dependency care.** Provides diagnosis and therapeutic services to patients with alcoholism or other drug dependencies. Includes care for inpatient/residential treatment for patients whose course of treatment involves more intensive care than provided in an outpatient setting or where patient requires supervised withdrawal.
14. **Psychiatric care.** Provides acute or long-term care to emotionally disturbed patients, including patients admitted for diagnosis and those admitted for treatment of psychiatric problems, on the basis of physicians' orders and approved nursing care plans. Long-term care may include intensive supervision to the chronically mentally ill, mentally disordered, or other mentally incompetent persons.
15. **Skilled nursing care.** Provides non-acute medical and skilled nursing care services, therapy, and social services under the supervision of a licensed registered nurse on a 24-hour basis.
16. **Intermediate nursing care.** Provides health-related services (skilled nursing care and social services) to residents with a variety of physical conditions or functional disabilities. These residents do not require the care provided by a hospital or skilled nursing facility, but do need supervision and support services.
17. **Acute long-term care.** Provides specialized acute hospital care to medically complex patients who are critically ill, have multisystem complications and/or failure, and require hospitalization averaging 25 days, in a facility offering specialized treatment programs and therapeutic intervention on a 24-hour/7 day a week basis.
18. **Other long-term care.** Provision of long-term care other than skilled nursing care or intermediate care for those who do not require daily medical or nursing services, but may requires some assistance in the activities of daily living. This can include residential care, elderly care, or sheltered care facilities for developmentally disabled.
18. **Other care.** (specify) Any type of care other than those listed above.
     __The sum of the beds reported in Section C 1-19 should equal what you have reported in Section D(1b) for beds set up and staffed.__
20. **Adult day care program.** Program providing supervision, medical and psychological care, and social activities for older adults who live at home or in another family setting, but cannot be alone or prefer to be with others during the day. May include intake assessment, health monitoring, occupational therapy, personal care, noon meal, and transportation services.

21. **Airborne infection isolation room.** A single-occupancy room for patient care where environmental factors are controlled in an effort to minimize the transmission of those infectious agents, usually spread person to person by droplet nuclei associated with coughing and inhalation. Such rooms typically have specific ventilation requirements for controlled ventilation, air pressure and filtration.

22. **Alcoholism-drug abuse or dependency outpatient services.** Organized hospital services that provide medical care and/or rehabilitative treatment services to outpatients for whom the primary diagnosis is alcoholism or other chemical dependency.

23. **Alzheimer center.** Facility that offers care to persons with Alzheimer's disease and their families through an integrated program of clinical services, research, and education.

24. **Ambulance services.** Provision of ambulance service to the ill and injured who require medical attention on a scheduled and unscheduled basis.

25. **Ambulatory surgery center.** Facility that provides care to patients requiring surgery that are admitted and discharged on the same day. Ambulatory surgery centers are distinct from same day surgical units within the hospital outpatient departments for purposes of Medicare payment.

26. **Arthritis treatment center.** Specifically equipped and staffed center for the diagnosis and treatment of arthritis and other joint disorders.

27. **Assisted living.** A special combination of housing, supportive services, personalized assistance and health care designed to respond to the individual needs of those who need help in activities of daily living and instrumental activities of daily living. Supportive services are available, 24 hours a day, to meet scheduled and unscheduled needs, in a way that promotes maximum independence and dignity for each resident and encourages the involvement of a resident's family, neighbor and friends.

28. **Auxiliary.** A volunteer community organization formed to assist the hospital in carrying out its purpose and to serve as a link between the institution and the community.

29. **Bariatric/weight control services.** Bariatrics is the medical practice of weight reduction.

30. **Birthing room/LDR room/LDRP room.** A single-room type of maternity care with a more homelike setting for families than the traditional three-room unit (labor/delivery/recovery) with a separate postpartum area. A birthing room combines labor and delivery in one room. An LDR room accommodates three stages in the birthing process--labor, delivery, and recovery. An LDRP room accommodates all four stages of the birth process--labor, delivery, recovery, and postpartum.

31. **Blood donor center.** A facility that performs, or is responsible for the collection, processing, testing or distribution of blood and components.

32. **Breast cancer screening/mammograms.** Mammography screening - The use of breast x-ray to detect unsuspected breast cancer in asymptomatic women. Diagnostic mammography - The x-ray imaging of breast tissue in symptomatic women who are considered to have a substantial likelihood of having breast cancer already.

33. **Cardiology and cardiac surgery services.** Services which include the diagnosis and treatment of diseases and disorders involving the heart and circulatory system.

    a-b Cardiology services. Adult Cardiology Services. An organized clinical service offering diagnostic and interventional procedures to manage the full range of adult heart conditions. **Pediatric Cardiology Services.** An organized clinical service offering diagnostic and interventional procedures to manage the full range of pediatric heart conditions.

    c-d. Diagnostic catheterization. (also called coronary angiography or coronary arteriography) is used to assist in diagnosing complex heart conditions. Cardiac angiography involves the insertion of a tiny catheter into the artery in the groin then carefully threading the catheter up into the aorta where the coronary arteries originate. Once the catheter is in place, a dye is injected which allows the cardiologist to see the size, shape, and distribution of the coronary arteries. These images are used to diagnose heart disease and to determine, among other things, whether or not surgery is indicated.

    e-f. Interventional cardiac catheterization. Nonsurgical procedure that utilizes the same basic principles as diagnostic catheterization and then uses advanced techniques to improve the heart's function. It can be a less-invasive alternative to heart surgery.

    g-h. Cardiac surgery. Includes minimally invasive procedures that include surgery done with only a small incision or no incision at all, such as through a laparoscope or an endoscope and more invasive major surgical procedures that include open chest and open heart surgery.

    i-j. Cardiac electrophysiology. Evaluation and management of patients with complex rhythm or conduction abnormalities, including diagnostic testing, treatment of arrhythmias by catheter ablation or drug therapy, and pacemaker/defibrillator implantation and follow-up.

    k. Cardiac rehabilitation. A medically supervised program to help heart patients recover quickly and improve their overall physical and mental functioning. The goal is to reduce risk of another cardiac event or to keep an already present heart condition from getting worse. Cardiac rehabilitation programs include: counseling to patients, an exercise program, helping patients modify risk factors such as smoking and high blood pressure, providing vocational guidance to enable the patient to return to work, supplying information on physical limitations and lending emotional support.

34. **Case management.** A system of assessment, treatment planning, referral and follow-up that ensures the provision of comprehensive and continuous services and the coordination of payment and reimbursement for care.

35. **Chaplaincy/pastoral care services.** A service ministering religious activities and providing pastoral counseling to patients, their families, and staff of a health care organization.

36. **Chemotherapy.** An organized program for the treatment of cancer by the use of drugs or chemicals.

37. **Children's wellness program.** A program that encourages improved health status and a healthful lifestyle of children through health education, exercise, nutrition and health promotion.

38. **Chiropractic services.** An organized clinical service including spinal manipulation or adjustment and related diagnostic and therapeutic services.

39. **Community outreach.** A program that systematically interacts with the community to identify those in need of services, alerting persons and their families to the availability of services, locating needed services, and enabling persons to enter the service delivery system.

40. **Complementary and alternative medicine services.** Organized hospital services or formal arrangements to providers that provide care or treatment not based solely on traditional western allopathic medical teachings as instructed in most U.S. medical schools. Includes any of the following: acupuncture, chiropractic, homeopathy, osteopathy, diet and lifestyle changes, herbal medicine, massage therapy, etc.

41. **Computer assisted orthopedic surgery (CAOS).** Orthopedic surgery using computer technology, enabling three-dimensional graphic models to visualize a patient's anatomy.

42. **Crisis prevention.** Services provided in order to promote physical and mental well being and the early identification of disease and ill health prior to the onset and recognition of symptoms so as to permit early treatment.

43. **Dental Services.** An organized dental service or dentists on staff, not necessarily involving special facilities, providing dental or oral services to inpatients or outpatients.

44. **Emergency services.** Health services that are provided after the onset of a medical condition that manifests itself by symptoms of sufficient severity, including severe pain, that the absence of immediate medical attention could reasonably be expected by a prudent layperson, who possesses an average knowledge of health and medicine, to result in placing the patient's health in serious jeopardy.

    a. Emergency department. Hospital facilities for the provision of unscheduled outpatient services to patients whose conditions require immediate care.

    b. Satellite Emergency Department. A facility owned and operated by the hospital but physically separate from the hospital for the provision of unscheduled outpatient services to patients whose conditions require immediate care. A freestanding ED is not physically connected to a hospital, but has all necessary emergency staffing and equipment on-site.

d. **Trauma center (certified).** A facility to provide emergency and specialized intensive care to critically ill and injured patients. Level 1: A regional resource trauma center, which is capable of providing total care for every aspect of injury and plays a leadership role in trauma research and education. Level 2: A community trauma center, which is capable of providing trauma care to all but the most severely injured patients who require highly specialized care. Level 3: A rural trauma hospital, which is capable of providing care to a large number of injury victims and can resuscitate and stabilize more severely injured patients so that they can be transported to level 1 or 2 facilities. Please provide explanation on page 13 if necessary.

45. **Enabling services.** A program that is designed to help the patient access health care services by offering any of the following: transportation services and/or referrals to local social services agencies.

46. **Endoscopic services.**
   a. **Optical colonoscopy.** An examination of the interior of the colon using a long, flexible, lighted tube with a small built-in camera.
   b. **Endoscopic ultrasound.** Specially designed endoscope that incorporates an ultrasound transducer used to obtain detailed images of organs in the chest and abdomen. The endoscope can be passed through the mouth or the anus. When combined with needle biopsy the procedure can assist in diagnosis of disease and staging of cancer.
   c. **Ablation of Barrett's esophagus.** Premalignant condition that can lead to adenocarcinoma of the esophagus. The nonsurgical ablation of premalignant tissue in Barrett's esophagus by the application of thermal energy or light through an endoscope passed from the mouth into the esophagus.
   d. **Esophageal impedance study.** A test in which a catheter is placed through the nose into the esophagus to measure whether gas or liquids are passing from the stomach into the esophagus and causing symptoms.
   e. **Endoscopic retrograde cholangiopancreatography (ERCP).** A procedure in which a catheter is introduced through an endoscope into the bile ducts and pancreatic ducts. Injection of contrast material permits detailed x-ray of these structures. The procedure is used diagnostically as well as therapeutically to relieve obstruction or remove stones.

47. **Enrollment assistance services.** A program that provides enrollment assistance for patients who are potentially eligible for public health insurance programs such as Medicaid, State Children's Health Insurance, or local/state indigent care programs. The specific services offered could include explanation of benefits, assist applicants in completing the application and locating all relevant documents, conduct eligibility interviews, and/or forward applications and documentation to state/local social service or health agency.

48. **Extracorporeal shock wave lithotripter (ESWL).** A medical device used for treating stones in the kidney or urethra. The device disintegrates kidney stones noninvasively through the transmission of acoustic shock waves directed at the stones.

49. **Fertility clinic.** A specialized program set in an infertility center that provides counseling and education as well as advanced reproductive techniques such as: injectable therapy, reproductive surgeries, treatment for endometriosis, male factor infertility, tubal reversals, in vitro fertilization (IVF), donor eggs, and other such services to help patients achieve successful pregnancies.

50. **Fitness center.** Provides exercise, testing, or evaluation programs and fitness activities to the community and hospital employees.

51. **Freestanding outpatient care center.** A facility owned and operated by the hospital, that is physically separate from the hospital and provides various medical treatments and diagnostic services on an outpatient basis only. Laboratory and radiology services are usually available.

52. **Geriatric services.** The branch of medicine dealing with the physiology of aging and the diagnosis and treatment of disease affecting the aged. Services could include: Adult day care; Alzheimer's diagnostic-assessment services; Comprehensive geriatric assessment; Emergency response system; Geriatric acute care unit; and/or Geriatric clinics.

53. **Health fair.** Community health education events that focus on the prevention of disease and promotion of health through such activities as audiovisual exhibits and free diagnostic services.

54. **Community health education.** Education that provides health information to individuals and populations as well as support for personal, family and community health decisions with the objective of improving health status.

55. **Genetic testing/counseling.** A service equipped with adequate laboratory facilities and directed by a qualified physician to advise parents and prospective parents on potential problems in cases of genetic defects. A genetic test is the analysis of human DNA, RNA, chromosomes, proteins, and certain metabolites in order to detect heritable disease-related genotypes, mutations, phenotypes, or karyotypes for clinical purposes. Genetic tests can have diverse purposes, including the diagnosis of genetic diseases in newborns, children, and adults; the identification of future health risks; the prediction of drug responses; and the assessment of risks to future children.

56. **Health screening.** A preliminary procedure such as a test or examination to detect the most characteristic sign or signs of a disorder that may require further investigation.

57. **Health research.** Organized hospital research program in any of the following areas: basic research, clinical research, community health research, and/or research on innovative health care delivery.

58. **Hemodialysis.** Provision of equipment and personnel for the treatment of renal insufficiency on an inpatient or outpatient basis.

59. **HIV-AIDS services.** Could include: HIV-AIDS unit-Special unit or team designated and equipped specifically for diagnosis, treatment, continuing care planning, and counseling services for HIV-AIDS patients and their families. General inpatient care for HIV-AIDS-Inpatient diagnosis and treatment for human immunodeficiency virus and acquired immunodeficiency syndrome patients, but dedicated unit is not available. Specialized outpatient program for HIV-AIDS-Special outpatient program providing diagnostic, treatment, continuing care planning, and counseling for HIV-AIDS patients and their families.

60. **Home health services.** Service providing nursing, therapy, and health-related homemaker or social services in the patient's home.

61. **Hospice.** A program providing palliative care, chiefly medical relief of pain and supportive services, addressing the emotional, social, financial, and legal needs of terminally ill patients and their families. Care can be provided in a variety of settings, both inpatient and at home.

62. **Hospital-based outpatient care center-services.** Organized hospital health care services offered by appointment on an ambulatory basis. Services may include outpatient surgery, examination, diagnosis, and treatment of a variety of medical conditions on a nonemergency basis, and laboratory and other diagnostic testing as ordered by staff or outside physician referral.

63. **Immunization program.** Program that plans, coordinates and conducts immunization services in the community.

64. **Indigent care clinic.** Health care services for uninsured and underinsured persons where care is free of charge or charged on a sliding scale. This would include "free clinics" staffed by volunteer practitioners, but could also be staffed by employees with the sponsoring health care organization subsidizing the cost of service.

65. **Linguistic/translation services.** Services provided by the hospital designed to make health care more accessible to non-English speaking patients and their physicians.

66. **Meals on wheels.** A hospital sponsored program which delivers meals to people, usually the elderly, who are unable to prepare their own meals. Low cost, nutritional meals are delivered to individuals' homes on a regular basis.

67. **Mobile health services.** Vans and other vehicles used to delivery primary care services.

68. **Neurological services.** Services provided by the hospital dealing with the operative and nonoperative management of disorders of the central, peripheral, and autonomic nervous system.

69. **Nutrition programs.** Those services within a health care facility which are designed to provide inexpensive, nutritionally sound meals to patients.

70. **Occupational health services.** Includes services designed to protect the safety of employees from hazards in the work environment.

71. **Oncology services.** Inpatient and outpatient services for patients with cancer, including comprehensive care, support and guidance in addition to patient education and prevention, chemotherapy, counseling and other treatment methods.

72. **Orthopedic services.** Services provided for the prevention or correction of injuries or disorders of the skeletal system and associated muscles, joints and ligaments.
73. **Outpatient surgery.** Scheduled surgical services provided to patients who do not remain in the hospital overnight. The surgery may be performed in operating suites also used for inpatient surgery, specially designated surgical suites for outpatient surgery, or procedure rooms within an outpatient care facility.
74. **Pain management program.** A recognized clinical service or program providing specialized medical care, drugs or therapies for the management of acute or chronic pain and other distressing symptoms, administered by specially trained physicians and other clinicians, to patients suffering from an acute illness of diverse causes.
75. **Palliative care program.** An organized program providing specialized medical care, drugs or therapies for the management of acute or chronic pain and/or the control of symptoms administered by specially trained physicians and other clinicians; and supportive care services, such as counseling on advanced directives, spiritual care, and social services, to patients with advanced disease and their families.
76. **Palliative care inpatient unit.** An inpatient palliative care ward is a physically discreet, inpatient nursing unit where the focus is palliative care. The patient care focus is on symptom relief for complex patients who may be continuing to undergo primary treatment. Care is delivered by palliative medicine specialists.
77. **Patient controlled analgesia (PCA).** Patient-controlled analgesia (PCA) is intravenously administered pain medicine under the patient's control. The patient has a button on the end of a cord than can be pushed at will, whenever more pain medicine is desired. This button will only deliver more pain medicine at pre-determined intervals, as programmed by the doctor's order.
78. **Patient education center.** Written goals and objectives for the patient and/or family related to therapeutic regimens, medical procedures, and self care.
79. **Patient representative services.** Organized hospital services providing personnel through whom patients and staff can seek solutions to institutional problems affecting the delivery of high quality care and services.
80. **Physical rehabilitation services.** Program providing medical, health-related, therapy, social, and/or vocational services to help disabled persons attain or retain their maximum functional capacity.
    a. **Assistive technology center.** A program providing access to specialized hardware and software with adaptations allowing individuals greater independence with mobility, dexterity, or increased communication options.
    b. **Electrodiagnostic services.** Diagnostic testing services for nerve and muscle function including services such as nerve conduction studies and needle electromyography.
    c. **Physical rehabilitation outpatient services.** Outpatient program providing medical, health-related, therapy, social, and/or vocational services to help disabled persons attain or retain their maximum functional capacity.
    d. **Prosthetic and orthotic services.** Services providing comprehensive prosthetic and orthotic evaluation, fitting, and training.
    e. **Robot-assisted walking therapy.** A form of physical therapy that uses a robotic device to assist patients who are relearning how to walk.
    f. **Simulated rehabilitation environment.** Rehabilitation focused on retraining functional skills in a contextually appropriate environment (simulated home and community settings) or in a traditional setting (gymnasium) using motor learning principles.
81. **Primary care department.** A unit or clinic within the hospital that provides primary care services (e.g. general pediatric care, general internal medicine, family practice, gynecology) through hospital-salaried medical and/or nursing staff, focusing on evaluating and diagnosing medical problems and providing medical treatment on an outpatient basis.
82. **Psychiatric services.** Services provided by the hospital that offer immediate initial evaluation and treatment to patients with mental or emotional disorders.
    a. **Psychiatric child-adolescent services.** Provides care to emotionally disturbed children and adolescents, including those admitted for diagnosis and those admitted for treatment.
    b. **Psychiatric consultation-liaison services.** Provides organized psychiatric consultation/liaison services to nonpsychiatric hospital staff and/or departments on psychological aspects of medical care that may be generic or specific to individual patients.
    c. **Psychiatric education services.** Provides psychiatric educational services to community agencies and workers such as schools, police, courts, public health nurses, welfare agencies, clergy, and so forth. The purpose is to expand the mental health knowledge and competence of personnel not working in the mental health field and to promote good mental health through improved understanding, attitudes, and behavioral patterns.
    d. **Psychiatric emergency services.** Services of facilities available on a 24-hour basis to provide immediate unscheduled out-patient care, diagnosis, evaluation, crisis intervention, and assistance to persons suffering acute emotional or mental distress.
    e. **Psychiatric geriatric services.** Provides care to emotionally disturbed elderly patients, including those admitted for diagnosis and those admitted for treatment.
    f. **Psychiatric outpatient services.** Provides medical care, including diagnosis and treatment, of psychiatric outpatients.
    g. **Psychiatric partial hospitalization program.** Organized hospital services of intensive day/evening outpatient services of three hours or more duration, distinguished from other outpatient visits of one hour.
83. **Radiology, diagnostic.** The branch of radiology that deals with the utilization of all modalities of radiant energy in medical diagnoses and therapeutic procedures using radiologic guidance. This includes, but is not restricted to, imaging techniques and methodologies utilizing radiation emitted by x-ray tubes, radionuclides, and ultrasonographic devices and the radiofrequency electromagnetic radiation emitted by atoms.
    a. **CT Scanner.** Computed tomographic scanner for head or whole body scans.
    b. **Diagnostic radioisotope facility.** The use of radioactive isotopes (Radiopharmaceuticals) as tracers or indicators to detect an abnormal condition or disease.
    c. **Electron beam computed tomography (EBCT).** A high tech computed tomography scan used to detect coronary artery disease by measuring coronary calcifications. This imaging procedure uses electron beams which are magnetically steered to produce a visual of the coronary artery and the images are produced faster than conventional CT scans.
    d. **Full-field digital mammography (FFDM).** Combines the x-ray generators and tubes used in analog screen-film mammography (SFM) with a detector plate that converts the x-rays into a digital signal.
    e. **Magnetic resonance imaging (MRI).** The use of a uniform magnetic field and radio frequencies to study tissue and structure of the body. This procedure enables the visualization of biochemical activity of the cell in vivo without the use of ionizing radiation, radioisotopic substances or high-frequency sound.
    f. **Intraoperative magnetic resonance imaging.** An integrated surgery system which provides an MRI system in an operating room. The system allows for immediate evaluation of the degree to tumor resection while the patient is undergoing a surgical resection. Intraoperative MRI exists when a MRI (low-field or high-field) is placed in the operating theater and is used during surgical resection without moving the patient from the operating room to the diagnostic imaging suite.
    g. **Multi-slice spiral computed tomography (<64+slice CT).** A specialized computed tomography procedure that provides three-dimensional processing and allows narrower and multiple slices with increased spatial resolution and faster scanning times as compared to a regular computed tomography scan.
    h. **Multi-slice spiral computed tomography (64+ slice CT).** Involves the acquisition of volumetric tomographic x-ray absorption data expressed in Hounsfield units using multiple rows of detectors. 64+ systems reconstruct the equivalent of 64 or greater slices to cover the imaged volume.

i. **Positron emission tomography (PET).** A nuclear medicine imaging technology which uses radioactive (positron emitting) isotopes created in a cyclotron or generator and computers to produce composite pictures of the brain and heart at work. PET scanning produces sectional images depicting metabolic activity or blood flow rather than anatomy.

j. **Positron emission tomography/CT (PET/CT).** Provides metabolic functional information for the monitoring of chemotherapy, radiotherapy and surgical planning.

k. **Single photon emission computerized tomography (SPECT).** Single photon emission computerized tomography is a nuclear medicine imaging technology that combines existing technology of gamma camera imaging with computed tomographic imaging technology to provide a more precise and clear image.

l. **Ultrasound.** The use of acoustic waves above the range of 20,000 cycles per second to visualize internal body structures.

84. **Radiology, therapeutic.** The branch of medicine concerned with radioactive substances and using various techniques of visualization, with the diagnosis and treatment of disease using any of the various sources of radiant energy. Services could include: megavoltage radiation therapy; radioactive implants; stereotactic radiosurgery; therapeutic radioisotope facility; X-ray radiation therapy.

a. **Image-guided radiation therapy (IGRT).** Automated system for image-guided radiation therapy that enables clinicians to obtain high-resolution x- ray images to pinpoint tumor sites, adjust patient positioning when necessary, and complete a treatment, all within the standard treatment time slot, allowing for more effective cancer treatments.

b. **Intensity-Modulated Radiation Therapy (IMRT).** A type of three-dimensional radiation therapy, which improves the targeting of treatment delivery in a way that is likely to decrease damage to normal tissues and allows varying intensities.

c. **Proton beam therapy.** A form of radiation therapy which administers proton beams. While producing the same biologic effects as x-ray beams, the energy distribution of protons differs from conventional x-ray beams in that they can be more precisely focused in tissue volumes in a three-dimensional pattern resulting in less surrounding tissue damage than conventional radiation therapy permitting administration of higher doses.

d. **Shaped beam radiation system.** A precise, non-invasive treatment that involves targeting beams of radiation that mirrors the exact size and shape of a tumor at a specific area of a tumor to shrink or destroy cancerous cells. This procedure delivers a therapeutic dose of radiation that conforms precisely to the shape of the tumor, thus minimizing the risk to nearby tissues.

e. **Stereotactic radiosurgery.** Stereotactic radiosurgery (SRS) is a radiotherapy modality that delivers a high dosage of radiation to a discrete treatment area in as few as one treatment session. Includes gamma knife, cyberknife, etc.

85. **Retirement housing.** A facility that provides social activities to senior citizens, usually retired persons, who do not require health care but some short-term skilled nursing care may be provided. A retirement center may furnish housing and may also have acute hospital and long-term care facilities, or it may arrange for acute and long-term care through affiliated institutions.

86. **Robotic surgery.** The use of mechanical guidance devices to remotely manipulate surgical instrumentation.

87. **Rural health clinic.** A clinic located in a rural, medically under-served area in the United States that has a separate reimbursement structure from the standard medical office under the Medicare and Medicaid programs.

88. **Sleep center.** Specially equipped and staffed center for the diagnosis and treatment of sleep disorders.

89. **Social work services.** Could include: organized services that are properly directed and sufficiently staffed by qualified individuals who provide assistance and counseling to patients and their families in dealing with social, emotional, and environmental problems associated with illness or disability, often in the context of financial or discharge planning coordination.

90. **Sports medicine.** Provision of diagnostic screening and assessment and clinical and rehabilitation services for the prevention and treatment of sports-related injuries.

91. **Support groups.** A hospital sponsored program that allows a group of individuals with the same or similar problems who meet periodically to share experiences, problems, and solutions in order to support each other.

92. **Swing bed services.** A hospital bed that can be used to provide either acute or long-term care depending on community or patient needs. To be eligible a hospital must have a Medicare provider agreement in place, have fewer than 100 beds, be located in a rural area, do not have a 24 hour nursing service waiver in effect, have not been terminated from the program in the prior two years, and meet various service conditions.

93. **Teen outreach services.** A program focusing on the teenager which encourages an improved health status and a healthful lifestyle including physical, emotional, mental, social, spiritual and economic health through education, exercise, nutrition and health promotion.

94. **Tobacco treatment/cessation program.** Organized hospital services with the purpose of ending tobacco-use habits of patients addicted to tobacco/nicotine.

95. **Transplant services.** The branch of medicine that transfers an organ or tissue from one person to another or from one body part to another to replace a diseased structure or to restore function or to change appearance. Services could include: Bone marrow transplant program; heart, lung, kidney, intestine, or tissue transplant. Please include heart/lung or other multi-transplant surgeries in 'other'.

96. **Transportation to health facilities.** A long-term care support service designed to assist the mobility of the elderly. Some programs offer improved financial access by offering reduced rates and barrier-free buses or vans with ramps and lifts to assist the elderly or handicapped; others offer subsidies for public transport systems or operate mini-bus services exclusively for use by senior citizens.

97. **Urgent care center.** A facility that provides care and treatment for problems that are not life threatening but require attention over the short term.

98. **Virtual colonoscopy.** Noninvasive screening procedure used to visualize, analyze and detect cancerous or potentially cancerous polyps in the colon.

99. **Volunteer services department.** An organized hospital department responsible for coordinating the services of volunteers working within the institution.

100. **Women's health center/services.** An area set aside for coordinated education and treatment services specifically for and promoted to women as provided by this special unit. Services may or may not include obstetrics but include a range of services other than OB.

101. **Wound management Services.** Services for patients with chronic wounds and nonhealing wounds often resulting from diabetes, poor circulation, improper seating and immunocompromising conditions. The goals are to progress chronic wounds through stages of healing, reduce and eliminate infections, increase physical function to minimize complications from current wounds and prevent future chronic wounds. Wound management services are provided on an inpatient or outpatient basis, depending on the intensity of service needed.

102a. **Physician arrangements.** An integrated healthcare delivery program implementing physician compensation and incentive systems for managed care services.

a. **Independent practice association (IPA).** AN IPA is a legal entity that holds managed care contracts. The IPA then contracts with physicians, usually in solo practice, to provide care either on a fee-for-services or capitated basis. The purpose of an IPA is to assist solo physicians in obtaining managed care contracts.

b. **Group practice without walls.** Hospital sponsors the formation of, or provides capital to physicians to establish, a "quasi" group to share administrative expenses while remaining independent practitioners.

c. **Open physician-hospital organization (PHO).** A joint venture between the hospital and all members of the medical staff who wish to participate. The PHO can act as a unified agent in managed care contracting, own a managed care plan, own and operate ambulatory care centers or ancillary services projects, or provide administrative services to physician members.

d. **Closed physician-hospital organization (PHO).** A PHO that restricts physician membership to those practitioners who meet criteria for cost effectiveness and/or high quality.

e. **Management services organization (MSO).** A corporation, owned by the hospital or a physician/hospital joint venture, that provides management services to one or more medical group practices. The MSO purchases the tangible assets of the practices and leases them back as part of a full-service management agreement, under which the MSO employs all non-physician staff and provides all supplies/administrative systems for a fee.

f. **Integrated salary model.** Physicians are salaried by the hospital or another entity of a health system to provide medical services for primary care and specialty care.

g. **Equity model.** Allows established practitioners to become shareholders in a professional corporation in exchange for tangible and intangible assets of their existing practices.

h. **Foundation.** A corporation, organized either as a hospital affiliate or subsidiary, which purchases both the tangible and intangible assets of one or more medical group practices. Physicians remain in a separate corporate entity but sign a professional services agreement with the foundation.

102b. Of all physician arrangements listed in question 102a (a-i), indicate the total number of physicians (count each physician only once) that are engaged in an arrangement with your hospital that allows for joint contracting with payers or shared responsibility for financial risk or clinical performance between the hospital and physician (arrangement may be at the hospital, system or network level). *Joint contracting* does not include contracting between physicians participating in an independent practice.

103a. **Joint venture.** A contractual arrangement between two or more parties forming an unincorporated business. The participants in the arrangement remain independent and separate outside of the ventures purpose.

106. **Percentage of hospital's net patient revenue.**

a. **Capitation.** An at-risk payment arrangement in which an organization receives a fixed prearranged payment and in turn guarantees to deliver or arrange all medically necessary care required by enrollers in the capitated plan. The fixed amount is specified within contractual agreements between the payor and the involved organization. The fixed payment amount is based on an actuarial assessment of the services required by enrollees and the costs of providing these services, recognizing enrollees' adjustment factors such as age, sex, and family size.

b. **Shared risk payments.** A payment arrangement in which a hospital and a managed care organization share the risk of adverse claims experience. Methods for sharing risk could include: capitation with partial refunds or supplements if billed hospital charges or costs differ from capitated payments, and service or discharge-based payments with withholds and bonus payouts that depend on expenditure targets.

SECTION D
TOTAL FACILITY BEDS, UTILIZATION, FINANCES, AND STAFFING

Instructions and Definitions

For the purposes of this survey, nursing home type unit/facility provides **long-term care for the elderly or other patients requiring chronic care** in a non-acute setting in any of the following categories: *Skilled nursing care *Intermediate care *Other Long-term Care (*see page 16 definitions)The nursing home type units/facilities are to be owned and operated by the hospital. Only one legal entity may be vested with title to the physical property or operate under the authority of a duly executed lease of the physical property.

a. **Total licensed beds** is the total number of beds authorized by the state licensing (certifying agency).

b. Report the number of **beds** regularly available (those **set up and staffed for use**) at the end of the reporting period. Report only operating beds, not constructed bed capacity. Include all bed facilities that are set up and staffed for use by inpatients that have no other bed facilities, such as pediatric bassinets, isolation units, quiet rooms, and reception and observation units assigned to or reserved for them. Exclude newborn bassinets and bed facilities for patients receiving special procedures for a portion of their stay and who have other bed facilities assigned to or reserved for them. Exclude, for example, labor room, post anesthesia, or postoperative recovery room beds, psychiatric holding beds, and beds that are used only as holding facilities for patients prior to their transfer to another hospital.

c. Report the number of normal newborn **bassinets**. Do not include neonatal intensive care or intermediate care bassinets. These should be reported on page 2, C6 and C7.

d. Total **births** should exclude fetal deaths.

e. Include the number of adult and pediatric **admissions** only (exclude births). This figure should include all patients admitted during the reporting period, including neonatal and swing admissions.

f. Report the number of adult and pediatric **days of care** rendered during the entire reporting period. Do not include days of care rendered for normal infants born in the hospital, but do include those for their mothers. Include days of care for infants born in the hospital and transferred into a neonatal care unit. Also include swing bed inpatient days. **Inpatient day** of care (also commonly referred to as a **patient day** or a **census day**, or by some federal hospitals as an **occupied bed day**) is a period of service between the census-taking hours on two successive calendar days, the day of discharge being counted only when the patient was admitted the same day.

g. **Emergency department visits** should reflect the number of visits to the emergency unit. Emergency outpatients can be admitted to the inpatient areas of the hospital, but they are still counted as emergency visits and subsequently as inpatient admissions.

h. An **Outpatient visit** is a visit by a patient who is not lodged in the hospital while receiving medical, dental, or other services. Each appearance of an outpatient in each unit constitutes one visit regardless of the number of diagnostic and/or therapeutic treatments that the patient receives. Total outpatient visits should include all clinic visits, referred visits, observation services, outpatient surgeries (also reported on line D1J), home health service visits, and emergency department visits (also reported on line D1g).

Clinic visits should reflect total number of visits to each specialized medical unit that is responsible for the diagnosis and treatment of patients on an outpatient, nonemergency basis (i.e., alcoholism, dental, gynecology, etc.). Visits to the satellite clinics and primary group practices should be included if revenue is received by the hospital.

Referred visits should reflect total number of outpatient ancillary visits to each specialty unit of the hospital established for providing technical aid used in the diagnosis and treatment of patients. Examples of such units are diagnostic radiology, EKG, pharmacy, etc.

Observation services are those services furnished on a hospital's premises, including use of a bed and periodic monitoring by a hospital's nursing or other staff, which are reasonable and necessary to evaluate an outpatient's condition or determine the need for a possible admission to the hospital as an inpatient. Observation services usually do not exceed 24 hours. However, there is no hourly limit on the extent to which they may be used.

Home health service visits are visits by home health personnel to a patient's residence.

i. **Inpatient surgical operation.** Count each patient undergoing surgery as one surgical operation regardless of the number of surgical procedures that were performed while the patient was in the operating or procedure room.

j. **Operating room.** A unit/room of a hospital or other health care facility in which surgical procedures requiring anesthesia are performed.

k. **Outpatient surgical operation.** For outpatient surgical operations, please record operations performed on patients who do not remain in the hospital overnight. Include all operations whether performed in the inpatient operating rooms or in procedure rooms located in an outpatient facility. Include an endoscopy only when used as an operative tool and not when used for diagnosis alone. Count each patient undergoing surgery as one surgical operation regardless of the number of surgical procedures that were performed while the patient was in the operating or procedure room.

2a2. Managed Care Medicare Discharges. A discharge day where a Medicare Managed Care Plan is the source of payment.

2b2. Managed Care Medicare Inpatient Days. An inpatient day where a Medicare Managed Care Plan is the source of payment.

2c2. Managed Care Medicaid Discharges. A discharge day where a Medicaid Managed Care Plan is the source of payment.

2d2. Managed Care Medicaid Inpatient Days. An inpatient day where a Medicaid Managed Care Plan is the source of payment.

3a. Net patient revenue. Reported at the estimated net realizable amounts from patients, third-party payors, and others for services rendered, including estimated retroactive adjustments under reimbursement agreements with third-party payors. Retroactive adjustments are accrued on an estimated basis in the period the related services are rendered and adjusted in future periods, as final settlements are determined.

3b. Tax appropriations. A predetermined amount set aside by the government from its taxing authority to support the operation of the hospital.

3c. Other operating revenue. Revenue from services other than health care provided to patients, as well as sales and services to nonpatients. Revenue that arises from the normal day-to-day operations from services other than health care provided to patients. Includes sales and services to nonpatients, and revenue from miscellaneous sources (rental of hospital space, sale of cafeteria meals, gift shop sales). Also include operating gains in this category.

3d. Nonoperating revenue. Includes investment income, extraordinary gains and other nonoperating gains.

3e. Total revenue. Add net patient revenue, tax appropriations, other operating revenue and nonoperating revenue.

3 f. Payroll expenses. Include payroll for all personnel including medical and dental residents/interns and trainees.

3g. Employee benefits. Includes social security, group insurance, retirement benefits, workman's compensation, unemployment insurance, etc.

3h. Depreciation expense (for reporting period only) report only the depreciation expense applicable to the reporting period. The amount also Should be included in accumulated depreciation (D7b).

3i. Interest expense. Report interest expense for the reporting period only.

3j. Supply expense. The net cost of all tangible items that are expensed including freight, standard distribution cost, and sales and use tax minus rebates. This would exclude labor, labor-related expenses and services as well as some tangible items that are frequently provided as part of labor costs.

3k. Total expenses. Includes all payroll and non-payroll expenses (including bad debt) as well as any nonoperating losses (including extraordinary losses).

4a. Total gross inpatient revenue. The hospitals full-established rates(charges) for all services rendered to inpatients.

4b. Total gross outpatient revenue. The hospitals full-established rates(charges) for all services rendered to outpatients.

4c. Total gross patient revenue. Total gross patient revenue (add total gross inpatient revenue and total gross outpatient revenue).

5. Uncompensated care. Care for which no payment is expected or no charge is made. It is the sum of bad debt and charity care absorbed by a hospital or other health care organization in providing medical care for patients who are uninsured or are unable to pay.

5a. Bad debt expense. The provision for actual or expected uncollectibles resulting from the extension of credit. Because bad debts are reported as an expense and not a deduction from revenue, the gross charges that result in bad debts will remain in net revenue (D3a).

5b. Charity care. Health services that were never expected to result in cash inflows. Charity care results from a provider's policy to provide health care services free of charge to individuals who meet certain financial criteria. For purposes of this survey, charity care is measured on the basis of revenue forgone, at full-established rates.

6. REVENUE BY PAYOR

6a1 Medicare. Should agree with the Medicare utilization reported in questions D21-Db2.

6a1a Fee for service patient revenue. Include traditional Medicare fee-for-service.

6a1c. Total. Medicare revenue (add Medicare fee for service patient revenue and Medicare managed care revenue).

6a2. Medicaid. Should agree with Medicaid utilization reported in questions D2c1-D2d2.

6a2a. Fee for service patient revenue. Do not include Medicaid disproportionate payments(DSH) or Medicaid supplemental payments that are non-Medicaid disproportionate payments (DSH).

6a2c. Medicaid disproportionate share payments. DSH minus associated provider taxes or assessments.

6a2d. Medicaid supplemental payments. Not including Medicaid DSH payments (these are supplemental payments the Medicaid program pays the hospital that are NOT Medicaid DSH) and minus associated provider taxes or assessments.

7. Fixed Assets. Represent land and physical properties that are consumed or used in the creation of economic activity by the health care entity. The historical or acquisition costs are used in recording fixed assets. Net plant, property, and equipment represent the original costs of these items less accumulated depreciation and amortization.

7d. Gross Square Footage: Include all inpatient, outpatient, office, and support space used for or in support of your health care activities. Exclude exterior, roof, and garage space in the figure.

8. Capital Expenses. Expenses used to acquire assets, including buildings, remodeling projects, equipment, or property.

9. Energy Consumption.

   a. Total energy usage includes electricity, natural gas, fuel oil, district stream, district chilled water, diesel (no. 2) and coal. Total energy usage is the sum of all MMBTUs.

CONVERSION CHART TO MMBTU:

Electric	Number of kW h x .0034 = Number of MMBTU
Natural Gas	Number of Therms x .1 = Number of MMBTU
	or
	Number of MCF x 1.03 = Number of MMBTU

   b. Energy Star rating is a national energy performance rating system, which utilizes a 1-100 scale to give meaning to the energy usage. To qualify, each building must meet specific guidelines in four areas: energy performance; thermal comfort; indoor air quality; illumination levels.

10. Information Technology.

   a. **IT Operating expense.** Exclude department depreciation and operating dollars paid against capital leases.

   b. **IT Capital expense.** Include IT capital expense for the current year only. Any capital expense that is carried forward from the previous year should be excluded from this figure. Include IT related capital included in the budget of other departments. (i.e. lab, radiology, etc., if known or can be reasonably estimated.) Include the total value of capital leases to be signed in the current year.

   c. **Number of Employed IT staff (in FTEs).** Number of full-time equivalent (FTE) staff employed in the IT department/organization and on the hospital payroll.

   d. **Total number of outsourced IT staff.** (i.e. contracted staff).

   e. **Electronic Health Record.** An electronic health record (EHR) integrates electronically originated and maintained patient-level clinical health information, derived from multiple sources, into one point of access. An EHR replaces the paper medical record as the primary source of patient information.

STAFFING

1. Full-Time Equivalent (FTE) is the total number of hours worked by all employees over the full (12 month) reporting period divided by the normal number of hours worked by a full-time employee for that same time period. For example, if your hospital considers a normal workweek for a full-time employee to be 40 hours, a total of 2,080 would be worked over a full year (52 weeks). If the total number of hours worked by all employees on the payroll is 208,000, then the number of Full-Time Equivalents (FTE) is 100 (employees). The FTE calculation for a specific occupational category such as Registered nurses is exactly the same. The calculation for each occupational category should be based on the number of hours worked by staff employed in that specific category.

  a. Physicians and dentists. Include only those physicians and dentists engaged in clinical practice and on the payroll. Those who hold administrative positions should be reported in "All other personnel."

  c. Other trainees. A trainee is a person who has not completed the necessary requirements for certification or met the qualifications required for full salary under a related occupational category. Exclude medical and dental residents/interns who should be reported on line 7b.

  d. Registered nurses. Nurses who have graduated from approved schools of nursing and who are currently registered by the state. They are responsible for the nature and quality of all nursing care that patients receive. Do not include any registered nurses more appropriately reported in other occupational categories, such as facility administrators, and therefore listed under "All other personnel."

  e. Licensed practical (vocational) nurses. Nurses who have graduated from an approved school of practical (vocational) nursing who work under the supervision of registered nurses and/or physicians.

  f. Nursing assistive personnel. Certified nursing assistant or equivalent unlicensed staff assigned to patient care units and reporting to nursing.

  g. Radiology Technicians. Technical positions in imaging fields, including, but not limited to, radiology, sonography, nuclear medicine, radiation therapy, CT, MRI.

  h. Laboratory professional/technical. Professional and technical positions in all areas of the laboratory, including, but not limited to, histology, phlebotomy, microbiology, pathology, chemistry, etc.

  i. Pharmacists, licensed. Persons licensed within the state who are concerned with the preparation and distribution of medicinal products.

  j. Pharmacy technicians. Persons who assist the pharmacist with selected activities, including medication profile reviews for drug incompatibilities, typing labels and prescription packaging, handling of purchase records and inventory control.

  l. All other personnel. This should include all other personnel not already accounted for in other categories.

  m. Total facility personnel. This line is to include the total facility personnel - hospital plus nursing home type unit/facility personnel (for those hospitals that own and operate a nursing home type unit/facility).

  n-o. Nursing home type unit/facility personnel. These lines should be filled out only by hospitals that own and operate a nursing home type unit/facility, where only one legal entity is vested with title to the physical property or operates under the authority of a duly executed lease of the physical property. If nursing home type unit/facility personnel are reported on the total facility personnel line, but cannot be broken out, please write "cannot break out" on this line.

12. Privileged Physicians. Report the total number of physicians (by type) on the medical staff with privileges except those with courtesy, honorary and provisional privileges. Do not include residents or interns.

  Employed by your hospital. Physicians that are either direct hospital employees or employees of a hospital subsidiary corporation. Physicians that are employed for non-clinical services (administrative services, medical director services, etc.) should be excluded.

  Individual contract. An independent physician under a formal contract to provide services at your hospital including at outpatient facilities, clinics and offices. Physicians that are contracted only for non-clinical services (administrative services, medical director services, etc.) should be excluded.

  Group contract. A physician that is part of a group (group practice, faculty practice plan or medical foundation) under a formal contract to provide services at your hospital including at inpatient and outpatient facilities, clinics and offices. Physicians that are contracted only for non-clinical services (administrative services, medical director services, etc.) should be excluded.

  Not employed or under contract. Other physicians with privileges that have no employment or contractual relationship with the hospital to provide services.

    The sum of the physicians reported in 12a-12f should equal the total number of privileged physicians in the hospital.

  a. Primary care. A physician that provides primary care services including general practice, general internal medicine, family practice, general pediatrics, obstetrics/gynecology and geriatrics.

  b. Emergency medicine. Physicians who provide care in the emergency department.

  c. Hospitalist. Physician whose primary professional focus is the care of hospitalized medical patients (through clinical, education, administrative and research activity).

  d. Intensivist. A physician with special training to work with critically ill patients. Intensivists generally provided medical-surgical, cardiac, neonatal, pediatric and other types of intensive care.

  e. Radiologist/pathologist/anesthesiologist
    Radiologist. A physician who has specialized training in imaging, including but not limited to radiology, sonography, nuclear medicine, radiation therapy, CT, MRI.
    Pathologist. A physician who examines samples of body tissues for diagnostic purposes.
    Anesthesiologist. A physician who specializes in administering medications or other agents that prevent or relieve pain, especially during surgery.

  f. Other specialist. Other physicians (not included above) that specialize in a specific type of medical care.

15. Advanced Practice Registered Nurses. Registered nurses with advanced didactic and clinical education, knowledge, skills, and scope of practice. Includes: **Physician assistant.** A healthcare professional licensed to practice medicine with supervision of a licensed physician.

  Nurse practitioner. A registered nurse with at least a master's degree in nursing and advanced education in primary care, capable of independent practice in a variety of settings. **Clinical nurse specialist (CNS).** A registered nurse who, through a formal graduate degree (masters or doctorate) CNS education program, is prepared as CNS with expertise in a specialty area of nursing practice. CNSs are clinical experts in the diagnosis and treatment of illness, and the delivery of evidence-based nursing interventions. Services provided include:

  Primary care. Medical services including general practice, general internal medicine, family practice, general pediatrics, obstetrics/gynecology.

  Emergency department care. The provision of unscheduled outpatient services to patients whose conditions require immediate care in the emergency department setting.

  Other Specialty care. A clinic that provides specialized medical care beyond the scope of primary care.

  Patient education. Goals and objectives for the patient and/or family related to therapeutic regimens, medical procedures and self care.

  Case management. A system of assessment, treatment planning, referral and follow-up that ensures the provision of comprehensive and continuous services and the coordination of payment and reimbursement for care.

  Other. (specify) Any type of care other than those listed above.

16. Foreign-educated nurses. Individuals who are foreign born and received basic nursing education in a foreign country. In general many of these nurses come to the US on employment-based visas which allow them to obtain a green card.

SECTION E. SUPPLEMENTAL INFORMATION
DEFINITIONS

1a. Mission statement. A general statement that describes a company's reason for existence, its vision and direction, its areas of expertise and its goals.

1h. Self-assessment. An evaluation of an organization's management system through achievements in areas such as: leadership, strategic planning, human resource management, information management, process management, customer focus and satisfaction, and business results.

1i. Health status indicators. Measures used to quantify various aspects of a populations health status.

2c. Leadership development program. A program that is designed to increase the leadership skills of manager level personnel for eventual placement in a more senior level position. This program focuses on two classes of personnel. Of greatest importance is the Mid-careerist that has been working in a hospital setting for 7-12 years and is stuck at the Manger level. The other category of a good Leadership Development program focuses on increasing the number of minorities at the Senior Executive level. This would include all titles *above* Department Director, including Administrator, Associate Administrator, and the various levels of Vice President.

2d. Diversity plan. A set of goals and objectives that are linked to the organization's Strategic Plan to promote the elimination of disparities and identify strategies to ensure the ethnic and racial composition of the workforce better reflects the composition of the communities being served.

2e. Leadership Succession planning. The deliberate use of mentoring, coaching and grooming of individuals inside the organization that have been identified as having the potential to advance when vacancies occur at the senior executive level.

2f. Career development resources. Tools, training programs, financial aid, executive coaching and other resources that can be used to prepare individuals to compete for advancement opportunities in an organization.

3a. Satellite facility(s). Satellite Services are available at a facility geographically remote from the hospital campus.

3c. Distributor. An entity that typically does not manufacture most of its own products but purchases and re-sells these products. Such a business usually maintains an inventory of products for sales to hospitals and physician offices and others.

NOTES

NOTES